CHRISTIANITY
THROUGH
THE CENTURIES

CHRISTIANITY

THROUGH

THE CENTURIES

A HISTORY
OF THE
CHRISTIAN CHURCH

EARLE E. CAIRNS

Revised and Enlarged Edition

Academie
Books
Grand Rapids, Michigan
Zondervan Publishing House

CHRISTIANITY THROUGH THE CENTURIES
Copyright © 1954, 1981 by The Zondervan Corporation
Grand Rapids, Michigan

ACADEMIE BOOKS are published by Zondervan
Publishing House, 1415 Lake Drive, S.E.,
Grand Rapids, Michigan 49506

Library of Congress Cataloging in Publication Data

Cairns, Earle Edwin, 1910–
    Christianity through the centuries.

    Includes index.
    1. Church history. I. Polcyn, Dick. II. Terpstra, Gerard. III. Title.
BR145.2.C28 1981   270   80-39597
ISBN 0-310-38360-9

Edited by Dick Polcyn and Gerard Terpstra

Designed by Stanley N. Gundry

Printed in the United States of America

85 86 87 88 89 90 91 92 93 / 40 39 38 37 36 35 34 33 32

To
Helen and Bruce

CONTENTS

ANCIENT CHURCH HISTORY
5 B.C.–A.D. 590

MEDIEVAL CHURCH HISTORY
590–1517

MEDIEVAL SUNSET AND MODERN SUNRISE,
1305–1517

MODERN CHURCH HISTORY
1517 and After

REFORMATION AND COUNTER REFORMATION,
1517–1648

RATIONALISM, REVIVALISM, AND DENOMINATIONALISM,
1648–1789

REVIVALISM, MISSIONS, AND MODERNISM,
1789–1914

CHURCH AND SOCIETY IN TENSION SINCE 1914

CHARTS

MAPS

PICTURES AND CREDITS

PREFACE

An examination of available church history texts reveals that most of them reflect a particular denominational or theological bias. This text was written from a conservative, nondenominational perspective. A Christian philosophy of history underlies the presentation.

Because one can never understand the history of Christianity effectively without some conception of the political, economic, social, intellectual, and artistic movements in each era of history, the events of church history are related to their secular environment. The treatment of persons, places, dates, events, ideas, and trends or movements in their proper temporal and geographical setting helps one grasp the flow of church history. I have given attention to the impact of Christianity on its times and to the mark of the times on Christianity. I have attempted to link information, understanding, and interpretation in a relevant synthesis that has value in the present.

I am grateful that after twenty-five years of the use of this text both by teachers and students in the classroom and by the Christian public its continued demand has made an extensive revision desirable and feasible. Constructive suggestions from several people have been most helpful in improving the accuracy and clarity of this work.

Several new maps and diagrams have been added to aid in understanding historical movements and relationships. Several new pictures have also been included. Bibliographies in the introduction, at the beginning of each of the three major eras of church history, and at the end of each chapter have been expanded and updated to make the best primary and secondary materials available to the reader. Many sections have been expanded and rewritten, for example, those on Scholasticism, the Radical Reformation, Roman Catholicism, and the Eastern churches. The account of the era since World War I has been extensively revised and expanded to take into account new developments in the ecumenical movement, in Roman Catholicism, and especially among Evangelicals.

I hope that through this book many will become aware of their spiritual heritage and ancestry in a day of existentialism and be constrained to serve God and their contemporaries better by life, word, and deed. I am deeply conscious of the part colleagues, teachers, students, other writers, and many others have played in the development of this text. I trust that through it the cause of Christ may be advanced and the church edified.

EARLE E. CAIRNS
Wheaton, Illinois

INTRODUCTION

Curiosity concerning the past has long characterized man, from Nabonidus, who lived in Babylon in the sixth century before Christ, to the present-day archaeologist and historian. Christians have a special interest in history because the very foundations of the faith that they profess are rooted in history. God became man and lived in time and space in the person of Christ. Christianity has become the most nearly global and universal of all the religions that emerged in the past in the Near and Far East. In addition, it has become increasingly influential in the history of the human race. Church history is thus a matter of profound interest to the Christian who desires to be enlightened concerning his spiritual ancestry, to emulate the good examples of the past, and to avoid errors that the church has frequently made.

I. WHAT IS CHURCH HISTORY?

The German noun *Geschichte*, a form of the verb *geschehen*, which means to happen, refers to history as *event* rather than as a process or a product. Thus history may be defined first as an *incident*, an actual event or happening in time and space as the result of human action. Such an incident is absolute and objective and can be known only directly and fully by God. Such history cannot be exactly repeated later in another place. Parallels and patterns may appear to the historian because people may behave in similar fashion in different times and places and because they are people who can be affected by good and evil.

Information about an incident is a second meaning for the word *history*. This usually indirect information about the past may be in the form of a document or object relating to the incident. Unlike the scientist who can study his material objectively and directly, the historian is subjectively limited because he is a part of what he studies and has to take God's actions in time and space into account, consider man's role in history as a freewill agent, and realize his data is indirect. Saint Peter's in Rome, the catacombs, a papal bull, and mosaics in Ravenna are examples of history as information.

The English word for history came from the Greek word *historia*, which is derived from the Greek verb *historeō*. This word was used by the Attic Greeks and originally meant to learn by inquiry or investigation. The word was used by Paul in Galatians 1:18 to describe his interview with Peter in Jerusalem. This leads to a third meaning of history as *inquiry* or research to check as well as find data about the past. History is a distinct discipline with a process for research. The historian tests the authenticity, genuineness, and integrity of his information by careful study of the background and text of his material. Valid inductions can also be developed as the scholar sees patterns objectively appearing in his material.

The historian who thus far seeks answers to such questions as who or what and when and where must then consider the question why or the meaning of his data. The Greeks who used the word *histoikos* as another term for history thought of history in this sense as the product of inquiry. This suggests *interpretation* as a fourth meaning for history. This is the subjective reconstruction of the past in the light of the data, the historian's own biases as well as the "climate of opinion" of his time, and the element of freedom of the human will. Such reconstruction can never fully tell the past as it was but must be partial, subject to error and human bias. A consensus about the past will emerge, however, as historians check one another's work. Students in classes usually study history of this type. Though absolute truth about the past may elude the historian, he will, as far as his information permits, present truth about the past objectively and impartially.

From this discussion the student will be aware that history may be event or incident, information, inquiry or process and product, or interpretation. History as event is absolute, occurring only once in time and space; but history as information, inquiry, and interpretation is relative and subject to change.

History may be defined as the interpreted record of the socially significant human past, based on organized data collected by the scientific method from archaeological, literary, or living sources. The church historian must be just as impartial in his collection of the data of history as the secular historian is, even though the church historian recognizes the fact that neither of them will be neutral to the data but each will approach the material with a framework of interpretation.

Church history, then, is the interpreted record of the origin, progress, and impact of Christianity on human society, based on organized data gathered by scientific method from archaeological, documentary, or living sources. It is the interpreted, organized story of the redemption of man and the earth. Only if this definition is fulfilled will the Christian student of history have an accurate record of the story of the faith that he professes. The children of light in this instance must not lag behind the children of darkness. God is transcendent in creation but immanent in history and in redemption.

II. THE WRITING OF CHURCH HISTORY

A. The Scientific Element

Church history will have a scientific element in that the historian of the church uses the scientific method also. The historian uses the scientific work of the archaeologist, who makes available information from the material remains of the past that he has unearthed. Study of the art of the catacombs of Rome has taught us much about the early church. The writer of church history will also make use of the techniques of literary criticism to evaluate the documents of the history of the church. He will have a decided preference for original sources, whether they be those of the archaeologist, the document, or the living person who took part in the event. All this material and the evaluation of it will give him information concerning the important questions of historical method—who, what, when, and where. The last two questions are important to the historian because historical events are conditioned by time and place.

The historian's work will be scientific in method but will not result in exact science because his information about the incidents of the past may be incomplete or false, biased by his own outlook and that of his time and affected by great men. He is also a freewill agent who is a part of his data. God as an actor in history will preclude the idea of history as an exact science.

B. The Philosophic Element

Historians divide into schools of history and philosophies of history as they pursue meaning in history. The former claim to find objective, scientific causation in man, nature, or process in time; but the latter rationally seek to relate the data to a timeless ultimate or absolute.

Geographic and economic determinists and biographical interpreters constitute three of the more important schools of history. William W. Sweet, of the frontier school of interpretation of church history, in his books on American church history made geography in the form of the frontier the determinative factor. Carlyle's work on Cromwell illustrates the biographical or "great man" school of history as he made the mid-sixteenth-century English Civil War the reflection of Cromwell. Max Weber's *The Protestant Ethic and the Spirit of Capitalism*,[1] in which he claimed that Protestantism led to the rise of capitalism, is an example of the economic school of interpretation. Such interpreters of history look for the answers to history in man, nature, or process.

Philosophies of history can best be considered under three categories.

1. One group may be classed as *pessimists.* Seeing history only "under the sun," they often adopt a materialistic approach to reality. They are obsessed with the failure of man in history. Oswald Spengler's *The Decline of the West*[2] is an illustration of this approach to history. Spengler was concerned with civilizations rather than with nations. Each civilization, he maintained, goes through a cycle of birth, adolescence, maturity, decay, and death. Western civilization, the most recent of civilizations, is in its period of decay. It will soon die and along with it Christianity will die. Obsessed with man's failure, men such as Spengler can see no progress in history. Their views may be symbolized by a series of identical circles, superimposed on one another, in which time is cyclical.

2. A second group may be called *optimists.* Their view of history can be symbolized by an ascending graph or successively rising levels of a spiral. Most optimistic interpreters are humanists: they see man as the main and determinative factor in history. They also usually accept biological and social evolution and see time as linear. The work of Arnold Toynbee, a great modern philosopher of history, serves to illustrate this philosophy of history. Toynbee agreed with Spengler that one should study the history of civilizations; but, unlike Spengler, he believed that each civilization makes progress toward its goal—the earth as a province of the kingdom of God. In spite of his more spiritual approach to history, he accepted modern biblical criticism and the theory of evolution.

Another optimist, Georg W. F. Hegel, the famous German philosopher of the nineteenth century, believed history to be the unfolding of the Absolute Spirit in the development of human freedom. Progress is by a process in which successive series of contradictions are reconciled until the Absolute is fully manifested in history.

Karl Marx, another nineteenth-century thinker, also belonged to the optimistic school. Borrowing Hegel's logic, he disavowed Hegel's view of reality. Marx taught that matter in flux is the only reality and that all human institutions, including religion, are determined by the economic processes of production. He maintained that a series of class struggles will end with the victory of the workers and the establishment of a classless society. Notice that Marx emphasized man's power to redeem himself and his world in the same way that Toynbee and Hegel did.

3. The third group of interpreters, in which the writer places himself, may be described as *pessimistic optimists*. These historians agree with the pessimists in emphasizing the failure of unregenerate man; but in the light of divine revelation and grace, they are optimistic concerning man's future. The pessimistic optimists approach history as biblical theists and seek to find the glory of God in the historic process. History becomes a process of conflict between good and evil, God and the devil, in which man is helpless apart from the grace of God. The work of Christ on the cross is the final guarantee of the eventual victory of the divine plan for man and the earth, when Christ returns.

The City of God, a defense and explanation of Christianity by Augustine, one of the church fathers, is an excellent illustration of this approach, though many Christians do not agree with Augustine's equation of the Millennium with the present period of the church. The grandeur of Augustine's conception grows out of its ascription of *creation* to the sovereign God. The *compass* or scope of Augustine's view of history includes the whole of the human race in contrast with the favored German nation of Hegel or the favored working class of Marx. There is, however, a temporal dualism in history because sin divides men in the City of God and the City of Earth. Augustine argued that the *course* of human history proceeds to and from the Cross; and the grace flowing from it is seen as operative within the Christian church, the invisible body of Christ. Christians, with divine grace to strengthen them, engage on the side of God in the conflict with evil until history reaches its cataclysmic *consummation* at the return of Christ.

My book *God and Man in Time* [3] is a contemporary attempt to set forth a Christian approach to history.

C. The Artistic Element

Finally, the maker of history as record must seek to be as artistic as possible in his presentation of the facts. Modern historians have not stressed an interesting literary presentation of history as much as they should have.

III. THE VALUE
OF CHURCH HISTORY

Church history is only a dreary academic exercise in the remembering of facts unless some thought is given to the matter of its value to the Christian. The ancient historians had a much higher appreciation of the pragmatic, didactic, and moral values of history than many modern historians have. The student who is conscious of the values to be achieved in the study of the history of the Christian church has a powerful motivation to study this particular area of human history.

A. Church History as a Synthesis

One of the primary values of church history is that it links the past factual data of the Christian gospel with the future proclamation and application of that gospel in a present synthesis that creates understanding of our great heritage and inspiration for its further proclamation and application. Church history shows the Spirit of God in action through the church during the ages of its existence. Exegetical theology is linked in a meaningful pattern with practical theology as the student sees how systematic theology has made an impact on previous human thought and action.

B. Church History as an Aid to Understanding the Present

Church history has great value as an explanation of the present. We can understand the present much better if we have some knowledge of its roots in the past. The answer to the puzzling query concerning the presence of over two hundred and fifty religious groups in the United States is to be found in church history. The principle of separation found a place early in the history of the church, and the Reformation accentuated it. It is interesting to trace the Protestant Episcopal Church in the USA back to England and to note the origin of the Anglican church in the struggle of the royal power with the papacy. The Methodist is interested in the beginnings of his church in the Wesleyan revival, which finally brought separation of Methodism from the Anglican church. Those of the Reformed or Presbyterian faith will take delight in tracing the origin of their church to Switzerland. Thus we become aware of our spiritual ancestry.

Different beliefs and liturgical practices become more understandable in the light of past history. Methodists kneel at the rail for Communion because for many years the Methodists constituted a church within the Anglican church; and Wesley, who was reluctant to break with the Anglican church, followed its liturgical customs. In contrast, Presbyterians are served the Communion in their seats. The difference in Methodist and Presbyterian theology becomes much plainer when one studies the views of Calvin and Arminius.

Present-day problems of the church are often illuminated by study of the past, because patterns or parallels exist in history. The refusal of most modern dictatorial rulers to permit their people to have any private interests separate from their public life in the state is more easily understood if one remembers that the Roman emperors did not think that one could have a private religion without endangering the existence of the state. The relationship between the church and state has again become a real problem in Russia and its satellite states; and it is to be expected that the state will persecute Christians just as Decius and Diocletian did in their day. The danger inherent in the union of the church and state through the state support for parochial schools and through the sending of envoys to the Vatican is illuminated by the slow decline of spirituality in the church and the interference with the church by the temporal power beginning with the control of the Council of Nicaea by Constantine in 325. Tennyson, in his poem *Ulysses*, reminds us that we are "a part of all that we have met."

C. Church History as a Guide

The correction of existing evils within the church or the avoidance of error and false practice is another value of the study of the past of the church. The present is usually the product of the past and the seed of the future. Paul reminded us in Romans 15:4 and 1 Corinthians 10:6, 11 that the events of the past are to help us avoid the evil and emulate the good. Study of the hierarchical, medieval Roman Catholic church will point out the danger in the modern ecclesiasticism that seems to be creeping into Protestantism. New sects will often be revealed as old heresies in a new guise.

Christian Science can be understood better after a study of Gnosticism in the early church and the ideas of the Cathari in medieval times. Ignorance of the Bible and the history of the church is a major reason why many advocate false theologies or bad practices.

D. Church History as a Motivating Force

Church history also offers edification, inspiration, or enthusiasm that will stimulate high spiritual life. Paul believed that knowledge of the past would give hope to the Christian life (Rom. 15:4). No one can study the brave stand of Ambrose of Milan, in refusing Emperor Theodosius the Communion until he repented of his massacre of the Thessalonian crowd, without being encouraged to stand for Christ against evil in high political or ecclesiastical circles. The industry and drive that enabled Wesley to preach over ten thousand sermons during his life and to travel thousands of miles on horseback is bound to be a rebuke and a challenge to Christians who have much better means for travel and study than Wesley had but who do not make adequate use of them. One may not agree with Rauschenbusch's theology, but one cannot help but be inspired by his passion to apply the gospel to social problems. The story of Carey's life was and is an inspiration to missionary service. The biographical aspect of church history is bound to bring inspiration and challenge to the student.

There is also edification in the process of becoming aware of one's spiritual ancestry. There is as much need for the Christian to become aware of his spiritual genealogy as there is for the citizen to study the history of his land in order that he might become an intelligent citizen. In showing the genetic development of Christianity, church history is to the New Testament what the New Testament is to the Old Testament. The Christian ought to be as aware of the main outlines of the growth and development of Christianity as he is of biblical truth. Then he will have a sense of being a part of the body of Christ, which includes a Paul, a Bernard of Clairvaux, an Augustine, a Luther, a Wesley, and a Booth. The sense of unity that comes from a knowledge of the continuity of history will lead to spiritual enrichment.

One who is fearful for the future of the church in countries where it is now persecuted will become more hopeful as he realizes the indestructible character of the church in past ages. Neither external persecution, internal unfaithful officialdom, nor false theology could stand against the perennial power of renewal that is revealed in the history of revival in the church. Even secular historians give credit to the Wesleyan revival as the agency that saved England from the equivalent of the French Revolution. The study of church history offers a stabilizing influence in an age of secularism, for one sees the power of God operating through the lives of people transformed by the gospel.

We should remember, though, that the church can be destroyed in a particular area by internal decay and unbearable external pressure. The fine church in old Carthage, the Nestorians in seventh-century China, and the Roman Catholic church in sixteenth-century Japan did disappear.

E. Church History as a Practical Tool

The reading of the history of the church has many practical values for the Christian worker, whether he or she is evangelist, pastor, or teacher. The writer has derived pleasure from seeing how much more intelligible systematic theology has become to the student who has studied its historical development. The doctrines of the Trinity, Christ, sin, and soteriology will never be properly understood unless one is aware of the history of the period from the Council of Nicaea to the Council of Constantinople in 680.

An abundance of illustrative material for his sermons also awaits the efforts of the diligent student of church history who intends to preach. Is he seeking to warn of the dangers of a blind mysticism that puts Christian illumination on a level with the inspiration of the Bible? Then let him study the mystical movements of the Middle Ages or early Quakerism. If he seeks to warn of the dangers of an orthodoxy unaccompanied by a study and application of the teachings of the Bible, then let him give attention to the period of cold orthodoxy in Lutheranism after 1648, which created a reaction known as Pietism, a movement that stressed earnest study of the Bible and practical piety in daily life.

F. Church History as a Liberalizing Force

Finally, church history has a cultural value. The history of Western civilization is incomplete and unintelligible without some understanding of the role of Christian religion in the development of that civilization. The history of man can never be divorced from the history of his religious life. The efforts of despots throughout the ages to eliminate Christian religion have always resulted in the substitution of some false religion. Both Hitler and Stalin gave their systems of statism a religious element by their respective emphasis on race and class.

One who has studied the history of the church will never again be denominationally provincial. He will sense the unity of the true body of Christ throughout the ages. He will also be humble as he encounters the giants of his spiritual past and realizes how much he owes to them. He will become more tolerant of those who differ with him on nonessentials but who, with him, accept the great basic doctrines of the faith, such as the vicarious death and resurrection of Christ, which were emphasized by Paul in Acts 17:2–3 and 1 Corinthians 15:3–4.

IV. THE ORGANIZATION OF CHURCH HISTORY

A. Branches of Church History

For the sake of convenience, church history can be organized under the following topics:

1. The *political* element involves the relations between the church and the state and the secular environment of the church. No one can understand the reversal of policy in France involved in the change from the situation created by the Civil Constitution of the Clergy of 1790 to the situation created by the Concordat of Napoleon in 1801 unless he has some knowledge of how Napoleon destroyed the democratic element in the French Revolution and set up a new authoritarian system in which only the Roman Catholic church was to play a part because it was the religion of "the majority of Frenchmen." An understanding of the political, social, economic, and aesthetic forces at work in history is essential if one is going to interpret church history properly. Such background will be provided at the points where it is appropriate.

2. The *propagation* of the Christian faith cannot be ignored. This involves the study of world missions, home missions, city missions, and the story of any special technique by which the gospel has been carried to others. The story of missions has its heroes and martyrs and is an integral part of the story of the church. The essential person-to-person nature of the spread of Christianity and the unlimited possibilities for a church faithful to its Lord is shown in a study of the propagation of the faith.

3. This propagation has many times brought *persecution* to the church. This persecution was begun by the political-ecclesiastical Jewish state, was organized on an imperial basis by Decius and Diocletian, was often made a part of Muslim policy, and has been revived by the modern secular totalitarian state. Study of persecution reveals the truth of Tertullian's dictum that "the blood of Christians is seed" (of the church). This branch of church history, far from leading to discouragement, shows rather that the church has made its greatest advances in periods of persecution or immediately after.

4. *Polity* is another branch of church history. It is the study of the government of the church. It necessitates consideration of the government of the church by bishops (episcopacy), elders (presbyterianism), the congre-

gation in a system of direct rather than representative democracy (congregationalism), or modifications of these three systems. Consideration of the position of the minister and the growth of the distinction between clergy and laity is also a part of this topic. Discipline and forms of worship (liturgy) are related to polity.

5. *Polemics*, which concerns the struggle of the church to fight heresy and to think out its own position, is an important aspect of the development of the church. It involves study of the opposing heresies and of the formulation of dogma, creeds, and Christian literature in answer to heresies. The literature of the church fathers is a particularly rich field for the study of polemics—whether that literature be the writings of Justin Martyr, answering the contention that the state must be all in life, or of Irenaeus, exposing the heresies of the various types of Gnosticism. Most theological systems have been born in a period of struggle to meet existing needs. The eras between 325 and 451 and between 1517 and 1648 especially involve the problem of polemics. Calvin developed his system of theology in an attempt to provide a scriptural theology that would avoid the errors of Romanism.

6. Still another branch of our study may be called *praxis*. It is the consideration of the practical outworking in life of the Christian faith. The home life, charitable work, and influence of Christianity on the life of the day are parts of this branch of church history, which involves the lifestyle of the church.

7. Christianity could not continue to grow unless it gave attention to the problem of *presentation* of truth. Presentation involves study of the educational system of the church, its hymnology, liturgy, architecture, art, and preaching.

These branches will be discussed in the eras in which each is most important, but not all will be developed in detail in every one of the periods. Each can be the center of fascinating studies that the individual can carry on for himself once he has the necessary general background.

B. Periods of Church History

The student must remember that history is "a seamless garment." By this Maitland meant that history is a continuous stream of events within the framework of time and space. For that reason periodization of church history is merely an artificial device to cut the data of history into easily handled segments and to aid the student in remembering the essential facts. The people of the Roman Empire did not go to sleep one night in the ancient era and wake up the next morning in the Middle Ages. There is instead a gradual transition from a view of life and human activity that characterizes one era of history to a view that characterizes another. Because the division of history into periods does aid the memory, does help one to deal with one segment at a time, and does present the view of life in that period, it is worthwhile to organize history chronologically.

ANCIENT CHURCH HISTORY, 5 B.C. –A.D. 590

The first period of church history reveals the growth of the apostolic church into the Old Catholic Imperial church and the beginning of the Roman Catholic system. The center of activity was the Mediterranean basin, which includes parts of Asia, Africa, and Europe. The church operated within the cultural environment of Greco-Roman civilization and the political environment of the Roman Empire.

The Spread of Christianity in the Empire to 100

In this section attention is given to the environment in which Christianity emerged. The foundation of the church in Christ's life, death, and resurrection and its founding among the Jews is important to an understanding of the genesis of Christianity. The gradual growth of Christianity within the swaddling bands of Judaism and the bursting of those bands at the Council of Jerusalem preceded the carrying of the gospel to the Gentiles by Paul and others and the emergence of Christianity as a sect distinct from Judaism. Attention is also called to the leading role of the apostles in this period.

The Struggle of the Old Catholic Imperial Church for Survival, 100–313

In this period the church was concerned with continued existence in the face of opposition from without —persecution by the Roman state. Martyrs and apologists were the answer of the church to this *external* problem. The church also had to deal with the *internal* problem of heresy at the same time, and the polemical writers of the church provided the answers to heresy.

The Supremacy of the Old Catholic Imperial Church, 313–590

The church faced the problems that arose out of its reconciliation with the state under Constantine and its union with the state in the time of Theodosius. Soon it was dominated by the state. The Roman emperors demanded a unified dogma in order to have a unified state to save Greco-Roman culture. But the Christians had not had time to work out a body of dogma in the period of the persecution. There followed then a long period of creedal controversy. The writings of the more scientifically minded Greek and Latin church fathers were a natural outcome of the theological disputes. Monasticism arose, partly as a reaction from and partly as a protest against, the increasing worldliness of the organized church. During this period of institutional development, the office of bishop was strengthened and the Roman bishop grew in power. As the period ended, the Old Catholic Imperial church virtually became the Roman Catholic church.

Medieval Church History, 590–1517

The scene of action moved from southern Europe to northern and western Europe—the Atlantic seaboard. The medieval church sought to win the migrating hordes of Teutonic tribes to Christianity and to integrate Greco-Roman culture and Christianity with Teutonic institutions. In so doing, the medieval church still further centralized its organization under papal supremacy and developed the sacramental-hierarchical system characteristic of the Roman Catholic church.

The Rise of the Empire and Latin-Teutonic Christianity, 590–800

Gregory I worked hard at the task of evangelizing the hordes of Teutonic invaders within the Roman Empire. The Eastern church in this period faced the threat of Islam, a rival religion that took away much of its territory in Asia and Africa. Gradually the alliance between the pope and the Teutons took place in the organization of the Teutonic successor to the old Roman Empire, the Carolingian Empire of Charlemagne. This was a period of heavy losses.

Ebb and Flow in Relationships Between Church and State, 800–1054

The first great schism within the church occurred during this period. The Greek Orthodox church after 1054 went its own way with the static theology created by John of Damascus in the eighth century. The Western church during this time became feudalized and tried without much success to work out a policy of relations between the Roman church and the state acceptable to the pope and the emperor. At the same time the Cluniac reformers aimed at the correction of evils within the Roman church.

The Supremacy of the Papacy, 1054–1305

The medieval Roman Catholic church reached the peak of its power under the leadership of Gregory VII (Hildebrand) and Innocent III and successfully enforced its claims to supremacy over the state by the humiliation of the most powerful sovereigns of Europe. The Crusades brought prestige to the pope; monks and friars spread the Roman Catholic faith and reclaimed dissenters. The Greek learning of Aristotle, brought to Europe by the Arabs of Spain, was integrated with Christianity by Thomas Aquinas in an intellectual cathedral

that has become the authoritative expression of Roman Catholic theology. The Gothic cathedral expressed the supernatural, otherworldly outlook of the era and provided a "Bible in stone" for the faithful. The Roman Catholic church was to tumble from this peak of power in the next era.

Medieval Sunset and Modern Sunrise, 1305–1517

Internal attempts to reform a corrupt papacy were made by mystics, who sought to personalize a religion too institutionalized. Attempts at reform were also made by early Reformers, such as the mystics John Wycliffe and John Hus, reform councils, and biblical humanists. An expanding geographical world, a new secular intellectual outlook in the Renaissance, the rising nation-states, and an emerging middle class were *external* forces that would not long brook a decadent and corrupt church. The refusal by the Roman Catholic church to accept internal reform made the Reformation a probability.

Modern Church History, 1517 and After

This era was ushered in by schisms that resulted in the origin of the Protestant state-churches and the world-wide spread of the Christian faith by the great missionary wave of the nineteenth century. The scene of action was no longer the Mediterranean Sea or the Atlantic Ocean but the world. Christianity became a universal and global religion.

Reformation and Counter Reformation, 1517–1648

The forces of revolt held back by the Roman church in the previous period

CHRONOLOGY OF CHURCH HISTORY

ca.30	Pentecost—Founding of Church
49 or 50	Jerusalem Council
64	Neronian Persecution
ca. 200	The Catholic Church
313	Edict of Milan
325	Council of Nicaea (Nicene Creed)
381	Christianity State Religion of the Empire
445	Valentinian's Edict
451	Council of Chalcedon
ca. 529	Benedictine Rule, Founding of Monte Cassino
590	Gregory I
597	Augustine Converts English
622	Islam, Christianity's New Foe, Appears
663	Synod of Whitby—England Under Papacy
ca. 750	Donation of Constantine
754	Beginning of Papal States by Donation of Pepin
800	Charlemagne's Roman Empire
962	Holy Roman Empire (Till 1806)
ca. 988	Russia Accepts Orthodox Christianity
1054	Schism—Orthodox Churches
1059	College of Cardinals—to Elect Pope
ca. 1095	Crusades and Scholasticism Begin
1215	Transubstantiation
1210–16	Franciscans and Dominicans
1309–77	Babylonian Captivity at Avignon
1378	Great Schism to 1417
1409	Reform Councils
1449	
1453	Fall of Constantinople
1516	Erasmus's Printed Greek New Testament
1517	Ninety-five Theses
1521	Melanchthon's *Loci Communes* and Diet of Worms

Ecumenical Councils and Theological Controversy *(bracketing entries 325–451)*

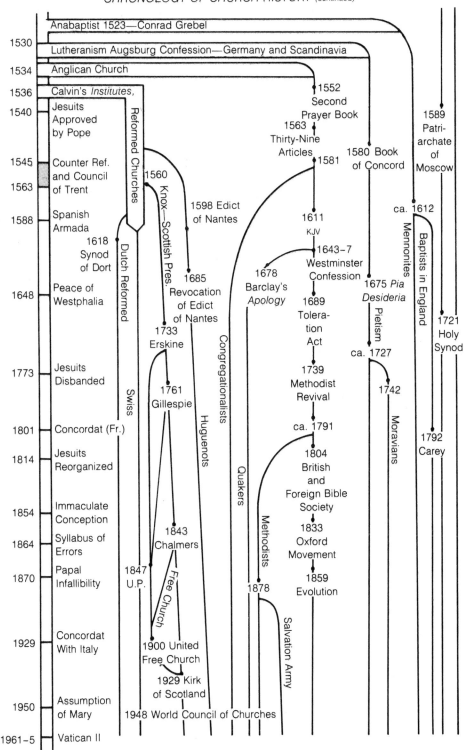

Anabaptist 1523—Conrad Grebel

1530 Lutheranism Augsburg Confession—Germany and Scandinavia

1534 Anglican Church

1536 Calvin's *Institutes,*

1540 Jesuits Approved by Pope

Reformed Churches

1545 Counter Ref. and Council
1563 of Trent

1560 Knox—Scottish Pres.

1588 Spanish Armada

1618 Synod of Dort

Dutch Reformed

1598 Edict of Nantes

1685 Revocation of Edict of Nantes

1648 Peace of Westphalia

1733 Erskine

Swiss

1761 Gillespie

Huguenots

1773 Jesuits Disbanded

1801 Concordat (Fr.)

1814 Jesuits Reorganized

Congregationalists

1843 Chalmers

1854 Immaculate Conception

1864 Syllabus of Errors

1870 Papal Infallibility

1847 U.P.

Free Church

Quakers

1929 Concordat With Italy

1900 United Free Church

1929 Kirk of Scotland

1950 Assumption of Mary

1948 World Council of Churches

1961–5 Vatican II

1552 Second Prayer Book

1563 Thirty-Nine Articles

1581

1580 Book of Concord

1589 Patri- archate of Moscow

ca. 1612

1611 KJV

1643–7 Westminster Confession

1678 Barclay's *Apology*

1689 Tolera- tion Act

1675 *Pia Desideria*

Mennonites

Baptists in England

Pietism

1739 Methodist Revival

ca. 1727

1742

ca. 1791

1721 Holy Synod

Moravians

1804 British and Foreign Bible Society

1833 Oxford Movement

1792 Carey

Methodists

1859 Evolution

1878

Salvation Army

broke forth in this period, and new national and free Protestant churches emerged—Lutheran, Anglican, Calvinist, and Anabaptist. As a result, the papacy was forced to consider reformation. In the Counter Reformation movements of the Council of Trent, the Jesuits, and the Inquisition, the papacy was able to halt the spread of Protestantism in Europe and make gains in Central and South America, in the Philippines, and in Vietnam and experience renewal. Only after the Treaty of Westphalia (1648) ended the bitter Thirty Years' War did the two movements settle down to consolidate their gains.

Rationalism, Revivalism, and Denominationalism, 1648–1789

During this period the Calvinist views of the Reformation were brought to North America by the Puritans. England passed on to the Continent a rationalism that had its religious expression in Deism. On the other hand, Pietism on the Continent proved to be the answer to cold orthodoxy. It expressed itself in England in the Quaker and Wesleyan movements.

Revivalism, Missions, and Modernism, 1789–1914

During the early part of the nineteenth century there was a revival of Catholicism. This was matched by a Protestant revival that created a surge of missionary endeavor abroad and that brought social reform at home in European countries. Later in the period the eroding forces of rationalism and evolution led to a "break with the Bible" that expressed itself in religious liberalism.

Church and Society in Tension Since 1914

The church in much of the world faces the problem of the secular and often totalitarian state. The sentimental modernism of the early twentieth century has given way to neoorthodoxy and its successors. The movement toward reunion of the churches continues. A rising evangelical tide is emerging.

It will be helpful to learn and periodically review these basic divisions of church history. The chronological chart is a helpful device to relate the events, persons, and movements to one another.

SUGGESTED READING

This reading list is confined to the more general literature of church history that should be available to the teacher or student of church history who desires to have the basic works in the field.

A. Church History Bibliography

American Historical Association. **Guide to Historical Literature.** *New York: Macmillan, 1961. This is a selected, classified, and critical bibliography which has a useful section that deals with church history.*

Case, Shirley J., ed. **A Bibliographical Guide to the History of Christianity.** *Chicago: University of Chicago Press, 1931. This is the most inclusive bibliography for the average student of church history. It should be supplemented by relevant bibliographical articles in the periodical* **Church History** *for books published since 1931.*

B. General Source Collections

Ayers, David, and Fisher, R. S. T. Records of Christianity. *New York: Barnes and Noble, 1971–. This series gives firsthand knowledge of the past.*

Baillie, John; McNeill, John T.; and Van Dusen, H. P., eds. The Library of Christian Classics. *26 vols. Philadelphia: Westminster, 1953–69. This series contains the major theological treatises from the early church fathers through the Reformation.*

Baldwin, Marshall W. Christianity Through the Thirteenth Century. *New York: Harper, 1970. This is an excellent collection of significant documents to 1300.*

Barry, Colman J. Readings in Church History. *3 vols. Westminster, Md.: Newman, 1965. This series has the documents from the apostolic times to the present that are important to Roman Catholics.*

Bettenson, Henry, ed. Documents of the Christian Church. *2nd ed. New York: Oxford University Press, 1963. This book is the best single-volume collection of primary materials. It includes an excellent selection of documents for the period up to the Reformation, but it shows a preference for the documents of Anglican church history from then to the present. This little work makes an excellent supplementary volume to be used with a regular text.*

Defarrari, Roy J., ed. The Fathers of the Church. *60 vols. Washington: Catholic University of America Press, 1947–. This will take its place beside the Schaff series when completed.*

Kidd, Beresford J. Documents Illustrative of the History of the Church. *3 vols. London: SPCK, 1920–41. This work contains more documents than Bettenson's, but it ends at 1500.*

Leith, John H., ed. Creeds of the Churches. *Rev. ed. Richmond, Va.: John Knox, 1973. This book includes important doctrinal sources and creeds.*

Petry, Ray C., and Manschreck, Clyde L., eds. A History of Christianity. *2 vols. Englewood Cliffs, N.J.: Prentice-Hall, 1964. Each volume includes useful historical introductions, important documents, bibliography, and chronology in each chapter.*

Roberts, Alexander, and Donaldson, James, eds. The Ante-Nicene Fathers. *10 vols. Grand Rapids: Eerdmans, 1951.*

Schaff, Philip. Creeds of Christendom. *3 vols. 6th ed. New York: Scribner, 1890. This is an excellent study of the creeds and confessions of the church. Volume 1 deals with the history of creeds; volume 2 gives the ecumenical, Roman Catholic, and Greek Orthodox creeds; volume 3 consists of the Protestant creeds and confessions.*

_____, ed. A Select Library of the Nicene and Post-Nicene Fathers of the Church: First Series. *14 vols. Buffalo: Christian Literature, 1886–90. This is a somewhat old but still useful collection of the writings of the church fathers.*

_____, and Wace, Henry, eds. A Select Library of Nicene and Post-Nicene Fathers of the Christian Church: Second Series. *14 vols. Buffalo: Christian Literature, 1890–1900.*

Stevenson, A. J., ed. A New Eusebius. *New York: Macmillan, 1957. This and the following work have partially replaced Kidd's series.*

_____. Creeds, Councils, and Controversies. *New York: Seabury, 1966.*

C. History of Church History

Barnes, Harry E. A History of Historical Writings. *Norman Okla.: University of Oklahoma Press, 1937. This book includes good evaluations of the various writers of church history.*

Cairns, Earle E. God and Man in Time. *Grand Rapids: Baker, 1979. This is an introduction to historiography with much material useful to the student of church history.*

Foakes-Jackson, Frederick J. **A History of Church History.** *Cambridge, England: Heffer, 1939. This is a treatment of church historians from Philo to Bede.*

Guilday, Peter, ed. **Church Historians.** *New York: Kennedy, 1926. This work has some good essays by Roman Catholic writers concerning church historians who may be classed as writers of source works.*

Jedin, Hubert, and Dolan, John, eds. **The Handbook of Church History.** *New York: Herder, 1965. An excellent section on the historiography of church history is found in pages 1–56.*

D. Periodicals

American Catholic Historical Association. **The Catholic Historical Review.** *Washington: Catholic University of America Press, 1915–. This official organ gives the results of the work of Roman Catholic church historians.*

American Society of Church History. **Church History.** *Chicago: American Society of Church History, 1932–. The files of this publication are rich with bibliographical and special topical articles of value to the teacher of church history.*

E. Encyclopedias and Dictionaries

Brauer, Jerald, ed. **The Westminster Dictionary of the Christian Church.** *Philadelphia: Westminster, 1971. This work is weak on data concerning evangelicals.*

Cross, Frank L., and Livingstone, E. A., eds. **The Oxford Dictionary of the Christian Church.** *2nd ed. London: Oxford University Press, 1974. This volume has good bibliographies but is more oriented to the English and European churches.*

Douglas, James, ed. **The New International Dictionary of the Christian Church.** *Rev. ed. Grand Rapids: Zondervan, 1978. This work gives adequate attention to evangelicalism in modern times.*

Eggenberger, David, ed. **The New Catholic Encyclopedia.** *16 vols. Washington, D.C.: Catholic University of America Press, 1967–74. This is most useful for the Roman Catholic viewpoint.*

Hastings, James, ed. **Encyclopedia of Religion and Ethics.** *13 vols. New York: Scribner, 1908–26.*

Moyer, Elgin S. and Cairns, Earle E. **Wycliffe Biographical Dictionary of the Church.** *Rev. and enl. ed. Chicago: Moody, 1982.*

Wace, Henry, and Piercy, William C., eds. **A Dictionary of Christian Biography and Literature.** *London: Murray, 1911.*

F. Atlases

Anderson, Charles. **Augsburg Historical Atlas.** *Minneapolis: Augsburg, 1967. This work contains clear maps and interpretative text for the Medieval and Reformation eras.*

Gaustad, Edwin S. **Historical Atlas of Religion in America.** *Rev. ed. New York: Harper, 1976. The fine maps, pie and bar diagrams, statistics, and interpretative text make this a very useful volume.*

Jedin, Hubert; Latourette, Kenneth S.; and Martin, J. **Atlas Zur Kirchengeschichte.** *Freiburg: Herder, 1970. This is helpful for those who read German.*

Littel, Franklin H. **The Macmillan Atlas History of Christianity.** *New York: Macmillan, 1976, Clear maps with helpful legends, pictures, and explanatory text mark this work.*

Shepherd, William R. **Historical Atlas.** *8th ed. New York: Barnes and Noble, 1956. This is probably the best general historical atlas relative to church history.*

G. Outlines of Church History

Cameron, Richard M. Outlines of the Early and Medieval History of the Christian Church. Boston: published privately, 1943.

_____. Outlines of the Reformation and Modern History of the Christian Church. Boston: published privately, 1943. *Cameron's outlines contain fine bibliographies and organize church history chronologically and topically with references to relevant pages in the best texts. They are especially useful to the teacher.*

McGlothin, William J. A Guide to the Study of Church History. New York: Doran, 1914.

H. Church History Texts

Bainton, Roland H. Christendom: A Short History of Christianity and Its Impact on Western Civilization. Rev. ed. New York: Harper, n.d.

Broadbent, E. H. The Pilgrim Church. London: Pickering and Inglis, 1931. *The author traced through history those groups that he felt followed the New Testament pattern, but he overlooked the fact that some of the groups were heretical on some accounts.*

Bruce, F. F., ed. The Advance of Christianity Through the Centuries. 8 vols. Grand Rapids: Eerdmans, 1958–68. *This is a scholarly series done by evangelical scholars.*

Chadwick, Owen, gen. ed. History of the Christian Church. 6 vols. Harmondsworth, Middlesex: Penguin, 1960–70 (distributed in the United States by Eerdmans). *Students will find this to be a scholarly series with helpful insights.*

Clarke, C. P. S. A Short History of the Christian Church. London: Longmans, 1929. *This work presents church history from the Anglican viewpoint.*

Daniel-Rops, Henri. The History of the Christian Church. 10 vols. New York: Dutton, 1957–67. *This series provides a recent, occasionally inaccurate survey of church history from a Roman Catholic viewpoint.*

Dolan, John P. Catholicism. Woodbury, N.Y.: Barron's Educational Series, 1968. *This Roman Catholic scholar has surveyed the rise and development of the Roman Catholic church with relevant sources.*

Dowley, Tim, ed. Eerdmans' Handbook to the History of Christianity. Grand Rapids: Eerdmans, 1977. *Church history and a church dictionary are combined; and there are excellent illustrations in color, good maps, and time charts, but a bibliography is lacking.*

Fisher, George P. History of the Christian Church. New York: Scribner, 1887. *This well-organized volume has long been a favorite of many teachers, but, of course, it has none of the history of the church in the twentieth century.*

Jacobs, Charles M. The Story of the Church. Rev. ed. Philadelphia: Muhlenberg, 1947. *This is little more than an outline, but it would be most useful to a Lutheran layman seeking information on the growth of his church.*

Johnson, Paul. A History of Christianity. New York: Atheneum, 1977. *This is a church history survey with stress on the role of the Roman Catholic church from a liberal viewpoint but with much illustrative detail.*

Kromminga, D. H. A History of the Christian Church. Grand Rapids: Eerdmans, 1945. *The book is designed primarily for high-school students, but it has some useful syntheses of ideas.*

Latourette, Kenneth S. A History of Christianity. New York: Harper, 1953. *This is a detailed, one-volume general church history by an eminent scholar, with selected, critical bibliographies of value to the teacher.*

_____. A History of the Expansion of Christianity. 7 vols. Grand Rapids: Zondervan, 1970. *This work goes into greater detail than the preceding.*

_____. Christianity in a Revolutionary Age. 5 vols. Grand Rapids: Zondervan, 1969.

Manschreck, Clyde L. **A History of Christianity in the World.** *Englewood Cliffs, N.J.: Prentice-Hall, 1974. The author discusses the events and men of church history with considerable reference to theological thought.*

Meyer, Carl S. **Church History From Pentecost to the Present.** *Chicago: Moody, 1970. This is a useful, basic text.*

Nagler, Arthur W. **The Church in History.** *New York: Abingdon, 1929. This book reflects a liberal Methodist viewpoint, but it has a fine general chronological treatment of church history. Following this, there are several chapters that trace specific topics.*

Newman, Albert H. **A Manual of Church History.** *2 vols. Rev. ed. Chicago: American Baptist Publication Society, 1931–33. The author sets forth the Baptist viewpoint clearly, but he devotes too much of the first volume to the apostolic period. This somewhat mars the balanced treatment.*

Nichols, Robert H. **The Growth of the Christian Church.** *Philadelphia: Westminster, 1930. Church history is treated from the Presbyterian viewpoint, though somewhat sketchy in places.*

Pope, Edward M. **The Church and Its Culture.** *St. Louis: Bethany, 1965. The author gives many interesting insights as he relates the church to its culture.*

Qualben, Lars P. **A History of the Christian Church.** *New York: Nelson, 1933. The Lutheran approach to church history is emphasized. While the organization is not always clear, the book has many excellent features, such as bibliographies at the end of each chapter, helpful maps, and many excellent charts and graphs. The treatment also gives full attention to the biblical viewpoint.*

Rowe, Henry K. **History of the Christian People.** *New York: Macmillan, 1931. The liberal point of view is followed, but the book is useful for the excellent background material it presents.*

Schaff, Philip. **History of the Christian Church.** *8 vols. Reprint. Grand Rapids: Eerdmans, 1960. This is the work of the acknowledged dean of American church historians of the past and present generations. It is an interesting and accurate portrayal of the drama of church history to the end of the Reformation. The reprinting of this work is a real service to church historians.*

Sweet, William W. **Makers of Christianity.** *3 vols. New York: Henry Holt, 1934–37. Short biographical sketches of Europeans important in church history are found in volumes 1 and 2 and, of Americans, in volume 3.*

Walker, Williston. **A History of the Christian Church.** *3rd ed. New York: Scribner, 1970. This book has been revised by three professors of Union Theological Seminary, New York. Though it is not conservative in interpretation, it has an excellent presentation of the basic factual material of church history.*

I. History of Doctrine

Gonzalez, Justo. **The History of Christian Thought.** *3 vols. Nashville: Abingdon, 1975.*

Kerr. Hugh T., ed. **Readings in Christian Thought.** *Nashville: Abingdon, 1966. This work has brief introductions and the significant part of each source for theology from Justin Martyr to John XXIII.*

Neve, Juergen L., and Heick, Otto W. **A History of Christian Thought.** *Rev. ed. 2 vols. Philadelphia: Fortress, 1965–66. This is a most useful treatment of the history of doctrine, although it is primarily from the Lutheran viewpoint. There are several older works, such as those by G. P. Fisher, A. Harnack, C. Sheldon, and especially the fine work by Reinhold Seeberg.*

Pelikan, Jaroslav. **The Christian Tradition: A History of the Development of Doctrine.** *Chicago: University of Chicago Press, 1971–.*

J. History of Missions

Glover, Robert. The Progress of Worldwide Missions. *Rev. and enl. ed. by J. Herbert Kane. New York: Harper, 1960. This is an excellent manual to supplement the brief treatment that missionary history is given in a church history text.*

Kane, J. Herbert. A Global View of Missions. *Grand Rapids: Eerdmans, 1971. This supplements Glover's book. It surveys missions to 1800 and gives extended treatment to the era since 1800.*

Latourette, Kenneth S. A History of the Expansion of Christianity. *7 vols. New York: Harper, 1937–45. This is the most inclusive history of missions available and is written by an acknowledged authority in the field.*

Neill, Stephen S. Christian Missions. *Baltimore: Penguin, 1964. This is a helpful volume for the student of missions.*

Thiessen, John C. A Survey of World Missions. *3rd ed. Chicago: Moody, 1961.*

K. Christian Literature

Hurst, George I. An Outline of the History of Christian Literature. *New York: Macmillan, 1926. This work contains listings of the important writings of the great figures of the church with a statement concerning the nature of each writing.*

L. Christian Art and Architecture

Gardner, Helen. Art Through the Ages. *Rev. ed. New York: Harcourt, Brace, 1959. This useful volume will help the layman understand the development of Christian art and architecture in the various periods.*

This general list, which is selective and critical, is supplemented by the citation of primary and secondary works at the end of each chapter. The student will find much pleasure and profit in the use of the source works cited.

ANCIENT CHURCH HISTORY, 5 B.C.–A.D. 590

THE SPREAD OF CHRISTIANITY IN THE EMPIRE TO 100

THE STRUGGLE OF THE OLD CATHOLIC IMPERIAL CHURCH
FOR SURVIVAL, 100–313

THE SUPREMACY OF THE OLD CATHOLIC IMPERIAL CHURCH,
313–590

Chapter 1

The Fullness of the Time

In Galatians 4:4, Paul called attention to the historical era of providential preparation that preceded the coming of Christ to earth in human form: "When the fulness of the time was come, God sent forth his Son." Mark also emphasized the coming of Christ when all was made ready on earth (Mark 1:15).[1] Consideration of the events that preceded the appearance of Christ on earth lead the sober student of history to acknowledge the truth of the statements of Paul and Mark.

In most discussions of this subject it has been forgotten that not only the Jew but also the Greek and the Roman contributed to the religious preparation for the appearance of Christ. Greek and Roman contributions aided in bringing historical development to the point where Christ could make the maximum impact on history in a way not possible before or since the time of His birth. Let us consider these various contributions.

I. THE ENVIRONMENT

A. Political Contributions of Romans

The political contribution to history preceding the coming of Christ was primarily the work of the Romans. This people—who followed the way of idolatry, mystery religions, and emperor worship—were used by God, of whom they were ignorant, to bring about the fulfillment of His will.

1. The Romans, as no other people up to their time, developed a sense of the unity of mankind under a universal law. This sense of the solidarity of man within the empire created an environment favorable to the reception of a gospel that proclaimed the unity of the human race in the fact that all men are under the penalty of sin and in the fact that all are offered a salvation that makes them a part of a universal organism, the Christian church, Christ's body.

No empire of the ancient Near East, not even that of Alexander, had succeeded in bringing to men a sense of their unity in a political organization. Political unity was to be the peculiar task of Rome. The application of the Roman law to citizens in all parts of the empire was daily pressed upon the Romans and the subjects of the empire by the impartial justice of Roman courts. This Roman law grew out of the customary law of the early monarchy. During the early republic, in the fifth century before Christ, this law was codified in the Twelve Tables, which became an essential part of the education of every Roman boy. The realization that great principles of Roman law were also a part of the laws of all the nations of men grew upon the Romans as the *praetor peregrinus*, who was charged with the task of dealing with court cases in which foreigners were involved, became acquainted with the national legal systems of these foreigners. Thus the code of the Twelve Tables, based on Roman custom, was enriched by the laws of other nations. Philosophically inclined Romans explained these similarities by borrowing the Greek concept of a universal law whose principles were written into man's nature and could be discovered by rational processes.

A further step in the fostering of the idea of unity was the granting of Roman citizenship to non-Romans. This process was started in the period preceding the birth of Christ and was completed when Caracalla in 212 admitted all freemen in the Roman Empire to Roman citizenship. Because the Roman Empire included all the Mediterranean world that counted in the history of that day, for all practical purposes, all men were under one system of law and citizens of one kingdom.

Roman law, with its emphasis on the dignity of the individual and his right to justice and Roman citizenship, and with its tendency to fuse men of different races into one political organization, anticipated a gospel that proclaimed the unity of the race both in setting forth the penalty for sin and the Savior from sin. Paul reminded the people of the Philippian church that they were members of a heavenly commonwealth (Phil. 3:20).

2. Free movement about the Mediterranean world would have been most difficult for the messengers of the gospel before the reign of Augustus Caesar (27 B.C.–A.D. 14). The division of the ancient world into small jealous units, city states or tribes, hindered travel and the spread of ideas. With the extension of Roman imperial power during the period of empire building, a period of peaceful development occurred in the countries surrounding the Mediterranean. Pompey had swept the pirates from the Mediterranean, and Roman soldiers kept the peace on the roads of Asia, Africa, and Europe. This relatively peaceful world made it easy for the early Christians to move from place to place so that they could preach the gospel to all men everywhere.

3. The Romans developed an excellent system of roads radiating out from the golden milestone in the Roman forum to all parts of the empire. The main roads were built of concrete to serve for ages. They went straight over hill and dale to the farthest point of the empire. A study of the journeys of Paul indicates that he made great use of the excellent road system to get from strategic center to strategic center of the Roman Empire. Roman roads and strategic cities located on these roads were an indispensable aid in the realization of Paul's mission.

4. The role of the Roman army in the development of the ideal of a universal organization and in the spread of the gospel should not be ignored. The Romans adopted the custom of using provincials in the army as the supply of Roman citizens declined because of war and easy living. These provincials were brought into contact with Roman culture and helped to spread its ideas throughout the ancient world. Moreover, some of these men became converts to Christianity and spread the gospel to areas where they were assigned for military duty. It is probable that the earliest introduction of Christianity to Britain was a result of the efforts of Christian soldiers who were stationed there.

5. Roman conquests led to a loss of belief by many peoples in their gods because the gods had not been able to keep them from defeat by the Romans. Such people were left with a spiritual vacuum that could not be filled satisfactorily by the religions of the day.

In addition, the substitutes that Rome had to offer for the lost religions could do no more than make people realize their need of a more spiritual religion. The cult of Roman emperor worship, which made its appearance early in the Christian Era, made an appeal to people only as a means of making the concept of the Roman Empire tangible.

The various mystery religions seemed to offer more than this in the way of spiritual and emotional aid, and in them Christianity was to find its greatest rival. The worship of Cybele, the great earth mother, was brought to Rome from Phrygia. The worship of this goddess of fertility had in it rites, such as the drama of the death and resurrection of Cybele's consort, Attis, that seemed to meet the emotional needs of people. The worship of Isis, imported from Egypt, was similar to that of Cybele, with its emphasis on death and resurrection. Mithraism, an import from Persia, made a special appeal to the soldiers of the Roman Empire. It had a December festival, an evil one, a miraculously born savior —Mithra, a savior-god—and chapels and worship.

All these religions emphasized the savior-god. The worship of Cybele called for the sacrifice of a bull and the baptism of worshipers with the bull's blood. Mithraism involved, among other things, sacrificial meals. Because of the influence of these religions, there seemed little odd in the demands of Christianity upon the individual. When many found that the bloody sacrifices of these religions could do nothing for them, they were led by the Holy Spirit to accept the reality offered to them in Christianity.[2]

Consideration of such factors as those that have been discussed leads one to the conclusion that the Roman Empire provided a political environment favorable to the spread of Christianity in the days of its infancy. Even the church of the Middle Ages was never able to rid itself of the glory of imperial Rome and sought to perpetuate its ideals in an ecclesiastical system.

B. Intellectual Contributions of Greeks

Great as the preparation by Rome for the coming of Christianity was, it was overshadowed by the intellectual environment that the Greek mind

Mithraism spread from Persia to Rome. Here Mithra, the god of light and fire, is shown sacrificing a bull. The scorpion at the testicles and the serpent and dog ready to lap up the blood probably symbolize fertility and rejuvenation. The cult was especially popular among Roman soldiers.

provided. The city of Rome may be associated with Christianity's political environment, but it was Athens that helped to provide an intellectual environment that aided the propagation of the gospel. The Romans may have been the political conquerors of the Greeks, but, as Horace indicated in his poetry, the Greeks conquered the Romans culturally. The practical Romans may have built good roads, mighty bridges, and fine public buildings, but the Greeks reared lofty edifices of the mind. Under Greek influence the plain rural culture of the early republic gave

way to the intellectual culture of the empire.

1. The universal gospel was in need of a universal language if it was to make maximum impact on the world. Just as English has become the universal language in the modern world and just as Latin was such in the medieval scholarly world, so Greek had become the universal tongue in the ancient world. By the time the Roman Empire appeared, most cultured Romans knew both Greek and Latin.

The process by which Greek became the vernacular of the world is of interest. The Attic dialect used by the Athenians came into wide usage in the fifth century B.C. with the growth of the Athenian Empire. Even though the empire was destroyed by the end of the fifth century, the dialect of Athens, which was that of classical Greek literature, became the language that Alexander, his soldiers, and the merchants of the Hellenistic world between 338 and 146 B.C. modified, enriched, and spread throughout the Mediterranean world.

It was this dialect of the common man, known as Koine and differing from classical Greek, through which Christians were able to make contact with the peoples of the ancient world and in which they were to write their New Testament and the Jews of Alexandria were to write their Old Testament, the Septuagint. Not until recently was it known that the Greek of the New Testament was the Greek of the common man of Christ's day, because of the marked difference between it and the Greek of the classics. One German theologian even went so far as to say that the Greek of the New Testament was a special Greek given by the Holy Spirit for the writing of the New Testament. Adolf Deissman made the discovery near the end of the last century that the Greek of the New Testament was the same Greek used by the ordinary man of the first century in the papyri records of his business and the documents essential to his daily life. Since that time such scholars as Moulton and Milligan have put Deissman's discovery on a sound scientific foundation by comparative study of the vocabulary of the papyri and that of the New Testament. This discovery has fostered the rise of numerous modern speech translations. If the gospel was written in the tongue of the common man in the period of its inception, the translators reason, it should be put in the vernacular of the common man of our day.

2. Greek philosophy prepared for the coming of Christianity by destroying the older religions. Whoever came to know its tenets, whether Greek or Roman, soon found that this intellectual discipline made his polytheistic religion so rationally unintelligible that he turned away from it to philosophy. But philosophy failed to satisfy his spiritual needs; so he either became a skeptic or sought comfort in the mystery religions of the Roman Empire. At the time of Christ's advent, philosophy had declined from the peak reached by Plato to a system of self-centered individualistic thought such as Stoicism or Epicureanism. Moreover, philosophy could only seek for God and posit Him as an intellectual abstraction; it could never reveal a personal God of love. This bankruptcy of philosophy by the time of the coming of Christ disposed men's minds toward a more spiritual approach to life. Christianity alone was capable of filling the vacuum in the spiritual life of the day.

Another way in which the great Greek philosophers served Christianity was to call the attention of the Greeks of their day to a reality that transcended the temporal and relative world in which they lived. Both Socrates and Plato in the fifth century B.C. taught that this present temporal world of the senses is but a shadow of the real world in which the highest ideals are such intellectual abstractions as the good, the beautiful, and the true. They insisted that reality was not temporal and material but spiritual and eternal. Their search for truth never led them to a personal God, but it demonstrated the best that man can do in seeking God through the intellect. Christianity offered to those who accepted Socrates' and Plato's philosophy the historical revelation of the good, the beautiful, and the true in the person of the God-man, Christ. Greeks also held to the immortality of the soul but had no place for a physical resurrection of the body.

Greek literature and history also convince the reader that the Greeks were concerned about questions of right and wrong and man's eternal future. Aeschylus in his drama *Agamemnon* came close to the biblical dictum "Be sure your sin will find you out" (Num. 32:23) in his insistence that Agamemnon's troubles were the result of his wrongdoing. However, the Greek never saw sin as more than a mechanical and contractual matter. It was never seen as a personal failure that affronted God and injured others.

At the time when Christ came, people realized, as never before, the insufficiency of human reason and polytheism. The individualistic philosophies of Epicurus and Zeno and the mystery religions all testify to man's desire for a more personal relationship to God. Christianity came with the offer of this personal relationship and found that Greek culture, because of its own inadequacy, had created many hungry hearts.

3. The Greek people also contributed in a religious way to making the world ready to accept the new Christian religion when it appeared. The advent of materialistic Greek philosophy in the sixth century B.C. destroyed the faith of the Greek peoples in the old polytheistic worship that is described in Homer's *Illiad* and *Odyssey*. Although elements of this worship lived on in the mechanical state worship, it soon lost its vitality.

After this the people turned to philosophy; but it, too, soon lost its vigor. Philosophy became a system of pragmatic individualism under the successors of the Sophists or a system of subjective individualism, such as is seen in the teachings of Zeno the Stoic and Epicurus. Lucretius, the poetic exponent of Epicurus's philosophy, founded his teaching of disregard for the supernatural on a materialistic metaphysic that considered even the spirit of man as merely a finer type of atom. Stoicism did consider the supernatural, but its god was so closely identified with creation that it was pantheistic. While Stoicism taught the fatherhood of God and the brotherhood of man and held to a highly desirable code of ethics, it left man by rational processes to work out his own obedience to the natural laws that he was to discover with his unaided reason.

Both the Greek and Roman systems of philosophy and religion thus made a contribution to the coming of Christianity by destroying the old polytheistic religions and by showing the inability of human reason to reach God. The mystery religions, to which many turned, accustomed the people to think in terms of sin and redemption. Thus when Christianity appeared, people within the Roman Empire were more receptive to a religion that seemed to offer a spiritual approach to life.

II. RELIGIOUS CONTRIBUTIONS OF THE JEWS

Religious contributions to the "fulness of the time" include those of the Greek and Roman as well as those of the Jew. But however great may have been the contributions of Athens and Rome to Christianity by way of environment, the contributions of the Jew stand forth as the *heredity* of Christianity. Christianity may have developed in the political milieu of Rome and may have had to face the intellectual environment created by the Greek mind, but its relationship to Judaism was much more intimate. Judaism may be thought of as the stalk on which the rose of Christianity was to bloom.

The Jewish people, in contrast to the Greeks, did not seek to discover God by processes of human reason. They assumed His existence and readily granted to Him the worship that they felt was His due. They were influenced toward this course by the fact that God sought them and revealed Himself to them in history by His appearances to Abraham and the other great leaders of the race. Jerusalem became the symbol of a positive religious preparation for the coming of Christianity. Salvation was to be, indeed, "of the Jews," as Christ told the woman at the well (John 4:22). From this tiny captive nation, situated on the crossroads of Asia, Africa, and Europe, a Savior was to come. Judaism provided the heredity of Christianity and, for a time, even gave the infant religion shelter.

A. Monotheism

Judaism existed in striking contrast to the generality of pagan religions by its emphasis on a sound spiritual monotheism. Never again after the return from the Babylonian captivity did the Jews lapse into idolatry. The message of God through Moses to them was allegiance to the one true universal God of all the earth. The gods of the pagans were merely idols, which the Jewish prophets condemned in no uncertain terms. This lofty monotheism was spread by numerous synagogues scattered throughout the Mediterranean area during the three centuries preceding the coming of Christ.

B. Messianic Hope

The Jews offered to the world the hope of a coming Messiah who would bring righteousness to the earth. This messianic hope was in sharp contrast with the nationalistic aspiration that Virgil depicted in the poem in which he described an ideal Roman ruler who was to come—the son to be born to Augustus. The hope of a Messiah had been popularized in the Roman world by its steady proclamation by the Jews. Even the disciples after the death and resurrection of Christ were still looking for a messianic kingdom on earth (Acts 1:6). Certainly the wise men who appeared in Jerusalem shortly after the birth of Christ had gained some knowledge of this hope. The expectancy of many Christians today regarding the coming of Christ helps one to realize the atmosphere of expectancy in the Jewish world concerning the coming of the Messiah.

C. Ethical System

In the moral part of the Jewish law, Judaism also offered to the world the purest ethical system in existence. The high standard of the Ten Commandments was in sharp contrast with the prevailing ethical systems of the day and the still more corrupt practice of those moral systems by those who professed them. To the Jews sin was not the external, mechanical, contractual failure of the Greeks and Romans; but it was a violation of the known will of God, a violation that expressed itself in an impure heart and then in overt external acts of sin. This moral and spiritual approach of the Old Testament made for a doctrine of sin and redemption that really met the problem of sin. Salvation came from God and was not to be found in rationalistic systems of ethics or subjective mystery religions.

D. Old Testament Scriptures

The Jewish people still further prepared the way for the coming of Christianity by providing the infant church with its message, the Old Testament. Even a casual study of the New Testament will reveal Christ's and the apostles' deep indebtedness to the Old Testament and their reverence for it as the Word of God to man. Many Gentiles also read it and became familiar with the tenets of the Jewish faith. This fact is indicated by accounts of the numerous proselytes to Judaism. Many of these proselytes were able to move from Judaism to Christianity because of the Old Testament, the sacred Book of the newborn church. Many religions, Islam for example, look to their founder for their sacred book; but Christ left no sacred writings for the church. The books of the Old Testament and the books of the New Testament, given under the inspiration of the Holy Spirit, were to be the literature of the church.

E. Philosophy of History

The Jews made possible a philosophy of history by insisting that history had meaning. They opposed any view that made history a meaningless series of cycles or a mere process of linear evolution. They upheld a linear and cataclysmic view of history in which the Sovereign God who created history would triumph over man's failure in history to bring about a golden age.

F. The Synagogue

The Jews also provided an institution that was most useful in the rise and development of early Christianity. This institution was the Jewish synagogue. The Jews' enforced absence from the temple at Jerusalem during the Babylonian captivity gave rise to the synagogue, and it became an integral part of Jewish life. Through it Jews and also many Gentiles were made familiar with a higher approach to life. It was also the place to which Paul first went to preach in all the cities he reached in the course of his missionary journeys. It became the preaching house of early Christianity. Judaism was indeed the *paidagōgos* to lead men to Christ (Gal. 3:23–25).

The matters that have been discussed show how favored Christianity was, both as to time and region, in the period of its emergence. At no other time in the world's history before the coming of Christ was such a large region under one law and government. The Mediterranean world also had one culture, centering in Rome.

One universal language made it possible to give the gospel to most of the people of the empire in a tongue common to them and to the preacher. Palestine, the birthplace of the new religion, had a strategic location in this world. Paul was right in emphasizing that Christianity was not something "done in a corner" (Acts 26:26), because Palestine was an important crossroads linking the continents of Asia and Africa with Europe by a land route. Many of the most important battles of ancient history were fought for possession of this strategic area. In the period of Christianity's birth and during the first three centuries of its existence, conditions were more favorable for its spread throughout the Mediterranean world than at any other time in the ancient or medieval eras. Such is also the opinion of the world's leading scholar of missions.[3]

Through the contribution of the Greek and Roman environment and through the heritage of Judaism, the world was prepared for "the fulness of the time" when God sent forth His Son to bring redemption to a war-torn and sin-weary humanity. It is significant that of all the religions practiced in the Roman Empire at the time of Christ's birth, only Judaism and Christianity have been successful in surviving the changing course of human history.

SUGGESTED READING

Any standard edition of the Old Testament and the Apocrypha constitutes the main source material for Judaism. Titles marked with an asterisk cover the entire period of ancient church history.

Ayer, Joseph C., Jr. A Source Book for Ancient Church History. New York: Scribner, 1913. This work, which has an explanatory preface to each document, is particularly useful for the period between 100 and 590.

Boak, Arthur E.R., and Sinnigen, William G. A History of Rome to A.D. 565. 5th ed. New York: Macmillan, 1965.

Botsford, George W., and Robinson, Charles A. Hellenic History. 4th ed. New York: Macmillan, 1956. *This has authoritative information on most phases of Greek history.*

Breed, David. A History of the Preparation of the World for Christianity. 2nd ed. New York: Revell, 1893.

Bright, William. The Age of the Fathers. 2 vols. New York: Longmans, 1903. This has detailed, scholarly accounts of the era from 300 to 500.

Bruce, F. F. The Spreading Flame. Grand Rapids, Eerdmans, 1958. This surveys church history to 590.

Chadwick, Henry. The Early Church. Grand Rapids: Eerdmans, 1968. This is another useful survey of the period.

Clarke, C. P. S. Church History From Nero to Constantine. Milwaukee: Morehouse, 1920. This is a survey from the Anglican viewpoint.

Cochrane, Charles S. Christianity and Classical Culture. New York: Oxford University Press, 1944. The author has given an excellent interpretation of the intellectual struggle of Christianity with classicism.

Davies, John G. The Early Christian Church. New York: Doubleday, Anchor, 1967. This is a well-balanced, scholarly account based on sources, and it has helpful information on early Christian architecture.

*Duchesne, Louis. **Early History of the Christian Church.** 3 vols. London: Murray, 1909-24. The liberal Roman Catholic viewpoint is presented here.*

Finegan, Jack. **Light From the Ancient Past.** 2nd ed. Princeton: Princeton University Press, 1959. This work provides the archaeological background for Judaism and early Christianity.

*Foakes-Jackson, Frederick J. **The History of the Christian Church From the Earliest Times to A.D. 461.** 6th ed. Cambridge, Eng.: Deighton, Bell, 1947. The student will find this a useful volume for ancient church history.*

*Freemantle, Anne, ed. **A Treasury of Early Christianity.** New York: Viking, 1953. This edited work has sources to 500.*

Howe, George, and Harrer, Gustave A. **Greek Literature in Translation.** New York: Harper, 1924.

_____. **Roman Literature in Translation.** New York: Harper Brothers, 1924. This set contains excellent selections of source material relevant to the theme of the chapter.

*Kidd, Beresford J. **A History of the Christian Church to A.D. 461.** 3 vols. Oxford: Clarendon, 1922. The author gives full references to sources and detailed background material.*

*Lietzmann, Hans. **A History of the Early Church.** 4 vols. Translated by B. L. Woolf. New York: Scribner, 1938–50. This set can be consulted with profit for further details on certain points.*

*Schaff, Philip. **History of the Christian Church.** New York: Macmillan, 1913. This fine work can always be consulted with profit for the details of ancient church history.*

Schurer, Emil. **History of the Jewish People in the Time of Jesus Christ.** 2nd ed. 5 vols. New York: Scribner, 1891. This is an older standard work concerning the Jewish heredity of Christianity.

Scramuzza, Vincent M., and Mackendrick, Paul L. **The Ancient World.** New York: Holt, Rinehart, and Winston, 1958. This is an excellent survey that incorporates recent historical research.

*Stevenson, A. J., ed. **A New Eusebius.** New York: Macmillan, 1959. This work contains important documents based on Kidd's collection up to 337.*

*_____. **Creeds, Councils, and Controversies.** New York: Seabury, 1966. This extends the previous work to 461.*

*Stob, Ralph. **Christianity and Classical Civilization.** Grand Rapids: Eerdmans, 1950. This is an able presentation of the relationship between Christianity and its classical environment.*

Tenney, Merrill C. **New Testament Times.** Grand Rapids: Eerdmans, 1965. This work provides a helpful account of the intertestamental era and New Testament backgrounds.

*Van der Meer, F., and Mohrmann, Christine. **Atlas of the Early Christian World.** Translated and edited by Mary F. Hedlund and H. H. Rowley. New York: Nelson, 1958. This atlas contains excellent maps, relevant quotations from the sources, and superbly printed pictures that illustrate the history and environment of the church up to A.D. 600.*

*Wand, J. W. C. **A History of the Early Church to A.D. 590.** London: Methuen, 1949.*

Chapter 2

On This Rock

Christ is the Rock on which the church is founded. Through Him comes faith in God for salvation from sin; and from Him comes love to the human heart, which makes men view personality as sacred because God is the Creator of both man's physical and spiritual being and because He is the basis for hope concerning the future.

Luke (1:1–4) and John (20:30–31) in their Gospels revealed that Christianity is a historical religion and cannot exist apart from the Christ of history. Our calendar, the church itself, Sunday as a day of rest, and the remarkable changes in lives of followers of Christ are historical testimony to Christ in history.

I. THE HISTORICITY OF CHRIST

Christianity has its beginnings, from the subjective human side, in temporal history. Because these values are inextricably linked with the person, life, and death of Christ, some consideration must be given to the evidence for the historical existence of Christ.

Many have denied the fact that Christ was manifested in human history (John 1:14).[1] It is fortunate that there is extrabiblical historical evidence for the existence of Christ.

A. Pagan Testimony

Tacitus (55–117), the dean of Roman historians, linked the name and origin of Christians with "Christus," who in the reign of Tiberius "suffered death by the sentence of the Procurator, Pontius Pilate."[2]

Pliny, who was propraetor of Bithynia and Pontus in Asia Minor, wrote to Emperor Trajan about 112 for advice as to how he should deal with the Christians. His epistle gives valuable extrabiblical information concerning Christ. Pliny paid high tribute to the moral integrity of the Christians by writing of their unwillingness to commit theft or adultery, to falsify their word, or to repudiate a trust given to them. He went on to say that they "sing a song to Christ as to a God."[3]

According to Luke, John the Baptist began his ministry of preparing the way for Jesus in the fifteenth year of the reign of Tiberius Caesar. The Roman historian Tacitus placed the death of Jesus Christ in the reign of Tiberius. The coin portrayed above bears the likeness of this same Tiberius.

Suetonius, in his *Lives of the Twelve Caesars: Vita Claudius* (25.4), mentioned that the Jews were expelled from Rome because of disturbances over Chrestos (Christ).

Another rather satirical and, for that reason, valuable witness is Lucian (ca. 125–ca. 190), who in about 170 wrote a satire on Christians and their faith. Lucian described Christ as the one "who was crucified in Palestine" because He began "this new cult." He wrote that Christ had taught the Christians to believe that they were brothers and should observe His laws. He also ridiculed them for "worshipping that crucified sophist."[4]

These testimonies are highly valuable historical evidence, coming as they did from cultured Romans who despised the Christians and were hostile toward them. On the basis of these testimonies, apart from the Bible, which is also a historical work, one can conclude that there is valid evidence for the historical existence of Christ.

B. Jewish Testimony

Josephus (ca. 37–ca. 100) the wealthy Jew who tried to justify Judaism to the cultured Romans by his writings, also mentioned Christ. Josephus wrote of James, "the brother of Jesus, the so-called Christ."[5] In another passage, which is often condemned as an interpolation by Christians, but which many still think is authentic in part, Josephus wrote of Christ as "a wise man" condemned to die on the cross by Pilate.[6] Even granting some interpolation by Christians, most scholars agree that this basic information just mentioned is most likely a part of the original text. Certainly Josephus was not a friend of Christianity, and thus his mention of Christ has more historic value.

C. Christian Testimony Apart From the Bible

Many apocryphal gospels, acts, letters, and apocalypses are predicated on the historicity of Jesus Christ. These are collected in Montague R. James's *The Apocryphal New Testament* (New York: Oxford University Press, 1924). Inscriptions and pictures of the dove, the fish, the anchor, and other Christian symbols in the Catacombs give witness to belief in a historic Christ as well as the existence of the Christian calendar, Sunday, and the church.

Unfortunately, in choosing a date to begin the Christian calendar, the Scythian abbot Dionysius Exiguus (d. ca. 550) in his *Cyclus Paschalis* chose 754

Two examples of early Christian catacomb art testifying to belief in the historical Christ. This symbolic representation of the miraculous multiplication of the loaves and fishes is from the Catacomb of Callistus. In the center of the illustration from the catacomb of Priscilla, Christ is depicted as the Good Shepherd.

A.U.C. (from the founding of Rome) instead of the more accurate 749 A.U.C. for the date of Christ's birth.

Matthew in his Gospel (2:1) stated that Jesus was born "in the days of Herod the king." Josephus in his *Antiquities* (18.6.4) mentioned an eclipse of 750 A.U.C. before the death of Herod. Because the slaughter of the Jewish babies and the flight to Egypt preceded the death of Herod, this brings us to a possible 749 A.U.C., or about 5 B.C., for the date of Christ's birth.

The Jews in John 2:20 said that the temple was forty-six years in building to that time. Josephus and the Roman historian Dio Cassisus made 779 A.U.C. the date the building began. Jesus was "about thirty years of age" according to Luke 3:23, which subtracted from 779 gives 749, or 5 B.C., as the most likely date for His birth, or about five years earlier than our dating for the Christian Era.

II. THE CHARACTER OF CHRIST

The Bible does give some indications as to Christ's personality and character. Even a casual reading of the Gospels leaves a powerful impression of His originality. Where Jewish and modern authorities quote others as authorities for various statements, Christ simply uttered the words, "I say." Statements following the use of this phrase and like phrases in the Gospels indicate the creativity and originality of Christ's thought, which astonished the people of His day (Mark 1:22; Luke 4:32).

Christ's sincerity also stands out in the biblical records. He was the only human being who had nothing to hide, and so He could be completely Himself (John 8:46).

The Gospels also give an impression of balance in His character. Boldness of character usually is associated with Peter, love with John, and meekness with Andrew. No one facet of character is in excess in Christ; rather, the records reveal a balance and unity of character. This balance, originality, and transparency can be adequately explained only by the historical account of the virgin birth of Christ.[7]

III. THE WORK OF CHRIST

The transcendent importance of the personality of Christ must never be dissociated from His work. This work was both active and passive. During His three-year ministry Christ gave evidence of a righteousness demanded by the law—a righteousness that was in addition to His intrinsic righteousness as the Son of God. This extrinsic, earned righteousness qualified Him to die for men who could never earn such a righteousness and who needed a righteous Substitute if their sins were to be forgiven by God. This active work had its counterpart in His so-called passive work, His voluntary death on the cross (Phil. 2:5–8). These two historic phases of the work of Christ are summed up in His statement concerning His mission of service and suffering (Mark 10:45).

A. The Ministry of Christ

Except for the description of Christ's visit to Jerusalem with His parents at the age of twelve (Luke 2:41–50) and a few scattered references to His mother and brothers, little is known of Christ's many years of residence in Nazareth. Most likely He was given a biblical education at home and in the synagogue school for children. He also learned the trade of His father, because every Jewish child was given instruction in some manual trade. Since Nazareth was on a main trade route, Christ would have opportunity to observe the life of the outside world as it passed through Nazareth. His parables and sermons show that He was a keen observer of nature. He knew God both from God's revelation of Himself in nature and from the Old Testament. During these years He developed physically, socially, mentally, and spiritually (Luke 2:52) in preparation for the great work ahead.

Christ's ministry was preceded by the brief ministry of His forerunner, John the Baptist. Christ's first public appearance at the beginning of His ministry was associated with His baptism by John. The careful student of the ministry of Jesus will notice that after this event He usually worked in Jewish centers throughout His ministry. This policy was in keeping with His own assertion that He came to help "the lost sheep of the house of Israel" (Matt. 15:24).

After His temptation in the wilderness, Christ chose some of the disciples who were to continue His work under the leadership of the Holy Spirit after His resurrection and ascension. A visit to Cana marked the occasion of His first miracle, the turning of water into wine. This was followed by a brief visit to Jerusalem, during which He cleansed the temple and had His momentous interview with Nicodemus. This interview revealed the spiritual nature of His ministry (John 3:3, 5, 7). He returned to Galilee by way of Samaria, where His interview with the woman of Samaria (John 4) demonstrated that His ministry was not going to be limited by national or sex barriers even though His mission was primarily to the Jews.

After His rejection in Nazareth, Christ made Capernaum the base for the Galilean ministry; and this ministry constituted the greatest portion of His earthly service to men. From here He made three tours of Galilee. The first tour, mainly in eastern Galilee, was marked by healing of the paralytic, the lame man, and many others as well as by the raising from the dead of the widow's son at Nain and the completion of the task of choosing His disciples. The miracles were matched by the superb presentation of the principles that He declared should govern human conduct. These principles are contained in the Sermon on the Mount. The theme of the sermon is that true religion is of the spirit rather than of external acts demanded by the law.

The high point of Christ's second tour of southern Galilee was His parabolic teaching concerning His kingdom (Matt. 13). Additional miracles, such as the healing of the Gadarene demoniac and the daughter of Jairus, testified to His power to back up His words with deeds. The third tour was a continuation of this work of teaching, preaching, and healing.

The three tours of Galilee were followed by brief periods of retirement during which Christ's main emphasis seemed to be instruction for His disciples. Nevertheless, He still found time to meet the needs of those who came to Him, for He fed the five thousand during His first retirement. He also demonstrated His lordship over nature by walking on the Sea of Galilee. This miracle impressed on His disciples the reality of His claims to be the Son of God. He brought healing, during the second withdrawal, to the daughter of the "Syrophoenician" woman who demonstrated remarkable faith in Christ (Mark 7:26). The third retirement was a still further revelation of His power to heal and bless.

The extended ministry in Galilee was followed by a short ministry in Jerusalem at the Feast of Tabernacles, during which Christ faced and met boldly the rising opposition from religious leaders—the Pharisees and the Sadducees. Because of this opposition, Christ withdrew east of the Jordan to Perea, where He taught and healed. This Perean ministry was succeeded by the short ministry of the last week in Jerusalem, during which He publicly met the rising antagonism of the Jewish national and ecclesiastical leaders. He rebuked their mechanical and external approach to religion in His parabolic teaching. The sad weekend, during which He gave His life on the cross, ended His active ministry to the world. After His glorious resurrection—an established historical fact based on documentary evidence in the New Testament (Acts 1:3; 1 Cor. 15:4–8)—He appeared only to His own followers. The culmination of His ministry came with His ascension into heaven in the presence of His disciples. This ascension was prefaced by His promises to send the Holy Spirit in His place and personally to return again to this earth.

The Christian church is fortunate to possess four sources for Christ's ministry on earth. Each of the authors presented his account from a different viewpoint. Matthew emphasized Christ's kingly activity as the promised Messiah who fulfilled the Old Testament prophecies. He did this by the constant use of the phrase "that it might be fulfilled which was spoken by the prophet." Mark, who wrote to appeal to the Roman mind, stressed the pragmatic side of Christ's ministry as Son of man. The sense of action and power is heightened by his constant use of the Greek word translated variously as "straightway" or "immediately." Luke the historian (Luke 1:1–4) gave us the human side of the ministry of Christ. The apostle John presented Christ as the Son of God with power to bring blessing to those who accept Him by faith (John 1:12, 20:30–31).

B. The Mission of Christ

The active phase of the ministry of Christ, which extended over three years, was but preparatory to the passive phase of His work, His suffering on the cross. His suffering and death was the great event foretold by the prophets (Isa. 53)—an event that was to bring about the final defeat of all the forces of evil and to release from sin (Gal. 3:10, 13) those who accept Him and appropriate all the spiritual power of His work on the cross (Eph. 1:19–23; 3:20). It was for this important temporal and eternal purpose that He came to earth. The Gospels emphasize this fact by the sense of climax in such references as Matthew 16:21; Mark 8:31; and Luke 9:44.

C. The Message of Christ

Although the Cross was the primary mission of Christ on earth, it was not His main message, nor was it considered as an end in itself. Any careful study of the Gospels will reveal that the kingdom was the primary message of the teaching of Christ. Two phrases were used by Christ: "the kingdom of God" and "the kingdom of heaven." The latter designation was used mostly by Matthew.

Both of the major interpretations of these phrases accept the fact that the kingdom of God refers to the rule of God over all beings in the universe who give to Him a voluntary allegiance. This kingdom, which is spiritual and which embraces time and eternity, is entered by human beings subsequent to a spiritual rebirth (Matt. 6:33; John 3:3, 5, 7). Never is there suggestion of evil in this realm in which Christ Himself will finally become subject to the Father (1 Cor. 15:24–28). All groups believe that in the present this kingdom is ethical and spiritual, that the church is a part of it; and that its full eschatological realization is yet future.

Discussion of the phrase "kingdom of heaven" brings a division of opinion. Some feel that the "kingdom of heaven" and the "kingdom of God" refer to two separate realms, though there is a measure of overlapping. The major reason for making a distinction between the two arises out of the fact that Christ used and interpreted the parables of the tares and dragnet in describing the kingdom of heaven, but He never used them in describing the kingdom of God. Since these two parables posit a mixture of good and evil men in the kingdom of heaven, and since all references to the kingdom of God refer only to those voluntarily subject to the will of God, many feel that there must be some distinction between the two terms and that they cannot, therefore, be synonyms. They note that the "kingdom of God" is related to God, is marked by goodness, and is cosmic and eternal as well as in time; on the other hand, the phrase "kingdom of heaven" is related to Christ's rule in time on earth and has both good and bad in it (Matt. 8:11–13).

Those premillennialists who hold that the two terms are not identical believe that the kingdom of heaven is linked with Christ's rule on the present earth, and they identify the kingdom of God with the eternal rule of God the Father. During the present period of the church, the kingdom of heaven is equivalent to Christendom, which consists of a mixture of Christians, professing Christians, unbelievers, and Jews. At the return of Christ the kingdom of heaven will be purged of unbelieving Jews and Gentiles and will be ruled for a thousand years by Christ and His church. This will be the kingdom foretold by the prophets in which Israel was to be blessed in the land of Palestine. After a short rebellion, to be led by Satan, following his release from his imprisonment of one thousand years during the Millennium, Christ will hand His authority over to God; and the pure part of the kingdom of heaven will be merged finally with the kingdom of God after the final judgment.

Many who hold that the two terms are synonymous and may be equated with the church think that the kingdom will be realized by an evolutionary historical process in which the church does the work of preparing the way for a kingdom that Christ will receive at His return. Social action to create a better environment for people is an important part of their plan. Christianity is often interpreted in ethical terms at the expense of the atoning work of the cross. This is liberal postmillennialism.

Some people, especially nineteenth-century thinkers, such as Charles Finney, the Hodges, B. B. Warfield, and A. H. Strong have also held to a postmillennial eschatology, but of a conservative, orthodox variety. They believed that church of regenerate persons under the guidance and power of the Holy Spirit would make such an impact on their society that there would emerge a perfect millennial order among people. When Christ comes at the end of the millennium, there would be a godly society. Augustine's equating the Millennium with the church age has given much support to this view.

Others, who do not subscribe to the above interpretation, but who think that the two terms are synonymous, believe that the final realization of the kingdom is yet future and that it will be consummated supernaturally and cataclysmically at the return of Christ. They do not accept the evolutionary approach of the postmillennialists. They are usually known as amillennialists. They do not accept the idea of a future millennial kingdom of Christ, nor do they usually relate Jews to Christ's kingdom.

Whether one believes that the two phrases are synonymous or not is not so important an issue as the agreement of evangelicals concerning certain points about which there can be no disagreement if one rightly interprets the Scriptures. The fact that sin is hereditary and personal rather than environmental and corporate precludes the postmillennial view of the kingdom. Man has to reckon with original sin. Hence, the primary task of the church is not world conversion by preaching and social action but the evangelization of the world by the proclamation of the gospel so that those who are to make up the true church may have an opportunity to respond to that message as the Holy Spirit brings conviction to their hearts. This is the specific task of the church in this period of human history, but it does not preclude making Christianity practical in daily life in society by the Christian who is also a citizen. Christ taught that the kingdom will never be realized by a historical evolutionary process in which the church by social action prepares the world for His coming. The Scriptures plainly teach that the future eschatological—as distinguished from the present ethical and spiritual—phase of the kingdom will be realized supernaturally and cataclysmically at the coming of Christ rather than as a result of the work of the church.

D. The Miracles of Christ

Christ's miracles were numerous and constituted an important part of His ministry. They were to reveal the glory of God and to show that Christ was the Son of God (John 2:22–23; 3:2; 9:3), in order that belief might follow and God be glorified. They are variously called power, works, wonders, or signs. Rationalists and empiricists have denied their possibility and have sought to explain them by natural law or to explain them away as myths. The latter necessarily involves a denial of the records as historical. Miracles may be defined as phenomena not explicable by known natural law but wrought by a special intervention of Deity for moral purposes.

The possibility and probability of miracles is demonstrated by the supernatural, creative Christ and by the existence of historical records that give accounts of such miracles as historical facts. The person and work of Christ received authentication in the eyes of many in His day because of the miracles He wrought.

E. The Meaning of Christ

There have been many different views of the Christ who is brought before us so graphically in the Gospels. During the great periods of theological controversy, between 325 and 451 and between 1517 and 1648, people sought to interpret Christ primarily in terms of the creeds. The mystics thought of Him as the Christ of immediate personal experience. Others in the late eighteenth and early nineteenth centuries spoke of Him as the Christ of history and sought to explain away the supernatural so that they might think of Christ as only an unusual man. The true Christian has always thought of Him as the Christ of God.

The historical significance of Christ is revealed in the development of a new value placed on human personality. The Greeks insisted on the dignity of human personality because man was a rational being, but the church has always insisted that human personality has dignity because man is a potential or actual child of God through faith in Christ. The Christian conception has resulted in the humanizing of life. Class, sexual, and racial barriers have been set aside in the church, and social reform has brought about better conditions of life for all people. It was the Evangelicals who were leaders in social reform in nineteenth-century England. Above all, the emphasis on an inner ethical code of love for conduct rather than external legal rules is a result of the contact of human personality with the Christ of Calvary. Christ's impact in the arts and literature is immense.

Christ's character, work, teachings, and, above all, His death and resurrection mark the beginning of Christianity. Many religions could exist without their human founders, but the removal of Christ from Christianity would leave a lifeless, empty shell. Christ gave to His church its two ordinances, the apostles, its basic message of the kingdom of God, its primary discipline (Matt. 16:16–19; 18:15–20), and the Holy Spirit to be the One to work through the church in the evangelization of the world. He left no basic organization, well-defined system of doctrine, or sacred books. These were to be worked out by the apostles, including Paul, under the guidance of the Holy Spirit whom Christ sent to the earth to minister in His absence. The true church, with Christ as the foundation and the Holy Spirit as the founder, was to march forward triumphantly, exalting its crucified, risen, and ascended Lord from the day of Pentecost to the present.

SUGGESTED READING

The Gospels are the primary sources for the study of Christ in history. The use of a harmony of the Gospels is an invaluable aid to a systematic, chronological study of the life of Christ.

Aland, Kurt. **Synopsis of the Four Gospels: Greek-English Edition.** 2nd ed. *New York: UBS, 1976.*

Case, Shirley J. **The Historicity of Jesus.** 2nd ed. *Chicago: University of Chicago Press, 1928. The author has ably criticized the evidence of those who deny the historicity of Christ and has presented positive evidence to demonstrate His historical existence.*

Edersheim, Alfred. **The Life and Times of Jesus the Messiah.** 3rd ed. *New York: Longmans, 1900. This is still an excellent work on the life of Christ. It throws much light on the historical background of Christ's day.*

Guthrie, Donald. **A Shorter Life of Christ.** *Grand Rapids: Zondervan, 1970.*
_____ . **Jesus the Messiah.** *Grand Rapids: Zondervan, 1972.*

Hoehner, Harold W. **Chronological Aspects of the Life of Christ.** *Grand Rapids: Zondervan, 1977.*

Robertson, Archibald T. **Syllabus for New Testament Study.** 5th ed. *London: Hodder & Stoughton, 1923. On pages 89 to 133 there is a fairly extensive bibliography for a study of the life of Christ.*

Smith, David. **The Days of His Flesh.** *London: Hodder & Stoughton, 1924. This is one of the best works on the life of Christ despite the author's inclusion of many liberal interpretations.*

Thomas, Robert L., and Gundry, Stanley N. **A Harmony of the Gospels.** *Chicago: Moody, 1978.*

Vollmer, Philip. **The Modern Student's Life of Christ.** *New York: Revell, 1912. This little manual is a useful companion volume to illuminate the study of the harmony of the Gospels.*

Chapter 3

To the Jew First

That Christ was the foundation rather than the founder of the church is evident from His use of the future tense in Matthew 16:18, in the statement, "Upon this rock I *will* build my church." Luke claimed that he was informing us in his Gospel concerning "all that Jesus began both to do and to teach" (Acts 1:1) while in the Acts he recorded the account of the founding and early spread of the Christian church by the apostles under the leadership of the Holy Spirit. Even the disciples misunderstood the spiritual nature of Christ's mission because they wanted to know whether, after His resurrection, He would restore the messianic kingdom (Acts 1:6). Christ, instead, told them that after they were empowered by the Holy Spirit their task was to witness to Him "in Jerusalem, and in all Judea, and in Samaria, and unto the uttermost part of the earth" (Acts 1:8).

It will be noticed that Christ gave priority to the proclamation to the Jew. This was the order followed by the early church. The gospel was first proclaimed in Jerusalem by Peter on the day of Pentecost; then it was carried by the Christian Jews to other cities of Judea and Samaria. Consequently, the early church was primarily Jewish and existed within Judaism. The early development of Christianity within Judaism and its progress to Antioch is described by Luke in the first twelve chapters of Acts.

I. THE FOUNDING
OF THE CHURCH IN JERUSALEM

That the very center of bitterest enmity to Christ should have become the city where the Christian religion first emerged seems paradoxical, but such was the case. From A.D. 30 to approximately 44 the church in Jerusalem held a leading position in the early Christian community.

The Holy Spirit was given the position of prominence in the founding of the Christian church. This was in accord with Christ's promises in the last weeks of His life that He would send "another Comforter" who would give leadership to the church after His ascension. A careful study of John 14: 16–18, 15:26–27, and 16:7–15 will make the function of the Holy Spirit in the early church quite clear. In fact, the foci of the Book of Acts are the resurrection of Christ, as the subject of apostolic preaching, and the Holy Spirit as the empowerer and guide of the Christian community from the day of Pentecost. The Holy Spirit became the agent of the Trinity in mediating the work of redemption to men.

Jews from all parts of the Mediterranean world were present at Jerusalem to observe the Feast of Pentecost at the time of the founding of the church (Acts 2:5–11). The supernatural manifestation of divine power in the speaking with tongues, which occurred in connection with the origin of the church and the coming of the Holy Spirit, brought to the Jews present the declaration of God's wonderful works in their own tongue (Acts 2:11). Peter made this the occasion for the first and possibly the most fruitful sermon ever preached, the declaration of Christ's messiahship and saving grace. At least three thousand accepted the word that he declared and were baptized (Acts 2:41). In this manner that spiritual entity or organism, the invisible church, the body of the resurrected Christ, came into being.

Growth was rapid. The total number of those baptized soon reached five thousand (Acts 4:4). Multitudes were later mentioned as becoming a part of the church (Acts 5:14). It is rather interesting that many of these were Hellenistic Jews (Acts 6:1) of the Dispersion who were in Jerusalem to celebrate the great festivals associated with the Passover and Pentecost. Not even the priests were immune from the contagion of the new faith. "A great company of the priests" (Acts 6:7) was mentioned as among the members of the early church in Jerusalem. Perhaps some of them had seen the rending of the great veil of the temple that had accompanied the death of Christ, and this, coupled with the preaching of the apostles, had caused them to give willing allegiance to Christ.

Such rapid growth was not without much opposition on the part of the Jews. Quickly the ecclesiastical authorities realized that Christianity offered a threat to their prerogatives as interpreters and priests of the law, and they rallied their forces to combat Christianity. Persecution came first from a politico-ecclesiastical body, the Sanhedrin, which, with Roman permission, supervised the civil and religious life of the state. Peter and John were hailed before that august body at least twice and were forbidden to preach the gospel, but they refused to accede to the demand. Later persecution became primarily political. Herod killed James and imprisoned Peter (Acts 12) in this period of persecution. Since then, persecution has followed this ecclesiastical or political pattern.

This early persecution provided Christianity with its first martyr, Stephen. He had been one of the most outstanding of the seven men chosen to administer the charitable funds of the Jerusalem church. False witnesses, who could not gainsay the spirit and logic with which he spoke, had him hailed before the Sanhedrin to answer for his offense. After a discourse in which he denounced the Jewish leaders for their rejection of Christ, he was taken out and stoned to death. The death of the first martyr of the Christian faith was a valuable factor in the spread and growth of Christianity. Saul, later to be Paul the apostle, kept the outer garments of those who stoned Stephen. There is little doubt but that Stephen's bravery and his forgiving spirit in the face of a cruel death made an impact on the heart of Saul. The words of Christ to him in Acts 9:5, "It is hard for thee to kick against the pricks," seem to indicate this. The persecution that followed was most severe and was the means of scattering and purifying the infant church so that the message could be carried to other parts of the country (Acts 8:4).

However, not all converts to Christianity had an undivided heart. Ananias and Sapphira became the first objects of discipline in the Jerusalem church because of their sin of deceit. Swift and terrible, such discipline was exercised through the apostles who were the leaders of this early organization.

The account of the visitation of discipline on this guilty pair raises the question whether or not the early church in Jerusalem practiced communism. A young Communist tried hard on one occasion to demonstrate to the writer that the church did practice communism. Passages such as Acts 2:44–45 and 4:32 seem to suggest the practice of a utopian type of socialism based on the favorite socialistic maxim, "From each according to his ability; to each according to his need." But it will be noticed in the first place that this was a *temporary* measure, possibly designed to meet the needs of the many from outside Jerusalem who would be desirous of instruction in the new faith before they returned to their homes. The fact that this was *voluntary* is much more important. It was by group cooperation rather than by enforcement of the state. Peter clearly stated in Acts 5:3–4 that Ananias and Sapphira had liberty either to hold or to sell their property. Common sharing was a purely voluntary matter. The Bible cannot be used as a scriptural warrant for state capitalism.

But early Christianity did promote great social change in certain areas. The early Jerusalem church insisted on the spiritual equality of the sexes and gave much consideration to the women of the church. Dorcas's leadership in the promotion of charitable works was noted by Luke (Acts 9:36). The creation of a group of men to take care of the needy was another remarkable social phenomenon that occurred in the early years of the church. Charity was to be handled by an organized body, the deacons. In this way the apostles were free to give their whole time to spiritual leadership. Necessity, because of the rapid growth and possibly imitation of the practices of the Jewish synagogue, led to the multiplication of offices and officials early in the history of the church. Sometime later elders were added to the number of officials so that finally apostles, elders, and deacons shared the responsibility of leadership in the Jerusalem church.

The nature of the preaching of the leaders of the early Jerusalem church stands out in the account of the rise of Christianity. Peter's sermon (Acts 2:14–36) is the first by an apostle. It will be noticed that Peter appealed to the prophets of the Old Testament who foretold a suffering Messiah. He then advanced the idea that Christ was this

Messiah because He had been raised from the dead by God. Consequently, He was able to bring salvation to those who would accept Him by faith. The main arguments of early sermons by the apostles are summarized in Acts 17:2–3. The necessity of Christ's death for sin was foretold in the prophets, and the resurrection of Christ was proof that He was the Messiah who could save men. Paul also followed this same technique (1 Cor. 15:3–4). The resurrected, crucified Christ was the content of their preaching both to Jews and, later, to Gentiles (John 5:22, 27; Acts 10:42; 17:31).

The Jewish church in Jerusalem, whose history has just been described, soon lost its place of leadership in Christianity to other churches. The decision at the council in Jerusalem not to bind the Gentiles to obedience to the law opened the way for spiritual emancipation of the Gentile churches from Jewish control. During the siege of Jerusalem in 69 by Titus, the members of the church were forced to flee from Jerusalem to Pella across the Jordan.[1] Jerusalem was no longer looked upon as the center of Christianity after the destruction of the temple and the flight of this Jewish church, and the spiritual leadership of the Christian church was centered in other cities, such as Antioch. This removed the possible danger that Christianity might never outgrow the swaddling clothes of Judaism.

II. THE CHURCH IN PALESTINE

Interest in the activities of the church in Jerusalem holds the attention of the readers of Luke's history of the early church up to the end of chapter 7 of Acts. The center of interest widens to include Judea and Samaria in chapters 8 to 12. Christianity was carried to people of other races. True Christianity has always been mission oriented.

Philip's visit to Samaria (Acts 8:5–25) brought the gospel to a people who were not of pure Jewish blood. The Samaritans were the descendants of those of the ten tribes who were not carried away to Assyria after the fall of Samaria and the settlers whom the Assyrians brought in from other parts of their empire in 721 B.C. The Jews and Samaritans became bitter enemies from that time. Peter and John were asked to come down to Samaria to help Philip when the work grew so rapidly that he found himself unable to meet all the demands. This revival was the first breach in the racial barrier to the spread of the gospel. Philip was led by the Holy Spirit after the completion of his work in Samaria to preach the gospel to an Ethiopian eunuch who was a high official in the government of Ethiopia.

Peter, who had been the first to preach the gospel to the Jews, was also the first to bring the gospel officially to the Gentiles. After a vision, which made clear to him that the Gentiles also had a right to the gospel, he went to the home of Cornelius the Roman centurion and was amazed when the same manifestations that had occurred on the day of Pentecost occurred in the home of Cornelius (Acts 10–11). Peter was willing from that time on to have the Gentiles hear the word of grace. The Ethiopian eunuch and Cornelius were the first Gentiles to have the privilege of receiving the message of Christ's saving grace.

Although those who had been forced out of Jerusalem preached only to the Jews at first (Acts 11:20), it was not long before a large Gentile church sprang up in Antioch in Syria. Here the name Christian, first given in ridicule by the witty Antiochians, originated and became the honored designation of the followers of Christ. It was at Antioch that Paul began his active public ministry among the Gentiles and it was from there that he started on the missionary journeys that were to carry him to his goal, the city of Rome. The church at Antioch was so large that it was able to give relief to the Jewish churches when they faced famine. It was the main center of Christianity from 44 to 68.

But the task of carrying the gospel to Gentiles in "the uttermost parts" was still to be done. That task, begun by Paul, is still the unfinished mission of the church of Christ.

SUGGESTED READING

Chapters 1 to 12 of the Book of Acts constitute the primary material for this period.

Bruce, F. F. **Commentary on the Book of Acts: The English Text.** *Grand Rapids: Eerdmans, 1954.*

Guthrie, Donald. **The Apostles.** *Grand Rapids: Zondervan, 1974.*

Kidd, Beresford J. **A History of the Christian Church to** A.D. **461.** *3 vols. Oxford: Clarendon University Press, 1922. The work with its full reference to sources is a useful and authoritative guide to information concerning this early period.*

Lenski, Richard C. **The Interpretation of the Acts of the Apostles.** *Columbus, Ohio: Wartburg, 1954. This includes useful historical and exegetical material for chapters 3 and 4.*

Longenecker, Richard N., "The Acts of the Apostles," **The Expositor's Bible Commentary.** *Vol. 9. ed. Frank E. Gaebelein. Grand Rapids: Zondervan, 1980.*

Purves, George T. **Christianity in the Apostolic Age.** *New York: Scribner, 1902. This is a brief but useful manual.*

Schaff, Philip. **History of the Apostolic Church.** *New York: Scribner, 1869. This is still an excellent volume for this period.*

Chapter 4

Also to the Greek

The early Jewish-Christian church seemed slow to apprehend the universal character of Christianity even though Peter had been instrumental in giving the gospel to the first Gentile converts. It was Paul who had by revelation of God the largeness of vision to see the need of the Gentile world and to spend his life carrying the gospel to that world. As no other in the early church, Paul realized the universal character of Christianity and dedicated himself to the propagation of it to the ends of the Roman Empire (Rom. 11:13; 15:16). One might well wonder whether he did not have in his mind the slogan "The Roman Empire for Christ" as he slowly made his way westward with the message of the Cross (Rom. 15:15–16, 18–28; Acts 9:15; 22:21). He did not spare himself in achieving this end, but he did not neglect his own people, the Jews. This is evidenced by his seeking out the Jewish synagogue first in every town he came to and by proclaiming the gospel to the Jews and Gentile proselytes as long as they would listen to him.

I. PAUL'S ENVIRONMENT

Paul was conscious of three temporal loyalties during the course of his life. He had as a young man the training accorded only to promising young Jews and had sat at the feet of the great Jewish teacher Gamaliel. Few could boast of having better training than Paul as far as Jewish religious education was concerned, and few had profited as thoroughly from their training as had Paul (Phil. 3:4–6). He was also a citizen of Tarsus, the leading city of Cilicia, "no mean city" (Acts 21:39). He was also a freeborn Roman citizen (Acts 22:28) and did not hesitate to make use of the privileges of a Roman citizen when such privileges would help in the carrying out of his mission for Christ (Acts 16:37; 25:11). Judaism was his religious environment prior to his conversion. Tarsus, with its great university and intellectual atmosphere, was the scene of his earlier years; and the Roman Empire was the political milieu in which he lived and did his work. Thus Paul grew up in an

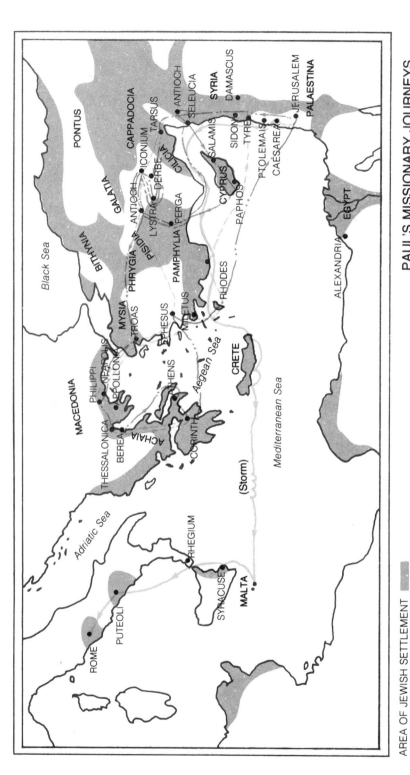

PAUL'S MISSIONARY JOURNEYS
AND TRIP TO ROME

AREA OF JEWISH SETTLEMENT
PAUL'S FIRST MISSIONARY JOURNEY
PAUL'S SECOND MISSIONARY JOURNEY
PAUL'S THIRD MISSIONARY JOURNEY
PAUL'S JOURNEY TO ROME

urban cosmopolitan culture.

This political environment did not seem to be too promising a one for the proclamation of the gospel. Caesar Augustus had brought about the downfall of the republic, except as a political form, when he set up a dyarchy in 27 B.C., in which he nominally shared control of the state with the senate. Unfortunately, his successors had neither the ability nor the character of Augustus, and they were guilty of misrule. Caligula (37–41) was insane during part of his reign; and Nero (54–68), under whom Paul was martyred and the church endured its first persecution, was a cruel and bloody man who did not hesitate to kill members of his own family. However, Claudius (41–54) was an excellent administrator, and the empire was fairly stable during his reign. It was in his reign that Paul made most of his missionary journeys.

The social and moral situation was much more unpromising than the political. Booty from the empire created a wealthy upper class of new aristocrats who had slaves and wealth to pander to their every legitimate and illegitimate desire. This class was somewhat contemptuous of the new religion and saw in its appeal to the poorer classes a threat to their superior position in society. But even some of this class were won by the preaching of the gospel when Paul was a prisoner in Rome (Phil. 1:13).

Paul also faced the rivalry of competing systems of religion. The Romans were somewhat eclectic in their religious outlook and were willing to give toleration to any faith that would not prevent its worshipers from taking part in the state system of worship, which combined emperor worship with the old republican state worship and claimed the allegiance of all the people in the empire except the Jews, who were exempt by law from its rites. Christians could not, of course, do this and so they faced the problem of opposition from the state. The more subjective mystery religions of Mithra, Cybele, and Isis claimed the allegiance of many others in the empire. Judaism, as Christianity was distinguished from it as a separate sect, offered increasing opposition.

Roman intellectuals accepted philosophical systems, such as Stoicism, Epicureanism, and Neo-Pythagoreanism, that suggested philosophical contemplation as the way to salvation. Stoicism, with its pantheistic view of God, its conception of natural ethical laws to be discovered by reason, and its doctrine of the fatherhood of God and the brotherhood of man, seemed to provide a philosophical foundation for the Roman Empire. Some of the emperors, such as Marcus Aurelius (161–80), found its ethical standards appealing. It was this confused religious scene that Paul had to face with the simple redemptive gospel of the death of Christ.

Archaeology helps us to date key points in Paul's life and work. Paul had been in Corinth eighteen months when Gallio became proconsul (Acts 18:12–13). An inscription on stone discovered at Delphi mentions that Gallio began his duties in Achaia in the twenty-sixth year of Claudius, which was A.D. 51–52. Thus Paul's visit would have begun eighteen months before, in A.D. 50. Other dates in his life can be calculated from this date with relative accuracy.[1]

Paul's conversion was also an objective historical event. He spoke of it as such in 1 Corinthians 9:1 and 15:8 and in Galatians 1:11–18. This was brought about by his contact with Christ on the road to Damascus (Acts 9; 22; and 26). This experience was vital to his later missionary work, teaching, writings, and theology.

II. PAUL'S WORK

Paul's genius was so many-sided that it is necessary to give consideration to his work under different categories. Each of the discussions will emphasize the magnitude of the task that God gave him and the devotion with which he worked to accomplish the appointed task.

A. The Propagator of the Gospel

Paul was a wise as well as devoted missionary, and his life illustrates the use of principles that have served many well in seeking to carry out Christ's great commission to the church. A consideration of the maps of his journeys reveals the advance of the gospel under his preaching along a great *semicircle* reaching from Antioch to Rome. Paul adopted as a basic principle the expansion of the gospel to the West, and it must have been with delight that he first caught sight of his goal, Rome, even if it was as a prisoner of the Roman government.

Paul also thought in terms of areas that could be reached from *strategic* urban centers. He always started his work in a new area in the most strategic city and used the converts to carry the message to the surrounding towns and countryside. Because of this practice it is not likely that he visited Colosse (Col. 2:1) but rather that the strong church in that town was founded by those whom he sent from Ephesus.

Paul began his work in strategic Roman centers by going first to the *synagogue*, where he proclaimed his message as long as he was well received. When opposition arose, he turned to a direct proclamation of the gospel to the Gentiles in any place that he found suitable. His principle was to preach to the Gentile after he had given the message to the Jew. This principle may be seen by a study of accounts of the journeys recorded in Acts (Rom. 1:16).

After founding a church, Paul would organize it with elders and deacons so that the church might be *self-governing* after his departure. He sought to build on solid foundations.

Paul's desire not to be a burden to the infant churches led him to assume the responsibility of supporting himself while he preached in a new area. He worked at his trade of tentmaking while he preached to the people in Corinth (Acts 18:1–4; cf. 1 Thess. 2:9). He did not make this a rule for others but felt that it was a necessity for his work. The church was also to be *self-supporting*.

His dependence on the Holy *Spirit's* guidance in his work is clearly evident in both the Acts and his epistles (Acts 13:2, 4; 16:6–7). He did not wish to go to any place unless there was clear evidence that it was the field in which God would have him labor. He sought to reach the areas untouched by others so that he might be a pioneer of the gospel (Rom. 15:20). This pioneering spirit was productive in that it resulted in his carrying the gospel from Antioch to Rome and, possibly, as far west as Spain during his lifetime.

These principles that the apostle followed served him well in the development of churches that were organized centers for the continued preaching of the gospel. He did not leave them without *supervision,* for he made a practice of revisiting or writing letters to the churches that he founded in order to encourage and to strengthen them (Acts 15:36). One does not wonder at the rapid growth of Christianity under such sane yet inspired leadership. The church was *self-propagating* also.

B. Paul's Publications

Paul made a practice of keeping in touch with the local situation in each church through visitors from that church (1 Cor. 1:11) or through the reports of agents whom he sent to visit the churches (1 Thess. 3:6). Whenever the local situation seemed to demand it, he wrote letters under the guidance of the Holy Spirit to deal with particular problems. He wrote twice to the Thessalonian church to clear up misunderstandings concerning the doctrine of the second coming of Christ. The Corinthian church faced the problems of a church in a large pagan city, and Paul addressed his first letter to the solution of their problems. Questions concerning human and spiritual wisdom peculiar to a church in a cultured Greek city (1 Cor. 1–4), the problem of morality in a pagan environment (chap. 5), lawsuits between Christians before pagan judges (6), marriage problems (7), and the problem of social relationships with pagan idolaters (8–10) were some of the matters with which Paul had to deal by correspondence. His Second Epistle to the Corinthians grew out of the need to assert his apostleship so that his

authority to act as stated in the first letter would be confirmed. The letter to the Galatians was made necessary by the problem of the relation of the Jewish law to Christianity so that faith rather than the works of law might be seen as the actuating principle of Christianity. The letter to the Romans is a systematic exposition and explanation of the gospel. The four epistles written during his imprisonment in Rome were occasioned by the special problems in the churches of Ephesus, Colosse, and Philippi. The personal epistle to Philemon is concerned with the problem of the Christian master and the slave who became a Christian. The three pastoral letters to Timothy and Titus are concerned with the problems facing a young pastor.

It will be noticed that each of these letters grew out of a definite historical crisis in one of Paul's beloved churches. The greatness of these "tracts for the times" is revealed by the fact that the principles that Paul developed to meet emergencies in first-century churches are still relevant to the church in modern times. Human beings face similar problems, and similar principles are useful even if the temporal and spatial environment is different. The Pauline Epistles are of value to any church in the solution of its problems. Paul always balanced theological formulas by practical application.

C. The Principles of Paul's Thought

No historical discussion of Paul can afford to ignore the basic doctrines that are developed in his letters, particularly in the letter to the Roman church. Christ left no well-defined body of dogma. The formulation of this was to be the work of Paul, guided by the Holy Spirit. This body of theology was not, however, in contrast to the teachings of Christ; rather, it grew out of the teachings and death of Christ.[2] Paul's education at home, in the synagogue, and under Gamaliel; his observation of nature (Rom. 1:19–20); his experience of conversion; his creative mind; and, above all, divine revelation were important in the development of his theology.

The essence of the Pauline gospel may be simply summarized. Paul realized that happiness and usefulness are basic goals to which all men aspire. Happiness and usefulness in this and the next life are dependent on the achievement of God's favor. God's favor can be granted only to the one who does God's will. Paul and his Jewish compatriots believed that observance of the law of Moses, which was an expression of God's holiness, should guarantee a happy and useful life. However, Paul found to his sorrow that the works of the law only result in the knowledge of sin and leave man helpless to fulfill the will of God as expressed in that law (Rom. 7). The experience on the Damascus road revealed to Paul that not the law but the Cross of Christ is the starting point for spiritual life. Christ, who had kept the Jewish law perfectly, could as perfect man and God offer Himself on the cross on behalf of sinful man and assume the burden of man's sin (Gal. 3:10, 13). People need only accept by faith (Rom. 5:1) the work that Christ has done for them.

Paul's ethical system grew out of this personal union of the believer with Christ by faith. This vertical relationship is to be balanced by a horizontal relationship in which one is united with fellow believers by Christian love expressed in a moral life (Eph. 1:15; 1 John 3:23). Neither the legalism of Judaism nor the rationalism of Stoicism, but Christian love is to be the spring of Christian conduct. The mystic union of the believer with his Lord is to be the source of love. This life of love involves separation from personal defilement growing out of idol worship, sexual impurity, or drunkenness —the major sins of heathendom. It results, positively, in loving service to others and steadfastness in the matter of personal integrity.

Such a system of ethics did not mean repudiation of the Jewish moral law, but rather it meant its fulfillment on the higher level of love in the family, household, and the state. The high ethical standards of the Christians impressed their pagan neighbors with the greatness of the Christian faith. Paul's own life of selfless service was a revelation to both Jew and Gentile of what God could do in the development of a Christian personality devoted to service for the glory of God and the good of man.[3]

Paul's philosophy of history is closely related to his ethical and theological views. He rejected the cyclic theory of history, which was so characteristic of the ancient world, and the modern theory of indefinite evolutionary progress, in favor of a cataclysmic supernatural view of history that takes into account unregenerate man's failure and God's power to fulfill His divine plan. This view is not limited to nations but encompasses the human race. According to it, progress can come only through spiritual conflict in which man is given strength through the grace of God. Ultimately God will be victor over all the forces of evil that were provisionally defeated on the cross of Calvary by Christ (Rom. 11:36; Eph. 1:10 *Weymouth*).

D. Paul as a Polemicist

Paul was never content merely to present Christianity; threats to the purity of Christian doctrine brought him into the fight against the foe. By voice and pen he fought for purity of Christian doctrine in his day. No deficient view of the person or work of Christ escaped his castigation, nor did he fail to try to win the erring one back to the faith.

The problem of the scope and means of salvation was the first difficulty to which Paul addressed himself during the Jerusalem Council at the end of his first missionary journey. The church, born in the bosom of Judaism, had developed into two groups. One group of Jewish Christians with a Pharisaic background believed that Gentiles as well as Jews must keep the law of Moses for salvation. They wanted to make Christianity a particularistic sect of Judaism. The other group realized that salvation came by faith in Christ alone and that the offer of salvation was for all rather than for Jews only, and that by works.

The visit of Judaizers to Antioch, ostensibly with authority from James to preach the former view (Acts 15:24), was the occasion for the meeting at Jerusalem in 49 or 50 to settle this problem. Commissioned by the church at Antioch (Acts 15:2) and assured by revelation (Gal. 2:2), Paul and Barnabas made their way to Jerusalem to the first and, possibly, the most important church council in church history.

They described their activities to a general public meeting of the church (Acts 15:4–5), after which they met with the apostles and elders in a special private meeting to discuss the problem in detail and to try to work out a solution (Acts 15:6; Gal. 2:2–10).[4] This private meeting seems to have been followed by another meeting of the whole church in which a decision was reached that was agreeable to all those present (Acts 15:7–29). The commendation of Paul's work among the Gentiles (Acts 15:25–26; Gal. 2:9) and the freeing of the Gentiles from keeping the Jewish law (Acts 15:19) were the immediate results of the conference. Minor demands to conciliate Jewish believers, such as refraining from eating blood or things strangled, were stated. Gentile converts were also asked to avoid the sins of idolatry and immorality—sins that would be a special temptation to converts from a sinful pagan environment (Acts 15:20–21). It will be clearly seen that these requests had nothing to do with the basic principle of how people are justified. They were designed simply to facilitate good relations between Jewish and Gentile converts to Christianity.

The happenings at the Jerusalem Council revealed Paul's doggedness where a matter of principle was concerned. Not for one moment would he consider the circumcision of Titus at the council (Gal. 2:3), but at the beginning of his second journey, when Timothy became his helper, he had Timothy circumcised (Acts 16:1–3) in order that the lack of this rite might not be a barrier in the presentation of the gospel. Paul was willing to make harmless concessions, such as this one, in order to facilitate his work; but he would not permit Titus to be circumcised at Jerusalem because Gentile freedom from observance of the Jewish ritual law was the principle for which he was fighting.

The liberation of Christianity from observance of the ceremonial Jewish law was the long-range result of the council. Henceforth, faith is the only means by which salvation comes to man. Because this faith is for all peoples, Christianity is freed from the danger of becoming only a sect of Judaism. The new law of love, which leads to the keeping of the Jewish moral law out of love to God rather than out of a sense of duty, becomes the basis for Christian ethics. It is also interesting to note the democratic fashion in which the church met its great problem. The decision was made by the church and its leaders under the guidance of the Holy Spirit. Jewish Christians, who had been saved by faith, were left free to observe the law of Moses as a voluntary task if they so desired.

Christianity must never forget the Jerusalem Council. The same problem was faced by the Reformers, who saw that the Roman church was demanding man-made works in addition to faith as the condition for salvation. Modern liberals with their emphasis on pleasing God by ethical deeds make the same mistake. The problem of the Jerusalem Council is a perennial one, and the principles that were victorious there are principles that have relevance throughout the history of the church.

Paul also faced the challenge of Greek rationalism when he fought an incipient Gnosticism in the church. Some men sought to make the means of salvation *intellectual* as the Jewish

Christians had sought to make them *legalistic.* Gnosticism developed with particular danger in the Colossian church.

The Gnostics held to a dualistic philosophy that made a sharp distinction between spirit as good and matter as evil. According to them, the link between pure spirit and evil matter is a hierarchy of celestial beings. Christ is considered one of this hierarchy. Angels are to receive worship because they have a part in this hierarchy (Col. 2:8, 18–19). Salvation is to be achieved mainly by ascetic acts to deny the desires of the material and evil body (Col. 2:14–17, 20–23) and by a special gnosis or knowledge accessible only to the elite among Christians. Faith is relegated to a subordinate position in this system that panders to human pride.[5]

Paul answered this heresy by unqualifiedly asserting the all-sufficiency of Christ as Creator and Redeemer (Col. 1:13–20). Christ is the full manifestation of God and is in no way inferior to God (Col. 1:19; 2:9). Only in this doctrine did Paul feel that man had any assurance of a Savior adequate to meet the problem of sin.

Gnosticism was the first heresy to be met by the church, but it was by no means the last. Error is perennial and usually springs from the same causes in every age. Man's pride in reason and his rationalizing tendency can still lead to heresy as it did in the Colossian church. Retention of the religious heritage of the pre-Christian period in the individual life may lead to a mixture of truth and error with dire consequences for salvation. That was the mistake made by the Judaizers. Misuse or overemphasis of some Scripture may lead to error. Sometimes a leader with mistaken enthusiasm, who seeks to protect the truth, may subvert it. Such was the case of Montanus in the second century.

With such faith and courage, it is little wonder that Paul was able to carry the message of salvation to the Gentile nations of the Roman Empire and to start Christian culture on its triumphant westward march across Europe. He was the unique interpreter of the meaning of Christ's life and death in terms of salvation for sinful man. He kept the faith free from admixture of legalism and rationalism. He worked out the details of organization in the Christian churches and was in constant correspondence with them to help them solve their problems in a Christian manner. As no one else did, Paul realized the cosmic significance of Christ for time and eternity: and, as the "apostle of the nations" (Rom. 11:13; 15:16), he interpreted Christ to the Gentile world.

SUGGESTED READING

Burton, Ernest D. The Records and Letters of the Apostolic Age. *New York: Scribner, 1895. The primary biblical sources for Paul's life and work are integrated in an interesting way in this work.*

Conybeare, William J., and Howson, John S. The Life and Epistles of St. Paul. *2 vols. New York: Scribner, 1854. This work is still a standard classic of Paul's life and work, though in some areas it must be supplemented by more recent works.*

Deissmann, Gustav. The Religion of Jesus and the Faith of Paul. *New York: Doran, n.d. Paul's theology is presented as an outgrowth of his experience of God's revelation and his consciousness of the indwelling Christ.*

Goodman, Frank J. A Harmony of the Life of Paul. *Grand Rapids: Baker, 1951. This work integrates the Acts and Paul's Epistles in an account of his life in the words of Scripture.*

Greenslade, S. L. Schism in the Early Church. *London: SCM, 1953. This is a helpful little book.*

Guthrie, Donald. The Apostles. *Grand Rapids: Zondervan, 1974.*

Longenecker, Richard N. The Ministry and Message of Paul. *Grand Rapids: Zondervan, 1971.*

Machen, J. Gresham. The Origin of Paul's Religion. *New York: Macmillan, 1923. The author has ably presented proof that Paul's message was not derived from the pagan mystery religions.*

Moe, Olaf. The Apostle Paul, His Life and His Work. *Translated by L. A. Vigness. Minneapolis: Augsburg, 1950.*

———. The Apostle Paul, His Message and Doctrine. *Translated by L. A. Vigness. Minneapolis: Augsburg, 1954.*

Smith, David. The Life and Letters of Saint Paul. *London: Hodder & Stoughton, 1919.*

Stevens, George B. The Pauline Theology. *New York: Scribner, 1892. The author has produced a useful outline of the biblical theology of Paul, but care should be exercised in its use because of the deficiencies in the author's theology at some points.*

Stewart, James S. A Man in Christ. *London: Hodder & Stoughton, 1935.*

Chapter 5

The Books and the Parchments

The New Testament is not an isolated mountain peak of religious literature; it is rather the highest peak of a mountain range of religious literature produced by the early church. Its basic literary forms—Gospels, Acts, Epistles, and Apocalypse—became the models on which the early fathers of the church based their writings. One is not so much amazed at the large number of books in the New Testament as one is at the small number in view of the abundance of religious literature in the early church. Luke hinted at the numerous gospels that were in circulation in the day when he took pen in hand to give his Spirit-inspired account of the life of Christ (Luke 1:1).

The writings of the Fathers do much to fill the gap in historical knowledge between the New Testament period and the latter part of the fourth century. The leading men of the church, by pen as well as by voice, formulated apologetic and polemical literature as they faced external persecution and internal heresy. Creeds were formed to give accurate statements of faith. Hence, the Fathers are of tremendous value in the study of the development of Christian life and thought in this period. This literature is far from dull, and the reading of it will repay the student with inspiration as well as with knowledge. The writers quote and use the language of Scripture.

The title "father of the church" has its origin in the use of the title "father," which was given to bishops, especially in the West, to express affectionate loyalty. It was increasingly used from the third century on to describe the orthodox champions of the church and exponents of its faith. These men were usually bishops. Patrology or patristics is the name of the study of the life and works of these men, most of whom lived in the period between the end of the apostolic age and the Council of Chalcedon (451). The diagram on page 72 will give some indication of who they were, their period, their major works, and the most important characteristics of their writings.

THE CHURCH FATHERS

West	East

FIRST CENTURY (95–ca. 150)
APOSTOLIC FATHERS—TO EDIFY—TYPOLOGICAL INTERPRETATION

EDIFICATION

West	East
Clement of Rome	Ignatius Polycarp Pseudo-Barnabas The Epistle to Diognetus The Second Epistle of Clement Papias *Shepherd of Hermas* (apocalyptic) *Didache* (catechetical manual)

SECOND CENTURY (120–220) APOLOGISTS—TO DEFEND CHRISTIANITY

EXPLANATION

West	East
Tertullian	Aristides Justin Martyr Tatian Athenagoras Theophilus

THIRD CENTURY (180–250) POLEMICISTS—TO FIGHT FALSE DOCTRINE

REFUTATION

Practical (polity)	Alexandrian School (Allegorical and speculative)	Antiochene School (Grammatico- historical)
Irenaeus vs. Gnostics Tertullian—founder of Western theology, "Trinity," vs. Praxeas Cyprian on Episcopacy and primacy of honor of Roman bishop	Pantaenus Clement Origen—*Hexapla* (text of Old Testament) *De Principiis* (first systematic theology) used allegorical method of interpretation)	

FOURTH CENTURY (325–460) GOLDEN AGE OF SCIENTIFIC BIBLE STUDY

EXPOSITION

West	East	
Jerome—translator of Bible Ambrose—preacher Augustine—philosophy of history in *City of God;* theologian.	Athanasius Basil of Caesarea	Chrysostom— preacher (Christian conduct) Theodore (use of context)

There is now reasonable assurance that the writings of the New Testament were completed just before the end of the first century after Christ. Men who knew the apostles and apostolic doctrine continued the task of writing Christian literature. These men are known as the apostolic fathers. Most of their literary works were produced between 95 and 150.

Certain well-defined characteristics appear in their writings. Their utterances are informal, simple statements of sincere faith and piety and show little evidence of the philosophical training in pagan philosophy that one notices in the writings of Origen or Clement of Alexandria. The apostolic fathers had a great reverence for the Old Testament, and they leaned heavily on it for support of their ideas. For this reason one notes in some cases an almost excessive use of typological interpretation. Christianity is declared to be the fulfillment of Old Testament prophecies and types. These men were also acquainted with the literary forms of the New Testament and used them as models for their work. Pastoral and practical edification of the church stands out above all else as the major objective of their writings.

I. EPISTOLARY LITERATURE

A. Clement of Rome (ca. 30–100)

About the year 95 a serious disturbance occurred in the church at Corinth. A little later Clement, the leading elder in the church at Rome, wrote his first epistle to the Corinthian church to urge the Christians who were in revolt against the elders to end their disturbance and to be in subjection to these elders (1:1; 14:1–2; 46; 47:3–6). This epistle has been assigned a prominent place among the writings of the apostolic fathers in recent times because it is the earliest Christian writing apart from the books of the New Testament.

After an introduction in which he called to their remembrance the fine spirit of their church in former times (chaps. 1–3), Clement launched into a series of exhortations concerning such Christian virtues as love, penitence, and humility in order to inspire obedience to his later admonitions (4–38). These exhortations, based on the citation of numerous examples from the Old Testament, are divided by a short parenthesis (24–26) concerning the certainty of future resurrection. It is interesting to note that Clement used the pagan story of the Phoenix in chapter 25 as an illustration of the resurrection. More direct attention is given to the troubles at Corinth in chapters 39 to 59:2. The idea of apostolic succession appears in chapters 42–44 and centers around the fact that the elders and deacons were provided for by the apostles, who in turn were sent out by Christ, and Christ was sent out by the Father. Clement then urged obedience to these democratically appointed leaders (44:3). This section is followed by a long prayer (59:3–chap. 61) in which his intense desire for the unity of the church is clear. A final exhortation to unity (62–65) concludes the work.

This letter is valuable for its information concerning the exalted position of the bishops or elders in the church at the end of the first century. Obedience to the bishop is to be the practical guarantee of Christian unity. Clergy are separated from laity (40:5). Clement's letter is also interesting because of its profuse quotations (about 150) from the Old Testament. In addition, it contains a widely quoted reference to Paul's career (5:5–7). The theory of two imprisonments at Rome and a period of release in the interim is built mainly on this reference. Christ's blood is said to be the means of salvation (7:14).

B. Ignatius (1st–2nd c.)

Another apostolic father is Ignatius, bishop of Antioch in Syria, who was arrested by the authorities because of his Christian testimony and sent to Rome to be killed by beasts in the imperial games. He was allowed to have visitors from the churches of the towns along the way, and before his martyrdom he addressed letters of thanks to these churches for their kindness to him. The letter to the Romans is primarily a plea that they should make no efforts to save him from his martyrdom in Rome. Ignatius welcomed his coming martyrdom and sought to prevent any action that might hinder him from becoming "pure bread of Christ" by the grinding of the teeth of the beasts (2, 4). These seven letters must have been written about 110. Though the authenticity of some of the letters is in question, those accepted make his teaching clear.

In his letters Ignatius sought to warn the churches he had visited on the way to Rome about the heresies that threatened the peace and unity of those churches. He opposed Gnostic and Docetic tendencies. The Docetists sought to keep Christ a purely spiritual being, free of any contamination by a material body. This led them to deny the reality of Christ's material body and to state that only a phantom suffered on the cross (Epistle to Smyrna, chap. 1). Ignatius insisted on the reve-

lation of Christ in the flesh as an antidote to this false teaching (Epistle to Smyrna, chap. 1, and Trallians, 9–10).

This early church father also lays great emphasis on subjection to the bishop as the way to achieve unity and to avoid the growth of heresy. There is considerable evidence in his letters that by this time one of the elders in each church had become a monarchical bishop to whom fellow elders were obedient.[1] Ignatius compared obedience of the elders to the bishop with the accord of the strings of a harp (Eph. 4:1) and urged all Christians to obey the monarchical bishop and the elders (20:2). He was the first to place the office of the bishop in contrast with the office of the presbyter and to subordinate the presbyters or elders to the monarchical bishop and the members of the church to both. The hierarchy of authority in the church is, according to him, bishop, presbyter, and deacon. However, Ignatius did not exalt the bishop of Rome as superior to other bishops even though he was the first to use the word *catholic* (Smyrna 8). The only superiority is that of the bishop to the presbyters within each church. Ignatius believed that without this threefold order there is no church (Trallians 3).

C. Polycarp (ca. 70–155)

Polycarp, the writer of a letter to the Philippians that is reminiscent of Paul's letter to that church, had special opportunities to know the mind of the disciples because he had been a disciple of John. Bishop of Smyrna for many years, Polycarp was martyred in 155 by being burned at the stake. During his trial before the Roman proconsul he said that he could not speak evil of Christ whom he had served eighty-six years and who had given him nothing but good.[2]

Polycarp wrote his letter in 110 in answer to one from the Philippians. In his letter Polycarp did not exercise much originality, for he quoted often, directly and indirectly, from the Old and New Testaments and gave much information that he had derived from the apostles, especially John. He was, however, a valuable second-century witness to the life and belief of the early church. He exhorted the Philippians to virtuous living, good works, and steadfastness even to death, if necessary, because they had been saved by faith in Christ. About sixty New Testament quotations, of which thirty-four are from Paul's writings, show Polycarp's acquaintance with Paul's Epistle to the Philippians and other Epistles, as well as with the other writings of the New Testament. Polycarp was not interested in church polity, as Ignatius was, but was interested in strengthening the practical daily life of Christians.

D. The Epistle of Barnabas

This letter is often known as *Pseudo-Barnabas* because it was evidently written by someone other than the Barnabas of the New Testament. Evidence within the epistle itself would confirm this view, although many of the fathers of the church associate it with the Barnabas of the New Testament. It is believed that the letter was written about 130 by some Christian from Alexandria.

The letter was intended to help converts from paganism whom some Jewish Christians were trying to persuade that the law of Moses should be observed because it was still, so they thought, in force. The writer disposed of this claim in the first seventeen chapters by showing that the life and death of Christ are completely adequate for salvation and that Christians are not bound to observe the law. The Mosaic covenant has ended with the death of Christ. The last four chapters present the contrast between two ways of life: "The Way of Light" and "The Way of the Black One." The reader is urged to follow the first way of life. These two ways are reminiscent of the two ways of the *Didache*, with which they probably had a close relationship.

The writer of this letter used Old Testament typology (119 quotations) to the point where it becomes allegory.[3] He allegorized the 318 servants of Abraham (9:9) as a reference to Christ's death on the cross on the basis that the Greek letter for 300 is cross-shaped and the Greek numerals for 18 are the first two letters of the name Jesus. The writer was very proud of this unique interpretation (9:9) of Genesis 14:14. He constantly went beyond legitimate typology to allegory in order to derive the meaning he wanted from the Old Testament Scriptures. This practice, derived from Philo of Alexandria, who sought to reconcile Greek philosophy and the Old Testament by it, was later developed into an organized method of interpretation by Origen. It has done much harm to sound interpretation of the Bible.

E. The Epistle to Diognetus

The tutor of Marcus Aurelius, whose name was Diognetus, may be the man to whom this letter was written by some anonymous writer in the late second or early third century. It is ranked among the writings of the apostolic fathers only by custom because its nature is apologetic, and it could well be considered one of the apologetic writings.

The writer presented a rational defense of Christianity by showing the folly of idolatry (chaps. 1–2), the inadequacy of Judaism (3–4), the superiority of Christianity in its beliefs, the character it builds, and the benefits it offers to the convert (5–12). He also likened the role of Christians in the world to that of the soul in the body in a series of interesting comparisons (6).

F. The Second Epistle of Clement to the Corinthians

This work is usually considered with the writings of the apostolic fathers, although it is not a letter but a sermon or homily (19:1) and was not written by Clement. It was written about 150.

The writer was interested in a sound view of Christ, a belief in the resurrection of the body, and purity of life on the part of the Christian. After a preliminary assertion of the utility of salvation (chaps. 1–4), he urged the Christian to enter the conflict against the world (5–7) by practicing Christian virtues (8–17) and working out the salvation that has become his through Christ (18–20). The letter is an interesting illustration of the content of preaching during the second century.

G. Papias (ca. 60–ca. 130)

The *Interpretations of the Sayings of the Lord* was written about the middle of the second century by Papias, the bishop of Hierapolis in Phrygia, in order to record the information that he had received from older Christians who had known the apostles. It is possible that Papias had been a disciple of John. The document deals with the life and words of Christ. Although it has disappeared, fragments of it are available in the writings of Eusebius and Irenaeus. The fragment preserved in Irenaeus's writings[4] gives clear evidence of Papias's strong millennial views. The section preserved by Eusebius[5] throws interesting light on the origin of the Gospels. He stated that Mark was the interpreter of Peter and that Matthew wrote his work in the Hebrew language. These little excerpts are tantalizing to the student who realizes the light that his complete work would throw on the beliefs, life, and literature of the New Testament.

II. APOCALYPTIC LITERATURE

The Shepherd of Hermas, modeled after the Book of Revelation, was probably written about 150 by Hermas, who was considered by the writer of the Muratorian Canon to be the brother of Pius, the bishop of Rome between 140 and 155.[6] The author's use of vision and allegory reminds one of John Bunyan's work, but, unfortunately, Hermas had little of the ability that that Puritan writer had.

Although the work is written in the form of a revelation abounding in symbols and visions, its aim is both moral and practical. The writer had been the slave of Rhoda, a Christian woman of Rome. She had freed him, and he had become a rich businessman. But in the process he had neglected his own family, and his family consequently fell into vile sin. He and his wife repented and confessed their sin, but his children turned against the faith. Then he lost all his possessions. Out of this experience came this work, which is designed to call sinners to repentance. Repentance and holy living are the keynotes of the work (mandate 4). The messages of the work are given to Hermas by a woman and an angel. The first section consists of five visions that emphasize the need of repentance in symbols. This is followed by twelve mandates or commandments depicting the code of ethics that the repentant one should follow in order to be pleasing to God. The final section is made up of ten similitudes or parables in which the main theme is the significance of repentance in life. The writer of *The Shepherd* is much concerned with the individual in relation to the Christian society, the church.

III. CATECHETICAL LITERATURE

The little book the *Didache* (the *Teaching of the Apostles*) came to light in the year 1873, when a man named Bryennios Philotheus discovered it in an ecclesiastical library in Constantinople and published it in 1883. This manual of church instruction was most likely composed before the middle of the second century in the form in which it has come down to us. However, many contend for a date at the end of the first century because of the resemblance of much in it to the practices of the New Testament.

Even the casual reader can pick out the clearly defined four parts of the work. The first section, which closely resembles the two ways of life in the *Pseudo-Barnabas*, consists of a discussion of the Ways of Life and Death (chaps. 1–6). Here the ethical action consistent with a Christian life is set forth in contrast with the deeds of those who follow the Way of Death. The writer then discussed such liturgical problems as baptism, fasting, and the Communion (7–10). Instruction on how to distinguish false prophets from true, how to find worthy officials, and disciplinary matters forms the burden of the third section (11–15). The document wryly points out the false prophet as one who seeks food and lodging without giving anything in return to the church in the form of spiritual inspiration. The need for a watchful and consistent life in view of the coming of the Lord is the burden of the last chapter. This discussion should make clear the importance of the *Didache* as a picture of life in the early church between 95 and 150.

The diligent reader of the literature that has been discussed will find much reward in the way of knowledge and inspiration. It seems somewhat a pity that these writings of edification should have been neglected by the church throughout the ages.

SUGGESTED READING

Goodspeed, Edgar. A History of Early Christian Literature. *Revised and enlarged by Robert Grant. Chicago: University of Chicago Press, 1946. This work has illuminating introductions to and discussions of the nature and value of the writings of the Fathers.*
Lake, Kirsopp. The Apostolic Fathers. *Loeb Classical Library. New York: Putnam, 1930. These two volumes of this series contain a good translation of the Fathers' writings on*

the right-hand page and the original text on the left-hand page. This is one of the best translations of these primary sources.

Newman, Albert. A Manual of Church History. Rev. and enlarged ed. Philadelphia: American Baptist Publication Society, 1933. The student will find pages 211 to 290 of volume 1 helpful for its presentation of the theology of these writers as well as for introductions to their writings.

Quasten, Johannes. Patrology. 3 vols. Westminster, Md.: Newman, 1950-63. This series has scholarly accounts of the lives, works, and theologies of the Fathers.

Swete, Henry B. Patristic Study. 3rd ed. New York: Longmans, 1904. Many will find this little manual useful in providing a historical background.

Tixeront, J. A Handbook of Patrology. Translated by S. A. Raemers. St. Louis: Herder, 1947. There are many excellent introductions to, and analyses of, the writings and the lives of the Fathers in this Roman Catholic work.

Williams, Robert R. A Guide to the Teachings of the Early Church Fathers. Grand Rapids: Eerdmans, 1960. The author quotes copiously from the sources on the major ideas of the church fathers in the context of their times and lives.

Chapter 6

With the Bishops and Deacons

The church exists on two levels. On one level it is an eternal, invisible, biblical *organism* that is welded into one body by the Holy Spirit. On the other it is the temporal, historical, visible, human, institutional *organization*. The first is the end, the second the means.

The development of the church as an organization was left to the apostles to work out under the guidance of the Holy Spirit. Any large corporate body must of necessity have leadership; and, as it grows, the division of functions and consequent specialization of leadership must come if it is to function effectively. A liturgy to guide the worship of the church in an orderly fashion (1 Cor. 14:40) is another logical outcome of the growth of the church as an organization. The eventual aim of the church as a worshiping organism is the achievement of quality of life. Thus, the Christian is part of an organism and of an organization.

I. THE GOVERNMENT OF THE CHURCH

The origin of church polity is to be credited to Christ because He chose the twelve apostles who were to be the leaders of the infant church. The apostles took the initiative in the development of other offices in the church when they were so directed by the Holy Spirit. This does not by any means imply a pyramidal hierarchy, such as the Roman Catholic church has developed, because the new officials were to be chosen by the people, ordained by the apostles, and have special spiritual qualifications that involved leadership by the Holy Spirit. Thus there was an inward call by the Holy Spirit to the office, an external call by the democratic vote of the church, and the ordaining to office by the apostles. There was to be no special class of priests set apart to minister a sacerdotal system of salvation because both the officials and the members of the church were spiritual priests with the right of direct access to God through Christ (Eph. 2:18).

These officials may be divided into two classes. The *charismatic officials* (Greek *charisma* means gift) were chosen by Christ and endowed with special spiritual gifts (1 Cor. 12–14; Eph. 4:11–12). Their function was primarily inspirational. The *administrative* officials constituted the second class. Their functions were mainly administrative; although after the death of the apostles, the elders took over many spiritual responsibilities. These officials were chosen by the congregation after prayer for the guidance of the Holy Spirit and appointed by the apostles.

A. Charismatic Officials

These men, whose main responsibilities were the guarding of the truth of the gospel and its initial proclamation, were specially selected by Christ through the Holy Spirit to exercise leadership within the church. There were four or five such offices designated by Paul—apostles, prophets, evangelists, pastors, and/or teachers. Many think that pastor and teacher may be designations for the same man.

The apostles were men who had been witnesses to Christ's life, death, and particularly His resurrection (Acts 1:22; cf. 1 Cor. 1:1; 15:8) and who had been personally called by Christ. Paul based his apostleship on a direct call from the living Christ. These men, who were the first officials of the early church, had combined in their work all the functions later carried on by various officials when the apostles were unable to take care of the needs of the rapidly expanding early church.

Peter is the dominant figure among the apostles in the first twelve chapters of Luke's record of the history of the early church. Not only did he make the first official proclamation to the Jews in Jerusalem on the day of Pentecost, but he also first introduced the gospel among the Gentiles by his preaching to the household of Cornelius. Despite this leadership, nothing of the hierarchical, authoritarian concept of the medieval Roman Catholic church is to be seen in the New Testament account of his activities. Tradition dating from the early church fixes Rome as the place of Peter's death. One rather interesting tradition describes Peter's escape from prison in Rome and flight from the city. Confronted by Christ, Peter asked Him where He was going. Christ replied that He was going to Rome to be crucified again. Smitten with remorse, Peter hastened back to the city where he was crucified at his own request, according to one tradition, with his head down because he did not feel worthy to die in the same way his Lord had died.

James, the son of Zebedee, was present at the Transfiguration and in Gethsemane. He was the first of the Twelve to be martyred, being beheaded by Herod Agrippa I in 44. The Spanish consider him as their patron saint.

James, the brother of Christ (Gal. 1:19), ranked next to Peter as the leader of the church in Jerusalem. His prominence in the church is clearly evident from his position of leadership at the Jerusalem Council. While closer to the legalism of Judaism than most of the leaders of the early Jerusalem church, he occupied a mediatorial position between Jewish and Gentile Christians at the Jerusalem Council. He had such a desire for holiness and a devout life of prayer that, according to tradition, his knees became calloused like those of a camel because of his constant kneeling. He was martyred by being clubbed to death after he had been thrown down from the pinnacle of the temple. All the while he uttered words of forgiveness similar to those used by Stephen.[1] He was not one of the Twelve.

John is ranked along with Peter as a leader in the early church. Tradition associates his later labors with the city of Ephesus. He was banished by Domitian to the island of Patmos, a solitary, barren rocky island off the western coast of Asia Minor. Here he wrote the Book of Revelation. After the death of Domitian, he was allowed to return to Ephesus, where he remained, ministering to the churches of Asia until his death at an advanced age.[2] His Gospel, his three epistles, and Revelation are a rich part of the literary heritage of the church in the New Testament.

Peter's brother Andrew preached in sections of the Near East and Scythia. According to later tradition, he was crucified on an X-shaped cross—the form of cross that has since been known by his name.

Little is known of Philip's later life except that he most likely died a natural death at Hierapolis after the destruction of Jerusalem. Nothing is known of the later labors and death of James the Less, the son of Alphaeus. Tradition concerning Thaddaeus assigned his labors to Persia, where he was martyred. Matthias, who took the place of Judas, labored in Ethiopia and was there martyred, according to one account. Simon Zelotes was also martyred. Tradition is not clear concerning the mode of martyrdom of Bar-

tholomew, but his name is linked with the proclamation of the gospel in India by one tradition. Matthew was supposed to have also labored in Ethiopia. The name of the most skeptical of the disciples, Thomas, is associated with labor in Parthia, but other accounts link his work and martyrdom with India. The silence of the New Testament and even tradition concerning these men[3] is remarkable compared with the later medieval tendency to glorify the death of the notable men of the church.

Prophets appeared to be among the more influential leaders of the New Testament church. They exercised the function of forthtelling or preaching the gospel (Acts 13:1; 15:32) as well as foretelling or predicting the future. Agabus is credited with having successfully predicted a coming famine and Paul's imprisonment at the hands of the Jews (Acts 11:28; 21:10–14). Evidently the early church was plagued with many who falsely pretended to be prophets because the *Didache* gives clear instruction as to how to distinguish the false prophet from the genuine prophet (10:7; 11:7–12).

Philip exercised the gift of evangelism (Acts 21:8), but little is known of this office and its specific functions. Perhaps it had special reference to work of the itinerant missionary whose main task was to proclaim the gospel in new, hitherto-untouched areas.

There is also the problem concerning whether the separate offices of pastor and teacher existed in two persons or were simply designations for two functions that one man specially gifted by God was to fill. The New Testament is less obscure concerning the test of a genuine teacher. No one who denied the personal advent of Christ into the world as man in human flesh could be a true teacher, according to John (2 John 1–11). The character of a true teacher is pointed out in the *Didache* (11:1–2).

B. Administrative Officials

All the officials who have been discussed were specially appointed to their offices by God rather than man. There was another class of officials who were democratically chosen "with the consent of the whole church."[4] Their task was to carry out governmental functions within a given church. The apostles laid down their qualifications and put them in office after their selection by the congregation. Unlike the apostles and other charismatic officials, these men, and in some cases women, worked and exercised their authority in the local church or congregation rather than in the church of Christ as a whole. These offices grew by division of function and specialization as necessity dictated aid to the overworked apostles faced with the problem of a growing church. Perhaps the example of the synagogue with its elders who presided over local affairs was a factor in the creation of these offices.

The office of the elder or presbyter ranked highest in the local congregation. Those who hold to a threefold organization in the church contend that the names elder (*presbyteros*) and bishop (*episkopos*) are not synonymous terms but represent the separate offices of bishop and presbyter. The New Testament, however, is quite clear in its association of these two names with the same office (Acts 20:17, 28; Phil. 1:1; Titus 1:5, 7). The growth of the office of the monarchical bishop did not come until after the end of the apostolic age in the second century.

The qualifications of an elder are clearly outlined at least twice in the New Testament (1 Tim. 3:1–7; Titus 1:5–9). Elders must be men of good reputation among the members of the church and outsiders. Conduct of public worship seems to have been one of their main functions (1 Tim. 5:17; Titus 1:9) along with the responsibility for the good government and orderly discipline of the church.

The deacons had a subordinate position to the elders, but those who filled the office faced the same rigid qualifications for office that the elders had to meet (Acts 6:3; 1 Tim. 3:8–13). The procedure for democratic election was also prescribed by the apostles in Jerusalem (Acts 6:3, 5). The dispensing of charity by the church was the major task of the deacons. Later, they aided the elders by giving the elements of the Communion to the people.

Women seem to have been admitted to this office in apostolic times, for Paul mentioned Phoebe the deaconess with approval (Rom. 16:1). The daughters of Philip the evangelist also fulfilled the functions of a prophet (Acts 21:9), but Paul was specific in his assertion that women could not be teachers in the church (1 Cor. 14:34; 1 Tim. 2:12).

The emergence of a set of officials for the congregation and the definition of their qualifications and duties were completed by the end of the first century. With salvation by faith in Christ as its gospel, a growing literature written by the apostles, and a form of organization to meet its needs, Christianity grew rapidly in the late first and early second centuries.

II. THE WORSHIP
OF THE EARLY CHURCH

The question of an orderly form of worship seems to have been a matter of some concern from the time of the apostles. Paul had to urge the Corinthian church to conduct its worship in an orderly, dignified manner (1 Cor. 14:40). Christ earlier had stated the essence of true worship when He declared that because God was a spirit, true worship was a matter of the spirit (John 4:24). Worship is really the upward reach of the human spirit through religious exercises that bring the soul into the presence of God.

The early Christians did not think of a church as a place of worship according to the common usage of the word today. A church signified a body of people in personal relationship with Christ. Such a group met in homes (Acts 12:12; Rom. 16:5, 23; Col. 4:15, Philem. 1–4), the temple (Acts 5:12), public auditoriums of schools (Acts 19:9), and in the synagogues as long as they were permitted to do so (Acts 14:1, 3; 17:1; 18:4). The place was not as important as the matter of meeting for fellowship with one another and for worship of God.

During the first century, two services were held on the first day of the week. That day was adopted as the day of worship because it was the day on which Christ rose from the dead (Acts 20:7; 1 Cor. 16:2; Rev. 1:10). The morning service most likely included the reading of Scripture (Col. 3:16), exhortation by the leading elder, prayers, and singing (Eph. 5:19). The love feast (1 Cor. 11:20–22), or agapē preceded the Communion during the evening service. By the end of the first century the love feast was generally dropped and the Communion celebrated during the morning service of worship. Pliny described the Christians to Trajan as those who met before daybreak, sang hymns, and took vows to lead an ethical life.[5]

Information concerning the order of worship in the middle part of the second century is much more complete and is to be found in the *First Apology* of Justin Martyr and the *Didache*.[6] The service, which was held on "the day of the sun," started with reading of the "memoirs of the apostles" or "the writings of the prophets" for a period "as long as time permits." An exhortation or homily based on the reading was then given by the "president." The congregation then stood for prayer. The celebration of the Lord's Supper followed the kiss of peace. The elements of bread and "water and wine" were dedicated by thanksgiving and prayers to which the people responded by an "Amen." The deacons then distributed them to the homes of those unable to be present at the meeting. They finally took up a collection for aid to widows and orphans, the sick, prisoners, and strangers. The meeting was then dismissed, and all the people made their way to their homes.

The Lord's Supper and baptism were the two sacraments that the early church used because they had been instituted by Christ. Immersion seems to have been widely practiced in the first century; but, according to the *Didache*, baptism could be performed by pouring water over the head of the one being baptized if no stream of running water or large amount of water were available.[7] Only those who were baptized could partake of the Communion.

From the Catacomb of Callistus, a representation of a convert being baptized.

III. THE LIFE OF THE CHURCH

The early church had no benevolent welfare state to give aid to the poor and sick. A church took that responsibility on itself. The money collected from those able to give in the offering following the celebration of the Communion was dispensed to meet such needs. Paul also mentioned the practice of collecting the gifts of the faithful each Sunday (1 Cor. 16:1–2). The deacons would then use it to care for those who were in need. The women of the churches also aided in this charitable work by making clothes for those with such a need (Acts 9:36–41).

The church did not attack the institution of slavery directly; nor was the ownership of slaves forbidden to Christians. However, Christianity soon undercut the institution of slavery by bidding the Christian master and slave to remember that they were brother Christians. Paul's tactful letter to Philemon, the leader of the church in Colosse, leaves one with the impression that Philemon as a sincere Christian would most likely give Onesimus his freedom.

The early church insisted on separation from the pagan practices of Roman society, but it did not insist on separation from pagan neighbors in harmless social relationships. In fact, Paul by inference made provision for such social mingling as long as it did not involve the compromise or sacrifice of Christian principles (1 Cor. 5:10; 10:20–33). He did, however, urge complete separation from any practice that might be related to idolatry or pagan immorality. The Christian should follow the principles of doing nothing that would harm the body that Christ owned (1 Cor. 6:12), of doing nothing that would keep people from coming to Christ or lead other weak Christians astray (1 Cor. 8:13; 10:24), and of avoiding all that would not bring glory to God (1 Cor. 6:20; 10:31). These principles precluded attendance at the pagan theaters, stadiums, games, or temples.

Despite this attitude of moral and spiritual separation, the Christians were willing and were even urged by Paul to fulfill their civic obligations of obedience to and respect for civil authority, payment of taxes, and prayers for those in authority (Rom. 13:7; 1 Tim. 2:1–2). They made excellent citizens so long as they were not asked to violate the precepts of God, the higher authority to whom their primary allegiance was due.

The purity of life, love, and courage

of the early church in standing and dying for principle made such an impact on the pagan society of imperial Rome that it was only three centuries after the death of Christ that Constantine gave official recognition to the importance of Christianity in the state by calling and presiding over the Council of Nicaea.

SUGGESTED READING

Schaff, Philip. **History of the Apostolic Church.** *New York: Scribner, 1869. Pages 433–92 and 545–86 have excellent discussions of the topics considered in this chapter.*

Chapter 7

Christ or Caesar

Christianity has always faced both external and internal problems in every period of its history. The church had to face the serious *internal* problem of *heresy* and deal with it between 100 and 313 and, at the same time, it had to solve the *external* problem of *persecution* from the Roman state.

Christians in the Roman Empire, Nestorians in China in the ninth and tenth centuries, and Roman Catholics in Japan in the seventeenth century, as well as Christians in the Nazi and Communist states, have had the common experience of state hostility even to the point of martyrdom. Christians have also faced attacks from pagan intellectuals, such as Lucian, Fronto, and Celsus.

Many have a confused idea of the number, duration, scope, and intensity of the persecutions that the church suffered. Before 250 persecution was mainly local, sporadic, and more often the result of mob action than the result of definite civil policy. After that date, however, persecution became at times the studied policy of

the Roman imperial government and, hence, widespread and violent. During that time Tertullian's idea that "the blood of Christians is seed" (of the church) became a terrible reality to many Christians. The church continued to develop in spite of or, perhaps, partly because of persecution until at the end of the period it won freedom of worship under Constantine.

I. CAUSES OF PERSECUTION

A. Political

The church endured little persecution as long as it was looked upon by the authorities as a part of Judaism, which was a *religio licita*, or legal sect. But as soon as Christianity was distinguished from Judaism as a separate sect and might be classed as a secret society, it came under the ban of the Roman state, which would brook no rival for the allegiance of its subjects. It then became an illegal religion, which was considered a threat to the safety of the Roman state. The state was the highest good in a union of the state

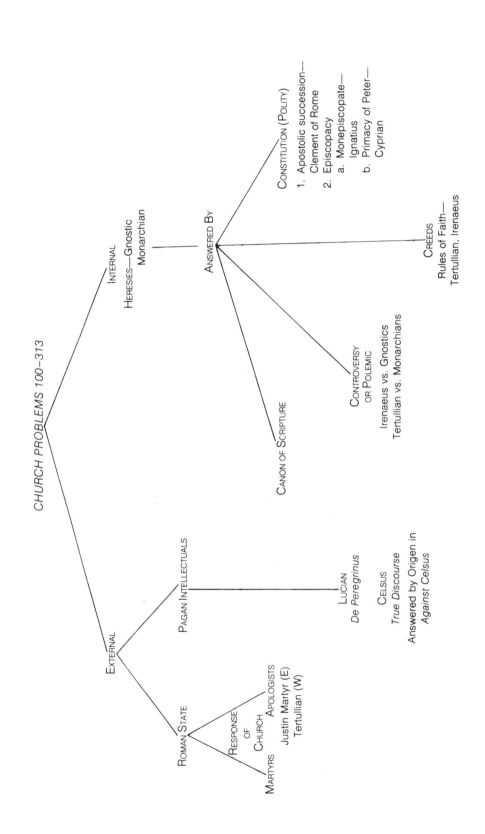

CHURCH PROBLEMS 100–313

EXTERNAL

PAGAN INTELLECTUALS

LUCIAN
De Peregrinus

CELSUS
True Discourse
Answered by Origen in
Against Celsus

ROMAN STATE

RESPONSE
OF
CHURCH

MARTYRS

APOLOGISTS
Justin Martyr (E)
Tertullian (W)

INTERNAL

HERESIES—Gnostic
Monarchian

ANSWERED BY

CONSTITUTION (POLITY)

1. Apostolic succession—
   Clement of Rome
2. Episcopacy
   a. Monepiscopate—
      Ignatius
   b. Primacy of Peter—
      Cyprian

CANON OF SCRIPTURE

CONTROVERSY
OR POLEMIC

Irenaeus vs. Gnostics
Tertullian vs. Monarchians

CREEDS
Rules of Faith—
Tertullian, Irenaeus

and religion. There could be no private religion.

Religion could be tolerated only as it contributed to the stability of the state. Since the rapidly growing Christian religion was exclusive in its claims on the moral and spiritual loyalty of those who accepted Christ, when a choice had to be made between loyalty to Christ and loyalty to Caesar, Caesar was bound to take second place. This was conceived by the Roman leaders, bent on preserving classical culture within the framework of the Roman imperial state, as disloyalty to the state; and they saw Christians as those who were trying to set up a state within a state. Either the universal state or the universal church, the body of Christ, must give way. The exclusive sovereignty of Christ clashed with Caesar's proud claims to exclusive sovereignty.

Many Christian practices seemed to confirm the Roman authorities' suspicions of the basic disloyalty of the Christians to the state. The Christians consistently refused to offer incense on the altars devoted to the genius of the Roman emperor, with whom the welfare of the state was inextricably mingled in the minds of the people during the imperial period from Caesar Augustus to Constantine. If one would sacrifice on these altars, he could then practice a second private religion. The Christians would not make such sacrifices, and, consequently, it was thought that they were disloyal. The Christians also held most of their meetings at night and in secret. To the Roman authority this could mean nothing else than the hatching of a conspiracy against the safety of the state. Christians would not serve as soldiers until after 313.

B. Religious

In addition to the basic political cause for persecution, there was a religious reason. Roman state religion was mechanical and external. It had its altars, idols, priests, processionals, rites, and practices that the people could see. The Romans were not averse to adding a new idol to the group in the Pantheon as long as that deity was subordinate to the prior claims of the Roman state religion. The Christians had no idols and little visible paraphernalia of worship. Their worship was spiritual and internal. When they stood and prayed with eyes closed, there was no visible object to which those prayers were addressed. This could mean nothing else but atheism to the Romans, who were accustomed to symbolic, material manifestations of their god.

The secrecy of the meetings of the Christians also brought moral charges against them. Public rumor made them guilty of incest, cannibalism, and unnatural practices. Misunderstanding concerning the meaning of "eating and drinking" the elements representing Christ's body and blood easily led to the rumor that the Christians killed and ate infants in sacrifice to their God. Word of "the kiss of peace" was easily twisted into charges of incest and other types of immoral conduct repugnant to the cultured Roman mind. It made little difference that there was no truth in these rumors.[1]

C. Social

Social problems also made their contribution to the cause of Roman persecution of the church. The Christians, who had great appeal for the lower classes and slaves, were hated by the influential aristocratic leaders of society. These leaders looked down on them with contempt but were fearful of their influence on the lower class. The Christians upheld the equality of all men (Col. 3:11); paganism insisted on an aristocratic structure for society in which the privileged few were served by the lower class and slaves. Christians separated themselves from pagan gatherings at temples, theaters, and places of recreation. This nonconformity to accepted social patterns brought down on them the dislike that the nonconformist always faces in any period of history. The purity of their lives was a silent rebuke to the scandalous lives that people of the upper class were leading. The Christians' nonconformity to existing social patterns led the pagans to believe that they were a danger to society and to characterize them as "haters of mankind" who might incite the masses to revolt.

D. Economic

It must not be forgotten that economic considerations played a part in the persecution of the Christians. The opposition that Paul received from the idol makers of Ephesus, who were more concerned over the danger of Christianity to their craft than to the damage it might cause Diana worship (Acts 19:27), is a clue to the feelings of those vested interests whose livelihood was threatened by the spread of Christianity. Priests, idol makers, soothsayers, painters, architects, and sculptors would hardly be enthusiastic about a religion that was threatening their means of livelihood.

The year 250, when persecution became general and violent instead of local and spasmodic, was, according to the reckoning of the Romans, about one thousand years after the founding of Rome. Since plague, famine, and civic unrest plagued the empire at this time, popular opinion ascribed these troubles to the presence of Christianity within the empire and to the consequent forsaking of the older gods. There is always a good deal of superstition concerning the end of a millennium, and the Romans were no better in this regard than people in the Middle Ages just before 1000. Persecution of the Christians seemed a logical way for the Romans to overcome their troubles.

All these considerations combined to justify the persecution of the Christians in the minds of the authorities. Not all were present in each case, but the exclusiveness of the claims of the Christian religion on the life of the Christian conflicted with pagan syncretism and the demand for exclusive loyalty to the Roman state in most instances. Persecution followed naturally as a part of imperial policy to preserve the integrity of the Roman state. Christianity was not a licensed religion with a legal right to existence. Martyrs and apologists were its answer to mobs, the state, and pagan writers.

II. PERSECUTION OF THE CHURCH

Persecution of the Christians was both ecclesiastical and political. The Jews were the persecutors during the infancy of the church in Jerusalem. Only in the reign of Nero (54–68) did organized persecution begin to come from the Roman state. Even these persecutions were local and sporadic until 250, when they became general and violent, beginning with that under Decius.

A. Persecution to 100

Nero has the dubious distinction of being the first major persecutor of the Christian church. Tacitus recorded the rumor that Nero had ordered the fire that destroyed part of the city of Rome. This rumor was so widely accepted by the people that Nero had to find a scapegoat. He diverted feeling against himself to the Christians by accusing them of arson and by engaging in a saturnalia of destruction of the Christians. Apparently the persecution was confined to Rome and its environs.[2] Peter and Paul died in this period.

Persecution broke out again in 95 during the reign of the despotic Domitian. The Jews had refused to pay a poll tax that had been levied for the support of Capitolinus Jupiter. Because the Christians continued to be associated with the Jews, they also suffered the effects of the emperor's wrath. It was during this persecution that the apostle John was exiled to the Isle of Patmos, where he wrote the Book of Revelation.

B. Christianity Under State Ban, 100–250

The first organized persecution, which brought Christians into the courts as defendants, took place in Bithynia during the governorship of Pliny the Younger, about 112. Pliny wrote a rather interesting letter to Emperor Trajan, in which he gave information about the Christians, outlined his policy, and asked Trajan for his judgment concerning the matter. He wrote that "the contagion of this superstition" (Christianity) had spread in the villages and rural areas as well as in the larger cities to such an extent that the temples had been almost deserted and the sellers of sacrificial animals impoverished. Pliny went on to inform Trajan of his procedure in treating Christians. When someone informed on a Christian, Pliny brought the Christian before his tribunal and asked him whether he was a Christian. If he still admitted the charge after three such questions, he was sentenced to death. In his answer Trajan assured Pliny that he was following the correct procedure. No Christians were to be sought out; but if someone reported that a certain individual was a Christian, the Christian was to be punished unless he recanted and worshiped the gods of the Romans.[3] It was during this persecution that Ignatius lost his life.

Another persecution took place at Smyrna about the middle of the second century. It was at this time that Polycarp was martyred as an enraged mob brought the Christians before the authorities.[4]

Local calamity, such as the fire in Rome, or the activity of a conscientious governor were the causes of persecution up to the reign of Marcus Aurelius. Marcus Aurelius was a devout Stoic who had been biased against Christianity by his teacher Fronto. Inclined to ascribe the natural and man-made calamities of his reign to the growth of Christianity, he gave orders for the persecution of the Christians. Justin Martyr, the great apologetic writer, suffered martyrdom in Rome during this persecution.

C. Universal Persecution After 250

Emperor Decius took the imperial throne about the time Rome was reaching the end of the first millennium of her history and at a time when the empire was reeling under natural calamities and internal and external attacks on its stability. He decided that if classical culture were to be saved, it would have to be with a strong arm. The Christians were picked out as a peculiar threat to the state because of their rapid increase in numbers and their seeming attempt to set up a state within a state.

Decius issued an edict in 250 that demanded, at the least, an annual offering of sacrifice at the Roman altars to the gods and the genius of the emperor. Those who offered such sacrifices were given a certificate called a *libellus*.[5] The church was later agitated by the problem of how to deal with those who denied their Christian faith to get such certificates. Fortunately for the church, the persecution lasted only until the death of Decius in the next year; but the tortures that Origen suffered later caused his death.[6]

Although there were periods of state persecution by order of the emperors, no major persecution occurred after that of Decius and Valerian, under whom Cyprian was martyred, until the reign of Diocletian (245–313). Diocletian was a strong military leader who came to the imperial throne at the end of a century that was marked by political disorder in the Roman Empire. He decided that only a strong monarchy could save the empire and its classical culture. In 285 he ended the dyarchy of the principate, created by Caesar Augustus in 27 B.C., by which the emperor and senate had shared authority.

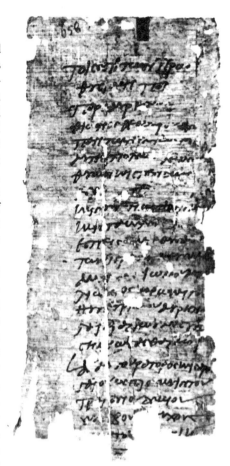

A photograph of an actual *libellus* from the reign of Decian. Translated from Greek, this document reads: "To the superintendents of offerings and sacrifices at the city from Aurelius . . . thion son of Theodorus and Pantonymis, of the said city. It has ever been my custom to make sacrifices and libations to the gods, and now also I have in your presence in accordance with the command poured libations and sacrificed and tasted the offerings together with my son Aurelius Dioscorus and my daughter Aurelia Lais. I therefore request you to certify my statement. The 1st year of the Emperor Caesar Gaius Messius Quintus Trajanus Decius Pius Felix Augustus, Pauni 20."

A powerful, orientalized monarchy seemed in his opinion to offer the only alternative to chaos. In such a despotic empire there was no place for democratic elements in government or for the toleration of faiths hostile to the state religion. Out of this historical situation came the most severe persecution that the Christians ever endured.

The first edicts calling for persecution of the Christians came in March 303. Diocletian ordered the cessation of meetings of the Christians, the destruction of the churches, the deposition of officers of the church, the imprisonment of those who persisted in their testimony to Christ, and the destruction of the Scriptures by fire. This last order was to give the church trouble later on when the Donatist controversy broke out in North Africa over how the *traditores*, those who had given up copies of the Scriptures to persecutors, were to be treated when they asked to be readmitted to the church after the persecution was over. A later edict ordered Christians to sacrifice to the pagan gods on pain of death if they refused.[7] Eusebius pointed out that prisons became so crowded with Christian leaders and their congregations that there was not even enough room for criminals.[8] Christians were punished by loss of property, exile, imprisonment, or execution by the sword or wild beasts. The more fortunate were sent to the Roman equivalent of a totalitarian labor camp where they were worked to death in the mines. The pace of the persecution slackened when Diocletian abdicated and retired in 305.

After other periods of persecution, Galerius issued an edict from his deathbed in 311 that gave toleration to Christianity, provided the Christians did not violate the peace of the empire. Persecution did not cease completely until Licinius and Constantine issued the Edict of Milan in 313. This edict brought freedom of worship, not only to Christianity but to all religions.[9] Because Constantine believed that "the worship of God" should be the "first and chiefest care" of the ruler, he thought that there could be no alternative to freedom of religion as the policy of the empire. Perhaps the vision of the Cross, which he is traditionally believed to have seen and which gave him the assurance of victory over his rivals, had something to do with his tolerant policy. Certainly he was ahead of his times, for not until the modern period has freedom of religion become a settled policy, even of democratic states. From that time on, Christians had freedom to worship and to propagandize others in order to win them for Christ.

In our day, this same issue of church and state has again been revived, and in many countries Christians are tolerated only under law. In other countries they face persecution from a state that will brook no rival. The early struggle of the church with persecution helps to point up the importance of the modern concept of the separation of the church and state. Only where people are permitted to have private interests apart from public interests can there be religious freedom.

III. RESULTS OF PERSECUTION

The rapid spread of Christianity, even during the periods of heaviest persecution, proved that indeed the blood of the martyrs was the seed of the church. During the apostolic period Christianity had been largely an urban movement. The number of active believers in Jerusalem after the

Resurrection was estimated at approximately five hundred by Paul (1 Cor. 15:6). Pliny's letter proved that Christianity was strong in Asia Minor shortly after the beginning of the second century. During the first century it had been confined largely to the eastern section of the empire, with the Jews being given the first chance to accept Christianity as the gospel reached new cities. During the second century, expansion was rapid among the Greek-speaking Gentile population of the empire. The church in Alexandria became the chief church of Egypt. Christians could be found in all parts of the empire by 200. The emphasis during the third century was on the spread of the gospel to the Latins of the western section of the empire. A powerful church with Carthage as its intellectual center grew up in North Africa. Estimates of the size of the church by 300 vary between 5 and 15 percent of the population of the empire, which was between 50 million and 75 million.

Persecution, however, did create internal problems that had to be solved. Two severe controversies broke out in North Africa and Rome concerning the manner of treatment those who had offered sacrifices at pagan altars in the Decian persecution and those who had given up the Scriptures in the Diocletian persecution should receive from the church when they repented. Some desired to exclude them from any fellowship with the church; others would receive them after a period of probation. The Donatist controversy, which grew out of the Diocletian persecution, was not settled by the time of Constantine (see chap. 8, pp. 103–4).

The Diocletian persecution forced upon the church the problem of the canon of the New Testament (see chap. 10, p. 118). If the possession of letters might mean death, the Christians wanted to be sure that the books that they would not give up on pain of death were really canonical books. This consideration contributed to the final decisions as to what literature was canonical. Apologetic literature was also created.

The era of persecution is interesting for the light it throws on the perennial problem of the relation of the church to the state. Christianity claimed the exclusive loyalty of its followers in moral and spiritual matters. The Christian was to be obedient to the state as long as it did not ask him to violate his moral and spiritual allegiance to God. Christians who live in states where they are now persecuted for their faith may take the history of early persecution as a guide. The problem of obedience to Christ or Caesar is perennial in the history of the church.

SUGGESTED READING

Ayer, Joseph, Jr. **A Source Book for Ancient Church History.** *New York: Scribner, 1913. This compilation contains much primary material concerning the causes and the story of the major persecutions.*

Frend, W. H. C. **Martyrdom and Persecution in the Early Church.** *New York University Press, 1967. This work is both scholarly and detailed.*

Grant, Robert M. **The Sword and the Cross.** *New York: Macmillan, 1955. This is a helpful survey of the relationship of religion to the Roman state.*

Norwood, Frederick. **Strangers and Exiles.** *2 vols. Nashville: Abingdon, 1969. The author has given a comprehensive account of persecution and refugees from the New Testament era to the present.*

Workman, Herbert B. **Persecutions in the Early Church.** *London: Epworth, 1923. This is a useful work for the student of the history of persecution of the church.*

Chapter 8

Fables or Sound Doctrine

The Christians of the second and third centuries had to fight what every strategist tries to avoid—a war on two fronts. While the church was fighting to preserve its existence in the face of attempts by the Roman state to abolish it, it was also fighting to preserve purity of doctrine within the church. Converts to the Christian faith either came from a Jewish background of salvation by works or from the intellectual environment of Greek philosophy. Many of these converts, until the church could instruct them properly, tended to carry their old ideas into their new environment. Others tried to make Christianity appear intellectually respectable to the upper classes in the state. The threat of legalistic or philosophical perversions of Christianity was very real in the church during this era. In some instances overzealous leaders developed a particular interpretation to correct real or fancied evils in the church and got many to follow their heretical ideas until heresies finally resulted in schisms, and from schisms came new sects.

I. LEGALISTIC HERESIES

One would have thought that the decision at the Jerusalem Council to free the Gentiles from the ceremonial and ritualistic demands of the Jewish law as requirements for salvation would have been final. Converts from Judaism, however, looked back to monotheism and, in thinking of Christ and salvation, tended to dilute the faith with their Jewish heritage. Moreover, groups of Ebionites persisted in Palestine and nearby countries for some time after the suppression by the Roman authorities of the rebellion of Jews under Bar Kochba between 132 and 135. These people emphasized the unity of God and His creatorship of the universe. They believed that the Jewish law was the highest expression of His will and that it was still binding on man. They believed that Jesus was Joseph's son who attained a measure of divinity when the Spirit came upon Him at baptism. They upheld, therefore, the teachings of Matthew's Gospel, but they disliked the writings of Paul. They insisted that Gentile as well as Jewish Christians were still bound by the law of Moses and that there was no salvation apart from circumcision and the law of Moses. After the destruction of Jerusalem by the Romans in 135, they ceased to have much influence; but their existence and beliefs showed that the church had repeatedly to fight for the principle that faith in Christ alone justifies the individual before God.

II. PHILOSOPHICAL HERESIES

A far greater threat to the doctrinal purity of the Christian faith came from Greek philosophy. Many more Gentiles than Jews were won to Christianity. Among these there were many philosophers who wanted to dilute Christianity with philosophy or to dress pagan philosophy in Christian garb.

A. Gnosticism

Gnosticism, the greatest of the philosophical threats, was at its peak of power about 150. Its roots reached back into New Testament times. Paul seemed to have been fighting an incipient form of Gnosticism in his letter to the Colossians. Christian tradition related the origin of Gnosticism to Simon Magus,[1] whom Peter had had to rebuke so severely.

Gnosticism sprang from the natural human desire to create a theodicy, an explanation of the origin of evil. The Gnostics, because they associated matter with evil, sought a way to create a philosophical system in which God as spirit could be freed from association with evil and in which man could be related on the spiritual side of his nature to Deity. It was also a logical or rational system that illustrated the human tendency to seek answers to the great questions of the origin of man. It sought to do this by synthesizing Christianity and Hellenistic philosophy. The Gnostics, like the Greeks of the first two chapters of 1 Corinthians, sought by human wisdom to understand the ways of God with man and to avoid what seemed to them to be the stigma of the Cross. If the Gnostics had succeeded, Christianity would have been simply another philosophical religion of the ancient world.

Discovery of nearly one thousand pages of documents about Egyptian and Syrian Gnosticism at Nag Hammadi in Upper Egypt in 1946 gives us some idea of their doctrines. Dualism was one of their main tenets. The Gnostics insisted upon a clear separation between the worlds of the material and the spiritual because to them matter was always associated with evil and spirit with good. Hence God could not have been the Creator of this material world.

The gap between God and the world of matter was bridged by the idea of a demiurge who was one of a series of emanations from the high god of Gnosticism. These emanations were beings with less of spirit and increasingly more of matter. The demiurge, as one of these emanations, had enough of spirit in him to have creative power and enough of matter to create the evil material world. This demiurge the Gnostics identified with the Jehovah of the Old Testament, whom they heartily disliked.

To explain Christ, they adopted a doctrine known as Docetism. Because matter was evil, Christ could not be associated with a human body despite the Bible's teaching to the contrary. Christ as absolute spiritual good could not unite with matter. Either the man Jesus was a phantom with the seeming appearance of a material body (Docetism), or Christ came upon the human body of Jesus only for a short time—between the baptism of the man Jesus and the beginning of His suffering on the cross. Then Christ left the man Jesus to die on the cross. It was the task of Christ to teach a special gnosis or knowledge that would help man save himself by an intellectual process.

Salvation, which was only for the soul or spiritual part of man, might begin with faith, but the special gnosis, which Christ imparted to the elite, would be far more beneficial, according to the Gnostic, in the process of the salvation of his soul. Since the body was material and was destined to be cast off, it might be kept under by strict ascetic practices or be given over to libertinism. Only the pneumatic Gnostics, those possessing the esoteric gnosis, and the psychic group, those having faith but no access to the gnosis, would get to heaven. The hylic would never enjoy the heavenly state, for they were destined to eternal loss. There was no place for the resurrection of the body.

This description of the major tenets held in common by the Gnostics should not mislead one as to the existence of numerous Gnostic sects with special doctrines of their own. Even a casual reading of the first few books of Irenaeus's *Against Heresies* will show the reader how numerous were the groups and how varied their ideas. Saturninus headed a Syrian school of Gnosticism; in Egypt, Basilides led

another school. Marcion and his followers seem to have been the most influential of the groups linked by some with Gnosticism.

Marcion left his native Pontus about 140 and went to Rome, where he became influential in the Roman church. He felt that Judaism was evil and, therefore, he hated the Jewish Scriptures and the Jehovah described therein. He set up his own canon of Scripture, which included a truncated Gospel of Luke and ten of the letters of the New Testament associated with the name of Paul. Although his business made him wealthy enough to be a real help to the Roman church, Marcion was expelled for holding to these ideas. He then founded his own church.

A critique of Gnosticism from a scriptural viewpoint will soon make it clear that the church was wise to fight this doctrine. It posited two gods, the evil one of the Old Testament to create and the good one to redeem. Consequently, it pandered to anti-Semitism in the church. It also rejected the reality of the humanity, sacrificial death, and physical resurrection of Christ, whom John claimed dwelt among us to reveal the glory of God. Little wonder that Paul asserted the fulness of God in Christ in his letter to the Colossian church (Col. 1:19; 2:9). Gnosticism also pandered to spiritual pride with its suggestion that only an aristocratic elite would ever enjoy the pleasures of dwelling with Deity in heaven. It had no place for the human body in the future life. In this respect it resembled the thinking of Greek mythology and philosophy that also had no future for the human body beyond this life. Its asceticism was a contributing factor to the medieval ascetic movement that we know as monasticism.

It did, however, contribute unwittingly to the development of the church. When Marcion formed his canon of New Testament Scriptures, the church was forced in self-defense to give attention to the problem of what books were to be considered canonical and thus authoritative for doctrine and life. The development of a short creed to test orthodoxy was speeded up to meet a practical need. The bishop's prestige was enhanced by emphasis on his office as a center of unity for the faithful against heresy. This in turn led to the later rise to prominence of the Roman bishop. Polemicists such as Tertullian, Irenaeus, and Hippolytus engaged in literary controversy to refute Gnostic ideas. Gnostic teachings reappeared to some extent in the doctrines of the seventh-century Paulicians, the eleventh- and twelfth-century Bogomils, and the later Albigenses in southern France.

B. Manicheanism

Manicheanism, which was somewhat similar to Gnosticism, was founded by a man named Mani or Manichaeus (216–76) of Mesopotamia, who developed his peculiar philosophical system about the middle of the third century. Mani worked a curious combination of Christian thought, Zoroastrianism, and other oriental religious ideas into a thoroughgoing dualistic philosophy. Mani believed in two opposing and eternal principles. Primitive man came into being by emanation from a being who in turn was a higher emanation from the ruler of the kingdom of light. Opposed to the

king of light was the king of darkness, who managed to trick primitive man so that man became a being with mingled light and darkness. Man's soul linked him with the kingdom of light, but his body brought him into bondage to the kingdom of darkness. Salvation was a matter of liberating the light in his soul from its thralldom to the matter of his body. This liberation could be accomplished by exposure to the Light, Christ. The elite or perfect ones constituted the priestly caste for this group. They lived ascetic lives and performed certain rites essential to the release of light. The auditors or hearers shared in the holiness of this elect group by supplying their physical needs. In this way the hearers might also participate in salvation.

Manicheanism laid so much stress on the ascetic life that it looked on the sex instinct as evil and emphasized the superiority of the unmarried state. Manicheanism may also have contributed to the development in the church of a priestly class apart from the rest of the believers, who were considered uninitiated laymen.

Manicheanism had much influence for a long time after the death of Mani in Persia. So great a thinker as Augustine, during the years he was seeking for truth, was a disciple of the Manicheans for twelve years. After his conversion, Augustine devoted much energy to refuting it.

C. Neoplatonism

Too often the average person thinks of mysticism only in connection with the medieval mystics. The fact is that there have been mystical tendencies in the church throughout the ages.

Mysticism may be thought of as

existing in three forms. There may be an *epistemological* type of mysticism in which the emphasis is on how man comes to know God. Those devoted to this type of mysticism think that all our knowledge of God is immediate and comes directly to us by intuition or spiritual illumination. Reason and, in some cases, even the Bible are subordinated to the inner light. Most medieval mystics, the Roman Catholic Quietists of the seventeenth century, and the Quakers held to this view. Others emphasize a *metaphysical* type of mysticism in which the spiritual essence of man is thought to be absorbed mystically into the divine being in occasional experiences here and now. Following the extinction of his separate personality by death, man's spirit becomes a part of the divine being. The Neoplatonists, some of the more extreme mystics of the Middle Ages, and Buddhists held to this type of mysticism. The Bible in contrast emphasizes an *ethical and spiritual* type of mysticism in which the individual is related to God through his identification with Christ and the indwelling Holy Spirit.[2]

Neoplatonism is a good illustration of the ontological type of mystical philosophy. It originated in Alexandria as the brainchild of Ammonius Saccas (ca. 174–ca. 242), who was born of Christian parents. Origen, the Christian church father, and a man named Plotinus studied under Saccas. Plotinus (ca. 205–70) then became the real leader and taught this doctrine in a school at Rome during the third quarter of the third century. The work of producing the literary statement of Neoplatonism was done by Porphory (232–305) from the collected writings of Plotinus. The resulting compilation, known as the *Enneads,* has been preserved. It teaches a metaphysical monism rather than dualism.

The Neoplatonists thought of Absolute Being as the transcendent source of all that is and from which all was created by a process of overflow. This overflow or emanation finally resulted in the creation of man as a reasoning soul and body. The goal of the universe was reabsorption into the divine essence from which all had come. Philosophy contributes most to this process as one engages in rational contemplation and by mystical intuition seeks to know God and to be absorbed into the One from whence all has come. The experience of ecstasy was the highest state one could enjoy in this life. These ideas influenced Augustine.

Emperor Julian, who was known as "the Apostate," embraced this rival of Christianity and during his short reign from 361 to 363 tried to make it the religion of the empire. Augustine embraced it for a time during the period of his quest for truth. The movement no doubt contributed to the rise of mysticism in Christianity and offered an attractive substitute for Christianity to the pagan unwilling to face the high ethical and spiritual demands of the Christian religion. It died out early in the sixth century.

III. THEOLOGICAL ERRORS

Certain views may be thought of as misinterpretations of the meaning of Christianity, overemphases, or as movements of protest. They were, however, harmful to Christianity; and some of the energy that might have gone into the work of evangelization had to be directed to the task of refutation of these errors. Montanism and Monarchianism are examples of two such errors.

A. Montanism

Montanism emerged in Phrygia after A.D. 155 as an attempt on the part of Montanus to meet the problems of formalism in the church and the dependence of the church on human leadership instead of on the guidance of the Holy Spirit. He was opposed to the rise to prominence of the bishop in the local church. This attempt to combat formalism and human organization led him to a reassertion of the doctrines of the Second Advent and the Holy Spirit. Unfortunately, as so often happens in such movements, he swung to the opposite extreme and developed fanatical misinterpretations of Scripture.

In the development of his peculiar doctrine concerning inspiration, Montanus contended that inspiration was immediate and continuous and that he was the paraclete or advocate through whom the Holy Spirit spoke to the church as He, the Spirit, had spoken through Paul and the other apostles. Montanus also had an extravagant eschatology. He believed that the heavenly kingdom of Christ would soon be set up at Pepuza in Phrygia and that he would have a prominent place in that kingdom. In order that they might be prepared for that coming, he and his followers practiced strict asceticism. There was to be no second marriage if a mate died, many fasts were to be observed, and dry foods were to be eaten.[3]

The church reacted against these extravagances by condemnation of the movement. The Council at Constan-tinople in 381 declared that the Montanists should be looked upon as pagans. But Tertullian, one of the greatest of the church fathers, found the doctrines of the group appealing and became a Montanist. The movement was strongest in Carthage and Eastern lands. It represented the perennial protest that occurs in the church when there is overelaboration of machinery and lack of dependence on the Spirit of God. The Montanist movement was and is a warning to the church not to forget that its organization and its formulation of doctrine must never be divorced from the satisfaction of the emotional side of man's nature and the human craving for immediate spiritual contact with God.

B. Monarchianism

If Montanus was overzealous in his presentation of the doctrines of the Holy Spirit and inspiration, the Monarchians may be said to have erred because of their excessive zeal in emphasizing the unity of God in opposition to any attempt to conceive of God as three separate personalities. They were concerned with an assertion of monotheism but ended up with an ancient form of Unitarianism, which denied the real deity of Christ. Their problem was how to relate Christ to God.

During the third century a man named Paul of Samosata was bishop of Antioch.[4] In addition to this office, he held an important political post in the government of Zenobia, queen of Palmyra. He often played the demagogue in the Antioch church by preaching to the gallery with violent bodily gestures and asking for applause and for the waving of handkerchiefs. On occasion he had a female choir sing hymns praising him. Because he neither inherited a fortune nor was engaged in business, there was some suspicion as to the sources of his large fortune. This able but unscrupulous man taught that Christ was not divine but was merely a good man who, by righteousness and by the penetration of his being by the divine Logos at baptism, achieved divinity and saviorhood. This attempt to uphold monotheism robbed the Christian of a divine Savior. The doctrine set forth by Paul of Samosata became known as Dynamic or Adoptionist Monarchianism.

The proponent of Modal Monarchianism was a man named Sabellius, who decided that he wished to avoid any danger of tritheism. After 200 he formulated the teaching that goes by his name. He taught a trinity of manifestation of forms rather than of essence. God was manifested as Father in Old Testament times, later as the Son to redeem man, and as the Holy Spirit after the resurrection of Christ. Thus there were not three persons in the Godhead but three manifestations. His view may be illustrated by the relationships that a man may have. In one relationship he is son; in another, brother; and in a third, father. In all these relationships there is but one real personality. This view denied separate personality to Christ. It has been revived in the New Issue or Jesus Only form of Pentecostalism.

IV. ECCLESIASTICAL SCHISMS

A. Easter Controversy

Certain schisms concerning matters of discipline and ritual also developed in the church during its infancy. The Easter controversy arose about the middle of the second century over the question of what was the proper date to celebrate Easter. The church in the East held that Easter should be celebrated on the fourteenth day of Nisan, the date of the Passover according to the Jewish calendar, no matter what day of the week it fell on. Polycarp of Asia was opposed in this view in 162 by the Roman bishop Anicetus, who believed that Easter should be celebrated on the Sunday following the fourteenth of Nisan. When in 190 Victor, bishop of Rome, excommunicated the churches of Asia as he opposed Polycrates of Ephesus, Irenaeus rebuked him for his pretensions to power. The Eastern and Western segments of the church could not arrive at any agreement until the Council of Nicaea in 325, when the viewpoint of the Western church was adopted.

B. Donatism

The Donatist controversy developed after 300 as a result of the persecution of the church by Diocletian. Most of the controversy was centered in North Africa. A churchman named Donatus wanted to exclude Caecilian from his office as bishop of Carthage because Caecilian had been consecrated by Felix, who was accused of being a traditor during the Diocletian persecution. Donatus argued that the failure to remain true during the persecution invalidated the power of Felix to ordain because he had thus committed an unpardonable sin. Donatus and his group elected Majorinus as bishop; and, after the death of Majorinus in 313, Donatus became bishop. When Constantine gave money for the African church, the Donatists complained because they received none. A synod held at Rome decided that the validity of a sacrament does not depend on the character of the one administering the sacrament. Hence the Donatists had no right to any of the aid. Another council of Western bishops, held at Arles in 314, again decided against the Donatist position. This controversy became a matter of some concern to Augustine, and, as a result of his concern, he wrote much on the question of the authority of the church.

It may be said in conclusion that the results of the controversies, errors, and heresies were not always destructive. The church was forced to develop an authoritative canon of Scripture, and creeds, such as the rules of faith of Tertullian and Irenaeus, that summarized the essential teachings of the Bible. The necessity of answering the false theologies stimulated the rise of Christian theology. The position of the bishop was strengthened by the emphasis on his office as a rallying point against heresy or error. False teachings arose through the attempts of ambitious men to assert their authority, through overemphasis and consequent misinterpretation of certain Scriptures, and through loveless treatment shown to an erring minority by the church. But these did not finally weaken the church; instead, they forced it to think out its belief and to develop organization.

Suggested Reading

Any one of the many good histories of doctrine may be consulted with profit for more information on the doctrines discussed.

Frend, W. H. C. **The Donatist Church.** *Oxford: Clarendon University Press, 1952. This is a full, scholarly discussion of Donatism.*

Neve, Juergen L., and Heick, Otto W. **A History of Christian Thought.** *2 vols. Philadelphia: Fortress; 1965–66. Although its emphasis is Lutheran, the work is still widely useful.*

Chapter 9

Earnestly Contending for the Faith

During the second and third centuries the church expressed its emerging self-consciousness in a new literary output—the writings of the apologists and the polemicists. Justin Martyr was the greatest of the former group; Irenaeus was the outstanding man of the latter group. The apologists faced a hostile government, which they tried to win with the arguments of their literary productions. They tried to convince the leaders of the state that the Christians had done nothing to deserve the persecutions being inflicted on them. The polemicists, such as Irenaeus, tried to meet the challenge of heretical movements. Whereas the apostolic fathers wrote only to and for Christians, these writers wrote to and for the leaders of the Roman state or to heretics in an effort to win them back to the truth of the Scriptures by literary argument. Apologists used the pagan literary form of the dialogue and the legal form of the *apologia*.

I. THE APOLOGISTS

The apologists had a negative and a positive aim in their writings. Negatively, they sought to refute the false charges of atheism, cannibalism, incest, indolence, and anti-social action that pagan neighbors and writers, such as Celsus, leveled against them. They also developed a positive, constructive approach by showing that in contrast to Christianity, Judaism, pagan religions, and state worship were foolish and sinful.

Their writings, known as apologies, made a rational appeal to the pagan leaders and aimed to create an intelligent understanding of Christianity and to remove legal disabilities from it. One of their major arguments was that since the false charges could not be substantiated, the Christians were entitled to civil tolerance under the laws of the Roman state.

These men, writing as philosophers rather than theologians, stressed the priority of Christianity as the oldest religion and philosophy because such writings as the Pentateuch predated the Trojan wars and because whatever truth could be found in Greek thought was borrowed from Christianity or Judaism. Much was made of the pure life of Christ, His miracles, and the fulfillment of Old Testament prophecies concerning Him as proofs of the fact that Christianity was the highest philosophy. Trained for the most part in Greek philosophy before their acceptance of Christianity, these writers looked upon Greek philosophy as a means to lead men to Christ. They used the New Testament more than the apostolic fathers did.

A. Eastern Apologists

About 140, Aristides, a Christian philosopher of the city of Athens, directed an apology to the Emperor Antoninus Pius. J. Rendel Harris discovered a complete Syriac version of this work in 1889 in the Monastery of Saint Catherine on Mount Sinai. The first fourteen chapters contrast Christian worship to Chaldean, Greek, Egyptian, and Jewish worship to prove the superiority of the Christian form of worship. The last three chapters give a clear picture of early Christian customs and ethics.

Justin Martyr (ca. 100–165) was the foremost apologist of the second century. Born of pagan parents near the biblical town of Shechem, he early became a wandering philosopher in search of truth. He tried Stoic philosophy, the noble idealism of Plato, Aristotle's ideas—marred for him by the exorbitant fees demanded by Aristotle's peripatetic successors—and the numerical philos-

ophy of Pythagoras. Not until one day, when he was walking along the seashore and an old man directed him to the Scriptures as the true philosophy, did Justin find the peace he craved (*Dialogue with Trypho*, chaps. 2–8). Then he opened a Christian school in Rome.

Shortly after 150 Justin Martyr addressed his *First Apology* to Emperor Antoninus Pius and his adopted sons. In it he urged the emperors to examine the charges against the Christians (chaps. 1–3) and to free them from legal disabilities if they were innocent. He proved that Christians were not atheists or idolaters (4–13). The major section of the work (14–60) is devoted to a discussion of the morals, dogmas, and Founder of Christianity. He sought to show that Christ's superior life and morality had been foretold in the Old Testament prophecies. Persecution and error he attributed to the work of demons. The last chapters (61–67) are given over to an exposition of the worship of the Christians. He argued that since examination would show that the Christians were blameless concerning the charges against them, they should have freedom from persecution.

The so-called *Second Apology* is in the nature of an appendix to the *First Apology.* In it Justin cited illustrations of cruelty and injustice to Christians and, after a comparison of Christ and Socrates, pointed out that the good in men is due to Christ.

In the *Dialogue with Trypho* Justin endeavored to convince the Jews of the messiahship of Jesus Christ. He allegorized Scripture and emphasized prophecy in this attempt. The first eight chapters of the work are autobiographical and constitute an excellent source of information concerning the life of this great writer. The largest section (chaps. 9–142) is a development of three ideas: the relation of the decline of the law of the old covenant to the rise of the gospel; the linking of the Logos, Christ, with God; and the calling of the Gentiles as the people of God. To him Christ was the fulfillment of Old Testament prophecies.

Tatian (ca. 110–72), the widely traveled Eastern scholar who was a pupil of Justin in Rome, wrote a work known as *Address to the Greeks* after the middle of the second century. It is a denunciation of Greek pretensions to cultural leadership couched in apologetic form. Its main interest, for us, is in the fact that it is addressed to a whole people, the Greeks. Tatian argued that since Christianity is superior to Greek religion and thought, Christians should be given fair treatment. The second section (chaps. 5–30) is devoted to a comparison of Christian teachings with Greek mythology and philosophy. In the next section he asserted that Christianity is far more ancient than Greek thought and religion because Moses antedated the Trojan wars (31–41). He also gave an interesting discussion of the Greek statuary that he had seen (33–34) in the city of Rome. In addition to being the author of the *Address*, Tatian was the compiler of the *Diatessaron*, the earliest harmony of the Gospels.

Athenagoras was a professor of Athens who had been converted by reading the Scriptures. About 177 he wrote a work called *Supplication for the Christians*. After stating the charges against the Christians in the introductory chapters, he refuted the charge of atheism made against the Christians by showing that the pagan gods are merely human creations (chaps. 4–30) and that the pagan gods are guilty of the same immoralities as their human followers (31–34). Because the Christians are guilty neither of incest nor of eating their children in sacrificial feasts (35–36), he concluded in the final chapter that the emperor should grant them clemency.

Theophilus of Antioch, who also was converted by the reading of the Scriptures, sometime after 180 wrote the *Apology to Autolycus*. Autolycus was apparently a learned pagan magistrate whom Theophilus hoped to win to Christianity by rational arguments. In the first book, Theophilus discussed the nature and superiority of God. In the second, he compared the weaknesses of the pagan religion to Christianity. In the final book he answered the objections of Autolycus to the Christian faith. He was the first to use the word *trias* of the Trinity.

B. Western Apologists

The Western apologetic writers laid a greater emphasis on the distinctiveness and finality of Christianity than they did on the similarities between the Christian faith and the pagan religions.

Tertullian was the outstanding apologist of the Western church. About 160 he was born into the home of a Roman centurion on duty in Carthage. Trained in both Greek and Latin, he was at home in the classics. He became a proficient lawyer and taught public speaking and practiced law in Rome, where he was converted to Christianity. His fiery nature and fighting spirit inclined him toward the

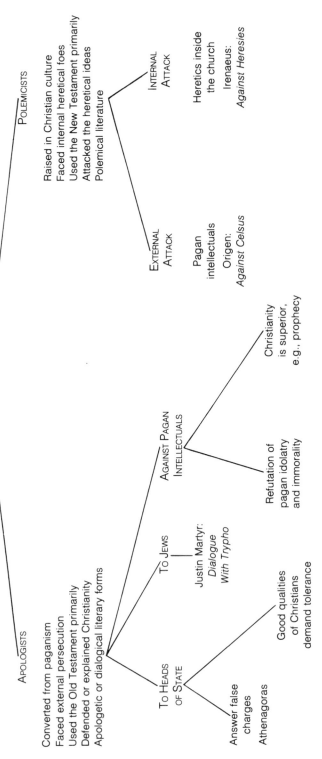

DEFENSE OF THE FAITH

APOLOGISTS

Converted from paganism
Faced external persecution
Used the Old Testament primarily
Defended or explained Christianity
Apologetic or dialogical literary forms

TO HEADS
OF STATE

Answer false
charges
Athenagoras

Good qualities
of Christians
demand tolerance

TO JEWS

Justin Martyr:
*Dialogue
With Trypho*

AGAINST PAGAN
INTELLECTUALS

Refutation of
pagan idolatry
and immorality

Christianity
is superior,
e.g., prophecy

POLEMICISTS

Raised in Christian culture
Faced internal heretical foes
Used the New Testament primarily
Attacked the heretical ideas
Polemical literature

EXTERNAL
ATTACK

Pagan
intellectuals
Origen:
Against Celsus

INTERNAL
ATTACK

Heretics inside
the church
Irenaeus:
Against Heresies

puritan approach to life of Montanism, and he became a Montanist about 202. His logical Latin mind was devoted to the development of a sound Western theology and the defeat of all false philosophical and pagan forces opposed to Christianity.[1]

In the *Apology*, addressed to the Roman governor of his province, he refuted the old charges against the Christians and argued that they were loyal citizens of the empire. He pointed out that persecution is a failure anyway because the Christians multiply every time the authorities try to down them by persecution.[2] Revealing the influence of his legal training, he argued that the state was persecuting the church on dubious legal grounds because the associations, doctrines, and morals of the Christians were of a higher caliber than those of their pagan neighbors.

Minucius Felix, about 200, wrote a dialogue called *Octavius.* This was an apology designed to win his friend Caecilius to the Christian faith from paganism.

It has often been asserted that the attempt to win the favor of the pagan world by this moral-rational approach led to a syncretism that made Christianity only another, although superior, philosophy. The fact is that while the apologies are philosophical in form, they are basically Christian in content. This can be verified by even a casual reading of the actual works of these men. The apologies are valuable to us for the light they throw on Christian thought in the middle of the second century. Whether they accomplished the purpose their authors intended for them, the ending of the persecution of the Christian church, is open to question.

II. THE POLEMICISTS

While the apologists of the second century sought to give a rational explanation and justification of Christianity to the authorities, the polemicists of the late second and the early third centuries endeavored to meet the challenge of false teaching by heretics with an aggressive condemnation of these false teachings and the heretical teachers. One notes again the difference in the approach used by the Eastern and Western churchmen in meeting the problems of heresy and the theological formulation of Christian truth. The Eastern mind busied itself with speculative theology and gave most attention to metaphysical problems; the Western mind was more concerned with aberrations of the polity of the church and endeavored to formulate a sound practical answer to the questions involved in this problem.

The apologists, who had been newly converted from paganism, wrote concerning the external threat to the safety of the church, namely, persecution. The polemicists, who had had a background of Christian culture, were concerned with heresy, an internal threat to the peace and purity of the church. The polemicists, unlike the apologists, who had laid much stress on the Old Testament prophecies, emphasized the New Testament as a source for Christian doctrine. The polemicists sought to condemn by argument the false teachings that they opposed. The apologists sought to explain Christianity to their pagan neighbors and rulers. The apostolic fathers had earlier sought to edify the Christian church. Note the chart on page 72.

A. Iranaeus, the Anti-Gnostic Polemicist

Irenaeus, who was born in Smyrna, had been influenced by Polycarp's preaching while Polycarp was bishop of Smyrna. From there Irenaeus went to Gaul, where he became a bishop before 180. He was a successful missionary bishop, but his greatest work was done in the field of polemical writing against Gnosticism.

His work *Adversus Haereses*, an attempt to refute Gnostic doctrines by use of the Scriptures and the development of a body of related tradition, was written about 185. Book I, which is primarily historical, is our best source of knowledge concerning the teachings of the Gnostics. It is a philosophical polemic against Valentinian, the leader of the Roman school of Gnosticism. In Book II Irenaeus insisted on the unity of God in opposition to the Gnostic idea of the demiurge as distinct from God. The more negative approach of the first two books gives way to a positive exposition of the Christian position in the last three books. Gnosticism is refuted by the Scriptures and relevant tradition in Book III; Marcion is condemned in Book IV by the citation of the words of Christ that are in opposition to Marcion's position; and the final book is a vindication of the doctrine of the Resurrection, which the Gnostics opposed because, according to their views, it associates the evil material body with spirit.

It should be noted that in Book III Irenaeus emphasized the organic unity of the church through the apostolic succession[3] of leaders from Christ and a rule of faith.[4] He was conscious of the unity that could be achieved by a closely knit church and felt that such a church could easily resist the blandishments of heretical ideas and their teachers.

B. The Alexandrian School

About 185 a catechetical school to instruct converts from paganism to Christianity was opened in Alexandria. Its earliest leader was Pantaenus, an able convert from, according to some, Stoicism. Clement and then Origen succeeded him as leaders of that influential school of Christian thought. The men of the Alexandrian school were anxious to develop a system of theology that by the use of philosophy would give a systematic exposition of Christianity. They had been trained in the classical literature and philosophy of the past and thought that it could be used in the formulation of Christian theology.

Thus, instead of emphasizing a grammatico-historical interpretation of the Bible, they developed an allegorical system of interpretation that has plagued Christianity since that time. This type of interpretation is based on the supposition that Scripture has more than one meaning. Using the analogy of man's body, soul, and spirit, they argued that Scripture had a literal, historical meaning that corresponded to the human body; a hidden moral meaning that corresponded to the soul; and a deeper, underlying spiritual meaning that only the more spiritually advanced Christians could understand. This system of interpretation grew out of the technique employed by Philo, the Alexandrian Jew, who tried to link Judaism and Greek philosophy by finding hidden meanings in the language of the Old Testament that could be related to Greek philosophy. Instead of being concerned with the meaning of the writer of Scripture for those to whom he was writing and its application to present circumstances, the men of the Alexandrian school were ever seeking hidden meanings. This method of interpretation has done much harm to the cause of correct interpretation of the Scriptures and has resulted in absurd and often unscriptural theological ideas.

Clement of Alexandria—not to be confused with Clement of Rome, one of the apostolic fathers—was born after 150 in Athens of pagan parents. He traveled widely and studied philosophy under many masters before he began to study with Pantaenus. Before 190 he was associated with Pantaenus as leader of the school at Alexandria, and from 190 to 202 he was head of the school until persecution forced him to leave.

Clement had the ideal of a Christian philosopher as his goal. Greek philosophy was to be related to Christianity so that one could see that Christianity was the great and final philosophy. He was widely read in Greek pagan literature and quoted something like five hundred authors in his works.

His *Protrepticus*, or *Address to the Greeks*, is an apologetic missionary document written about 190 to show the superiority of Christianity as the true philosophy so that pagans might be influenced to accept it. Another work, the *Paidagogos*, or the *Tutor*, is a moral treatise of instructions for young Christians. Christ is presented as the true teacher who has given rules for the Christian life. The *Stromata*, or *Miscellanies*, reveals Clement's wide acquaintance with the pagan literature of his day. In Book I Christianity is presented as the true knowledge and the Christian as the true Gnostic. Clement believed that Greek philosophy borrowed what truth it had from the Old Testament and that it was a preparation for the gospel.[5] In Book II he showed that Christian morality is superior to pagan morality. Book III is an exposition concerning Christian marriage. In Books VII and VIII, which are the most interesting, he pictured the development of the religious life of the Christian.

There is no doubt that Clement favored Greek learning, but any careful study of his works leaves one with the impression that for him the Bible comes first in the life of the Christian. At the same time, since all truth belongs to God, what truth there is in Greek learning should be brought into the service of God. The danger in this position is that one may imperceptibly synthesize Christianity and Greek learning until Christianity is only a syncretism of Greek philosophy and biblical teaching.

Clement's pupil and successor to leadership of the catechetical school was Origen (ca. 185–254). Origen took over the care of a family of six at the age of sixteen when his father Leonides was martyred. According to one account, he wished to be martyred with his father, but his mother hid his clothes so that he had to stay home. He was so capable and learned that in 203, at the age of eighteen, he was chosen to be Clement's successor as leader of the school, a position that he held until 231. A wealthy man named Ambrose, a convert from Gnosticism, became Origen's friend and arranged for the publication of his many works.

According to one estimate, Origen was the author of six thousand scrolls. In spite of his exalted position and wealthy friend, Origen lived a simple ascetic life that included sleeping on bare boards.[6]

Origen may be compared with Augustine in the scope of his work. The earliest beginnings of textual criticism of the Scriptures can be traced to the *Hexapla*, in which several Hebrew and Greek versions of the Old Testament are arranged in parallel columns.[7] In this work Origen sought to establish a text that Christians could be assured was a correct representation of the original. This interest in the text led him to do more exegetical work than anyone did before the Reformation. Another work, *Against Celsus*, is a statement of and an answer to the charges that the Platonist Celsus had made against the Christians in his *True Discourse*. Origen dealt with Celsus' charges concerning the irrationality of Christians and the lack of apparent historical foundations for Christianity by emphasizing the change in conduct that Christianity produces in contrast with paganism; the open-minded investigations of truth by Christians; and the purity and influence both of Christ, the leader of the Christians, and His followers.

Perhaps Origen's greatest contribution to Christian literature is his work entitled *De Principiis* (230), which has come down to us only in a Latin version by Rufinus. This work is the first Christian treatise of systematic theology. In the fourth book of this work, Origen developed his allegorical system of interpretation at great length. Unfortunately, though he thought of Christ as "eternally generated" by the Father, he thought of Him as subordinate to the Father. He also held the ideas of the preexistence of the soul, the final restoration of all spirits, Christ's death as a ransom to Satan, and, he denied a physical resurrection.

C. The Carthaginian School

The Western or Latin mind was more interested in practical matters of church organization, government, and doctrines relating to the church than in the speculative type of theology that attracted such a scholar as Origen, for example. This difference of viewpoint can be seen by contrasting the work of Origen with that of Tertullian and Cyprian of North Africa.

Tertullian wrote widely and well, though often intolerantly, on many different subjects. His *Apology*, in which he defended the Christian against false charges and persecution, has already been discussed (see p. 109). He also wrote on practical as well as apologetic matters. In special pamphlets he urged simplicity of dress and ornament for women and urged Christians to separate themselves from pagan amusements, immorality, and idolatry. These practical works seem to have been an outcome of his Montanist puritanism.

It is Tertullian's work as a theologian, however, that is most outstanding. He was the founder of Latin theology and was the first to state the theological doctrine of the Trinity and to make use of that term to describe that doctrine. He did this in *Against Praxeas* (chaps. 2–3), written about 215. He seemed to emphasize the distinction that must be made between the persons of the Father and the Son. In *De Anima*, regarding the soul, he emphasized the traducian doctrine of the transmission of the soul from the parents to the child in the reproductive process. He laid great emphasis on the rite of baptism in his *Of Baptism*, believed that postbaptismal sins were mortal sins, and opposed infant baptism.

Cyprian was born of well-to-do pagan parents shortly after 200 in the same city as Tertullian and was given a good education in rhetoric and the law. He became a successful teacher of rhetoric but did not find the satisfaction his soul craved until he became a Christian about 246. About 248 he became the bishop of Carthage, a position that he held for nine years until his martyrdom about 258. He was a great organizer and administrator. He opposed the claims of Stephen, the bishop of Rome, to supremacy over all bishops.

Though he looked up to Tertullian as his master, according to Jerome, Cyprian was calm, whereas Tertullian was passionate. His most important work was the *De Unitate Catholicae Ecclesiae*, (chap. 4), which was directed against the schismatic followers of Novatian, who seemed bent on the destruction of the unity of the church. Cyprian made a clear distinction between bishop and elder and emphasized the bishop as the center of unity in the church and a guarantee against schism. While he did not assert the supremacy of Peter's episcopal see in Rome, he did assert the primacy of honor of Peter in tracing the line of apostolic succession down through the early history of the church. If one can say that Tertullian helped to formulate the doctrine of the Trinity and gave a name to that doctrine, one can also say that Cyprian gave the earliest formulation of the doctrines of apostolic succession and the primacy of honor of the Roman bishop in the church.

Cyprian tended to think of the clergy as sacrificing priests in offering up Christ's body and blood in the Communion service.[8] This idea later was developed into the concept of transubstantiation.

SUGGESTED READING

The student will find most of the readings listed at the end of chapter 5 useful for this era also.

Farrar, Frederick W. **Lives of the Fathers.** 2 vols. New York: Macmillan, 1889. Volume 1 is a useful work on the lives and work of the leading Fathers of this period.

Leigh-Bennet, Ernest. **Handbook of the Early Christian Fathers.** London: Williams & Norgate, 1920. This handbook contains good biographical material and discussions of the works and theological ideas of the leading church fathers in this period.

Chapter 10

The Church Closes Ranks

During the period between 100 and 313, the church was forced to give consideration to how it could best meet the external persecution from the Roman state and the internal problem of heretical teaching and consequent schism. It sought to close its ranks by the development of a *canon* of the New Testament, which gave it an authoritative *Book* for faith and practice; by the creation of a *creed*, which gave it an authoritative statement of *belief*; and by obedience to the monarchical *bishops*, among whom the Roman bishop took a place of leadership. The last gave it a bond of unity in the *constitution* of the church. Polemicists wrote *books* in *controversy* with heretics. Around 170 the church was calling itself the "catholic," or universal, church, a term first used by Ignatius in his *Epistle to Smyrna* (chap. 8).

I. THE MONARCHICAL BISHOP

Practical and theoretical necessities led to the exaltation of one bishop's position in each church until people came to think of him and to acknowledge him as superior to the other elders with whom his office had been associated in New Testament times. The need of leadership in meeting the problems of persecution and heresy was a practical need that dictated an expansion of the bishop's power. The development of the doctrine of apostolic succession and the increasing exaltation of the Lord's Supper were important factors in his rise to power. It was but a short step to the recognition that the monarchical bishops of some churches were more important than others. The exaltation of the monarchical bishop by the middle of the second century soon led to recognition of the special honor due to the monarchical bishop of the church in Rome.

Several considerations brought extra prestige to the bishop of Rome. The first and most important argument that had been advanced since early in the history of the church was the argument that Christ gave to Peter, presumably the first bishop of Rome, a position of primacy among the apostles by His supposed designation of Peter as the rock on which He would build His church (Matt. 16:18). According to Matthew 16:19, Christ also gave Peter the keys to the kingdom and later specially commissioned him to feed His sheep (John 21:15–19).

It should be borne in mind that in the account in Matthew, Christ used two words for rock; and it is by no means clear that the rock on which He said He would build His church is Peter the rock. Christ called Peter a *petros*, or stone, but He spoke of the rock on which He would build His church as *petra*, a living rock. The word "rock" that is applied to Peter is masculine in gender, but the "rock" on which Christ said he would build His church is feminine in gender. There is good reason to believe that the correct interpretation is that Christ was by the word "rock" referring to Peter's confession of Him as "the Christ, the Son of the living God."

One cannot help but remember, too, that Christ told Peter he would fail Him in the crisis in the garden, that Satan would defeat him (Luke 22:31–32), and that Christ had to urge upon him the care of His flock after the Resurrection and His forgiveness of Peter for betraying Him. One also notices that powers similar to those mentioned in connection with Peter in Matthew 16:19 were also conferred on the other apostles equally with Peter (John 20:19–23). Peter himself in his first letter made it abundantly clear that not he but Christ was the foundation of the church (1 Peter 2:6–8). Paul had no conception of Peter's superior position, for he rebuked him when Peter temporized and cooperated with the Judaizers in Galatia.

In spite of these facts, the Roman church has insisted from earliest times that Christ gave to Peter a special rank as the first bishop of Rome and the leader of the apostles. Cyprian and Jerome did the most to advance this position by their assertion of the primacy of the Roman see to the other ecclesiastical seats of authority.[1]

Extra prestige would accrue to the Roman bishop because Rome was linked with many apostolic traditions. Both Peter and Paul had suffered martyrdom in Rome for their faith. Because both were outstanding leaders of the early church, it was not strange that the church and bishop of the church in Rome would have added prestige. The church at Rome had been the center of the earliest persecution by the Roman state under Nero in 64. The longest and possibly the most important of Paul's letters had been addressed to this church. It was one of the largest and wealthiest of the Christian churches by 100. The historical prestige of Rome as the capital of the empire led to a natural exaltation of the position of the church in the capital city. It had a reputation for unswerving orthodoxy in facing heresy and schism. Had not Clement, one of its early leaders, written to the church in Corinth to urge upon that church a unity that centered in the person of the bishop? Many Western church fathers, such as Clement, Ignatius, Irenaeus, and Cyprian, had pressed the importance of the position of bishop and, in the case of Cyprian, that of the bishop of Rome. Though all bishops were equal, and though all were in the line of apostolic succession of bishops from Christ Himself, Rome deserved special honor, it was believed, because its bishop was in the line of succession from Peter.

It must be remembered that some of the five important bishops of the church lost their seat of authority for various reasons. After 135, with the destruction of Jerusalem by the Romans, the bishop of Jerusalem ceased to count as a rival bishop of Rome. The bishop of Ephesus lost prestige as Asia was torn by the Montanist schism in the second century.

By the end of the period three things concerning the Old Catholic church became clear-cut realities. The doctrine of apostolic succession, which linked each bishop in an unbroken line with Christ through the apostles, was accepted. In each church one bishop stood out among his fellow elders as a monarchical bishop. The Roman bishop came to be recognized as the first among equals because of the importance of the weight of tradition associated with his see. This primacy was later to be developed into supremacy of the Roman bishop as pope of the church. Apostolic succession in the hierarchy as a guarantee against schism and to promote unity had been developed by Clement, Ignatius, and Irenaeus. The hierarchy, according to Ignatius and Irenaeus, would also be the best defense against heresy and would promote true doctrine.

II. THE DEVELOPMENT OF THE RULE OF FAITH

The role of the bishop as a bond of unity in the church was reinforced by the development of a creed. A creed is a statement of faith for public use; it contains articles needful for salvation and the theological well-being of the church. Creeds have been used to test orthodoxy, to recognize fellow believers, and to serve as a convenient summary of the essential doctrines of faith. They presuppose a living faith of which they are the intellectual expression. Denominational creeds appeared during the Reformation period. Conciliar or universal creeds made by representatives of the whole church emerged during the period of theological controversy between 313 and 451. The earliest type of creed was the baptismal creed of which the Apostles' Creed may serve as an example.[2] It must always be remembered that creeds are relative and limited expressions of the divine and absolute rule of faith and practice within the Scriptures. Statements in the New Testament that savor of a creed are found in Romans 10:9–10, 1 Corinthians 15:4, and 1 Timothy 3:16.

Irenaeus and Tertullian developed Rules of Faith to be used in recognizing the true Christian from the Gnostic. They were a summary of the major biblical doctrines.[3]

The Apostles' Creed is the oldest summary of the essential doctrines of Scripture that we have. Some think the Apostles' Creed grew out of the brief statement of Peter concerning Christ in Matthew 16:16 and that it was used as a baptismal formula from very early times. The oldest form, similar to the one used by Rufinus about 400, appeared in Rome about 340. This creed, which is definitely Trinitarian, gives attention to the person and work of each of the three persons of the Trinity. It emphasizes the universal nature of the corporate church and, after linking salvation with Christ, has an explicit eschatology centering in the resurrection of the believer and his goal of eternal life. Many churches still find the Apostles' Creed useful as a convenient summary of the main points of the Christian faith.

III. THE NEW TESTAMENT CANON

To the authoritative bond in the bishop and to the authoritative belief of the creed, the canon, a listing of the volumes belonging to an authoritative book, came as a reinforcement. People often err by thinking that the canon was set by church councils. Such was not the case, for the various church councils that pronounced upon the subject of the canon of the New Testament were merely stating publicly, as we shall see later, what had been widely accepted by the consciousness of the church for some time. The development of the canon was a slow process substantially completed by A.D. 175 except for a few books whose authorship was disputed.

Certain practical reasons made it essential that the church develop the list of books that should comprise the New Testament. Heretics, such as Marcion, were setting up their own canon of Scripture and were leading people astray. In persecution men were not willing to risk their lives for a book unless they were sure it was an integral part of the canon of Scripture. Because the apostles were slowly passing from the scene, there was need for some records that could be recognized as authoritative and fit for use in worship.

The major test of the right of a book to be in the canon was whether it had the marks of apostolicity. Was it written by an apostle or one who was closely associated with the apostles, such as Mark, the writer of the Gospel of Mark, written with the aid of the apostle Peter? The capacity of the book to edify when read publicly and its agreement with the rule of faith served as tests also. In the final analysis, it was the historical verification of apostolic authorship or influence and the universal consciousness of the church, guided by the Holy Spirit, that resulted in the final decision concerning what books should be considered canonical and worthy of inclusion in what we know as the New Testament.

Apparently the Epistles of Paul were first collected by leaders in the church of Ephesus. This collection was followed by the collection of the Gospels sometime after the beginning of the second century. The so-called Muratorian Canon, discovered by Lodovico A. Muratori (1672–1750) in the Ambrosian Library at Milan, was dated about 180. Twenty-two books of the New Testament were looked upon as canonical. Eusebius about 324 thought that at least twenty books of the New Testament were acceptable on the same level as the books of the Old Testament. James, 2 Peter, 2 and 3 John, Jude, Hebrews, and Revelation were among the books whose place in the canon was still under consideration.[4] The delay in placing these was caused primarily by an uncertainty concerning questions of authorship. Athanasius, however, in his Easter letter of 367 to the churches under his jurisdiction as the bishop of Alexandria, listed as canonical the same twenty-seven books that we now have in the New Testament. Later councils, such as that at Carthage in 397, merely approved and gave uniform expression to what was already an accomplished fact generally accepted by the church over a long period of time. The slowness with which the church accepted Hebrews and Revelation as canonical is indicative of the care and devotion with which it dealt with this question.

IV. LITURGY

Emphasis on the monarchical bishop who, it was believed, derived his authority by apostolic succession, led many to think of him as a center of unity, the depository of truth, and the dispenser of the means of the grace of God through the sacraments. Converts from the mystery religions may also have aided in the development of the concept of the separation of the clergy and laity as they emphasized the holiness of the bishop's position. The Lord's Supper and baptism came to be rites that could be performed adequately only by an accredited minister. As the idea of the Communion as a sacrifice to God developed, it enhanced the superior sanctity of the bishop as compared with the rank and file of the ordinary church members.

Baptism as an act of initiation into the Christian church was usually performed at Easter or Pentecost. At first apparently faith in Christ and the desire for baptism were the only requirements, but by the end of the second century a probationary period as a catechumen was added to test the reality of the experience of the convert. During this period of probation the catechumen attended services in the narthex of the church building and was not allowed to worship in the nave. Baptism was normally by immersion; on occasion affusion, or pouring, was practiced. Infant baptism which Tertullian opposed and Cyprian supported, and clinical baptism, the baptism of the sick, devel-

The catacombs of Rome consist of more than sixty miles of underground galleries similar to these; more than half a million tombs have been excavated. Although Christians did meet in the catacombs and bury their dead there, others also used them. (See page 120.)

Excavations at Dura-Europa reveal a private house that had been converted to the use of a Christian congregation. The small room shown here has been set up in the Art Museum of Yale University. On the left is a baptistry. The main feature in the scene behind the baptistry is Jesus the Good Shepherd with a flock of sheep. On the upper half of the side wall Jesus is shown raising the paralytic, and the ship apparently contains the disciples. Peter is walking toward the ship on the waves. The lower half of the wall shows three women coming to the empty tomb. Dura-Europa was destroyed in A.D. 258, so this house church predates that event.

oped in this period. The church increasingly hedged the two sacraments of the Lord's Supper and baptism around with requirements and rites that a priest alone could perform.

The emergence of a cycle of feasts in the church year may be noted in this era. Easter, originating in the application of the Jewish Passover to the resurrection of Christ, seems to have been the earliest of the festivals. Not until about 350 was Christmas adopted as a Christian festival and purged of its pagan elements. Lent, a forty-day period of penitence and restraint on bodily appetites preceding Easter, had been accepted earlier as a part of the churches' cycle of worship before the adoption of Christmas.

The Christians met even before 313 in the catacombs of Rome and there often made themselves places for interment of their dead. These places were made up of miles of underground passages, often on different levels below the surface of the ground. Evidences of Christian art, such as symbols of the fish, dove, and figures associated with Christianity, have been found in some of the graves.[5] They were rediscovered in 1578. The oldest surviving building used as a church was a house-church at Dura-Europa, dating from about 232, that was excavated by a Yale University expedition.

Near the end of the period the Christians began to build churches patterned after the Roman basilica. The basilica-church was an oblong building with a porch or narthex at the west end where the catechumens worshiped, a semicircular apse at the east end where the altar and bishop's seat were placed, and a long central nave with aisles on either side. Usually these churches were fairly simple during this period, but they became increasingly ornate after 313 as the church found itself in favor with the state.

Pagans still looked upon worshipers in the churches or catacombs as antisocial because the Christians, urged by writers such as Tertullian, avoided the worldly amusements of their day and refused to become involved in political life. Apart from this, the Christians were willing to play their part in society when they could do so without denying their Lord. Their love for one another, revealed in a pure and happy family life and philanthropic activity for the needy, made an impression on their pagan neighbors. The emperors of the Roman state, finding that they could not stamp out Christianity, finally realized that they had come to terms with it. Despite external problems, created by persecution by the state, and the internal threat of dissension and schism because of heresy, the church came through all its difficulties with flying colors. Its closer association with the Roman state during the period between 313 and 590 was to bring into it many flaws that had not been problems during the periods of persecution.

SUGGESTED READING

Hardman, Oscar. A History of Christian Worship. *London: Hodder & Stoughton, 1937. This work has helpful chapters on the liturgy and worship of each important era of church history.*

Schaff, Philip. The Creeds of Christendom. *3 vols. 6th ed. New York: Scribner, 1890. This is still the best work to consult for the historical background and the text of the various creeds.*

Souter, Alexander. The Text and Canon of the New Testament. *New York: Scribner, 1923. This is a brief but excellent historical treatment that includes quotations from many of the relevant documents.*

Westcott, Brooke F. The Bible in the Church. *London: Macmillan, 1913. This work has an excellent chronological and topical discussion of the growth of the canon.*

Chapter 11

The Church Faces the Empire and the Barbarians

Between 375 and 1066, during the period of the so-called Dark Ages, in which the mass movement of the barbarian Teutonic tribes took place in western Europe, the church faced a twofold problem. The decline of the Roman Empire placed before her the task of being "salt" to conserve the Helleno-Hebraic culture, which was threatened with destruction. The monasteries, centers where manuscripts were carefully preserved and copied, were a great aid in her fulfillment of this function. Confronting her also was the task of being a "light" to give the gospel to the peoples making up the masses of wandering tribesmen. This she did through the work of missionary monks, and she succeeded in the mighty task of winning the tribes to the Christian faith. However, secularization and the voice of the state in the affairs of the church were part of the price she had to pay for her success in conserving culture and converting tribes. Institutional development and doctrine were adversely affected.

I. THE CHURCH AND THE STATE

If one is to understand relationships between church and state after the granting of freedom of religion by Constantine, it is necessary to give some attention to the political problems that the emperor faced at this time. The anarchy of the century of revolution, which wrecked the Roman Republic between 133 and 31 B.C., had been ended by the powerful principate that Augustus created after he destroyed Antony's army. But the principate, in which the emperor as princeps shared authority with the senate, proved to be too weak to meet the challenge of internal decay and barbarians on the borders of the empire; and the prosperity and peace of the early era of the principate gave way to another century of revolution between 192 and 284. Diocletian in 285 reorganized the empire along more autocratic lines, copied from oriental despotisms, in an attempt to create security for Greco-Roman culture. Because Christianity seemed to threaten this culture, he, under Galerius' urging, made an unsuccessful attempt to wipe it out between 303 and 305. His more astute successor, Constantine, realized that if the state could not wipe out Christianity by force, it might make use of the church as an ally to save classical culture.[1] The process by which the church and the state came to terms began with Constantine's winning complete control in the state. Although he officially shared authority with his coemperor Licinius between 311 and 324, he made most of the real decisions in matters of state.

Constantine (ca. 274–337) was the illegitimate son of the Roman military leader Constantius and a beautiful Christian Oriental freedwoman named Helena. When his enemies seemed about to overwhelm him in 312, he had a vision of a cross in the sky with the words "in this sign conquer" in Latin. Taking it as a favorable omen, he went on to defeat his enemies at the battle of the Milvian bridge over the Tiber River. Though the vision may have occurred, it is likely that Constantine's favoritism to the church was a matter of expediency. The church might serve as a new center of unity and save classical culture and the empire. The fact that he delayed baptism till shortly before his death and kept the position of *Pontifex Maximus*, chief priest of the pagan state religion, would seem to support this view. Moreover, his execution of the young men who might have had a claim to his throne was not in keeping with the conduct of a sincere Christian. Perhaps there was a mixture of superstition and expediency in his policy.

Whether or not this interpretation of his motives is correct, Constantine embarked on a policy of favoring the Christian church. In 313 he and Licinius granted all freedom of worship by the Edict of Milan. During the next few years Constantine issued edicts that brought about the restoration of confiscated property to the church, the subsidization of the church by the state, the exemption of the clergy from public service, a ban on soothsaying, and the setting apart of the "Day of the Sun" (Sunday) as a day of rest and worship.[2] He even assumed a position of theological leadership at Arles in 314 and at Nicaea in 325, when he proposed to arbitrate the Donatist and Arian controversies. Even though the number of Christians could not have been much above one-tenth of the population of the empire at this time, they exercised an influence in the state far in excess of their numbers.

In addition to granting freedom and favors to the church and bending it to the service of the empire, Constantine in 330 founded the city of Constantinople. This act helped to divide East and West and open the way for the Schism of 1054, but it did provide a haven for Greco-Roman culture when the West fell to the German tribes in the fifth century. It became the center of political power in the East, and the bishop of Rome was left after 476 with political as well as spiritual power.

The sons of Constantine continued his policy of favoring the church and even went beyond it to such an extent that they forced paganism onto the defensive by such procedures as edicts banning pagan sacrifices and attendance at pagan temples. Just when it looked as if Christianity would shortly become the state religion, it received a setback by the accession of Julian (332–363) in 361 to the imperial throne. Julian had been forced to accept Christianity outwardly, but the death of his relatives at the hands of the Christian ruler and his study of philosophy at Athens inclined him to become a follower of Neoplatonism. He took away from the Christian church her privileges and restored full freedom of worship. Every facility was given to aid the spread of pagan philosophy and religion. Fortunately for the church, his reign was short; and the setback to the development of the church was only temporary.[3]

Later rulers continued the process of granting privileges to the church until Christianity finally became the state religion. Emperor Gratian renounced the title of *Pontifex Maximus.* Theodosius I in 380 and 381 issued edicts that made Christianity the exclusive religion of the state. Any who would dare to hold to any other form of worship would suffer punishment from the state.[4] The Edict of Constantinople in 392 prohibited paganism. Justinian in 529 struck paganism a further blow by ordering the closing of the school of philosophy at Athens.

Looking back at the steps by which Christianity, a despised sect with small numbers, became the official religion of the mighty Roman Empire, one might well believe, with the advantage of the perspective of time, that this victorious march was detrimental to the church. It is true that Christianity had raised the moral tone of society so that, for example, the dignity of women was given more recognition in society, gladiatorial shows were eliminated, slaves were given milder treatment, Roman legislation became more just, and the spread of missionary work was speeded up; but the church also found that, while there were advantages to close association with the state, there were also marked disadvantages. The government in return for position, protection, and aid demanded the right to interfere in spiritual and theological matters. Constantine at Arles in 314 and at Nicaea in 325 arrogated to himself the right to arbitrate the dispute in the church, even though he was only the temporal ruler of the empire. The long vexatious problem of the struggle between the church and state had its beginnings in this era. Unfortunately, the church, when it gained the power, too often became as arrogant a persecutor of paganism as the pagan religious authorities had ever been of the Christians. It would appear on balance that the rapprochement between church and state brought more drawbacks than blessings to the Christian church.

II. THE CHURCH AND THE BARBARIANS

It was well that the church had been able to come to terms with the empire in the early part of the fourth century because the latter part of the century brought a new problem to the fore, the problem of how to win to Christianity the masses of people who started the migrations in Europe that were to continue until the eleventh century. There were mass migrations of Teutonic, Viking, Slav, and Mongol peoples into and within Europe between 375 and 1066.

A. The Spread of the Barbarians

Barbarian Goths first appeared on the Danube frontier of the empire in the latter part of the fourth century; and, pressed by Mongol tribes behind them, they asked permission of the Roman authorities to move into the

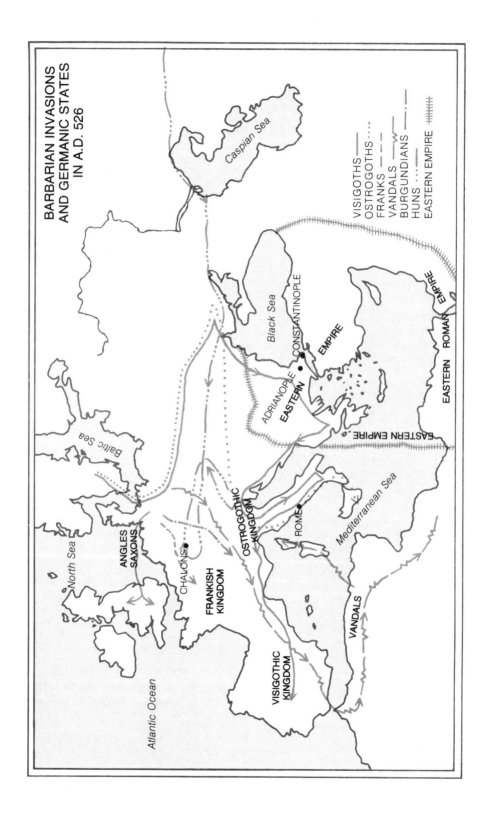

BARBARIAN INVASIONS
AND GERMANIC STATES
IN A.D. 526

VISIGOTHS
OSTROGOTHS
FRANKS
VANDALS
BURGUNDIANS
HUNS
EASTERN EMPIRE

Caspian Sea

Black Sea

CONSTANTINOPLE

ADRIANOPLE

EASTERN
EMPIRE

EASTERN ROMAN EMPIRE

EASTERN EMPIRE

Baltic Sea

North Sea

ANGLES
SAXONS

CHALONS

FRANKISH
KINGDOM

OSTROGOTHIC KINGDOM

ROME

Mediterranean Sea

Atlantic Ocean

VISIGOTHIC
KINGDOM

VANDALS

empire. The battle of Adrianople between them and the Romans in 378 resulted in the death of the emperor Valens and the influx of the Arian Visigoths (West Goths) into the eastern section of the empire. Many crossed the Danube after that battle and started their migrations within the empire. After sacking Rome in 410, they finally founded a kingdom about 426 in Spain. They were followed by the Arian Vandals from east of the Rhine, who finally settled in North Africa. The Arian Ostrogoths, coming later, took over the leadership of the bankrupt Roman Empire under Theodoric. The Arian Lombards and Burgundians and pagan Franks crossed the Rhine and settled during the fifth century in the area of what is now modern France, and Anglo-Saxons settled in England. In the same century the church in the West had also to face the temporary, yet terrible, threat created by the invasion of Europe by the Mongol Huns under the leadership of Attila. The Huns were finally driven back by the victory at Chalons in 451. Just as the church seemed to be winning many of the Teutonic peoples to Christianity, new threats from Muslims and the Arian Lombards became a reality in the sixth century.

The greatness of the civilization that western Europe was to develop was not so much due to the irruption of fresh, vigorous barbarians into the empire as it was to the mass conversions of these barbarians of northwest Europe to Christianity.

B. The Evangelization of the Barbarians

Armenia was won for the gospel by Gregory the Illuminator, when, in about 300, King Tiridates was converted and baptized. The New Testament was translated into Armenian. Some claim that about 2.5 million were won by 410. Armenia was the first state to become officially Christian, and in spite of persecution through the centuries, the Armenians have held tenaciously to the Christian faith.

Frumentius (ca. 300–ca. 380) and his brother, through a shipwreck, landed in Ethiopia and preached the gospel. Athanasius of Alexandria consecrated Frumentius as a bishop to head the Coptic Ethiopian church, which only in recent times has become independent of Egypt.

The British Isles were also won for Christianity in this period. We do not have much information about the introduction of Christianity to Celtic Britain, but it is more than likely that it was planted there by Roman settlers and merchants. We do know that Celtic bishops represented the British church at the Council of Arles in 314. Pelagius, Augustine's opponent, also came from the British church and began to teach the heresy known by his name on the continent about 410. This primitive Celtic church in Britain did not recognize either the jurisdiction or the primacy of the Roman bishop. It also followed the practice of the Eastern church in determining the date of Easter. There were other differences of a minor character. This Celtic church was left defenseless when the Roman armies were withdrawn from Britain at the beginning of the fifth century to meet the threat of the barbarians on the eastern frontier of the empire. The Celtic peoples were exterminated or driven into the western and northern hills by the pagan Angles, Saxons, and Jutes.

Missionary work among the Goths began before the Visigoths poured over the Danube into the Roman Empire. Ulfilas (ca. 310–80), an Arian Christian, felt the call to missionary work among these people. Consecrated bishop of the Gothic Christians, he went to live among them. His work was so successful that when the Goths came into the Roman Empire, many of them came as Christians. As the first outstanding missionary translator, he reduced the language of the Goths to writing, after creating an alphabet, and gave them the Scriptures in their own tongue. Because the Goths were so warlike, he felt justified in not translating the books of Kings and Samuel into their language. The Goths were thus won to the Arian form of Christianity that Ulfilas professed. This fact was later to give the church in the West the difficult task, not only of converting many tribes from paganism, but also of converting the Visigoths of Spain and the Lombards from Arianism to orthodox Christianity.

The pagan Teutonic invaders from across the Rhine presented a more immediate and pressing problem for the Western church. Martin of Tours (ca. 335–ca. 400), now the patron saint of France, felt called to preach to the Burgundians who had settled in southern Gaul. Adopting rather rough and ready pioneering tactics in carrying the gospel to these people, he organized his soldier monks into bands and led them in the destruction of the groves where the people worshiped their pagan gods. His work did not have the impact on subsequent history that the work of Augustine had, because the Burgundians were brought under the sway of their Frankish cousins who also settled in Gaul.

Gregory of Tours in his interesting *History of the Franks* described the settlement, history, and conversion of the Franks. Near the end of the fifth century, Clovis (481–511), king of the Franks, married Clotilda, a Christian princess of Burgundy. Clotilda's influence, combined with what Clovis believed was divine aid in battle, led to his conversion in 496.[5] When he became a Christian, the mass of his people also accepted Christianity.

Whether all conversions were genuine or not, the formal acceptance of Christianity by Clovis was to have far-reaching effects on the history of the church. All the Franks who dominated Gaul, the area of modern France, were now within the Christian church. Gaul became a base from which missionaries could go into Arian Spain to win the Arian Goths who had settled there back to Christianity of the orthodox persuasion. Most important of all, the Frankish monarchy became the ardent supporter of the papacy during the early Middle Ages. Frankish kings crossed the Alps many times to save the Roman bishop from his enemies in Italy.

Patrick (ca. 389–461), who later became the patron saint of Ireland, was taken from Britain to Ireland by pirates at the age of sixteen. He lived there, tending cattle, for six years. Upon his return to his homeland, he felt called to labor among the people of Ireland as a missionary. From 432 to 461 he worked among the Celts of Ireland and, despite the efforts of the priests of the Druid religion, managed to make the island a strong center of Celtic Christianity. During the time of the Dark Ages in Europe, Ireland was a center of culture from which monks as missionaries and scholars were sent to work on the Continent. It was from Ireland that Columba set forth to win the Scots to Christianity.

Columba (521–97) was the apostle of Scotland as Patrick had been the apostle of Ireland. In 563, on the island of Iona, he founded a monastery that became a center for the evangelization of Scotland. It was from here that Aidan in 635 set out to carry the gospel to the Anglo-Saxon invaders of Northumbria. The Celtic church in Ireland and Scotland was above all a missionary church.

At the end of the period under discussion, Celtic Christianity had been victorious in Scotland and Ireland. It had been all but exterminated in England. The Celtic Christians and the Roman Christians were to become rivals for the allegiance of the Anglo-Saxons, whom both groups helped to win to Christianity.

By 590 the church had not only been freed from persecution by the Roman state but had also become closely linked with that state. It had also done its part in converting the Teutonic invaders of the empire to Christianity and in passing on to them the elements of Greco-Roman culture. But in the process, masses of pagans had been won to the Christian religion too quickly for the church to train them and to guide them through a period of probation. Many of them brought old patterns of life and customs with them into the church. Saint worship was substituted for the old hero worship. Many ritualistic practices that savored of paganism found an open door into the church. The church, in attempting to meet the need of the barbarians, was itself partially paganized.

Suggested Reading

Baynes, Norman H. **Constantine the Great and the Christian Church.** *New York: Gordon, 1974.*

Edman, V. Raymond. **The Light in the Dark Ages.** *Wheaton, Ill.: Van Kampen, 1949. This is a scholarly work on this and later eras.*

King, Noel Q. **The Emperor Theodosius and the Establishment of Christianity.** *Philadelphia: Westminster, 1960. This work ably describes the relation of the emperor and the church.*

McNeill, John T. **The Celtic Churches (200–1200).** *Chicago: University of Chicago Press, 1974. This has a good treatment of the rise and influence in Europe of Celtic Christianity in Britain.*

Moorman, John R. H. **A History of the Church in England.** *New York: Morehouse-Gorham, 1954.*

Robinson, Charles G. **The Conversion of Europe.** *London: Longmans, 1917. The writer has given interesting and scholarly accounts of the work of the men cited in this chapter.*

Chapter 12

Conciliar Controversy
and Creedal Development

Between 313 and 451 theological controversies resulted in councils attempting to resolve the issues by formulating creeds. There have been two great eras of theological controversy in the history of the church. The great creeds of Protestantism were hammered out in the period of theological dispute at the time of the Reformation. The earlier period of theological controversy occurred between 325 and 451, when universal or ecumenical councils of leaders of the church were held to resolve conflicts. These councils brought about such great universal formulations of the Christian church as the Nicene and Athanasian creeds. It was the era when the main dogmas of the Christian church were developed. The word *dogma* came through the Latin from the Greek word *dogma*, which was derived from the verb *dokeo.* This word means to think. The dogmas or doctrines formulated in this period were the result of intense thought and searching of the Bible and the writings of the Fathers in order to interpret correctly the meaning of the Scriptures on the disputed points and to avoid erroneous opinions.

The era is also an excellent illustration of how intense zeal for a doctrine may unwittingly lead an individual or church into error unless there is a balanced study of the Bible. Just as Sabellius was led to a denial of the essential Trinity by his attempt to safeguard the unity of the Godhead, so Arius became involved in an antiscriptural approach to the relation of Christ to the Father in his attempt to escape what he thought was the danger of polytheism.

One might wonder why major controversy over theological questions came so late in the history of the ancient church; but, in the era of persecution, allegiance to Christ and the Scriptures took precedence over the meaning of particular doctrines. The threat from the state forced the church to internal unity in order to present a united front. Then, too, Constantine's attempt to unify the empire in order to save classical civilization meant that the church must have a unified body of dogma if it were to be the cement to

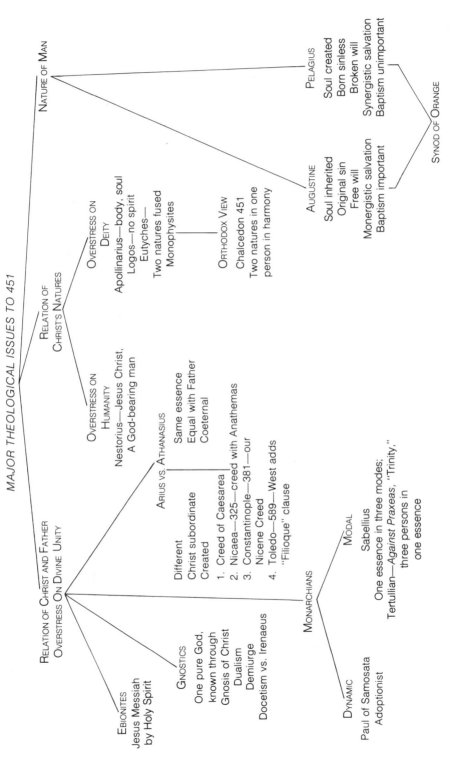

MAJOR THEOLOGICAL ISSUES TO 451

NATURE OF MAN

RELATION OF CHRIST AND FATHER
OVERSTRESS ON DIVINE UNITY

RELATION OF CHRIST'S NATURES

EBIONITES
Jesus Messiah
by Holy Spirit

GNOSTICS
One pure God,
known through
Gnosis of Christ
Dualism
Demiurge
Docetism vs. Irenaeus

MONARCHIANS

DYNAMIC
Paul of Samosata
Adoptionist

MODAL
Sabellius
One essence in three modes;
Tertullian—Against Praxeas, "Trinity,"
three persons in
one essence

ARIUS VS. ATHANASIUS

Different
Christ subordinate
Created

1. Creed of Caesarea
2. Nicaea—325—creed with Anathemas
3. Constantinople—381—our
   Nicene Creed
4. Toledo—589—West adds
   "Filioque" clause

Same essence
Equal with Father
Coeternal

OVERSTRESS ON
HUMANITY

Nestorius—Jesus Christ,
A God-bearing man

OVERSTRESS ON
DEITY

Apollinarius—body, soul
Logos—no spirit
Eutyches—
Two natures fused
Monophysites

ORTHODOX VIEW
Chalcedon 451
Two natures in one
person in harmony

AUGUSTINE
Soul inherited
Original sin
Free will
Monergistic salvation
Baptism important

PELAGIUS
Soul created
Born sinless
Broken will
Synergistic salvation
Baptism unimportant

SYNOD OF ORANGE

hold the body politic together. One empire must have one dogma.

The method adopted by the church to resolve the vital differences of opinion concerning the teachings of the Scriptures was the ecumenical or universal council, usually called and presided over by the Roman emperor. There were seven councils that were representative of the whole Christian church.[1] Great church leaders mainly from the eastern parts of the empire represented their respective localities and gave their assistance in the working out of solutions to the theological problems that dominated the thinking of Christians in this era.

I. THEOLOGY— THE RELATIONSHIPS OF THE PERSONS IN THE TRINITY

A. The Relationship of the Son to the Father in Eternity

The problem of the relationship between God the Father and His Son Jesus Christ became an acute problem in the church soon after the cessation of persecution. In western Europe, Tertullian, for example, insisted on the unity of essence in three personalities as the correct interpretation of the Trinity. Hence the dispute centered in the eastern section of the empire. It must be remembered that the church has always had to fight Unitarian conceptions of Christ. Modern Unitarianism has had its forerunners in Arianism and sixteenth-century Socinianism.

In 318 or 319, Alexander, the bishop of Alexandria, preached to his presbyters on "The Great Mystery of the Trinity in Unity." One of the presbyters, Arius, an ascetic scholar and popular preacher, attacked the sermon because he believed that it failed to uphold a distinction among the persons in the Godhead. In his desire to avoid a polytheistic conception of God, Arius took a position that did injustice to the true deity of Christ.

The issue was soteriological in nature. Could Christ save man if He were a demigod, less than true God, and of a similar or different essence from the Father as Eusebius and Arius respectively asserted? Just what was His relationship to the Father? The controversy became so bitter that Alexander had Arius condemned by a synod. Arius then fled to the friendly palace of Eusebius, the bishop of Nicomedia, who had been his schoolmate. Since the dispute centered in Asia Minor, it threatened the unity of the empire as well as that of the church. Constantine tried to settle the dispute by letters to the bishop of Alexandria and Arius, but the dispute had gone beyond the power even of a letter from the emperor. Constantine then called a council of the bishops of the church to work out a solution to the dispute. This council met at Nicaea in the early summer of 325. Between two and three hundred bishops of the church were present, but fewer than ten were from the western section of the empire. The emperor presided over the first session and paid all costs. For the first time the church found itself dominated by the political leadership of the head of the state. The perennial problem of the relationship between church and state emerged clearly here, but the bishops were too busy dealing with theological heresy to think of that particular problem.

Three views were put forth at the council. Arius, who was backed by Eusebius of Nicomedia (to be distinguished from Eusebius of Caesarea) and a minority of those present insisted that Christ had not existed from all eternity but had a beginning by the creative act of God. Arius believed that Christ was of a *different (heteros)* essence or substance from the Father. Because of the virtue of His life and His obedience to God's will, Christ was to be considered divine. But Arius believed that Christ was a being created out of nothing, subordinate to the Father, and of a different essence from the Father. He was not coequal, coeternal, or consubstantial with the Father. To Arius He was divine but not deity.[2]

Athanasius (ca. 295–373) became the chief exponent of what became the orthodox view. His wealthy parents had provided for his theological education in the famous catechetical school of Alexandria. His work *De Incarnatione* presented his idea of the doctrine of Christ. At the council this young man, slightly over thirty, insisted that Christ had existed from all eternity with the Father and was of the same essence *(homoousios)* as the Father, although He was a distinct personality. He insisted on these things because he believed that if Christ were less than he had stated Him to be, He could not be the Savior of men. The question of man's eternal salvation was involved in the relationship of the Father and the Son according to Athanasius. He held that Christ was coequal, coeternal, and consubstantial with the Father; and for these views he suffered exile five times.

The largest party was led by the gentle scholar and church historian Eusebius of Caesarea, whose dislike of controversy led him to propose a view that he hoped would be an acceptable compromise. He proposed a moderate view that would combine the best ideas of Arius and Athanasius. Over two hundred of those present followed his views at first. He taught that Christ was not created out of nothing as Arius had insisted but that He was begotten of the Father before time in eternity. Christ was of a like *(homoi)* or similar essence to the Father. His creed became the basis of the creed that was finally drawn at Nicaea, but that one differed from his in its insistence on the unity of essence of substance of the Father and the Son.[3]

Orthodoxy gained a temporary victory at Nicaea by the assertion of the eternity of Christ and the identity of His substance with that of the Father. However, the creed formulated here must not be confused with the Nicene Creed used by the church today, although that creed is similar to the one formulated at Nicaea. The creed of 325 stops with the phrase "and in the Holy Spirit" and is followed by a section condemning Arius' views.[4]

Between 325 and 361 under Constantine and his sons orthodoxy had to face a reaction that led to its defeat and the temporary victory of Arianism. A second reaction against orthodoxy, with orthodoxy's final victory in 381, came between 361 and 381. Theodosius in 381 defined as the faith of true Christians the views formulated by the orthodox at Nicaea, but the years between 325 and 381 were marked by bitterness and contention.

The Council of Constantinople in 381 stated in canon 1 of its decisions that the faith of the 318 fathers at Nicaea "shall not be set aside but shall remain dominant." The present Nicene Creed, approved at Chalcedon in 451, is in all probability based on

Syro-Palestinian creeds such as the Jerusalem Creed of Cyril's writings. This creed, the Apostles' Creed, and the Athanasian Creed are the three great universal creeds of the church.[5] Arianism, to which modernism and Unitarianism are both related, was rejected as unorthodox doctrine, and the true deity of Christ was made an article of Christian faith. Arianism did spread among Goths, Vandals, and Lombards. Though the decision at Nicaea became a factor in the eventual split between the Eastern and Western churches, that must not blind us to the value of that decision for our faith. Nicaea cost the church its independence, however, for the church became imperial from this time and was increasingly dominated by the emperor. The church in the West was able to rise above this domination, but the church in the East never freed itself from domination by the political power of the state.

B. The Relationship of the Holy Spirit to the Father

Macedonius, bishop of Constantinople between 341 and 360, most likely taught that the Holy Spirit was "a minister and a servant" on a level with the angels and that the Holy Spirit was a creature subordinate to the Father and Son. This was a denial of the true deity of the Holy Spirit and would be as harmful to the conception of the Holy Spirit as the views of Arius were to the conception of Christ. The ecumenical Council of Constantinople condemned these views in 381. When the creed of Constantinople, our Nicene Creed, was recited at the third Council of Toledo in 589, the words "and the Son" (filioque) were added to the statement "that proceedeth from the Father," which is concerned with the relationship between the Holy Spirit and the Father and the Son. The Western churches since then have insisted on the true deity and the personality of the Holy Spirit as coequal, coeternal, and consubstantial with the Father and the Son.[6]

II. CHRISTOLOGY— CONTROVERSIES CONCERNING THE RELATIONSHIP BETWEEN THE NATURES OF CHRIST

The settlement of the theological question concerning the eternal relationship of the Son to the Father at Nicaea raised new problems concerning the relationship between the human and divine natures of Christ in time. Before the orthodox doctrine of the relationship of the two natures was finally formulated, many scenes of passion and violence occurred. In general, those theologians linked with Alexandria emphasized the deity of Christ; those with Antioch, His humanity at the expense of His deity.

A view of the two natures of Christ that did injustice to Christ's true manhood was developed by Apollinarius, a converted teacher of rhetoric and bishop of Laodicea. Apollinarius developed his peculiar doctrine concerning the natures of Christ when he was about sixty. Until that time he had been a good friend of Athanasius and had been one of the leading champions of orthodoxy. In an attempt to avoid the undue separation of the human and divine natures of Christ, Apollinarius taught that Christ had a true body and soul but that the spirit in man was replaced in Christ by the *logos*. The *logos* as the divine element actively dominated the passive element, the body and soul, in the person of Christ. He stressed the deity of Christ but minimized His true manhood. His view was officially condemned at the ecumenical Council of Constantinople in 381.[7]

In contrast to the view of Apollinarius was the view developed by Nestorius (ca. 381–ca. 452), a scholarly monk who became patriarch at Constantinople in 428. Nestorius disliked the use of the term *theotokos* (God-bearer) as a name for Mary, the mother of Jesus, because it seemed to exalt her unduly. He offered the word *Christotokos* as an alternative, arguing that Mary was only the mother of the human side of Christ. By so arguing, he made Christ out to be a man in whom, in Siamese twin fashion, the divine and human natures were combined in a mechanical union rather than in an organic union of natures. Christ was in effect only a perfect man who was morally linked to deity. He was a God-bearer rather than the God-man. Leaders of the church gathered at Ephesus in 431 and, led by Cyril of Alexandria, condemned this doctrine; but the followers of Nestorius continued their work in the eastern section of the empire and carried the gospel as they conceived it to Persia, India, and even China in 635 by Alopen.[8] It was destroyed in China by the end of the ninth century.

In reaction to views of such men as Nestorius, emphasis was again laid on the divine nature of Christ to the neglect of His human nature. Eutyches, archimandrite of a monastery at Constantinople, insisted that after the Incarnation the two natures of Christ, the human and the divine, were fused into one nature, the divine. This view resulted in the denial of the true humanity of Christ. It was condemned in a long letter, known as the *Tome*,[9] by Leo I, the bishop of Rome between 440 and 461, and by the Council of Chalcedon held in 451. The Council of Chalcedon went on to promulgate a Christology that would be in accord with the Scriptures. The council held that Christ was "complete in Godhead and complete in manhood, truly God and truly man," having "two natures, without confusion, without change, without division, without separation." These two natures were brought together harmoniously in one person with one essence by the Incarnation. This formulation has been the view of the orthodox on this point since the time of the council.[10]

The views of Eutyches were revived in the Monophysite controversy that disturbed the peace of the eastern empire until the middle of the sixth century. Over 15 million Monophysites still exist in the Coptic churches of Egypt, Ethiopia, Lebanon, Turkey, and Russia.

The settlement of the relation between the human and divine natures of Christ was followed by discussion of the relationship of the wills of Christ. Did He have both a divine and human will? If so, were they equal or was one subordinate to the other? This dispute was finally settled at the Council of Constantinople (680–81) with the assertion that the two wills of Christ exist in Him in a harmonious unity in which the human will is subject to the divine will.

The settlement of these various issues in the Eastern church left the Eastern section of Christianity with little further contribution to make to the main stream of Christianity. Except for the word of John of Damascus in the eighth century, Eastern theology remained stagnant until modern times.

III. ANTHROPOLOGY—THE MANNER OF MAN'S SALVATION

The heresies and controversies so far discussed were problems mainly in the Eastern wing of the church. Theology and Christology were not grave problems in the West where such leaders as Tertullian had led the church to the orthodox view of the relationship of Christ to the Father and of His two natures to each other. The Western church was not as concerned with speculative metaphysical theology as the more rationalistic Greek thinkers of the Eastern church were. Instead, the thinkers of the church in the West were concerned with more practical problems. This distinction becomes quite clear to any student of ancient history. The Greek mind made its contribution in the field of thought, whereas the more practical Roman mind was more concerned with matters of practice in the church. For example, Augustine and Pelagius were concerned with the problem of the nature of man and how man is saved. Was man to be saved by divine power only, or was there a place in the process of salvation for the human will?

Pelagius (ca. 360–ca. 420), a British monk and theologian whom Jerome described as "weighed down with the porridge of the Scots," came to Rome about 400 where, with the help of Celestius, he formulated his idea of how man is saved. He soon found that Augustine would have no part of his ideas. He left Rome in 409. Pelagius, a cool, calm individual, had known nothing of the struggle of soul through which Augustine had gone before he was saved. Hence, Pelagius was more willing to give the human will a place in the process of salvation. But Augustine had found his will helpless to extricate him from the morass of sin in which he found himself because of his sinful nature.

Pelagius believed that each man is created free as Adam was and that each man has the power to choose good or evil. Each soul is a separate creation of God and, therefore, uncontaminated by the sin of Adam. The universality of sin in the world is explained by the weakness of human flesh rather than by the corruption of the human will by original sin. Man does not inherit original sin from his first ancestor, although the sins of individuals of the past generation do weaken the flesh of the present generation so that sins are committed unless the individual wills to cooperate with God in the process of salvation. The human will is free to cooperate with God in the attainment of holiness and can make use of such aids to grace as the Bible, reason, and the example of Christ. Because there is no original sin, infant baptism is not an essential element in salvation.[11]

Augustine, the great bishop of Hippo, opposed what he believed was a denial of the grace of God by insisting that regeneration is exclusively the work of the Holy Spirit. Man was originally made in the image of God and free to choose good and evil, but Adam's sin bound all men because Adam was the head of the race. Man's will is entirely corrupted by the Fall so that he must be considered totally depraved and unable to exercise his will in regard to the matter of salvation.

Augustine believed that all inherit sin through Adam and that no one, therefore, can escape original sin. Man's will is so bound that he can do nothing to bring about his salvation. Salvation can come only to the elect through the grace of God in Christ. God must energize the human will to accept His proffered grace, which is only for those whom He has elected to salvation.[12]

Pelagius's views were condemned at the Council of Ephesus in 431, but neither the Eastern nor the Western churches ever fully accepted Augustine's views. John Cassian (ca. 360–ca. 435), a monk, endeavored to find a compromise position by which the human will and the divine will could cooperate in salvation. He taught that all men are sinful because of the Fall and that their wills are weakened but not totally corrupted. Man's partially free will can cooperate with divine grace in the process of salvation. He feared that the doctrines of election and irresistible grace taught by Augustine might lead to ethical irresponsibility. The view of Cassian was condemned at the Synod of Orange in 529 in favor of a moderate Augustinian view.[13]

The problem raised by Pelagius and Augustine has, however, been perennial in the Christian church. Twentieth-century liberal thought is only a resurgence of the Pelagian idea that man can achieve salvation by cooperation with the divine will through his own efforts. The problem is whether Christianity is a matter of morals or religion; man's free will or God's grace; character development by culture or by a conversion that makes such development possible; a matter of man's rational powers or God's revelation. The church has always been closer to Augustine's view than to that of Pelagius or John Cassian, although the views of the medieval church on this point were similar to those of the semi-Pelagians who followed John Cassian.

Most of the major controversies were ended by 451, but they left a definite impact on the Christian church. The unity of the church was preserved but at the expense of the freedom of spirit that was so characteristic of the early church. Christians were now in possession of authoritative statements regarding the sense in which the Scriptures were to be interpreted on major doctrinal issues. But there were also some disadvantages that must be considered. The emphasis on the theological led to a danger that people might be orthodox in faith but not live up to the ethical implications of that faith. Creed and conduct must always go hand in hand. It was also sad that many Christians felt that the church might properly resort to violence and persecution in its attempt to keep the faith pure. The emperor as an arbiter of the differing viewpoints at councils was able to assert the power of the state in religious matters and end the separation of church and state. But we can be grateful to those who risked life as well as position to get the church to accept doctrines that are true to the Scriptures, and we can unite in praise to God for His providential guidance in all these matters.

The books mentioned in the reading for chapter 8 will be found useful references for the material discussed in this chapter.

Arpee, Leon. A History of Armenian Christianity. New York: Armenian Missionary Association of America, 1946.

Atiya, Aziz S. A History of Eastern Christianity. London: Methuen, 1968. This work describes the progress of the Monophysite churches to the present.

Baker, George P. Constantine the Great and the Christian Revolution. London: Nash & Grayson, 1931.

Evans, Robert F. Pelagius. New York: Seabury, 1968.

Ferguson, John. Pelagius. Cambridge: Heffer, 1956. This is a sympathetic treatment.

Frend, W. H. C. The Rise of the Monophysite Movement. Cambridge: Cambridge University Press, 1972.

Jedin, Hubert. Ecumenical Councils of the Catholic Church. Translated by Ernest Graf. New York: Herder and Herder, 1960.

Kelly, J. N. D. Early Christian Doctrine. 2nd ed. New York: Harper, 1960.

Landon, Edward H. A Manual of Councils of the Holy Catholic Church. 2 vols. Edinburgh: Grant, 1909.

Newman, Albert. A Manual of Church History. 2 vols. Rev. Ed. Chicago: American Baptist Publication Society, 1931–33. See volume 1, pages 320–92, for a good discussion of the controversies mentioned.

Schaff, Philip. Creeds of Christendom. 3 vols. 6th ed. New York: Scribner, 1890. See volumes 1 and 2 for discussions of the rise of the creeds as well as the relevant documents.

Sellers, R. V. The Council of Chalcedon. London: SPCK, 1953. This is a helpful treatment of the history and doctrine of Chalcedon.

Wand, John W. C. The Four Great Heresies. London: Mowbray, 1955.

Chapter 13

The Golden Age of Church Fathers

The church fathers whose work came before the Council of Nicaea were known as the ante-Nicene fathers, whether they were apostolic fathers, apologists, or polemicists. Between the Councils of Nicaea (325) and Chalcedon (451) several of the most able Fathers of the Christian church did their greatest work. They endeavored to study the Scriptures along more scientific lines in order to develop their theological meaning. Because of the sheer weight of his work and his influence on the church of his day, Augustine was the greatest of these fathers.

I. EASTERN POST-NICENE FATHERS

The Fathers of the Eastern wing of the church belonged to what have been called the Alexandrian and Antiochene schools of interpretation. Such men as Chrysostom or Theodore of Mopsuestia followed the Antiochene or Syrian school of interpretation, emphasizing a grammatico-historical study of the Scriptures in order to discover the meaning that the sacred writer had for those to whom he was writing. They avoided the allegorizing tendency practiced by the men of the Alexandrian school, who followed the example of Origen.

A. Chrysostom (ca. 347–407)— Expositor and Orator

John, who was called Chrysostom shortly after his death because his eloquence was literally that of one who deserved the name "golden-mouthed," was born about 347 into a wealthy aristocratic family of Antioch. His mother, Anthusa, reminds one of Augustine's mother because, though she was widowed at the age of twenty, she refused to remarry in order that she might devote all her time to her son's education. Chrysostom was a student of the sophist Libanius, who had been a friend of Emperor Julian. This man gave him a good training in the Greek classics and the rhetoric that laid the foundation for his excellent speaking ability. For a time he practiced law, but after his baptism in 368 he became a monk. After his mother's death in 374, he practiced a severely ascetic life until 380. During this time he lived in a cave on a mountain near Antioch. Ill health stopped this severe regimen. Ordained in 386, he preached some of his best sermons in Antioch until 398. In that year he was made a patriarch of Constantinople. He held this position until Empress Eudoxia finally banished him in 404 because he had denounced her extravagant dress and her placing a silver statue of herself near Saint Sophia, where he preached. He died in exile in 407.

Chrysostom lived a pure, simple life that was a rebuke to his highly placed wealthy parishioners in Constantinople. Extremely ascetic in his insistence on simplicity of life and inclined to mysticism, he did not always possess tact; but he did have a courteous, affectionate, kindly nature. Though he was a giant in moral and spiritual stature, he was short and thin. His emaciated but pleasant face, wrinkled forehead, bald head, and piercing bright eyes made a lasting impression on his hearers.

Perhaps some years of study under Diodorus of Tarsus had something to do with his ability as an expositor. About 640 of his homilies are still extant, and even a reading of the cold print gives one some idea of his oratorical ability. Most of his homilies or sermons are expositions of Paul's Epistles. Not knowing Hebrew, he could not make a critical investigation of the Old Testament Scriptures; but he kept the importance of the context in mind and sought to discover the literal meaning of the writer and to make a practical application of that meaning to the problems of the people of his day. These practical applications of the gospel were given with great moral earnestness. He taught that there must be no divorce of morals and religion; the Cross and ethics must go hand in hand. It is little wonder that he was and still is hailed as the greatest pulpit orator the Eastern church ever had.[1]

B. Theodore (ca. 350–428)—Exegete

Another noted church father is Theodore of Mopsuestia. He, too, studied the Scriptures—for about ten years—under Diodorus of Tarsus. This good education was made possible by his birth into a wealthy family. He was ordained a presbyter in Antioch in 383 and became the bishop of Mopsuestia in Cilicia about 392.

Theodore has been rightly called "the prince of ancient exegetes." He opposed the allegorical system of interpretation and insisted on a thorough understanding of the grammar of the text and the historical background of the text in order to discover the meaning of the writer. He also gave careful attention to the text in its immediate and its more remote contexts. This type of study made him an able commentator and theologian. He wrote commentaries on such books of the Bible as Colossians and the letters to the Thessalonians. Both he and Chrysostom had a healthy influence on the interpretation of the Bible in their day. Their work was a marked contrast to the strained interpretations of Scripture that resulted from the use of the allegorical method of interpretation.

C. Eusebius (ca. 265–ca. 339)— Church Historian

One of the most widely studied of the church fathers is Eusebius of Caesarea, who has as much right to the title of Father of Church History as Herodotus has to the title Father of History. After having a good education under Pamphilus at Caesarea, he helped his friend Pamphilus build up his library in that city. Eusebius was an assiduous student and read everything he could obtain that might help him in his research. He excerpted widely from both profane and sacred literature. Much literature of his day that might otherwise have been lost has been preserved because these excerpts were quoted in his works.

Eusebius's personality was one that fitted him for such scholarly pursuits. He was of a gentle and agreeable disposition and disliked the quarrels engendered by the Arian heresy. He was given a place of honor at the right hand of Constantine at the Council of Nicaea and, like him, preferred a compromise between the parties of Athanasius and Arius. It was the Caesarean Creed, put forth by Eusebius of Caesarea, that the Council of Nicaea modified and accepted.

His greatest work is *Ecclesiastical History*, a survey of the history of the church from apostolic times until 324. His purpose was to make a record of the past trials of the church at the end of its long period of struggle and the beginning of its era of prosperity. This work is especially valuable today because Eusebius had access to the fine library at Caesarea and the imperial archives. He made a great effort to be honest and objective in his use of the best and most reliable of the primary sources that were available to him.[2] In his critical use of many reliable documents Eusebius anticipated something of the careful scientific study that the modern historian does in evaluating the sources of his knowledge. It is little wonder that Eusebius is our best source of knowledge concerning the history of the church during the first three centuries of its existence, but scholars regret that he did not make careful footnotes of his sources of knowledge after the manner of the modern historian. Sometimes, too, his work becomes little more than a collection of facts and extracts with no orderly view of cause and effect. Despite these defects and the monotonous rambling and desultory style, the work has been of inestimable value to the church all through the ages.

Eusebius wrote the *Chronicle*, a universal history from the time of Abraham until 323. The "Chronological Canons," which is a part of the *Chronicle*, provided the conventional chronological framework for medieval history. His *Life of Constantine* was written somewhat as an appendix to this *History* and is an excellent, though somewhat laudatory, source of information concerning the doings of Constantine as they were related to the church. He also wrote a laudatory biography of Constantine.

The historical work of Eusebius was continued by two successors who did not always measure up to the high standard of reliability set by him. It must be said, however, that these laymen, Socrates and Sozomen, both trained for the legal profession, showed a lack of bigotry even in dealing with those who were opposed to them. Socrates' work carries the story of Christianity from 305 to 439 in an attempt to complete the task begun by Eusebius. Sozomen was much more credulous than Socrates and often plagiarized his work. He also often digressed in favor of asceticism. His work covers the period from 323 to 425. Together with Eusebius, these men are the chief ecclesiastical authorities for the history of the ancient church.

II. WESTERN POST-NICENE FATHERS

The fathers of the Western church in this period excelled in different fields from those of the East. The translation of the Scriptures, the writings of pagan philosophers, and the writing of theological treatises were important parts of their work. The practical bent of the Latin in contrast with the interest in speculation of the Greek may be seen in the work of Jerome, Ambrose, and Augustine.

A. Jerome (ca. 347–420)— Commentator and Translator

Jerome, a native of Venetia, was baptized in 360 and for several years was a wandering student in Rome and the cities of Gaul. During the next decade he visited Antioch and followed the monastic life while he learned Hebrew. He became secretary to Damasus, bishop of Rome, in 382; and Damasus suggested to him that he might profitably make a new translation of the Bible.[3] In 386 Jerome went to Palestine and there, through the generosity of Paula, a wealthy Roman lady whom he had taught Hebrew, he lived in a monastic retreat at Bethlehem. He led this retreat for nearly thirty-five years.

There are no known contemporary portrayals of Jerome; however, later editions of his works frequently represented him. These two from an Italian Renaissance translation of his life and letters show him first with his many books and then with Marcella who, with Jerome's mother and sister, assisted him in his work on Scripture. Jerome is pointing at his critics, who apparently took a dim view of his talking to a woman.

Jerome's greatest work was a Latin translation of the Bible known as the Vulgate. Before 391 he had completed the revision of the Latin New Testament. He went beyond the Greek of the Septuagint version of the Old Testament to make a Latin translation from the Hebrew, finishing his work around 404 or 405. Jerome's version of the Bible has been widely used by the Western church and has been, until recently, the only official Bible of the Roman Catholic church since the Council of Trent.

Jerome was also an able commentator and wrote many commentaries that are still helpful today. His early love for and knowledge of the classics was a help in the interpretation of the Scriptures, although in later years he disavowed classical learning. He wrote a fine work, *De Viris Illustribus*, after the model of ancient biographers. It contains brief biographical and bibliographical sketches of leading Christian writers and their works from the time of the apostles until his day. His love of the ascetic life caused him to champion it with his pen, and the later medieval popularity of the ascetic life in the West owed much to the writings of Jerome on this subject.

B. Ambrose (ca. 340–97)— Administrator and Preacher

Ambrose demonstrated his ability in the areas of church administration, preaching, and theology. His father had held the high position of prefect of Gaul; and his family, high in imperial circles in Rome, educated him in law for a political career. He soon rose to the position of imperial governor of the area around the city of Milan. Upon the death of the bishop of Milan in 374, the people unanimously wanted him to take that position. Believing this to be the call of God, he gave up his high position, distributed his money to the poor, became a bishop, and began an intensive study of the Scriptures and theology.

Ambrose proved to be a fearless and able administrator of the affairs of the church. He spoke against the powerful Arian groups and did not even hesitate to oppose Emperor Theodosius. In 390 Theodosius had gathered the people of Thessalonica, whose governor had been slain, into the square in that city

A mosaic of Ambrose—bishop of Milan, powerful preacher, theologian, and able administrator. This mosaic comes from the first half of the fifth century and may be a somewhat fanciful representation of his actual appearance.

and had ordered their massacre. When he came to church to take the Communion, Ambrose refused him admission to the Lord's Supper until he humbly and publicly repented of this deed.[4] Ambrose wanted to make the state and its rulers respect the church so that they would not transgress on the rightful claims of the church in the spiritual realm.

Even though his practical expositions of Scripture were marred by his use of the allegorical method, Ambrose was an able preacher. His preaching in the cathedral at Milan was instrumental in bringing Augustine to a knowledge of Christianity that later resulted in his salvation. He introduced congregational singing of hymns and antiphonal psalmody into the Western church. He also became a theologian of no mean ability, although he had not studied theology until his consecration as bishop.

C. Augustine (ca. 354–430)— Philosopher and Theologian

Although Jerome and Ambrose were honored with the title of doctor by the medieval church, their fame is small compared to the reputation of Augustine. Both Protestantism and Roman Catholicism pay tribute to the contribution of Augustine to the cause of Christianity. He was an able polemicist, a good preacher, a fine episcopal administrator, a superb theologian, and the creator of a Christian philosophy of history that is still valid in its essentials. Living at a time when the old classical civilization seemed to be doomed to fall before the barbarians, Augustine stood between two worlds, the classical and the new medieval. He insisted that people must look forward to the "City of God," a spiritual civilization, because the old classical civilization was passing.

Augustine was born in 354 into the home of a Roman official in the North African town of Tagaste. His mother, Monica, prayed much for his conversion to the Christian faith. He received his early education in the local school, where he learned Latin to the accompaniment of many beatings and hated Greek so much that he never learned

to use it proficiently. He was sent to school in nearby Madaura and from there to Carthage to study rhetoric. Freed from the restraint of home, Augustine followed the pattern of many students of his day and indulged his passions by an illegitimate union with a concubine. His son Adeodatus was born of this union in 372. In 373 Augustine adopted Manichean teaching in his search for truth; but, finding it insufficient, he turned to philosophy after a reading of Cicero's *Hortensius* and the Neoplatonic teachings. He taught rhetoric in his hometown, Carthage, and in Rome until he went to Milan about 384.

In 386 came the crisis of conversion. Meditating on his spiritual need one day in a garden, he heard a voice next door saying, "Take up and read." Augustine opened his Bible to Romans 13:13–14, and the reading brought to his soul the light he had been unable to find either in Manicheanism or Neoplatonism. He dismissed his concubine and gave up his profession of rhetoric. His mother, who had prayed long for his conversion, died shortly after his baptism. Returning to Carthage, he was ordained priest in 391. In 396 he was consecrated bishop of Hippo. From that time until his death in 430 he gave his life to episcopal administration, studying, and writing. He is acclaimed as the greatest of the Fathers of the church.[5] He left over one hundred books, five hundred sermons, and two hundred letters.

Perhaps the most widely known work from the pen of Augustine is his *Confessions*, one of the great autobiographical works of all time. It was completed by 401. Like all his major works, it came out of crises he or the church faced. In the course of his work he laid bare his soul. Books 1 to 7 describe his life before conversion; Book 8 describes the events surrounding his conversion; and the next two books recount the events after his conversion, including the death of his mother and his return to North Africa. Books 11 to 13 are a commentary on the first chapters of Genesis, in which Augustine often resorted to allegory.

Christians throughout the ages have found spiritual blessing in the reading of this work that Augustine wrote to God to praise Him for the grace that He had extended to such a sinner as he. The book contains the often quoted "Thou madest us for thyself, and our heart is restless, until it repose in thee" in the very first paragraph. The sense of his sin and the power of evil revealed by his passionate, immoral life caused him to cry out, "Give me chastity and continency, only not yet." That need was finally met by his experience of the grace of God.[6]

Augustine wrote another autobiographical work, *Retractationes*, or *Revisions*, shortly before his death. He discussed his works in chronological order and pointed out the ways his mind had changed over the years. He particularly regretted his early connection with pagan philosophy, because it can never bring man to the truth as it is in Christianity.[7] This is his intellectual biography.

Augustine also wrote philosophical works in dialogue form. *Contra Academicos* is the most interesting of these works. In it he tried to demonstrate that man can achieve probable truth through philosophical study but that certainty comes only by the revelation in the Bible.

His *De Doctrina Christiana* is the most important of his exegetical works. It is a small manual dealing with his views on hermeneutics or the science of interpretation. In it he developed the great principle of the analogy of faith. He meant by it that no teaching contrary to the general tenor of the Scriptures should be developed from any particular passage. Failure to keep this in mind has led many into fields of error and, often, heresy. With this principle in mind, he wrote many exegetical commentaries on the Old and New Testaments.

Augustine also wrote theological treatises of which his *De Trinitate*, concerning the Trinity, is the most significant. The first seven books of the work are devoted to a scriptural exposition of that doctrine. His *Enchiridion ad Laurentium* is a small manual of his theological views. This work, coupled with his *Retractationes*, will give the reader a clear picture in small compass of the theological views of Augustine. He also wrote many polemical works to defend the faith from the false teachings of the Manicheans, the Donatists, and particularly the Pelagians. His *De Haeresibus* is a history of heresies.

He wrote several practical and pastoral works and many letters, of which we have over two hundred still available. These works and letters deal with the many practical problems that a church administrator or pastor faces over the years of his ministry.

His greatest apologetic work and, in the minds of many, his greatest work, on which his enduring fame rests, is the treatise *De Civitate Dei*, popularly known as *The City of God* (413–26). Augustine himself was of the opinion that it was his great work.[8] Shocked by the sack of Rome by Alaric in 410, the Romans made the charge that this disaster had come upon them because they had forsaken the old classical Roman religion and had adopted Christianity. Augustine set out to answer this charge at the request of his friend Marcellinus. Books 1 to 10 constitute the apologetic part of this work. He tried to demonstrate in Books 1 to 5 that the prosperity of the state was not dependent on the old polytheistic worship, because the Romans had suffered catastrophes long before the advent of Christianity, and what success they had attained was due to the providence of God of whom they had been ignorant. In the next five books Augustine demonstrated that the worship of the Roman gods was not necessary in order to attain eternal blessing. Neither in the temporal nor spiritual realms could the gods aid their devotees, but Christianity could give them and had given them what temporal blessings they had enjoyed.

Augustine's philosophy of history, the first real philosophy of history ever to be developed, is to be found in Books 11 to 22 of this great work. The origin of the two cities is discussed in books 11 to 14. The central idea of the work is developed in chapter 28 of Book 14. The first city, the City of God, consisted of all human and celestial beings united in love to God and seeking His glory alone. The City of Earth is composed of those beings who, loving only self, seek their own glory and good. The dividing principle is that of love. Augustine did not have the Roman Empire or the Church of Rome in mind when he spoke of these two cities. His outlook was much more universal and opposed to the prevailing cyclical view of history. In Books 15 to 18 he traced the growth and prog-

ress of the two cities through biblical and secular history. The remaining books give an account of the destiny of the two cities. After judgment the members of the City of God share in eternal happiness and those of the City of Earth in eternal punishment. Augustine did not take into account the place of the Jew in the future and believed that the present age of the church is the Millennium. He asserted that the dualism of the two cities is only temporal and permissive and will be ended by the act of God. Though the work is heavy and tedious, a careful student will have a better grasp of the plan and purpose of God after reading it.

The development of a Christian interpretation of history must be considered one of the abiding contributions made by this great Christian scholar. Neither Greek nor Roman historians had been able to achieve any such universal grasp of man's history. Augustine exalted the spiritual over the temporal in his assertion of the sovereignty of the God who became the *Creator* of history in time. God is Lord over history and is not bound up in history as the philosopher Hegel later taught. History is linear, not cyclical. All that comes into being does so as a result of His will and action. Even before creation, God had a plan in mind for His creation. This plan will be partially realized in time in the struggle between the two cities on earth and finally realized beyond history by the supernatural power of God. Augustine also had a wider *compass* to his view of history than any man before him. He saw history as universal and unitary in that all men were included in it. Herodotus, in writing of the Persian War, limited his work to the struggle between the Greeks and the Persians. Augustine instead asserted the solidarity of the human race. Moreover, he believed that progress was primarily along moral and spiritual lines and was the result of *conflict* with evil, a conflict in which man had God's grace on his side. The *consummation* of this conflict would dissolve the sin-caused temporal dualism of the struggling cities in the final victory of the City of God. In this way Augustine avoided the error of Marx and others who try to make a temporal relative scene of history absolute and eternal by finding solutions to man's problems in temporal history. The end or goal of history, for Augustine, is beyond history, in the hands of an eternal God. This inspiring philosophy sustained the church through the dark half-millennium before 1000.

Augustine is looked upon by Protestants as one who was a forerunner of Reformation ideas in his emphasis on salvation from original and actual sin as a result of the grace of a sovereign God who irresistibly saves those whom He has elected. But in his discussion of how man is saved, Augustine so emphasized the church as a visible institution with the true creed, sacraments, and ministry that the Roman church considers him the father of Roman ecclesiasticism. It should be remembered that he made these emphases to defeat the claims of the Pelagians on the one hand and the Donatists on the other. His insistence on consideration of the whole tenor of Scripture in interpreting a part of Scripture has been a principle of lasting value in the church.

In spite of these abiding values, Augustine brought some errors into the stream of Christian thought. He helped to develop the doctrine of purgatory with all its attendant evils. He so emphasized the value of the two sacraments that the doctrine of baptismal regeneration and sacramental grace were logical outcomes of his views. His interpretation of the Millennium as the era between the Incarnation and Second Advent of Christ in which the church would conquer the world led to the Roman emphasis on the Church of Rome as the universal church destined to bring all within its fold and to the idea of postmillennialism.

These emphases of Augustine should not blind one to his significance for the Christian church. The Reformers found Augustine an invaluable ally in their belief that man bound by sin needs salvation by God's grace through faith alone. Between Paul and Luther the church had no one of greater moral and spiritual stature than Augustine.

SUGGESTED READING

Many of the items enumerated in the reading for chapter 5 may be profitably consulted for information concerning the Fathers of this period.

Battenhouse, W., ed. A Companion to the Study of Saint Augustine. *New York: Oxford University Press, 1955. This gives helpful background information.*

Bourke, Vernon J. Augustine's Quest of Wisdom. *Milwaukee: Bruce, 1945. The author has given a helpful, scholarly, and detailed account of Augustine's life and work from the Roman Catholic viewpoint.*

Brown, Peter. **Augustine of Hippo.** *Berkeley and Los Angeles: University of California Press, 1967.*

Dudden, F. Homes. **The Life and Times of Saint Ambrose.** *2 vols. Oxford: Clarendon University Press, 1935. This is well documented.*

Farrar, Frederick W. **Lives of the Fathers.** *2 vols. New York: Macmillan, 1889. Volume 2 has lengthy accounts of the lives and works of Jerome, Chrysostom, and Augustine.*

Kelly, J. N. D. **Jerome.** *New York: Harper and Row, 1975.*

Leigh-Bennett, Ernest. **Handbook of the Early Christian Fathers.** *London: Williams & Norgate, 1920. There are excellent chapters on most of the Fathers discussed in this chapter.*

Oates, Whitney J., ed. **Basic Writings of St. Augustine.** *2 vols. New York: Random, 1948.*

Paredi, Angelo. **Saint Ambrose.** *Notre Dame: University of Notre Dame Press, 1964. This is a scholarly work that is well documented and fairly recent.*

Van der Meer, Frederick. **Augustine the Bishop.** *Translated by Brian Battershaw and G. R. Lamb. London: Sheed and Ward, 1961. This is a literary mosaic of Augustine's life and work based on his writings and on recent research and archaeology.*

Wallace-Hadrill, David S. **Eusebius of Caesarea.** *London: Mowbray, 1960.*

Chapter 14

The Christianity of the Cloisters

Throughout history men have renounced society in times of worldliness and institutionalism and have retired into solitude to achieve personal holiness by contemplation and asceticism apart from the society they believe to be decadent and doomed. During the period of the gradual internal decay of the Roman Empire, monasticism made a powerful appeal to many, who renounced society for the cloister. This movement had its origins in the fourth century, and laymen in increasing numbers retired from the world from that time on. By the end of the sixth century monasticism had deep roots in the Western as well as in the Eastern sections of the church. A second era of greatness for monasticism occurred in the monastic reforms of the tenth and eleventh centuries. The era of friars in the thirteenth century was a third period. And the emergence of the Jesuits in the Counter Reformation of the sixteenth century constituted the final period in which monasticism deeply affected the church. This countercultural movement still has an important place within the life of the Roman Catholic church.

I. THE CAUSES OF MONASTICISM

Several influences contributed to the rise of monasticism within the ancient church. The dualistic view of flesh and spirit, with its tendency to consider flesh evil and spirit good—so characteristic of the Orient—influenced Christianity through the Gnostic and Neoplatonic movements. Retirement from the world would, it was thought, help the individual to crucify the flesh and to develop the spiritual life by meditation and ascetic acts.

One should also remember that some Scriptures seem to support the idea of separation from the world. Paul's apparent advocacy of the celibate life in 1 Corinthians 7 is a case in point. The early church fathers such as Origen, Cyprian, Tertullian, and Jerome urged celibacy as the correct interpretation of such Scriptures.

Certain psychological tendencies

strengthened the desire for a monastic life. In periods of crisis there is always a tendency to retreat from the harsh realities about one. The late second and third centuries saw the beginning of civil disorder that was to become so prevalent in the later history of the empire. Many left society for the monastery as a means of escape from harsh reality and the moral contamination of the times. With the union of church and state the possibility of martyrdom was lessened, but those who desired martyrdom as a pledge of their faith could find a psychological substitute in the ascetic practices of monasticism. Monasticism also offered a more individualistic approach to God and salvation than the formal corporate worship of the times.

History also played a part in the decision of many to accept the life of the cloister. The increasing number of barbarians crowding into the church brought many semipagan practices within the church, and puritanical souls revolted against them. The increasing moral deterioration, especially of the upper classes in Roman society, caused many to despair of social reform. Monasticism became a haven for those in revolt against the growing decadence of the times. It was a living criticism of the society of the day.

Geography merits some consideration as a factor responsible for the rise of monasticism. It would have been much more difficult to carry on the monastic life in areas where the climate was more severe than in Egypt, where the monastic life had its beginnings. The warm, dry climate and the multitude of caves in the hills along the banks of the Nile were conducive to separation of the individual from society. Small gardens, along with the resources of food provided by the nearby Nile, made securing of food by the individual fairly easy. Nearness to the desolate, forbidding scenery of the desert stimulated meditation.

II. THE DEVELOPMENT OF MONASTICISM

Monasticism went through four main stages during the period of its emergence in Western civilization. At first, ascetic practices were carried on by many within the church. Many later withdrew from society to live as anchorites or hermits. The holiness of these hermits attracted others, who would then take up residence in nearby caves and look to them for leadership in what was called a *laura*. A cloister for common exercises might be built. In the final stage organized communal life within a monastery appeared. This process had its beginnings in the East in the fourth century, and from there it spread to the church in the West.

A. In the East

Anthony (ca. 251–ca. 356) is usually regarded as the founder of monasticism. At the age of twenty he sold all his possessions, gave the money to the poor, and retired to a solitary cave to lead a life of meditation. His life of holiness gave him such a reputation that others also went to live near him in numerous caves that were not far from his habitation. He never organized these followers into a community; rather, each practiced the ascetic life of a hermit in his own cave.[1]

Not all the hermit monks were as sane as Anthony and his followers.

A balanced view of monasticism must keep in mind its motivations, positive contributions, and excesses. Macarius, shown in this woodcut, is said to have been so penitent for having killed a mosquito that he lived six months in a swamp, allowing himself to be stung by insects.

living twelve years with a hermit, organized the first monastery about 320 at Tabennisi on the east bank of the Nile. He soon had several thousand monks under his direct control in Egypt and Syria. Simplicity of life, work, devotion, and obedience were the keynotes of his organization.[2]

Basil of Caesarea (ca. 330–79) did much to popularize the communal type of monastic organization. Having had an excellent education in Athens and Constantinople, at the age of twenty-seven he gave up worldly advancement for the ascetic life. He was made a bishop of a large area in Cappadocia in 370, a post he held until his death. He gave a more utilitarian and social expression to the monastic spirit by insisting that the monks under his rule work, pray, read the

One, known as Saint Simeon Stylites (ca. 390–459), after having lived buried up to his neck in the ground for several months, decided to achieve holiness by becoming an ecclesiastical "pole sitter." He spent over thirty-five years on the top of a sixty-foot pillar near Antioch. Others lived in fields and grazed grass after the manner of cattle. A certain Ammoun had a particular reputation for sanctity because he had never undressed or bathed after he became a hermit. Another wandered naked in the vicinity of Mount Sinai for fifty years. These, however, were only the fanatic fringe of the movement and were to be found in the East more than in the West.

The communal or social type of monasticism, often called cenobite monasticism, also made its appearance first in Egypt. Pachomius (ca. 290–346), a discharged soldier, after

Monks regarded females as the sources of temptation and sin and consequently withdrew from their companionship. The irony is that sex then tended to become an obsession with them. To dispel his temptation, the monk is burning away his fingers. Nothing remains on his left hand except a stump, and on his right hand only the thumb and forefinger remain.

Bible, and perform good deeds. He discouraged extreme asceticism. The monasticism of the church in Eastern Europe today owes much to the rule that he developed for the guidance of his monks.[3] More and more people were swept into the movement until there were nearly a hundred monasteries in Europe at the accession of Justinian to the throne of the Eastern empire.

B. In the West

Monasticism in the West differed considerably from that in the East. The colder climate made communal organization much more essential in order that warm buildings and food for the winter season might be provided. Monasticism was also much more practical in its expression. It rejected idleness and deplored purely ascetic acts. Work as well as devotion was emphasized.

Athanasius is traditionally credited with the introduction of monasticism to the West during one of his periodic exiles from Alexandria. Pilgrims to Palestine came in contact with it there and in Syria and were attracted to it. Martin of Tours, Jerome, Augustine, and Ambrose wrote in favor of it and helped to popularize it within the Roman Empire. Jerome's writings on asceticism ranked next to the Bible and Benedict's Rule in the medieval monk's library.

The greatest leader of Western monasticism was Benedict of Nursia (ca. 480–ca. 542). Shocked by the vice of Rome, he retired to live as a hermit in a cave in the mountains east of Rome about 500. About 529 he founded the monastery of Monte Cassino, which survived until World War II, when it was destroyed by bombardment. Soon several monasteries were under his control and following his plan of organization, work, and worship, that is, his Rule. Each monastery was considered a self-sufficient, self-supporting unit or garrison of the soldiers of Christ. The day was divided into periods in which reading, worship, and work had important roles. The regulations that he drew up provided little meat for the monks but allowed plenty of fish, oil, butter, bread, vegetables, and fruit in their diet. This Rule, which emphasized poverty, chastity, and obedience, was one of the most important in the Middle Ages.[4] It was carried to England, Germany, and France by the seventh century and became almost universal in the time of Charlemagne. It was the standard rule in the West by the year 1000.

III. EVALUATION OF MONASTICISM

Casual students of church history often dismiss the work of the monk as of little value or evince a hostility that does not take into account the contribution made by the monk in his own day, a contribution that still affects modern civilization.

The local monastery often served as the medieval equivalent of a modern experimental farm in demonstrating better methods of agriculture. The monks cleared the forests, drained the marshes, made roads, and improved seeds and breeds of livestock. Nearby farmers often emulated the better techniques that they saw the monks using.

Monasteries helped to keep scholarship alive during the Dark Ages between 500 and 1000, when urban life was disrupted as the barbarians took over the Roman Empire. Monastery schools provided education on the lower levels for those nearby who were desirous to learn. Monks busied themselves copying precious manuscripts, which were thus preserved for posterity. In the middle of the sixth century, Cassiodorus, (478–573), a high government official under the Ostrogoths, retired from government service to devote himself to the task of collecting, translating, and copying patristic and classical literature. He was aided in this task by the monks of a monastery that he founded. The Book of Kells, a lovely illuminated manuscript of the Gospels in Latin, done about the seventh century by Irish monks, is an example of the beauty of the monks' work. Monks, such as Bede, Einhard, and Matthew Paris, wrote historical records, which are primary sources of information concerning the history of the period.

Monks, particularly from Britain, became the missionaries of the medieval church. They went out as fearless soldiers of the Cross to found new monasteries, and these became centers from which whole tribes were won to Christianity. Columba, a monk from Ireland, won the Scots; and one of his followers, Aidan, won the people of northern England. Unfortunately, much of their missionary work was marred by their mass methods of conversion. If a ruler accepted Christianity, he and his people were baptized whether or not they fully understood the meaning of the act or the implications of Christianity for their lives.

The monasteries provided a refuge for the outcast of society who were in need of help. Those in need of hospitalization would usually find loving care in the monastery. The weary traveler could be sure of food and bed in the hospice of the monastery. Those who tired of the worldliness of their day could find in the monastery a refuge from the cares of life. Some of the best leaders of the medieval church, such as Gregory VII, came from monasteries.

But there is also a debit sheet that must be considered in any evaluation of early medieval monasticism. Too many of the best men and women of the empire were drained off into the monasteries, and their abilities were lost to the world, which was so badly in need of such leaders. Moreover, the celibate life kept these able men and women from marriage and the rearing of able children. This led to one standard of morality for the monks (celibacy) and another for the ordinary individual.

Too often monasticism merely pandered to spiritual pride as monks became proud of ascetic acts performed to benefit their own souls. As the monasteries became wealthy because of community thrift and ownership, laziness, avarice, and gluttony crept in.

Monasticism aided in the rapid development of a hierarchical, centralized organization in the church because the monks were bound in obedience to superiors who in turn owed their allegiance to the pope. We can but deplore these tendencies while at the same time we admire the fine contributions that the monks made to medieval life.

SUGGESTED READING

Hannah, Ian. **Christian Monasticism.** *New York: Macmillan, 1925.*

La Carriere, Jacques. **Men Possessed of God.** *Translated by Roy Monkcom. Garden City, N.Y.: Doubleday, 1964. This work discusses the more ascetic Eastern monasticism.*

Zarnecki, George. **The Monastic Achievement.** *New York: McGraw, 1972.*

Chapter 15

Hierarchical and Liturgical Developments

Between 313 and 590 the Old Catholic church, in which each bishop had been an equal, became the Roman Catholic church, in which the bishop of Rome won primacy over other bishops. The ritual of the church also became much more elaborate. The Roman Catholic church in its structure and canon law reflects imperial Rome.

I. THE DOMINANCE OF THE ROMAN BISHOP

The bishop in the early church was considered one of many bishops who were equal to one another in rank, power, and function. Between 313 and 450 the Roman bishop came to be acknowledged as the first among equals. But, beginning with Leo I's accession to the episcopal throne in 440, the Roman bishop began to claim his supremacy over other bishops. The need for efficiency and coordination led naturally to centralization of power. The bishop was also considered the guarantor of orthodox doctrine. In addition, some of the Roman bishops of this period were strong men who missed no opportunity to increase their power.[1]

Historical events during this era conspired to enhance the reputation of the bishop of Rome. Rome had been the traditional center of authority for the Roman world for half a millennium and was the largest city in the West. After Constantine moved the capital of the empire to Constantinople in 330, the center of political gravity shifted from Rome to that city. This left the Roman bishop as the single strongest individual in Rome for great periods of time, and the people of that area came to look to him for temporal as well as spiritual leadership whenever a crisis faced them. He was a tower of strength during the sacking of Rome in 410 by Alaric and his Visigothic followers, and his clever diplomacy had at least been able to save the city from the torch. The emperor at Constantinople was remote from Rome and its problems, but the bishop was near at hand to exercise effective authority in meeting political as well as spiritual crises. When the imperial throne in the West fell into the hands of the barbarians after 476, and other Italian cities became the seat of temporal power, the people of Italy came to look to the Roman bishop for political as well as spiritual leadership.

The Petrine theory, based on such Scriptures as Matthew 16:16–18, Luke 22:31–32, and John 21:15–17, was generally accepted by 590. According to this theory, Peter had been given "ecclesiastical primogeniture" over his fellow apostles, and his superior position had been passed on from him to his successors, the bishops of Rome, by apostolic succession. About 250 Stephen had used these Scriptures.

Such great theologians as Cyprian, Tertullian, and Augustine were outstanding men of the Western church under the leadership of the bishop of Rome. The domains of the Roman bishop had never suffered from heretical disputes such as those that had divided the East—for example, those of Arius. Indeed, the bishop of Rome had held synods in which he had been able to develop clearly what was to be the orthodox position.

Of the five great patriarchs of the church—in Jerusalem, Antioch, Alexandria, Constantinople, and Rome—only the patriarch of Constantinople and the bishop of Rome lived in cities of world consequence by 590. The bishop of Jerusalem lost prestige after the Jewish rebellion against Rome during the second century. Alexandria and Antioch rapidly declined in importance when they were overrun by the Muslim hordes in the seventh century. The bishop of Rome and of Constantinople were left as the two most prominent clerical leaders by 590. The Council of Constantinople in 381 recognized the primacy of the Roman see. The patriarch of Constantinople was given "the primacy of honor next after the Bishop of Rome," according to the third canon of the Council of Constantinople.[2] This was a practical recognition of the primacy of the Roman bishop by a group of leading clerics of the church. Emperor Valentinian III, in an edict in A.D. 445, recognized the supremacy of the bishop of Rome in spiritual affairs. What the bishop would enact was to be "law for all."[3] Thus both ecclesiastical and temporal authorities in the fourth and fifth centuries recognized the claims of the bishop of Rome to primacy in the church.

The effective missionary work of monks loyal to Rome also enhanced the authority of the Roman bishop. Clovis, the leader of the Franks, was a loyal supporter of the authority of the bishop of Rome. Gregory I sent Augustine to England, and that monk and his successors were able to bring Britain under the sway of Rome. Wherever missionary monks went, they insisted that their converts yield allegiance to the bishop of Rome.

Above all, the Roman church was blessed with many able bishops during this era, and these men lost no chance to strengthen their power. Damasus I (366–84) was apparently the first bishop of Rome to describe his see as the "apostolic see." The Vulgate translation of the Bible, which Jerome began at Damasus' request while he was his secretary, added to the prestige of the occupants of the episcopal chair in Rome. Jerome's high opinion of the authority of his employer can be read in a letter that he wrote to Damasus in which he categorically stated that the chair of Peter is the rock on which the church was built.[4]

Leo I, who occupied the episcopal throne in Rome between 440 and 461, was the ablest occupant of that chair until Gregory I took that position in 590. His abilities won for him the name "great." He made much use of the title *papas* from which our word "pope" is derived. In 452 he was able to persuade Attila the Hun to let the city of Rome alone. Again in 455, when Gaiseric and his Vandal followers from North Africa came to sack Rome, Leo persuaded them to save the city from fire and pillage; he had to agree, however, that the city would be given over to a two-week period of sacking by the Vandals. Gaiseric kept his word, and the Romans looked up to Leo as the one who had saved their city from complete destruction. His position was further strengthened when Valentinian III recognized his spiritual supremacy in the West by an edict in 445. Leo insisted that appeals from the church courts of bishops should be brought to his court and that his decision should be final. He defined orthodoxy in his *Tome* and wrote against the heresy of the Manicheans and the Donatists.[5] Even if we do not consider Leo the first pope, it is fair to say that he made the claims and exercised the power of many later incumbents of the Roman bishopric. Gelasius I, pope from 492 to 496, wrote in 494 that God gave both sacred and royal power to the pope and the king. Because the pope had to account to God for the king at the judgment, the sacred power of the pope was more important than the royal power. Hence, rulers should submit to the pope. Perhaps such power was useful in this early period in dealing with the barbarians, but later it led to corruption within the Roman church itself.

II. THE GROWTH OF THE LITURGY

The practical union of the church and the state under Constantine and his successors led to the secularization of the church. The patriarch of Constantinople came under the control of the emperor, and the Eastern church became a department of the state. The influx of pagans into the church through the mass conversion movements of the era contributed to the paganization of worship as the church tried to make these barbarian converts feel at home within its fold. This influx of pagans, many of whom did not become more than nominal Christians, caused the church to call upon the state to help enforce discipline by the use of its temporal power to punish ecclesiastical offenses. In 529 Justinian, emperor of the Eastern segment of the empire, ordered the closing of the Academy at Athens. Up until that time pagan Greek philosophy had been taught there. Discipline became lax within the church because its resources were overtaxed in handling the many barbarians who had been only partially converted from paganism.

The influx of barbarians and the growth of episcopal power also brought changes in the worship of the church. If the barbarians who had been used to worshiping images were to find any real help in the church, many church leaders believed that it would be necessary to materialize the liturgy to make God seem more accessible to these worshipers. The veneration of angels, saints, relics, pictures, and statues was a logical outcome of this attitude. Connection with the monarchical state also led to a change from a simple democratic worship to a more aristocratic, colorful form of liturgy with a sharply drawn distinction between the clergy and the laity.

Sunday became one of the major days in the church calendar after Constantine decided that it was to be a day of civic as well as religious worship. The festival of Christmas became a regular practice in the West about the middle of the fourth century, with the adoption of the December date that had been previously used by the pagans. The Feast of Epiphany, which in the West celebrated the coming of the Magi to see Christ and in the East Christ's baptism, was also brought into the church calendar. Accretions from the Jewish sacred year, the gospel history, and the lives of saints and martyrs led to a steady expansion of the number of holy days in the church calendar.

There was also an increase in the number of ceremonies that could be ranked as sacraments. Augustine was inclined to believe that marriage should be regarded as a sacrament. Cyprian held that penance was vital to the Christian life. With the increased gap between the clergy and the laity it was almost necessary to consider ordination in the light of a sacrament. Confirmation and extreme unction came to be looked on as having sacramental value about 400. The early theological development of the doctrine of original sin contributed to the importance of infant baptism. By the beginning of the third century, Tertullian and Cyprian considered infant baptism an accepted fact. Augustine especially emphasized the importance of baptism. The Lord's Supper

occupied the central place in the thinking of the worshiper and the order of the liturgy. In fact, it was in process of becoming a sacrifice as well as a sacrament. Cyprian thought that the priest acted in Christ's place at Communion and that he offered "a true and full sacrifice to God the Father."[6] The *Canon of the Mass*, which Gregory I altered slightly, emphasized the sacrificial nature of the Communion service.[7] By the end of the sixth century all the seven acts that the Roman Catholic church regards as sacraments were in use and had an exalted position in worship. Sacerdotalism, the belief that the substance of the ordinance is efficacious through the priestly celebrant, steadily gained ground. This led to an increasing emphasis on the separation of the clergy and the laity.

The veneration of Mary, the mother of Jesus, developed rapidly by 590 and led to the adoption of the doctrines of her immaculate conception in 1854 and her miraculous assumption to heaven in 1950. The false interpretation of Scripture and the mass of miracles associated with Mary in the apocryphal gospels created great reverence for her. The Nestorian and other christological controversies of the fourth century resulted in the acceptance of her as the "Mother of God" and entitled her to special honors in the liturgy.

Clement, Jerome, and Tertullian had ascribed perpetual virginity to Mary. Augustine believed that the mother of the sinless Christ had never committed actual sin. Monasticism, with its emphasis on the virtue of virginity, strengthened the idea of the veneration of Mary. These and other considerations led the Roman church to give special honor to Mary. What at first was merely acknowledgment of her exalted position as Christ's mother soon became belief in her intercessory powers because it was thought that the Son would be glad to listen to the requests of His mother.

The prayer of Ephraim Syrus before 400 is an early instance of a formal invocation to her. By the middle of the fifth century she was placed at the head of all the saints. Festivals associated with her also sprang up in the fifth century. The Feast of the Annunciation on March 25, which celebrated the angelic announcement of the birth of a son to her; Candlemas on February 2, the celebration of her purification after the birth of Christ; and the Assumption on August 15, which celebrates her supposed ascension to heaven, were the principal festivals. In the sixth century Justinian asked her intercession on behalf of his empire. By 590 she had a unique position in the worship of the Roman church.

The veneration of saints grew out of the natural desire of the church to honor those who had been martyrs in the days when the church had been severely persecuted by the state. Furthermore, the pagans had been accustomed to the veneration of their heroes; and when so many pagans came into the church, it was almost natural for them to substitute the saints for their heroes and to give them semidivine honors. Up to the year 300, celebrations at the grave involved only prayers for the repose of the soul of the saint; but by 590 prayer *for* them had become prayer to God *through* them. This was accepted at the Second Council of Nicaea. Churches and chapels were built over their graves, festivals associated with their death gained a place in the church calendar, and legends of miracles associated with them developed rapidly. The traffic in relics, such as bodies, teeth, hair, or bones, became so great a problem that it was ordered stopped in 381.

The use of images and pictures in worship expanded rapidly as more and more untutored barbarians came into the church. Both images and pictures materialized the invisible reality of deity for these worshipers. They also had a decorative function in beautifying a church. The Fathers of the church tried to make a distinction between reverence of these images— reverence that was a part of the liturgy—and the worship of God; but it is doubtful whether this subtle distinction prevented the ordinary worshiper from offering to them the worship that the Fathers would reserve for God alone.

Thanksgiving or penitential processions became a part of worship after 313. Pilgrimages, at first to Palestine and later to the tombs of notable saints, became customary. Constantine's mother, Helena, visited Palestine in her old age and was supposed to have found the true cross.

Government aid and freedom of worship under Constantine led to extensive building of churches. The Christians borrowed the basilica type of architecture that the Romans had developed for public buildings devoted to business or pleasure. The basilica was a long rectangular, cruciform building with two aisles, a portico at the west end for the unbaptized, a nave for the baptized, and a chancel at the east end where the choir, the priests, and, if it was a cathedral church, the bishop officiated during the service. This chancel was usually separated from the nave by a screen of ironwork.

The earliest singing in the church had been conducted by a leader to whom the people gave response in song. Antiphonal singing, in which two separated choirs sing alternately, developed at Antioch. Ambrose introduced the practice of antiphonal singing at Milan, from whence it spread through the Western church.

This was also an era of great preachers. Ambrose in the West and Chrysostom in the East were the leading preachers. Until that time these preachers wore no special vestments. Special vestments for the priests were to come as the people gave up the Roman type of dress, while the clergy retained it in the church services.

During this era there arose a special sacerdotal hierarchy under a dominant Roman bishop, the tendency to increase the number of sacraments and to make them the main avenues of grace, and the movement to elaborate the liturgy. These things helped to lay the foundation for the medieval Roman Catholic church.

SUGGESTED READING

Freemantle, Anne. **The Papal Encyclicals.** *New York: Mentor, 1956.*

Gontard, Friedrich. **The Chair of Peter.** *Translated by A. J. and E. F. Peeler. New York: Holt, Rinehart, and Winston, 1964. This is a scholarly history of the popes by a Protestant.*

Hardman, Oscar. **History of Christian Worship.** *London: Hodder & Stoughton, 1937.*

Jalland, Trevor. **The Life and Times of Saint Leo the Great.** *New York: Macmillan, 1941. This is scholarly and well documented.*

Miegge, Giovanni. **The Virgin Mary.** *Philadelphia: Westminster, 1955. This is a scholarly survey from the sources of the development of the doctrine of Mary.*

MEDIEVAL CHURCH HISTORY, 590–1517

THE RISE OF THE EMPIRE
AND LATIN-TEUTONIC CHRISTIANITY, 590–800

EBB AND FLOW IN RELATIONSHIPS
BETWEEN CHURCH AND STATE, 800–1054

THE SUPREMACY OF THE PAPACY, 1054–1305

MEDIEVAL SUNSET
AND MODERN SUNRISE, 1305–1517

Chapter 16

The First Medieval Pope

The consecration of Gregory I as the bishop of Rome constitutes a watershed that divides the ancient period of church history from that of the medieval period of church history. One should always remember, however, that periodization in history is an artificial mechanism to organize the God-guided order of history into manageable segments. Some begin medieval church history in 313 with the grant of freedom of religion. Others begin at the Council of Nicaea in 325. Others prefer 378 because the battle of Adrianople resulted in the migration of the Visigoths into the empire. Still others think that the ancient period of church history ended with the fall of the last Roman emperor in 476. The year 590 is chosen for this work because Gregory I ushered in a new era of power for the church in the West in that year.

The end of the Middle Ages of the history of the church is also debatable. It has been variously set at 1095, the beginning of the era of the Crusades; at 1453, the fall of Constantinople; and at 1648, the Peace of Westphalia. The writer has chosen 1517 because the activities of Luther in that year ushered in an entirely different era, in which the emphasis was not so much on the church as an institution as it was on the church constituted as a body of individual believers by a personal faith in the redemptive work of Christ.

In the Medieval Era the Roman Empire fragmented into Muslim North Africa, Asiatic Byzantine, and European papal areas. Church-state relations became very important. A distinct Western European civilization emerged from Christian and classical foundations.

The name Middle Ages was originated by Christopher Kellner (1634–80) in a handbook published about 1669. He thought of three divisions in the history of the West. Ancient history, for him, ended at 325. Modern history, he thought, had its beginning in 1453 when the Fall of Constantinople brought a flood of Greek scholars and manuscripts to the West. He characterized the years between these two dates as the Middle Ages because of their apparent sterility and the absence of the classical influence. Since that time historians have used the term Middle Ages as a convenient designation for that era. However, only the first five centuries of the era, from about 500 to 1000, may be designated as the Dark Ages, and even in that period western Europe was not totally lacking in culture because the monasteries made intellectual contributions. The men of the Renaissance thought that this era was a chasm separating the brilliant classical and modern periods of humanism. To them, this period could be only an age of darkness. But modern historians of the period have been able to show that the Medieval Era was one of slow growth in which the church in the west fulfilled useful cultural and religious functions by bridging the gap between the ancient city-state and the modern nation-state.

If the men of the Renaissance thought of the years between 500 and 1000 as the Dark Ages, the Roman Catholic church thought that this era was the Golden Age of human history. It was preceded by classical paganism and followed by the disintegrating forces of Protestantism, which created the chaos of the modern religious scene—according to the Roman Catholic thinkers.

Protestant historians considered the Middle Ages the valley of shadow in which the pure church of the ancient era of church history was corrupted. The modern era of church history, which began with Luther, was to them one of reformation in which the church regained the ideals of the New Testament.

All these views must be tempered by the fact that the Middle Ages was not a static but a dynamic period. Development under divine direction was continuous even in the Middle Ages.

The medieval history of the church took place in a wider arena than did that of the ancient church. After the Teutonic tribes were won to Christianity, the Baltic basin became as important as the Mediterranean basin.

The Modern Era is deeply indebted to the Middle Ages. In the Middle Ages men attempted to set up a Christian civilization in which the past was integrated with the present in a meaningful synthesis. The classic culture of the past, transmuted by Christianity, was given to the Teutonic tribes by the church. The Modern Era thus far lacks such a synthesis for life; and, as a result, modern man is struggling against confusion and the prospect not only of intellectual, moral, and spiritual, but also of material chaos.

With this in mind, the importance of Gregory I becomes obvious. He stood, as Augustine did in his day, at the divide between the two worlds of classicism and medieval Christianity and became the symbol of the new medieval world in which culture was institutionalized within the church dominated by the bishop of Rome.

Gregory (540–604), often called the Great, was born in the troublous times when the Eastern empire under Justinian was seeking to regain the section of the Western empire that had been lost to the Teutonic tribesmen. Pillaging bands, disease, and famine were often the order of the day.

Born into one of the old, noble, and wealthy families of Rome, Gregory was given a legal education to fit him for government service. He studied Latin literature extensively but knew no Hebrew or Greek. He was familiar with the writings of Ambrose, Jerome, and Augustine but knew little of the classical literature or philosophy of Greece. About 570 he was made prefect of Rome, a position of importance and honor. Shortly thereafter he gave up the fortune that he had inherited from his father—his mother, Silvia, entered a convent after the death of his father—and used the proceeds to build seven monasteries in Italy, the most important of which was set up in his father's palace. Here he became a monk. Between 578 and 586 he was an ambassador representing the Roman bishop at Constantinople. Upon his return to Rome, he was made abbot of Saint Andrew's monastery, which he had founded after his father's death. If Augustine became a monk for intellectual purposes, it is fair to say that Gregory became a monk because he thought asceticism was a way to glorify God. When Pope Pelagius died of the plague in 590, Gregory was chosen to take his place.

This man, whose epitaph was "God's Consul," was one of the noblest of the leaders of the Roman church. His renunciation of great wealth impressed the people of his day. He was a man of humility who thought of himself as the "servant of the servants of God." He was a zealous missionary and was instrumental in winning the English to Christianity. His legal training, tact, and common sense made him one of the ablest administrators the Roman church had during the Middle Ages. But like many men of his age, he was unduly superstitious and credulous. His *Dialogues* (593) display his unbounded credulity in what seemed to be miraculous to the medieval mind.[1] Moreover, though he had

some training in sacred learning, his scholarship was marred by a lack of knowledge of the original languages of the Bible. During the seven years when he was ambassador in Constantinople, he did not even learn Greek.

Gregory's greatest work was to expand the power of the Roman bishop. Though he disclaimed the title of pope, he exercised all the power and prerogatives of the later popes. This he did to assert the spiritual supremacy of the bishop of Rome. He exercised episcopal care over the churches of Gaul, Spain, Britain, Africa, and Italy. He appointed bishops and sent the pallium, the scarf of office, to those whose appointments he had made or ratified.

When John the Faster, the patriarch of Constantinople, claimed the title of "ecumenical" or universal bishop, Gregory immediately gave battle. He was willing to accept a coordinate status for the patriarchs of the church, which would put them on a level as heads of the great sections of the church, but he was not willing to let anyone have the title of universal bishop. But neither the patriarch nor the Eastern emperor would give in, and Gregory had to bide his time. When in 602 revolution brought a new emperor, Phocas, to the throne in Constantinople, Gregory sought to be on friendly terms with him, although this vulgar upstart had murdered the wife and family of the former emperor. In return, Phocas sided with Gregory against the patriarch and acknowledged the bishop of Rome as the "head of all the churches." Gregory did not, however, accept the title "universal pope," which the patriarch of Alexandria wanted to give to him. He preferred to be called the "servant of the servants of God." But while he disclaimed the title of supreme head of the church, he would let no one else lay claim to the title and exercised the papal power in fact. No bishop or metropolitan in the West dared to go against his will, and he permitted no one elsewhere in the world of that day to assert universal supremacy over the church.

Gregory's deep interest in missionary work is shown by the fine story that Bede told in his history. According to the story, when Gregory was told that the fair-haired, blue-eyed boys up for sale as slaves in Rome were Angles, he said that they were not "Angles" but "angels." When told that they were from Deiri (Yorkshire), he decided that they must be delivered from the wrath (*de ira*) of God by missionary work.[2] He therefore commissioned the monk Augustine, who must not be confused with Augustine of Hippo, to go to Britain and give the message of the gospel to the British. Augustine landed in England in 597 and soon won the king of Kent to Christianity. But the Roman missionaries quickly ran into competition from the Celtic church, which was slowly evangelizing to the south. In 663 the Roman faith finally won. Thus Gregory may be considered the instrument in bringing the English under the sway of the Church of Rome. He made careful plans for the development of the English church.[3]

Gregory made the bishopric of Rome one of the wealthiest in the church of his day by his excellent work as an administrator. The papal possessions in Italy and nearby areas had never before yielded such a golden harvest as they did under Gregory's careful administrative policies. With this money he was able to act as the protector of the peace in the West. When the Arian Lombard king threatened Rome on one occasion during Gregory's pontificate, Gregory was able to raise troops and force the Lombard ruler to make peace and to win them from Arianism.

He was also the organizer of the Gregorian chant, which came to have a more important place in the Roman Catholic church than that developed by Ambrose. This chant involved the use of a stately and solemn monotone in that part of the worship that was chanted.

Gregory was a good preacher, too, with a real message for the time of crisis in which he lived. His sermons were practical and stressed humility and piety, but they were often marred by an excessive use of allegory, a common fault of preaching in his day.[4]

More outstanding than his sermons are his other literary works. In the *Magna Moralia*, a commentary on the Book of Job, he emphasized moral interpretation and resorted to allegorizing in order to derive his ethical formulas. He pictured Job as a type of Christ, his wife as a type of the carnal nature, the seven sons as types of the clergy, and the three daughters as types of the faithful laity. He wrote other commentaries, but none of them are as extensive as his work on the Book of Job. He also wrote the *Book of Pastoral Care*, which concerns pastoral theology. He emphasized the prerequisites for the bishopric, the virtues a bishop needs, and the need for introspection. The work made a great appeal to the monks of his day because of its ascetic nature.[5] There are also over eight hundred of his letters extant.

Gregory the Great was so highly respected as a teacher in the Western church that in pictures he was always portrayed with a dove, representing the Holy Spirit, perched on his shoulder and communicating divine truth into his ear.

Gregory was also an outstanding theologian. He is ranked with Jerome, Ambrose, and Augustine as one of the four great doctors of the Western church. He laid the groundwork of the theology that was held by the Roman church throughout the Middle Ages until Thomas Aquinas formulated his *Summa.* He believed that man was a sinner by birth and choice, but he softened Augustine's view by asserting that man did not inherit guilt from Adam but only sin, as a disease to which all were subject. He maintained that the will is free and that only its goodness has been lost. He believed in predestination, but he limited it to the elect. Grace is not irresistible, he believed, because it is based on both the foreknowledge of God and, to some extent, the merits of man. He upheld the idea of purgatory as a place where souls would be purified prior to their entrance to heaven. He held to verbal inspiration of the Bible but, strangely, gave tradition a place of equality with the Bible. The Canon of the Mass, which he changed somewhat, was widely used in his day; and it revealed the growing tendency to consider the Communion as a sacrifice of Christ's body and blood each time it is performed.[6] He also emphasized good works and the invocation of the saints in order to get their aid. It may safely be said that medieval theology bore the stamp of Gregory's thought.

The pontificate of Gregory is indeed a landmark in the transition from ancient to medieval church history. Later successors built on the foundation that he had laid as they created the sacramental hierarchical system of the institutionalized church of the Middle Ages. He systematized doctrine and made the church a power in politics.

SUGGESTED READING

Titles marked with an asterisk cover the entire period of medieval church history.

*Anderson, Charles S. **The Augsburg Historical Atlas of Christianity in the Middle Ages and Reformation.** *Minneapolis: Augsburg, 1967. This atlas has clear, simple maps and helpful texts for these eras.*

*Cannon, William R. **History of Christianity in the Middle Ages.** *New York: Abingdon, 1960. This book surveys the era with above-average coverage of the Eastern churches.*

*Deanesley, Margaret. **A History of the Medieval Church, 590–1500.** *7th ed. London: Methuen, 1951. This work provides much additional material for the period.*

*Downs, Morton. **Basic Documents in Medieval History:** *Princeton, N.J.: Van Nostrand, 1959.*

Dudden, Frederick H. **Gregory the Great.** *2 vols. New York: Russell & Russell, 1905. Though old, this work is based on sources.*

*Edman, V. Raymond. **The Light in the Dark Ages.** *Wheaton, Ill.: Van Kampen, 1950. The work on medieval missions gives a good account of missionary work in this era.*

*Foakes-Jackson, Frederick J. **An Introduction to the History of Christianity, A.D. 590–1314.** *New York: Macmillan, 1928. I have found this to be a more detailed and very interesting history of the period.*

*Kidd, Beresford J. **Documents Illustrative of the History of the Church.** *3 vols. London: SPCK, 1920–41. Documents specifically dealing with church history will be found in volume 3.*

*Latourette, Kenneth S. **The Thousand Years of Uncertainty: A History of the Expansion of Christianity.** *Vol. 2. New York: Harper, 1938. This is an even more detailed history of medieval missions. The complete seven-volume work has been republished by Zondervan, Grand Rapids, Michigan.*

*Ogg, Frederic A. **A Source Book of Medieval History.** *New York: American, 1907. This contains many interesting documents.*

*Paetow, Louis J. **A Guide in the Study of Medieval History.** *New York: Crofts, 1931. The teacher or student who desires to pursue the study of medieval church history in more detail will find this biographical work a useful guide to other works.*

*Scott, Jonathon F.; Huma, Albert; and Noyes, Arthur H. **Readings in Medieval History.** *New York: Appleton-Century-Crofts, 1933.*

*Southern, R. W. **Western Society and the Church in the Middle Ages.** *Harmondsworth, Middlesex: Penguin, 1970. This work has many helpful insights.*

*Thatcher, Oliver J., and McNeal, Edgar H. **A Source Book for Medieval History.** *New York: Scribner, 1905.*

*Ullman, Walter. **A Short History of the Papacy in the Middle Ages.** *London: Methuen, 1972. This is a useful, factual survey of the medieval papacy.*

*Walker, G. S. M. **The Growing Storm.** *Grand Rapids: Eerdmans, 1961. This covers the era from 600 to 1350 from an evangelical viewpoint, with stress on the rise and fall of the medieval papacy.*

Chapter 17

Christian Losses and Expansion

The Middle Ages is often thought to be a period in which society was static and in which people moved around very little. A casual study of the movement of people during the Middle Ages will show that there has never been an era in the history of Europe when there were greater mass migrations than those following the breakup of the Roman Empire. The movement of the Mongol Huns and the Germanic Goths and Teutons from the Northeast into the Roman Empire after 375 has already been noticed. After 590 Christianity faced new dynamic movements of people. During the seventh and later centuries the church in the East had to face the threat of Islam. Islam was also a matter of concern to the Western church until it was turned back at Tours in 732. The renewed movement of Vikings out of the Scandinavian Peninsula after the eighth century also threatened the Western church with destruction. Later the Slavs, the Magyars, and the Mongols threatened the church in the East.

In addition to meeting the challenge of these migrants, the Western church had also to take on the task of evangelizing the Teutonic tribes within the bounds of the old empire. Those who had accepted an Arian form of Christianity and who had settled in Spain, North Africa, and Italy presented a further challenge to Christianity. This task of winning the pagans and the heterodox Arians and the challenge of the rival religion of Islam taxed the growing resources of the church to the limit. Between 590 and 800 the Western church made great gains in the northern and western areas of Europe; but in contrast, Eastern Christianity, which had become static, did little more than hold its own against the Muslims who, at times, knocked against the gates of Constantinople.

The work of missions was put on a professional basis during this period. Bands of monks went out to proclaim the gospel to the groups to whom the highest authority in the church, the pope, had sent them.

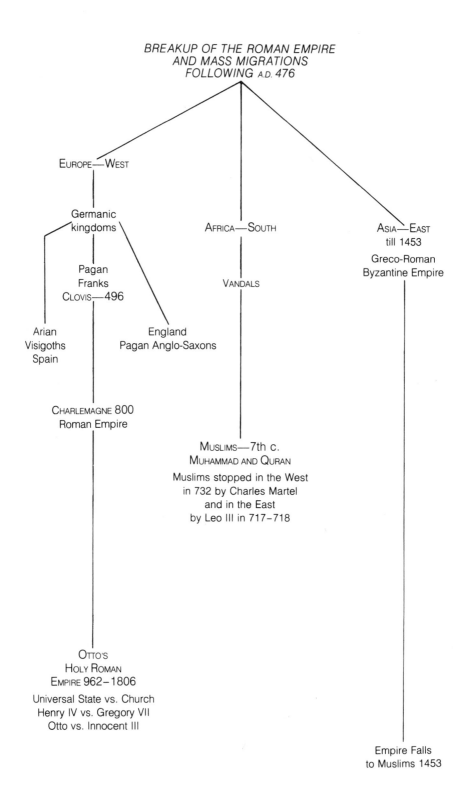

BREAKUP OF THE ROMAN EMPIRE
AND MASS MIGRATIONS
FOLLOWING A.D. 476

EUROPE—WEST

Germanic
kingdoms

Pagan
Franks
CLOVIS—496

Arian
Visigoths
Spain

England
Pagan Anglo-Saxons

CHARLEMAGNE 800
Roman Empire

OTTO'S
HOLY ROMAN
EMPIRE 962–1806

Universal State vs. Church
Henry IV vs. Gregory VII
Otto vs. Innocent III

AFRICA—SOUTH

VANDALS

MUSLIMS—7th c.
MUHAMMAD AND QURAN

Muslims stopped in the West
in 732 by Charles Martel
and in the East
by Leo III in 717–718

ASIA—EAST
till 1453

Greco-Roman
Byzantine Empire

Empire Falls
to Muslims 1453

I. THE RISE AND IMPACT OF ISLAM

The Muslims, energized by the dynamic of a newfound faith, the hope of plunder in the name of religion, and a zeal to convert the unbelievers to their faith, rapidly expanded from Arabia into North Africa, Asia, and even Europe by way of Spain. Founded by a personal leader, their religion was the latest of the three great monotheistic religions of the world. It, too, claimed to be a universal religion for all peoples. The Muslims finally wiped out the church in North Africa and weakened the church in other areas of Africa. They eventually brought about the downfall of the Eastern empire in 1453 and put the Eastern church under Muslim political control.

Islam had its origins in the Arabian Peninsula, a piece of land relatively isolated from the surrounding world by water or trackless desert except on the northwestern border. The area is inhospitable, and man is forced to struggle in the midst of barren rocks, sand, and hot sun to maintain his existence. When faced by the powers of nature, man is inclined to recognize a supreme being greater than himself.

At the time of the rise of Islam, Semitic Bedouin tribesmen wandered from oasis to oasis with their camels, flocks, and herds, doing only what trading was necessary with the townsmen of Mecca and Medina. Tribal warfare was frequent except during the periods of truce each year when the tribes went to worship the black stone in the Kaaba at Mecca.

One of these tribesmen was Muhammad (ca. 570–632), who made his living as a camel driver. Going with his uncle on one trip to Syria and Palestine, he came into contact with Christianity and Judaism. He then married a rich widow named Khadijah and gained the wealth whereby he could be free to devote his time to religious meditation. In 610 he felt divinely called to proclaim monotheism and in the course of three years won twelve converts, mostly among his own kinsmen. Stirring up opposition with his preaching against idolatry, he was forced to flee in 622 to Medina from Mecca. The year of this flight, known as the Hegira, became the first year of the Muslim calendar. By 630 the movement had grown so much that Muhammad was able to capture Mecca. Two years later, at the time of his death, his followers were ready to expand outside the Arabian Peninsula.

The greatest gains of this new dynamic faith took place between 632 and 732. Syria and Palestine were won by 640, and the Mosque of Omar was soon erected in Jerusalem. Egypt was won in the next decade, and Persia fell under Muslim control by 650. The crescent-shaped expansion to the West and the East threatened Christianity with a great pincers, but expansion at the eastern end of the crescent was stopped by the brave defense of the Eastern empire under Leo the Isaurian in 717 and 718. Muslim expansion on the Western wing of the crescent was halted by the defeat of the Muslims by the armies of Charles Martel at Tours in 732. But the church had already undergone great losses as the conquered people were faced with the choice of the sword, tribute, or Islam. Muslims were not always intolerant, however, for they often permitted people in tribute-paying areas to practice their faith. By 750 the era of conquest came to an end, and the Muslims, influenced by Greek cul-

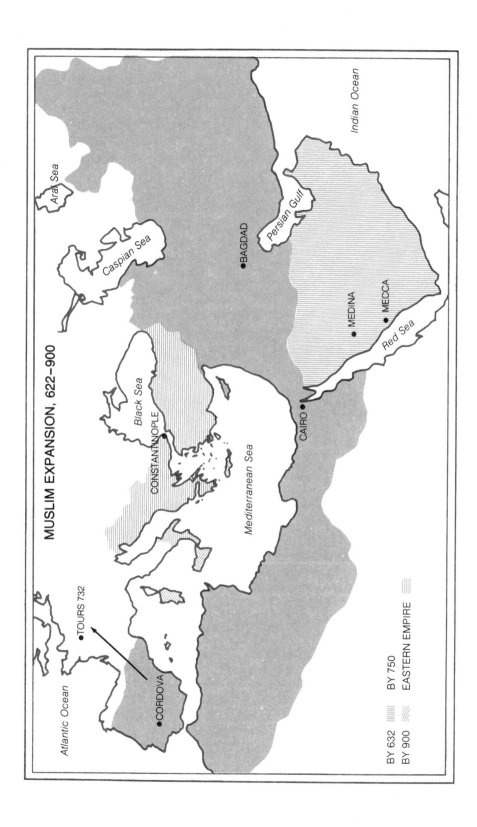

MUSLIM EXPANSION, 622–900

Aral Sea

Caspian Sea

Indian Ocean

Persian Gulf

●BAGDAD

●MEDINA

MECCA
●

Red Sea

Black Sea

CONSTANTINOPLE
●

Mediterranean Sea

CAIRO ●

Atlantic Ocean

●TOURS 732

●CORDOVA

BY 632

BY 900

BY 750

EASTERN EMPIRE

ture, set out to build a splendid Arabic civilization centered in Bagdad. The peak of culture came under Haroun-Al-Raschid (786–809), the ruler of the eastern section of Muslim territory.

The main source of the Muslim religion is the Quran. This work, two-thirds the length of the New Testament, is arranged in 114 chapters. The longest chapter comes at the beginning of the book, and the chapters become successively shorter until the last chapter consists of only three verses. It is repetitious and unorganized.

Belief in one God known as Allah is the central theme of Islam. Allah made his will known through twenty-five prophets, including biblical characters such as Abraham, Moses, and Christ; but Muhammad was the latest and greatest of these prophets. Muslims deny both Christ's deity and His death on the cross. The religion is fatalistic with its idea of passive submission to the will of Allah. After judgment men will enjoy a rather sensual paradise or face the terrors of hell. The good Muslim prays five times daily, facing toward Mecca. He also recites his creed daily. Fasting and almsgiving are important, and the holiest Muslims are those who, at least once during their life, make a pilgrimage to Mecca.

Islam has had a marked cultural and religious significance for western Europe. It assimilated and passed on to western Europe through Arabic Spain the Greek philosophy of Aristotle. The medieval scholastics attempted to integrate Greek scientific thought with Christian theology by use of the deductive method of Aristotle, which they had come to know in Spain through Averroes's translation of Aristotle's writings. So great was this influence in Europe during the twelfth century that Haskins called the period the "Twelfth Century Renaissance."[1]

Both the Eastern and Western sections of the church were weakened by losses of people and territory to Islam, but the losses of the Eastern churches were greater than those of the West. The strong North African church disappeared, and Egypt and the Holy Land were lost. The Eastern churches were able to do little more than hold back the Muslim hordes from sweeping past Constantinople. Consequently, missionary activity, which was carried on mainly by the Western church, centered in northwestern Europe. The Eastern churches also had to deal with the problem of whether images as well as pictures could be used in the church. This issue, known as the iconoclastic controversy, came about partly because the Muslims were accusing the Christians of being idolaters, because they had pictures and images in the church.

This weakening of the Eastern churches was balanced by the stronger position of the bishop of Rome. Rival patriarchs of the church in Alexandria and Antioch were under Islamic domination and were unable any longer to speak for the church at large. The pope was not slow to make the most of this opportunity to strengthen his own position. Islam stubbornly resisted the efforts of the papacy and Crusaders to regain the Holy Land and since that time has strongly resisted every attempt of Christian missionaries to propagate Christianity among Muslims.

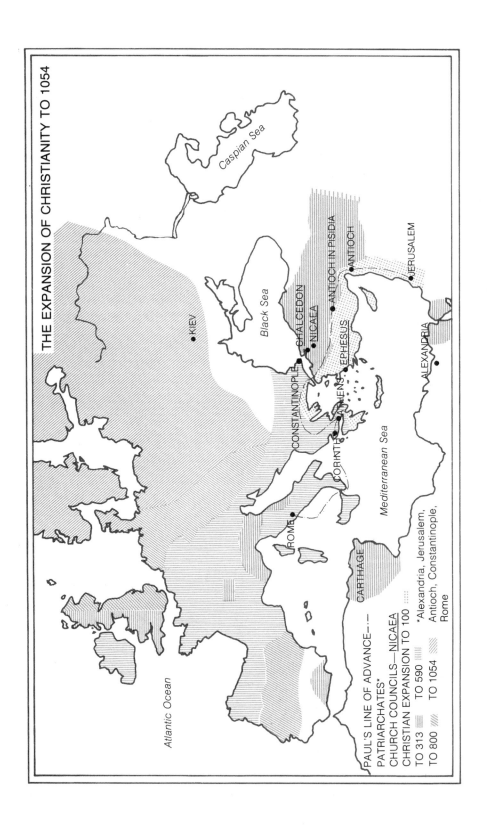

THE EXPANSION OF CHRISTIANITY TO 1054

Caspian Sea

Black Sea

• KIEV

CONSTANTINOPLE
CHALCEDON
NICAEA
ANTIOCH IN PISIDIA
ANTIOCH
EPHESUS
ATHENS
CORINTH
JERUSALEM
ALEXANDRIA

ROME

CARTHAGE

Mediterranean Sea

Atlantic Ocean

PAUL'S LINE OF ADVANCE-----
PATRIARCHATES*
CHURCH COUNCILS—NICAEA
CHRISTIAN EXPANSION TO 100
TO 313   TO 590
TO 800   TO 1054

*Alexandria, Jerusalem,
Antioch, Constantinople,
Rome

II. MISSIONARY ACTIVITY
IN THE WEST

A. In the British Isles

The Irish church, which had been planted by Patrick, was the brightest spot culturally in northern Europe between 590 and 800. It had sent Columbanus to the Swiss and Columba to the Scots. Irish monks had engaged in the work of preserving, copying, and beautifully illuminating manuscripts at a time when learning on the Continent was in eclipse. Not until the beginning of the eighth century did the Irish church accept Roman control. The eighth- and ninth-century invasions of the Vikings so weakened it that in the tenth century it fell into decay, but earlier it had led in scholarship and the evangelization of Europe.

The Irish church was also indirectly responsible for the evangelization of northern England because it was under influences from Columba's monastery on the Island of Iona that Aidan carried the message of the gospel to the Northumbrians of the northeast coast of England. Oswald, an Anglo-Saxon ruler, had spent some time in exile among the Irish and Scottish Christians and had seen the attractiveness of the life of these Celtic Christians. Oppressed by the spiritual darkness of the Anglo-Saxons, who had driven the Celts and their Christianity out of England in the fifth century after the withdrawal of the Roman armies, he called upon the Scottish church for missionaries.

Aidan went to the people of Northumbria in 635 and set up his headquarters on the Island of Lindisfarne, known also as Holy Island. There he built a monastery that became a center of evangelism. He enjoyed the full cooperation of Oswald, who often acted as his interpreter when he made his journeys on foot among Oswald's people. Aidan gave considerable attention to education in order that the church in Northumbria might have an able leadership. When he died in 651, Celtic Christianity had been firmly established in northern England.

Some years before the beginning of Celtic missionary activities in the north, the Roman church had begun missionary activity among the Anglo-Saxons of southern England. Gregory appointed Augustine, the prior of Saint Andrew's monastery in Rome, as the leader of a band of monks from that monastery. They were ordered to proceed to southern England and to win the Anglo-Saxons to the Christian faith. Augustine and his band of monks landed in the Island of Thanet off the Kentish coast in the spring of 597. Bertha, the Gallic wife of Ethelbert, the king of Kent, had been converted before she became Ethelbert's wife; and she influenced her husband in favor of the missionaries. After the first interview between Augustine and Ethelbert, which was held in the open air where Ethelbert thought Augustine's magic might not affect him, the king gave Augustine permission to preach the gospel.[2] Ethelbert soon submitted himself for baptism, and large numbers of his people followed him in the acceptance of Christianity.

The Christianity planted in the north by the Celtic Christians soon came into contact with the Roman Catholic Christianity expanding northward from the south of England. The two forms of Christianity differed on many matters. The Celtic Christians did not acknowledge the authority of the pope. They did not always

TWO EVANGELIZATIONS OF BRITISH ISLES

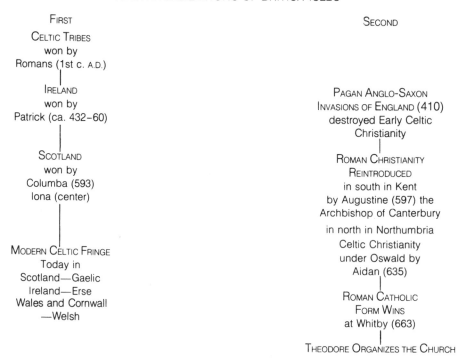

FIRST

CELTIC TRIBES
won by
Romans (1st c. A.D.)

IRELAND
won by
Patrick (ca. 432–60)

SCOTLAND
won by
Columba (593)
Iona (center)

MODERN CELTIC FRINGE
Today in
Scotland—Gaelic
Ireland—Erse
Wales and Cornwall
—Welsh

SECOND

PAGAN ANGLO-SAXON
INVASIONS OF ENGLAND (410)
destroyed Early Celtic
Christianity

ROMAN CHRISTIANITY
REINTRODUCED
in south in Kent
by Augustine (597) the
Archbishop of Canterbury

in north in Northumbria
Celtic Christianity
under Oswald by
Aidan (635)

ROMAN CATHOLIC
FORM WINS
at Whitby (663)

THEODORE ORGANIZES THE CHURCH

have Easter on the same day of the week each year as the Roman church did. Celtic monks might marry; Roman monks were not permitted to do so. Celtic monks had a different type of tonsure or haircut. These differences caused such confusion and rivalry between the two forms of Christianity that Oswy, who had united most of Anglo-Saxon England under himself, called a meeting at Whitby in 663 to decide which form of Christianity his people would follow. Roman Christianity won the day because Oswy, according to Bede, preferred the religion that claimed to have the keys to heaven.[3] In 668 Theodore was then sent to England to organize English Christians under the Roman banner and to set up dioceses and archbish-oprics, which, in many cases, still exist in the Anglican church.

English Christianity was soon noted for its scholarship because Theodore started schools. The schools of Jarrow and York were outstanding. When, after 781, Charlemagne wanted someone to help him to develop an educational system in his domain, he got Alcuin from the school at York to do the task. Bede was another outstanding scholar, spending most of his life at Jarrow. His history of England, written from the ecclesiastical viewpoint, is one of the best sources of information concerning English life and history before 731.

The church in England also sent to the continent of Europe missionaries who were instrumental in winning their Teutonic kinsmen to Roman Christianity. Because the English had a filial loyalty to the Roman see that persisted until the time of the Reformation, the church in England became a bolster to the papacy as did the Franks in Europe.

B. Germany

Boniface (680–754), also known as Winfrid, brought the Teutonic tribes, who occupied most of the area of modern Germany, under the influence of the gospel. At the same time he made sure that they would become loyal subjects of the pope. After he became a learned and devout priest with considerable business ability, he decided to consecrate his life to missionary activity. He went to Rome in 718 and got authority from the pope to preach the gospel in Germany. He cut down an oak at Geismar, which was sacred to Thor, a German god, and made a chapel from the timber. Quickly he won Hesse to Roman Christianity. He next turned his attention to Thuringia and planted the gospel there. In 732 he was elevated to the rank of archbishop by Pope Gregory III. During this part of his missionary career he began to use devoted women as missionaries. These women were among the first in a long line of women who have served Christ bravely and well throughout the history of the church in the missionary fields of the world. Boniface next turned to Bavaria, and he established the church there on strong foundations. Charlemagne "converted" the Saxons on the eastern border of his empire by force of arms.

Such sweeping conquest, amounting at times to mass conversions and baptism of whole tribes and nations, raised the problem of baptism without a real experience of faith. This has been a perennial problem of missionary effort wherever the conversion of an influential leader has resulted in such wholesale acceptance of Christianity that there has not been help enough to see that the converts have had a genuine experience of salvation.

C. The Low Countries

Wilfrid (634–709), an English churchman, landed in Friesland in 678 and preached the gospel to the people of that area. Willibrord (658–79) later succeeded in planting Christianity on sounder foundations and won Friesland to allegiance to the papacy about 690.

D. Italy

Between 568 and 675 the Lombards, who had been converted to Arian Christianity, got control of southern Italy and offered opposition to the papacy within its own land. Gregory I was able to prevent trouble during his pontificate through his influence on the Bavarian princess Theudelinda, who had been successively the wife of two Lombard kings. The visit of the Irish monk Columbanus about 610 was instrumental in bringing many Lombards to a renunciation of their Arian faith. By 675 the Lombard rulers and most of their people had accepted the orthodox faith of Rome.

E. Spain

The Arian Visigoths of Spain offered another challenge to the Roman church. Recared II announced at the

Third Council of Toledo in 589 that he had renounced Arianism in favor of orthodox Christianity. Many of his nobles and Arian bishops followed suit. But the conquest was never complete, and dissension between the orthodox and the Arians of Spain made the area an easy prey for the Muslims who overran Spain in the eighth century.

By 800 the authority of the papacy was firmly established in the British Isles and in much of the area of modern Germany. The threat to the papacy from Arianism in Italy and Spain was nullified. But in the Eastern church little missionary work was done except for the conversion of the Bulgarians and Moravians by Cyril and Methodius about the middle of the ninth century. The Moravians later came under papal jurisdiction. Most of the energies of the Eastern church were thrown into the struggle to prevent the Muslims from capturing Constantinople.

Suggested Reading

Addison, J. T. The Medieval Missionary. New York: International Missionary Council, 1931. This is a careful study of missionary techniques.

Bodley, Ronald U. C. The Messenger. Garden City, N.Y.: Doubleday, 1946. A good edition of the Quran also helps in understanding the Muslim faith.

Crawford, Samuel J. Anglo-Saxon Influence in Western Christendom, 600–800. Oxford: Oxford University Press, 1933. The author shows how in the Dark Ages the Celtic churches busied themselves with missions and manuscripts.

Deanesley, Margaret. Augustine of Canterbury. London: Nelson, 1964.

Emerton, Ephraim, trans. The Letters of Saint Boniface. New York: Columbia University Press, 1940.

Godfrey, John. The Church in Anglo-Saxon England. Cambridge: Cambridge University Press, 1962.

Hilgarth, J. N. The Conversion of Western Europe, 350–750. Englewood Cliffs, N.J.: Prentice-Hall, 1969. This volume contains many primary documents.

Robinson, Charles. The Conversion of Europe. London: Longmans, 1917. This detailed work provides more background for missions than is possible within the scope of this text.

Talbot, C. H., ed. and trans. The Anglo-Saxon Missionaries in Germany. London: Sheed and Ward, 1954. The primary documents contained in this work emphasize especially the work of Willibrord and Boniface.

Chapter 18

The Revival of Imperialism in the West

The popes found themselves subject to pressures that threatened the increasingly strong claims to power they made after 590. The emperors in Constantinople, who believed that the church should be subordinated to the ruler of the state, were steadily encroaching on what the bishop of Rome thought were his prerogatives and possessions. The Lombards, who held to the Arian form of Christianity, knocked on the gates of Rome more than once during this period. These difficulties forced the pope to look around for a powerful ally who would support his claims to spiritual power and to temporal possessions in Italy. The Frankish rulers seemed to be the most promising allies, and with them the popes made an alliance that was to influence both ecclesiastical and political affairs during the Middle Ages. The new political empire in the West, to which the pope gave his assent in 800, revived the imperial idea of the Roman Empire; but the rulers of this new empire were to be Teutons rather than Romans. The glory of reviving the Roman Empire went to the Carolingian rulers.

I. THE MEROVINGIAN DYNASTY

The importance of the conquest and civilization of Gaul by Caesar in the middle of the first century before Christ now became apparent because it was to the Franks in this territory that the pope turned for aid. These Franks had come to France from their homelands along the eastern bank of the Rhine River and had conquered Gaul, but at the same time they had accepted the Roman culture of their victims.

Clovis (ca. 466–510) was the first leader to unify the Franks and to complete the conquest of the territories of what would be the major part of modern France. He married a Burgundian princess, Clotilda (474–545), and linked the Burgundian territories won by this marriage with others won in battle. The union of all the Frankish tribesmen from the Rhine under his leadership was a great contribution to

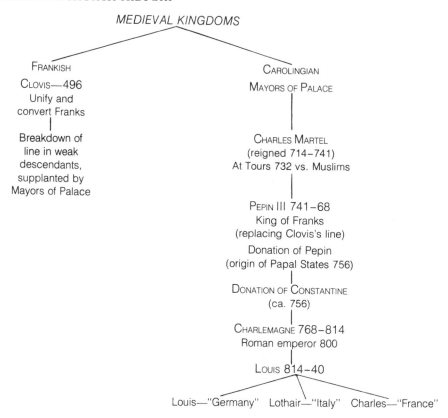

MEDIEVAL KINGDOMS

FRANKISH

CLOVIS—496
Unify and
convert Franks

Breakdown of
line in weak
descendants,
supplanted by
Mayors of Palace

CAROLINGIAN
MAYORS OF PALACE

CHARLES MARTEL
(reigned 714–741)
At Tours 732 vs. Muslims

PEPIN III 741–68
King of Franks
(replacing Clovis's line)

Donation of Pepin
(origin of Papal States 756)

DONATION OF CONSTANTINE
(ca. 756)

CHARLEMAGNE 768–814
Roman emperor 800

LOUIS 814–40

Louis—"Germany"   Lothair—"Italy"   Charles—"France"

stability in the area. Clovis accepted Christianity, partly through the influence of his wife, and partly because of what appeared to be providential aid given to him in battle. His acceptance of Christianity in 496 makes that year significant in the history of western Europe because the Franks, whom he had united, and their rulers were to become the bulwark of the papacy against its temporal foes and to give to the papacy the territories that it held as temporal possessions for over a millennium.

As is so often the case, Clovis's sons did not have the ability of their father; and control of the affairs of state passed into the hands of an official, known as the mayor of the palace, who held the reins of government, while the weak successors of Clovis enjoyed life in the palace. These mayors of the palace made up what is known as the Carolingian dynasty, which was to reach its zenith of power under Charlemagne.

II. THE CAROLINGIAN RULERS

Pepin of Heristal was the first of these mayors of the palace to reunite the divided possessions of Clovis, and from 687 to 714 he controlled the Franks for the degenerate descendants of Clovis. He made the office of mayor of the palace a hereditary position to be filled by his descendants.

Charles Martel (689–741) (the Hammerer), an illegitimate son of Pepin, took over the duties of mayor of the palace after 714. His abilities as a warrior were badly needed because the Muslims, who had overrun Spain, were now threatening to take over all of western Europe. Charles defeated them at the battle of Tours near Poitiers in 732 and obligated the Roman church to him because he had apparently saved western Europe for orthodox Christianity. He supported the work of Boniface in evangelizing the tribes beyond the Rhine, knowing that if they were won to Christianity, he would not have difficulty with them on the western bank of the Rhine.

Charles's successor as mayor of the palace was his son Pepin (ca. 714–68), known as Pepin the Short or Pepin the Great, who ruled jointly with his brother from 741 until 747, when the brother withdrew to a monastery. Pepin was the first real Carolingian king because he took the title of king (751) as well as exercising the authority of mayor of the palace. The occasion for this extension of his authority was a request from Pope Zacharias for aid against the Arian Lombards who were threatening the authority of the papacy in Italy. Pepin was consecrated by Boniface as the king of the Franks. Childeric III, the last of the Merovingians, was deposed and compelled to spend the rest of his life in a monastery. Pepin redeemed his promise to aid the pope by expeditions against the Lombards in 754 and 756. He promised land in central Italy from Rome to Ravenna to Pope Stephen II in 754. This grant, known as the Donation of Pepin, had special significance for the people of Rome because 754 B.C. was the traditional date for the founding of the city of Rome. This allotment

was the foundation for the papal states that the pope held uninterruptedly in Italy from 756 until the union of the Italian people in 1870. It is little wonder that the reigning pope, Stephen II, crowned Pepin for the second time as the "King of the Franks and Patrician of the Romans" in 754. Stephen received the promised grant in 756.

For some centuries an account had been developing concerning the supposedly miraculous healing and conversion of Constantine by the bishop of Rome. The grateful Constantine was supposed to have made liberal grants of rights and territories to the bishop. These stories were combined in a document known as the *Donation of Constantine* and given wide circulation during the Middle Ages. The document was used by the popes to buttress their claims to temporal possessions and to power in both the temporal and spiritual realms.[1] The authoritative formulation seems to have been made about the middle of the eighth century so that it was in circulation at the time Pepin made his grant of land in Italy to the papacy.

In the document Constantine greeted Sylvester and the bishops of the church and went on to relate that he had been healed from leprosy and baptized by Sylvester. In return, he declared that the church at Rome was to have precedence over all other churches and that its bishop was the supreme bishop in the church. He gave territories throughout his empire, the Lateran Palace, and the clothing and insignia of the imperial rank to Sylvester. Constantine then withdrew to Constantinople so that he would not interfere with the imperial rights of the pope.

Though the facts just described

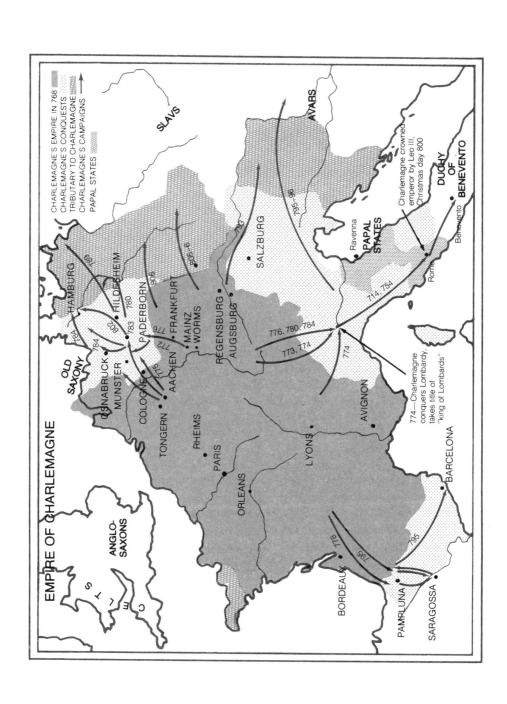

EMPIRE OF CHARLEMAGNE

CHARLEMAGNE'S EMPIRE IN 768
CHARLEMAGNE'S CONQUESTS
TRIBUTARY TO CHARLEMAGNE
CHARLEMAGNE'S CAMPAIGNS
PAPAL STATES

SLAVS

AVARS

DUCHY OF BENEVENTO

Charlemagne crowned emperor by Leo III, Christmas day 800

Ravenna
PAPAL STATES
Rome
Benevento

714, 754

795-96

795

805-6

789

806

776, 780, 784

773, 174

774

SALZBURG

HAMBURG
HILDESHEIM
PADERBORN
FRANKFURT
MAINZ
WORMS
REGENSBURG
AUGSBURG

783
780
776
772

784
782
799

OLD SAXONY

OSNABRUCK
MUNSTER
COLOGNE
TONGERN
AACHEN
775

774—Charlemagne conquers Lombardy, takes title of "king of Lombards"

AVIGNON

RHEIMS
PARIS

LYONS

ORLEANS

ANGLO-SAXONS

CELTS

BARCELONA

BORDEAUX

778
795
795

PAMRLUNA
SARAGOSSA

were in the document, they were not historically correct. No other record of any such facts exists. Moreover, Lorenzo Valla in 1440 showed in his book, the first document of real historical criticism, that the *Donation* was a forgery made some centuries after the events it purported to describe. Few spurious documents have exercised so potent an influence on history as this one did.

The next ruler over the Franks was Charlemagne, son of Pepin the Short. Charlemagne (742–814) came to the throne in 768 and in 800 he became emperor in the West when the pope crowned him *Imperator Romanorum* (Emperor of the Romans). His influence was felt in every area of human endeavor in western Europe.

Much information about Charlemagne is derived from Einhard, sometimes incorrectly known as Eginhard, writer of a biographic sketch of Charlemagne.[2] Charlemagne was about seven feet tall and had a proportionately large body. His bright face and long white hair, coupled with such height, gave him an air of dignity. He delighted in hunting, riding, and swimming but also had a real interest in culture; and this interest led him to combine the pleasure of the table with listening to music or having someone read to him. He was also devoted to religion. However, his religion did not carry over into his domestic life because he kept concubines as well as his legal spouse in his palace.

Charlemagne was also a man of war. He engaged in over fifty campaigns during the course of his reign in an attempt to end anarchy within his kingdom and to expand its borders into Italy, where he completed the defeat of the Lombards, and into Germany, where he conquered the Saxons. He spread Christianity among the Saxons by force of arms. He was able to double his father's possessions until he held all of Italy as far south as Rome, most of the area of modern Germany, and all of the area of modern France. So much land in western Europe had not been under one jurisdiction since the time of the Roman Empire. Because this kingdom was held together by the genius of Charlemagne, it did not last long after his death in 814.

Charlemagne developed an able bureaucracy and a good system of imperial government to administer his large empire. The empire was divided into different areas, each of which comprised several counties, under a duke. The emperor sent men known as *missi dominici* to the courts of these dukes at unexpected times to inspect their accounts, to announce new capitularies or laws, and to check on how well they were keeping order.

He was also friendly to the church. He thought that the church might be compared to the soul and the state to the body of man. Church and state had their respective spheres of responsibility. While on a visit to Rome to finish the work of defeating the Lombards in 774, he reconfirmed the donation of lands that Pepin had made to the pope in 756. He believed, however, that the ruler of the church should not dispute the decision of the ruler of the state and that bishops should also be subordinated to the head of the state.

When Pope Leo III was set upon by a faction in Rome and nearly killed, he left Rome for the court of Charlemagne. Charlemagne went back to Rome with him, and at a council the pope was cleared of the charges

One version of the relationship between the pope and the emperor is depicted in this mosaic. Peter, seated on the throne, is shown conferring the pallium on Pope Leo III and giving a banner to Emperor Charlemagne, showing that each derived his authority directly from Peter and independently of the other.

against him. At a holy mass in the cathedral on Christmas Day in 800, while Charlemagne knelt before the altar, the pope put the crown on Charlemagne's head and declared that he was the emperor of the Romans. Thus was the Roman Empire revived in the West; and new Rome, led by a Teuton, took the place of the old Roman Empire. A universal empire existed beside a universal church. The classical and Christian heritage were not linked in a Christian empire.

The human dream of unity of men seemed again to be realized, for Charlemagne had the largest territory under his control that any man held since the fall of the empire. The universal spiritual empire of the papacy over men's souls now had its counterpart in the revived Roman Empire that Charlemagne had over the bodies of men.

The kingdom of God was thought to have two arms: the spiritual, presided over by the pope, was to have responsibility for men's souls; the temporal was to have responsibility for the physical well-being of man. The pope and the emperor were to give each other mutual support. Of course, such a view was bound to bring conflict between the rulers of the church and the new Teutonic Roman Empire. Was the emperor given power from God over men, and did the pope exercise delegated power from the emperor over men's souls? Or did God give supreme authority to the church, and did the pope delegate authority over men's bodies to the emperor? Or did they hold coordinate positions in which God gave to each one directly supremacy within his respective sphere? The answer to this problem occupied the energies of popes and emperor during the Middle Ages until the popes finally succeeded in bringing the emperor under their control.

After the death of Charlemagne, his empire declined under his weak son and warring grandsons until the grandsons divided it among themselves in the Treaty of Verdun in 843, after a long period of war. The imperial idea was again revived by a German prince named Otto, in 962; and from 962 until 1806 the Holy Roman Empire was an honored institution in Europe in spite of Voltaire's jibe that it was neither holy, Roman, nor an empire.

Charlemagne was deeply devoted to cultural progress, and his imperial reign from 800 to 814 was a period of cultural development that has since become known as the "Carolingian Renaissance." Not since the work of Boethius and Cassiodorus during the reign of Theodoric, the Ostrogothic ruler of the land of Italy in the sixth century, had there been such cultural progress. In order to effect his cultural renaissance, Charlemagne turned to the scholars of the church in England and persuaded the great scholar Alcuin (ca. 735–804) to come to his court from York and to assume the leadership of his palace school at Aachen, where the children of the royal family and leading nobles might be educated. Alcuin had the assistance of Paul the Deacon, Einhard, and other able scholars in this work.

The palace school of Charlemagne was an integral link in the chain of men and schools responsible for passing on to the medieval university the basic outlines of its curriculum, the trivium, and the quadrivium that had been derived from Roman higher education by Martianus Capella in the fifth century. The cultural activities of

Charlemagne were an important step in the process by which the German people assimilated classical and Christian learning. Charlemagne himself delighted to listen to the reading of great books from the past and, according to his biographer Einhard, particularly liked Augustine's works, especially the *City of God.* He also insisted that the abbots set up monastery schools so the interpreters of Scripture might be learned men who would understand and rightly interpret the Bible.[3]

Considerable emphasis should be given to the significance of Charlemagne in medieval history. His coronation marked the reconciliation and union of the population of the old Roman Empire with its Teutonic conqueror. It ended the dream of the Eastern emperor to regain for the Eastern segment of the Roman Empire the areas lost to the barbarians in the West in the fifth century. Because the pope had crowned Charlemagne, his position was enhanced as one to whom rulers owed their crowns; and the emperor was bound to aid him when he was in difficulty. Charlemagne's coronation marked the peak of Frankish power that began with Clovis's decision to become a Christian.

III. THE CHURCH
AND EMPIRE IN THE EAST

Charlemagne was also interested in the Eastern empire and church and even made attempts to unite the East and West into one empire that would embrace most of the territories of the old Roman Empire. One must not forget that the Eastern emperors held back the Muslim hordes from sweeping over Europe until the West could recover from the confusion and chaos created by the fall of the empire and the influx of the barbarians.

The East was particularly troubled by the iconoclastic controversy from 726–843. Leo III in decrees of 726 and 730 had banned the use of images in the church and ordered their destruction. Charlemagne made a statement opposing worship of images about the time Irene became the empress of the Eastern empire. He even offered to marry Irene in order to reunite the areas of the old Roman Empire under one crown with the capital in the West. But Irene refused his advances, and the division of the empire, first started when Constantine moved the capital to Constantinople from Rome in 330, continued. The Second Council of Nicaea in 787 permitted veneration rather than worship of images.

The Eastern church, except for the work of John of Damascus, remained static in the development of theology from the period of theological controversy in the fourth to the sixth centuries until the Modern Era. John (ca. 675–ca. 749) formulated theological ideas into what became the Eastern equivalent of the *Summa* of Thomas Aquinas. His *Fountain of Wisdom* in three books became the authority for theologians in the Eastern church as the work of Thomas Aquinas became the authority in the Western church. The third book, *Of the Orthodox Faith,* is a summation of the theology developed by the Fathers and councils from the fourth century up to his own day; and it became the standard expression of orthodoxy in the eastern part of the empire. Perhaps the fact that the church at Constantinople was subordinated to the authority of the emperor accounted for the static position of Eastern Christianity after the middle of the eighth century. In the East the church was virtually a department of the state whereas in the West the pope had been able to gain freedom from temporal control and was even able at a later date to control the temporal power.

By the end of the era between 590 and 800, some of the confusion attendant upon the fall of the Roman Empire in the West had been cleared. The Eastern Asiatic section of the empire continued under the rule of the emperor at Constantinople. The Frankish kingdom of Clovis grew into the Christian empire under Charlemagne and united the now Christian Teutons and the inhabitants of the old empire in the West. The southern shore of the Mediterranean, formerly territory held by the Roman Empire, was lost to Islam by Rome and Constantinople, but further Muslim expansion was stopped in the East and West by 732. The old territories of Rome were now divided into three areas, and church history of the era between 800 and 1054 is mainly concerned with the struggle between the pope and the ruler of the Frankish Empire.

Suggested Reading

Duckett, Eleanor S. Alcuin, Friend of Charlemagne. *New York: Macmillan, 1951.*

Chapter 19

The Emergence
of the Holy Roman Empire

The history of the church in this era involves discussion of the complex web of relationships that existed between the church and the imperial states in the East and the West. It was the period when the first great schism in the church occurred. The Western and Eastern sections of the church separated to go their respective ways as the Roman Catholic church in the West and the Greek Orthodox church in the East. And the gloom of the Dark Ages was being slowly dispelled by a revival of learning that began under Charlemagne.

I. THE DECLINE
OF THE CAROLINGIAN EMPIRE

A. The Weak Successors of Charlemagne

The brilliant imperial structure established by the coronation of Charlemagne by Leo III on Christmas Day of the year 800 did not long survive its great founder. Because the empire had been dependent on his personal genius, his death was the signal for the

beginning of its dissolution. Neither his son nor his grandson had the energy and ability that he had, and the splendid Frankish Empire broke up rapidly.

B. Teutonic Principle of Inheritance

An even more important factor in the decline of the Frankish phase of the Holy Roman Empire was the fragmentation introduced into the imperial structure by the fatal Teutonic principle that prescribed the division of the lands of the father among his sons. This principle was put into operation even during the lifetime of Louis the Pious (778–840), Charlemagne's immediate successor. The concept of an indivisible empire, held by the Romans, was foreign to the Teutonic mind. Furthermore, even if Louis had held this concept, he lacked the personal genius of his father Charlemagne to work it out. He was unable to control the strong aristocracy, and his indulgent nature weakened his control of his turbulent family.

191

Shortly after he took over the imperial throne, Louis announced his plans for the division of his empire among his sons. When another son, Charles the Bald, was born to him and to his second wife Judith, he had to change his plans so as to include Charles among his heirs in the event of his death.

When Louis died in 840, after a troubled reign that had begun in 814, the quarrels of his sons made the decline of the great Carolingian Empire inevitable. His son Louis inherited the eastern section; Charles the Bald inherited the western section; and the long central section, stretching from the North Sea to the Adriatic Sea, and the imperial title of emperor went to Lothair. Lothair wished to extend his control over the whole area of his father's empire, but his two brothers, Charles the Bald and Louis the German, united against him. The latter two met at Strasbourg in 842 and took an oath in the vernaculars of their respective peoples to be loyal to each other until they had defeated Lothair. This meeting had significance for the history of modern France and Germany because Louis, whose possessions included most of the area of modern Germany, and Charles, whose possessions included most of the area of modern France, each recognized the common tongue of his subjects by taking his oath in it.[1]

This alliance was too strong for Lothair, and in 843 the three brothers agreed to the Treaty of Verdun.[2] The area of modern France was granted to Charles the Bald, and the area of modern Germany was to belong to Louis. Lothair was given the title of emperor and a strip between the two kingdoms that was a thousand miles long and over a hundred miles wide. This event marked the birth of the modern states of France and Germany; and rivalry between them for possession of the area between the two kingdoms has continued until modern times and has been a source of trouble in the affairs of western Europe. By the Treaty of Mersen in 870, the rulers of the eastern and western Frankish kingdoms divided the central area between their two kingdoms and confined the descendants of Lothair to Italy.

C. The Rise of Feudalism

Fragmentation of the great empire that Charlemagne had built up was also hastened by the rise of feudalism. Feudalism in one form or another always arises when a central government becomes weak and can no longer exercise effective authority over the areas under its control. The decline of city life and trade after the fall of the Roman Empire forced people back to the land to make a living. Feudalism had precedents both in Roman and German customs concerning the holding of land and service. These and other chaotic conditions of the ninth century encouraged the rise of the feudalistic way of life in western Europe. It put public power into private hands.

Society was divided horizontally rather than vertically in the Middle Ages so that there was little social mobility. A person usually lived his life in the social rank in which his father had lived. Society was divided after the rise of feudalism into a group of protectors, the feudal knights, who had the privilege of land ownership in return for their services; into a group of producers, the serfs on the manors, who became the economic foundation of feudalism; and into a group of prayers, the priestly class of the universal church. The individual was subordinated to the corporate or group interest, and every man had his master in such a hierarchical society.

Feudalism may be defined as a system of political organization based on possession of land. The local lord gave good government in the immediate area where he owned the land. Until nation-states could emerge in England, France, and Spain in the late Middle Ages, this was the only way in which justice and order could be maintained during the period of weak centralized authority after the decline of the Roman Empire, the failure of the Merovingian kingdom, and the breakup of Charlemagne's Empire.

Manorialism was also an economic system that provided a living for all classes of society after the breakdown of international trade, another result of the fall of the Roman Empire. Both the lord and serf got their living from the soil, and each manor was self-sufficient except for a few items such as salt, millstones, or iron bars for the smith to work into tools. The manor, an area that could support an armed knight, was the land unit in the feudal system. Some feudal lords might own several manors. Thus the manor was the basic economic unit that made the feudal system possible.

Land tenure was the link that tied the manorial and feudal systems together. The knight, the lowest link in the feudal pyramid, was dependent for his living on the serfs who worked the land for him. In return he gave them protection.

Feudalism also involved personal relationships of loyalty between the vassal and the lord, such as the obligation of forty days of military service each year, the provision of food, and prayers, if the vassal was a churchman. Ideally, society was pyramidal, with each vassal having a lord; and the lord at the top of the pyramid, the king, was a vassal of God. Only in England under William the Conqueror in the eleventh century was the feudal pyramid realized. In what is now modern France and Germany, the tie between the feudal vassal and the ruler was weak.

This somewhat lengthy discussion of feudalism has been made necessary by the importance of feudalism as the political and economic system that gave law and order in the era of decentralization and chaos that followed the dissolution of the Carolingian Empire and the invasions of western Europe and England by the Vikings in the ninth and tenth centuries and by Slavs and Magyars.

The influence of feudalism on the church in this period is even more important. A large amount of the land of western Europe was held by the church during the late Middle Ages. Because the gifts of land by pious or repentant men, seeking to atone for a life of sin, remained in the hands of the Roman church as a corporate body from generation to generation, that church as a great landowner could not help but be influenced by the feudal system. These gifts were held in feudal tenure by abbots and bishops. The clergy as servants of God could not render military service to their feudal lord and therefore they either had to give part of their lands to vassal knights who could render military service for them or devise other services. This feudalization of church land tended to secularize the church and to distract its attention from spiritual to mundane interests. The ecclesiastical vassal faced the problem of divided allegiance. Should his primary allegiance be to the temporal lord, to whom he owed feudal dues, or to the pope, the spiritual overlord, from whom his spiritual authority came? This division of allegiance hindered the development of the sound spiritual life essential to the success of the church.

Since the younger sons of the nobles could gain land and prestige through service in the church, great nobles often interfered with elections to get an abbey or bishopric for their relatives. Many of these men were worldly and little interested in the spiritual matters that went with the ecclesiastical position.

The investiture controversy, the dispute as to whether the feudal lord or the pope should grant an ecclesiastical feudal vassal the symbols of his authority, embittered relationships between the church and the state during the eleventh and twelfth centuries. The ring, staff, and pallium were the symbols of spiritual authority; and the sword and scepter were the symbols of feudal authority. At times both the feudal lord and the pope claimed the right to give all these symbols. Such controversy led to a loss of spiritual life on the part of the leaders of the church, the neglect of their spiritual duties, and the secularization of their interests as they gave more attention to control of their land and local feudal squabbles than they did to the affairs of the church. The church in the West had to fight feudalization while that in the East unsuccessfully fought imperial control.

The secularization of the church, because of its involvement in the feudal system, must be balanced against the attempts of the church to mitigate the evils of feudal warfare. Early in the eleventh century the church was able to get the feudal lords to accept the Peace of God and the Truce of God. The Peace of God was an agreement to ban private quarrels, to attack no unarmed persons, to permit no robbery or violence, and to pillage no sacred place. This agreement was needed because the feudal lord felt no obligation not to fight his feudal neighbor. The Truce of God by 1031 bound the feudal class not to fight from sunset on Wednesday to sunrise on Monday of each week and not to fight on the day of church festivals. This left less than one hundred days in the year open to feudal fighting. It also provided that churches, cemeteries, monasteries, and convents should be sanctuaries where refugees could find a safe asylum in time of trouble. Women, peasants, and clergy were not to be harmed. These agreements[3] did much to lessen the brutalities of feudal warfare in the Middle Ages.

D. Viking, Slav, and Magyar Invasions

While feudalism was both effect and cause in the decline of the Carolingian Empire, the Viking, Slav, and Magyar invasions were definite factors in its rapid dissolution. These Vikings, or Northmen, who came from what is now modern Sweden, Denmark, and Norway, were a problem in western Europe from the late eighth century until the tenth century. Any town or monastery along the coast or on the shores of a navigable river could expect a visit from these bold sea rovers.

Many of them finally settled in England and, after much fighting, merged with their kinsmen, the Anglo-Saxons, who had come to England earlier. In the process the fine Christian culture that had been built up in Ireland and England during the Dark Ages was destroyed or set back. Other Vikings settled in Normandy, from whence they came to conquer England under the leadership of William the Conqueror in 1066. Some trekked south across eastern Europe and laid the foundations of the Russian state. Others settled in Sicily and southern Italy, where for a time they presented a threat to the temporal power of the papacy. The Slavs and Magyars settled in south-central Europe.

II. THE IMPORTANCE OF THE CAROLINGIAN EMPIRE

Preoccupation with the reasons for and the decline of the Carolingian Empire must not blind us to its importance in western European history. The French and German states emerged from its ruins. Although the German state, with its later claims to universal empire, as the legitimate successor to the Roman and Carolingian Empires never succeeded in working out a centralized nation-state until nineteenth-century nationalism welded the Germans into one nation-state, it became the successor to the imperial Frankish state in the tenth century. Instead of aiding the pope as the Frankish emperors had done, it fought with the papacy for supremacy until its ruling line was defeated by Innocent III.

The ideal of a revived Roman Empire was never given up after the fall of Charlemagne's empire. The German emperors of the tenth century took over from the west Frankish state the tradition of empire, and the empire founded by Otto I was known as the Holy Roman Empire.

The Carolingian Empire also created the problem of whether the church or the state was the representative of Deity on earth. The issue of whether God had delegated sovereignty to the pope or to the emperor so that one derived his authority from the other was a heritage of Charlemagne's empire. That issue embittered relationships between church and state for some centuries during the Middle Ages.

The beginning of the pope's claim to be a temporal ruler dated from the grant of lands in Italy to the pope by Pepin, the ancestor of Charlemagne, in 756. The pope as a temporal as well as a spiritual ruler made claims on national rulers during the Middle Ages—claims they would not admit were justified.

The impetus given to culture by Charlemagne must be counted as one of the great marks of his empire. His reign was a bright light illuminating by contrast the cultural darkness of the Dark Ages elsewhere in western Europe. One cannot but be impressed with the significance of Charlemagne and his empire for the subsequent history of the church and state in western Europe.

III. THE TENTH-CENTURY REVIVAL OF THE ROMAN EMPIRE

Even though the empire created by Charlemagne disappeared, the ideal of a universal political empire, which western Europe had inherited from Rome, remained. It was not to be

EMPIRE OF OTTO THE GREAT
962–73 AND HIS SUCCESSORS

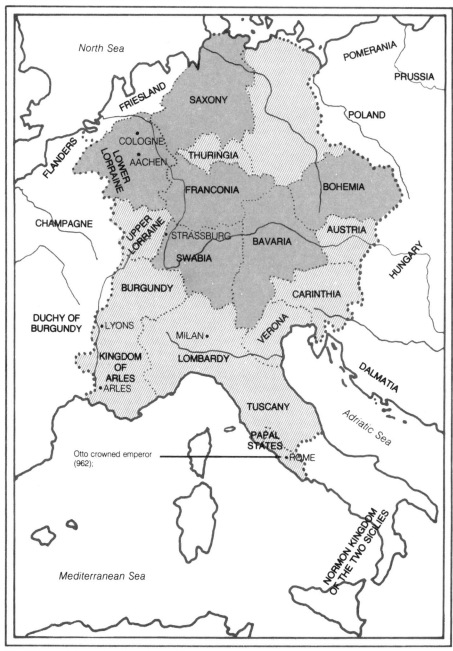

North Sea

POMERANIA

PRUSSIA

FRIESLAND

SAXONY

POLAND

FLANDERS

COLOGNE

LOWER LORRAINE

AACHEN

THURINGIA

FRANCONIA

BOHEMIA

CHAMPAGNE

UPPER LORRAINE

STRASSBURG

AUSTRIA

BAVARIA

SWABIA

HUNGARY

BURGUNDY

CARINTHIA

DUCHY OF BURGUNDY

LYONS

MILAN

VERONA

DALMATIA

KINGDOM OF ARLES

LOMBARDY

ARLES

Adriatic Sea

TUSCANY

PAPAL STATES

Otto crowned emperor (962);

ROME

NORMON KINGDOM OF THE TWO SICILIES

Mediterranean Sea

EMPIRE UNDER OTTO (936–73)
ACQUIRED BY OTTO

realized again by the Franks but was to be realized in the eastern section of Charlemagne's empire, which had gone to Louis the German in 843. Some consideration must be given to the rise, growth, and significance of this new claimant to the power of imperial Rome in the West.

Unification in Germany has always been more difficult than unification in France. The physical geography of France provides her with the natural boundaries of the Mediterranean Sea, the Atlantic, the Pyrenees Mountains, and the Alps. Only on the Rhine does she face frustration, because she has never been able to make it a natural boundary for the French state. Geography works against German unity because rivers in Germany flow north to the North or Baltic Seas, and in the southern part of the country they flow east. Northern Germany is mostly plain, whereas southern Germany is mountainous. This makes for different interests among the people. Moreover, the traditional tribal divisions, coupled with later feudal states, led to decentralization of authority. Even after Germany was made one in name under the emperors of the Holy Roman Empire, the interest of the emperor in the affairs of the church across the Alps was not shared by his people. But in spite of these problems the eastern part of Charlemagne's old empire became the center of the imperial power that had once been wielded in the West by the Franks.

The tribal dukes of Germany, faced with the need of unity for defense against the Northmen and the Slavic Magyars, selected Henry the Fowler, the duke of Saxony, as their ruler in 919. He drove back the Northmen and was able to defeat the Slavic invaders.

Henry was succeeded as king of the Germans by his son Otto (912–73) in 936. Otto made the dukes his vassals and took over supervision of the affairs of the church by naming bishops and abbots of his choosing to take care of ecclesiastical interests in Germany. If he had been willing to confine his efforts to Germany, he might have built up a powerful centralized monarchy similar to that which later English, French, and Spanish kings were to create. But he became interested in affairs across the Alps, and for centuries problems of the church and state in Italy became a drain on German resources. He went to Italy to aid the pope against a powerful ruler who had risen to threaten the papal power in Italy, and Pope John XII crowned him as emperor of the Holy Roman Empire in 962. Once again there was a Roman emperor to claim jurisdiction over the people of Europe as Charlemagne and the Roman emperors had done earlier. All central Europe from the North Sea to the Adriatic was united under the German Roman Empire, which was to last until Napoleon brought about its dissolution in 1806.

During the next two centuries the Roman see had weak incumbents, and the German emperors often crossed the Alps to bring order out of chaos and to extend their own interests in Italy. For example, Otto III in 996 entered Rome and, after putting down a faction of Roman nobles, forced the election of his own cousin Bruno as Pope Gregory V. This constant interference by the German rulers in the affairs of the papacy in Italy led to a struggle between the emperor and the pope until Innocent III humiliated and defeated the emperor and ended German interference in Italy.

Chapter 20

Revival and Schism in the Church

Although the Western church was under the shadow of the Holy Roman Empire during the latter part of the period between 800 and 1054, it experienced an inner renewal that gave it the strength to cope with imperial interference. The Eastern church during this era became conscious of such differences between itself and the Western church that the period ended with a schism resulting in the creation of the Greek Orthodox church in the East.

I. RENEWAL IN THE WEST

Although the renewal in the Western church was not always a renewal of spirit, there was a renewal of strength that helped it in its struggle with the state, represented by the German Holy Roman Empire. Several things strengthened the power of the pope.

A. Documents Supporting the Papacy

The *Donation of Constantine* (see chap. 18, p. 183) became the legal ground for the possession of land by the pope. The greatest grant of land, which this document was used to justify, was given by Pepin in 756. In 865 Pope Nicholas I who was pope from 858 to 867, first made use of a collection of the decrees of the various pontiffs of Rome. This collection is known as the False Decretals, or the Pseudo-Isidorian Decretals. The remarkable document included the *Donation of Constantine*, the real and some forged decrees or decretals of the popes of Rome from the time of Clement of Rome, and some of the canons of the great councils of the church. The collection was associated with the name of Isidore of Seville (ca. 560–636), head of the Spanish church during the first part of the seventh century. One cannot be dogmatic about the authorship of the Decretals, but it is certain that from the middle of the ninth century they played an important part in the claims of the Roman bishop to supremacy within the church.

The *Donation of Constantine*, which was first used in the eighth century, was used to buttress the claims of the popes to land in Italy; but the Decretals were used to support the power of the pope within the church. The Decretals asserted the supremacy of the pope over all ecclesiastical leaders of the church and gave any bishop the right to appeal directly to the pope over the head of his archbishop. The right of the church to be free from secular control was also claimed. Although it is not likely that any pope created the forgery, many popes made use of the collection to support their claims to power within the church. The *Dictatus* of Gregory VII later reinforced these claims.

B. The Conversion of Scandinavia

The power of the Roman bishop was strengthened in this era by the acceptance of the gospel by the people of Scandinavia. Anskar (801–65), a native of Flanders, deserves much of the credit for this gain. When the Danish king Harald asked for a missionary in 826, Anskar felt that he should answer the call and devoted the rest of his life to missionary activity in northern Europe. Denmark was not finally won to Christianity until the eleventh century, in the days of Canute. Christianity was permanently established in Norway about 1000, and about the same time it was made the state religion in Sweden and Iceland. The work, begun by Anskar,[1] bore fruit by 1000 that strengthened the power of Rome in northern Europe.

C. The Doctrine of the Mass

The controversy regarding the nature of Christ's presence in the Communion agitated the Western church early in the ninth century. Any acceptance of the idea of the Lord's Supper as a sacrifice by the priest was a gain for the power of the papacy because the pope headed the hierarchy of clergymen who alone had the power to perform this miracle of the Mass. About 831 Paschasius Radbertus (ca. 785–860), abbot of the monastery of Corbie near the city of Amiens, began to teach that by a divine miracle the substance of the bread and the wine were actually changed into the body and blood of Christ. Although he did not call this change transubstantiation, his teaching amounted to the same thing. He set forth these views in 831 in a book entitled *Of the Body and Blood of the Lord*.[2] Such a view was bound to strengthen the power of the priest and his superior in the hierarchy, the pope, even though the Roman church did not officially accept the doctrine of transubstantiation until 1215 nor fully define it until the Council of Trent (1545).

D. Monastic Reform

The monastic reforms carried out by the Cluniac monasteries in the tenth and eleventh centuries made a great contribution to the supremacy of the papacy. By the tenth century the monasteries had become wealthy and corrupt and were badly in need of reform. The earlier ideal of service had been replaced by the ideal of individual salvation coupled with an easy life in a wealthy monastery. The papacy itself experienced a period of serious decline between Nicholas I and Leo IX (see p. 202). The reform movement originating at Cluny was the first of several successive reform movements in Roman monasticism.

It had far-reaching effects.

The monastery at Cluny came about this way. In 909, Duke William of Aquitaine, "for the good" of his soul, gave a charter to Berno,[3] who had already made a record as abbot of another monastery, for founding a new monastery at Cluny in eastern France.[4] The charter provided that the monastery was to be free from all secular or episcopal control and that it was to exercise self-government under the protection of the pope. Berno, abbot from 910 to 926, and Odo, abbot from 927 to 944, were both men of ability and character. They did their work so well that many monasteries of the Benedictine order, including the monastery of Monte Cassino, were reorganized along the same lines as the one at Cluny.

Under the older system of monasticism, each monastery had its own abbot and was independent of other monasteries of the same order. The abbot of Cluny, however, appointed the priors of new monasteries founded by himself or others and made them subject to himself. This innovation created an order that was centralized under one head, the abbot of Cluny, who worked in close harmony with the papacy. By the twelfth century over eleven hundred monasteries were under the leadership of the abbot of Cluny.

The Cluniac leaders called for reform in clerical life. Their Cluniac platform condemned simony (the practice of buying and selling church offices for money) and nepotism (the practice of showing favoritism to relatives in appointments to office). Celibacy was the third plank in their platform. Clergymen were neither to marry nor keep concubines in order that their whole attention would be given to the affairs of the church. These monks also insisted that the church should be free from temporal or secular control by king, emperor, or duke. This program was put into effect by a series of reforming popes with the aid of the Cluniac monasteries. The ascetic life also received a new emphasis.

The reforming enthusiasm of the Cluniac movement made itself felt in many other areas. The men of Cluny created good monastic schools, and these schools helped to make Latin the common tongue of the Middle Ages. The movement that resulted in the Crusades being launched against the Muslims in the Holy Land owed much to monks from Cluniac monasteries. Cluniac monasteries on the frontiers of civilization became centers of missionary effort. The order came to an end legally in 1790.

E. Capable Leaders

Although many of the popes in the era between 800 and 1054 were corrupt or incompetent, there were several able leaders who helped to consolidate the strength of the papacy. Nicholas I, who was pope from 858 to 867, was one of the ablest of these men. Both in writing and in practice, he insisted on the supremacy of the pope within the church as one who was responsible for the spiritual welfare of the faithful and on the supremacy of the pope over temporal rulers in matters of morals or religion. The Pseudo-Isidorian Decretals were often mentioned by him as a justification for this claim.[5]

Nicholas I successfully exerted his power over both bishops and the temporal ruler in the case of Lothair II of

Lorraine. Lothair had married Teutberga mainly for political reasons. Becoming enamored with Waldrada, he put his legal wife aside. He got a divorce from Teutberga by calling a synod in which the bishops granted him a divorce. Appeal was made to Nicholas by both parties; but, in the meantime, Lothair had married Waldrada. Determined to bring under control the bishops who had acted so hastily and to discipline Lothair for immorality, Nicholas forced Lothair to set aside Waldrada and to restore Teutberga to her place as his rightful wife.

Nicholas also was successful in upholding the right of a bishop to appeal directly to the pope. When Hincmar, archbishop of Rheims, removed Rothad, bishop of Soissons, from his position, Nicholas reversed Hincmar's decision and forced him to restore Rothad to his bishopric.

Nicholas even tried to assert his authority over the patriarch and the Eastern emperor at Constantinople. Emperor Michael, who had been corrupted by his uncle Bardas, deposed the patriarch Ignatius when he refused to administer the sacrament to Bardas, and in 858 he appointed the learned Photius in his place. Ignatius asked Nicholas for aid. Nicholas declared Photius deposed, but an Eastern synod under the leadership of Photius accused the Western church of heresy for adding to the creed the statement that the Holy Spirit proceeds from the Son as well as from the Father.[6] Ill will between the two sections of the church was augmented, and Nicholas, though successful in asserting his supremacy over temporal and ecclesiastical rulers in the West, was unsuccessful in the East.

Between the pontificates of Nicholas I and Leo IX there were few good leaders on the papal throne. This was not for lack of popes, because over forty popes occupied the episcopal throne in Rome during that period. A particularly bad scandal developed in the middle of the eleventh century. Benedict IX, an unworthy pope, was driven from Rome, and Sylvester III was placed on the papal throne. Benedict returned to Rome and sold the papal throne for a large sum of money in 1045 to a man who became Gregory VI. During the course of events, however, Benedict refused to lay down the papacy. There were now three popes, each claiming to be the rightful pope. Henry III, (ca. 1017–56), emperor of the Holy Roman Empire, then called a synod at Sutri in 1046. Benedict and Sylvester were deposed, and Gregory was forced to resign in favor of Clement II. Clement soon died, and his successor, another one of Henry's appointees, was also short-lived. Henry later appointed his cousin Bruno as Pope Leo IX.

With the coming of Leo IX, the long era of poor popes between Nicholas I and Leo IX came to an end because Leo and his successors were strong men who were interested in reform along the lines of the Cluniac platform. The synod of Sutri thus marked the lowest ebb in the power of the papacy in the medieval period. Under Nicholas II, aided by Humbert and the able Hildebrand, who was to become Gregory VII, the election of the pope was taken out of the hands of the Roman populace and put under the control of the church leaders in the college of cardinals in 1059. From that time until the papacy reached a peak of power under Innocent III there was steady advance in the influence of the papacy in European affairs.

The church in the East, harassed by the fight to restrain the Muslims from overrunning the Eastern empire, weakened by the control of its affairs by the emperor of that empire, and frustrated by the theological stagnation that set in after the great work of John of Damascus, was not in a position to offer much opposition to the rise in temporal as well as spiritual power of the Roman bishop. The growing antagonism between the two sections of the church, which rose out of historic roots, led to a break in 1054. With the break, two great divisions of the Christian religion appeared, and they have had few official contacts with each other since that time.

II. THE ORIGIN OF THE GREEK ORTHODOX CHURCH

The church in the East was never able to be as independent as that in the West because it was under the eye of the emperor and because it had to cope with the Greco-Roman tradition of culture, which was preserved in the East during the time the West was going through the cultural chaos of the Dark Ages. After the fall of the Roman Empire, the church in the West faced no great political rival on the imperial throne and grew stronger as it faced the problems associated with the cultural chaos that surrounded the fall of the empire.

A. Differences and Causes for Separation of East and West

When Constantine moved his capital to Constantinople in 330, he paved the way for political and, finally, ecclesiastical separation of the church into the East and the West. Theodosius put the administration of the Eastern and Western areas of the empire under separate heads in 395. With the fall of the Roman Empire in the West, in the late fifth century, this division was completely realized. The church in the East was under the jurisdiction of the emperor, but the pope in Rome was too far away to be brought under his control. In the absence of effective political control in the West, the pope became a temporal as well as spiritual leader in times of crisis. Emperors were almost popes in the East, and in the West popes were almost emperors. This gave the two churches an entirely different outlook concerning temporal power.

The intellectual outlook of the West also differed from that of the East. The Latin West was more inclined to consider practical matters of polity and had little trouble formulating orthodox dogma. The Greek mind of the East was more interested in solving theological problems along philosophical lines. Most of the theological controversies between 325 and 451 arose in the East, but in most cases the same problems caused little difficulty in the West.

Another difference between the two churches concerned celibacy. Marriage of all parish clergy below the rank of bishop was permitted in the East, but in the West the clergy were not allowed to marry. Disputes even arose on some occasions over the wearing of beards. The priest in the West might shave his face, but the clergymen in the East had to wear a beard. Also, the West stressed the use of Latin while the Eastern churches used Greek. This occasionally led to misunderstanding.

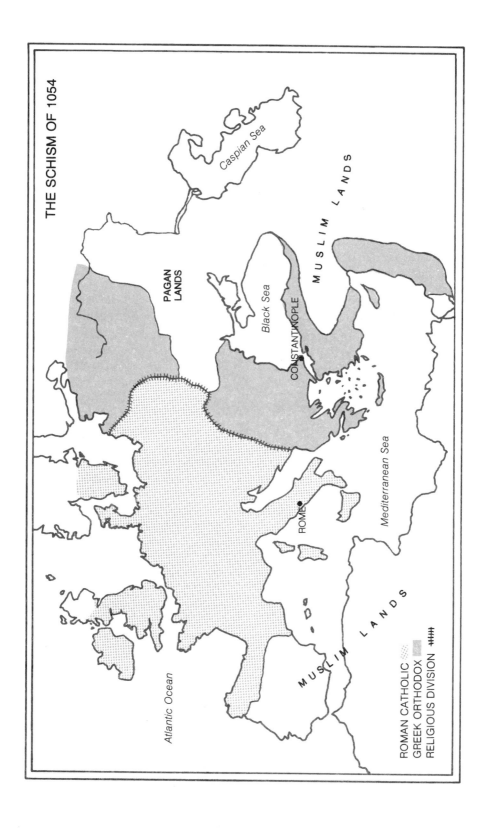

THE SCHISM OF 1054

Caspian Sea

PAGAN
LANDS

MUSLIM LANDS

Black Sea

CONSTANTINOPLE

ROME

Mediterranean Sea

Atlantic Ocean

MUSLIM LANDS

ROMAN CATHOLIC
GREEK ORTHODOX
RELIGIOUS DIVISION

Though these and similar matters may seem trivial now, they were of great importance at that time to both sections of the church.

The two churches clashed over theological matters. In 867 Photius, the patriarch in the East, charged Nicholas I and the church in the West with heresy because the West had the *filoque* clause in its form of the Nicene Creed. The West accepted the procession of the Holy Spirit from the Son, but this was rejected by the East.

Then a series of controversies embittered relations between the East and West. With each dispute the hostility increased.

About the middle of the second century, the problem of when to celebrate Easter had arisen to mar relations between the two sections of the church (see chap. 8, p. 97). Differences of opinion regarding this question always made amicable relations between the two groups difficult.

The iconoclastic controversy in the Eastern church in the eighth and ninth centuries caused many hard feelings. In 726, Leo III, as emperor of the East, forbade any kneeling before pictures or images and in 730 he ordered all except the cross removed from the churches and destroyed to limit the power of the monks and to refute Muslim charges of idolatry. This attempt at lay revival in the Eastern church ran into the vested opposition of the parish and monastic clergy. In the West the pope and even the emperor Charlemagne took a stand in favor of the use of visible symbols of divine reality. This interference by the West in the affairs of the church in the East increased the antagonism between the two areas. The church in the West continued to use pictures and statues in worship; the church in the East, however, finally eliminated statues but kept icons, usually pictures of Christ which were to be accorded reverence but not worship, which belongs to God alone.

The people of the East particularly resented the attempt by Pope Nicholas I in the middle of the ninth century to interfere with the appointment of the patriarch of the church in the East, even though it may have been justified on moral grounds (see p. 202). Though Nicholas was not successful, his interference, in what many in the East felt was a matter for the East alone, intensified the bad feeling between the two churches.

B. The Schism of 1054

In 1054, the final controversy revolved around what was apparently a minor matter. Michael Cerularius, patriarch of Constantinople from 1043 to 1059, condemned the church in the West for the use of unleavened bread in the Eucharist. Such use had been a growing practice in the West since the ninth century. Pope Leo IX sent Cardinal Humbert and two other legates to the East to end the dispute. The differences of opinion widened as the discussions went on. On July 16, 1054, the Roman legates finally put a decree of excommunication of the patriarch and his followers on the high altar of the cathedral church of Saint Sophia.[7] The patriarch was not to be outdone, and thereupon in synod he anathematized the pope of Rome and his followers. The first great schism in Christianity broke the unity of the church. From this time the Roman Catholic church and the Greek Orthodox church went their separate ways. This mutual excommunication was not removed until December 7, 1965, by Paul VI and Athenagoras.

C. The Consequences of Schism

Any ecumenical movement was difficult after the bitter events that separated the church in the East and the church in the West. The modern ecumenical movement aimed at the reunion of the churches of Christendom has had little support from the Roman Catholic church and from the Greek Orthodox church. The movement has been primarily a Protestant movement until recently. Neither of the two churches desires any ecumenical church except on its own terms, although the church of the East has been willing to confer with Protestant churches concerning reunion.

Separation shut the church in the East off from many of the vitalizing influences that strengthened the church in the West. The rise of towns, nations, and the middle class, the cultural movements of the Renaissance, and the Reformation passed by the church in the East; but the Roman Catholic church in the West was subjected to their influence and made stronger, either by assimilation of helpful features or by reaction against what appeared to Rome to be harmful.

The church in the East did, however, engage in some missionary work in this era. The Bulgarians were won to Christianity in 864, under Boris, who reigned from 852 to 889, and they adopted the faith of Constantinople. Though Cyril and Methodius won the Moravians to Christianity, the Moravians finally came under Roman jurisdiction instead of that of Constantinople. The patriarch had more success with missionary work in Russia. A princess named Olga accepted Christianity in 955 and was able to influence her grandson Vladimir (956–1015) so that he accepted Christianity about 988. This event marked the beginning of the triumph of Eastern Christianity in Russia. Russia, along with much of eastern and central Europe, followed the patriarch of Constantinople.[8] The Magyars also were converted.

The shock of Islam in the seventh century and the loss of people and land to the Muslims, coupled with the two centuries of unrest concerning the use of images, left Christianity in the East to become stagnant. Little change in ritual, polity, or theology has appeared in that church until the present time. Consequently it has not had the influence on the world that Christianity in the West has had, although in the ancient period of church history it had led in the formulation of theology.

SUGGESTED READING

Adeney, Walter F. **The Greek and Eastern Churches.** *New York: Scribner, 1908. This is still a useful survey for more detail concerning the history of the church in the East.*

Benz, Ernest. **The Eastern Orthodox Church: Its Thought and Life.** *Chicago: Aldine, 1963,*

Meyendorff, John. **The Orthodox Church.** *New York: Pantheon, 1962.*

Runciman, Steven. **The Eastern Schism.** *Oxford: Clarendon University Press, 1955. This is a scholarly study of the schism of 1054.*

_____. **The Great Church in Captivity.** *Cambridge: Cambridge University Press, 1968. Both of Runciman's books are excellent.*

Spinka, Matthew. **Christianity in the Balkans.** New York: Archon, 1968.

Chapter 21

The Zenith of Papal Power

The papacy exercised great temporal power between 1054 and 1305. Hildebrand was able to humble the emperor of the Holy Roman Empire; Innocent III was powerful enough to force rulers of rising nation-states to do his will; and the papacy inspired the early Crusades. The rise of universities and Scholasticism strengthened the intellectual foundations of papal power. Monastic reform added to papal power by giving the pope many zealous monks, who were his obedient servants. It is doubtful whether the papacy has ever exercised such absolute power over all phases of life as it did in medieval Europe during this era. However, it would soon find nationalism in France and England and conciliarism harder to handle.

I. GREGORY VII
ASSERTS PAPAL SUPREMACY

A. The Power Behind the Papal Throne

The pontificates of Gregory VII and Innocent III easily dominate the history of the medieval papacy. Both men were unwilling to accept the idea that God had given the pope and the temporal ruler coordinate sovereignty over the souls and bodies of men. The pope would not accept the idea that he derived his control over men's souls from the temporal ruler to whom God had given sovereignty, and the ruler would not willingly consent to the idea that he exercised sovereignty over men's bodies by a gracious grant of power from the pope. No subsequent pope has ever been able to enforce this last claim as successfully as these two popes did. Hildebrand (ca. 1021–85) laid the foundations on which Innocent was able, at a much later date, to build in making claims to supreme power.

Hildebrand's career readily divides itself into two periods. He was the power behind the papal throne for over twenty years before he became pope in 1073, and from 1073 until his death in 1085 he exercised the powers that he had obtained for the popes while he was a humble supporter of

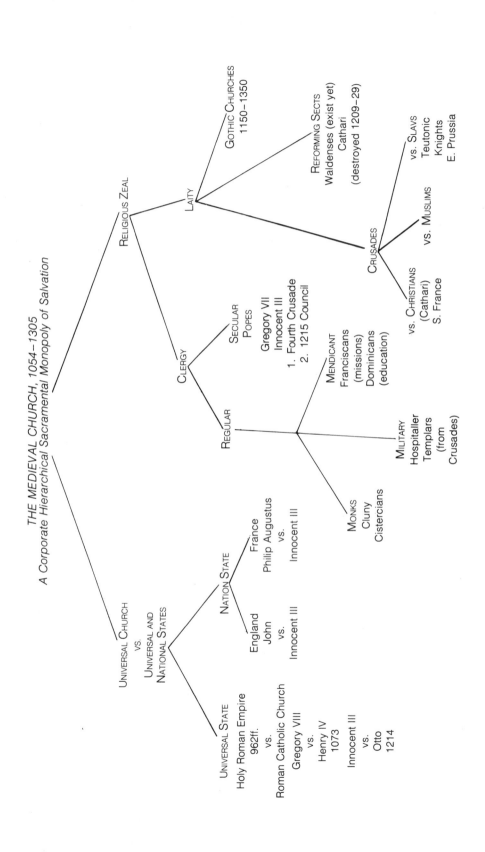

THE MEDIEVAL CHURCH, 1054–1305
A Corporate Hierarchical Sacramental Monopoly of Salvation

RELIGIOUS ZEAL

LAITY

GOTHIC CHURCHES
1150–1350

REFORMING SECTS
Waldenses (exist yet)
Cathari
(destroyed 1209–29)

CRUSADES

vs. SLAVS
Teutonic
Knights
E. Prussia

vs. MUSLIMS

vs. CHRISTIANS
(Cathari)
S. France

CLERGY

SECULAR
POPES

Gregory VII
Innocent III
1. Fourth Crusade
2. 1215 Council

MENDICANT
Franciscans
(missions)
Dominicans
(education)

REGULAR

MILITARY
Hospitaller
Templars
(from
Crusades)

MONKS
Cluny
Cistercians

UNIVERSAL CHURCH
vs.
UNIVERSAL AND
NATIONAL STATES

NATION STATE

France
Philip Augustus
vs.
Innocent III

England
John
vs.
Innocent III

UNIVERSAL STATE
Holy Roman Empire
962ff.
vs.
Roman Catholic Church
Gregory VIII
vs.
Henry IV
1073
Innocent III
vs.
Otto
1214

the papacy. He was able to influence the formulation of papal policy under five popes before he finally became pope.

This small ungainly man with a weak voice had all the zeal of the best of the reformers of the Cluniac monasteries, with whose program of reform he sympathized. He also opposed simony, clerical marriage, and lay investiture.

Leo IX gave Hildebrand his chance to become the power behind the papal throne by Leo's selection of him and other good men from outside Rome to fill important positions in the papal curia. About the beginning of the fourth century certain churches in Rome and its environs had been designated as exclusive sites for baptisms. Pastors of these churches became known as cardinal priests. The division of Rome into districts for works of charity had been made somewhat earlier, and the priests of these areas were known as cardinal deacons. Bishops near Rome were known as cardinal bishops. These men were the nucleus of what was to become the college of cardinals. Hildebrand was placed in charge of finances of the Roman see and thus became a cardinal.

Hildebrand exercised still greater power during the rule of Nicholas II (1058–61), when he helped to have ecclesiastical legislation passed that took the power of electing the pope out of the hands of the populace of the Roman bishopric. The bishops of Rome had been elected from the earliest time by popular vote, although the emperors of the Holy Roman Empire had often interfered in elections, and in the days of Hildebrand the aristocracy of Rome had come to exercise corrupt control over the elections. At the Lateran Council of 1059, Nicholas, counseled by Humbert and Hildebrand, had the method of electing popes changed so that Roman lay aristocratic or German imperial influence might be eliminated. When a pope died, the cardinal bishops would meet to consider his successor. They would then consult the cardinal priests and cardinal deacons. Only then were the people of the Roman bishopric to be permitted to vote on the nominee of the cardinals. For all practical purposes, this put the election of the pope under the control of the college of cardinals. A clergyman from anywhere in the Roman Catholic church might be selected as pope, and, in case of unrest, the election might be held outside of Rome. The new pope was to take office immediately after his election. This change in electoral procedure placed the choice of the pope within the power of the clergy and eliminated lay control.[1] The significance of this legislation for the rise of papal power must not be overlooked.

B. Pope Gregory VII

Hildebrand was unanimously elected as Pope Gregory VII in 1073 as a result of the people shouting, "Let Hildebrand be bishop." He was now in a position to work directly for his ideal of a theocracy in which temporal as well as spiritual power would be exercised by the pope as the vice-regent of God. He wanted no civil power to dominate the Roman church; instead, the church was to control the civil power. For this reason, he dedicated himself to the abolition of lay investiture, the practice by which clerical leaders received the symbols of their office from their feudal lord, who was usually a layman. He was also interested in the abolition of simony and the enforcement of clerical celibacy as the best way to reform the Roman church.

This ideal of papal supremacy within the Roman church and over temporal rulers is clearly developed in the *Dictatus Papae*, a document that was found *among* the letters of Hildebrand after his death. Even if Cardinal Deusdedit, who is often credited with its authorship, wrote it, the document clearly expresses Gregory's ideal for the papacy. It made the most sweeping claims for papal supremacy that have thus far been noticed. It averred that the Roman church owed its foundation to "God alone"; that its pontiff was "alone to be called universal"; that he had full power over all bishops; that only his feet should be kissed by "all princes"; that he could "depose emperors"; and that he might absolve subjects of evil temporal rulers "from their allegiance." The peak of papal pretension to supremacy was reached in the twenty-second article of the *Dictatus* with the statement that there had never been error in the Roman church and that, according to the Bible, it would never err.[2] Gregory was fully prepared to enforce these claims to temporal as well as spiritual supremacy. He asserted that countries such as England, Hungary, Russia, and Spain had been put under the control of Peter and his successors.

While Gregory warred successfully against clerical marriages and simony, the claims of the *Dictatus* indicated that his greatest problem would be to bring temporal rulers under his control. The major struggle of his pontificate, the struggle over the question of lay investiture, was a heritage from his predecessor, Alexander II. The important archbishopric of Milan was vacant, and the emperor of the Holy Roman Empire, Henry IV, selected a man named Godfrey to fill the office. The electoral body of the archbishopric, however, chose a man named Atto. Alexander II recognized Atto, and just before he died he excommunicated Godfrey. His successor, Hildebrand, gladly took up the struggle with Henry. In 1075 a Roman synod forbade any high clergyman to receive investiture to a church office from a layman.

Henry also was ready for the struggle with the spiritual power of the papacy, but he had not been schooled to discipline himself. This flaw led him to take unwise courses of action in the struggle with the pope, and he soon faced the rebellious feudal lords of Saxony who resented his attempts to create a centralized state in Germany. After making a temporary peace with the Saxon nobles, Henry, five of whose councilors had been excommunicated by Gregory in 1075 for simony, called a council in January 1076 at Worms. The council rejected papal authority.[3] Gregory met this bitter denunciation and rejection of his authority by excommunicating Henry and releasing all his subjects from allegiance to him.[4] This was as bold a step as any pope had ever taken in a dispute with the temporal power, but Henry's weakness at home gave Gregory hopes of success.

In the fall of 1076, Henry's Saxon and other enemies declared that if he did not get release from Gregory's sentence of excommunication against him, they would depose him. They also invited Gregory to a synod that

This illustration from the Chronicle of Otto of Freising represents the controversy between Henry IV and Gregory VII over lay investiture. From left to right are Henry IV; Guibert, the anti-pope whom Henry set up; and Gregory VII, being driven out by the sword.

was to meet at Augsburg in the winter. Faced with the danger of losing his throne and humiliation within his own realm if Gregory came to Augsburg, Henry capitulated and, with his wife and his baby son, crossed the Alps in the winter of 1077 to meet Gregory at Canossa. It was a difficult journey; and when Henry finally reached Canossa, Gregory let him stand barefoot in the snow outside the gates of the palace on three successive days before he would admit him to his presence. He then released him from his sentence of excommunication.

Though the greatest ruler in Christendom was thus humiliated by the pope, Henry gained much by his submission, for he had kept Gregory from coming to a meeting at Augsburg and had defeated his German foes. The struggle continued throughout the remainder of Gregory's pontificate. Gregory later excommunicated and deposed Henry a second time; but, with Germany supporting him, Henry invaded Italy and selected Wibert as pope. After he was crowned by Wibert,

Henry left Italy. Gregory then asked the Normans of southern Italy to help him. They did, but they also pillaged in the area around Rome, and Gregory was forced to flee to Salerno. There this great pope died in exile because, according to him, he "loved righteousness, and hated iniquity."

The warfare over lay investiture continued until a compromise agreement was made in the Concordat of Worms between Emperor Henry V and Pope Calixtus II in 1122. Free elections of church officers by churchmen were to be held in the presence of the king. The ring and staff, symbols of spiritual power, were to be given to church officials by the pope or his agent, and the church official was to take an oath of loyalty to the temporal ruler who happened to be his feudal overlord. The Roman Catholic church had the better of the king in spite of the compromise reached[5] because it had at least asserted equality with the state and had freed itself of imperial control in Italy. In addition, by his enforcement of clerical celibacy after the ban on clerical marriage in 1074, Gregory had prevented the clergy from degenerating into a hereditary cast and had created a class of men loyal to their spiritual superior, the pope. This settlement solved the issue of lay investiture. Though he died in exile, Gregory had done his work, and later popes built on the foundations that he had laid.

II. PAPAL SUPREMACY UNDER INNOCENT III

Elected as pope in 1198, Innocent III (1161–1216) brought the medieval papacy to the zenith of its power. He was the son of a Roman noble and was given a fine education in theology at Paris and in law at Bologna. His personal humility and piety were balanced by vigor, common sense, and a strong sense of the moral force that the papacy had.

Innocent believed that he was "the vicar of Christ," with supreme authority on earth. He believed that kings and princes derived their authority from him and that he could therefore excommunicate, depose them, or lay an interdict, which forbade the clergy to perform any but the most essential services of the church, upon their state. He believed that God had given the successor of Peter the task of "ruling the whole world" as well as the church. The pope stood above man and below God. The state should be related to the church as the moon is to the sun. The moon shines by the reflected light of the sun; the state was to bask in the glory of the papacy and derive its power from the pope.[6] It is little wonder that, with this view of his authority and all the power and prestige of the papacy under his control, Innocent was able to bring the rulers of the rising nation states of England and France under his control and to defeat the emperor of the Holy Roman Empire.

The position of the papacy had been further strengthened by the publication of an authoritative edition of the canon law of the Roman church about 1140 by Gratian, a teacher monk at Bologna. This edition, known as the *Decretum*, provided a complete statement of canon law that could be used in all the courts of the Roman church. It must be remembered that Roman law, which was the foundation on which canon law was built, supported the idea of centralization of authority in one individual. The pope made full use of this system to buttress his authority and to find legally trained administrators.

A. Temporal Vs. Spiritual Rulers

Innocent III quickly took up the challenge of the rulers of the rising nation-states of France and England and of the Holy Roman Empire after his accession to the chair of Peter. He used his power first against Philip Augustus of France in order that he might demonstrate that not even a king could flout the moral law of God concerning marriage. Philip had married Ingeborg of Denmark after the death of his first wife in 1193. When his bride came to France, he took a dislike to her and claimed that he had been bewitched. He forced the French bishops to annul the marriage and he took Agnes into his home as his wife. Ingeborg appealed to the pope for redress. Innocent thereupon ordered Philip to put away Agnes and to restore Ingeborg to her place as his lawful wife. When Philip refused to do so,

Innocent placed France under an interdict in 1200. The interdict, which affected everyone in the nation, closed all churches, except for the baptism of infants and the granting of extreme unction to the dying; forbade the celebration of the mass, except for those who were sick or dying; and banned burial in the consecrated ground. The priest was not allowed to preach except in the open air.[7] The uproar that the interdict created all over France forced Philip to submit to the pope, and with bad grace he sent Agnes away and brought Ingeborg back into the palace as his wife. Ingeborg's life was still not happy, but Innocent, by the use of spiritual weapons had forced the ruler of one of the great new nation-states to obey the moral law.

Between 1205 and 1213 Innocent was able to defeat John of England in a contest over the election of an archbishop to the vacant archbishopric of Canterbury. Both the archbishop, elected by the clergy of the archbishopric, and the nominee forced on them by John were set aside by Innocent when the question of his confirmation of the appointment arose. He appointed Stephen Langton instead. John refused to accept Langton. Innocent then excommunicated John in 1209, after placing an interdict upon England in 1208. John was forced to humble himself because the English were opposed to him, and Philip of France, at the invitation of the pope, was only too happy to have an excuse to invade England. John acknowledged in 1212 that he held his kingdom as the feudal vassal of the pope and agreed to pay a thousand marks annually to the pope.[8] This payment was not finally repudiated until the time of the English Reformation.

Having successfully humiliated the rulers of the two most important emerging national states, Innocent III decided that it was time to deal with the problem of the ruler of the Holy Roman Empire. In 1202 he asserted the right of the pope to approve or disapprove the emperor elected by the German electors of the empire.[9] The compromise of Worms had created what was an uneasy armistice between emperor and pope, and the Italian people were anxious to cooperate with the pope to end imperial interference by the emperor in Italy. Henry VI, emperor between 1190 and 1197, had married a Norman princess named Constance. Through his marriage to her, he laid claim to Sicily as part of his dominion. This gave him control of lands to the north and south of the papal states. His son, Frederick, was made king of Sicily, and Innocent was made his guardian after the death of Constance. When Otto IV forgot the promises that he had made to Innocent at the time of his coronation as Holy Roman Emperor, Innocent supported the claims of Frederick to the imperial throne and was able to secure his election to that office as Emperor Frederick II in 1212. Innocent then called in the armies of Philip II of France and defeated Otto at Bouvines in 1214.

Thus, by clever political maneuvering, Innocent had dictated the imperial succession. But, while his reign marked the peak of medieval papal power, the great pope had unwittingly created a problem for his successors. Twice, in the case of John of England and Otto of the empire, Innocent had asked the king of France to help him win his struggle. By so doing he had destroyed the power of the Holy Roman Empire and left his successors without a balance against the powerful French state. Before this time the pope could play the French king and the emperor against each other. One does not wonder that later Boniface VIII suffered humiliation at the hands of the rulers of the powerful nation-states of England and France.

B. Innocent III as a Crusader

The Fourth Crusade, to recover Palestine from the Muslims by capturing Egypt as a base for later actions, was instigated by Innocent and several French priests. It was largely a French crusade under papal direction. When boats were needed to transport the Crusaders to their objective, the Doge of Venice agreed to supply transports and supplies in return for a large sum of money. The Crusaders came to Venice but without enough money. Thereupon the Venetians asked their aid to regain Zara, which had once belonged to Venice, from the Christian king of Hungary. After the sack of Zara, the Crusaders sailed to Constantinople instead of Alexandria and, after a siege, captured the city in 1204. A Latin kingdom, which lasted until 1261, was set up at Constantinople. Although Innocent had not officially sanctioned the diversion of the crusading Christians against their fellow Christians in Zara and Constantinople, he accepted the results because it brought the Eastern empire under his control and because Constantinople could serve as a base for the Fifth Crusade that he was planning against the Muslims. The Eastern empire as well as the rulers of the West now were under his control.[10] He stood forth as the leading figure in medieval Europe.

Innocent also sponsored a crusade under the leadership of Simon de Montfort against the Albigenses of southern France in 1208. The Albigenses were members of a heretical sect known as the Cathari. Because they claimed their beliefs were based on the Bible, the Roman church later forbade the people to possess the Bible. The crusade got under way in 1209 and virtually exterminated the Cathari in southern France after many bloody battles. This crusade was strongly supported by both the Dominican and Franciscan orders. Heretics as well as temporal rulers had to bow to the supreme head of the Roman church.

C. The Fourth Lateran Council of 1215

Having abolished heresy by force, Innocent attempted to make a positive statement of truth. In order to do this, he called a general council in Rome. This council, known as the Fourth Lateran Council, made an annual confession to a priest by all the laymen mandatory and declared that all must be at the Mass at least at Easter. The declaration of the dogma of transubstantiation, which all members of the Roman church had to accept as authentic doctrine from this time on, was more important. It was the teaching that the substance of the bread and wine became the actual body and blood of Christ after the words of consecration by the priest. The accidents or outward form of the elements still appeared to the senses as bread and wine, but a metaphysical change had taken place in the substances so that the bread and wine became respectively the body and blood of Christ. Thus the priest performed a sacrifice each time he held a mass. Small wonder that medieval men feared the clergy, who had power to give or withhold the life-giving sacraments.

III. DECLINE OF PAPAL POWER UNDER BONIFACE VIII

The pontificate of Innocent III marked the peak of papal power in Europe. Sordid stories of nepotism, simony, drunkenness, and neglect of their people by the priests antagonized many in the century following Innocent's death in 1216. Rulers of such rising nation-states as England and France were more inclined to dispute with the papacy because they had a national army and a wealthy middle class to back them. The humiliation of the Holy Roman Empire by Innocent III left the pope with little support against the French ruler.

If the pontificate of Innocent III was the zenith of papal power in the Middle Ages, that of Boniface VIII between 1294 and 1303 may be said to be the nadir of papal power. On more than one occasion Boniface suffered humiliation from the temporal power. The greatest struggle took place between Boniface and Philip the Fair of France. To help pay the costs of a war between their two countries Philip of France and Edward I of England taxed the clergy. In 1296 Boniface issued the bull *Clericis Laicos*, [11] which forbade the priest to pay taxes to a temporal ruler without papal consent. Edward met the challenge by outlawing the clergy and by having Parliament pass an act forbidding them to acknowledge the pope's claims to temporal power

in England. Philip met the challenge by forbidding the export of money from France to Italy and thus deprived the papacy of its French revenues.

The struggle between Philip and Boniface was renewed in 1301 when Philip arrested a papal legate for treason against the king. When the pope ordered Philip to release him and to come to Rome to explain his conduct, Philip called the French legislative body, the Estates General, which upheld Philip's resistance to the demands of Boniface. Boniface then issued the papal bull known as *Unam Sanctum*. He claimed that "neither salvation nor remission of sins" could be found outside the Roman church, that the pope as head of the Roman church had spiritual and temporal authority over all, and that submission to the pope was "necessary to salvation." [12] These ideas were repeated in *Quanto Conficiamur* issued by Pious IX in 1863. Boniface could not, however, back up his claims with armies; and Philip temporarily made Boniface a prisoner to prevent his proclamation of excommunication of the king.

Clement V became pope after the death of Boniface, and he transferred the papal court in 1309 to Avignon, where he and his court were under pressure from the king whose territories were all around them. This was Canossa in reverse with a vengeance. The removal of the papal seat from Rome in 1309 was the beginning of the era known as the Babylonian Captivity of the papacy. Until 1377 the papacy was under the influence of the French monarchs and lost the tremendous moral and temporal power it had had in Europe during the pontificate of Innocent III.

SUGGESTED READING

The readings cited at the end of chapter 16 are also useful for the period from 1054 to 1305.

Clayton, Joseph. **Pope Innocent III and His Times.** *Milwaukee: Bruce, 1941. Though written from the Roman Catholic viewpoint, this is an interesting biography of that great medieval pope.*

Cowdrey, H. E. J. **The Cluniacs and the Gregorian Reform.** *Oxford: Clarendon University Press, 1970.*

Emerton, Ephraim, ed. **The Correspondence of Pope Gregory VII.** *New York: Columbia University Press, 1932. Much insight into the activities of Gregory VII can be gained from this volume.*

MacDonald, Allan J. **Hildebrand.** *London: Methuen, 1932.*

Stevens, R. W. **Hildebrand and His Times.** *New York: Randolph, ca. 1888. This little work is a useful summary of the imperial papal conflict with the empire, with an emphasis on Hildebrand's work.*

Chapter 22

Crusaders and Reformers

Christianity in western Europe was marked by bursts of crusading and reforming zeal during the twelfth and thirteenth centuries. Expeditions of Christian knights fought for religious ends instead of private gain or political ends. Between 632 and 750 Muslims had aggressively threatened the West, but between 1095 and 1291 crusades against Muslims in Europe and Asia and heretics in Europe were carried on, for the most part under the aegis of the Roman church. The Cistercian, the Dominican, and the Franciscan orders appeared as reform movements to rejuvenate medieval monasticism. Spiritual zeal spurred laymen to engage in the Albigensian and Waldensian movements. The energy expended in the building of the great Gothic cathedrals of Europe was also a testimony to the spiritual zeal of the era.

I. THE CROSS VS. THE CRESCENT, 1095–1291

Christians had carried on crusades against the Moors in Spain and the Muslims in Sicily for some time before the Crusades to the Holy Land. This Western wing of the crusading movement was aimed at expelling the Muslims from territory that they held in western Europe. The Crusades to Palestine, which were the Eastern and great wing of this crusading movement against the Muslims, had for their aim the recapture of Palestine from the more brutal Muslim Seljuk Turks. The whole movement may be characterized as a holy war against the enemies of the Cross by the spiritual forces of Western Christendom. Already in 1074 Gregory VII had called for a crusade against the Muslims in Palestine who were harassing the Eastern empire and who were persecuting pilgrims,[1] but the struggle with Henry IV over lay investiture kept him from being the pope who started the Crusades.

A. Causes of the Crusades

One should always remember that although the Crusaders had economic

219

or political interests, the primary motive of the Crusades was religious. The Seljuk Turks, who had replaced the Arabs, were much more fanatical and brutal than those whom they had replaced, and European pilgrims were subjected to persecution when they landed in Palestine. Moreover, Alexius, the emperor at Constantinople, had asked the aid of western European Christians against these Muslim Asiatic invaders who were threatening the security of his kingdom. This religious motivation gave the Crusades the nature of a mass pilgrimage to Palestine. The movement of people was comparable in its scope to the barbarian migrations into the Roman Empire shortly before its fall. It has been estimated that nearly a million people took part in the activities associated with the First Crusade. The movement was also an attempt to solve the problem of who should control the Near East, a problem that has always been a matter of concern to Europe.

Economic considerations led many to take the Cross. Famine was a common phenomenon in western Europe in the century preceding the Crusades. The Venetians were interested in the stimulation of the trickle of trade with the Near East; and the Normans were apparently as much interested in plunder or setting up feudal fiefs as they were in rescuing the holy places from the Muslims.

The love of military adventure, which was sanctified by the Roman church, also drew many of the feudal nobles and knights into the armies of the Crusades. Others took the Cross to escape from domestic boredom or the punishment for crimes.

B. The Crusades

The direct cause of the First Crusade was the preaching of a crusade against the Muslims by Urban II at a synod at Clermont in November 1095. He urged the Crusade as an answer to

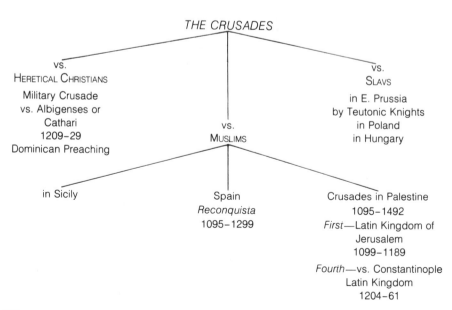

Alexius' appeal for aid, but in Urban's mind the grander concept of the rescue of the holy places from Muslim hands took priority over aid to the eastern Empire.[2] The assembled crowd, mostly Frenchmen, replied with an enthusiastic *Deus vult* (God wills it) to the proposal of Urban, who was a Frenchman.

The enthusiasm was so great that masses of peasants, aroused by the preaching of Peter the Hermit and Walter the Penniless, started to march through Germany, Hungary, and the Balkans in 1096 to Palestine. Because they were unorganized and undisciplined, the emperor at Constantinople was glad to let those still alive cross the straits to Asia Minor, where they were either massacred by the Turks or taken prisoners and sold as slaves.

This unorganized lay crusade of French peasants was only a prelude to the organized effort of the First Crusade led by nobles from France, Belgium, and Norman Italy. The various armies and their leaders arrived at Constantinople by the spring of 1097. The Crusaders took Nicaea after a short siege and by fall found themselves before Antioch, which they captured in the spring of 1098. Finally, in June 1099 they captured Jerusalem. These Crusaders, who had been feudal lords back in Europe, succumbed to the temptation to set up feudal fiefs in areas they had captured, and many of the castles in the Near East date from this period. Jerusalem and the surrounding country was finally organized into the kingdom of Jerusalem under Godfrey of Bouillon, who had been the moral leader of the Crusade. In this fashion the objectives of the First Crusade were achieved. The pressure against Constantinople

by the Muslims was relaxed, and Jerusalem was again in the hands of Christian rulers. The Knights Templars and Hospitallers were organized to provide protection and aid to pilgrims and to fight the Muslims.

The occasion for the Second Crusade was the Muslim threat to the northeastern flank of the kingdom of Jerusalem after the Muslims had captured the feudal fief of Edessa. In 1146 the saintly mystic, Bernard of Clairvaux, preached the Second Crusade. The king of France and the emperor of the Holy Roman Empire led the crusade, but it proved to be a failure. This failure was followed by the recapture of Jerusalem by Saladin, the Muslim leader, in 1187.

The Third Crusade (1189–92), known as the King's Crusade, was under the leadership of Philip Augustus of France, Richard of England, and Emperor Frederick. Frederick was accidently drowned on the way to Palestine, and Philip Augustus after a quarrel with Richard went home. Richard went on fighting. Although he was unsuccessful in recapturing Jerusalem, he did get Saladin to agree to give pilgrims access to Jerusalem. Forced to be content with this, Richard made his way home to England.

Innocent III, who was anxious to retrieve the failure of the Third Crusade, ardently preached the need of a crusade, the Fourth, to capture Egypt as a base for operations against Palestine.[3] An important result of this crusade was that the Greek church and the Eastern empire were again made subject to the pope from 1204 to 1261, after a century and a half of religious independence. This crusade helped to weaken the Eastern empire and to deepen the hatred between

Latin and Greek Christians (see chap. 21, p. 216).

Frederick II, the leader of the Sixth Crusade, was successful in negotiating a treaty that brought Jerusalem, Bethlehem, Nazareth, and a corridor to the sea under control of the Christians; but the Muslims kept the Mosque of Omar. Jerusalem was once again temporarily under a Christian king. But, in spite of several later crusades, the territories captured by the Crusaders fell once more into the hands of the Saracens, who had succeeded the Seljuk Turks as overlords in Palestine.

The Children's Crusade of 1212 was the saddest incident in the history of the Crusades. Children of France and Germany, led by two boys not yet in their teens named Stephen and Nicholas, marched across southern Europe to Italy, supposing that the purity of their lives would bring them success in a venture in which their more sinful parents had failed. Many perished on the way, and the rest were sold into slavery in Egypt. The crusading era ended with the fall of Acre to the Muslims in 1291.

C. Consequences of the Crusades

The Crusades had important political and social results in western Europe. Feudalism was weakened because many knights and nobles who went as Crusaders never returned and because many sold their lands to peasants or wealthy middle-class townsmen to raise money for the Crusades. Cities controlled by feudal lords often were able to buy charters providing them with self-government. Kings were able to centralize their control with the aid of the middle class, which favored a strong centralized nation-state under a monarch in order to provide the conditions of security and order so essential to business.

Some of the religious results were that the papacy enhanced its prestige during the Crusades, but the channeling of the energies of nations into the Crusades led to a rise of national feeling that eventually weakened the papal power. The creation of the Latin Kingdom of Constantinople deepened the religious antagonism between East and West and weakened the Eastern kingdom so that its eventual fall in 1453 was assured. The emergence of the military orders gave the pope additional bands of loyal monks.

Persuasion replaced power as a technique to deal with the Muslims. Raymond Lull (ca. 1235–1315), of a noble Minorcan family, learned Arabic and the Arab culture from a slave whom he bought for that purpose. So that prospective missionaries to the Muslims might know the Arab language, literature, and culture, he set up a training college in 1276 at Miramir, in southeast Spain, and created books of apologetic arguments to win Muslims. He was martyred in North Africa.

Economic results were equally important. The Italian cities, led by Venice, started trade with the Near East as soon as possible after the successful First Crusade. The trade in luxury products from the Near East, such as silks, spices, and perfumes, laid the economic foundations for the patronage of art in Renaissance Italy. People who returned from the Crusades wanted to buy the luxuries that they had seen in the Near East.

Although the Crusades failed to accomplish the permanent freedom of Jerusalem from Muslim control, they did bring many benefits to western Europe and helped to dissipate its cultural provincialism. Arabic learning, science, and literature were brought to western Europe and were studied by the Scholastics, who tried to synthesize this learning with Christian revelation.

II. MONASTIC REFORM

Many new monastic organizations emerged in the twelfth century as an expression of the same spiritual zeal that displayed itself in the Crusades and that was also manifested in the great wave of cathedral building. The reforming zeal of the Cluniac movement of the tenth century disappeared as the order became wealthy; but new reforming groups, such as the Cistercians, arose to do in the twelfth century what Cluny had done in the tenth century. The orders of Dominicans and Franciscans came into being to meet the problem of winning Muslims and heretics to the faith by persuasion, through education, or by missionary effort. The spiritual zeal of the Crusaders resulted in the founding of lay military orders. All these orders willingly subjected themselves to the papacy, the vow of obedience including obedience to the pope as well as to the abbot or head of the order. The movement also satisfied the medieval desire for the ascetic life and provided those interested in learning with an opportunity to engage in scholarly studies.

Attempts were made to reform the Benedictine order during the eleventh century by a renewed emphasis on that movement's earlier asceticism, which had expressed itself in work

and prayer. The decentralization of the older order, which gave autonomy to the local abbot, was replaced by centralization of authority. The Carthusian monasteries, which were organized by Bruno in 1084, followed this pattern.

The order of Augustinian canons began as an attempt to bring the canons, secular clergymen of a cathedral who aided the bishop in his work, under the rules of the regular clergy. The Rule of Saint Augustine was adopted, and common dress and community of goods and residence were adopted about 1119.

A. The Cistercian Order

The Cistercian order was founded at Citeaux in France in 1098 by a Benedictine monk named Robert, who wanted to correct the lack of discipline in contemporary monasticism. The Cistercian monks differed from those of Cluny by their greater emphasis on ascetic self-denial, the simplicity of the architecture of their buildings, and centralized organization. The abbots of the daughter monasteries met with the abbot of Citeaux in a yearly assembly to consider the problems of the group. Though the abbot of Citeaux exercised authority over the sister houses, he did not exercise the power of the abbot of Cluny but presided over an annual council of abbots. Whereas the Cluniacs were mainly aristocratic in background, the Cistercians attracted more adherents from the peasant class. The Cistercians also gave more attention to agriculture than to scholastic pursuits. Their reforming program made such an appeal that the order included 530 houses by 1200, and from that point it grew rapidly. It brought a fresh spirit of zeal to a decadent monasticism.

Much of the fame of the organization was a result of the efforts of Bernard (1090–1153) of the monastery at Clairvaux. He was of noble birth and owed much to his godly mother, Aletta. He founded the monastery at Clairvaux in 1115 at the age of twenty-five and, with the aid of thirty companions and his five brothers, he was able to make it one of the most famous centers of the Cistercian order.[4] Though he was humble and inclined to a mystical life, Bernard could be practical and courageous. In the heyday of his rule at Clairvaux, the pope as well as the rulers were glad to listen to his counsel. His preaching, which emphasized the suffering of pilgrims to Palestine and the profanation of the holy places, was largely responsible for the Second Crusade. His great ability in homiletics and his delight in mysticism are revealed in his *Homilies on the Song of Solomon*. His mystical tendencies produced such great hymns as "Jesus, Thou Joy of Loving Hearts" and "Jesus, the Very Thought of Thee." Not deficient in theology, when Abelard's conceptualist views seemed to be subverting the foundation of theology, Bernard came forth as the champion of the orthodox position. His intellectual, mystical, oratorical, and practical abilities made him the spiritual leader and second founder of the Cistercian movement, as well as a power in the affairs of church and state in medieval Europe.

B. The Military Orders

The Crusades gave rise to a military type of monasticism that combined the art of war with the monastic life.

The order of the Knights of Saint John, or the Knights Hospitallers, was founded early in the twelfth century to defend pilgrims and to care for the ill. In the early period of its history, it was the medieval equivalent to the modern Red Cross. The monks took the threefold monastic vow but did not give up the profession of arms. In fact, the order later became a strictly military organization to defend the Holy Land from the infidels. The Knights Templars, whose name was derived from their headquarters near the temple in Jerusalem, was founded as an order about 1118. The order was recognized officially in 1128 and brought under the Cistercian rule for the monastic life in 1130. It was primarily pledged to defend the Holy Land from the onslaughts of the Muslims. The order was dissolved in 1312 because it was dabbling too much in French politics. Subject only to the papacy and dedicated to the advance of its interests, these two organizations formed a standing army of monk-knights.

C. The Friars

The friars represented still another type of twelfth-century reforming monasticism. They took vows of poverty, chastity, and obedience as did the monks; but instead of living in monastic communities to pray and labor apart from the secular world, they went among the people of the cities to help them and to preach to them in the vernacular. The monasteries had property, and the monks supported themselves by work; but the friars were supported by the alms and gifts that the people gave them. They were more directly under the leadership of the pope than the orders before the twelfth century had been. In addition to the more important Franciscan and Dominican Friars, the Carmelite and Austin Friars were organized in this period.

The Franciscan order was founded by Francis of Assisi (1182–1226), the pleasure-loving son of a rich merchant. He was converted during an illness and left his father's home to consecrate himself to poverty and the service of God. Gathering several young men of like interest around himself,[5] he drew up a rule to govern their lives. This rule involved poverty, chastity, and obedience; but obedience to the papacy was emphasized.[6] The organization was approved verbally by Innocent III in 1209. The Franciscan order became so popular that in 1212 the pope permitted a girl of eighteen named Clare to organize a companion order for women known as the Poor Clares. In 1221 the Tertiaries, or third order, was founded for those laymen and laywomen who lived by the rules of the order but could not leave their secular life because of family or business ties.

The name *friar*, derived from the Latin word for brother, *frater*, was synonymous not only with spiritual development but also service to the Roman church. The Franciscans have always been in the van of the missionary effort of the Roman church. During his lifetime Francis preached in Spain and Egypt. Others also went to the Near East and even to the Far East. John de Monte Corvino (1246–1328) reached Peking before 1300.[7] He baptized six thousand in Peking alone and had thirty thousand converts by 1300, but the Ming dynasty destroyed the church in 1368. When Spain and France opened up the lands of the Western Hemisphere, most of the missionary work in the new world was done by the Franciscans. The ruins of the eighteenth-century Franciscan missions along the King's Road in California testify to their activity.

As the order grew, it became more centralized under a general appointed by the pope. The order also had many scholars, such as Roger Bacon, Bonaventura, Duns Scotus, and William of Ockham. Bacon became a pioneer in scientific experiment, and the ideas of Ockham concerning the nature of reality had an influence on the spiritual development of Luther and strengthened the experimental approach to life during the Renaissance.

The Dominicans were also mendicants, that is, members of a religious order who lived by alms. Whereas the Franciscans were great missionaries, winning men by example and emotional appeal, the Dominicans were great scholars who tried to win men from heresy by intellectual persuasion. The appeal of the Dominicans was to man's head, that of the Franciscans to his heart.

Dominic (1170–1221), a Spanish priest of noble birth, on a visit to southern France pitied the Albigensian heretics of that area and developed the idea of fighting heresy with the weapons of austerity of life, simplicity, and argument. For this reason the Dominican "Hounds of the Lord" emphasized preaching. The Dominican order was approved by the pope in 1216, and a highly centralized organization was developed. Each of the separate groups was under a prior who, in turn, was subject to a prior in charge of a province. Over the general convocation of the order was placed a master-general, who was responsible to the pope. They were missionaries and educators.

Thomas Aquinas and his teacher, Albertus Magnus, were the outstanding scholars of the order. The present system of theology of the Roman Catholic church was developed by Aquinas. The Dominicans also engaged in missionary activity. It was the Dominican order that in 1233 was given the task of running the machinery of the Inquisition after it was organized. Several of the leading mystics, such as Meister Eckhart and John Tauler, were Dominican friars; and Savonarola, the famous Florentine reformer, belonged to this order.

The friars strengthened religion among the people of the parishes by their unselfish service. Their good deeds and preaching in the vernacular were practical manifestations of the church that the people readily understood. In fact, preaching was restored to its proper place in the Roman church by the friars. Directly responsible to the pope, they tended to strengthen the power of the papacy over local bishops and lay rulers. Both orders provided many fine missionaries to all parts of the world. Franciscan hospitals ministered to the physical as well as to the spiritual needs of the people. Nearly ten thousand friars died while ministering to the people during the Black Death of 1348 and 1349. Above all, they made tremendous contributions to the field of learning, particularly in the realm of theology, where the name of Thomas Aquinas stands out as the best scholar of the mendicant movement.

The activities of the Dominicans in operating the Inquisition for the popes is another and blacker side to the pic-

ture. By the middle of the fourteenth century the mendicant movement formed corporations to hold wealth, and the spiritual zeal of the first generation of friars disappeared.

III. LAY REFORMING MOVEMENTS

Unity was the keynote of medieval society; and this unity was achieved by the universal institutions of the Holy Roman Empire, by the hierarchical Roman church and allegiance to it, and by the spiritual standardization of the sacraments and the creeds; but underneath this unity there were always rumblings of dissent. These rumblings were to become at the time of the Reformation a volcanic explosion that would tear asunder the fabric of medieval religion. Unlike the monks and friars, who sought to bring about internal reform, the Cathari or Albigenses, the Waldenses, and other sects arose as an external revolt to purify religion in the late twelfth century. The frequency of corruption in the life and practice of the papal hierarchy and the secular activities of the papacy made many react against the lack of spiritual power that they often saw in their parish churches. More information concerning these medieval sects has been preserved by their enemies than by their friends, and therefore accurate information about them is scarce. Both the Albigenses and the Waldenses sought to return to the purer form of religion they saw in the New Testament. They were forerunners of the Reformation.

A. The Philosophic Albigenses

The Cathari, or Albigenses, so-called because they were most numerous around Albi in southern France, used the New Testament as a basis for their ideas; but the heretical ideas that they formulated resembled the dualistic and ascetic ideas of the Gnostic, Paulician, and Bogomil movements. The Albigenses believed that there was an absolute dualism between the good God, who made the souls of men, and the bad god, who was given a material body after he was cast out of heaven. Following his expulsion, the bad god made the visible world. Consequently matter is evil, and therefore the Cathari (literally, the pure) were opposed to reproduction of the race, to the sacraments, particularly the Mass with its emphasis on the physical presence of Christ in the elements, the doctrines of hell and purgatory, and a physical resurrection. Salvation involved repentance, the rite of *consolamentum*—performed by the laying of hands and the Gospel of John on the head of the candidate—and an ascetic avoidance of marriage, oaths, war, milk, meat, cheese, and eggs. They condemned the use of anything material in worship. The elite, called the *perfecti*, had forgiveness of sins and an assurance of restoration to the kingdom of God. Because flesh cannot inherit heaven, the believers who lacked this rite of *consolamentum* had to receive it before death. The Albigenses, by making the New Testament the authoritative expression of their faith, offered a challenge to the Roman church, which claimed authority, through the lines of popes, from Christ Himself. Persecution and the Albigensian crusade led by Simon de Montfort and sponsored by Innocent III in 1208 were the answers of the medieval Roman church to this affront to its authority.

B. The Puritan Waldenses

The Waldensian movement, which emerged during the last quarter of the twelfth century, was much more like the Protestant and Puritan movements. About 1176 Peter Waldo, a rich merchant of Lyons, read a translation of the New Testament and was so impressed with the claims of Christ that he gave up all his property except enough to feed his family. He then organized a band known as the "Poor Men." They wished to preach as laymen, but they were forbidden to do so by the pope. In 1184 they were excommunicated for their refusal to stop preaching. As is so often the case, a minority desiring reform was forced out of the organized church by a loveless majority who lost the values that such a zealous group might have supplied.

The Waldensians believed that every man should have the Bible in his own tongue and that it should be the final authority for faith and life. Following the example of Christ, they went out by twos, laymen dressed in simple clothes, to preach to the poor in the vernacular. They accepted the standard ecumenical confessions, the Lord's Supper and baptism, and lay ordination to preach and administer the sacraments. Their society had its own clergy, with bishops, priests, and deacons. Waldo was the head of the society up to the time of his death in 1217. Others, known as friends, were secret associates of the Waldensian groups, but they were permitted to remain within the Roman church. The Waldensians anticipated in many respects the ideas of the Protestants of the Reformation. They still exist as an earnest band of about thirty-five thousand believers in northern Italy.

C. The Eschatological Joachimites

Joachim (ca. 1132–1202), a Cistercian monk, believed that the Father was important in the Old Testament period of law stressed by Peter, the Son in the New Testament era of Paul until 1260, and in the era of the Holy Spirit after 1260 a new age of love as seen in John's writings would come after a short period of Antichrist.

The response of the Roman church to these affronts to its authority, especially by the Cathari, was varied. The Dominican friars by preaching made every effort to win the Cathari back to the faith. Another answer was the crusade that practically exterminated the Albigenses in southern France. Still another answer was given at the Synod of Toulouse in 1229. This synod forbade laymen the use of vernacular translations of the Bible. In this way invidious comparisons between the New Testament church and the Roman Catholic church might be avoided. Still another answer was the development of the Inquisition, a secret ecclesiastical court that used torture and withheld the names of accusers in its judgment of heretics and turned them over to the state for punishment in the form of loss of property or burning at the stake. At first the Inquisition was in episcopal hands; but, as the number of heretics increased, the papacy assumed control, and in 1233 Gregory IX commissioned the Dominicans to punish heresy and in this way to eliminate the Cathari.

These procedures for dealing with heresy brutalized the clergy and laymen engaged in dealing with the heretics. Fear of punishment for thought other than that prescribed by the Roman church brought intellectual stagnation. Persecution, however, often brought more people to an acceptance of heretical doctrine. The unwillingness of the Roman Catholic church to meet the need for the spiritual reform desired by the sects tended toward an ossification that made the Reformation inevitable.

The twelfth and thirteenth centuries were marked by movements of internal and external reform. The Cistercian movement, symbolized in the person of Bernard of Clairvaux, and the mendicant movements were attempts to purify the Roman church by a renewal of spiritual zeal. Laymen who attempted to reinstate the Bible as authority found themselves balked in their attempts and therefore set up movements outside the Roman church in order to practice the Christianity that they saw in the Bible. Though the zeal of monk, friar, and crusader was associated with an institution rather than a divine Person, the period was one of spiritual enthusiasm that the Roman church might have put to a more constructive use than she did.

SUGGESTED READING

Numerous volumes of source materials of the period have been edited and are available in most good libraries.

Barker, Ernest. **The Crusades.** *London: Oxford University Press, 1923. This little volume is an excellent manual with a fine bibliography.*

Brundage, James A. **The Crusades.** *Milwaukee: Marquette, 1962. The Crusaders tell their own story through the author's selection of documents.*

Bruno, James S. **The Letters of Saint Bernard of Clairvaux.** *Chicago: Regnery, 1953.*

Coulton, George G. **Five Centuries of Religion.** *4 vols. Cambridge: Cambridge University Press, 1923–50.*

Daniel-Rops, Henri. **Bernard of Clairvaux.** *New York: Hawthorne, 1964.*

Jarrett, Bede. **Life of Saint Dominic 1170–1221.** *Westminster, Md.: Newman, 1955.*

Lamb, Harold. **The Crusades, Iron Men, and Saints.** *New York: Doubleday, 1930. This popular account of the Crusades expresses the spirit of the Crusades.*

Lea, Henry C. **A History of the Inquisition of the Middle Ages.** *3 vols. New York: Harper, 1887. This is a standard work based on scholarly research in the primary documents.*

Runciman, Steven. **A History of the Crusades.** *3 vols. Cambridge: Cambridge University Press, 1951–54. This is an excellent work on the Crusades.*

Setton, Kenneth M., ed. **The History of the Crusades.** *6 vols., 4 completed. Madison: University of Wisconsin Press, 1969–.*

Seward, Desmond. **The Monks of War.** *Hamden, Conn.: Shoestring, 1972.*

Smith, John H. **Francis of Assisi.** *New York: Scribner, 1972.*

Storrs, Richard S. **Bernard of Clairvaux.** *New York: Scribner, 1893. This is a good biography of the outstanding monk of the period.*

Wakefield, Walter L., and Evans, Austin P. **Heresies of the High Middle Ages.** *New York: Columbia University Press, 1969.*

Warner, H. J. **The Albigensian Heresy.** *New York: Russell and Russell, 1967.*

Zwemer, Samuel L. **Raymond Lull.** *New York: Funk and Wagnalls, 1902.*

Chapter 23

Medieval Learning and Worship

The church can practice *diastasis*, i.e., separation from culture, or it can practice synthesis. The Scholastics did the latter. The Scholastic intellectual movement developed between 1050 and 1350 and paralleled the development of the mendicant and heretical movements of the same period. It found a home at first in the cathedral and monastic schools and later, with the rise of universities in the thirteenth century, it dominated the curriculum of European universities. After 1050 the Scholastics replaced the fathers of the church as the main guardians of the truth, and *doctor* became as great a term of honor as *father* had been earlier in the history of the church.

I. SCHOLASTICISM

A. Definition of Scholasticism

The terms *Scholasticism* and *Scholastic* came through the Latin from the Greek word *scholē*, which signifies a place where learning takes place. "Scholastic" was applied to teachers in Charlemagne's court or palace school and to the medieval scholars who used philosophy in the study of religion. These scholars sought to prove existing truth by rational processes rather than to seek new truth. Scholasticism may be defined as the attempt to rationalize theology in order to buttress faith by reason. Theology was to be treated from a philosophical point of view rather than from a biblical point of view. The data of revelation were to be organized systematically by the use of Aristotelian deductive logic and were to be harmonized with the newly rediscovered philosophy of Aristotle. The Scholastics faced a similar problem to that which the church faced in the nineteenth century when the new discoveries of science had to be harmonized with religion. They had to reconcile the general natural philosophy of Aristotle, gained by rational processes, with the special revealed

SCHOOLS OF SCHOLASTICISM

	REALISM	MODERATE REALISM OR CONCEPTUALISM	NOMINALISM
Relation of faith and reason	I believe in order that I may know	I know in order that I may believe	I believe—separated from I know
Nature of reality	*universalia ante rem*	*universalia in re*	*universalia post rem*
Men	Anselm	Aquinas and Abelard	William of Ockham and Roscellinus
Works	Proslogion Monologion	Summa Theologiae	
Modern proponents	Evangelicalism	Roman Catholic Church	Renaissance and Enlightenment

theology of the Bible, accepted by faith.

B. Causes for the Rise of Scholasticism

The major cause for the rise of Scholasticism was the emergence in Europe of the philosophy of Aristotle. Except for some translations of parts of Aristotle's philosophy made in the fifth century by monks, led by Boethius, little was known of his philosophy until Latin translations by William of Moerbeke (1215–86) from Jewish or Arabic sources began to appear in western Europe in the twelfth century. The translations of Aristotle by Averröes (1126–98), the great Arabic philosopher, were introduced into the West through Spain by 1200. About the same time translations by Moses Maimonides (1135–1204), the famous Jewish rabbi and philosopher, were appearing in the West. Men like Alexander of Hales (ca. 1186–1245) welcomed this philosophy and attempted to relate it to theology.

Still another cause for the expansion of the Scholastic movement was the interest of the new mendicant orders in the use of philosophy in the study of revelation. Thomas Aquinas, the greatest Scholastic of all, and Albertus Magnus, his teacher, were Dominicans; and William of Ockham and Bonaventura were Franciscans.

The expansion of the university movement, which began in the twelfth century, provided a home for the new intellectual movement; and the universities rapidly centered their curriculum around the study of theology by the aid of logic and reason. The University of Paris in Abelard's time became the leading center of Scholasticism.

C. Content of Scholasticism

The student of church history must always remember that the Scholastics were not so much seeking truth as they were trying rationally to organize a body of accepted truth so that truth, whether it came by faith from revelation or by reason from philosophy, might be a harmonious whole. The medieval mind sought intellectual as well as political and ecclesiastical unity. The appearance of Aristotelian philosophy in the twelfth century forced men to take up this great task. For the Scholastics the data or content of their study was fixed, authoritative, and absolute. The content of their study was the Bible, the canons and creeds of the ecumenical councils, and the writings of the fathers of the church. The question that they wished to settle involved whether or not the faith was reasonable.

D. Methodology of Scholasticism

Scholastic methodology was as much subjected to the authority of Aristotle's dialectic or logic as the content was to the authoritative theology of the Roman Catholic church. Both content and method were fixed. The modern scientist follows the empirical method of inductive logic and enunciates a general truth on the basis of facts only after he has observed and experimented for a long time. Aristotle's dialectic or logic is deductive rather than inductive and emphasizes the syllogism as the instrument of deductive logic. The deductive thinker starts with a general truth or law that he does not prove but that he takes for granted. He relates this general law to a particular fact and from the relationship between the general law and the particular fact derives a conclusion that in turn becomes a new general law or truth to be related to new facts. This method was taken by the Scholastics from Aristotle. The general truths of philosophy were taken from revealed theology; and using Aristotelian methodology, the Scholastics sought to draw legitimate conclusions in order to develop a harmonious system. Passages from the Bible, the Fathers, the canons and creeds of the councils, and papal decretals were concatenated in logical order.

E. The Schools of Scholasticism

Both in content and method, then, the Scholastics consented to the authority both of the church and of Aristotle. The philosophic framework into which most of the Scholastics may be fitted was based on Greek philosophy and depended on whether a Scholastic followed the general position of Plato or of Aristotle with respect to the problem of the nature of universals or ultimate reality and the relation of faith and reason.

1. *Realism.* Plato had insisted, as did also his master Socrates and Aristotle, that universals, such as church and man, have an objective existence. In contrast to Aristotle, Plato insisted that these universals or Ideas exist apart from particular things or individuals. For example, he believed that there are universals of truth, beauty, and goodness that exist apart from individual human acts of truth, beauty, and goodness. This view was summed up in the Latin phrase *universalia ante rem;* that is, universals exist before created things. A good deed, for example, is simply a shadow or reflection of the reality of goodness that exists ob-

jectively apart from that deed. Plato thus insisted that men must look beyond this life for ultimate reality. Earlier Augustine and now Anselm were the leading thinkers who applied this view to theology. This view is known as realism, which in less temperate realists often became pantheism, which merged everything into the universal.

a. Anselm (ca. 1033–1109), who was born in northern Italy, received his education in the Abbey of Bec. Elected as prior of the abbey, he held that position until he became archbishop of Canterbury in 1093. He fought against the practice of lay investiture, which was practiced by the English kings; but his enduring fame rests on his intellectual activities in theology.

Anselm's idea of the relationship of reason and faith was summed up in the statement *Credo ut intelligam* (I believe in order that I may know). Faith must be primary and must be a foundation for knowledge. This was essentially the position that Augustine had held some centuries before. Anselm applied reason to the verification of faith in two great works. The *Monologion* is really an inductive argument from effect to cause for the existence of God. This argument, a form of the cosmological argument, may be stated as follows. Man has many goods that he enjoys in life. These goods are simply reflections of the one supreme Good through whom all exist. Because infinite regress is unthinkable, the cause of all must be the One whom we call God. Anselm's *Proslogion* is a deductive argument for the existence of God. This argument, known as the ontological argument, is based on the doctrine of correspondence. Anselm wrote that everyone has an idea of a perfect supreme being in his mind. This idea must correspond to a reality that has an objective existence, for such a being lacking existence would not be perfect nor would it be that than which a greater cannot be conceived. Because no greater idea than that of God as the perfect Supreme Being can be conceived, God must exist in reality.[1]

Though these and other intellectual arguments for the existence of God do not conclusively demonstrate His existence, they have a cumulative value in showing an intelligent person that nothing is really explicable if God's existence is rejected.

Anselm also developed a theory of the Atonement in his work *Cur Deus Homo* (Why God Became Man). Man, he wrote, owed absolute obedience to God. This obedience had been withheld by natural man since the sin of Adam, and man was in debt to a God who demanded payment of the debt or satisfaction by punishment. The God-man, Christ, by His death on the cross, paid the debt that man could not pay. Thus man was freed from that obligation. Anselm's view of the Atonement was commercial, but his view dominated orthodox thinking until the time of Thomas Aquinas in the thirteenth century; and it ended the patristic view of the Atonement as a ransom paid to Satan.

b. Textbooks, such as Gratian's *Decretum*, a text on canon law, had an important place in the life of the medieval scholar. Peter Lombard (ca. 1100–ca. 1160), a brilliant theological teacher of the University of Paris, wrote what became the theological textbook of the Middle Ages. This was his *Four Books of Sentences*, known usually as *Sentences*, concerning the Trinity, the Incarnation, the sacraments, and eschatology. Lombard emphasized the seven sacraments that were finally accepted as authoritative at the Council of Florence in 1439.

2. *Moderate Realism.* Aristotle held a more moderate view of the nature of reality. He insisted that universals have an objective existence but that they do not exist apart from individual things but rather in them and in their minds. This view was summed up in the Middle Ages by the phrase *universalia in re*. The medieval Scholastic who accepted Aristotle's framework was known as a moderate realist. Abelard and Thomas Aquinas may be classed as moderate realists or, as they are sometimes called, conceptualists.

a. A native of Brittany, Abelard (1079–1142) early became famous for his intellectual ability. His lectures on theology at the University of Paris became so famous that he had thousands of students in his classes at times. He fell in love with one of his private pupils, Heloise, the niece of a fellow canon named Fulbert. When their love affair and subsequent marriage became known, Fulbert took brutal revenge by having some ruffians emasculate Abelard. Abelard then persuaded Heloise to go into a convent. His theological views opposed successfully by Bernard of Clairvaux, the defeated Abelard was forced to retire to a friendly monastery until his death.[2]

Abelard's theological position was that of moderate realism. He believed that reality existed first in the mind of God, then here and now in individuals and things rather than above and beyond this life, and finally in man's mind. In contrast to Augustine and Anselm, he held to the idea of *intelligo*

Thomas Aquinas synthesized faith and reason and systematized theology in his *Summa Theologiae*. It became the classical exposition of the prevailing medieval Roman Catholic theology. In this portrayal, Aristotle is on Thomas's right and Plato on his left; the Islamic philosopher Averroës, who wrote commentaries on Aristotle, lies vanquished by a ray of light coming from the *Summa Theologiae*.

ut credam (I know in order that I may believe). Emphasizing the position of reason in the development of truth, he constantly appealed to it from authority. He believed that doubt would lead to inquiry and inquiry to truth. He thought that the death of Christ was not to satisfy God but to impress man with the love of God so that man would be morally influenced to surrender his life to God. This view of the Atonement is known as the moral influence theory.

Abelard's outstanding work is *Sic et Non*. This book consists of 158 propositions arranged to show the views of the Fathers pro and con with regard to certain ideas. Thus Abelard was able to point out the contradictions that existed among the Fathers, hoping his method would solve them.[3] He did not reject the stated theology of the Roman Catholic church, but his methods made many feel that he was overemphasizing reason and was, therefore, a danger to the truth.

b. Albertus Magnus (ca. 1193–1280), known as the "Universal Doctor" because of the tremendous scope of his knowledge, taught at the University of Paris, but his greatest work was done at Cologne in his homeland. His chief works, compendiums of theology and of creation, treat respectively theological and natural science in an effort to reconcile science and religion. This reconciliation was to be finally accomplished for that era by Albert's pupil Thomas Aquinas.

c. Thomas Aquinas (1225–74), known as the "Angelic Doctor," was of noble birth, his mother being the sister of Frederick Barbarrossa. Educated at Monte Cassino and at the University of Naples, he became a Dominican monk against the wishes of his parents and devoted himself to study. He was a large, shambling, taciturn, somewhat absent-minded man. When his classmates at Cologne teased him about being a "dumb ox," the teacher Albert remarked that one day the lowing of this ox would fill the world.

The prodigious learning of Thomas was applied to the problem of integrating the new (for that day) natural philosophy of Aristotle with the revealed theology of the Bible as interpreted by the church. In so doing, he took the position of moderate realism and became the leading Scholastic thinker to uphold that position. He believed that in the realm of natural philosophy, comparable to modern science, man by the use of reason and the logic of Aristotle could gain such truths as those of God's existence, providence, and immortality. Beyond this realm, concerning such ideas as the Incarnation, the Trinity, creation in time, sin, and purgatory, man could only get truth through faith in God's revelation in the Bible as interpreted by the Fathers and the councils. Reality existed in God's mind before it existed in things or in man's mind. Thomas endeavored to synthesize the two areas of faith and reason into a totality of truth in his great work called *Summa Theologiae*.[4] Because both are from God, there can be no essential contradiction between them, according to Aquinas. His *Summa . . . contra Gentiles* was a handbook of arguments from natural revelation to train missionaries to the Muslims.

The *Summa Theologiae* consists of three thousand articles including over six hundred questions in three major sections. It was intended to be a systematic exposition of the whole of theology. It has become, rather, the classic exposition of the system of theology held by the Roman Catholic church. Neo-Thomistic scholars today study Thomas's great intellectual cathedral with as much interest as medieval scholars did. The first part, which discusses the existence and nature of God, emphasizes God's being. The Trinity and the work of the Trinity in creation are also discussed. The second section discusses man's "advance toward God." Thomas took note of the nature of morality and the virtues and pointed out that man's will is bent by sin, although it is not completely determined to evil. Here he broke with Augustine who believed that the human will is helpless to help man move toward God. The third section concerns Christ as our Way to God and stresses Christ's incarnation, life, death, and resurrection. It concludes with a discussion of the seven sacraments as channels of grace instituted by Christ. Thomas shared with other medieval men belief in a hierarchy of truth and order. His view was later expressed poetically by Dante in his *Divine Comedy* and reasserted by Leo XIII in 1879.

Aquinas rationalized the idea of indulgences, created to free one from the satisfaction normally necessary in the sacrament of penance, by his emphasis on the availability of the extra merits of Christ and the saints. These merits can be drawn upon by the church for the penitent. His moderate realism led him to emphasize the church as a corporate institution at the expense of the freedom of the individual. There is also the danger that his postulate of the two realms of knowledge, natural philosophy and biblical revelation interpreted by the church, may lead to a belief in double truth and the separation of knowledge into two realms.

3. *Nominalism.* The medieval Scholastics known as nominalists were opposed both to the realists and the moderate realists. Roscellinus and, later, William of Ockham were outstanding examples of nominalistic thinking. Their view was expressed in the phrase *universalia post rem.* General truths or ideas have no objective existence outside the mind; rather, they are merely subjective ideas of common characteristics developed by the mind as a result of the observation of particular things. Universals are only class names. Justice is simply the composite idea that man derives from a consideration of justice in action. The nominalists gave much attention to individuals, whereas the realists and moderate realists were more concerned with the group and the institution. The nominalists were the medieval forerunners of the empiricists of the seventeenth and eighteenth centuries and the positivists and pragmatists of our day. The nominalists did not deny revelation; rather, they asserted that it must be believed merely on authority apart from reason, for much that was stated by the church to be authoritative could not be demonstrated by reason.

a. The Franciscans soon began to criticize the work of the great Aquinas, who was a member of the rival Dominican order. This criticism led to the development of a nominalistic position that became dominant during the fourteenth century, a time of decline for Scholasticism. Although John Duns Scotus (ca. 1265–1308) laid more emphasis on the individual than on the institution, he was not a nominalist. It was William of Ockham (ca.

1280–ca. 1349) who developed full-fledged nominalism. Ockham insisted that theological dogmas were not rationally demonstrable and that they must be accepted on the authority of the Bible. This view separated faith and reason and denied Aquinas's synthesis of the realms of reason and revelation. Ockham also denied the existence of objective universals and held that the universals are only names for the mental concepts that men develop in their minds. The individual was real and much more important than the institution, according to him. Ockham's undermining of the authority of the church as a rationally derived institution aroused Luther's interest in his work.

b. Roger Bacon (ca. 1214–92) belonged to the same tradition as Ockham but devoted his time to scientific experiments. In so doing, he laid the foundation for experimental science, the method of which Francis Bacon was to develop in the seventeenth century. This approach to truth through the realm of nature by experiment was in full accord with the nominalistic position.

This intellectual speculative movement of the medieval Roman church concerned itself with the problem of unity in man's intellectual life so that his spiritual and rational knowledge could be harmonized to give him certainty both in the realm of faith and in the realm of reason. The conflict between nominalism and realism was the great problem that the Scholastics faced in the early period of Scholasticism between 1050 and 1150. In this era the realism championed by Anselm and Bernard was victorious. During the period of High Scholasticism, between 1150 and 1300, the moderate realism championed by Aquinas won out over nominalism. But in the years after 1300, nominalism gained ground in the thinking of theological leaders of the church.

F. Results of Scholasticism

Realism and moderate realism buttressed the sacramental and hierarchical system of the Roman church by an emphasis on universals that led to the subordination of the individual to the more real corporate group or institution. Aquinas's emphasis on the sacraments as the channels of grace strengthened the hold of the Roman Catholic church on the individual, for there could be no salvation apart from the sacraments dispensed by the hierarchy.

Aquinas's view that reason precedes revelation as a means of knowledge but is completed by revelation led to a danger that people might separate truth known by these two methods into two spheres, the secular and sacred. The actual divorce is apparent in the thinking of the nominalists, who believed that there is a realm of scientific truth and another of theological truth instead of seeing that the two are simply parts of a greater whole that is unified in God as the Creator.

Nominalism created a new interest in man since, according to it, the individual was more real than the institution. This interest sponsored much of the materialism of the Renaissance as people began to think of man as autonomous, and it led to an exaltation of the experimental method as the main avenue to truth. Others who followed the nominalistic views moved in the direction of mysticism as a way by which the individual could come directly into the presence of God.

Above all, in the *Summa Theologiae* of Aquinas, Scholasticism furnished the medieval and modern Roman Catholic church with an authoritative, integrated synthesis that harmonized philosophy and religion. The Neo-Thomists seek today in a restudy of the work of Aquinas to furnish an integration of science and religion for the modern Roman Catholic. One cannot dismiss the Scholastics as hair-splitting dialecticians any more than one can condemn modern scientists as grubbers for facts who have no sense of integration or morality in the use of their facts.

II. THE RISE OF UNIVERSITIES

The university as a center for teaching and research developed about 1200. By 1400 there were over seventy-five European universities. In these schools Scholastic studies formed a large part of the curriculum. Most of the great universities of modern Europe had their beginnings in this period. Teaching on the higher level had gone on before the development of the universities, but after their rise most of higher education, which had centered in monastic and cathedral schools, was given in university classrooms.

A. Reasons for the Rise

Several reasons account for the rapid rise of universities before 1200. Martianus Capella about 425 adapted the Roman quadrivium and trivium to the use of religion. Grammar, rhetoric, and logic made up the trivium; geometry, arithmetic, astronomy, and music were included in the quad-rivium. The trivium was useful for training the clergy in public speaking so that they could fulfill their preaching function effectively; the quadrivium was useful in the establishment of the dates of the sacred festivals of the church. These studies were used in Charlemagne's palace school and were based on the model of monastery schools for learning between 550 and 1100. Other centers for higher learning sprang up in connection with the cathedral church of the bishop or archbishop. The University of Paris developed from the cathedral school connected with Notre Dame cathedral.

A second reason for the rise of universities was the presence of a great teacher in a school. In the eleventh century, Irnerius developed a reputation as a great scholar of Roman law, and students flocked to Bologna to hear him. Soon there was a thriving university at Bologna. Abelard's fame as a teacher contributed greatly to the development of the University of Paris.

Other universities came into being as a result of student revolts or migrations. Because the English and French kings were quarreling shortly after the middle of the twelfth century, English students, who felt that they were mistreated at the University of Paris, revolted against conditions there and moved in 1167 or 1168 to Oxford in England. From this revolt grew the great University of Oxford. Cambridge grew out of a student revolt and exodus from Oxford to Cambridge in 1209.

B. Organization of the Universities

Medieval university organization differed considerably from that of modern times. The *universitas*, from which our word for university is derived, was a guild or corporation of students or teachers set up for purposes of common protection while the group went on with its work. The phrase *studium generale* was used to describe this group in its educational function. The universities of southern Europe followed the practice of Bologna, where the corporation was made up of students who organized for mutual protection against abuses from the towns where they were located or from failure on the part of their teachers. From a king or other overlord of the area the university received a charter that set forth its rights, privileges, and responsibilities. Bologna was noted for the study of law, but Salerno gained its fame as a university of advanced medical teaching and research. The universities of northern Europe were organized on the model of Paris. Here the guild, which received the charter, was made up of teachers.

The university usually had four faculties. The arts were the general course for all. Theology, law, and medicine were more advanced studies. The student in the general curriculum of the arts studied the trivium, which led to the bachelor's degree. Further study of the quadrivium gave him a master's degree, which was essential if he desired to become a teacher. Continued study in other faculties might give him a doctorate in law, theology, or medicine.

Students in the medieval university began their studies as early as their fourteenth birthday, although they were usually between sixteen and eighteen when they entered the university. They had the privileges of clergymen. Examinations were oral, comprehensive, and public; and during the course of an examination the student had to defend a thesis against teachers or students. Instruction was in Latin. Because there were textbooks only for the teachers, the student had to do a good deal of memorizing. A good memory and the use of logic were as important then as reading and research are in the modern university. Learning was to be by lecture and debate.

Most of the paraphernalia of modern university life comes from medieval times. The nomenclature of many degrees, examinations, gowns, hoods, and basic elements of the curriculum were created in medieval times. The teaching of successive generations of students and the advancement of learning by research are functions that the modern university has inherited from its medieval ancestor. Above all, the university in medieval times kept alive and developed the study of theology. The great Scholastics were also the greatest university teachers. Universities served the interests of the church in medieval times by preparing men for service in it instead of preparing them for service in the fields of science and industry as the modern university does. Scholasticism and the universities were closely associated in the service of the church. They poured a steady stream of personnel trained in arts, law, and theology into its hierarchy.

III. MEDIEVAL LIFE AND WORSHIP

Gothic architecture was preceded by a Byzantine style in which great domes on pendentives and decorative mosaics were used in Saint Sophia and Saint Marks. Later Romanesque architecture from 1100 to 1150 had heavy round arches and a cruciform shape. Durham Cathedral is an example of this later architecture.

Medieval university towers, representative of Scholasticism, had their counterpart in the spires of the Gothic cathedral that has often been described as a "Bible in stone." The great medieval cathedrals, emphasizing vertical lines, often took about a century to build. They expressed the spiritual nature of the age as much as the skyscraper expresses the materialistic spirit of the twentieth century. Many of these great churches were raised in northern and western Europe between 1150 and 1550. Gothic architecture like Scholasticism, at its peak during the thirteenth century, was pioneered by Suger, the abbot of Saint-Denis.

Although the earth-bound Renaissance architect thought of medieval architecture as barbaric and, therefore, Gothic, later ages have not sustained his viewpoint. Gothic buildings have certain characteristics that show the skill of the medieval builders. On going into a Gothic cathedral, one notices the cross-shaped floor plan of the building, expressive of the central symbol of the Christian church. The use of the pointed arch instead of the rounded Roman arch is instantly noticeable and leads the eye and aspirations upward from the earth. Ribbed vaulting and flying buttresses—long ribs attached to the roof and to separate pillars—or buttresses built into the walls of the cathedral convey the weight of the roof to the earth so that the upper walls could be thin and windows could be put in to admit light, so badly needed in the gloomy days of northern European winters. Usually there are three doors at the west end of the church. All ornamentation, whether stained-glass windows or statues, was subordinated to the design of the whole building. A statue, seen on the ground, might seem grotesquely out of proportion; but the same statue in its niche above the doors blends into the design of the building harmoniously. Colors were used by the worker in stained glass to illustrate stories as clearly as possible.

The best examples of the medieval Gothic cathedral were built within a hundred-mile radius of Paris. The cathedral of Notre Dame is noted for its beautiful facade. Both the cathedrals at Chartres and Notre Dame have outstanding rose windows above the main entrance that show the skillful use of colored glass by the medieval artisan.

The significance of the Gothic cathedral is much more important than its characteristics. The cathedral represented the supernaturalistic spirit of the age clearly by its dominating posi-

A nineteenth-century engraving of Notre Dame, clearly showing the typical structural features of a Gothic cathedral.

tion in the town and by its symbolic expression of biblical truth. The social solidarity of medieval man was expressed by the fact that the great cathedrals were built as community enterprises extending over decades, with all ranks and classes taking part in the work. Cologne cathedral was built from about 1248 to 1880. The cathedral also had a real educational value because in stained-glass window and statue the illiterate peasant might see for himself the truth of the Bible. Often a center for social and many other activities of the town, the cathedral was, above all, a place where the soul might come into contact with God in the act of worship.

All the ceremonies important to the religious life of the individual occurred in the cathedral, and one who lived in a cathedral town was considered fortunate. He was baptized, confirmed, and married in the church. He was buried from the church in the cemetery within the grounds of the church. But the most important part of worship, whether the building was a cathedral or a simple church, was the Mass. After the Fourth Lateran Council of 1215, it was a part of Roman Catholic dogma that the priest's words of consecration changed the bread and the wine into the actual body and blood of Christ. Christ was sacrificed afresh by the priest for the benefit of the believers. It did not matter that the cup was withheld from the believer after the twelfth century, for the body and blood were, according to Roman dogma, in each element. The practice of elevating the elements by the priest

became a custom in the thirteenth century in order that the faithful might worship Christ in the Mass.

The development of polyphonic music, which consisted of many melodic lines and hence was better sung by trained choirs, ended the practice of congregational singing in unison. Music became elaborate and colorful as a proper accompaniment to the sacred mysteries of the Mass.

One cannot overlook the real and positive contributions of the Roman church between 590 and 1305, despite the many evidences of failure in personal and institutional practices. It gave Greco-Roman culture and the Christian religion to the Germans who took over the Roman Empire. It provided the only real culture and scholarship, which kept learning alive through the work of such scholars as Bede, Alcuin, Einhard, and others. The moral tone of society was improved by the mitigation of the evils of slavery, the elevation of the position of women, and the softening of the horrors of feudal war. The Roman church sponsored what relief and charitable work was done in the Middle Ages. It provided an intellectual synthesis for life in the theological system that the Scholastics developed and it impressed on men their solidarity as members of the church, despite the decentralizing tendencies of feudalism, God used the Roman Catholic church to further His own ends in spite of its failure at so many points when it is compared with the true church, depicted in the New Testament.

Suggested Reading

Artz, F. B. The Mind of the Middle Ages. *New York: Knopf, 1953. See pages 253–69 for the pertinent discussion.*

Clayton, Joseph. Saint Anselm. *Milwaukee: Bruce, 1933.*

De Wulf, Maurice M. C. J. An Introduction to Scholastic Philosophy. *Translated by P. Coffey. New York: Dover, 1956. This is useful for the beginning student.*

Fairweather, Eugene R., ed. and trans. A Scholastic Miscellany: Anselm to Ockham. *Philadelphia: Westminster, 1956.*

Gardner, Helen. Art Through the Ages. *Rev. ed. New York: Harcourt, Brace, 1936. There is a useful section on Gothic architecture on pages 303–34.*

Jansen, H. W., with Jansen, Dora J. A History of Art. *Englewood Cliffs, N.J.: Prentice-Hall and New York: Abrams, n.d. This work has a clear, helpful text and many pictures both in black and white and in color.*

————. Key Monuments of the History of Art. *Englewood Cliffs, N.J.: Prentice-Hall and New York: Abrams, 1962. This work has hundreds of pictures to illustrate the above book.*

Kessel, Dimitri. Splendors of Christendom. *Lausanne: Edita Lausanne, 1964. This is a folio with helpful text and splendid color illustrations of Byzantine, Romanesque, Gothic, and Baroque architecture.*

Neve, Juergen L., and Heick, Otto W. A History of Christian Thought. *Philadelphia: Fortress, 1965. A helpful discussion of Scholasticism is given in vol. 1, pp. 265–309.*

Simson, Otto G. von. The Gothic Cathedral. *New York: Pantheon, 1956.*

Short, Ernest. The House of God. *London: Eyre and Spottiswood, 1955. This is a useful history of religious architecture.*

Southern, Richard W. Saint Anselm and His Biographer. *Cambridge: Cambridge University Press, 1963.*

Thorndyke, Lynn. University Records and Life in the Middle Ages. *New York: Columbia University Press, 1944. This work has a fine collection of documents relating to the universities of medieval Europe. Matters such as curriculum, fees, charters, rules, and student life are illustrated from contemporary documents.*

Weinberg, Julius R. A Short History of Medieval Philosophy. *Princeton: Princeton University Press, 1964.*

Chapter 24

Attempts at Internal Reform

The return to the Scriptures did not begin with such leaders of the Reformation as Luther and Calvin. There were earlier attempts to halt the decline in papal prestige and power by reforms of various kinds. From 1305 to 1517, protest and attempted reform challenged the authority of the Roman church. The corrupt, extravagant papacy that resided in France instead of in Rome and the schism that resulted from the attempts to get the pope to return to Rome provided the impetus that led mystics, reformers (such as Wycliffe, Hus, and Savonarola), the reform councils of the fourteenth century, and the biblical humanists to seek ways to bring about a revival within the Roman Catholic church.

I. THE PAPACY IN DECLINE, 1309–1439

A. Failure of the Clergy

Between 1309 and 1439 the Roman church sank to a new low in the estimation of the laity. The hierarchical organization, with its demand for celibacy and absolute obedience to the pope, and the feudalization of the Roman church led to a decline in clerical morals. Celibacy was opposed both to the natural instincts of man and to the biblical statements in favor of the married state. Many priests took concubines or indulged in illicit love affairs with the women in their congregations. Some had the problem of caring for children that were born to these unions and gave more attention to that problem than they did to their clerical duties. Others, especially during the Renaissance, enjoyed luxurious living. Feudalism was still a problem because the dual allegiance to the pope and the feudal lord created a division of interest in many cases. The cleric often gave more attention to his secular responsibilities than he did to his spiritual responsibilities.

B. The Babylonian Captivity and the Great Schism

The papacy itself lost the respect of the laity of the various areas under its

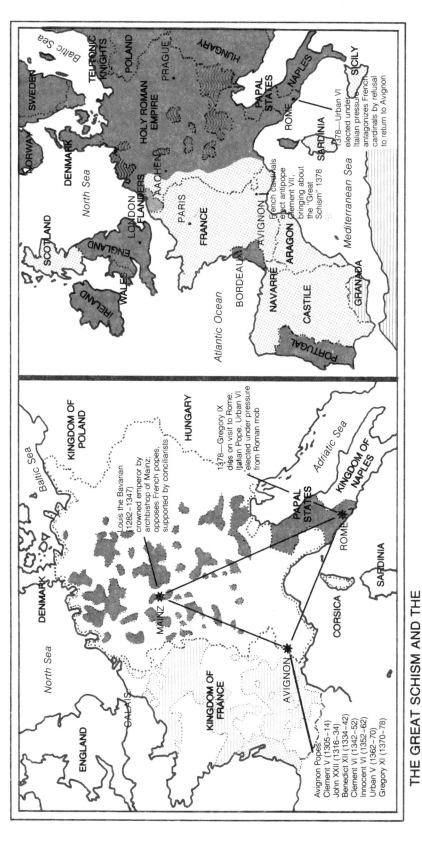

THE GREAT SCHISM AND THE
BABYLONIAN CAPTIVITY OF THE PAPACY

BOUNDARY OF THE HOLY ROMAN EMPIRE •••••

CHURCH LANDS

FRENCH ROYAL DOMAIN

ENGLISH DOMAIN IN FRANCE

ALLEGIANCE TO ROME

ALLEGIANCE TO AVIGNON

NEUTRAL   DISPUTED

MUSLIM TERRITORY

Left map labels:

KINGDOM OF POLAND

Baltic Sea

North Sea

DENMARK

HUNGARY

KINGDOM OF FRANCE

ENGLAND

CALAIS

MAINZ

Louis the Bavarian (1282–1347) crowned emperor by archbishop of Mainz; opposes French popes, supported by conciliarists

AVIGNON

Avignon Popes:
Clement V (1305–14)
John XXII (1316–34)
Benedict XII (1334–42)
Clement VI (1342–52)
Innocent VI (1352–62)
Urban V (1362–70)
Gregory XI (1370–78)

CORSICA

SARDINIA

PAPAL STATES

KINGDOM OF NAPLES

ROME

Adriatic Sea

1378—Gregory IX dies on visit to Rome; Italian Pope, Urban VI elected under pressure from Roman mob

Right map labels:

Baltic Sea

TEUTONIC KNIGHTS

POLAND

SWEDEN

NORWAY

PRAGUE

HUNGARY

DENMARK

North Sea

HOLY ROMAN EMPIRE

SCOTLAND

IRELAND

WALES

ENGLAND

LONDON

FLANDERS

AACHEN

PARIS

FRANCE

Atlantic Ocean

BORDEAUX

AVIGNON

ARAGON

NAVARRE

CASTILE

PORTUGAL

GRANADA

Mediterranean Sea

SARDINIA

SICILY

NAPLES

ROME

PAPAL STATES

French cardinals elect antipope Clement VII, bringing about the "Great Schism" 1378

1378—Urban VI elected under Italian pressure; antagonizes French cardinals by refusal to return to Avignon control. The "Babylonian Captivity" (1309–77) and the Great Schism (1378–1417), which must not be confused with the Schism of 1054, were the events responsible for the papacy's loss of prestige. The zenith of papal power was reached in the pontificate of Innocent III, but the papacy slid rapidly from that dizzy eminence of power after Boniface VIII was unsuccessful in his attempts to subjugate the rulers of England and France, who were supported by nationalism.

Clement V, a Frenchman chosen as pope by the cardinals in 1305, was a weak man of doubtful morality. Soon falling under the influence of the French king, he moved to France in 1305 from Rome and to Avignon in 1309. In the eyes of the people of Europe this put the pope under French control even though Avignon was not technically French territory. Except for a brief period between 1367 and 1370, the papal residence was maintained at Avignon until 1377 and was dominated by strong French kings. The godly mystic, Catherine of Siena (1347–80), strongly pressed Gregory XI (1329–78) to return to Rome to restore order there and to regain prestige for the papacy as an independent international authority. Early in 1377 he returned and ended the Babylonian captivity.

When Gregory XI died in the next year, the cardinals elected the man who became Urban VI. Urban's bad temper and arrogant manner soon won him their enmity, and they elected Clement VII in 1378. Clement dutifully removed the capital to Avignon for the second time. Both men, elected by the same body of cardinals, claimed to be the legitimate pope and the true successor to Peter. This forced the people of Europe into the dilemma of papal allegiance. Northern Italy, most of Germany, Scandinavia, and England followed the Roman pope; France, Spain, Scotland, and southern Italy gave allegiance to the pope at Avignon. This schism continued until it was resolved early in the next century by the reforming councils (see pp. 253–57). The captivity and the Great Schism strengthened the rising clamor for reform within the Roman church.

C. Papal Taxation

Papal taxation to support two papal courts became an onerous burden to the people of Europe. Papal income was made up of income from the papal estates; tithes, which the faithful paid; annates, which was the payment of the first year's salary by a church official to the pope; the right of purveyance, by which churchmen and their constituents had to pay the pope's traveling expenses while he was in their area; the right of spoil, by which the personal property of the upper clergy went to the pope upon their death; Peter's Pence, which was paid annually by the laity in many lands; and the income from vacant offices as well as numerous fees.[1] The now-powerful rulers of national states and the strong middle class that supported them resented the drain of wealth from the national treasury to the papal treasury. This was especially true of the rulers of England and France. During the long period of the "Captivity" in the fourteenth century, the English hated to pay money that they thought would only go to England's enemy France because the pope's residence was in territory dominated by the French king.

D. The Rise of Nation-States

A political factor that played an important part in the decline of papal influence in Europe was the rise of national states opposed to the idea of universal sovereignty inherent in the concepts of the Holy Roman Empire and the Roman Catholic church. King and middle class cooperated: the king with his national army gave security so that the middle class could carry on business safely; and the middle class in return gave money so that the king could run the state. The resulting strong, centralized nation-state was strong enough to defy the pope's dicta and to try to make the church subject to national interest in Bohemia, France, and England.

All this created a clamor for internal reform of the papacy in the fourteenth and fifteenth centuries. Leaders soon came to the fore. The mystical, biblical, evangelical, and conciliar reformers were the successors of the monastic reformers of the twelfth and thirteenth centuries.

II. THE MYSTICS

The recurrence of mysticism in eras when the church lapses into formalism testifies to the desire of the human heart to have direct contact with God in the act of worship instead of passively participating in the coldly formal acts of worship performed by the clergyman. The mystic desires direct contact with God by immediate intuition or contemplation. If the emphasis is on the union of the essence of the mystic with the essence of deity in the experience of ecstasy, which is the crown of mystical experience, then mysticism is philosophical. If the emphasis is on an emotional union with deity by intuition, then mysticism is psychological. The main objective in either case is immediate apprehension of God in an extrarational way as the mystic waits before Him in a passive, receptive mood. Both types were to be found in the mysticism of the fourteenth century.

A. Causes for the Rise of Mysticism

Scholasticism contributed to the rise of mysticism because it emphasized reason at the expense of man's emotional nature. Mysticism was a reaction against this rationalistic tendency. Movements emphasizing the subjective aspect of man's relation to God usually come as a reaction to movements that emphasize the intellectual aspect. In a similar manner, Pietism was to follow the period of cold orthodoxy in the Lutheranism of the seventeenth century. Scholastic nominalism led to an emphasis on the individual as the source of reality and on experience as the way to gain knowledge. In this way, one wing of nominalistic Scholastics turned to mysticism as a way to gain knowledge of God, while other nominalists were emphasizing materialism and experiment.

The movement was also one of protest and reaction against the troubled times and a corrupt church. Social and political upheaval in the fourteenth century was a common experience. The Black Death in 1348–49 took away by painful death about one-third of the population of Europe. The Peasants' Revolt of 1381 in England was an evidence of social unrest associated with the ideas of Wycliffe. The Babylonian Captivity and the Great Schism made many question their spiritual leadership and desire direct contact with God.

B. Outstanding Mystics

The mystics of this era fall into two major groups, the Latin and the Teutonic mystics. The Latin mystics, having a more emotional outlook on life than the Teutons, emphasized mysticism as a personal emotional experience of Christ. Such an emphasis had been true of Bernard of Clairvaux in the twelfth century. He had emphasized a oneness of will and affection with God rather than any oneness of essence. Most of the Teutonic mystics stressed a more philosophical approach to God, which in the case of Meister Eckhart led to a kind of pantheism.

Catherine of Siena represented Latin mysticism at its best. She firmly believed that God spoke to her in visions and she always seemed to use these visions to good practical ends. It was she who fearlessly denounced clerical evils and who, in the name of God, was able in 1376 to persuade Gregory XI to return to Rome from Avignon. Her courage[2] led her to oppose sin even in the papacy.

The mystical movement in Germany centered in the Dominican order. Meister Eckhart (ca. 1260–1327) was the Dominican who is usually credited with the founding of German mysticism. Before going to Cologne to preach, he studied at the University of Paris. Believing that only the divine was real, he taught that the aim of the Christian should be the union of the spirit with God by a fusion of the human essence with the divine essence during an ecstatic experience. He differentiated between the God-head which to him signified God in the absolute sense as the philosophical unity back of the universe, and God, who was the personal Creator and Ruler of the world. His aim was soul unity with the Godhead back of all creation. He is reputed to have said, "God must become I, and I God." Eckhart's beliefs came so close to Neoplatonism that charges of pantheism were brought against him, and his views were condemned as pantheistic in a papal bull issued after his death. It must be said that Eckhart also emphasized the need for Christian service as the fruit of mystical union with God.[3]

A group of Dominicans known as the Friends of God carried on the tradition of Eckhart's teaching. John Tauler (ca. 1300–61), more evangelical than his master, emphasized an inward experience of God as being much more vital to the soul's welfare than external ceremonies. He was associated with the Friends of God who made their headquarters in the Rhine valley. Heinrich Suso (ca. 1295–1366) was the poet of the group and expressed mystical ideas similar to those of Eckhart in poetical form. A banker named Ruleman Merswin (1307–82) was the good angel who provided a religious house where members of the group could take up residence. The little mystical volume entitled *Theologia Germanica (German Theology)* is usually associated with this group. Luther found this book a help in his struggle for salvation and had it issued in a German edition in 1516. It has, however, the same undertone of pantheism as is found in the writings of Meister Eckhart.

The movement in the Netherlands known as *Devotio Moderna*, or the

Brethren of the Common Life, which had its main center at Deventer, was a much more practical and, certainly, less pantheistic expression of lay mysticism than the Friends of God movement. John of Ruysbroeck (1293–1381), who had come under the influence of Eckhart's writings, and who knew some of the Friends of God, influenced the mystical movement in Holland. He helped Gerard Groote (1340–84) to emphasize the New Testament in the development of the mystic experience, and Groote became the leader of the Brethren of the Common Life at Deventer. Groote inspired his disciple Florentius Radewijns (1350–1400) to open a house for the Brethren of the Common Life at Windesheim. The order consisted of laymen who lived under a rule in community and devoted their lives to teaching and other practical service rather than to the passive experience of God that had been emphasized by Meister Eckhart. Both groups emphasized the education of young people and built large and excellent schools. Other houses of the group were founded all over the Netherlands.[4]

The *Imitation of Christ* has contributed more than anything else to the lasting reputation of the Brethren of the Common Life. This book is associated with the name of Thomas à Kempis (1380–1471) or, as he was known then, Thomas Hemerken of Kempen. Educated in Deventer under the kindly eye of Radewijns, he entered the Augustinian monastery near Zwolle. He was most likely the writer of the *Imitation of Christ*.[5] This work reflects the more practical emphasis of the Brethren. It does not stop with mere negative renunciation of the world but asserts the need of a positive love for Christ and service for Him in humble practical ways.

C. Consequences of the Rise of Mysticism

The mystical movement, the classical form of Roman Catholic piety, developed as a reaction against formal and mechanical sacerdotal ritual and dry Scholasticism in the church of the day. It reflected the perennial tendency toward the subjective aspect of Christianity, which always occurs when too much emphasis is laid on outward acts in Christian worship. In that sense mysticism may be thought of as anticipating the more personal approach to religion that was such an outstanding characteristic of the Reformation.

Tendencies to substitute a subjective inner authority for the Bible and to minimize doctrine were some of the dangers in such a movement. In its excesses there was danger of it being so passivist that its adherents became introspective and antisocial. In Eckhart's case it also led philosophically to a kind of pantheism that identified God with His creation and creatures.

III. FORERUNNERS OF THE REFORMATION

The mystics had attempted to personalize religion, but biblical and nationalistic reformers such as Wycliffe, Hus, and Savonarola were more interested in an attempt to return to the ideal of the church presented in the New Testament. Wycliffe and Hus were able to capitalize on nationalistic antipapal sentiment during the period of the Babylonian captivity, when the pope was resident in Avignon.

ROMAN CATHOLIC DECLINE

1. Babylonian Captivity 1309–77
2. Great Schism 1378–1414
vs.
Protest and Reform 1305–1517

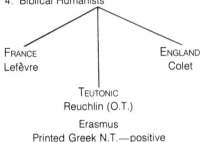

INTERNAL

1. Mystics—participants (13th C.)
   not spectators
2. Reformers—Wycliffe (14th C.)—Lollards
   Huss—United Brethren
3. Reform Councils (15th C.)
   Pisa, Constance
4. Biblical Humanists

EXTERNAL

1. Nation-State and Rulers and
2. Middle Class Resented
   a. church courts
   b. church taxes
   c. church lands
   d. clerical corruption
3. Printing Press

FRANCE
Lefèvre

ENGLAND
Colet

TEUTONIC
Reuchlin (O.T.)

Erasmus
Printed Greek N.T.—positive
The Praise of Folly—negative

A. John Wycliffe (ca. 1328–84)

The English people resented sending money to a pope in Avignon who was under pressure from England's enemy, the French king. This nationalistic feeling was augmented by royal and middle-class resentment over the money lost to the English treasury and to the service of the English state by papal taxation. The Statute of Provisors of 1351 banned appointment by the pope of clergymen to offices in the Roman church in England. The Statute of Praemunire of 1353 forbade the practice of taking cases concerning clergymen out of English courts for trial in the papal court in Rome. Payment of the annual tribute of one thousand marks, which had been begun by John, also was stopped by Parliament in this period. It was in this era of nationalistic reaction against ecclesiasticism that Wycliffe appeared on the scene. Aided by the powerful John of Gaunt, Wycliffe was able to defy the pope.

Wycliffe studied and taught at Oxford for the greater part of his life. Until 1378 he wanted to reform the Roman church by the elimination of immoral clergymen and by stripping her of property, which he felt was a root of corruption. In a work entitled *Of Civil Dominion* (1376) he asserted a moral basis for ecclesiastical leadership. God gave the use and possession of property, but not the ownership, to church leaders as a trust to be used for His glory. Failure on the part of ecclesiastics to fulfill their proper functions was a sufficient reason for the civil authority to take the property from them and to give it to someone else who would serve God acceptably. This view suited the nobles who were happy to seize the property of the Roman church. They and John of Gaunt championed Wycliffe so that the Church of Rome did not dare to touch him.

Wycliffe, disgusted with the Captivity and schism, was not satisfied with this more negative approach and after 1379 began to oppose the dogma of the Roman church with revolutionary ideas. He attacked the authority of the pope in 1379 by insisting in writing that Christ and not the pope was the head of the church. He asserted that the Bible instead of the church was the sole authority for the believer and that the church should model itself after the pattern of the New Testament. To support these beliefs, Wycliffe made the Bible available to the people in their own tongue. By 1382 the first complete manuscript translation into English of the New Testament was finished. Nicholas of Hereford completed the translation of most of the Old Testament into English in 1384. Thus, for the first time, Englishmen were able to read the whole Bible in their own tongue. Wycliffe went still further by 1382 by opposing the dogma of transubstantiation. Whereas the Roman church believed that the substance or essence of the elements changed while the outward form remained the same, Wycliffe argued that the substance of the elements was indestructible and that Christ was spiritually present in the sacrament and was apprehended by faith.[6] If adopted, Wycliffe's view would mean that the priest could no longer withhold salvation from one by withholding the body and blood of Christ in the Communion.

Wycliffe's views[7] were condemned in London in 1382, and he was forced to retire to his rectory at Lutterworth. He had made provision for the continued dissemination of his ideas, however, by the founding of a group of lay preachers, the Lollards, who preached his ideas all over England[8] until the Roman church, by forcing the statute *De Haeretico Comburendo* through Parliament in 1401, made the death penalty the punishment for preaching Lollard ideas.

Wycliffe's accomplishments were influential in paving the way for subsequent reformation in England. He gave the English their first Bible in the vernacular and created the Lollard group to proclaim evangelical ideas all over England among the common people. His teachings of equality in the church were applied to economic life by the peasants and contributed to the Peasants' Revolt of 1381. Bohemian students studying in England carried his ideas to Bohemia where they became the foundation for the teachings of John Hus.[9]

B. John Hus (ca. 1373–1415)

When Richard II of England married Anne of Bohemia, students from that land came to England to study. When they returned to Bohemia, they carried Wycliffe's ideas back with them. John Hus, pastor of the Bethlehem Chapel, who had studied in the University of Prague and had become its rector in about 1409, read and adopted the ideas of Wycliffe. His preaching of these ideas coincided with a rise of Bohemian national feeling against the control of Bohemia by the Holy Roman

Empire. Hus proposed to reform the church in Bohemia along lines similar to those proclaimed by Wycliffe. His views exposed him to papal enmity, and he was ordered to go to the Council of Constance under a safe-conduct from the emperor. But the safe-conduct was not honored. Both his and Wycliffe's views were condemned there. After Hus refused to recant, he was burned at the stake by order of the council; but his book *De Ecclesia* (1413) lived on.

Persecutors may destroy men's bodies, but they cannot destroy ideas, and the ideas of Hus[10] were spread by his followers. His more radical followers, known as the Taborites, rejected all in the faith and practice of the Roman church that could not be found in Scripture. The Utraquists took the position that only that which the Bible actually forbade should be eliminated and that the laity should receive both bread and wine in the Mass. Some of the Taborite group formed what was known as the *Unitas Fratrum* (United Brethren) or Bohemian Brethren about 1450. It was from this group that the Moravian church, which still exists, developed.

Even though the church took John Hus's life, it could not destroy his influence. The Moravian church became at a later date one of the most missionary-minded churches in the history of Christianity. John Amos Comenius (1592–1670), the progressive evangelical educator, was one of the Brethren. He wrote the *Great Didactic* on education. Hus may be said to have indirectly influenced Wesley because it was the Moravians who helped to lead Wesley to the light in London. The teachings and example of Hus were an inspiration to Luther as

he faced similar problems in Germany in his day.

C. Savonarola (1452–98)

Wycliffe and Hus were branded as heretics who made the Bible the first standard of authority, but Savonarola was more interested in reform within the church at Florence. Becoming a Dominican monk in 1474, he was assigned to Florence in 1490. He tried to reform both state and church in the city, but his preaching against the evil life of the pope resulted in his death by hanging. He never took the more advanced position that Wycliffe and Hus held, but he did demand reform in the church. All these men anticipated the spirit and work of the Reformers to such an extent that Wycliffe, as the outstanding exponent of reformation measures, has often been called the "Morning Star of the Reformation."

IV. THE REFORMING COUNCILS, 1409–49

Leaders of the councils of the fourteenth century sought reform by making church leadership represent the laity. Councils made up of representatives of the people of the Roman church were to eliminate corrupt church leaders. The councils did not emphasize the Scriptures to the extent that Hus and Wycliffe did, nor did they seek reform by the subjective religious expression favored by the mystics.

The need of reform within the Roman church became clear with the development of the Great Schism of 1378. In that year, Urban VI and Clement VII each claimed to be the legitimate successor to Peter. Since the countries of Europe had to choose

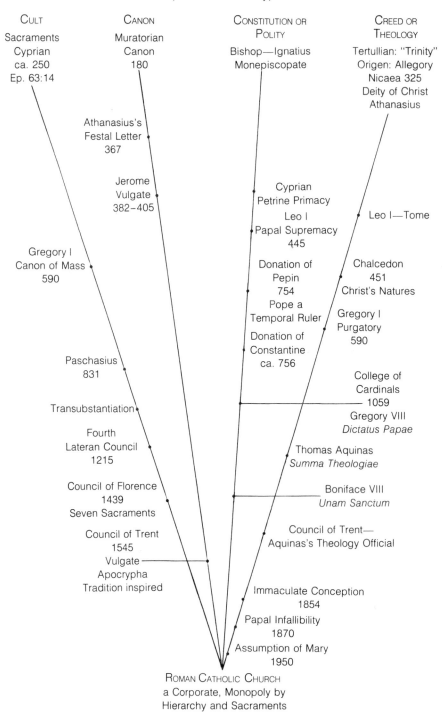

FROM NEW TESTAMENT TO ROMAN CATHOLIC CHURCH
(Bible Plus History)

CULT

Sacraments
Cyprian
ca. 250
Ep. 63:14

CANON

Muratorian
Canon
180

CONSTITUTION OR
POLITY

Bishop—Ignatius
Monepiscopate

CREED OR
THEOLOGY

Tertullian: "Trinity"
Origen: Allegory
Nicaea 325
Deity of Christ
Athanasius

Athanasius's
Festal Letter
367

Jerome
Vulgate
382–405

Cyprian
Petrine Primacy
Leo I
Papal Supremacy
445

Leo I—Tome

Gregory I
Canon of Mass
590

Donation of
Pepin
754
Pope a
Temporal Ruler
Donation of
Constantine
ca. 756

Chalcedon
451
Christ's Natures

Gregory I
Purgatory
590

Paschasius
831

College of
Cardinals
1059
Gregory VIII
Dictatus Papae

Transubstantiation

Fourth
Lateran Council
1215

Thomas Aquinas
Summa Theologiae

Council of Florence
1439
Seven Sacraments

Boniface VIII
Unam Sanctum

Council of Trent
1545
Vulgate
Apocrypha
Tradition inspired

Council of Trent—
Aquinas's Theology Official

Immaculate Conception
1854
Papal Infallibility
1870
Assumption of Mary
1950

ROMAN CATHOLIC CHURCH
a Corporate, Monopoly by
Hierarchy and Sacraments

whom they would follow, Europe became split ecclesiastically as well as politically. Both men had been chosen by the college of cardinals. Who was to decide their claims? Leading theologians of the University of Paris proposed that a council of the Roman Catholic church should decide the matter. They used the precedent of the ecumenical councils from 325 to 451. A council, representative of all the church, seemed to be the best solution, because neither pope would abdicate nor accept the decision of arbitrators.[11]

Justification for a council's deposing a pope was not wanting. Dante in his *Of Monarchy*, written after 1311, insisted that the state as well as the church was an arm of God. Both were given by God. The emperor was to secure man's happiness here; the pope to lead men to heaven. Neither was to seek supremacy over the other.

Most important of all the rationalizations of conciliar reform was set forth in the book *Defensor Pacis* (1324), by Marsilius of Padua (ca. 1275–1342) and John of Jandun. In this work they supported Louis of Bavaria against the pope. The book destroyed the idea of an absolute hierarchy in either the church or state. Marsilius believed that the people in the state and Christians in the church were the repository of sovereignty and that they could through representative bodies elect the emperor and the pope but that the emperor was above the pope. The church in a general council guided by the New Testament alone could proclaim dogma and appoint its officials. The church council and not the pope was thus the highest authority in the church, and it should act for the good of the whole body of Christians.[12] If

Marsilius's views had been victorious, the Roman Catholic church would have been transformed into a constitutional monarchy led by a pope appointed by a council, and the absolute papacy of the medieval church would have disappeared. But this view was not to triumph permanently, although the councils did some good in other areas.

The council was called to end the schism in the leadership of the Roman church, to reform that church from within, and to put down heresy. It might also put into practice a theory of government along the lines laid down by Marsilius.

A. The Council of Pisa (1409)

When the Council of Pisa met in the spring of 1409, Benedict XIII was safely in control of Avignon, and Gregory XII held the papal chair in Rome. The council, which was called by the cardinals, at once stated that the cardinals had the authority to call it and that it was competent even to call the popes to account for the Great Schism.[13] It deposed both Benedict XIII and Gregory XII and appointed the man who became Alexander V as the rightful pope.[14] But the other two popes refused to recognize the decision of the council. Now there were three popes instead of two. Alexander V was succeeded by John XXIII when the former died in 1410.

B. The Council of Constance (1414–18)

The Council of Constance was then called by Sigismund, the emperor of the Holy Roman Empire, and John XXIII. This council was called because of the precedent set by Constantine when he called the Council of Nicaea in 325. Over 350 high officials of the hierarchy met. In order to frustrate John's attempt to control the council through the use of a majority vote, which would have permitted his Italian followers to dominate the decisions of the council, the members of the council agreed to vote as national groups of clergymen. Each national group was allotted one vote, and a unanimous vote of the five nations represented was necessary for binding action by the council. The council declared its legality and its right to supreme authority in the Roman church.[15] This decree of the council, which substituted conciliar control of the Church of Rome for papal absolutism, was given the title *Sacrosanct.*

Presently Gregory XII resigned, and after much negotiation both Benedict XIII and John XXIII were deposed by 1415. Martin V was then elected by the council as the new pope. The council thus took the power of electing a pope from the college of cardinals. The council also dealt with the problem of heresy by condemning the ideas of Wycliffe and by burning Hus at the stake, in spite of the emperor's safe-conduct. It then went on to discuss the problem of reform, schism, and heresy. A decree of the council, called *Frequens*, provided for the meeting of general councils at stated times in the future as a technique to keep order in the Roman church. One was to be held five years after the close of the Council of Constance; a second after another seven years; and thereafter councils were to convene once every decade to deal with problems of schism, heresy, and reform.[16]

C. The Councils of Basel and Ferrara, (Florence) (1431–49)·

The unrest in Bohemia after the martyrdom of Hus and the need of continued reform brought about the Council of Basel in 1431. The council dragged on until 1449, but the strength of the reforming movement was matched by a resurgence of papal power. Eugenius IV, the pope at that time, was deposed by the council in 1439, just one year after the rival council, which he had called, met at Ferrara. Because of the plague, the rival council was moved to Florence in 1439. The Council of Florence made an unsuccessful attempt to reunite the Greek and Roman Catholic churches. It was this council that declared the seven sacraments to be accepted by the Roman church. This was promulgated by Eugenius IV in a papal bull in 1439. The Council of Basel acknowledged defeat by dissolving itself in 1449.

Thus the attempt to create a constitutional monarchy in the Roman church came to an end, and the papacy reverted to the system of papal despotism that it had followed for so many centuries. Pius II in a papal bull entitled *Execrabilis* issued in 1460 condemned any appeals to future general councils.[17] But the French clergy concurred with the French ruler in the proclamation of the Pragmatic Sanction of Bourges in 1438, which made the French church autonomous of the pope, but which in turn put it under the power of the state.[18]

Although the reforming councils had failed in the attempt to set up a constitutional monarchy in the Roman church, they had saved it from the disorder of the Great Schism. The lack of success in securing effective reform destroyed the last chance of reform of the Roman Catholic church from within by mystics, reformers, or councils. From this time the Protestant Reformation became inevitable.

Suggested Reading

Flick, Alexander. The Decline of the Medieval Church. *2 vols. London: Kegan, Paul, Trench, Truber, 1930. This work was a helpful discussion of this era.*

Gill, Joseph. The Council of Florence. *Cambridge: Cambridge University Press, 1959. This is a scholarly treatment of that council.*

Hyma, Albert. The Christian Renaissance. *New York: Century, 1924. This is a scholarly work on the Brethren of the Common Life.*

Leff, Gordon. Heresy in the Middle Ages. *New York: Barnes & Noble, 1967.*

Lucas, Henry S. The Renaissance and the Reformation. *2nd ed. New York: Harper, 1960. This work is still one of the most useful surveys of the era between 1305 and 1517 concerning such matters as the reforming councils, the rise of nations, and the Renaissance. The bibliography will be found helpful for information on the mass of literature available concerning the subjects discussed in this unit.*

MacKinnon, James. The Origin of the Reformation. *New York: Longmans, 1939.*

Mollatt, Guillaume. The Popes at Avignon 1305–78. *Translated by Janet Love. New York: Nelson, 1968.*

Mundy, John H., and Woody, Kennerly M., eds. The Council of Constance. *Translated by Louise R. Loomis. New York: Columbia University Press, 1961. Contemporary accounts of the Council of Constance are found in this work.*

Parker, Geoffrey H. W., The Morningstar: Wycliffe and the Dawn of the Reformation. *Grand Rapids: Eerdmans, 1965.*

Ridolfi, Roberto. The Life of Girolamo Savonarola. *Translated by Cecil Grayson. New York: Knopf, 1959. The author ably describes that reformer.*

Smith, John H. The Great Schism: The Disruption of the Papacy. *New York: Weybright and Tally, 1970.*

Spinka, Matthew. John Hus: A Biography. *Princeton: Princeton University Press, 1968.*

_____. John Hus at the Council of Constance. *New York: Columbia University Press, 1965. This and above work cover the life of Hus in scholarly fashion.*

_____, *trans.* The Letter of John Hus. *Manchester: Manchester University Press, 1972. This is a firsthand account of the thought of Hus.*

Stacey, John. John Wyclif and Reform. *Philadelphia: Westminster, 1964.*

Workman, Hebert B. The Dawn of the Reformation. *2 vols. London: Kelly, 1901–2.*

_____. John Wyclif. *2 vols. Oxford: Clarendon University Press, 1926.*

Chapter 25

The Papacy Faces
External Opposition

The work of the mystics, reformers, reforming councils, and humanists was an earnest attempt from different angles to bring about internal reform that would make religion more personal, the Scriptures the source of authority, and the Roman church more democratic in its organization. The defeat of these movements or their absorption by the Roman church ended all attempts at internal reform. At the same time external forces were creating opposition to the papal system. These forces were the humanistic spirit of the Renaissance, nationalism, and an expanding geographical world that was a result of exploration in the Far East and in the Western Hemisphere. These forces strengthened the movement that was eventually to break forth as the Protestant Reformation and to bring to an end the dominance of the papacy.

I. THE RENAISSANCE

The Renaissance, which took place in the important countries of Europe between 1350 and 1650, marks the transition from the medieval to the modern world. The name, which is derived from the Latin words for "birth" and "back," expresses the idea of a rebirth of culture. The name was first used about 1854 as a term descriptive of this era. In a narrower sense, the Renaissance has been linked with the fourteenth century in Italy, during which time men's minds were stimulated to literary and artistic production by the rediscovery of the treasures of the classical past. The classical spirit is apparent in the works of men like Petrarch (1304–74) and Boccacio (1313–75). This classical humanism south of the Alps was to be matched by the religious humanism of Reuchlin, Colet, Erasmus, and others north of the Alps in the early sixteenth century. The northern humanists went back to the Bible in the original, but the southern humanists emphasized the study of the classical literature and languages of Greece and Rome.

In a broader sense the Renaissance may be defined as that era of cultural reorientation in which men substituted a modern secular and individualistic view of life for the medieval religious and corporate approach to life. Attention was focused on the streets of Rome instead of on the streets of the New Jerusalem. The medieval theocentric conception of the world, in which God was the measure of all things, gave way to an anthropocentric view of life, in which man became the measure of all things. Emphasis was placed on the glory of man instead of on the glory of God. Urban middle-class society became more important than the old rural agrarian society of the feudal era. In this connection it must be remembered that the Renaissance was confined largely to a small upper-class society and that their ideas and way of living trickled down slowly to the lower segments of the social order. Commerce became more important than agriculture as the way to make a living. A humanistic, optimistic, and experimental approach to the things of this life became common. Although the age clung to religion, it was only as a mere formality on the holy days of the church; and the tendency was to forget the claims of God on the individual in daily life.

Several things contributed to the rise of this view of life. The Italian cities, where the movement first appeared, had become wealthy through serving as the middlemen in the rich commerce between western Europe and the Near East. The wealth provided leisure for study and enabled merchants to act as patrons to scholars and artists. The new middle class with money to spend was interested in that which would make life more pleasant and comfortable. Centralized government provided security and order. The advent of printing with movable type about 1456 in Germany made it possible to spread information quickly during the latter part of the Renaissance. Nominalism, with its interest in the individual and in the empirical approach as a way to truth, had stimulated tendencies that were to flower in the Renaissance.

A. The Italian Renaissance

The Renaissance appeared first in Italy during the fourteenth century because the classical tradition was stronger there than elsewhere. Italians were surrounded with the material remains of their past greatness, and the Italian spirit was sympathetic with an emphasis on the finer cultural values of this present life. Moreover, in Italy there were wealthy men who could give financial aid to artists so that they could be free to create. The great merchant Lorenzo de' Medici gave commissions to scholars and artists in order to create beautiful surroundings for himself. Popes of the Renaissance became interested in literature and the arts to such an extent that these interests took precedence over their spiritual functions. The fall of Constantinople in 1453 caused many Greek scholars to bring themselves and thousands of valuable Greek manuscripts to Italy in order to escape destruction by the Muslims.

Certain characteristics of the early Renaissance in Italy were interested in the classical or humanistic culture of Greece and Rome more than in theology. When Manuel Chrysoloras (1350–1415) came to Venice in 1393 as an ambassador to get aid for Constantinople against the Turkish threat, he remained in Florence three years teaching the Greek language to interested Florentines. Petrarch, the earliest of the Italian humanists, sought diligently to discover Greek and Roman manuscripts that he might study. These men found a new world as they studied these manuscripts, a world in which men were interested in the enjoyment of life here and now. The joys of this life appealed to these Italian scholars, and religion, which pertained to eternity, faded into the background.

Renaissance scholars and artists tended to be individualistic in their outlook. Cellini, who has left an interesting account of his life in his autobiography, was intensely individualistic in his enjoyment of life and gave primary consideration to his own desires. This attitude on the part of artists and scholars led to a secularization of society that was in strong contrast to the otherworldliness of medieval society. Something of this amoral secularization becomes apparent in Machiavelli's book *The Prince*. Machiavelli (1469–1527) advised the ruler of a state to subordinate absolute standards of conduct to expediency. If a lie or deceit would strengthen his position or his state, then he should not hesitate to use it.

The student is also impressed with the versatility of men of the Renaissance. Michaelangelo decorated the ceiling of the Sistine Chapel with magnificent paintings. He also became the able architect who supervised the completion of Saint Peter's in Rome and crowned the building with its lovely dome. He also designed the colorful uniform still used by the Swiss guard. Leonardo da Vinci painted the beautiful *Last Supper* and the *Mona Lisa* and drew sketches of machine guns and submarines that are remarkable in their similarity to modern machines.

The men of the Renaissance were lovers of beauty in nature or in man. In fact, they made a cult of beauty. Paintings of the era indicate increasing interest in the careful study of human anatomy so that pictures would be accurate. This love of beauty is to be seen in the skillful presentation of colorful rich fabrics in the pictures drawn by Titian, the great portrait painter of Venice. These pictures are in contrast to the emaciated, distorted figures and paintings of the Gothic era.

The dogmas of the church were accepted and the rites of worship were practiced, but there was a divorce between man's religious life and his daily life. This worldly spirit even affected the popes of the Renaissance. There were few heretics or atheists in the Latin countries, but spirituality took second place to formal religion.

A brief consideration of the activities of the leading Renaissance popes between 1447 and 1521 will show how the papacy capitulated to the secular and humanistic spirit of the age. Nicholas V (1397–1455) was a humanist who had risen through the ranks in the church until he became pope. His interest in the classical world made him seek to repair the buildings, bridges, aqueducts, and the great churches of Rome. His interest in the classical past was clearly shown in his giving up his own library to form the nucleus of the Vatican library, which was to be a treasure trove for future scholars. His secretary was Lorenzo Valla (1405–57), who, about 1440, after he had left the papal employ, wrote a treatise in which he exposed the *Donation of Constantine* as a forgery by his use of literary and historical criticism. He was thus the first to develop the rudiments of historical criticism. The fact that Lorenzo got into no trouble because of this daring act was a testimony to the indifference of the papacy to religion.

Julius II (1441–1513) spent much time in the political endeavor of unifying the papal states of Italy. He was also a patron of artists. He commissioned Michaelangelo to decorate the ceiling of the Sistine Chapel which Sixtus IV (1471–84) had built.

Leo X (1475–1521), who was pope when Luther took his stand against indulgences, was a member of the Medici family of Florence. He sanctioned the sale of indulgences to raise money for the building of the present Saint Peter's Cathedral in Rome. He was also a patron of the arts and letters. With such popes it is little wonder that Luther was scandalized at the formalism and lack of real spirituality when he made his famous visit to Rome in 1510–11.

B. The Biblical Humanists

Renaissance scholars north of the Alps had in common with their brethren south of the Alps a love for sources from the past, an emphasis on human beings as individual entities with a right to develop their own personalities, and an interest in the powers of the human mind to interpret the data that the senses brought to it. However, they were not so much interested in the classical past as they were in the Christian past. They studied the biblical documents in the original tongues as much as or more than they studied the writings of Plato or Aristotle. Their emphasis was on the Jewish-Christian heritage rather than on the Hellenic heritage of western Europe. They were essentially Christian humanists who applied the techniques and methods of humanism to the study of the Scriptures. They were more interested in man as a human being with a soul than they were in him as a rational creature. Their humanism was ethical and religious, whereas that of their Latin brethren to the south of the Alps was more aesthetic and secular.

1. Though what has been said of the Italian humanists was true of the majority, there was a small group in Florence, led by Marsilio Ficino (1433–99), that had fallen under the influence of Savonarola. Marsilio translated Plato's writings into Latin from 1463 to 1477. These humanists wished to integrate the Bible with Greek philosophy, particularly that of Plato. In an effort to achieve this aim, they began a study of the Bible from the literary viewpoint of the humanists. Financial aid from the de' Medici family made possible a Platonic Academy in Florence where Christian humanists might pursue their studies. John Colet from England, Jacques Lefèvre from France, and Reuchlin from Germany all spent some time at the academy.

2. Although Lefèvre (1455–1536) used a literal and spiritual interpretation of the Bible in writing his philological work on the Psalms, he did emphasize the study of the text of the Bible. About 1512 he published a Latin commentary on Paul's Epistles. His work helped to pave the way for the rise of the Huguenots when the influence of the Reformation reached France.

3. Jiminéz Francisco de Cisneros, better known as Cardinal Ximénes, the archbishop of Toledo, Spain, became Isabella's confessor and for some years the Grand Inquisitor of the Spanish Inquisition. He founded the University of Alcala to train clergy in the Bible and printed a Greek New Testament by 1514. In addition, he supervised the completion of the Complutensian Polyglot of the Bible.

4. John Colet (ca. 1467–1519) was one of a group in England who were known as the Oxford Reformers. After his visit to Italy, Colet began in lectures to develop the literal meaning of the Pauline Epistles. This was an innovation because former theologians had been more interested in allegory than they were in what the writer of the Scriptures was trying to say to his or a later day. The work of the Oxford Reformers was a contributing factor in the coming of the Reformation in England.

5. Reuchlin and Erasmus were, however, the most influential of the humanists because the influence of their work was felt all over Europe. John Reuchlin (1455–1522) had studied under Pico Della Mirandola in Italy and had developed a taste for Hebrew language, literature, and theology. The fruit of his scientific study of the Old Testament was a combined Hebrew grammar and dictionary that he called *Of the Rudiments of Hebrew*. This work, completed in 1506, helped others become familiar with the tongue of the Old Testament so that they could study that book in the original language. It is interesting that Reuchlin gave advice concerning the education of Melanchthon, Luther's right-hand man and the first theologian of the Reformation.

6. Desiderius Erasmus (ca. 1466–1536) was even more influential than Reuchlin. He had received part of his early education in the school of the Brethren of the Common Life in Deventer and later studied at many of the universities of Europe and England. He became a universal scholar who was at home in cultured circles in any land. His scholarly spirit inclined him to reform rather than revolution, and his negative opposition to the abuses of the Roman Catholic church was expressed in his books *The Praise of Folly* (ca. 1511) and *Familiar Colloquies* (1518).[1] In these books Erasmus attempted by clever satire to point out the evils of the life of the priestly and

Hans Holbein the younger, made woodcuts as marginal illustrations for *The Praise of Folly*, Erasmus's satire on the evils in the church. In the three reproduced here and on page 264, Holbein represents a fat monk, the soul of a monk entering the body of Folly, and an individual worshiping an icon.

monastic hierarchy. The humanists satirized and the Reformers denounced evils in the church. The positive aspect of his work was the Greek New Testament that was published in 1516 by the publisher Froben of Basel, who was desirous of getting the fame and market that would accompany the publication of the first printed and published Greek New Testament. The Spanish scholar Ximénes had had a Greek New Testament printed in 1514, but he could not sell it until the pope approved. In order to reach the market before him, Froben urged Erasmus on. Erasmus used four Greek manuscripts, which were available at Basel; but, when he found that the last few verses of Revelation were missing in all of them, he translated the Latin back into what he thought the Greek should be. The influence of the book was tremendous, for scholars were now in a position to make accurate comparison between the church that they saw in the New Testament and the church of their day. The comparison was decidedly unfavorable to the latter.

At first Erasmus sympathized with Luther, but later he opposed him because he did not desire the break with the Roman Catholic church that Luther was forced to make. Erasmus's *Handbook of the Christian Soldier* (1503) was an ethical approach to Christianity. He put his stress on ethics. Moreover, his theology differed greatly from that which Luther held. In his book *Free Will* (1524), he emphasized the reform of abuses rather than an attack on doctrine and upheld the freedom of the human will, which Luther said was completely bound as far as goodness and salvation were concerned.

In both northern and southern

Europe the Renaissance had lasting results. The study of the classical pagan past led to a secular approach to life in which religion was reduced to a formal affair or ignored until one came to the hour of death. The ideal of the person as an independent human being with the right to develop as his tastes led him took precedence over the medieval ideal of one who was to be saved by taking his humble place in the corporate hierarchical society of the Roman Catholic church. The impetus given to the use of the vernacular by the scholars and poets of fourteenth- and fifteenth-century Europe was helpful later in bringing to the people the Bible and the services of the church in their mother tongue. The return to sources of culture from the past and the scientific study of them made possible a far more accurate knowledge of the Bible than had been the case before this time. In the political realm the amoral note struck in Machiavelli's *Prince* led to the ignoring of moral principles in the conduct of the foreign affairs of the city-states of Italy and the rising nation-states of northern Europe. One who seeks a balanced view of the impact of the Renaissance can call it neither a tragedy nor an unmixed blessing but will have to consider it a mixture of blessing and bane to the people of Europe.

7. In addition to the development of man's interest in himself as an individual with a mind and a spirit, the Renaissance resulted in the development of a wider knowledge of man's physical universe. Man became interested in his environment as well as in himself, and scientific and geographical studies led to a new world of science and to an increased knowl-edge of how large man's world actually is. The beginning of geographical exploration was again the work of the Latin. Prince Henry of Portugal (1394–1460) sent out explorers from Portugal until Vasco da Gama discovered the way to India around the southern tip of Africa. Columbus (1445–1506) made the Western Hemisphere known to the world, and his work was speedily supplemented by that of French and English explorers, all of whom were seeking a shorter route to the wealth of the Far East. Copernicus and Galileo also made men conscious of the immensity of the universe about them, and the invention of the telescope and its increasingly effective use substantiated their earlier theories.

II. THE RISE OF NATION-STATES AND THE MIDDLE CLASS

The classical world had been dominated by the ideal of the city-state as the largest political unit into which men might organize themselves. Even the Roman Empire was simply an expansion of the city-state of Rome. Anyone who became a citizen became a citizen of Rome, no matter where he resided. The Middle Ages was dominated by the concept of political as well as spiritual unity, and, in theory, all men were to be united in a new Rome, the Holy Roman Empire. In practice, however, feudalism with all its decentralization gave security and order in chaotic periods. The revival of towns prior to the Renaissance created strong city-states in Italy. But the future in Europe was with the nation-state as a form of political organization. England, France, and Spain were pioneers in the development of such nation-states. The development in

England was along the lines of a constitutional monarchy in which sovereignty was shared by the monarch and parliament. The bodies representing the people in France and Spain never became as powerful as Parliament in England; and France and Spain developed as centralized nation-states in which the ruler was absolute. As cities grew and commerce developed, a middle class arose, and they wanted a share in political and religious life.

A. The Rise of the English Nation-State

The English Parliament grew out of the feudal assembly, known as the *curia regis*, that was introduced into England during the reign of William the Conqueror, after his successful invasion of England in 1066. This assembly of the feudal lords served as a high court, an advisory body to the king, and as a money-granting body when the king asked for more than the standard feudal grants. Its powers were strengthened by the signing of the Magna Charta by John in 1215. John agreed not to levy new taxes without the consent of the *curia regis* and to permit the barons to rise against him if he violated the charter. Justice was to be administered fairly, and people were given the right to be tried before those of their own class. Although this document benefited only the feudal class at the time, it did introduce the principles that the ruler was limited by the law and that taxes could be levied only by consent of those taxed. In 1295 Edward I called the Model Parliament in which representatives of the counties and the cities were present as well as the feudal lords and great churchmen.

The two former groups developed the House of Commons, and the last two groups eventually formed the House of Lords. During the fourteenth century the king's need of money led to the development of the law-making powers of Parliament since the members of Parliament would not grant the king desired revenues unless he would sign their petitions or bills, which then became law.

The representative Parliament, to which the king's ministers were responsible, was only one of the foundations of English constitutional monarchy. In the reign of Henry II the common law, which protects the liberties of the individual better than Roman law does, and the jury system were developed. The individual thus had protection against the arbitrary acts of the ruler.

The Hundred Years' War with France (1337–1453) served to create English national pride as the English yeomen-archers with their long bows found that the arrows could defeat the French mounted knight, and the final loss of territories held by the English ruler in France tended to draw the upper and lower classes together into national unity. The War of the Roses in the third quarter of the fifteenth century led to the wiping out of the old feudal nobility and made possible an alliance between the king and the middle class in the state. The middle class in return for order and security willingly granted money and authority to the rulers. The freedom of the fifteenth-century Parliament gave way to the veiled despotism of the Tudors, who ran the state along Machiavellian lines during the sixteenth century. They did, however, keep Parliament to secure popular backing for their acts.

B. The Rise of the French Nation-State

The French nation-state faced great obstacles in its development. English rulers held much territory in France, and the great feudal nobles were not controlled by the French king, who only held a small area of land around Paris. France had no racial or geographic unity because of the diverse racial elements in the population and the geographic composition of the country, which stimulated provincialism. In spite of these problems, the Capetian line of rulers in Paris, beginning with Hugh Capet in 987, was able to unify France. The Estates General, the French Parliament, never became as powerful as the English Parliament, and the ruler was consequently more absolute in his control of the state. Able rulers and hatred of the common enemy, England, during the Hundred Years' War did much to unify France. This war also gave the French their national heroine, Joan of Arc.

C. The Rise of the Spanish Nation-State

The marriage of Ferdinand of Aragon and Isabella of Castile in 1469 promoted Spanish unity. The development of the Spanish nation-state was given a religious aspect by the struggle to free the Iberian Peninsula of the Muslim invaders. The crusade, known as the *Reconquista*, was at its height during the eleventh century. The Roman Catholic faith and nationalism became partners in Spain, and the absolutism of the Roman church was paralleled by the political absolutism of the ruler. This manifested itself in the Spanish Inquisition led by Torquemada, under whom over ten thousand were killed, and Ximénes, under whom twenty-five hundred were killed.

The rise of the nation-state provided opposition to the Roman Catholic church, particularly in France and England, where rulers and the powerful middle class resented the flow of money from the state treasury or from their own pockets into the papal treasury. The noble class resented the control of so much land by the Church of Rome. The kings were not pleased with the divided sovereignty that caused their subjects to give allegiance to the pope as well as to themselves. Church courts, in which alone clergymen might be tried, were an affront to the royal system of courts; and appeals to the papal courts were particularly obnoxious. It will be remembered that in about 1300 the powerful rulers of England and France successfully defeated the efforts of Boniface VIII to control the clergy of their states and that France in the Pragmatic Sanction of Bourges in 1438 insisted that the Roman church in France must be controlled by the French ruler. England in two statutes, in 1351 and 1353 respectively, forbade the pope to fill vacancies in church offices in England without elections by the local clergy and the consent of the king and banned appeals from courts in England to the papal court. This tendency to resent ecclesiastical interference in affairs of state was an external force that fostered the work of the Reformers when they appeared on the scene.

It should be noted that the rulers of Europe could never have successfully fought the papacy if it had not been for the backing of the wealthy middle class that was created by commerce arising from the rebirth of towns and revival of trade after 1200. The middle-class merchants of the city and the wealthy middle-class land-owners backed the rulers in their opposition to the papal control of their lands. Sovereignty rested in the rulers of the nation-states rather than the pope.

III. THE GREEK ORTHODOX CHURCH, 1305–1517

While dynamic external forces of opposition and reform were building up in western Europe, forces that would shatter the unity of the medieval Roman Catholic church, the Eastern church remained static in its theological outlook and expanded very little. In fact, the importance of Constantinople as a religious center declined after its fall to the Ottoman Turks in 1453, and the Russian patri-archs became increasingly important in the leadership of the Greek Or-thodox church.

Two changes took place in Russia that deeply affected the future devel-opment of its Christianity. Between 1237, when Mongol invaders first came into Russia, and 1480, when they finally lost control of the state, Russia was under the control of Mongol Tar-tar invaders. Although this invasion put Russia back culturally, it worked to the advantage of the Russian church because the invasion cut the Russian church off from Constantinople and forced it to fall back on its own native leadership. Russian nationalism and religion were unified as the Russians strove to maintain their religion and culture in spite of their conquerors.

People turned to religion for solace as well as for leadership in their time of crisis.

In 1325 the metropolitan arch-bishop of the Orthodox church in Rus-sia moved his headquarters from Kiev, which was near Constantinople, to Moscow. Here he could be more inde-pendent of Constantinople, but at the same time he was more subject to sec-ular control by the rulers of the Rus-sian state. After 1453 the Russian met-ropolitan became independent of the patriarch at Constantinople because that city and the leader of the Or-thodox church were under the control of the Turks. Shortly after the fall of Constantinople, the Russian bishops elected the metropolitan as the "Met-ropolitan of Moscow and all Russia." Free to develop along independent lines, although its theology and liturgy were not changed appreciably, the Or-thodox church in Russia became a na-tional church in 1589 and, later, even became closely identified with the state. Moscow became the "third" Rome to replace Rome and Constan-tinople.

Between 1305 and 1517 forces pro-moting change were at work both in the church in the East and the church in the West. In the East, the changes were to be primarily along the lines of ecclesiastical leadership and organi-zation, but in the West, the Reforma-tion brought about fundamental changes that not only created the na-tional Protestant churches but also brought reformation within the Roman Catholic church so that it could meet the challenge of Protes-tantism.

SUGGESTED READING

Adeney, Walter F. **The Greek and Eastern Church.** *New York: Scribner, 1908. This will provide sufficient information concerning the church in the East in this period.*

Bainton, Roland H. **Erasmus of Christendom.** *New York: Scribner, 1969.*

Erasmus. **In Praise of Folly.** *The student should read this classical satirical work so that he can capture the critical spirit of the Christian humanists.*

Ferguson, Wallace. **The Renaissance.** *New York: Holt, 1940. This little volume is a helpful survey of the Renaissance.*

Froude, J. A. **Life and Letters of Erasmus.** *New York: Scribner, 1912.*

Green, Vivian H. H. **Renaissance and Reformation.** *London: Arnold, 1952.*

Hyma, Albert. **The Life of Desiderius Ersamus.** *Assen, Netherlands: Van Gorcurm, 1972.*

Lea, Henry C. **A History of the Inquisition in Spain.** *4 vols. London: Macmillan, 1906–7.*

Lucas, Henry S. **The Renaissance and Reformation.** *2nd ed. New York: Harper & Brothers, 1960. This is a helpful general treatment of the northern and southern Renaissance and also gives attention to the rise of nation-states and the middle class as important influences during the Reformation.*

Smith, Preserved. **Erasmus.** *New York: Harper, 1923. This is a scholarly and interesting account of the life and work of Erasmus.*

Thomson, S. Harrison. **Europe in Renaissance and Reformation.** *New York: Harcourt, Brace, 1963.*

MODERN CHURCH HISTORY, 1517 AND AFTER

Reformation and Counter Reformation, 1517–1648

Rationalism, Revivalism, and Denominationalism, 1648–1789

Revivalism, Missions, and Modernism, 1789–1914

Church and Society in Tension Since 1914

Chapter 26

The Background of Reformation

The unwillingness of the medieval Roman Catholic church to accept reforms suggested by sincere reformers such as the mystics, Wycliffe and Hus, the leaders of the reforming councils, and the humanists; the emergence of nation-states, which opposed the papal claim to have universal power; and the rise of a middle class, which disliked the drain of wealth to Rome, all combined to make a Reformation a certainty. Its gaze fixed on the pagan classical past, oblivious of the dynamic forces that were creating a new society, Italian society, of which the papacy was a part, adopted a corrupt, sensual, and immoral, although cultured, way of life.

I. THE EMERGENCE OF AN EXPANDING DYNAMIC WORLD

By 1500 the foundations of the old medieval society were breaking up, and a new society with a larger geographical horizon and with changing political, economic, intellectual, and religious patterns was slowly coming into being. The changes were so great as to be revolutionary, both in their scope and in their effects on the social order.

The medieval synthesis was challenged during the Reformation in its polity by the idea that the universal church should be replaced by national or state churches and free churches. Its Scholastic philosophy tied to Greek philosophy gave way to Protestant biblical theology. Justification by faith, sacraments, and works gave way to faith alone to justify. The Bible rather than the Bible and tradition as interpreted by the church became the norm. All this after 1650, in turn, was undermined by German idealistic philosophy and biblical criticism. Western civilization became increasingly secularized. As Europe expanded globally, all the world was affected.

A. Geographical Change

The geographical knowledge of the medieval man underwent remarkable changes between 1492 and 1600. The civilization of the ancient world has been characterized as potamic (from *potamos*, the Greek word for river) because it was linked with the river systems of the ancient world. The civilization of the Middle Ages has been called thalassic because it developed about seas—the Mediterranean and the Baltic. By 1517 the discoveries of Columbus and other explorers ushered in an era of oceanic civilization, in which the oceans of the world became the highways of the world. By the time Luther had translated the New Testament into German (1522), Magellan's ship had completed a voyage around the world. Southeastern and southwestern water routes opened cheaper routes to the riches of the Far East. The Roman Catholic countries of Portugal, France, and Spain were leaders in exploration, but the Protestant nations of England and Holland soon overtook them in geographical exploration and settlement. Two rich new continents in the Western Hemisphere were opened up for exploitation by the Old World. Spain and Portugal had a monopoly in South and Central America, but the greater part of North America, after a struggle between France and England, became a new home for Anglo-Saxons. Spain, Portugal, and later France exported a Latin culture with Counter Reformation Catholicism carried by conquistadors and clergy to Quebec and Central and South America to form a homogeneous culture. The people of northwestern Europe exported Anglo-Saxon or Teutonic culture and pluralistic Protestantism to form the culture of the United States and Canada. These have persisted to the present in the Western Hemisphere.

B. Political Change

Perspectives were also changing in the political realm. The medieval concept of a universal state was giving way to the new concept of the territorial, nation-state. Since the end of medieval times, states have been organized on a national basis. These centralized nation-states with powerful rulers, ably served by army and civil service, were nationalistic and opposed to domination by a universal state or a universal religious ruler. Some of them were consequently eager to support the Reformation in order that national churches might be more directly under their control. The theoretical political unity of the medieval world was replaced by nation-states, each of which was insistent on its independence and sovereignty. The practical feudal decentralization of the medieval world was replaced by a Europe made up of centralized nation-states. Because each state was independent, the new principle of balance of power as a guide in international relations became prominent in the religious wars of the sixteenth and early seventeenth centuries.

C. Economic Change

Startling economic changes were also taking place just before the Reformation. During the Middle Ages the economy of the countries of Europe was agricultural, and land was the basis of wealth. By 1500 the revival of towns, the opening of new markets, and the discovery of sources of raw materials in colonies in the newly discovered lands ushered in an age of commerce in which the middle-class merchant replaced the medieval feudal noble as a leader in society. Not until the advent of the Industrial Revolution about 1750 was this commercial pattern of economic life appreciably changed. Trade became international rather than interurban. An economy in which profits became important emerged. The rising capitalistic middle class resented the drain of their wealth to the international church under the leadership of the pope in Rome, and in northern Europe it threw its influence behind the Reformation.

D. Social Change

The horizontal social organization of medieval society, in which one remained in the class into which one was born, was to be replaced by a society organized along vertical lines. One might rise from a lower class in society to a higher class. In medieval times, if one were the son of a serf, there was little chance for him to be anything but a serf, except for service in the church. By 1500 men were rising, by dint of industry, to higher social rank. Serfdom was fast disappearing, and a new urban middle class, which had been missing in medieval society, and in this class the free farmer, the country gentry, and the merchant class of the town were most prominent. This strong middle class generally supported the changes made by the Reformation in northwestern Europe.

E. Intellectual Change

The intellectual changes wrought by the Renaissance both north and south of the Alps created an intellectual outlook that favored the development of Protestantism. The desire to return to sources of the past led the Christian humanists of the north to a study of the Bible in the original tongues of the Scriptures. Thus the difference between the church of the New Testament and the medieval Roman Catholic church became clear to them, and the difference was to the disadvantage of the medieval papal, ecclesiastical organization. Renaissance emphasis on the individual was a helpful factor in the development of the Protestant insistence that salvation was a personal matter to be settled by the individual in immediate relationship with his God without a priest standing by as a human mediator. The critical spirit of the Renaissance was used by the Reformers to justify observation of the hierarchy and sacraments of the medieval Roman church and a critical comparison of them with the Scriptures. Though the Renaissance in Italy proceeded along humanistic and pagan lines, the tendencies that it fostered were taken over in northern Europe by the Christian humanists and the Reformers and used by them to justify individual study of the Bible in the original as the source document of the Christian faith.

F. Religious Change

Medieval religious uniformity gave way in the early sixteenth century to religious diversity. The seamless garment of the international and universal Roman Catholic church, with its corporate, hierarchical, sacramental structure, was rent again, as it had been before in 1054, by schisms that resulted in the founding of national or free Protestant churches. Such churches were generally under the control of the rulers of the nation-states, particularly the Anglican and Lutheran churches. Not until after 1648 were denominations and freedom of religion to emerge. The authority of the Roman church was replaced by the authority of the Bible, which the individual was to be allowed to read freely. The individual believer could now be his own priest and conduct his own religious life in fellowship with God after he had accepted His Son as his Savior by faith alone.

Within the generation between Columbus's discovery of America (1492) and Luther's posting of the ninety-five theses on the door of the church in Wittenberg (1517), the startling changes that have been described took place or had their beginnings. The static patterns of medieval civilization were replaced by the dynamic patterns of modern society. The changes in the religious realm were by no means the least remarkable changes in the civilization of western Europe. The Christian is compelled to bow in reverence as he traces the hand of God in the affairs of men in this era.

II. NAME AND DEFINITION OF THE REFORMATION

Both the name and definition given to the Reformation are somewhat conditioned by the outlook of the historian. Some Roman Catholic historians look on it as a revolt by Protestants against the universal church. The Protestant historian considers it a reformation that brought religious life nearer to the pattern of the New Testament. The secular historian thinks of it more as a revolutionary movement.

If one considers the Reformation solely from the viewpoint of polity or church government, it may be considered a revolt against the authority of the church of Rome and its head, the pope. Though we thus concede that the Reformation had a revolutionary character, it does not necessarily follow that the true church was confined to Rome. The Reformers and many others who preceded them had tried unsuccessfully to bring reform to the medieval Roman Catholic church from within its fold, but they were forced out of the older organization because of their ideas of reform. In the Catholic Reformation, however, renewal came later.

The more familiar term "Protestant Reformation" has become hallowed by age; and because the Reformation was an attempt to return to the early purity of the Christianity of the New Testament, it is wise to continue to use the term to describe the religious movement between 1517 and 1545. The Reformers were anxious to develop a theology that was in complete accord with the New Testament and believed that this could never be a reality as long as the church instead of the Bible was made the final authority.

Many Protestants forget that the Protestant movement stimulated, partly as a reaction to check Protestant gains, a movement of reform within the Roman Catholic church that prevented the Reformation from making many new gains after it had once got under way. This reform movement that developed in the Roman Catholic church between 1545 and 1563 is known as the Counter Reformation or Catholic Reformation.

For the most part, the Reformation was confined to western Europe and to Teutonic middle-class peoples. Neither the Eastern church nor the

Latin peoples of the old Roman Empire accepted the Reformation. In those areas the medieval ideals of unity and uniformity still held sway, but in northern and western Europe the Teutonic peoples moved from religious unity and uniformity to the diversity of Protestantism.

The definition of the term "Reformation" is no easy task. If one considers the Reformation simply as the creator of national churches, it would be a religious movement between 1517 and 1648. Because only Holland was won to Protestantism after the Council of Trent, it would seem wise to limit the most important part of the Reformation to the years between 1517 and 1545. The Reformation is here defined as that movement of religious reform that resulted in the creation of the national Protestant churches between 1517 and 1545. Consequently, the Catholic Reformation may be defined as a movement of religious reform within the Roman Catholic church between 1545 and 1563 that stabilized and strengthened that church after its heavy losses to Protestantism and promoted a major Roman Catholic missionary movement in the sixteenth century that won Central and South America, Quebec, Indochina, and the Philippines to the church.

III. THE GENESIS OF THE REFORMATION

A. Interpretations of the Reformation

The interpretation that historians give to history has influenced their consideration of the causes of the Reformation. Emphasis on one or another factor in history is made, depending on what school of historical interpretation is followed.

Protestant historians—such as Schaff, Grimm, and Bainton—interpret the Reformation largely as a religious movement that sought to recover the purity of the primitive Christianity that is depicted in the New Testament. This interpretation tends to ignore the economic, political, and intellectual factors that helped to promote the Reformation. According to this interpretation, Providence is the primary factor that takes precedence over all other factors.

Roman Catholic historians interpret the Reformation as a heresy inspired by Martin Luther from base motives, such as his desire to marry. Protestantism is looked upon as a heretical schism that destroyed the theological and ecclesiastical unity of the medieval Roman church. It is true that, viewed from the Romanist viewpoint, Luther was a heretic and became a schismatic, but from such a viewpoint historians usually fail to see how far the medieval church had departed from the ideal of the New Testament. The Catholic Reformation was in itself an admission that all was not well in the medieval church.

Secular historians give more attention to secondary factors in their interpretation of the Reformation. Voltaire illustrated the rationalistic interpretation of the movement quite well. To him the Reformation was little more than the consequences of a monastic squabble in Saxony, and the religious Reformation in England was an outcome of the love affairs of Henry VIII. It is true that the Augustinian order of monks clashed with the Dominicans on the issue of indulgences and that the love of Henry VIII for Anne Boleyn made the early stage of the Reformation in England a matter of politics; but this type of interpretation ignores many other important factors, such as the essentially religious Reformation in England in the reign of Edward VI, the son of Henry VIII.

Historians who accept the Marxist concept of economic determinism cannot interpret the Reformation in any other way than in economic terms. The Reformation is looked upon as the result of the attempt of the Roman papacy to exploit Germany economically for the material benefit of the papacy. Political historians see the Reformation as a result of nation-states opposing an international church. To them the Reformation is simply a political event caused by the rise of nationalism.

Although there are elements of truth in all these interpretations, the student will notice that they emphasize, for the most part, secondary causes and, often, only one particular secondary cause. The causes of the Reformation were not simple and single but were complex and multiple. The Reformation was both derivative and determinative in its causation. Many causes had their roots in the centuries preceding the Reformation, when Rome had opposed any internal reform and had ignored the rising tide of external opposition that was to cause her so much trouble. The creative personalities of such leaders in the Reformation as Luther, Calvin, and others were determinative of the direction the Reformation took. The leaders of the Protestant Reformation usually came from the middle class, but those of the Catholic Reformation were aristocratic. For these reasons, the interpretation of the Reformation in this work is a synthesis; that is, religion is given primary consideration, but secondary political, economic, moral, and intellectual factors are not ignored.[1]

B. Causes of the Reformation

1. The political factor may be considered one of the important indirect causes for the coming of the Reformation. The new centralized nation-states of northwestern Europe were opposed to the concept of a universal church that claimed jurisdiction over the nation state and its powerful ruler. The ideal of such a universal church clashed with the rising national consciousness of the middle class in these new states.

This basic political problem was complicated by particular questions. It will be noticed that the nations that accepted Protestantism during the Reformation were located outside the orbit of the old Roman Empire and that the powerful middle classes in them had a different cultural outlook from that of the Latin nations. Some even think of the Reformation as a revolt of northern Teutonic nations against the Latin nations with their Mediterranean culture and with their concept of international organization that were their heritage from the old Roman Empire. Rulers of these nation-states resented the jurisdiction of the pope within their territory. This jurisdiction was often temporal as well as spiritual because the Roman church owned great tracts of land throughout Europe. Church ownership of land created a division of sovereignty within the state, and such despotic rulers as the English Tudors resented this. Appointments to important positions in the Roman church were made by a foreigner, the pope. Clerics were not subject to trial in civil courts but were tried in church courts rather than royal courts. Appeals could be carried from these courts to the papal court. Heavy church taxes also alienated the people and their rulers from Rome. The national ruler and his civil service were opposed to the international religious hierarchy of the Roman church. Henry VIII broke with the Church of Rome over the issue of whether the royal divorce was an international matter for the pope to decide or a national matter that the national clergy could settle.

2. The recent attention given to economics as a motivating factor in human affairs cannot be dismissed casually by the Christian historian even though he does not accept the materialistic interpretation of Marx or the economic determinists. The land possessed by the Roman church in western Europe was regarded with greedy eyes by the national rulers, nobles, and middle class of the new nation-states. The rulers resented the loss of the money that went to the papal treasury in Rome. Moreover, the clergy were exempt from the taxes of national states. The papal attempt to get more money out of Germany in the sixteenth century was bitterly resented by the rising middle class of such states as Saxony. This drainage of money from the state to Rome was complicated by inflation and the rising cost of living. Inflation had grown out of the great sums of money that Spain gathered by the exploitation of her possessions and subjects in the New World. This money Spain had poured into the economic blood stream of Europe. It was the abuse of the indulgence system as a tool to get wealth from Germany for the papacy that angered Luther.

3. The intellectual factor in the Reformation was that men with awakened minds and a secular outlook became critical of the religious life of their day as represented in the Roman Catholic church. As the middle class grew in numbers, it became individualistic in outlook and began to revolt against the corporate concept of medieval society that put the individual under authority. This tendency to individualism was reinforced by the rise of absolutist nation-states in which the interests of the international Roman Catholic church took second place to those of the nation and of the ruler and his loyal supporters of the middle-class business group. Renaissance humanism, especially in Italy, created a secular spirit similar to that which had characterized classical Greece. Even the popes of the Renaissance adopted the intellectual and secular approach to life. This spirit and approach grew out of the desire of scholars to go back to the sources of man's intellectual past. A comparison of the corporate hierarchical society of the day with the intellectual freedom and secularism of Greek society and with the principle of freedom for the individual seen in scriptural sources made men skeptical of the claims of the Church of Rome and its leaders. Men began to have wider intellectual horizons and began to be interested in secular rather than religious life.

4. The moral factor of the Reformation was closely allied to the intellectual. The humanistic scholars, who had the New Testament in Greek, clearly saw the discrepancies between the church about which they read in the New Testament and the Roman Catholic

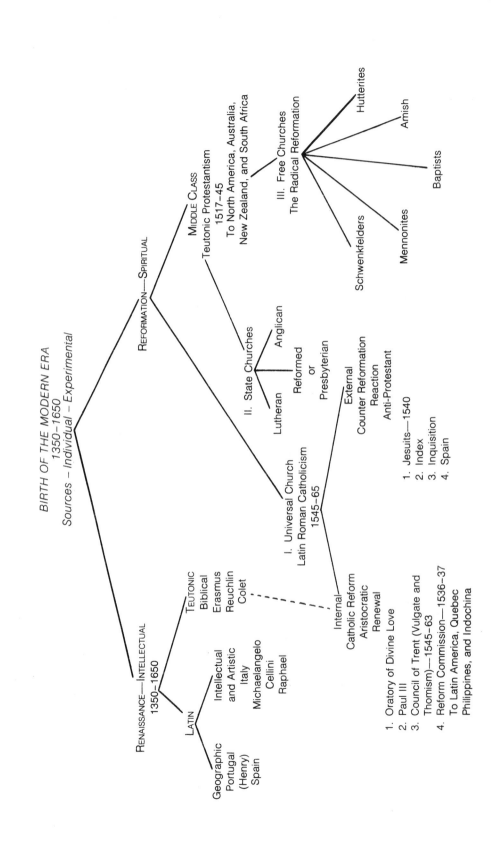

BIRTH OF THE MODERN ERA
1350–1650
Sources – Individual – Experimental

RENAISSANCE—INTELLECTUAL
1350–1650

REFORMATION—SPIRITUAL

LATIN

TEUTONIC
Biblical
Erasmus
Reuchlin
Colet

Geographic
Portugal
(Henry)
Spain

Intellectual
and Artistic
Italy
Michaelangelo
Cellini
Raphael

Internal—
Catholic Reform
Aristocratic
Renewal

1. Oratory of Divine Love
2. Paul III
3. Council of Trent (Vulgate and
   Thomism)—1545–63
4. Reform Commission—1536–37
   To Latin America, Quebec
   Philippines, and Indochina

I. Universal Church
Latin Roman Catholicism
1545–65

External
Counter Reformation
Reaction
Anti-Protestant

1. Jesuits—1540
2. Index
3. Inquisition
4. Spain

II. State Churches

Lutheran

Anglican

Reformed
or
Presbyterian

MIDDLE CLASS
Teutonic Protestantism
1517–45
To North America, Australia,
New Zealand, and South Africa

III. Free Churches
The Radical Reformation

Hutterites

Amish

Baptists

Mennonites

Schwenkfelders

church of their day. Corruption had spread through both head and members of the hierarchy of the Roman church. Self-seeking clerics bought and sold offices freely. Too many enjoyed sinecures, positions in which they received the salary but did none of the work usually associated with the office. Some held several offices at once, as did Albert of Mainz, whose agent Tetzel was so strenuously opposed by Luther in Saxony. Justice was bought and sold in the church courts. One could for a payment of money get a dispensation that would permit him to marry a close relative, even though the canon law forbade it. Many priests lived in open sin or kept concubines. The people of the dioceses were neglected by the bishops, who often failed to engage in the episcopal visitation necessary to supervise the clergy under them and to see that the clergy did not neglect their flocks. Many parish clergy consequently neglected preaching and visitation, being content to say the Mass, which they proclaimed as a magic rite that would bring grace to a person. Collections of relics, such as bits of the cross and bones of saints, became the vogue. A single viewing of the 5,005 relics of Frederick of Saxony was supposed to reduce one's time in purgatory by nearly two million years. People became tired of the ceaseless cry for money from the head of an institution that did not seem to be rendering that service to communities that one would associate with the church.[2]

5. Changes taking place in the social structure accelerated the disillusionment of medieval men with the Roman church. The rise of towns and a prosperous middle class within the towns created a new spirit of individ-ualism. The new money economy freed people from dependence on the soil as the main way they could make a living. Middle class burghers were not as tractable as their feudal forerunners had been, and even the artisans of the cities and the agricultural workers were beginning to realize that all was not well with a social order in which they were oppressed by those above them in society. Social discontent and the demand for reform was a definite social factor in the coming of the Reformation.

6. Behind the failure of the Roman church to meet the real needs of the people was the theological or philosophical factor of the Reformation. Some have so overemphasized this element that they can see the Reformation only in terms of a struggle between the theology of Thomas Aquinas and that of Augustine. It is true that the medieval church adopted the philosophy of Thomas Aquinas. It emphasized his teaching that man's will was not totally corrupted. By faith and the use of the means of grace in the sacraments dispensed by the hierarchy, man could achieve salvation. Augustine believed that man's will was so totally depraved that he could do nothing toward his salvation. God would extend the grace to man to energize his will so that he could by faith take the salvation that Christ proffered him. However, any careful study of the writings of the Reformers will indicate that the Reformers went to Augustine from the Bible to seek the aid of his powerful authority, but they did not arrive at the doctrine of justification by faith by studying the writings of Augustine. It was the Scriptures that brought home that profound truth to them. The theological

cause of the Reformation was the desire of the Reformers to go back to the classic source of the Christian faith, the Bible, in order to counter the claims of Thomistic theology that salvation was a matter of grace obtained through the sacraments dispensed by the hierarchy.

7. If discontent becomes extreme when people face adverse conditions, their dissatisfaction will usually express itself through some great leader who expresses their ideas for them. The refusal of the medieval Roman Catholic church to accept reform, indeed, the impossibility that it would reform itself, opened the way for the coming of a leader who would embody the desire for reform of abuses and who would be used to bring about revolutionary changes. Such was the function of Martin Luther in whom the spirit of Reformation, with its insistence on the right of the individual to go directly to God through the Christ revealed in the Scriptures, was embodied.

Glaring abuse of the indulgence system in Germany was the *direct* cause for the coming of the Reformation in that country. Archbishop Albert (1490–1545), a prince of the House of Hohenzollern, who was already in control of two provinces of the Roman church, cast covetous eyes on the vacant archbishopric of Mainz in 1514. Because Albert was only twenty-three, and because canon law also forbade one man to hold more than one office, he had to pay Pope Leo X for the dispensations necessary before he could fill the two offices. Fortunately for him, his desire for the archbishopric of Mainz and that of Pope Leo X for money to build the present Saint Peter's cathedral in Rome coincided.

Albert was to be permitted to become archbishop of Mainz if he would pay the pope a large sum of money in addition to the regular fees for taking over such an office. Because this sum was in the realm of high finance, the papacy suggested that Albert might borrow the money from the wealthy Fugger banking family in Augsburg. A papal bull, authorizing the sale of indulgences in Saxony, was granted as security, guaranteeing that Albert would repay his loan to the Fuggers. Leo got half the money and the other half went to repay the Fuggers.

Indulgences were associated with the sacrament of penance. After one had repented of sin and had confessed it, one was assured of absolution by the priest, provided satisfaction was made. It was thought that the guilt of sin and eternal punishment for sin were forgiven by God but that there was a temporal satisfaction that the repentant sinner must fulfill either in this life or in purgatory. This satisfaction might be a pilgrimage to a shrine, a payment of money to a church, or some meritorious deed. The indulgence was a document that could be bought for a sum of money and that would free one from the temporal penalty of sin. It was believed that Christ and the saints had achieved so much merit during their earthly lives that the excess merit was laid up in a heavenly treasury of merit on which the pope could draw on behalf of the living faithful.[3] This idea was first formulated by Alexander of Hales in the thirteenth century. Clement VI declared it to be dogma in 1343. A later papal bull of Sixtus IV in 1476 extended this privilege to souls in purgatory, provided their living relatives purchased indulgences for them.

Johannes Tetzel von Leipzig
S.S. Theol. Doctor und Professor, ein Bruder
des Dominicaner Ordens, Ketzer Meister, und
Päpstlicher Gnadenprediger, oder Ablas Cræmer.

In a contemporary line engraving Tetzel, the indulgence peddler, is shown with a price list of standard fees for indulgences and a cash box ready to receive the money.

It was this system for raising money that was so unblushingly abused in the papal bull issued to Albert. Albert's main agent was a Dominican monk named Johann Tetzel, who was paid nearly eleven hundred dollars a month and his expenses to sell these indulgences. With him and other sellers of indulgences went an agent of the Fuggers to see that half the money paid for each indulgence was turned over to the bank to discharge the loan that had been granted to Albert. Tetzel used high pressure sales methods to step up sales and promised remission of temporal punishment for the gravest of sins if the sinner would only buy an indulgence.[4] The amount charged was determined by the sinner's wealth and social position. Indulgences were given free to the destitute, but a king might pay more than three hundred dollars for his indulgence. It was Luther's famous protest in the Ninety-Five Theses against the abuse of indulgences that precipitated the train of events that resulted in the Reformation in Germany. From Germany the Reformation spread all over northern and western Europe.

The Reformation was not an isolated event but was closely related to the Renaissance and other movements that brought about the birth of the Modern Era in the sixteenth century. Its relationship to the Renaissance and to the Catholic Reformation can be more clearly seen by reference to the simple diagram on page 280.

The Protestant churches that came out of this upheaval differed in the extent to which they departed from the medieval church, but all of them accepted the Bible as the final authority. Luther retained many things in the ritual that were not prohibited in the Bible. The Anglican church departed little further from the ritual and practice of the medieval church than the Lutherans did, but it must be understood that both the Anglicans and Lutherans completely disavowed the hierarchical sacramental system of the Roman church. The Reformed and Presbyterian churches, which followed Calvin in France, Holland, Scotland, Switzerland, and Hungary, disavowed all practices that could not be proved to be in accordance with the New Testament. The Anabaptists made the most radical break of all the Reformation groups and sought to create a free believers' church patterned after the primitive New Testament churches. Only those peoples who were of Teutonic extraction in northern and western Europe accepted the Reformation; Latin nations in southern Europe generally remained true to the pope and the doctrine of merit. The Reformation ushered in startling changes by which the one universal Roman Catholic church was replaced in western Europe by national churches. These churches took the Bible as the final authority and believed that man needed no human mediator between himself and God to obtain the salvation that had been purchased for him by Christ on the cross.

SUGGESTED READING

Titles marked with an asterisk cover the entire period of modern church history.

Anderson, Charles S. **Augsburg Historical Atlas of Christianity in the Middle Ages and Reformation.** *Minneapolis: Augsburg, 1967. This work has clear, simple maps and helpful texts for these eras.*

Atkinson, James. **The Great Light.** *Grand Rapids: Eerdmans, 1968.*

Bainton, Roland. **The Reformation of the Sixteenth Century.** *Boston: Beacon, 1952. This book contains illuminating insights and has a good bibliography of the Reformation.*

———. **Women of the Reformation.** *2 vols. Minneapolis: Augsburg, 1971–73. These two volumes discuss the role of women in the German, Italian, French, and English Reformations very ably from the best sources.*

———. and Gritsch, Eric W. **Bibliography of the Continental Reformation.** *2nd rev. and enl. ed. Hamden, Conn.: Shoestring, 1972.*

Chadwick, Owen. **The Reformation.** *Grand Rapids: Eerdmans, 1964.*

*Cheetham, Samuel. **A History of the Christian Church Since the Reformation.** *London: Macmillan, 1907. This work can be consulted with profit.*

*Dillenberger, John, and Welch, Claude. **Protestant Christianity.** *New York: Scribner, 1954. This is a series of interpretative essays covering the era from 1650 on.*

Dolan, John P. **History of the Reformation.** *New York: Desclee, 1955. This is an irenic Roman Catholic interpretation.*

Elton, G. R. **The New Cambridge History of the Reformation, 1520–59.** *Cambridge: Cambridge University Press, 1958. Vol. 1 is a detailed account of the politics and culture of the Reformation.*

*Ferm, Vergilius. **Pictorial History of Protestantism.** *New York: Philosophical Library, 1957. The student will find this helpful in visualizing scenes and persons in Protestant church history.*

Fisher, George. **The Reformation.** *New York: Scribner, 1873. This is an older but able treatment of the Reformation by an outstanding church historian.*

Fosdick, Harry Emerson. **Great Voices of the Reformation.** *New York: Random, 1952. There is an excellent compilation of documents of the ideas of the Reformers in this book.*

Gee, Henry, and Hardy, William J. **Documents Illustrative of English Church History.** *London: Macmillan, 1921. The important documents of the English Reformation are in this work.*

Grimm, Harold J. **The Reformation Era.** *2nd ed. New York: Macmillan, 1973. This is an extensive and scholarly volume on the Reformation.*

Hillerbrand, Hans J. **Christendom Divided.** *New York: Corpus Instrumentorum, Inc., 1973.*

_____. **The Protestant Reformation.** *New York: Walker, 1968.*

_____. **The Reformation.** *New York: Harper, 1964. This gives the story of the Reformation by selections from the sources.*

_____. **The World of the Reformation.** *New York: Scribner, 1973.*

Hulme, Edward M. **Renaissance and Reformation.** *New York: Century, 1915. This older volume will repay study.*

Hyma, Albert. **Renaissance to Reformation.** *Grand Rapids: Eerdmans, 1951.*

Kidd, Beresford J. **Documents Illustrative of the Continental Reformation.** *Oxford: Clarendon University Press, 1911. Source materials of the Reformation are available in this work to the student who reads Latin and French.*

Lindsay, Thomas. **A History of the Reformation.** *2 vols. New York: Scribner, 1906–7. This work has a wealth of useful detail.*

Lucas, Henry S. **The Renaissance and the Reformation.** *2nd ed. New York: Harper, 1960. This good work has an interesting and authentic history of the Reformation in the various countries.*

*Manschreck, Clyde L., ed. **A History of Christianity.** *Englewood Cliffs, N.J.: Prentice-Hall, 1964. This is a collection of well-selected documents for church history since 1517.*

Neve, Juergen L., and Heick, Otto W. **A History of Christian Thought.** *2 vols. Philadelphia: Fortress, 1965. Volume 1, pages 313–467, has several fine chapters on the theology of the Reformers.*

*Nichols, James H. **History of Christianity, 1650–1950.** *New York: Ronald, 1956.*

*Norwood, Frederick A. **The Development of Modern Christianity Since 1500.** *New York: Abingdon, 1956. This is a brief yet helpful survey.*

*Pullan, Leighton. **Religion Since the Reformation.** *Oxford: Clarendon University Press, 1924. This is a useful series of lectures on modern church history that begins with the Counter Reformation, but it has no treatment of the Protestant Reformation.*

Schaff, Philip. **Creeds of Christendom.** *3 vols. 6th ed. New York: Scribner, 1890. Volume 1 gives the origin of the Protestant creeds and confessions, and volume 3 presents the creeds in the original language or translation.*

_____. **History of the Christian Church.** *8 vols. New York: Scribner, 1882–1910. The relevant volumes can be consulted with profit.*

Smith, Preserved. **The Age of the Reformation.** *New York: Henry Holt, 1920. At times this work is unsympathetic to the Reformers. It contains a wealth of valuable material based on an intensive study of the sources. It also has a good bibliography.*

Spitz, Lewis. **The Renaissance and Reformation.** *Chicago: Rand McNally, 1971. This has helpful concepts and syntheses.*

*Stearns, Raymond P. **Pageant of Europe.** *New York: Harcourt, Brace, 1947. This work has many useful documents relevant to modern church history.*

Steinmetz, David C. **Reformers in the Wings.** *Philadelphia: Fortress, 1971. This book presents the lesser, little-known medieval, Lutheran, Reformed, and radical Reformers.*

Todd, John M. **Reformation.** *Garden City, N.Y.: Doubleday, 1971.*

Walker, Williston. **The Reformation.** *New York: Scribner, 1900. This is a good, factual one-volume survey of the field.*

*Wand, J. W. C. **A History of the Modern Church.** *New York: Crowell, 1929. This is a useful survey of the entire field of modern church history.*

Ziegler, Donald J. **Great Debates of the Reformation.** *New York: Random, 1969.*

Chapter 27

Luther
and the German Reformation

Not enough emphasis has been given to the Reformation as a religious movement that took place, for the most part, among people of Germanic stock in northern and western Europe. Most of the nations that adopted the principles of the Reformation had never been a part of the old Roman Empire nor had they been border territories. The Latin nations of southern Europe did not accept the Reformation; rather, they remained true to the Roman Catholic system.

Perhaps the rationalistic and critical spirit of the Renaissance took so great a hold on the people of southern Europe that they were not concerned with matters of the spirit. It is likely that they were satisfied with a religion that was external and formal and that left them free to devote their lives to the enjoyment of material things. Even the Renaissance popes gave more time to cultural pursuits than they did to their religious functions. Whatever the ultimate reasons may be, the Protestant Reformation found no congenial home south of the Alps, but its principles were welcomed by the people of Teutonic descent.

Several reasons may account for this phenomenon. The German humanists with their negative satirical criticism of the Roman church in such books as Erasmus's *In Praise of Folly* and with their presentation of a more positive Christianity, which they saw in the Greek Testament, were widely read by the cultivated classes of northern Europe. Such reading created a spirit of discontent with the papal system and a desire to have reform in religion.

Another reason may be that the mystical tradition of religion was more strongly entrenched in Teutonic lands than in Italy or Spain. The student will remember that most of the important mystics were German or Dutch. The pious burgher read his *Imitation of Christ* and endeavored to make his religion practical. They were not at this time quite so sophisticated in their culture as the southern Europeans.

Because Germany had no powerful national ruler to protect her interests, it was easier for the papacy to get money from her. The opening up of new mines created new wealth in Germany, and the papacy wanted to tap this wealth. The Roman church also owned much land in Germany. In addition, the German middle classes were subjected to financial abuses by the hierarchy. Nationalism and resentment against the drain of wealth from Germany combined to create an atmosphere that would be favorable to whatever movement might lead a revolt against Rome. The main issue, however, was "How can I be saved?"

The man and the hour met in sixteenth-century Germany. Germany had her Luther in whom all the forces of opposition to Rome could be concentrated in a declaration of spiritual independence. Up to 1517 Luther went through a formative period. At the end of this period he was critical of the indulgence system; between 1518 and 1521 he was forced to break with the church; 1522 to 1530 was a period of organization; and from 1531 to the peace of Augsburg in 1555, Lutheranism, led by Luther and, after his death, by his friend Melanchthon, faced an era of conflict with Romanism and the consolidation of its gains.

I. LUTHER'S FORMATIVE YEARS TO 1517

Martin Luther was born on November 10, 1483, in the little town of Eisleben. His father, who was of free peasant stock, had migrated from the ancestral home some distance from Eisleben. He gained wealth from the copper mines of that area in which he had an interest and became a man of considerable wealth. Although he owned shares in six mines and two smelters by 1511, times were still difficult for the family when Luther was born. Luther was raised under the strict discipline of those times. He told of being whipped by his mother until the blood came because he had stolen a nut. One morning in the Latin school at Mansfeld he was whipped fifteen times. His peasant parents, particularly his pious but superstitious mother, inculcated many of the superstitions of their class in him. Some of these terrors haunted him as he struggled so long in seeking salvation for his soul. His love of hard work, his strong will, and his practical conservatism were present in him from the beginning.

After a short period in a school of the Brethren of the Common Life in Magdeburg, Luther was sent to school in

Lucas Cranach, the Elder, famous painter of the Reformation, probably produced this portrait of Martin Luther. It was painted in 1526, after Luther's marriage to Katherina von Bora, a former nun.

Eisenach between 1498 and 1501. He was given food and lodging by kindly friends, such as Ursula Cotta. Here he received the advanced instruction in Latin that was essential if he were to go on to the university. In 1501 at the University of Erfurt he began to study the philosophy of Aristotle under the influence of teachers who followed the nominalistic ideas of William of Ockham. William had taught that revelation was the only guide in the realm of faith; reason was the guide to truth in philosophy. Thus Luther's philosophical studies at Erfurt made him aware of the need of divine intervention if man were to know spiritual truth and to be saved. In 1502 or 1503 he received the bachelor of arts degree, and in 1505 he was granted the degree of master of arts.

His father wished him to study law, but in 1505 Luther became frightened during a severe thunderstorm on the road near Stotternheim and promised Saint Anne that he would become a monk if he were spared. Perhaps his growing concern about his soul was brought to a focus by this experience early in July of 1505, an experience that his father dryly suggested might be "a trick of the devil." About two weeks later he entered a monastery of the Augustinian order at Erfurt. Here, in 1507, he was ordained and celebrated his first mass.

During the winter of 1508 he taught theology one semester at the new university that had been founded in Wittenberg by Frederick, the elector of Saxony, in 1502. His studies at Erfurt were also mainly theological. These studies only made his soul struggle more intense, but he found some help in the admonitions of the godly Staupitz, the vicar-general of his order,

who urged him to trust God and to study the Bible.

During the winter of 1510 and 1511 he was sent to Rome on business for his order. There he saw something of the corruption and luxury of the Roman church and came to realize the need of reform. He spent much time visiting churches and viewing the numerous relics that were in Rome. He was shocked by the levity of the Italian priests who could say several masses while he said one.

In 1511 Luther was finally transferred to Wittenberg. Here, during the next year, he became a professor of Bible and received his doctor of theology degree. He held the position of lecturer in biblical theology until his death. At this time he was also given the office in the tower where he came to a realization of justification by faith. It was in this university that he and a loyal band of fellow professors and students accepted the faith that was to spread over Germany.

Luther began to lecture in the vernacular on the books of the Bible, and in order to do so intelligently, he began to study the original languages of the Bible. He gradually developed the idea that only in the Bible could true authority be found. From 1513 to 1515 he lectured on the Psalms, from 1515 to 1517 on Romans, and, later, on Galatians and Hebrews. Between 1512 and 1516, while preparing these lectures, he found the peace of soul that he had not been able to find in rites, acts of asceticism, or in the famous *German Theology* of the mystics which he published in German in 1516. A reading of Romans 1:17 convinced him that only faith in Christ could make one just before God. From that time on, *sola fide*, or justification by faith, and *sola*

A pro-Lutheran artist in 1617 shows Luther one hundred years earlier writing his Ninety-five Theses on the church door. Luther's pen pierces the ears of Pope Leo X, symbolized by the lion, and knocks the crown off the head of Charles V, emperor of the Holy Roman Empire. Further to the right, the Bible symbolically sheds light on Jesus in the clouds of heaven. The burning goose symbolizes the martyr John Hus, burned at the stake for his reforming ideas almost a hundred years before Luther by the Council of Constance. Luther originally wrote the Ninety-five Theses in Latin, but for the benefit of his German readership, the artist shows him writing in German on the church door.

scriptura, the idea that the Scriptures are the only authority for sinful men in seeking salvation, became the main points in his theological system. Staupitz, the visit to Rome, the writings of the mystics, and the writings of the Fathers, especially those of Augustine, had been formative influences in his life; but it was his study of the Bible that led him to trust in Christ alone for his salvation.

In 1517 Tetzel, the wily agent of Archbishop Albert, began his sale of indulgences at Jüterbock near Wittenberg. Luther and those who followed him in his new-found faith resented the exploitation of the people by this nefarious system; and he decided to make public protest. Tetzel claimed that repentance was not necessary for the buyer of an indulgence and that the indulgence gave complete forgiveness of all sin. On October 31, 1517, Luther posted his Ninety-Five Theses on the door of the Castle Church in Wittenberg. In them he condemned the abuses of the indulgence system and challenged all comers to debate on the matter. A reading of the Ninety-five Theses[1] will reveal that Luther was merely criticizing abuses of the indulgence system. However, during the years between 1518 and 1521 he was forced to accept the idea of separation from the Roman system as the only way to get a reform that would involve a return to the ideal of the church revealed in the Scriptures. The translation into German and the printing of the Theses spread Luther's ideas rapidly.

II. THE BREAK WITH ROME, 1518–21

After the publication of the Theses, Tetzel endeavored to use all the power of the Dominican order to silence Luther, who found support in the Augustinian order. It was this conflict in the early years of the Reformation that gave rise to the foolish charge of the rationalist that the Reformation was only "a squabble of monks." Luther was ordered to debate the problem before members of his order at Heidelberg in 1518, but little came of the debate except a widening of the circle of those who accepted Luther's ideas, including Martin Bucer (1491–1551).[2]

A valuable ally, who later supplemented Luther's bold courage with his gentle reasonableness, came to Wittenberg as professor of Greek in 1518. At the age of twenty-one Philipp Melanchthon (1497–1560) was already well trained in the classical languages and Hebrew. While Luther became the great prophetic voice of the Reformation, Melanchthon became its theologian. He and others of the Wittenberg faculty loyally supported Luther's views.[3]

By the fall of 1518 Luther was insisting that his only authority in the coming dispute would be neither the pope nor the church, but the Bible. He would have fallen before the Dominicans had it not been for the aid of Frederick, the elector of Saxony, who was one of those who elected the emperor of the Holy Roman Empire. When Luther was summoned to appear before the imperial Diet of Augsburg in 1518, Frederick promised that he would give his powerful support to this brave reformer. The pope did not seem to realize the extent of popular support for Luther in Germany. At the Diet Luther met Cardinal Cajetan, who demanded that he retract his views, but Luther refused to do this until he should become convinced of their falsity by Scripture. He also denied the pope as final authority in faith and morals and the usefulness of the sacraments without faith. Early in 1519 Luther promised the papal nuncio, Karl von Miltitz, that he would not proclaim his views if his opponents also kept silence.

In a sixteenth-century pro-Catholic cartoon, the devil calls the tune for Luther. Luther was equal to the occasion when he saw this cartoon. "I must be invincible," he said, "because they cannot overcome me when I have only one head."

Later Luther appealed for a general council to deal with the problem. In July 1519 he debated with John Eck at Leipzig.[4] The clever Eck was able to force Luther into an admission of the fallibility of a general council, his unwillingness to accept the decisions of the pope, and the validity of many of Hus's ideas.

In 1520 Luther decided to carry the issue to the German people by the publication of three pamphlets. The *Address to the German Nobility*[5] was aimed at the *hierarchy*. Rome claimed that spiritual authority was superior to temporal authority, that the pope alone could interpret the Scriptures, and that no one but the pope could call a council. After stating the arguments for these claims, Luther proceeded to demolish them from Scripture. He stated that princes should reform the church when necessary, that the pope should not interfere in civil affairs, and that all believers were spiritual priests of God who could interpret Scripture and had the right to choose their own ministers. In October he published his *Babylonian Captivity*.[6] In this pamphlet he widened his attack by challenging the *sacramental system* of Rome. The first document had been a historical attack on the hierarchy, but this pamphlet attacked the center of the Roman system—the sacraments as means of grace when dispensed by the priesthood. Luther emphasized the sure validity of only the Lord's Supper and baptism. Henry VIII won from the pope the title "Defender of the Faith" for himself and future English royalty by his attempt to answer this attack of Luther on the sacramental system. The third pamphlet, *The Freedom of the Christian Man*, really attacked the

theology of the Roman church by its assertion of the priesthood of all believers as a result of their personal faith in Christ. The issues were clearer than ever now that Luther had attacked the hierarchy, sacraments, and theology of the Roman church and was appealing for national reform.

Another contemporary pro-Catholic cartoonist caricatured Luther as having seven heads, portraying him, from left to right, as a sorcerer, a monk in a cowl, a turbaned infidel, a churchman, a fanatic with bees in his hair, a clown, and a Barabbas guilty of murder, sedition, and robbery.

In June 1520 Leo X issued the bull *Exsurge Domine*, and this eventually resulted in the excommunication of Luther. Luther's books were also burned at Cologne. Not to be outdone, Luther promptly burned Leo's bull publicly on December 10, 1520.[7] Charles V, the new emperor, now issued a summons for an imperial diet at Worms in the spring of 1521, at which Luther was to appear to answer for his views. Luther went to Worms with the assurance of protection by Frederick, who was the elector of Saxony and founder of Wittenberg University, and other German princes. He again refused to recant unless he could be convinced of fault by "the testimony of the Scriptures" or by reason. He said that he would take his stand on this alone and appealed to God for help.[8] His friends kidnapped him on the road back to Wittenberg and took him to Wartburg Castle, where he remained until 1522. After his departure from Worms, the Diet issued an edict that ordered any subject of the emperor to seize Luther and to turn him over to the authorities. The reading of his writings was also banned.

III. YEARS OF SEPARATION, 1522–30

During the trying year of May 1521 to March 1522, Melanchthon was not idle. His short work on the theology of the Reformers of Wittenberg, *Loci Communes*,[9] came out in 1521. This little work in Latin was the first major theological treatise of the Reformation and went through numerous editions during the lifetime of its author. It established Melanchthon as the theologian of the Lutheran movement.

Melanchthon rejected the authority of the Roman church, the Fathers, the canon law, and the Scholastics. He put the Bible above these as the final authority for Christians. His little book grew out of studies of Paul's Epistle to the Romans. In it, Melanchthon attempted to deal with the "most common topics of theological science" in a methodical fashion in order that he might "incite people to the Scrip-

tures." He pictured man bound by sin and unable to help himself. The law, he wrote, cannot help because its main function is to reveal sin. God must initiate the work of the salvation that the individual receives by faith in Christ. Luther, who recognized that he was bold and violent where Melanchthon was irenic and gentle, fully approved of this work as the theological expression of his ideas. He characterized it as "immortal."

Melanchthon also set up the German school system. He was responsible for the Augsburg Confession. For thirty years this irenic scholar was Luther's friend and colleague.

But neither had Luther been idle during his enforced residence at Wartburg Castle between May 1521 and March 1522. Making use of Erasmus's edition of the Greek Testament, he completed his German translation of the New Testament in less than a year. The whole Bible, including the Apocrypha, was translated from the original into German by 1534. When it was published, it not only gave the German people the Bible in their own tongue, but it also set the standard form of the German language. He also wrote *On Monastic Vows*, in which he urged monks and nuns to repudiate their wrongful vows, to leave the cloister, and to marry.

Luther was indeed a national hero and held in high regard by prince, peasant, humanist, and knight alike; but his policies in the subsequent years alienated some of those who had followed him so readily at first. While he was at Wartburg, Nicholas Storch and Markus Stübner, who were known as the Zwickau prophets, appeared at Wittenberg and began preaching ideas similar to some of the Anabaptists' ideas. They taught that the kingdom of God would soon appear on earth and that their followers would have special revelations. The usually unstable Carlstadt was influenced by them. At the risk of his life, Luther returned to Wittenberg in 1522. After eight fiery sermons, in which he stressed the authority of the Bible and the need for gradual change in the church, he defeated the Zwickau prophets. The radical wing of the Reformation, however, felt from this time that it could not count on help from Luther, and in 1535 Luther broke openly with the Anabaptist movement.

Luther also lost the support of the humanists, such as Erasmus, by 1525. Erasmus had supported Luther's demands for reform at first but recoiled when he saw that Luther's views would lead to a break with Rome. He also disagreed with Luther's view that man's will was so bound that the initiative in salvation must come from God. Erasmus emphasized the freedom of the human will in his book *The Freedom of the Will*, which he published in 1524 as an answer to Luther's denial of the freedom of the will.

The peasants also became hostile to Luther in 1525 when he opposed the Peasants' Revolt. The peasants had heard him denounce the authority of the church and assert the authority of the Scripture and the right of the individual to come directly to God for salvation, and they applied these arguments to their social and economic problems. Feudalism had caused much oppression of the peasants, and in their "Twelve Articles"[10] of 1525 they demanded the reform of feudal abuses that could be demonstrated as abuses on the authority of Scripture. At first, in his *Admonition to Peace* in April of 1525, he urged the peasants to patience and the lords to redress the grievances of the peasants. When Luther realized that this revolutionary social movement might endanger the Reformation and might subvert the foundations of orderly government even in Protestant provinces, he urged the princes in violent language, in his pamphlet *Against the Plundering Murderous Hordes of Peasants*, to put down disorder. The authorities needed no urging to use severe measures and slaughtered about one hundred thousand peasants. Southern German peasants remained in the Roman Catholic church partly because of this apparent betrayal of them by Luther.

Others felt that Luther's repudiation of monastic vows by his marriage to the escaped nun Katherine von Bora in 1525 was an abrupt break with the past that was not justified. Luther, however, always felt that he had done the right thing and derived much joy from his home life. His six children, as well as numerous students, graced his table to such an extent at times that his "Katie" was hard pressed to provide the necessary food.

It also was unfortunate that Luther could not see his way clear to join forces with Zwingli, who was leading the Reformation in the northern cantons of Switzerland. Luther and Zwingli met in the fall of 1529, in what was known as the Marburg Colloquy, at the Marburg Castle of Philip of Hesse. They agreed on over fourteen out of fifteen propositions but disagreed on how Christ was present in the elements. Zwingli contended that Communion was a memorial of Christ's death, but Luther argued that there was a real physical presence of

Christ in the Communion although the substance of bread and wine did not change. Just as iron remains iron but becomes cherry red when it is heated, so he contended that the substance of the bread and wine do not change but that around and under the symbols there is a real physical presence of Christ.[11]

Events in Germany forced Luther into a position where he had to develop church organization and liturgy suitable for his followers. At the Diet of Speier in 1526 the princely followers of Luther were able to get the Diet to agree that until a general council met, the ruler of each state should be free to follow what he felt was the correct faith. The principle of *cuius regio eius religio*—that the ruler should choose the religion of his state—was adopted for the time being. The fact that Emperor Charles V was fighting to prevent his French foe Francis I from gaining control of Italy during the 1520s, the eastern Turkish threat, and the absence of many Catholic German princes at the Diet may account for this decision and the later rapid growth of the Lutheran movement.

A second Diet at Speier in 1529 canceled the decision of the previous Diet and declared that the Roman Catholic faith was the only legal faith. The six princely followers of Luther and representatives of fourteen free cities read a *Protestation.* From then on, they were known as Protestants by their opponents. Such was the honored derivation of the word "Protestant."

In 1530 the Diet of Augsburg was held. Melanchthon with Luther's approval had drawn up the Augsburg Confession, which was presented at the Diet.[12] It became the official creed of the Lutheran church. It was the first of several creeds that made the period between 1517 and 1648 as great a period of Protestant creedal development as the period between 325 and 451 had been for the development of the ecumenical creeds of the church, such as the Nicene Creed. Only seven of the twenty-nine articles were negative, being repudiations of religious abuses; the remaining articles were positive statements of the Lutheran faith. Luther drew up the German Mass and Order of Service in 1526.

Luther had also drawn up the *Short Catechism* in 1529[13] as a concise statement of the Ten Commandments, the Apostles' Creed, the Lord's Prayer, and other matters of theology and liturgy. The Wittenberg faculty in 1535 began to examine and ordain ministerial candidates. The Lutheran movement then made rapid progress in northern Germany despite armed opposition from the emperor and the Catholic princes.

IV. THE ERA OF GERMAN RELIGIOUS WARS AND TERRITORIAL CHURCH ORGANIZATION, 1531–55

The Protestant princes decided to organize for mutual defense and formed the Schmalkaldic League early in 1531. They agreed to defend their faith by force of arms if necessary. But the emperor was kept busy with wars against the Turks and the French between 1532 and 1542, and the Protestant League did not have to fight. Thus Lutheranism was able to make great gains in northern Germany. The Lutheran order of ordination of 1535 meant an ecclesiastical break with the Roman hierarchy.

Luther's last years were troubled by the bigamy of Philip of Hesse (1504–67), one of his supporters, when he married Margaret von der Saale in 1540 without the formality of divorcing his first wife. Luther temporized at this point by consenting to the second marriage and by urging that it be kept secret. In 1546 he died, leaving the Lutheran movement to the leadership of Melanchthon.

Finally the emperor was ready for war with the German Protestants, and the Schmalkaldic wars occupied the stage of German history between 1546 and 1552. Fighting was finally ended by the Peace of Augsburg in 1555. The agreement put Lutheranism on a basis of legal equality with Roman Catholicism in Germany. The prince was to determine the religion in his territory, but any dissenters were to be given the right to emigrate. If a Catholic leader turned Protestant, he must give up his position. This agreement safeguarded the Roman Catholic control of the areas in southern Germany that were predominantly Roman Catholic. This was a step toward religious pluralism.

It will be noticed that the Peace of Augsburg made the prince a power in the religious affairs of the church. As early as 1539 a consistory was appointed by Elector John Frederick in Wittenberg to serve as a court in cases involving discipline and divorce. During the next decade the consistory became a governing body to govern the affairs of the church under the supervision of the prince. Superintendents, who had been used as early as 1527 in Saxony by the princes, were sent out to supervise the affairs of the local church. Luther believed in order and wrote that although the state had no right to interfere with the individual in

the matter of salvation, the state was given the sword by God to maintain order so that the godly might live their lives in peace. The ruler of the state was responsible to God for the manner in which he ruled the state. Luther was, however, opposed to revolution to overthrow an arbitrary and oppressive government, on the grounds that time or external enemies would correct the condition.[14] The territorial churches included all baptized persons, with superintendents appointed by and responsible to the prince for uniform worship and discipline of pastors.

Luther was indeed one of the titanic figures of the church because of his influence on later times as well as on his own era. The national Lutheran churches of Germany and the Scandinavian countries were a result of his work. To these churches he gave the *Large* and *Small Catechisms; Postils*, which were sermonic aids for the minister; a system of church government, which he, to a large extent, developed; the German Bible, which helped to standardize the German language; and beautiful and stately hymns, such as "A Mighty Fortress," which were to be sung in the vernacular by the whole congreation. He urged Melanchthon to set up a system of universal elementary education in Germany in order that the people might be taught to read the Bible in the vernacular. He urged this duty upon the governing bodies of German cities in a letter to them in 1524, and in 1530 he wrote concerning the duty of parents to send their children to school. Universal compulsory elementary education had its early beginnings in his efforts. He was also interested in secondary schools and university education.

Luther restored preaching to its rightful place in the church and thus recreated a medium of spiritual instruction that had been so widely used in the early church. Above all, he awakened his day to the fact that culture was not merely a matter of reason but of regeneration by faith in Christ. He did not repudiate the individualism of the Renaissance but made it a spiritual matter as the individual was brought into saving relationship with God by faith in Jesus Christ. In the place of an authoritative church he put an authoritative Bible as the infallible rule of faith and practice that each believer-priest should use for guidance in matters of faith and morals. Luther did not repudiate the necessity of a corporate relationship of the individual and others in the church; on the contrary, he was insistent on the importance of communion with other members of the body of Christ.

V. LUTHERANISM, 1555–80

From the Peace of Augsburg until the publication of the *Book of Concord* in 1580, the peace of the Lutheran churches was marred by internal doctrinal controversy. Most of the issues were similar to the points on which Melanchthon and Luther had had differences of opinion. One dispute concerned the place of the law in preaching. Luther had urged the preaching of the law as a means of revealing to men how sinful they were. Others urged that only the gospel should be preached because it was the gospel that brought salvation. The Majoristic controversy grew out of George Major's contention that good works were an important part of salvation even though one was saved by faith

alone. Those Lutherans who were close followers of Luther argued that this was really a return to the Roman doctrine of salvation by faith and works. Arguments also developed over the Lord's Supper and over whether or not the human will was able to cooperate with the divine grace in salvation.[15]

Because these disputes created political as well as religious disunity, the princes of Germany decided that the problems must be settled if the Lutheran movement was not to go to pieces. A document known as the Formula of Concord was completed by 1577 and published in 1580.[16] Most of the Lutherans of Germany accepted this expression of their theology. Lutheran theologians also took up the task of creating a complete statement of the Lutheran theology that would differentiate it from Roman Catholic theology. This was done by the preparation of the *Book of Concord* in 1580. The book contained the three great universal creeds of the early church and the various Lutheran formulas that had been drawn up between 1529 and 1580.

These disputes made the Lutherans very conscious of the importance of doctrine and brought about a viewpoint that emphasized correctness of doctrine. This emphasis at times led to a cold, scholarly orthodoxy that tended to ignore the more subjective spiritual aspects of Christianity. The Pietistic movement arose in the seventeenth century as a reaction to this strong intellectual emphasis.

VI. LUTHERANISM IN SCANDINAVIA

Church reform in Denmark began in the reign of a nephew of Frederick of

Saxony, Christian II (1513–23), who had strong humanistic sympathies and was anxious to free the crown from the control that a council of nobles and the clergy were able to exert over it. He wanted to create a state church that would be under royal control. His successor, Frederick I (1523–33), was favorably disposed to the Lutheran faith and permitted Hans Tausen (ca. 1494–1561) to do in Denmark what Luther had done in Germany. Tausen was helped greatly by the publication of a Danish translation of the New Testament in 1524. Frederick came out openly in favor of the Reformation in 1526 and made Tausen the royal Chaplain. He was loyally supported by the common people, who were disgusted with the corruption of the higher clergy and the indulgence traffic. By 1530 a Lutheran confession of faith was available. Frederick's successor, Christian III, had the Diet of 1536 abolish the Roman religion and confiscate all Roman church property. This property was then divided between the king and the nobles. From 1539 on, Lutheranism was the state religion of Denmark.

Because Norway was dominated by Denmark until 1814, it had to accept the religious changes that came in Denmark. Lutheranism was introduced into Norway during the reign of Frederick I and became the state religion in 1539 during the reign of Christian III.

A clergyman by the name of Gissur Einarsen, who had come under the influence of the Lutheranism of the University of Wittenberg during his stay in Germany, preached Lutheran doctrines in Iceland upon his return in 1533. When he became bishop in 1540, he introduced Lutheranism into his bishopric. He published the New Testament in Icelandic to promote the cause of Protestantism. By 1554 Lutheranism became the official religion of Iceland by royal decree.

Sweden became independent of Denmark in 1523 by the revolution of 1521, during the reign of Christian II; and that of her new reforming ruler Gustavus Vasa (1523–60) also favored the Reformation as a tool whereby he could confiscate the wealth of the Roman church. Olavus Petri (1493–1552), after three years' study in Wittenberg, did the work in Sweden that Luther had done in Germany and laid the popular base for reform. Petri's work enabled the ruler to bring Sweden into the Lutheran fold. A Swedish translation of the New Testament in 1526 made it possible for the reading public to compare the teaching of their clergy with the Bible so that they could see that the Lutheran doctrines of Petri were nearer to the Scriptures. Lutheranism was made the religion of the state at the Diet of Wësteras held in 1527 and was accepted gradually by the people. During Gustavus Vasa's long reign from 1523 to 1560, the Reformation was thoroughly established in the country.

The Reformation spread from Sweden to Finland because Finland was controlled by Sweden. Michael Agricola (1508–57) was its apostle in that country. He became archbishop about 1510 and produced a Finnish New Testament, by which he also made a written Finnish language. By 1530 the Lutheran faith became that of the Finnish people and their leaders.

Lutheranism was also influential in other countries. Lutheran ideas laid the groundwork for the Reformation in Scotland under John Knox. Lutherans also spread their teachings in England. Even though these countries finally adopted other forms of the Reformation, Lutheranism was a factor in the transition from Catholicism to Protestantism. Lutheranism was temporarily triumphant in Poland, but divisions among those favorable to the Lutheran faith and internal struggle enabled the Roman church to regain Poland for Catholicism. It was in Germany and the Scandinavian lands that Lutheranism made the greatest and most permanent gains. The authority of the Bible, which the Lutheran leaders translated into the vernacular of their countries, and justification by faith became the watchwords of those lands in the sixteenth century. Luther did an even greater work than he could ever have imagined when he first opposed Tetzel's traffic in indulgences in 1517.

SUGGESTED READING

Aland, Kurt. **Martin Luther's Ninety-Five Theses.** *St. Louis: Concordia, 1967.*

Bainton, Roland. **Here I Stand.** *Nashville: Abingdon, 1950. This is a popular and interesting account of the reformer.*

Carlson, Edgar. **The Reinterpretation of Luther.** *Philadelphia: Westminster, 1948.*

Doernberg, Edwin. **Henry VIII and Luther.** *Stanford: Stanford University Press, 1961.*

Drummond, Andrew L. **German Protestantism Since Luther.** *London: Epworth, 1951.*

Fife, Robert H. **The Revolt of Martin Luther.** *New York: Columbia University Press, 1957.*

Green, Vivian H. H. **Luther and the Reformation.** *New York: Putnam, 1964. This is a brief, scholarly account of the reformer's career.*

Hyma, Albert. **Luther's Theological Development From Erfurt to Augsburg.** *New York: Crofts, 1928. This little book gives insight from the sources into the development of Luther's theological ideas until 1530.*

Kerr, Hugh Thomson, Jr. **A Compend of Luther's Theology.** *Philadelphia: Westminster, 1943. This is a helpful compilation of Luther's theological views that the average student would not otherwise get.*

Luther, Martin. **Table Talks.** *Philadelphia: Fortress, 1967. This is an excellent source from which to obtain a knowledge of Luther's personality.*

Manschreck, Clyde L. **Melanchthon, the Quiet Reformer.** *New York: Abingdon, 1958.*

McGiffert, Arthur C. **Martin Luther, the Man and His Work.** *London: Unwins, 1911. This older biography is interestingly written and has many fine pictures of places of importance in Luther's life.*

Melanchthon, Philip. **Loci Communes.** *Translated by Charles L. Hill. Boston: Meador, 1944.*

Plass, Ewald. **This Luther.** *St. Louis: Concordia, 1948.*

Ruff, Ernest G., and Drenz, Benjamin., eds. **Martin Luther.** *London: Arnold, 1970. This is useful for Luther's life in terms of sources available in it.*

Schweibert, Ernest G. **Luther and His Times.** *St. Louis: Concordia, 1950. This should become the classic biography. It is the result of exhaustive study of the sources and shows the influence of the University of Wittenberg upon the Reformation in Germany.*

Smith, Preserved. **The Life and Letters of Martin Luther.** *New York: Houghton Mifflin, 1911. This work allows one to see Luther through his letters and work. It has a helpful chronology of Luther's life.*

Stupperich, Robert. **Melanchthon.** *Translated by Robert H. Fischer. Philadelphia: Westminster, 1965.*

Tillman, Walter G. **The World and Men Around Luther.** *Minneapolis: Augsburg, 1959. This is a helpful collection of biographical sketches.*

Chapter 28

The Reformation in Switzerland

Switzerland was the freest land in Europe at the time of the Reformation, although it was nominally a part of the Holy Roman Empire. As early as 1291 the three forest cantons of Schwyz, Uri, and Unterwalden had entered into a union that left each canton free to develop as a self-governing republic. By the time of the Swiss Reformation, there were thirteen cantons in the confederacy. The sturdy democratic Swiss were in demand throughout Europe as mercenary soldiers. They provided the armies that the pope engaged to protect his interests.

The government of each canton was in complete charge of local affairs, and for that reason the individual canton was free to accept the form of religion that it would follow. Hence, the Reformation in Switzerland was accomplished by the legal action of democratically elected local government.

The Swiss cities were also centers of culture, and humanism was able to establish itself in the city cantons. Basel had a famous university. It was here that Erasmus had edited his printed Greek New Testament. Because of these developments, the Swiss Reformation had humanism as one of its major sources.

Three types of Reformation theology developed in Swiss territories. The German-speaking cantons, of the northern part of the country, led by Zurich, followed Zwingli's view of the Reformation. The French-speaking cantons in the south, led by Geneva, followed the views of Calvin. In addition, the radicals of the Reformation, known as Anabaptists, developed as an extreme wing among those who at first worked with Zwingli. From Zurich the Anabaptist movement spread throughout Switzerland, Germany, and Holland. Under Menno Simons it had a steady development in Holland and northern Germany.

I. THE ZWINGLIAN REFORMATION IN THE GERMAN CANTONS OF NORTHERN SWITZERLAND

Huldreich Zwingli (1484–1531) was also of the first generation of the Reformers. In him the forces of discontent with Rome crystallized into a Reformation church. His father was a farmer and the chief magistrate of Wildhaus. The family had a good income, making it possible for Zwingli to have a good education for the priesthood. He attended the University of Vienna and in 1502 went to the University of Basel, where he received his bachelor of arts degree in 1504 and his master of arts degree in 1506. His teachers' emphasis on humanism appealed to him. Erasmus became his idol; the humanities were his chief desire; but theology had little interest for him.

Between graduation in 1506 and the year 1516, Zwingli served the pope well as a parish priest, chaplain, and an ardent Swiss patriot. His first parish was at Glarus. At this time his humanistic sympathies caused him to interpret the Pauline gospel by the philosopher Plato and Christ's Sermon on the Mount so that he emphasized the ethical aspects of Christianity. Study of Erasmus's teaching led him away from Scholastic theology to the study of the Bible. His patriotic tendencies led him to oppose mercenary service by Swiss young men, except for the pope. To get his support, the pope gave him a generous annual pension. In 1513 and 1515 he went with the mercenaries from Glarus to serve as their chaplain.

Between 1516 and 1518 he served as pastor at Einsiedeln, a center for pilgrims. There he began to oppose some of the abuses of the Roman system of indulgences and of the black image of the Virgin Mary by ridiculing them in the fashion of Erasmus. When Erasmus's Greek Testament came out in 1516, he copied the letters of Paul from a borrowed copy so that he might have his own copy. He was a biblical humanist when he left Einsiedeln. Called to be a pastor at Zurich, he began his work there early in 1519. It was at this time that he took a definite stand against the enlisting of the Swiss as mercenaries in foreign service because of the corrupting influences that he saw the men encounter in such service, and Zurich stopped the practice in 1521.

An attack of the plague in 1519 and contact with Lutheran ideas led him into an experience of conversion. Zwingli first raised the issue of Reformation when he declared that tithes paid by the faithful were not of divine authority and that their payment was a voluntary matter. This struck a blow at the financial basis of the Roman system. It seems odd that he should have entered into a secret marriage with the widow Anna Reinhard in 1522. Not until 1524 did he publicly legitimize their union by marrying her openly.

When citizens broke with the idea of the Lenten fast by eating two dried sausages during Lent in 1522 and cited Zwingli's assertion of the sole authority of the Bible to excuse themselves, and when changes were made that modified the Roman system of worship, the authorities decided to hold a public debate in which Zwingli would meet all comers. The elected authorities would then decide what faith the city and canton should adopt. Thus the Reformation in the northern Swiss cantons was put into effect by governmental action after debate. Before the debate against Johann Faber in 1523, Zwingli prepared the *Sixty-seven Articles*, which emphasized salvation by faith, the authority of the Bible, the headship of Christ in the church, and the right of clerical marriage. They also condemned unscriptural Roman practices.[1] The town council decided that Zwingli had won, and his ideas were rapidly given legal status. Fees for baptisms and burials were eliminated. Monks and nuns were allowed to marry. Images and relics were banned, and in 1525 the Reformation was completed in Zurich by the abolition of the Mass. Zwingli's belief that the ultimate authority resided in the Christian community, which exercised its authority through an elected civil government acting on the authority of the Bible, had borne fruit in the Zurich Reformation in which the church and the state were linked in a theocratic manner.

Bern was won over to the side of the Reformation by a debate similar to that in Zurich. Zwingli took part in the debate on the basis of his *Ten Theses*,[2] and, as a result, the city council ordered the acceptance of the principles of the Reformation in 1528. By 1529 the Mass was abolished also in Basel through the influence of Zwingli's warm friend Oecolampadius.

From 1522 on, Zwingli was hampered by followers who became known as Anabaptists because they insisted on the rebaptism of converts. In 1525 the city council forbade their meetings and banished them from the city. Felix Manz (1498–1527) in 1527 was executed by drowning.

Zwingli also lost the support of Luther at the Marburg Colloquy in 1529, when the two men could not come to an agreement over the presence of Christ in the Communion. Zwinglianism thus developed separately from Lutheranism.

The acceptance of the Zwinglian principles by several cantons made some kind of religious organization necessary, and in 1527 a synod of the Swiss evangelical churches was formed. About the same time the Bible was translated into the vernacular for the people. Up to this time the pope had not interfered because of his need of Swiss mercenaries, but the older rural cantons, faithful to the pope, decided to stop the march away from Rome. They organized a Christian Union of Catholic Cantons, and open war broke out between Protestant and Roman Catholic cantons in 1529. The two groups made a peace at Cappel by which the majority of citizens in each canton were to decide the form of religion and by which Protestants were to be tolerated in the papal cantons. When Zwingli forced reform in some cantons, war broke out again in 1531. Zwingli took the field as a chaplain with his soldiers and was killed in the fighting. As a result of the fighting, each canton was given full control over its internal affairs, and Zurich gave up its alliance with the Christian Civic League of Reformed Cantons. There was little change in the religious situation after this time in German Switzerland. Heinrich Bullinger (1504–75) became the able and conciliatory successor of Zwingli. Later the Zwinglian forces merged with the Calvinistic forces in the Reformed churches of Switzerland through the Consensus of Zurich in 1549.

Zwingli was the most humanistic of the Reformers. He believed that such Greeks as Socrates and Plato and such Romans as Cato, Seneca, and the Scipios would be in heaven. But, apart from this, he upheld the absolute authority of the Bible and would permit nothing in religion that could not be proved by the Scriptures. He accepted

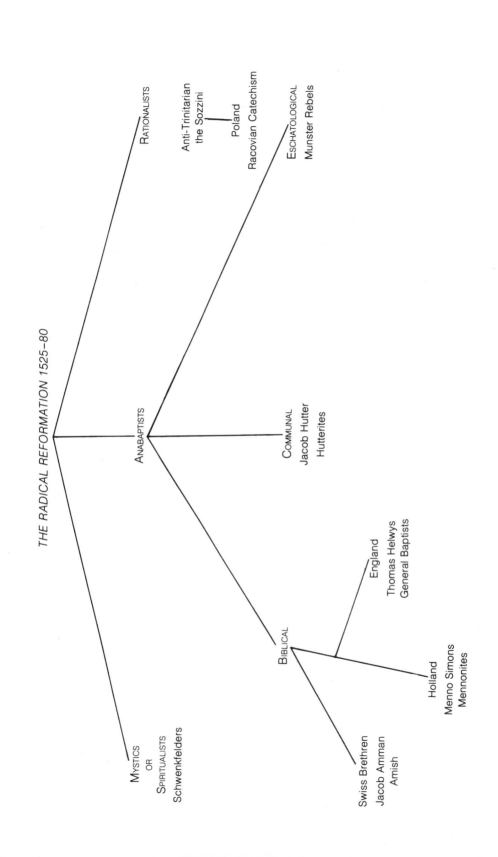

THE RADICAL REFORMATION 1525–80

RATIONALISTS

Anti-Trinitarian
the Sozzini

Poland
Racovian Catechism

ESCHATOLOGICAL
Munster Rebels

ANABAPTISTS

MYSTICS
OR
SPIRITUALISTS
Schwenkfelders

COMMUNAL
Jacob Hutter
Hutterites

BIBLICAL

England
Thomas Helwys
General Baptists

Holland
Menno Simons
Mennonites

Swiss Brethren
Jacob Amman
Amish

unconditional predestination to salvation but believed that only those who heard and rejected the gospel in unbelief were predestinated to condemnation. He believed that faith was the essential element in the sacraments, that the Lord's Supper was a symbolic "commemoration" rather than a "repetition" of the Atonement, and that the believer by reflection on Christ's death received spiritual blessing. He thought of original sin as a moral disease, but he did not think of it as guilt. Infants consequently could be saved by Christ without baptism. His *True and False Religion* (1525) expresses his biblical and Christocentric outlook.

Such were the views of the man who laid the foundation of the Reformed faith in German Switzerland. Though Calvin became the hero of the Reformed faith, the church should not forget the part that the cultured, democratic, and sincere Zwingli played in liberating Switzerland from the chains of the papacy. He was more liberal than Luther but no less courageous than he.

II. THE RADICAL REFORMATION, 1525–80

Treatment of the Anabaptists in a chapter devoted to the rise of the Reformed faith in Switzerland is justified by the fact that the Anabaptist movement was at first closely linked with the Zwinglian movement in northern Switzerland. From there it spread to Moravia, Holland, and other lands. It was the spiritual and lineal ancestor of the modern Mennonite, Amish, and Hutterite churches throughout the world. It appealed to workers in town and country.

A. The Anabaptists

Anabaptists appeared first in Switzerland because of the freedom that existed in that land. Neither feudalism nor the papacy had been able to gain a hold on this land of courageous mercenary soldiers. Zwingli's insistence on the Bible as the basis for the teaching of the preachers encouraged the rise of the Anabaptist concepts based on the Bible.

1. Conrad Grebel (1498–1526) may be regarded as the founder of the *Swiss* Anabaptist movement. He was born of an influential patrician family and received a good education at the universities of Vienna and Paris. After his conversion in 1522 he worked closely with Zwingli until he broke with him by 1525. Zwingli's early view that infant baptism had no biblical warrant had appealed to him. In 1525 the Zurich council ordered Grebel and Felix Manz, another well-educated Anabaptist leader, to desist holding meetings for Bible study. George Blaurock in 1525 was baptized by Grebel and then he baptized Grebel and several others. Because insistence on believer's baptism would deprive many of the franchise, Zwingli gave up his earlier stand based on the lack of a spiritual foundation for infant baptism. The more radical Anabaptists who opposed state control of religion were also endangering his plans for enlisting the slow-moving conservative authorities on the side of reform. At first Zwingli was willing to use his technique of debate to persuade them to give up their views; but, when this failed, the council adopted stronger measures, such as fines and exile. The movement was practically nonexistent in Zurich by 1535 because of cruel

treatment, and the lowly Christians fled to other lands. The Amish of Pennsylvania came out of this background.

2. Balthasar Hubmaier (ca. 1481–1528), one of the early *German* Anabaptists, had an excellent education and received a doctor of theology degree from the University of Ingolstadt, where he studied under Luther's opponent, John Eck. His pastorate at Waldshut, near the Swiss border, gave him contact with the Swiss radicals whose ideas he adopted. He and three hundred followers were baptized by affusion in 1525, and he had to flee to Zurich to escape the Austrian authorities. From there he was banished to Moravia, where he assumed leadership of those who fled from the Zwinglian persecution and of the thousands of Moravian converts to Anabaptist views. He was burned at the stake by order of the emperor in 1528, and his wife was drowned in the Danube by the Roman Catholic authorities. Throughout his career as an Anabaptist leader, he insisted on the separation of church and state, the authority of the Bible, and the baptism of believers.[3]

The radical fringe of the Anabaptist movement, because of their eschatology, helped to discredit the many sound believers in the ranks of the Anabaptists in Germany. The Zwickau prophets, who caused Luther trouble in 1522 in Wittenberg, were often, though perhaps mistakenly, associated with the movement to its discredit. The Münster rebellion of 1535, led by some radical, chiliastic Anabaptists, served to alienate Luther and his followers from these people.

Bernhard Rothmann, one of the canons of the cathedral of Münster,

Anabaptists were cruelly victimized by both Protestants and Catholics. They were forced to jump to their deaths from tops of haystacks and were drowned, burned, and hanged.

began an effort to win Münster to the evangelical faith. In 1532 the council allowed Lutheran ministers to man the pulpits, but the emperor ordered the bishop of Münster to drive out Rothmann and his followers, for they were becoming increasingly radical

—adopting Anabaptist ideas of socialism and proposing to sell property to aid the poor. At this point Melchior Hoffman (ca. 1495–1543), who had arrived in Strasbourg in 1529 to await the coming of the Millennium in 1533, was superseded as leader of the chiliastic Strasbourg Anabaptists by the baker Jan Matthys. Matthys proclaimed himself to be Enoch and sent emissaries to Münster in 1534. Later he decided that Münster and not Strasbourg was to be the New Jerusalem and moved there with his wife, the beautiful former nun Divara. When Matthys was killed in fighting, John of Leyden succeeded him and married Divara and fifteen additional wives. Polygamy was decreed because of the large surplus of unmarried women in Münster and the practice of some Old Testament patriarchs. Community of goods and a fanatical anticipation of the coming of the heavenly kingdom led to disorder. The bishop of the area, aided by a large fighting force and by treachery in the Anabaptist ranks, recaptured the city, and the Anabaptist leaders were executed. Anabaptist denial of the ideas of Luther and Zwingli, as well as the Münster incident, brought condemnation and persecution against the movement from both Protestants[4] and Roman Catholics.

A communal pattern based on the early church in Acts was developed by groups in Germany and Moravia, led initially by Jacob Hutter (d. 1536). Persecution drove them to Hungary and the Ukraine and after 1874 to South Dakota and the Canadian province of Manitoba, where they still practice agrarian communalism on a voluntary basis. They are known as Hutterites.

3. The wreckage of the Anabaptist movement by the Münster chiliasts was averted by the sane leadership of Menno Simons (1496–1561) in the *Netherlands.* Simons had embraced Anabaptist views and had given up his priesthood in the Roman church in 1536. He assumed leadership of the "brethren," the name that the Anabaptists of the Netherlands adopted in order to get rid of the stigma attached to the name "Anabaptist." After his death, the "brethren" were known as Mennonites. They were finally granted freedom of religion in 1676.

Because there were so many different Anabaptist groups with slightly different variations in belief—variations that grew out of the insistence on the believer's right to interpret the Bible as a literal and final authority—it is difficult to give an organized statement of Anabaptist beliefs. However, there were some doctrines that all Anabaptists held in common. They insisted on the authority of the Bible as a final and infallible rule for faith and practice. Many of them gave it a literal interpretation. They believed that the pure church was to be a free association of the regenerated rather than a state church with some unsaved in it. They also practiced the baptism of believers, at first by affusion or pouring and later by immersion. Their opposition to infant baptism as unscriptural and their insistence on rebaptism gave them the name of Anabaptists. Most of them insisted on the complete separation of church and state and would have nothing to do with state churches. The Schleitheim Confession[5] of 1527, mainly the work of Michael Sattler, expressed the major ideas of most Anabaptists. Some were inclined to pacifism and objected to the taking of oaths in court and to serving as magistrates. Some were millenarian in their view of the future and, partly because of that, practiced community of goods.

The Anabaptists appealed particularly to the workers and the peasants, who were not reached by the other Reformers. This fact, coupled with a frequent tendency to literal interpretation of the Bible by ignorant men, often led to mystical or chiliastic excesses. The hard times of the sixteenth century led many of the lower class to accept the consolation that they found in the views of the Anabaptists. The Anabaptists were not "Bolsheviks of the Reformation," nor were all of them "left wing" fanatical visionaries. They were simple Bible-believing people, some of whom were led astray by ignorant leaders, who interpreted the Bible literally to their own advantage. Neither the Mennonites nor the Baptists should be ashamed to count them among their spiritual ancestors. Their free-church concept influenced Puritan Separatists, Baptists, and Quakers.

B. The Mystical or Spiritual Radicals

Many followed the nobleman Kaspar Schwenkfeld (1489–1561). These people were more experientially oriented, were inclined to mysticism, and believed in inner spiritual guidance by the Holy Spirit. A small group still exists in Pennsylvania. Sebastian Franck (1499–ca. 1542) had similar ideas.

C. Rationalistic Socinian Radicals

The Socinians, the forerunners of the modern Unitarians, were another radical group of the Reformation. Socinian ideas developed in Italy. Lelio Sozzini (Socinus) (1525–62) of Siena was attracted to anti-Trinitarianism by the death of the anti-Trinitarian Servetus in Geneva. Fausto Sozzini (1539–1604), his nephew, moved to Poland in 1579 and remained there until his death. Socinianism developed rapidly in Poland, and Fausto gave the movement the Racovian Catechism, which was published in 1605. According to Socinianism, Christ is to be worshiped as a man who obtained divinity by his superior life. His death was simply an example of the obedience that God desires from His followers. Original sin, the deity of Christ, the Trinity, and predestination were denied. The Jesuits were able to suppress this movement in Poland, but Socinian ideas spread to Holland and to England, whence they spread to America. The modern Unitarian church is a lineal descendant of the Socinians of Poland, who were first called Unitarians in Transylvania about 1600.

III. THE CALVINISTIC REFORMATION IN GENEVA

The millions today in Switzerland, Holland, Scotland, the United States, and elsewhere who accept the Reformed faith as their doctrinal basis testify to the importance of the system of theology that John Calvin (1509–64) developed. The term "Calvinism" and the phrase "Reformed faith" have reference to the system of theology developed on the basis of Calvin's system. "Presbyterianism" is the word used to express the system of church government that Calvin developed. Geneva was the center where Calvin fully worked out his ideas. Calvin may be ranked as the leader of the second generation of Reformers.

A. Luther and Calvin

Calvin was an interesting contrast to Luther. Luther had been born of peasant stock, but Calvin's father was a notary. This made Calvin a member of the professional class. Luther had studied philosophy and theology during his university career, but Calvin had humanistic and legal training. Because of this he was more the organizer of Protestantism whereas Luther was its prophetic voice. Luther was physically strong, but Calvin fought illness during the period of his work in Geneva. Luther loved his home and family, but Calvin was essentially a lonely student. Luther, who lived in monarchical Germany, looked for aristocratic and princely support; Calvin, in republican Switzerland, was interested in the development of representative government in the church.

Luther and Calvin differed theologically as well as personally. Luther emphasized preaching, but Calvin was interested in the development of a formal system of theology. Both accepted the authority of the Bible; but Luther's main emphasis was on justification by faith, whereas Calvin stressed the sovereignty of God. Luther held to consubstantiation as the proper explanation of Christ's presence in the Lord's Supper, but Calvin rejected the physical presence of Christ in favor of the spiritual presence of Christ by faith in the hearts of the participants. Luther rejected only what the Scriptures would not approve, but Calvin refused everything of the past that could not be proved by the Scriptures. Luther believed in predestination of the elect but said little about election to condemnation. Calvin held to a double predestination—to salvation and to condemnation—based on the will of God, and he rejected any idea of merit on the part of the elect or foreknowledge on the part of God in the sense that God elected to salvation those whom He foreknew would believe.

B. Calvin's Life to 1536

Calvin's life can be readily divided into two major periods. Until 1536 Calvin was a wandering student; from 1536 until his death in 1564, except for a short period of exile to Strasbourg between 1538 and 1541, he was the leading citizen of Geneva. He was born at Noyon in Picardy in northeastern France, where his father was a respected citizen who was able to have the income from a church benefice set aside for his son's education. Two other better livings made it possible for Calvin to have the best preparation available before he went to the university. He studied for a time at the University of Paris, where he met the humanist Guillaume Cop. Here Calvin was introduced to Protestant ideas by his cousin Pierre Oliver. After he finished his humanistic studies, his father sent him to the university at Orleans to study law. He transferred to the University of Bourges in 1529. His successful completion of an able commentary on Seneca's *De Clementia* in 1532 marked the peak of humanistic influence on his life. Sometime between the completion of the commentary and the end of 1533 Calvin was converted and adopted the ideas of the Reformation. He gave up the income from the benefices. Forced to leave France in 1534 after he had collaborated with Nicholas Cop, the rector of the University of Paris, in an

An aging John Calvin as sketched with pen and ink by one of his students.

address that called for a biblical reformation like Luther's, he went to Basel.

In Basel Calvin completed his greatest work, *The Institutes of the Christian Religion*, in the spring of 1536 at the age of twenty-six. The little work was addressed to Francis I of France in an attempt to defend the Protestants of France, who were suffering for their faith, and to urge Francis to accept the ideas of the Reformation. The first edition was thus an apologetic in which Calvin developed his understanding of the Christian faith. The influence of Luther's *Catechism* can be discerned in the order of this first edition. Calvin first discussed the Ten Commandments; then, on the basis of the Apostles' Creed, the faith; next, prayer on the basis of the Lord's Prayer; the two sacraments; the evils of the Roman view of the Lord's Supper; and finally Christian liberty of the citizen, which he also related to political liberty. The work went through several

editions until the final edition of 1559. This final edition consists of four books and eighty chapters and is a large text on theology.[6]

C. Calvin's Theology

At the risk of oversimplification, one can summarize the essence of Calvin's theology by the use of a simple mnemonic device that has been developed in recent years and has often been used by students. The first letters of the main words of Calvin's theology spell the word *tulip*. The coordinating idea of his theology is the complete sovereignty of God. Calvin had the majestic conception of God and His glory that is so characteristic of some of the Old Testament prophets. He believed in the *t*otal depravity of all men. Man has through Adam inherited the guilt of Adam's sin and can do nothing for his own salvation because his will is totally corrupted. Calvin next taught that salvation is a matter of *u*nconditional election apart from human merit or divine foreknowledge. Election is based on the sovereign will of God and is a dual predestination of some to salvation and others to condemnation. Calvin also believed that the work of Christ on the cross is limited to those elected to salvation. This belief is his doctrine of a *l*imited atonement. The doctrine of *i*rresistible grace is an inevitable corollary to this. The elect will be saved apart from their own initial desire as the Holy Spirit irresistibly draws them to Christ. *P*erseverance (or preservation) of the saints is the final point of importance in his system. Those elect who are irresistibly saved by the work of the Holy Spirit will never be finally lost.[7] Although Calvin's theology has an emphasis similar to that of Augustine, Calvin owes his system to his study of the Scriptures rather than to Augustine. Like other Reformers, he went from the Bible to Augustine to seek the support of that prince of the Fathers rather than going from Augustine to the Bible and the doctrines of the Reformation.

D. Calvin's Life After 1536

While Calvin was thus engaged, the Reformation advanced into the French cantons of Switzerland. Guillaume Farel (1489–1565), a red-headed, hot-tempered, strong-voiced, prophetic individual, established the Reformation in Geneva. Farel was born into a middle-class French family and educated in French universities. Soon after 1521 he accepted Luther's idea of justification by faith. Protected by Bern, he helped spread Reformed ideas. In 1532 he began work in Geneva. In 1535 he won a dispute with those opposed to the Reformation, and the General Assembly of Citizens formally adopted the ideas of the Reformers in 1536. Farel realized that he needed someone with more organizing ability to help him to establish the Reformation in Geneva. During his travels, Calvin stopped in Geneva one night in 1536. Farel went to him and urged him to help him. When Calvin demurred because he loved the life of a student and writer of theology, Farel told him that the curse of God would be on him if he did not stay. Stricken by fear, as Calvin later confessed, he decided to remain. He and Farel cooperated until they were exiled in 1538. Calvin was ordained as a teaching minister of Geneva in 1536.

In 1537 Calvin and Farel succeeded in getting an ordinance passed that decreed that the Lord's Supper was to be celebrated at stated times, a children's catechism was to be prepared, congregational singing was to be adopted, and those under severe discipline could be excommunicated. The two introduced a catechism and a short confession of faith, but a dispute over the liturgy of the Lord's Supper led to their exile in 1538.

Between 1538 and 1541 Calvin ministered to French religious refugees in Strasbourg, where Martin Bucer (1491–1551) led the reform, and lectured on theology. In 1540 he married Idelette de Bure, the widow of an Anabaptist pastor. Their only son died in infancy, and in 1549 Idelette herself died.

In 1541 the reforming forces again gained control in Geneva, and Calvin was invited back there. That same year he had the *Ecclesiastical Ordinances*[8] promulgated. This outlined the activities of the four classes of office-bearers in the church. It provided for an association of pastors to preach and to administer discipline; a group of teachers to teach doctrine; a group of deacons to administer the work of charity; and, most important of all, the consistory, composed of ministers and elders, to supervise the theology and morals of the community and to punish when necessary the wayward members of the church by excommunication. In order to set up an effective system, Calvin used the state to inflict more severe penalties.

Such penalties proved to be much too severe, fifty-eight people being executed and seventy-six exiled by 1546. Servetus (1511–53), who questioned the doctrine of the Trinity, was executed in 1553. Though we cannot justify these procedures, we can understand that people of those days believed that one must follow the religion of the state and that disobedience could well be punished by death. This belief was held by both Protestants and Roman Catholics. Some of Calvin's regulations also would today be considered an unwarranted interference in the private life of the individual.

In 1564 Calvin died, worn out because of his weak body and arduous labors for the sake of the gospel. Theodore Beza (1519–1605), rector of the Genevan Academy, took over his work of leadership in Geneva.

E. Calvin's Contributions

Calvin's greatest contribution to the Reformed faith was his *Institutes*, which has been accepted as the authoritative expression of the Reformed theology. In this work he laid the foundation for the Reformed emphasis on the importance of doctrine and the centrality of God in Christian theology.

Calvin was also a voluminous letter-writer to the many who wrote to him for advice from all over Europe and the British Isles. His letters and other writings fill nearly fifty-seven volumes of the *Corpus Reformatorum*, and two thousand of his sermons are extant.

Calvin also encouraged education. He set up in Geneva a three-level system of education at the top of which was the Academy, now known as the University of Geneva, which was founded in 1559. His emphasis on education affected America later as the Calvinistic Puritans created colleges in the new world.

Geneva under Calvin's leadership became an inspiration and model to those of the Reformed faith elsewhere, and it provided a refuge for those who were oppressed for their Reformed faith. John Knox for a time sought refuge in Geneva and fell under the spell of Calvin's able preaching. Calvin's many commentaries on the books of the Bible have been studied by those who have adopted his ideas since his death. The government of the Genevan church became the model for Reformed churches.

Calvin also influenced the growth of democracy because he accepted the representative principle in government of the church and the state. He believed that both the church and the state were created by God for the good of men and that they should work together amicably in the furthering of Christianity. His emphasis on a divine call to a vocation and on thrift and industry stimulated capitalism.

Some have thought that Calvinistic theology cuts the nerve of evangelism and missionary effort. However, any study of the history of the propagation of the gospel will show that those who have professed the Reformed faith have had an important part in the great revivals of the past and in the modern missionary movement. The influence of this emaciated, temperate scholar and able preacher on the spiritual development of modern society has been out of proportion to his frail physique. Only the grace of God operative in his life is an adequate explanation of the work that he accomplished and that has gone on since his death. He was indeed an international reformer whose work influenced Presbyterians, Reformed, and Puritans.

SUGGESTED READING

In addition to the general works cited at the end of chapter 26, many fine biographies of the men discussed in this chapter are available.

Bender, Harold S. **Conrad Grebel.** *Goshen: Mennonite Historical Society, 1950. This is a useful biography of that leader.*

Bratt, John H., ed. **The Heritage of John Calvin.** *Grand Rapids: Eerdmans, 1973. This may be profitably used with McNeill's work.*

Claus-Peter, Asen. **Anabaptism, a Social History, 1525–1618.** *Ithaca: Cornell University Press, 1972. This is a scholarly account of Anabaptist groups, life, organization, and persecution.*

Courvoisier, Jacques. **Zwingli, a Reformed Theologian.** *Richmond, Va.: John Knox, 1963.*

Dakin, Arthur. **Calvinism.** *Philadelphia: Westminster, 1946.*

Dyck, Cornelius J., ed. **An Introduction to Mennonite History.** *Scottdale, Pa.: Herald, 1967.*

Epp, Frank H. **The Mennonites in Canada, 1786–1920.** *Toronto: Macmillan, 1974.*

Estep, William. **The Anabaptist Story.** *Nashville: Broadman, 1963. This is a short, popular account.*

Farner, Oskar. **Zwingli the Reformer.** *Translated by D. G. Sear. London: Lutterworth, 1952.*

Hostetler, John A. **Hutterite Society.** *Baltimore: Johns Hopkins, 1974.*

———. and Huntington, Gertrude E. **The Hutterites in North America.** *New York: Holt, Rinehart, and Winston, 1967.*

Hughes, Philip E., ed. and trans. **The Register of the Company of Pastors of Geneva in the Time of Calvin.** *Grand Rapids: Eerdmans, 1966. This is valuable for documents important to the Reformed faith.*

Hunt, Robert N. **Calvin.** *London: Geoffrey Bles, 1933. This is a useful account of the important events in Calvin's life.*

Jackson, Samuel M. **Huldreich Zwingli.** *New York: Putnam, 1901. This has excellent maps, several helpful appendices, and documents of importance.*

McNeill, John T. **The History and Character of Calvinism.** *Rev. ed. New York: Oxford University Press, 1964. This work gives excellent biographical sketches on Calvinistic leaders, the progress of Calvinism, and its relation to current issues.*

Parker, T. H. L. **John Calvin: A Biography.** *Philadelphia: Westminster, 1975.*

Reyburn, Hugh Y. **John Calvin.** *London: Hodder and Stoughton, 1914. This older work is still a useful biography of Calvin.*

Rilliet, Jean H. **Zwingli: Third Man of the Reformation.** *Translated by Harold Knight. Philadelphia: Westminster, 1964. This is a scholarly work.*

Ruth, John L. **Conrad Grebel.** *Scottdale, Pa.: Herald, 1975. This is a popular biography.*

Schaff, Philip. **Creeds of Christendom.** *3 vols. 6th ed. New York: Scribner, 1890. Volume 1, pages 423–66, has an excellent account of Calvin's life and work.*

Schultz, Selina G. **Caspar Schwenkfeld von Ossig, 1489–1561.** *Norristown, Pa.: Board of Publication of the Schwenkfeld Church, 1946. This is well documented.*

Vedder, Henry C. **Balthasar Hubmaier.** *New York: Putnam's, 1905. This is an interesting account of one of the early leaders of the Anabaptists.*

Walker, Williston. **John Calvin.** *New York: Shocken, 1906.*

Wenger, John C., ed. **The Complete Writings of Menno Simons.** *Translated by Leonard Verduin. Scottdale, Pa.: Herald, 1956. There is also a very useful biography by Harold S. Bender included in this volume.*

Wilbur, E. M. **A History of Unitarianism.** *Cambridge: Harvard University Press, 1945.*

Williams, George H. **The Radical Reformation.** *Philadelphia: Westminster, 1962. This work contains a scholarly synthesis of learning concerning the Anabaptists.*

Yoder, John H., ed. **The Legacy of Michael Sattler.** *Scottdale, Pa.: Herald, 1973.*

Zuck, Lowell H., ed. **Christianity and Revolution.** *Philadelphia: Temple University Press, 1975. This work contains documents concerning the radical wing of the Reformation.*

Chapter 29

The Reformed Faith Outside Switzerland

While the Lutheran faith made gains among the Scandinavians, Calvinism won adherents during the sixteenth century in the Rhine valley in Germany, in Hungary, in Moravia, in France, in the Netherlands, in Scotland, in northern Ireland, and, for a brief time, in Poland. Calvinism formed a bloc between the Lutheran north and the Roman Catholic south.

I. THE REFORMED FAITH IN FRANCE

Francis I, who ruled France between 1515 and 1547, engaged in an almost constant struggle with the Spanish ruler over Italy. French interference in Italian affairs brought about the rise of biblical humanism because Frenchmen studied in Italy and developed an enthusiasm for sources of knowledge from the past. Jacques Lefèvre (1455–1536) was one such Frenchman. Studying under the humanists of Italy who were interested in studying the Bible in the original, Lefèvre by 1525 completed a translation of the New Testament into French from the Vulgate version. Even Margaret, the sister of the ruler, became a member of the group around him that included Farel; Bude, the classicist; and Vatable, an able Hebraist. Meaux became the center of the teaching of these humanists, who wished to reform the Roman church from within so that it would more nearly correspond to the Scriptures.

Lutheran influence, chiefly through the import of Luther's writings, became another factor in the rise of the Reformation in France. The upper middle-class merchants of the town and the workers in town and country were dissatisfied with the monopoly of social and political position that the nobles and the clergy held and they were opposed to the corruption of the Roman church. The ideas of the biblical humanists of Meaux and the teachings of Luther made an appeal to them as a way by which reform could come.

Francis, alarmed at the rise of Protestant ideas, decided to use force to stop the continued spread of heretical ideas. In 1525 the group at Meaux was scattered, and many fled from France. The Sorbonne had also condemned Luther's writings as early as 1521, but it could not prevent the spread of Protestant ideas.

The movement in France lacked effective leadership, but those who adopted the principles of the Reformation emphasized the authority of the Bible for faith and morals and the doctrine of justification by faith. Lefèvre's Bible, which was based largely on the Vulgate, was distasteful to many; and Olivetan, who had influenced Calvin at Orleans, made a new translation, which was ready for use by 1535.

Though the strength of the French Reformation at first was drawn from the ideas of the biblical humanists and Luther, the conversion of John Calvin provided a writer who was able to popularize the Reformation faith, and in 1532 the Waldenses of southern France adopted Calvinism. It was persecution of French Protestants that caused Calvin to issue his first edition of the *Institutes* in 1536 as an apologetic to defend the French Christians as loyal subjects and to suggest that persecution stop. He was as much the leader of the French Protestants as he was of those in Geneva. Over 150 pastors, trained in Geneva, were sent to France between 1555 and 1556. Despite the wave of severe persecution that began in 1538, unorganized Protestants of different theological shades of opinion were consolidated into an organized, self-conscious group by 1559 with aid from Geneva. Early in the reign of Henry II (1547–59), about 400,000 of the French population were Protestant, according to one estimate. The great French admiral Coligny became a Protestant. In 1559 the first national synod, which marked the first evidence of national organization, was held in Paris. The synod adopted the Gallican Confession of Faith,[1] the first draft of which had been prepared by Calvin. The Confession was essentially a summary of his theology. After 1560 the French Protestants became known as Huguenots. The origin of the name is uncertain, but it became the badge of honor of French Calvinistic Protestants.

The Huguenots became so powerful and so well organized that they formed a kingdom within a kingdom. Realization of this situation by the government brought a transition from the government's policy of steady, fierce, bloody persecution between 1538 and 1562 to a policy of religious war to restore France to the bosom of Rome. Between 1562 and 1598 there were eight fierce wars and massacres. The terrible massacre of Saint Bartholomew was begun in 1572 by the murder of the godly Coligny. About two thousand were killed on the nights of August 23 and 24 in Paris, and in all about twenty thousand were massacred and their property seized by the Roman Catholics. The Roman Catholics had been inspired to this bloody deed by Catherine de' Medici, who had a strong influence over the king, Charles IX.

In 1593 Henry of Navarre, the leader of the Huguenots, became a Roman Catholic and ruled as Henry IV. He issued the Edict of Nantes in 1598,[2] which granted freedom of religion to the Huguenots so that they formed a tolerated state within the French state. They were allowed to keep garrisons in several of the two hundred towns in their hands. This charter of liberty protected Protestantism in France until the charter was revoked in 1685 by

Admiral Gaspard de Coligny, the political leader of the Huguenots, was the first victim of the St. Bartholomew's Day Massacre. He was murdered in his bedroom and his body dumped out the window. From an early-nineteenth-century American edition of *Foxe's Book of Martyrs.*

Louix XIV, who desired to have one state, one ruler, and one faith. Then about 400,000 Huguenots were forced to flee from France to England, Prussia, Holland, South Africa, and the Carolinas in North America. Because they were skilled artisans and professional men of the middle class, the loss of the Huguenots was a serious economic blow to France. This loss helped to bring about her defeat by England in the struggle for colonies in the eighteenth century. Since that time, Reformed Protestantism has not had much influence in France, and Protestants have been a small minority within the population.

Jansenism in the Roman Catholic church of France was the Continental counterpart of English Puritanism. Both found their main theological roots in Augustine's views. The Jansenist movement was a reaction from the Thomistic orthodoxy of the Council of Trent to a Bible-based Augustinianism that would vitalize personal life. The movement took its name from the bishop of Ypres, Cornelius Jansen (1585–1638), who had been a professor at Louvain. In 1640 his book *Augustinus* was published posthumously. In his book he taught that conversion came through grace, which was irresistible and which reason could not make known.[3] Jansen's views were widely received among devout Frenchmen, but at no place were they more strongly held than at the nunnery of Port Royal near Paris. His ideas were opposed by the Jesuits, whom he accused of a semi-Pelagianism because they emphasized human effort as well as grace in salvation.

Blaise Pascal (1623–62) supported the Jansenists. He had been a sickly but precocious child who had been

317

trained in mathematics by his father. When his father withheld geometry books to make him study languages, the boy worked out thirty-two of Euclid's propositions without previous knowledge of them. Pascal became the leading mathematician of France. In 1654 a profound religious experience made the teachings of Jansen and the Bible, which he had accepted about five years earlier, real to him; and he threw his efforts into the defense of Jansenism and Port Royal, where his sister Jacqueline had become a nun in 1652. He wrote a volume called *Provincial Letters* in 1656–57 in which he attacked the questionable moral code of the Jesuits. His famous *Pensées* appeared after his death in 1670. In it he emphasized the corruption of man and the redemptive power of God in Christ as over against the way in which the senses and reason might deceive man.

But not even Pascal's able defense could save the cause for which he fought. Port Royal was razed in 1710 by royal order; and Louis XIV, influenced by the Jesuits, persecuted the Jansenists. The new leader Pasquier Quesnel (1634–1719) had to flee to Holland. Clement XI, urged on by the Jesuits, condemned Quesnel's writings in a papal bull issued in 1713. In 1723 a Jansenist Catholic church was organized in Holland. Such was the end of attempts to promote Augustinianism in the Roman church.

II. THE REFORMED FAITH IN GERMANY

When Luther lost the support of the peasant class of the Rhine valley by his uncompromising opposition to the Peasant's Revolt, many peasants became Anabaptists. With the coming of Calvinism, those who were financially better off turned to Calvinism. Earlier, in 1530, three cities of the Rhine area and Strasbourg presented their Tetrapolitan Confession to the Diet of Augsburg.

Calvinism also made gains in the Palatinate, whose ruler, the elector Frederick III, was sympathetic toward Calvinistic theology and Presbyterian church government. After a public disputation in 1560, Frederick decided in favor of Calvinism. Zacharias Ursinus (1534–83) and Kaspar Olevianus (1536–87) were given the task of drawing up a catechism for the use of the church. They prepared the Heidelberg Catechism, which was officially adopted in 1563.[4] It became the official creed of the German Reformed churches. When the Reformed faith was finally established after a short Lutheran interlude, the University of Heidelberg became a center of Calvinism.

III. THE REFORMED FAITH IN HUNGARY

Few realize that between two and three million people in Hungary profess the Reformed faith. Because the Magyars disliked the Germans, Lutheranism did not receive a kindly reception. But after 1550 as Hungarians, who had studied at Geneva and Wittenberg, returned home to spread Protestant ideas and after the translation of the New Testament into the Magyar tongue by John Erdosi, the people of Hungary eagerly adopted Protestantism. By the end of the sixteenth century a large part of the people and the nobility had adopted the Reformed faith. Matthew Dévay

(1500–43) was largely responsible for this turn of events. By 1570 the Hungarian Confession, which had been prepared in 1558, was widely circulated. Because the Socinian or anti-Trinitarians were making such progress, the confession was preceded by a statement of the biblical arguments against Unitarianism.

After 1572 severe persecution became the lot of the Magyar Reformed church for about two centuries. The Jesuits also made strong efforts to win the Magyars back to the Roman system. In spite of this persecution, the Protestants remained firm and were granted toleration in 1781 and freedom of religion by 1848.

IV. THE REFORMED FAITH IN SCOTLAND

From about 1300, when Edward I tried unsuccessfully to bring Scotland under the English crown, Scotland made common cause with England's great enemy France. England could always count on a flank attack from the Scots in the north whenever she went to war with France. It was not until the Reformation, which brought both countries into the Protestant fold, that relations became better. The common fight between episcopacy and presbyterianism during the first half of the seventeenth century helped to heal the old breach between the two states after both were brought under one ruler in 1603.

Politics were dominated by religion during the Scottish Reformation, but in England religion had been secondary to political considerations. The barons and good burghers of the middle class in Scotland united under John Knox against the crown to bring about reform. In England the Reformation had been created from above by law of the ruler. It is little wonder that the Reformation in Scotland was more radical than that in England. In no other area, except Geneva, was the influence of Calvinism so strong.

Lack of a strong ruler in Scotland had created many local areas under the leadership of strong clan chieftains. Small wonder that in this anarchic situation morals and religion deteriorated. Concubinage, drunkenness, simony, and greed for wealth coupled with disregard for the people characterized the leaders of the Roman church in Scotland. This condition of the Roman church constituted the negative cause of the Reformation.

One positive cause of the Scottish Reformation was the Lutheran teaching of Patrick Hamilton (ca. 1503–28), who had studied at Marburg and Wittenberg. Hamilton's emphasis on justification by faith and his assertion that the pope was antichrist so aroused the authorities that he was burned in 1528. George Wishart (ca. 1513–46) also began teaching Protestant doctrine and was burned for his faith in 1546. He exerted considerable influence on the spiritual development of John Knox. Copies of Tyndale's New Testament, brought to Scotland by Scottish merchants, also had their effect in the promotion of Protestant ideas.

The Scots also were alienated from the royal family when Mary Stuart was sent to France for her education and when she married the young heir to the French throne. The Scots were worried lest Scotland should become a part of French dominions because of this marriage. They were also antagonized by the lax morality of the Frenchmen in Scotland. Failure of the Roman church and the spread of the theology of the Reformation created an atmosphere favorable to the coming of the Scottish Reformation.

In the meantime, the man who was to establish the Reformation in Scotland was being prepared for his task. John Knox (ca. 1514–72) was a courageous, sometimes harsh, man who feared no one except God. He was educated at the University of Saint Andrews and ordained to the priesthood in 1536. He became a follower of Wishart and preached to the Protestant soldiers in the garrison of Saint Andrews until the French captured him. For nineteen months he served as a galley slave in a French warship until he was released through an exchange of prisoners. Edward VI of England offered him the bishopric of Rochester, but Knox refused it. Knox then became a royal chaplain. When Mary Tudor ascended the English throne, he fled to Europe where he ministered to religious exiles at Frankfurt. He was much influenced by Calvin. To him, Calvin was "that notable servant of God."

A number of Scottish nobles, who were disgusted with French influence in Scotland and the "idolatry" of the "Congregation of Satan" (their name for the church of Rome), met in Edinburgh in December 1557. These lords made a covenant to use their lives and possessions to establish "the Word of God" in Scotland. At this juncture, Knox in 1559 returned to Scotland as a fiery prophet of Calvinistic thought. When Mary Stuart and her husband became rulers of France, and French soldiers were brought into Scotland, the Scots appealed to Elizabeth, the new queen of England, for aid.

Elizabeth, a skillful diplomat, hesitated to assist a people in revolt against their sovereign. Further, she disliked Knox because in 1558 he had published a tract against the Scottish lady-regent and Mary Tudor entitled *The First Blast of the Trumpet Against the Monstrous Regiment of Women* in which he argued that it was contrary to nature, God, and His Word to have a woman ruler, because it would mean "the subversion of good order, of all justice, and equity." However, because French troops in Scotland were a threat to English security, she sent money and a fleet in 1560. The Treaty of Edinburgh in 1560 provided that only a harmless token force of 120 French troops could stay in Scotland; that Frenchmen could not hold public office in Scotland; and that Francis II, Mary Stuart's husband, was not to engage in war against England. This ended French control of Scotland and left the Lords of the Congregation, as the Scottish nobility interested in reform were called, free to promote the cause of religious reformation.

The Scottish Parliament met in 1560 and, led by Knox, proceeded to the work of reformation. It ended the rule of the pope over the Scottish church, declared the Mass to be illegal, and repealed all statutes against heretics. It accepted the Scottish Confession of Faith that the "Six Johns," Knox and five other men with the first name of John, drew up in less than a week.[5] The Confession was definitely Calvinistic in tone and remained the major Scottish confession until the adoption of the Westminster Confession in 1647. Later the first *Book of Discipline* and in 1561 the *Book of Common Order* were drawn up. The Scottish church was also organized

This print appeared in a Catholic satire by Peter Frarin, *An Oration Against the Unlawful Insurrections of the Protestants of Our Time* (1566). On the left Christopher Goodman is shown blowing his blast *How Superior Powers Ought to be Obeyed*. On the right is John Knox blowing his blast entitled *The First Blast of the Trumpet Against the Monstrous Regiment* (i.e., rule) *of Women.* Knox had in mind the Catholic women rulers of Scotland and England.

into presbyteries, synods, and a national assembly, with the system of representative government of the church by elders as in the Reformed church in Geneva. Thus was the Reformation accomplished bloodlessly by the decree of the Scottish legislature, but Knox and his friends still faced severe tests before it was firmly established.

Mary Stuart (1542–87), whose husband, the French ruler, had died, landed in Scotland in 1561 during these changes. She was a beautiful and clever woman who was devoted to Catholicism. The dour, outspoken Knox had many tempestuous interviews with her, but he would not yield in any way despite her tears and blandishments. Mary's domestic problems led to her final defeat. In 1565 she married her cousin, the handsome but

vain and jealous Darnley, who murdered her Italian secretary in her presence because he thought Mary was in love with him. A son, who became James VI of Scotland and James I of England, was born to them; but after the murder of her secretary Mary had no use for Darnley and fell in love with Lord Bothwell. Darnley was blown up in a cottage in Edinburgh where he was staying. In 1567 Mary married Bothwell, and it was assumed that he had murdered Darnley. This so enraged the Scottish Parliament that it forced her to abdicate. She escaped to England and appealed to Elizabeth for protection in 1569. Elizabeth put her in protective custody until plots to put Mary on the English throne threatened Elizabeth with assassination. Elizabeth then reluctantly agreed to Mary's execution in 1587.

John Knox died in 1572. The middle class was firmly in political control, and the presbyterian system of church government and Calvinistic theology were adopted by the Scottish people. The French threat to English security through Scotland was forever ended, and the religious barrier to political union between England and Scotland was removed so that the two lands were united under the same ruler in 1603 and became one kingdom with one Parliament in 1707. Indirectly, the Scottish Reformation affected America because many Scottish Presbyterians migrated to northern Ireland early in the seventeenth century; and, from there, 200,000 migrated to America in the first half of the eighteenth century. Thus Presbyterianism in America is a lineal descendant of Scottish Presbyterianism.

In 1572 an attempt was made to establish episcopalian church government in Scotland. The battle against prelacy now took the place of the war against popery. Andrew Melville (1545–1622), the principal of Saint Andrews University, led the battle to restore the presbyterian system of church government. In 1581 presbyteries were again set up on an experimental basis. In 1592, despite opposition from King James VI, Presbyterianism became the established religion in Scotland. The early Stuarts unsuccessfully tried to reestablish the episcopal system between 1603 and 1640, but in 1690 Presbyterianism was established finally in Scotland.

V. THE REFORMED FAITH
IN IRELAND

Although the English were able to unite Wales and, finally, Scotland with England, they were never able to win the native Irish to unification except for brief periods. Even then unification was only imposed by force. This was the result of the hatred of the conquered race for the conquering race, Ireland's economic bondage to England, and the failure to win Ireland for Protestantism.

When the Irish revolted against England during the Reformation, Parliament in 1557 by law confiscated the land of the defeated rebels and granted two-thirds to English settlers. This inaugurated the policy of colonization that was to result in a divided Ireland in modern times. Plots between the Spanish and rebellious Irish leaders led to the revolt from 1598 to 1603 that marred the end of Elizabeth's reign. When James I ascended the English throne, he decided to colonize northern Ireland with Protestants. Most of the Protestants were Scottish Presbyterians, and they came to form the bulk of the population in the northern counties. Ulster became a Presbyterian county, and Belfast became the Presbyterian city. These Scotch-Irish Presbyterians were the ancestors of those now living in northern Ireland. When England placed economic disabilities upon them before 1700, about 200,000 migrated to North America. By 1750 they had planted Presbyterianism in America, particularly around what is now Pittsburgh. This colonization of Ireland by the Scottish Presbyterians was also one of the reasons why the northern part of Ireland is united with England and Scotland under one crown today while the southern part is a free republic. Southern Ireland did not accept the Reformation but remained loyal to the pope.

VI. THE REFORMED FAITH
IN HOLLAND

The revolt of the seven northern provinces of the Netherlands, later Holland, against the pope must not be dissociated from the political revolt of the Netherlands against Spanish domination. In this struggle England gave aid during the reign of Elizabeth in order to harass Philip II, who was supporting the Roman church and making a claim to the throne of England through his dead wife, Mary Tudor, the former queen of England. The Dutch people finally gained their freedom and adopted the Reformed faith.

Lutheranism failed to win the loyalty of the Dutch, although it contributed to religious revolt in Holland. However, after the Peasants' Revolt, Luther's insistence on the authority of the prince was distasteful to the Dutch who were to revolt against their Spanish ruler. The more democratic Calvinism appealed to them as a way to escape from the corruption of the Roman system.

It must also be remembered that this was the land of Erasmus and the Brethren of the Common Life. The first Dutch New Testament was also published in 1523 so that the Dutch could compare the Roman church in their land with the New Testament church.

All these forces coalesced in a political-ecclesiastical revolt against domination by the Spanish ruler and the pope. Holland was the only land gained for Protestantism after the Catholic Reformation got under way.

Up to 1525 those who accepted the Reformation followed Luther, but the Anabaptists gained a strong following from that date until about 1540. From 1540 the Reformation in Holland proceeded along Calvinistic lines. By 1560 the majority of Protestants were Calvinistic; a minority were Anabaptists, led by Menno Simons; and a small minority followed Luther's ideas. Neither the passive obedience of Lutheranism nor the revolutionary spirit of Anabaptism had the appeal for the independent Dutch burghers that Calvinism had with its insistence on freedom from tyranny. Protestantism spread in spite of the organization of the Inquisition by 1524 to stamp it out in these valuable Spanish possessions.

When Philip II, an earnest and devout Roman Catholic, ascended the throne of Spain after his father, Charles V, abdicated in 1555, he determined to bring the Spanish Netherlands back to the fold of the pope. His vacillation between indulgence and savage cruelty caused the Netherlanders to rise against him. Noblemen of the Netherlands formed the Compromise of Breda in 1565 and presented a petition asking for the suspension of the Inquisition and the laws against heretics. Uprisings in Flanders in 1565 and in Holland by Protestants in 1566 brought the plundering of four hundred Roman churches and the desecration of the host used in the Mass. This profanation caused Philip to take strong measures, and these he took through the Duke of Alva whom he made the regent of the Netherlands in 1569. Alva set up a special tribunal backed by the power of ten thousand Spanish soldiers and inaugurated a reign of terror. Between 1567 and 1573 he executed about two thousand people, and by the end of the century forty thousand had migrated to other countries.

Heavy taxation by the Spanish also threatened to impoverish the Netherlands.

Opposition to the Spanish policy came to be centered in William of Orange, known as the Silent. The standard of revolt was raised in 1568; but William's army was no match for Alva's trained soldiers, and he had to retire to Germany. Because war on land was hopeless, the Dutch became "Beggars of the Sea." They took to the sea by 1569 and preyed on Spanish commerce. After long sieges, Alva took the revolting cities and engaged in wholesale massacres. An attack on one city by the Spanish was stopped by the cutting of the dikes and the flooding of the countryside with sea water. In 1576 Antwerp was looted and seven thousand were killed by the Spanish soldiery under Alva's successor. This act, known as the "Spanish fury," aroused such nationalistic spirit that Holland and Zeeland, which were definitely Calvinistic, united with the other provinces in the Pacification of Ghent in 1576 to drive out the Spanish.

Differences of race, language, ways of making a living, and, above all, religion brought about a division between the Roman Catholic Flemish (modern Belgians) in the south and the Calvinistic Dutch in the northern provinces. The seven northern provinces signed the Union of Utrecht in 1579 and in 1581 formally repudiated the sovereignty of the Spanish king. The foundations of the modern state of Holland were laid under the leadership of William of Orange. The Dutch eventually won their war for freedom, but in the process they lost their great leader William to an assassin's dagger in 1584. English aid and England's defeat of the Spanish Armada in 1588 left the Dutch relatively free from Spanish efforts at recapture; but the end of the war and the independence of the Dutch Republic were not formally recognized until the Treaty of Westphalia in 1648. Holland became a sea power in the seventeenth century, built up a wealthy empire in the Far East and the Western hemisphere, and gave a king to England in 1689.

The Dutch did not neglect the development of church organization and theology during the struggle for national independence. At a national synod in Emden in 1571 it was decided that the church should adopt the presbyterian system of church government. The consistory, the classis, and the synod were to be the units of organization. The synod also adopted the Belgic Confession,[6] which had been prepared by Guido de Brès (1527–67) in 1561 and revised by Francis Junius, a Calvinistic pastor at Antwerp. The Confession was adopted by a synod at Antwerp as early as 1566 and received approval by the national synod at Dort in 1574. It and the Heidelberg Catechism became the theological standards of the Reformed church of Holland. The University of Leyden, which was formed in 1575 in gratitude for the freeing of the city from a siege, became a center for Calvinistic theological study. The Dutch Calvinists have always been sturdy defenders and exponents of Christianity.

Victorious Calvinism, however, found its first opposition in Holland in the development of Arminianism. James (Jacobus) Arminius (1559–1609), its exponent, was educated with funds given by friends and, later, by the civic authorities of Amsterdam. He studied at Leyden and at Geneva under Beza and traveled widely in

Italy. In 1603, after fifteen years as a pastor in Amsterdam, he became professor of theology at Leyden. His attempt to modify Calvinism so that, according to him, God might not be considered the author of sin, nor man an automaton in the hands of God, brought down upon him the opposition of his colleague Francis Gomar. Arminius asked the government to call a national synod concerning the matter, but he died before it was called. The supporters of Arminius, among whom were such men as Hugo Grotius, who wrote on international law, compiled their ideas in the *Remonstrance*[7] of 1610.

Both Arminius and Calvin taught that man, who inherited Adam's sin, is under the wrath of God. But Arminius believed that man was able to initiate his salvation after God had granted him the primary grace to enable his will to cooperate with God.[8] Calvin thought that man's will had been so corrupted by the fall that salvation was entirely a matter of divine grace. Arminius accepted election but believed that the decree to save some and damn others had "its foundation in the foreknowledge of God."[9] Thus election was conditional rather than unconditional. Calvin, on the other hand, accepted an unconditional election by a sovereign God to grace and condemnation. Arminius also believed that Christ's death was sufficient for all but that it was efficient only for believers. Calvin limited the atonement to those elected to salvation.[10] Arminius also taught that men might resist the saving grace of God,[11] whereas Calvin maintained that grace was irresistible.

Arminius answered the Calvinistic insistence on the perseverance of saints by stating that God would give the saints grace so that they need not fall but that the Scriptures seemed to teach that it was possible for man to fall away from salvation.[12] Arminius did not want to make God the author of sin[13] nor man an automaton. He thought that these modifications of Calvinism would eliminate those dangers to theology.

From 1618 to 1619 a synod was held at Dort. It was really an international Calvinistic assembly because twenty-eight of the one hundred thirty present were Calvinists from England, Bremen, Hesse, the Palatinate, Switzerland, and France. The Arminians came before the meeting in the role of defendants.

Five Calvinistic articles, the *Canons of Dort*, opposing the *Remonstrance* of 1610 were drawn up, and the clerical followers of Arminius were deprived of their positions. Not until 1625 did persecution of Arminians cease. Arminianism had considerable influence on one wing of the Anglican church in the seventeenth century, the Methodist movement of the eighteenth century, and the Salvation Army.

John Coeccius (1603–69), an able biblical scholar in Holland, developed the idea of a covenant of works with Adam that was replaced by a new covenant of grace in Christ. This idea is still held in the Dutch Reformed and the Christian Reformed Churches. Much later, Abraham Kuyper (1837–1920) founded the Free University of Amsterdam and promoted Calvinism.

SUGGESTED READING

The general works cited at the end of chapter 26 have useful sections on the development of the Reformed faith in the countries that have been discussed in the preceding chapter.

Bangs, Carl. **Arminius.** *Nashville: Abingdon, 1971. This is a well-documented biography that includes the ideas of Arminius.*

Brown, Peter H. **John Knox.** *2 vols. London: Black, 1895. This is an old but still helpful work.*

Burleigh, J. H. S. **A Church History of Scotland.** *Oxford: Oxford University Press, 1960.*

Caillet, Emile. **Pascal.** *Philadelphia: Westminster, 1945. The author has ably presented the work and contributions of Pascal.*

Classen, Claus Peter. **The Palatinate in European History, 1559–1660.** *Oxford: Blackwell, 1963.*

Cowan, Henry. **John Knox.** *New York: Putnam, 1905. This biography gives an excellent account of the life and work of John Knox.*

De Jong, Peter Y., ed. **Crisis in the Reformed Churches.** *Grand Rapids: Reformed Fellowship, 1968. This contains helpful data on the Synod of Dort.*

Dickinson, William C. **A New History of Scotland.** *London: Nelson, 1962.*

―――― et al., eds. **A Source Book of Scottish History.** *London: Nelson, 1962.*

Donaldson, Gordon. **The Scottish Reformation.** *Cambridge: Cambridge University Press, 1960.*

Knox, John. **History of the Reformation in Scotland.** *2 vols. Edited by William C. Dickinson. New York: Philosophical Library, 1950. This is an interesting, firsthand account.*

MacGregor, Geddes. **The Thundering Scot: A Portrait of John Knox.** *Philadelphia: Westminster, 1957.*

Renwick, A. M. **The Story of the Scottish Reformation.** *Grand Rapids: Eerdmans, 1960.*

Ridley, John. **John Knox.** *New York: Oxford University Press, 1968. This is about the best, well-documented introduction to the life of Knox.*

Roche, O. J. A. **The Days of the Upright.** *New York: Potter, 1965. This gives the Huguenot story.*

Romanes, Ethel. **The Story of Port Royal.** *London: Murray, 1907.*

Ziff, Otto. **The Huguenots.** *New York: Fischer, 1942.*

Chapter 30

The Reformation and Puritanism in England

The Protestant Reformation created the Lutheran, Anabaptist, and Reformed aspects of the Christian faith. The fourth and, for the United States and the Commonwealth nations of England, one of the most important, was the Anglican Reformation in England. It ranks with the Lutheran movement in its conservative approach to reform. Having no dominant ecclesiastical leader such as Calvin or Luther, it was dominated by the ruler who became the head of the national church. For that reason it began as a lay political movement, continued as a religious movement, and concluded with the Elizabethan settlement in the middle of the sixteenth century. It spread all over the world because of the worldwide extent of British settlement.

I. REFORMING THE CHURCH IN ENGLAND

A. Causes of the Reformation in England

The Lollards, who had been organized to spread the teachings of John Wycliffe, had never been stamped out. On the contrary, their teachings had circulated in the homes of the more humble people of England through a religious underground movement during the fifteenth century. Their emphasis on the authority of the Scriptures and the need of a personal relation to Christ was revived with the emergence of the political reformation in England in the first quarter of the sixteenth century.

One must also remember that the Tudor rulers, who ruled England between 1485 and 1603, had created a strong national state in which the ruler through the army and a bureaucracy was able to give to the rising middle class the security that was essential to business. In return, the middle class accepted restrictions on their liberty and cooperated with the ruler, who also used them in the government. The older feudal nobility had practically disappeared by 1485 because it had committed class suicide during the Wars of the Roses. King and middle class united in promoting the welfare of the land. Because of this, there was a rising tide of national consciousness that gave support to the ruler in his efforts to separate the English church from the papacy. Control of much land in England by the Roman church; papal taxation, which took good English money to Rome; and church courts, which were rivals of the royal courts, angered both ruler and subjects. These problems caused the nation to support Henry VIII when he decided to break with Rome.

The intellectual factor must not be ignored. The biblical humanists or Oxford reformers of Oxford University, such as John Colet (ca. 1466–1519), dean of Saint Paul's Church, began early in the sixteenth century to study the Bible in the original tongue through the medium of Erasmus's Greek New Testament and to expound the meaning of the Bible to their people. These humanists were extremely critical of the failure that they saw in the Roman church and were anxious to bring about reform. William Tyndale (ca. 1494–1536) and Miles Coverdale, who later made the Scriptures available to the English people in their own tongue, were also reformers. Tyndale published two editions, each of three thousand copies, of his English New Testament at Worms in 1525. This translation from Erasmus's Greek Testament was the first printed English New Testament. It was distributed in England by friendly merchants. Although Tyndale was martyred near Brussels in 1536, his work lived on and helped to stimulate religious reform in England. Miles Coverdale published the first complete printed English translation of the whole Bible in 1535. The student of the Reformation is always impressed with the way in which the fortunes of the Reformation were so closely identified with the translation of the Bible into the common tongue of the people.

Luther's writings were also circulated widely in England. Scholars at Oxford and Cambridge studied his *Babylonian Captivity* with relish because of its criticism of the abuses of the Roman church. In 1521 Henry VIII attacked this tract in a scurrilous work called *In Defence of the Seven Sacraments.*[1] The grateful pope gave him the title of "Defender of the Faith," and this title has been used by the Protestant rulers of England since that time. Public burning of Luther's books did not stop the spread of his ideas, and thus men such as Tyndale and Thomas Cranmer were attracted to Protestant ideas.

The direct cause of the coming of the Anglican Reformation was not so much the love affairs of Henry VIII as his desire to have a legitimate male heir. It seemed that he and Catherine could never have a son. In order to get a divorce from her and the right to marry Anne Boleyn, with whom he was in love, he had to bring the Roman church in England under his control. Henry's action constituted the direct and personal cause for the beginning of the Reformation.

B. Ecclesiastical Reformation Under Henry VIII (1509–47)

Henry VIII, who ruled from 1509 to 1547, was a handsome, generous, strong, cultured prince, who knew theology, was a good musician, and could speak Latin, French, and Spanish, as well as English. He enjoyed the chase, archery, and tennis, sports that helped to make him more popular

with the English people than his par-
simonious father Henry VII had been.
His father had endeavored to relate his
line to the important royal families of
Europe by strategic marriages. His
daughter Margaret was married to
James of Scotland. (Her great-
grandson, James VI of Scotland, became James I of England in 1603.) His
son Arthur was married to a Spanish
princess, Catherine of Aragon. When
Arthur died, the miserly king, in order
not to lose Catherine's dowry, persuaded Pope Julius II to grant a dispensation so that Catherine could be
married to Arthur's younger brother,
Henry in 1503. Henry and Catherine
had one child. Later this child ruled as
Mary Tudor.

When it became apparent that he
could not have a son by this marriage,
Henry became concerned, because he
believed that England would need a
male ruler after his death in order to
see the land through the period of
international turbulence. He also
thought that possibly God was punish-
ing him for marrying his brother's
widow, an action prohibited by both
canon law and Leviticus 20:21. Falling
in love with the pretty Anne Boleyn,
Henry ordered his adviser Cardinal
Wolsey to negotiate with Clement VII
for a divorce from Catherine. Clement
VII was unable to grant this request
because in 1527 he was under the
control of Catherine's nephew, the
powerful Charles V, the ruler of Spain
and the emperor of Germany. Henry
accused Wolsey of high treason when
he failed to get the divorce, but Wolsey
died before Henry could execute him.

Thomas Cromwell became Henry's
chief minister, and in 1532 Protestant
Thomas Cranmer (1489–1556) was
made archbishop of Canterbury. Be-

The papal bull ruling against Henry VIII's request for an annulment.

cause it was apparent that the pope
would not grant him a divorce, Henry
decided to get it through the English
clergy who could be coerced into
granting it by Parliament. The Tudor
Parliament was representative of the
people but was responsible to the king
rather than to the people because the
Tudors ruled as dictators, concealing
the iron fist in a velvet glove. Thus the
Reformation was initiated in England
by the lay authority of the ruler and
Parliament. The Reformation Parliament ended papal control and monasticism.

In 1531 Henry accused the English
clergy of violating a statute prohibiting
recognition of any appointee of the
pope without the ruler's consent because they had accepted Wolsey as a
papal legate, even though Wolsey had
been Henry's trusted adviser. Henry
had them accept himself as head of
the church in England "as far as the
law of Christ allows." He also fined
them over £118,000. He again fined
them in 1532 and forced the clergy in
convocation, the national meeting of

the Roman church in England, to agree in the *Submission of the Clergy* that they would promulgate no papal bull in England without the ruler's consent. In this manner the clergy accepted Henry as their head,[2] and his marriage to Catherine was declared invalid in 1533 by Cranmer in his church court. Henry married Anne that same year.

Henry then turned to Parliament for aid. Parliament prohibited residence of the English clergy outside the country. Another act forbade the payment of annates to the pope. Parliament banned appeals from church courts in England to the papal courts in Rome.[3] The most important step in the separation of the church in England from the papacy was then taken in the Act of Supremacy of 1534. The act declared that the king was "the supreme head of the church of England."[4] This constituted the political break with Rome. Parliament in the same year passed the Act of Succession, which gave the throne to the children of Henry and Anne. Subjects were to take an oath to observe the statute and to repudiate papal authority. When the courageous Thomas More refused to do so, he was executed. Henry was now head of the English church.

Henry evidently believed that his settlement would be final only if he could tie the middle class of England to the changes he had made by giving them an economic interest in the change. He cast covetous eyes on the property of the Roman church and had Cromwell gather evidence, some of it genuine, of the sins of the monks. In 1536 Parliament ordered the closing of all monasteries with less than two hundred pounds annual income. In all, 376 monasteries were closed, and

their property was taken over by the crown. In 1539 over 150 of the larger ones were closed by act of Parliament. Twenty-eight abbots disappeared from the House of Lords. The king kept part of the lands and wealth for himself; the rest he gave or sold cheaply to the middle-class landed gentry. These people became a new nobility and loyal supporters of the ecclesiastical changes that Henry and Parliament had made. Henry gained an income of approximately one hundred thousand pounds annually. Because the dispossessed monks had to be cared for, the state, for the first time, began to engage in relief by grants of aid to some of the monks.

The passage of the Six Articles by Parliament in 1539 was proof that Henry had broken only the ecclesiastical tie between the church in England and Rome. These Articles reaffirmed transubstantiation, Communion in one kind, celibacy, and auricular confession.[5] In theology the Church of England remained true to Rome. Henry had made concessions to reform in 1536 by issuing the Ten Articles and by authorizing an English translation of the Bible. Hence the Great Bible was issued in 1539 as a revision of the work of Tyndale and Coverdale. Cranmer wrote the preface. It was also known as the "Chained Bible" because it was chained to its stand in many churches. When the danger of foreign attack passed, Henry again enforced the reactionary Six Articles of 1539.

In the meantime, Henry had tired of Anne Boleyn, especially because their child had been a girl, whom they named Elizabeth. In 1536 Anne was tried and beheaded on charges of adultery. Henry next married Jane

Seymour, who bore the son he wanted before she died. Later Henry married Anne of Cleves, whom he divorced; Catherine Howard, whom he executed; and Catherine Parr, who had the singular fortune to outlive him.

Henry freed the church from the papacy and put it under royal control as a national church. In his will[6] he stated that after his death his son Edward should take the throne. Edward would be followed by Mary, the daughter of Catherine of Aragon, and Mary by Elizabeth, the daughter of Anne Boleyn. When Henry finally died, the English church was a national church with the ruler as its head, but it was Roman Catholic in doctrine. The Bible was, however, available to the people in their own tongue. Henry's son Edward was to carry out the Protestant phase of the Reformation that Henry had begun as an ecclesiastical movement between 1527 and 1547.

C. Protestant Reformation Under Edward VI

Because Edward VI was only nine when he came to the throne, his mother's brother, the duke of Somerset, was appointed regent. He was succeeded by the duke of Northumberland some two and a half years later. Somerset had Protestant sympathies and helped the young king to institute changes that would make the Reformation in England religious and theological. In 1547 Parliament granted the cup to the laity in the Communion service; repealed treason and heresy laws and the Six Articles; legalized the marriage of priests in 1549; and in 1547 ordered the dissolution of the chantries, which were endowed chapels for the saying of masses for the soul of the one who made the endowment.

Positive action was also taken by Somerset. Church services were to be in the common tongue rather than in Latin. An Act of Uniformity in 1549 provided for the use of a Book of Common Prayer, which was the work of Cranmer. The book emphasized the use of English in the services, the reading of the Bible, and the participation of the congregation in worship. The second and more Protestant edition, issued in 1552, reflected Calvinistic influences because of Bucer. The churches were ordered to use it by a second Act of Uniformity.[7] This prayer book, with slight modifications adopted in Elizabeth's reign, is the same one that the Anglican church has used since that time. Cranmer also engaged in the drawing up of a creed with the advice of various theologians, such as John Knox. The resulting Forty-Two Articles were made the creed of the Anglican church by royal assent in 1553. The Articles were somewhat Calvinistic in tone, especially in the matter of predestination and the view of the Communion. Signature of this act was followed by the death of Edward VI.

D. Roman Catholic Reaction Under Mary Tudor

Mary, who ruled from 1553 to 1558, was the daughter of Henry VIII by Catherine of Aragon. Her reign coincided with the development of the Counter Reformation in the Roman church on the Continent and may be thought of as the English parallel to the Counter Reformation on the Continent. Advised by Cardinal Reginald Pole, Mary, who was Roman Catholic to the core, forced Parliament to restore religious practices in England to what they were at the death of her father in 1547 and to repudiate the changes that had been made under Edward. Parliament agreed to the necessary measures, but it would not restore the lands that had been taken from the Roman church during the reign of Henry VIII. Mary married Philip II of Spain in 1554, but the marriage was unpopular with the English people, and Philip never requited Mary's love.

This sketch appeared in John Foxe's *Book of Martyrs* (originally published as *Actes and Monuments*) in 1563. The caption with the sketch read, "The description of Doctour Cranmer, howe he was plucked down from the stage, by Friers and Papists, for the true Confession of hys Faith."

About eight hundred of the English clergy refused to accept these changes and lost their parishes. They were forced to flee to Geneva and to Frankfort for refuge if they were not to perish in the persecution that Mary initiated. Nearly three hundred, mainly from the commercial areas of southeastern England, were martyred for their faith. Chief among them were Latimer, Ridley, and Cranmer. Latimer encouraged Ridley at the stake by his remark that their burning would light a candle in England that by God's grace would never be put out. Cranmer at first recanted but later recanted his recantation and, when he was burned, put the hand that had signed the recantation in the fire until it was burned. Nothing strengthened the cause of Protestantism more than the death of these brave martyrs. Their earnest conviction and courage convinced Englishmen of the truth of their opinions. Foxe's *Book of Martyrs* (1563) recounted these persecutions in gory detail and aroused sympathy for Protestantism. Mary's great mistakes were the Spanish marriage, the restoration of the authority of the pope, and this persecution. Englishmen have never favored extremes, and they reacted against Mary's extreme as some had against the extreme Protestant changes under Edward VI. The way was prepared for a compromise settlement with the accession of Elizabeth.

E. The Elizabethan Settlement

When Elizabeth ascended the throne at the age of twenty-five, she faced many problems: Mary Stuart had a valid claim to the throne; Spain was ready to intervene to substantiate Philip's claim to the English throne as the husband of the late Mary Tudor; and England was divided between the Protestant and Roman religious views. Elizabeth could hardly be other than a Protestant because the Roman clergy would not admit the legality of her parent's marriage, but she did not want to risk open conflict with the powers supporting the pope. For that reason she favored the course that would be acceptable to most of the

As the fire was being lighted, Latimer said, "Be of good comfort, Master Ridley, and play the man; we shall this day light such a candle by God's grace in England as I trust shall never be put out."

people of England, who favored a moderate settlement of religion that would avoid the extremes of either side.

Elizabeth had Parliament pass the Act of Supremacy in 1559,[8] which made the queen "the only supreme governor of this realm" in spiritual and ecclesiastical as well as temporal matters. This title gave less offense than that of "supreme head of the church," upon which Henry VIII had insisted, because, while it gave the queen administrative authority, it implied that matters of faith and morals should be settled by the Church of England.

An Act of Uniformity[9] provided for the use of the Prayer Book of 1552 with only slight modifications. Absence from church was to be punished by a shilling fine. The Forty-Two Articles were revised by the omission of articles condemnatory of the antinomians, Anabaptists, and millenarians and by the reorganization of others until there were thirty-nine articles. The Thirty-Nine Articles were accepted by Parliament in 1563 as the creed of the Anglican church,[10] and all pastors were required to subscribe to

it. This creed, with slight modifications in 1571, has been the creed of the Anglican church since that time.

These steps, even though moderate, aroused the undying enmity of the pope, and in 1570 Pope Pius V issued a bull excommunicating Elizabeth and freeing her subjects from allegiance to her.[11] Elizabeth retaliated by an act aimed at the Jesuits who planned to recapture England for the papacy. A seminary had been set up at Douai in Flanders in 1568 by William Allen, and here men could be trained by the Jesuits to minister secretly to the followers of the pope in England. About 125 Jesuits were executed in England. The pope then enlisted the aid of Philip of Spain to recover England for the Roman church. Philip was only too glad to do this because he was a loyal son of the Church of Rome and because he knew that Elizabeth was secretly aiding his rebellious Dutch subjects. In 1588 he gathered a great fleet known as the Spanish Armada and sailed against England. His fleet was ignominiously defeated by the English fleet, which consisted of smaller, more maneuverable ships manned by expert sailors. This victory established England as the champion of Protestantism in Europe and blasted the pope's last hope of regaining England for the Roman church.

The Reformation brought the Bible to the English people in their own tongue. England became the champion of Protestantism in Europe and aided the Dutch and French Calvinistic Protestants against their Catholic rulers. A state church was adopted. Irish bitterness toward England was intensified because Ireland remained loyal to the papacy. An Irish revolt near the end of her reign taxed Elizabeth's

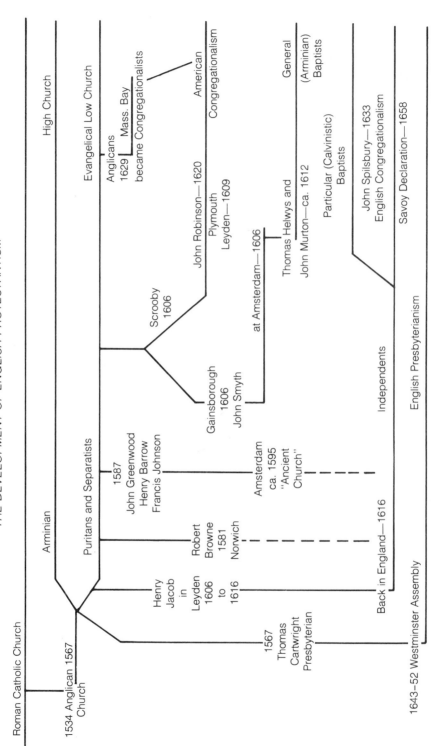

THE DEVELOPMENT OF ENGLISH PROTESTANTISM

Roman Catholic Church

1534 Anglican 1567 Church

Arminian

Puritans and Separatists

High Church

Evangelical Low Church

Anglicans 1629 Mass. Bay became Congregationalists

American Congregationalism

John Robinson—1620 Plymouth Leyden—1609

Scrooby 1606

Gainsborough 1606 John Smyth

at Amsterdam—1606

Thomas Helwys and John Murton—ca. 1612

General (Arminian) Baptists

Particular (Calvinistic) Baptists

1587 John Greenwood Henry Barrow Francis Johnson

Amsterdam ca. 1595 "Ancient Church"

Robert Browne 1581 Norwich

Henry Jacob in Leyden 1606 to 1616

Back in England—1616

Independents

John Spilsbury—1633 English Congregationalism

Savoy Declaration—1658

1567 Thomas Cartwright Presbyterian

English Presbyterianism

1643–52 Westminster Assembly

financial resources to the limit. The sale and gift of the land, taken from the Roman church, to the middle class created a new Tudor nobility. The abbots, who lost their monasteries, no longer met with the House of Lords. The need for an agency to take over the welfare work of the church led to an extension of the activities of the state in this area. The Elizabethan settlement did put England on the road to greatness and empire, but the road ahead was not to be without trouble. The defeat of Spain and the pope left the English rulers free to give attention to the problem of Puritanism. From 1567 to 1660 the Puritans were a dominant force in English domestic affairs. They sought to transform rather than overthrow the Anglican church.

II. PURITANS AND SEPARATISTS

A. The Puritans

Victory in the struggle with the papacy did not give the queen rest because of the rising power of the Puritans, who threatened to change the episcopal state church into a Presbyterian or Congregational church. The Puritans contended that too many "rags of popery" were still in the Anglican church; and they wanted to "purify" the Anglican church in accordance with the Bible, which they accepted as the infallible rule of faith and life. This desire led to their being nicknamed Puritans after 1560. Up until 1570 their main objections were directed against the continued use in the liturgy of the church of ritual and vestments that seemed popish to them. They opposed the use of saints' days, clerical absolution, the sign of the Cross, the custom of having godparents in baptism, kneeling for Communion, and the use of the surplice by the minister. They also deplored the loose observance of Sunday by the Anglicans. They followed William Ames's (1576–1633) and William Perkins's interpretations of Calvin. Cambridge became the university center where the Puritans had their greatest influence.

Puritanism continued to grow and won the support of many lawyers, merchants, and country gentry. After the ending of the danger from the pope, Elizabeth had an act passed against the Puritans in 1593.[12] This act gave the authorities the right to imprison the Puritans for failure to attend the Anglican church. It must be remembered that the Puritans were not dissenters but a party in the Anglican church who, in the case of Cartwright and his followers, wanted a Presbyterian or, as Jacob and his followers, a Congregational state church. The latter group formed the group of Puritans known as Independents. The Independents must be distinguished from the Separatists who wanted separation of church and state and congregational government of the church. Both groups continued to grow in strength in spite of opposition from the ruler and to give useful criticism to the Church of England. Extreme fashions in dress, laxity in keeping Sunday, and the lack of consciousness of sin were all condemned. The roots of English nonconformist sects and New England Congregationalism were in the Puritan movement.

A few years before his death, Richard Hooker (ca. 1554–1600), in order to meet the Puritan threat to the state church, wrote the *Treatise of the Laws of Ecclesiastical Polity*, a work primarily philosophical in nature. In it

Hooker maintained that law, given by God and discovered by reason, is basic. Obedience to the ruler, who rules by consent of the people and according to law, is necessary because the ruler is head of both state and church. Members of the state are also members of the state church and in both areas' are subject to divine law. Bishops, subordinate to the king, are to supervise the state church. Hooker was opposed both to the tendency of the Puritans to separate the church and the state and to the papal claims to power over the state. It was little wonder that the Puritan theologians opposed his ideas because they believed that the people, under God, were the source of sovereignty in the church.

The emergence of Thomas Cartwright (1535–1603) as professor of theology at Cambridge about 1570 shifted the emphasis in the Puritan efforts from reform of liturgy to reform in theology and church government. Insistence on the final authority of the Scriptures led his followers to adopt a Calvinistic theology that would make the Thirty-Nine Articles even more Calvinistic. In his lectures on the Book of Acts in 1570, Cartwright opposed government by bishops. The government of the church, he wrote, should be in the control of a presbytery of bishops or elders who had only spiritual functions. This system was essentially the Calvinistic system of church government by elders who were elected by the congregation. Later Cartwright translated Walter Travers's *Ecclesiastical Discipline* in which he advocated the setting up of a presbytery in every diocese of the church. He laid the foundations of the English Presbyterianism that was so influential between 1643 and 1648. Presbyterianism in modern England owes its existence to his initial work. The first Presbyterian church was at Wandsworth in 1572.

A number of the Puritans who did not follow the Presbyterian pattern of Cartwright adopted the ideas of Henry Jacob (1563–1624). Jacob may be considered the founder of the Independents or Puritan Congregationalists. The Independents were not so inclined to separatism as the followers of Robert Browne, who emphasized the church covenant as the link that bound Christians together. Jacob was one of the signers of the Millenary Petition to James I in 1603, which asked for a change from episcopacy in England. He was imprisoned for his view that each congregation was to be left free in the state church to choose its own pastor, determine its policies, and manage its own affairs. About 1606 Jacob migrated to Holland and became the minister of Englishmen in Middleburg. John Robinson, pastor of the Separatist congregation in Holland whose members later migrated to Plymouth, and Jacob had considerable influence on each other. Jacob returned to England in 1616 and became the pastor of a congregation of Independents in Southwark, London, from 1616 to 1622. Independent or Congregational Puritanism in England grew slowly from this humble beginning until under Oliver Cromwell it became more powerful than Presbyterianism. Cromwell and Milton were Independents.

In 1658 at Savoy in London, Congregationalist followers of Jacob and Separatist congregations formulated a Calvinistic creed known as the Savoy Declaration.[13] English Congregationalism is a lineal descendant of this Puritan Congregationalism rather than that of the Separatist Congregationalism of Robert Browne.

B. Separatist Puritans

The major point of difference between the Episcopal, Presbyterian, and Independent Puritans so far discussed and the Separatist Puritans was the idea of the church covenant by which the Separatists bound themselves in loyalty to Christ and one another apart from a state church. The following diagram will give some idea of the development of the various Puritan groups.

Christ and to one another by a voluntary covenant, that officers were to be chosen by the members, and that no congregation was to have authority over another. Unlike the Independent Congregationalists, the Separatists would have nothing to do with the state church. Browne returned to England and in 1591 was ordained in the Anglican church, which he served until his death. But the advanced principles that he had developed were to live on.

Browne's principles of advanced Congregationalism were somewhat modified by the congregation that appeared in London about 1586 under the leadership of John Greenwood

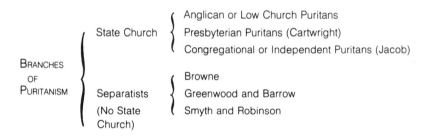

The earliest group of Separatists who set up a church based on a covenant was that organized by Richard Fitz about 1567. Robert Browne (ca. 1550–1633), who graduated from Cambridge in 1572, gathered together a group under a church covenant in Norwich in 1580 or 1581. From there he was forced to flee with his congregation to Holland, where he wrote three treatises elaborating the principles of Separatist Congregationalism. The most important was entitled *Reformation Without Tarrying for Anie.* In this work of 1582 Browne argued that believers were to be united to

and Henry Barrow, who were both hanged in 1593 by the authorities for their views. Francis Johnson became the pastor of the flock that migrated to Holland. By 1640 several hundred of these Barrowists were in England.

A third Separatist group of Congregationalists appeared in Gainsborough and Scrooby in 1606. The Scrooby group was led by John Robinson (ca. 1575–1625), under whose leadership the group finally settled in Leyden, Holland, in 1608. William Bradford (1590–1657), of later fame in Plymouth, became a member of this group. It was members of this group

The Anabaptiſt.   The Browniſt.

The Familiſt.   The Papiſt.

This cartoon from 1641 gives the Anglican perspective on Anabaptists, Brownists (early Independents), Familists (also known as the Family of Love), and Papists (Roman Catholics). Anglicans claimed that the sectaries as much as Roman Catholics had tossed the Bible up in a blanket, making sport of it.

who finally migrated to America in 1620 in the *Mayflower*. It is interesting to note that the immigrants applied the covenant idea to political life by entering into the Mayflower Compact before landing at Plymouth. Because of persecution the Gainsborough group also migrated to Amsterdam in 1606 or 1607 under the leadership of John Smyth (ca. 1565–1612). There they came under the influence of the Mennonites. In 1608 or 1609 Smyth baptized himself, Thomas Helwys (ca. 1550–ca. 1616), and other members of his flock by pouring. Part of his congregation became Mennonites after a long period of negotiation for inclusion in that body.

Thomas Helwys, John Murton, and their followers returned to England about 1612 and organized the first English Baptist church. This group practiced baptism by affusion and held to Arminian doctrines with which they had become familiar during the Arminian dispute in Holland. They were known as General Baptists because they held to general rather than particular atonement. Thus the first English Baptist church emerged from the Separatist Congregationalist group.

The stronger group of Calvinistic or Particular Baptists originated in a schism from Henry Jacob's congregation in London in 1633 and 1638. They held to the baptism of believers by immersion and a Calvinistic theology that emphasized a limited atonement. It was this congregation, first led by John Spilsbury, that in 1638 became the main influence in the English Baptist movement. The antecedents of the American Baptist movement are to be found in this group. Although Roger Williams was not a Baptist when he went to America, he had imbibed Baptist principles and he used these as soon as opposition to his preaching developed among the Congregationalists. The fires of Smithfield, the Spanish Armada, Foxe's *Book of Martyrs*, and the Guy Fawkes plot made the English anti–Roman Catholic.

C. The Puritan Struggle With the Stuarts

The religious forces generated by the exiles under Mary Tudor—exiles who had become acquainted with Calvinism in Europe—and by the Geneva Bible of 1560 resulted in the Puritanism that caused Elizabeth no little difficulty. When her successor, James VI of Scotland, became James I of England in 1603, the Puritans hoped that this Calvinistic king, who liked episcopacy, would set up a presbyterian government in the Anglican church. To emphasize their hope, they presented him with the Millenary Petition, signed by nearly a thousand Puritan ministers, upon his arrival in 1603 and asked that the Anglican church be completely "purified" in liturgy and polity.[14] The pudgy, ricket-deformed, vain, garrulous ruler called the Hampton Court Conference in 1604. When the Puritans again demanded reform, James became angry and said that he would "harry them out of the kingdom" if they would not conform; and, as for presbyterian polity in the state church, he said that presbyterianism "agreeth as well with monarchy as God and the devil." Permission to make a new English translation of the Scriptures was the net result of this meeting, and a group of fifty-four learned divines began work on the Bible popularly known as the Authorized or King James Version. This translation was completed in 1611 and in time replaced the Genevan Bible in the affections of the Anglo-Saxons.

The issues between James and the Puritans included more than the religious disagreement over presbyterian or episcopal forms of government for the state church. The judicial issue concerned the struggle between the legal, common-law courts of England and the extra-legal court system that the Tudors had set up to give them complete control of their subjects. Another problem concerned the question as to whether monarch or Parliament was sovereign. Was the king, the divinely appointed sovereign, responsible only to God, or was he appointed by the consent of the people in Parliament? The economic question involved the problem of whether the king could levy taxes or whether that was the exclusive prerogative of Parliament. Unfortunately for the Stuarts, neither James nor his three successors had any of the skill of the Tudors in hiding the iron fist in the velvet glove of a monarch apparently supported by Parliament. During Elizabeth's and James's reigns the Puritans had been winning adherents to their views among the merchants of the city and the country gentry. These groups were forced into opposition to the ruler on all the points just mentioned and bided their time until they could act.

Charles I, who ruled from 1625 until he was executed in 1649, was an honorable, brave, and able but weak man who believed more strongly in the marriage of divine right monarchy and episcopacy than his father did. He also insisted on a subservient Parliament and, when he could not get one, ruled without Parliament from 1629 until 1640. Many Puritans, wearied with his pro-Catholic policy and hoping for better conditions in England, migrated to America. At least twenty thousand left England for America between 1628 and 1640.

Charles' appointment of William Laud (1573–1645), a man of small stature and narrow mind, as the archbishop of Canterbury created a set of conditions that in time brought his downfall. Laud was favorable to uniformity in polity and to Arminian theology, which the Calvinistic Puritans disliked; and he appointed Arminians to the best church positions.

The attempt by Laud to force a new Book of Common Prayer on the Church of Scotland in 1637 proved to be the incident that started the struggle between the Puritans and their ruler. The Scots rebelled against this

Of God,   Of Man,   Of the Divell.

Archbishop Laud and the bishops are attacked in this 1641 woodcut from a Puritan tract. The figure on the left is a Puritan with a Bible. The two other figures are bishops with a service book and a book of superstition.

attempt to change their liturgy, polity, and faith in order to have religious uniformity in the two lands. This was the period when Jenny Geddes was supposed to have hurled the stool on which she was sitting at the head of the minister for daring to "say mass at my lug" (ear) in historic Saint Giles' Church in Edinburgh. In 1638 the Scottish people signed a national covenant to defend Presbyterianism and invaded England. Charles made an attempt to repel the invasion but finally had to buy them off. The Scots marched into England a second time and remained in the north as a threat. To get money, Charles called a Parliament in 1640, which was known as the Long Parliament because it was not replaced until 1660.

The Long Parliament, before granting any funds, imprisoned or executed Charles's advisers, abolished all the illegal courts, and took control of finance in the state; but it could not reach an agreement on the subject of religion. Moderates, who wanted to re-

tain episcopacy, were known as the Royalists or Cavaliers, and the Puritan country gentry and merchants, who desired Presbyterian or Congregational polity and doctrine, were known as Puritans or Roundheads. In 1642 the Royalists withdrew from Parliament after Charles tried unsuccessfully to arrest five members of the House of Commons for treason; and the Civil War, which was to last until 1646, began. Success in the conflict came to the Puritans of the Long Parliament because of the unexpected military skill of Oliver Cromwell (1599–1658). His well-trained and highly disciplined cavalry of godly Puritans, the Ironsides, became the model on which the victorious New Model army was organized. By 1646 the king was captured by Parliament and, after his subsequent escape and a short second civil war in 1648, he was executed in 1649.

Parliament, in the meantime, abolished episcopacy in 1643 and commissioned the Westminster Assembly, composed of 151 English Puritans. To secure Scottish aid in the war, Parliament accepted the *Solemn League and Covenant* of 1638 and added eight Scottish Presbyterians to advise it on the polity and creed of the national church.[15] The group held 1,163 daily sessions between 1643 and 1649, during which time its real work was done, although it did not end until 1652. The *Directory of Worship* along Presbyterian lines was completed in 1644 and accepted by both the Scottish and English Parliaments in 1645. The *Form of Government*, which advocated presbyterian polity for the national church, was completed by 1645 and adopted by Parliament in 1648. The Calvinistic Westminster *Confes-*

sion of Faith, the assembly's most important work, was completed by 1646 and adopted by the Scots in 1647 and by the English in 1648.[16] Thus the state church of England was a Calvinistic Presbyterian church by 1648. The Longer and the Shorter Catechisms were also completed by 1647. With these things done, the real work of the Westminster Assembly of divines was completed. The constitutions of the larger American Presbyterian churches include all the above documents.

The Presbyterians in Parliament had not paid as much attention as they should have to the army, which had become Congregationalist in sentiment. Tired of the Presbyterian refusal to pay arrears of wages to the army and of their unwillingness to have any but a Presbyterian state church, Cromwell, an Independent or Congregationalist, ordered a Colonel Pride to "purge parliament" in 1648. The Presbyterians were driven out, leaving a "rump" of Congregationalists in charge. Cromwell, after the execution of Charles in 1649, created a commonwealth headed by himself. He dismissed the Rump Parliament in 1653, set up a Protectorate, and until 1658 ruled as dictator with the aid of the army. He was tolerant in matters of religion. He permitted the Jews, who had been expelled in 1290, to return in 1656.

After Cromwell's death, the Long Parliament voted itself out of existence in 1660. The English, tired of the strict way of life of the Puritans, recalled Charles II to become their ruler and adopted episcopacy again. A stiff code of laws, known as the Clarendon Code,[17] put positions in the state church and state in the hands of Anglicans and forbade the meetings of Puritans. About two thousand Calvinistic clergymen were driven from their churches, and Puritanism became a part of the nonconformist tradition of England. Its most distinguished writers were John Milton (1608–74), whose epic poem, *Paradise Lost*, is a theological treatise in verse form and whose tract, the *Areopagitica*, defended freedom of thought, and John Bunyan (1628–88), whose allegory of the progress of the Christian life in *Pilgrim's Progress*, written in 1678, has brought help to many since that time. Not until James II was driven from England in the Glorious Revolution of 1689 was toleration granted to the nonconformists of England. Both England and Holland had an established church with toleration for others.

SUGGESTED READING

The general works on the Reformation mentioned in the Suggested Reading list at the end of chapter 26 have useful sections on religion in England between 1527 and 1689.

Burgess, Walter H. **The Pastor of the Pilgrims.** *New York: Harcourt, Brace, 1920. This work has helpful accounts of Robinson, Smith, Helwys, and others.*

Burrage, Champlin. **The English Dissenters.** *2 vols. Cambridge: Cambridge University Press, 1912. This is an excellent study of the various Presbyterian and Congregationalist groups that developed into Puritanism. Volume 2 contains important documents written by them. The writer has followed Burrage's interpretation of the relationships between the Puritans and the Separatists.*

Carruthers, Samuel W. The Everyday Life of the Westminster Assembly. *Philadelphia: Presbyterian Historical Society, 1943.*

Coffin, Robert P. T. Laud. *New York: Brentano, 1930.*

Collinson, Patrick. The Elizabethan Puritan Movement. *Berkeley: University of California Press, 1967.*

Clark, Henry W. History of English Nonconformity. *2 vols. New York: Russell & Russell, 1965.*

Dickens, A. G. The English Reformation. *New York: Shocken, 1964. This is an excellent survey.*

_____. and Carr, Dorothy, eds. The Reformation in England. *London: Arnold, 1967. Documents for the English Reformation are contained in this work.*

Douglas, James D. Light in the North. *Grand Rapids: Eerdmans, 1964. This is a scholarly history of seventeenth- and eighteenth-century Scottish Presbyterianism.*

Fraser, Antonia P. Cromwell the Lord Protector. *New York: Knopf, 1974.*

Gee, Henry, and Hardy, William J. Documents Illustrative of English Church History. *London: Macmillan, 1921. This contains most of the documents of interest to the student of this period.*

Haller, William. Elizabeth I and the Puritans. *Ithaca, N.Y.: Cornell University Press, 1964.*

_____. The Rise of Puritanism. *New York: Columbia University Press, 1938. This is a helpful study of the writings of the leading Puritans.*

Knappen, Marshall M. Tudor Puritanism. *Chicago: University of Chicago Press, 1939. This is an excellent study of the rise of Puritanism in Elizabeth's reign.*

Loades, D. M. The Oxford Martyrs. *New York: Stein and Day, 1970.*

Mattingly, Gerrett. Catherine of Aragon. *Boston: Little, Brown, 1941.*

Maynard, Theodore. The Life of Thomas Cranmer. *Chicago: Regnery, 1956.*

Moorman, John R. H. A History of the Church in England. *New York: Morehouse-Gorham, 1954. This is an able survey of English church history.*

Pearson, Andrew. Thomas Cartwright and Elizabethan Puritanism, 1553–1603. *Cambridge: Cambridge University Press, 1925. This authoritatively describes the rise of Presbyterian Puritanism.*

Plum, Harry G. Restoration Puritanism. *Chapel Hill: University of North Carolina Press, 1943. This book describes Puritanism after 1660.*

Porter, Harry C. Puritanism in Tudor England. *Columbia, S.C.: University of South Carolina Press, 1971.*

Prescott, H. F. M. The Life of Mary Tudor. *New York: Macmillan, 1962.*

Ridley, Jasper. Thomas Cranmer. *Oxford: Clarendon, 1962.*

Simpson, Alan. Puritanism in Old and New England. *Chicago: University of Chicago Press, 1955. This is a good synthesis.*

Wands, W. C. Anglicanism in History and Today. *New York: Nelson, 1962. This updates Moorman's book.*

Warfield, Benjamin B. The Westminster Assembly and Its Work. *New York: Oxford University Press, 1931. This is a most useful study of the Westminster Assembly.*

Chapter 31

Counter Reformation
and Evaluation

The magisterial or state church forms of the Lutheran, Anglican, and Reformed churches and the radical or free church forms of Anabaptism seemed to be well on the way to winning all Europe north of the Alps by 1545. They were firmly planted in Germany, Scandinavia, France, Scotland, Switzerland, and England. Protestantism won only Holland after 1560 because a wave of religious energy vitalized the Roman Catholic church. Indeed, Protestantism lost Poland and Belgium. This was the result of the Counter Reformation in the Roman Catholic church, under the leadership of the upper-class clergy and the papacy. It brought internal renewal and reform in the church and an external reaction in opposition to Protestantism. It also unleashed forces that led to the final struggle between Protestants and Roman Catholics in the empire during the Thirty Years' War from 1618 to 1648. Counter-Reformation Catholicism was carried by missionaries to Quebec, Latin America and Southeast Asia.

I. THE COUNTER REFORMATION

A. Renewal and Reform

Several causes prevented Protestantism from winning Italy. Italian disunity led to domination by Spain, the champion of Catholicism. Rome was also the seat of the papacy, and the papacy prevented the translation of the Bible into the vernacular.

1. A powerful factor in preventing the spread of Protestantism was the Oratory of Divine Love between 1517 and 1527. This informal organization of about sixty important churchmen and laymen was interested in deepening spiritual life by spiritual exercises. It also supported works of charity and reform. The most important members were Giovanni Pietro Caraffa (1476–1559), who became Pope Paul IV in 1555, and Gaetano di Tiene (1480–1547), who was a source of inspiration to the reforming popes. Caraffa was strongly attached to the medieval dogma of the Roman church. This group of spiritually minded churchmen sponsored any movement that

ROMAN CATHOLICISM
1545–63

COUNTER-REFORMATION
External Reaction to Protestantism

1. National Rulers
   a. Spain—Charles V,
      Philip II
   b. France—
      Catherine de Medici,
      Louis XIV

2. Jesuits—Loyola and
   Spiritual Exercises

3. Index of Prohibited
   Books   Paul III

4. Inquisition
   Spanish—Torquemada
   Roman Inquisition

Roman Catholic Church lost
only Holland after 1563 but
regained Belgium and Poland

ROMAN CATHOLIC REFORMATION
Internal Renewal and Reform

1. Monastic Orders—Jesuits,
   Theatines, Ursulines
2 Morals—Commission
   Paul III 1536–37
3. Men—Cardinal Contarini,
   Paul III
4. Mystics—St Teresa, Oratory of Divine Love
5. Meetings—Council of Trent 1545–63
      adopts:
   a. Thomistic Theology
   b. Vulgate
   c. Apocrypha
   d. Tridentine Profession
6. Missions
   Jesuits, Franciscans,
   and Dominicans to
   Central and South
   America, Quebec, China,
   India, Japan, Philippines,
   and Indochina
7. Music—Palestrina, Masses,
   Polyphony
8. Baroque Architecture
   II Jesu Church
   Bernini Columns
9. Myth—History
   Caesar Baronius
   Ecclesiastical History
   Church always one and the same

TRIUMPHALISM
1563–1648

would contribute to a return of personal conviction in their beloved church.

2. Pope Paul III made the most able of these earnest men cardinals. He put such men as Caraffa; Gasparo Contarini (1483–1542), who sympathized with the Protestant doctrine of justification by faith; Pole; and others on a commission in 1536 to report to him on a plan for religious reform. In 1537 they presented a report that pointed out that the abuses in the Roman church were the fault of former pontiffs and corrupt cardinals who had sold offices and dispensations indiscriminately.[1]

3. The Oratory of Divine Love also inspired the founding of new religious orders that helped to stop the spread of Protestantism. Gaetano di Tiene, aided by Caraffa, founded the Theatine order in 1524. This order bound secular priests to live under the threefold rule of poverty, chastity, and obedience in a religious community; but it left them free to serve the people just as parish priests did. The preaching, teaching, and social service of these priests led to a new respect for the Roman church in Italy; and the Theatine movement spread rapidly in that country.

Both the leadership and the membership of the Theatines were aristocratic, but the Capuchin order, founded by Matteo da Bascio (1495–1552) about 1525 as a reformed branch of the Franciscans, made an appeal to the peasants with its self-sacrificing spirit of service and its popular type of preaching. The order was easily recognizable by the pointed hood and bare feet of the monks. Their form of life and their chapels were much simpler and more austere than those of the Theatines. The pope approved the Capuchin order in 1528.

The Ursuline order for women was founded by Angela Merici (1474–1540) in 1535 to care for the sick and to educate girls, and it received papal approval in 1544. Many orders were organized in this period and they have served the Roman church well since that time. Many of them are still strong today. The most important order, to be discussed later, was the Society of Jesus. All these orders put at the disposal of the pope loyal and obedient men and women, dedicated to the service of the Church of Rome in the attempt to save souls and in social service to benefit the people of their day.

4. The fact that the luxury-loving, greedy, yet cultured popes of the Ren-

aissance were succeeded during the sixteenth century by many popes who zealously supported reform also helped to prevent the growth of Protestantism. Paul III (1534–49) was so favorable to the cause of reform that his pontificate marks an important point in the Counter Reformation. During his rule the Jesuit order was formed; the Inquisition was set up; the Index of Books, which listed the books that Catholics were not to read, was published; and the Council of Trent was opened in 1545. He had also permitted the commission of nine to make their famous report in 1537 on abuses in the Roman church. Cardinal Caraffa became Pope Paul IV (1555–59) and supported the Counter Reformation. As a cardinal he had encouraged Paul III to set up the Roman Inquisition and to publish the Index of Books in order to rid the church of heresy. As pope he made these two weapons even more powerful. He failed, however, to free the papacy of the political control of Spain, and he was even guilty of nepotism.

Pius IV, successor to Paul IV, succeeded in eliminating nepotism and in regulating the powers of the college of cardinals. Sixtus V was able to bring about financial reform. With renewed spiritual zeal and with these practical reforms, the Church of Rome, purged in its head, was able to undertake reform in its members throughout Europe and to try to win many Protestants back to the Roman fold. By 1590 the papacy had made considerable gains because of these reforms.

5. If, as Latourette suggested, the nineteenth century was the great century of Protestant missions, it can be said that, thanks to the Jesuits, the sixteenth century was the great century

of Roman Catholic missions. Spanish, Portuguese, and later French Jesuits carried their faith to Latin America, Quebec, and Southeastern Asia. Exploration and settlement of these areas by the above nations made this religious expansion possible. It was heartily approved by the pope. National patronage of missions by rulers of these states gave way in 1622 to the Sacred Congregation for the Propagation of the Faith, which was created by Gregory XV. The Dominican and Franciscan orders also participated in this work, and some were martyred.

China, which had received Nestorian Christianity in the seventh century and Roman Catholic Christianity about 1300 through John of Monte Corvino, received a third infusion of Christianity through the Jesuits. Matteo Ricci (1552–1610), with his knowledge of mathematics and astronomy, his gifts of clocks to the emperor, and his willingness to adapt to Chinese culture in dress and customs when he arrived at Peking in 1601, soon had about 6,000 followers. By 1700 the Jesuits in China claimed to have 300,000 followers. In the early eighteenth century the monks were expelled when the emperor turned against them.

Francis Xavier, who preached in many parts of the Far East, landed in Kagoshima in Japan in 1549; and by 1614 the monks claimed that 300,000 Japanese were won. Horrible persecution, with war and martyrdom, destroyed that effort early in the sixteenth century when the rulers Hideyoshi and Ieyasu turned against the monks because they thought they were agents of European imperialism.

Robert de Nobili (1577–1656), who dressed like upper-caste Indians and studied their culture, was instrumental in planting the Roman Catholic church in India. The Philippine people turned as a nation to the Roman Catholic faith in the second half of the sixteenth century, and that church still holds the allegiance of the majority of the people. Indochina was entered by the monks, and a strong Roman Catholic church was founded.

Central and South America, through the Spanish and the Portuguese, and Quebec, through the French, were added to the fold. Roman Catholicism is still dominant in those areas. Ecclesiastical imperialism of Spain, Portugal, and France went hand in hand with political imperialism. In all of this missionary expansion, the Jesuits had a leading role. The Dominican monk Bartolomé de Las Casas (1474–1566), early in the era of missionary expansion, wrote against the mistreatment of the Indians by the Spanish settlers and opposed making them slaves.

6. Cardinal Caesar Baronius (1538–1607), at the bidding of Philip Neri (1515–95), took upon himself the research for and writing of his twelve-volume *Ecclesiastical Annals* (1588–1607) to refute the *Magdeburg Centuries*, thirteen volumes under the editorship of Matthias Flacius (Illyricus). The latter set pictured the papacy as Antichrist, but Baronius argued that the Roman Catholic church had always been one and the same and true to the apostolic teaching.

7. Giovanni da Palestrina (ca. 1524–94), the choirmaster of Saint Peters, composed polyphonic music in which a mosaic of sound was created by choirs singing different melodic lines. He wrote ninety masses and about five hundred motets which pro-

claimed the triumphant spirit of the Counter Reformation.

8. Baroque architecture expressed the triumphalism of the church. Giovanni Bernini's (1598–1680) columns in front of Saint Peter's Church in Rome and the altar canopy inside the church proclaimed the majesty of the church. The Il Gesu Church in Rome and the El Escorial palace-monastery-church of Philip II north of Madrid are other examples.

B. Reaction Against Protestantism

1. Spain became the national leader in the work of the Counter Reformation because nationalism and religion had been united in the attempt to unify and consolidate the Spanish state by driving out the Muslim Moors and the Jews. After their marriage in 1469, the intensely religious Isabella of Castile and the equally religious Ferdinand of Aragon worked for a united Spain loyal to Rome. It was in Spain that the Inquisition was set up in 1480 and developed under the leadership of Thomas Torquemada into an organ to exterminate heretics. It was from Spain that the idea of the Roman Inquisition was borrowed by Paul III. It was also a Spaniard, Ignatius Loyola, who was instrumental in the founding of the Society of Jesus. Cardinal Ximénes, another Spaniard, revived the study of the Scriptures among the clergy trained at the University of Alcalá and was the first to have the Greek New Testament printed. He also led in the publication of the *Complutensian Polyglot* in 1520. This work gave the text of the Bible in the original languages as well as in the Latin of the Vulgate. Charles V and Philip II, successive rulers of Spain, the Nether-lands, and the Holy Roman Empire were earnest supporters of the papal system. Philip poured the treasure and blood of Spain into efforts to hold the Netherlands to the Roman Catholic faith and to regain England for the papal system. In these many respects Spain provided the dynamic that could be used to consolidate the position of the Roman church and to regain lost territories. She also organized and led the navy that at Lepanto in 1571 destroyed the Muslim naval power. Portugal and France also supported the papacy.

2. The most effective weapon of positive propaganda for the Church of Rome was provided by the Jesuit order, which emphasized preaching by well-educated monks as a means to win men back from Protestantism. The founder of the order, Ignatius Loyola (ca. 1491–1556), was born into a wealthy noble Basque family. After the usual fighting, gaming, and love-making antics as the son of a noble Spanish family, he became a soldier. His leg was smashed in a battle against the French in 1521, and for a long time he had to be in a hospital while his leg was improperly set, broken, and reset. During this period his reading of religious literature resulted in a spiritual experience in 1522 that led him to dedicate his life to the service of God and the church. He made a trip to the Holy Land in 1523 and returned from it to get an education. In 1528 he enrolled at the University of Paris. In 1534 he and six companions became the nucleus of an order that was given papal approval by Paul III in 1540. The little, deformed, scarred man became the general of the new order in 1541. By 1556 the order numbered about one thousand monks.

Earlier Loyola had written a work called *Spiritual Exercises* to guide the recruits into a spiritual experience that would make them faithful members of the order. Several weeks were to be spent in meditation on sin and the life, death, and resurrection of Christ. This long period of spiritual exercise made his recruits faithful to God and their human leadership.[2] The members finally had to take a vow of special obedience to the pope as well as to their general. Under the general were provincials in charge of districts. Loyola's rules for thinking with the church required absolute blind obedience to the pope in addition to purity, poverty, and chastity.[3]

The main functions of the organization were education, fighting heresy, and foreign missions. The order has always had control of the most important educational institutions of the Roman church. By way of preaching, large parts of Germany were regained for the Roman church. The order has also provided some heroic missionaries. Francis Xavier (1506–52) was an early outstanding missionary of the order. Traveling to the Far East, Xavier preached in India, the East Indies, and Japan and baptized many thousands in the Roman faith. The Jesuits were able to regain the southern provinces of the Netherlands and Poland for the Church of Rome, although Lutheranism seemed to be strongly established in Poland. But in these struggles the very efficiency of the Jesuits made them soulless; their ethical relativism made them justify any means to accomplish what seemed to be good ends; and their enlistment of the rulers of state in the fight against heresy led to an undue interference in politics that later made them unpopular.

3. The Roman church had two weapons of coercion to back up the propaganda of the Jesuits. These were the Inquisition and the Index. The Inquisition had originated in the struggle against the Albigenses in southern France early in the thirteenth century. It had been established in Spain by papal license in 1480 to deal with the problem of heresy in that land. Under Thomas Torquemada's (1420–98) leadership, ten thousand were executed; and under Ximénes, about two thousand died. Because of Caraffa's urging, the Roman Inquisition was proclaimed by a papal bull of Paul III in 1542 as an instrument to deal with heresy anywhere until it was abolished in 1854. Those accused were always presumed guilty till they proved their innocence; they were never confronted with their accusers; they could be made to testify against themselves; and they could be tortured to extract a confession. If sentenced, they were punished by loss of property, imprisonment, or burning at the stake, unless they confessed and recanted. These punishments were carried out by the secular authorities under the watchful eye of the inquisitors.

4. The development of printing in the middle of the fifteenth century helped the Protestants to disseminate their ideas. To counteract this, the Roman church developed the Index, a list of books that the faithful were not permitted to read. As Paul IV, Caraffa issued the first Roman Index of Prohibited Books in 1559. The books of Erasmus and some Protestant editions of the Bible appeared on the list. A special Congregation of the Index, created in 1571, was charged by the pope with the task of keeping the list up to date. The Index kept many

Roman Catholics from reading Protestant literature, and the Inquisition forced many to recant their Protestant views. The Index was abolished in 1966.

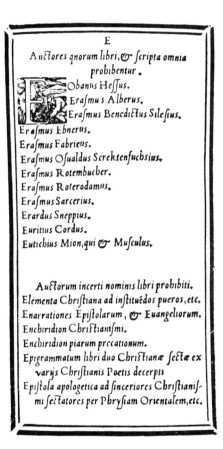

The *Index of Prohibited Books* listed the writings of reform-minded Catholics as well as Protestants. This page from the Index of 1559 identifies forbidden books by Erasmus and his pen names.

5. Paul III seemed to see the need for reform in the Roman church more than any other because it was he who authorized the Jesuit order in 1540, set up the Roman Inquisition in 1542, and issued the bull of 1544 that called the Council of Trent. The council opened December 13, 1545, and ran, with long periods when there were no sessions, until December 4, 1563. It was not permitted to state its superiority to the pope. Voting was by head and not by nations as had been the case at the Council of Constance. Italians always numbered about three-quarters of those present. Thus the papacy and the Italian hierarchy were assured of control of its actions. Paul wanted to consider the doctrine of the Church of Rome, reform of clerical abuses, and the possibility of a crusade against the infidel. Although the final decrees were signed by 255 churchmen, there were never more than about 75 present at most of the 25 sessions.

The first series of sessions between 1545 and 1547 was taken up with various doctrinal questions. The council declared that not the Bible alone but the canonical Scriptures and the Apocrypha in the Vulgate edition of Jerome and the tradition of the church constituted the final authority for the faithful.[4] The discussion of justification by faith resulted in the decision that man was justified by faith and subsequent works rather than by faith only. The seven sacraments were reaffirmed by the council, and decrees concerning reform of ecclesiastical abuses were formulated.

During the second series of sessions between 1551 and 1552 the dogma of transubstantiation was reaffirmed and further decisions on reform were formulated. The final series of sessions between 1562 and 1563 were occupied with detailed discussions concerning other sacraments, rules concerning marriage, decrees concerning purgatory, and various matters of reform.[5] The control of the pope over the council was demonstrated by its request that he confirm its work by a papal bull. Another papal bull, issued in 1564, contained a summary of the faith formulated at the Council of Trent. It was known as the Tridentine Profession of Faith. All Roman Catholic clergy and teachers must subscribe to it as well as converts to that faith from Protestantism. The individual so subscribing must swear "true obedience" to the pope.[6]

The real significance of the council was the transformation of medieval Thomistic theology into an authoritative dogma binding on all the faithful.[7] It rendered any chance of reconciliation with Protestantism impossible because the Protestants would not accept the equal authority of tradition and Scripture. It did, however, promote a higher moral standard among the clergy by needed reforms. It opened seminaries to train ministers, provided for the Roman Catechism of 1566, and adopted an authoritative version of the Bible, the Vulgate. It marked the final defeat of conciliarism and the triumph of curial or papal absolutism.

Armed with a system of dogma spread by faithful Jesuit educators such as Peter Canisius (1521–97) and missionaries and backed by the power of the Inquisition, the papacy was able to stop Protestant gains—except in Holland—after 1560 and to go on and regain territories, such as Poland, where it seemed that Protestantism would triumph. The peak of conquest and reform was reached about 1600.

The Reformation and Counter Reformation in the West had little effect on the church in the East. Cyril Lucar (1572–1638), who studied at Geneva and was elected patriarch at Constan-

tinople about 1620, was interested in the Calvinistic religious movement in the West but was opposed by his own people and by the Jesuits who did not want the Eastern church to become Protestant. He published his Confession of Faith in 1629 that was strongly tinged with Calvinistic views of doctrine. He also sent one of the three oldest manuscripts of the Bible, the Codex Alexandrinus, to England in the reign of Charles I. His enemies persuaded the Sultan to put him to death for supposedly instigating rebellion among the Cossacks, and a synod of Bethlehem in 1672 repudiated all the aspects of Reformation doctrine in his Confession and even claimed that he did not write it. In this humiliating fashion the attempt to make the Greek church Protestant failed.

II. THE THIRTY YEARS' WAR

Because many clerical rulers of Germany who became Protestants made their lands Protestant in spite of the Peace of Augsburg, which made it mandatory that they give up their lands if they became Protestant, both Roman Catholics and Lutherans became dissatisfied. Calvinism, which had not been recognized in the negotiations at Augsburg, had won areas in Germany, such as the Palatinate; and Calvinists desired legal recognition. The Jesuits lost no chance to interfere in political affairs in countries such as Bavaria and Bohemia in order to regain lost territories for the Roman church. Emperor Ferdinand II and Maximilian of Bavaria had been trained to hate Protestantism by the Jesuits. Lutherans of Donauwörth stoned a procession of monks in 1606. Even though the monks had agreed not to demonstrate their religion outside the monastery walls, Maximilian took their part, captured the city, and garrisoned it with soldiers. Fearing the breakdown of the Augsburg agreement, the Protestant rulers organized an Evangelical Union in 1608; and in 1609 the princes supporting the pope organized a Catholic League. Thus were the lines drawn in the empire for battle between the rival faiths. One notes that external war against Spain in Holland and England and internal conflict in Germany, France, Scotland, and Zurich preceded the final Reformation settlements in those lands.

The Defenestration of Prague in 1618 provided the spark to set off the Thirty Years' War. Ferdinand, who became emperor in 1619, was selected in 1617 to succeed the childless Emperor Matthias as ruler of Bohemia. In 1618 Protestants had thrown the representatives of Matthias out a window of a castle in Prague into the muddy moat. When Matthias died, the Bohemians elected Frederick, ruler of the Protestant Palatinate, as ruler of Bohemia.

The resulting war went through four phases. The Bohemian period lasted from 1618 to 1623 and was fought between Ferdinand the emperor and Maximilian of Bavaria on the one side and Frederick and the Bohemians on the other. The Battle of White Mountain outside Prague in 1620 led to the temporary defeat of Protestantism in Germany by Tilly.

The Danish phase of the war between 1625 and 1629 was fought to protect the northern German Protestant states from the fate of Bohemia. Christian IV of Denmark, as much to add to his own territories as to aid Protestantism, came to the aid of the German princes but was defeated by the forces of Emperor Ferdinand II, led by the able generals Tilly and Wallenstein. The emperor in the Edict of Restitution of 1629 ordered that all lands of the Roman church that had been taken by Protestants since 1552 should be surrendered, that Protestants should be expelled from areas ruled by Catholic princes, and that only Lutherans should have recognition and toleration.

Dissension among the Roman Catholic German princes over the spoil and the aid of Gustavus Adolphus of Sweden to the Protestants brought on the Swedish phase of the war between 1630 and 1635. The Swedish ruler wanted to make the Baltic a Swedish lake as well as to aid his fellow Protestants. In a battle at Lützen in 1632 the imperial forces of the Holy Roman Empire were defeated by the Protestants. Sweden got the territory that she desired on the shores of the Baltic; northern Germany was freed from domination by Roman Catholics; but southern Germany was not finally reconquered by the Protestants.

The final phase of the war between 1635 and 1648 involved the interference of Roman Catholic France on the side of the Protestants because Richelieu hoped to gain land for France and to harass the Hapsburg ruler of Spain and the Holy Roman Empire. The modern European system of states emerged.

The Peace of Westphalia ended the long bloody struggle in 1648. Holland and Switzerland were recognized as independent Protestant states. France, Sweden, and the tiny state that was to become Prussia made important gains of territory; and France became the dominant power in Europe. Both Lutheranism and Calvinism be-

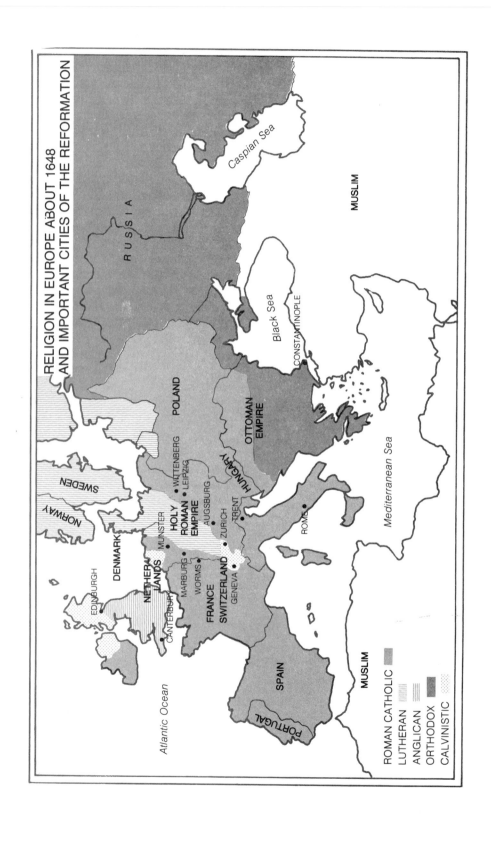

RELIGION IN EUROPE ABOUT 1648
AND IMPORTANT CITIES OF THE REFORMATION

Atlantic Ocean

RUSSIA

Caspian Sea

Black Sea

Mediterranean Sea

NORWAY

SWEDEN

DENMARK

NETHER-
LANDS

EDINBURGH

CANTERBURY

MÜNSTER

MARBURG

WORMS

FRANCE

SWITZERLAND

GENEVA

ZURICH

TRENT

HOLY
ROMAN
EMPIRE

AUGSBURG

LEIPZIG

WITTENBERG

POLAND

HUNGARY

OTTOMAN
EMPIRE

CONSTANTINOPLE

ROME

SPAIN

PORTUGAL

MUSLIM

MUSLIM

ROMAN CATHOLIC
LUTHERAN
ANGLICAN
ORTHODOX
CALVINISTIC

came recognized religions, and Protestants were given the right to hold offices in the state. Lands that were Protestant in 1624 were permitted to remain Protestant. This brought about the end of religious persecution. The Holy Roman Empire became a mere geographical term and lost its former political significance after the Peace of Westphalia because its only unity had been religious and the Reformation and the war had shattered that. This treaty stabilized the political and religious map of Europe.

The cost of the settlement was high. The population of Germany was cut by about one-third with a loss of several million lives. Property had been destroyed in the numerous battles and sackings of towns and villages. It took decades before Germany recovered from the devastation of property, the loss of life, and the breakdown of morals incurred in the Thirty Years' War.

III. THE REFORMATION IN RETROSPECT

The Reformation meant the end of the control by a universal church. The corporate Roman Catholic church was replaced by a series of national Protestant state churches in the lands where Protestantism was victorious. The Lutherans dominated the religious scene in Germany and Scandinavia. Calvinism had its adherents in Switzerland, Scotland, Holland, France, and Hungary. The English had set up the Anglican state church. The radicals of the Reformation, the Anabaptists, had not set up state churches but were strong especially in Holland, northern Germany, and Switzerland. They alone of the Reformation groups were opposed to the union of church

and state, but they were equally opposed to domination by the pope. They favored free churches of believers separated from any state.

Although great doctrinal changes were brought about by the Reformation, the student must not think that the new national churches broke completely with all that was handed down by the church from the past. Protestants and Roman Catholics alike accepted the great ecumenical creeds, such as the Apostles' Creed, the Nicene Creed, and the Athanasian Creed. They all held the doctrines of the Trinity and (except for the Socinians) the deity and resurrection of Christ, the Bible as a revelation from God, the fall of man, original sin, and the need of a moral life for the Christian. The Protestants had a common area of agreement concerning salvation by faith alone, the sole authority of the Scriptures as an infallible rule of faith and life, and the priesthood of believers. In addition, each denomination held to its own particular viewpoint that distinguished it from other Protestants, such as baptism by immersion in the case of the Baptists and predestination in the case of the Calvinists. This relationship can be illustrated by the diagram (see page 354) of the faith of any Protestant.

The student of church history will also notice that the Reformation constituted the second great period of creedal development. The ecumenical creeds were hammered out between 325 and 451, but between 1530 and 1648 many Protestant confessions and creeds were developed that are still held by the various branches of Protestantism today. The formulation of great Protestant theological systems, such as that of Calvin in his *Institutes*,

THE ELEMENTS IN A PROTESTANT'S FAITH

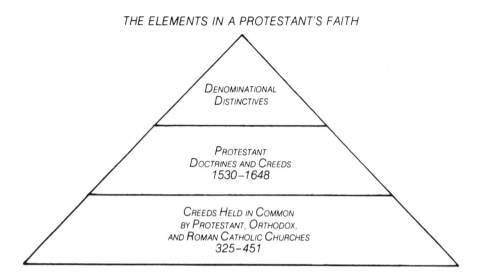

DENOMINATIONAL
DISTINCTIVES

PROTESTANT
DOCTRINES AND CREEDS
1530–1648

CREEDS HELD IN COMMON
BY PROTESTANT, ORTHODOX,
AND ROMAN CATHOLIC CHURCHES
325–451

is also closely related to the development of creeds.

Protestantism was also responsible for certain great doctrinal emphases that have had a marked effect on both man's temporal and spiritual interests. The assertion that justification was by faith alone marked the resurgence of religious individualism, which had been lost during the Middle Ages because of the view that man best developed as a part of the corporate organization of the church. Man now could have direct personal access to God. Such an assertion of the individual did not mean that the Reformers neglected the group aspect of life, for all of them, except the Anabaptists, laid great emphasis on the church, which was to be recognized by the preaching of the Word and the sacraments. But so far as salvation was concerned, man need not come to God by the sacraments of the Roman Catholic church.

The doctrine of the priesthood of believers struck at the importance of the hierarchical system of mediators between God and man, just as the doctrine of justification by faith had made the sacramental system unnecessary. No mediator was needed because each believer was a spiritual priest who offered spiritual sacrifices to God.

The assertion of the final authority of the Scriptures marked a repudiation of the authority of the church. The Bible, rather than the decrees of councils, the writings of the Fathers, and the bulls of the popes, was the final rule of faith and practice. Because individuals were thought to be able to interpret it for themselves by paying attention to the grammatical and historical background, the right of private interpretation was emphasized. Almost all the Reformers themselves or their colleagues translated the Bible into the vernacular.

The Reformation helped to create a demand for universal elementary education, for if everyone was to interpret the Bible for himself, he must have some knowledge of reading. All the Reformers gave considerable attention to the founding of schools on the three levels of elementary, secondary, and university education. The Reformation also stimulated the rise of empirical science.

Insistence upon the spiritual equality of men led to an insistence upon their political equality. In this way the Reformation, particularly where Calvinistic doctrines were accepted, promoted the rise of democracy in both the church and state. Laymen were given a greater share in the government of the church.

The Reformation also stimulated capitalism because the medieval opposition to usury was dropped by most of the Reformers. The insistence upon thrift, industry, and separation from costly worldly amusements resulted in the creation of savings that could be used as capital for new economic ventures. It is not fair, however, to say that any of the Reformers were responsible for the rise of capitalism because it was in existence long before the Reformation. The modern welfare state, which assumes responsibility for the economic welfare of its citizens,

also had its beginnings in the need of the state to provide for those who were dispossessed and impoverished by the confiscation of church property during the Reformation.

The Reformation also brought a much-needed revival of preaching. Men such as Luther excelled as preachers of the Word. Calvin spent much of his time in preaching as well as in teaching the Word.

The Reformation also had an impact on the Roman Catholic church through the reformation in morals and the clear statement of dogma of the Counter Reformation at Trent. The Jesuit order became the leader in Roman Catholic missionary work in Asia and the Western Hemisphere.

By 1648 the main churches of the Christian religion were in existence. The period from then to the present is concerned with the fortunes of these various forms of Christianity as they faced the secularism that first began to make a marked impression on western Europe during the seventeenth century.

Suggested Reading

Bangert, William H. **A History of the Society of Jesuits.** *St. Louis: Institute of Jesuit Sources, 1932.*

Brodrick, James. **The Origin of the Jesuits.** *New York: Longmans, 1940. This describes the beginning of the order.*

_____. **The Progress of the Jesuits 1556–1579.** *London: Longmans, 1947.*

_____. **Saint Francis Xavier.** *Garden City, N.Y.: Doubleday, 1957.*

_____. **Saint Ignatius Loyola.** *New York: Farrar, Strauss, 1956.*

Burns, Edward M. **The Counter-Reformation.** *Princeton: Princeton University Press, 1964.*

Cronin, Vincent. **The Wise Man From the West.** *London: Hart-Davis, 1955. This is a popular biography of Matteo Ricci.*

Daniel-Rops, Henry. **The Catholic Reformation.** *New York: Dutton, 1962.*

Dickens, Arthur G. **The Counter Reformation.** *New York: Harcourt, Brace, 1969.*

Dolan, John P. **History of the Reformation.** *New York: Desclee, 1955. This is a helpful survey by a Roman Catholic scholar.*

Dudon, Pere Paul. **Ignacio de Loyola, The Spiritual Exercises.** *Westminster, Md.: Newman, 1951. This is the author's main work on Loyola.*

_____. **Saint Ignatius of Loyola.** *Translated by William J. Young. Milwaukee: Bruce, 1949. This is a helpful biography.*

Hadjiantoniau, George A. **Protestant Patriarch.** *Richmond, Va.: John Knox, 1961. This is a biography of Cyril Lucar that is based on the sources.*

Janelle, Pierre. **The Catholic Reformation.** *Milwaukee: Bruce, 1949. The Catholic viewpoint is ably presented here.*

Jedin, Hubert. **A History of the Council of Trent.** *Translated by Ernest Graf. St. Louis: Herder, 1941.*

Kamen, Henry. **The Spanish Inquisition.** *London: Weidenfeld and Nicholson, 1965.*

Kidd, Beresford J. **The Counter-Reformation, 1550–1600.** *London: SPCK, 1933. This is an excellent history of the Counter Reformation.*

Lea, H. C. **The Inquisition in Spain.** *4 vols. London: Macmillan, 1906–7.*

Olin, John. **The Catholic Reformation.** *New York: Harper, 1969. This has many useful documents.*

Polisensky, Joseph V. **The Thirty Years' War.** *Translated by Robert Evans. Berkeley: University of California Press, 1971.*

Schroeder, Henry J. **Canons and Decrees of the Council of Trent.** *St. Louis: Herder, 1941. This work has the original text and an English translation of the canons and decrees of the council.*

Van Dyke, Paul. **Ignatius Loyola.** *New York: Scribner, 1926. This is an able and interesting biography of the founder of the Jesuits.*

Wedgwood, Cicely V. **The Thirty Years' War.** *New Haven: Yale University Press, 1939. This is a scholarly discussion of the war.*

Chapter 32

The Establishment of Christianity in North America

Modern culture has broken increasingly with Christian control and integration of life. The Peace of Westphalia in 1648 is a dividing point between religious patterns developed in the Reformation and tendencies in church history since that time. Recurrent revivalism and various manifestations of rationalism developed concurrently. Rationalism, which gave birth to liberalism in the church, led to a break with the Bible and the theology of the Reformation. Denominationalism grew out of the separation of church and state. The rise of toleration and freedom of religion brought about the necessity of voluntary support of the church and more democratic control over its affairs by the laity. The colonists accepted the fallibility of man and his institutions and the need to limit power because of sin. Because people were not born into a state church, evangelism became important as a means of winning them to Christianity. Unfortunately, separation of church and state often meant not merely the refusal to favor one religion

above another but an irreligious attitude in affairs of state. Separation has created the secular state of the twentieth century, which in some lands threatens the existence of the church. The tendency to denominationalism has been somewhat offset in the twentieth century by tendencies toward reunion and ecumenical movements. Today fusion or reunion seems to have replaced the fission of post-Reformation Protestantism. A great Protestant missionary movement since 1792 and philanthropy to meet social needs have been definite parts of modern Christianity. The church has also faced attack from biblical critics, evolutionists, and totalitarian states.

Nowhere have these characteristics of modern church history been so pronounced as in America. One cannot but be impressed with the fact that Columbus's discovery of America and the beginning of the Reformation took place within twenty-five years of each other. Nearly every one of the Protestant churches of the Reformation and

THE HERITAGE OF THE REFORMATION IN THE UNITED STATES

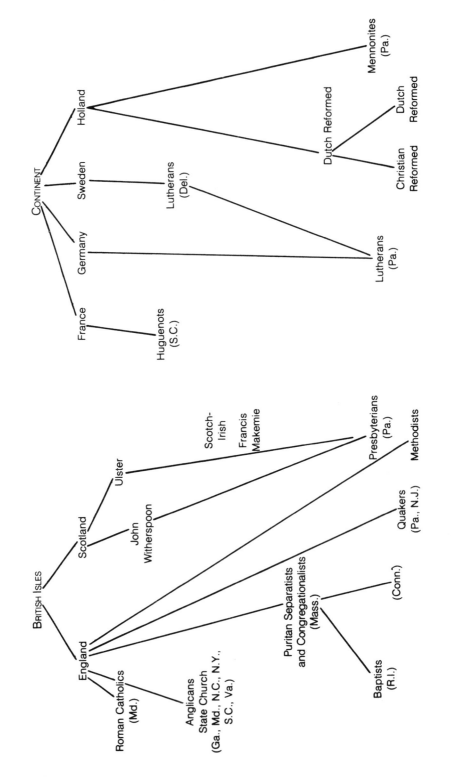

later the Roman Catholic church came to be represented in America. Distance from Europe, the early rise of voluntarism and consequent lay control of the church, recurrent revivals, the influence of the frontier, and the relative religious radicalism of the sects who came to America have made American Christianity quite creative in its activities. Camp meetings, mass evangelism, generous giving, the temperance movement, the institutional church to provide for social and cultural as well as religious needs, youth work, city missions, and the ecumenical movement illustrate this creative aspect of American Christianity.

I. THE PLANTING OF AMERICAN CHRISTIANITY

The motives stimulating Anglo-Saxon colonization along the Atlantic seaboard of North America varied. Many of the colonists hoped to find the western sea route to the riches of Asia, valuable raw materials, and markets for profitable trade. Others were sent because it was believed that the colonies could absorb the surplus population of the homeland. The planting of the colonies would also help to meet the military threat from Spain in the New World. But the religious motivation was extremely important in the founding of the colonies. Most of the charters mention the desire of the stockholders to convert the natives and to extend Christ's dominion.[1] In other cases, such as those of the Puritans of Plymouth and Salem, the colonists were interested in worshiping in their own way. Thus the transplanting of English, French, Spanish, Swedish, and Dutch settlers to North America cannot be dissociated from the transplanting of their religion to the same land. Most of these were oriented to Calvinism. The instrument used in this transplanting of people was the joint stock company, the forerunner of the modern corporation. It made possible the gathering together of the great sums of money needed to finance such undertakings.

A. The Anglican Church in America

The Virginia Company, which was given a charter in 1606 to settle and to exploit land in America, sent out settlers to Jamestown in 1607. This settlement of gentry and workers was organized on a communal basis, and provision was made for the establishment of the Anglican church. Among the settlers was Robert Hunt, a chaplain, who first gave the Lord's Supper to the colonists under the protection of an old sail while the worshipers sat on logs. John Rolfe, who married Pocahontas, laid the foundation for the early wealth of the colony by successfully growing tobacco in 1612. The colony did not prosper economically until the communal experiment ended in 1619, and land and the privilege of electing a representative governing body were granted to the colonists by the company. Increasing numbers of Puritan Anglicans migrated to the colony. Alexander Whitaker, who had Puritan leanings, became the leading minister of the Anglican church in Virginia between 1611 and 1617. Slavery was established with the purchase of slaves from Dutch traders in 1619 to work the tobacco plantations. In 1624 the company was dissolved, and Virginia became a royal colony ruled for the king by a governor. The Anglican church remained as the established church of the new colony. Its pastors gave indifferent service until James Blair (ca. 1655–1743), pastor of Bruton parish from 1710 to 1743, came to Virginia as commissary in 1689 to inspect the churches and to work out reforms. He founded the College of William and Mary in 1693.

The Anglican church also finally became the established church of Maryland in 1702, despite the opposition of the Roman Catholics, who had been permitted to settle there by Lord Baltimore. The religious toleration that the first Lord Baltimore had permitted was thus ended. It was made the established church in parts of New York in 1693 in spite of opposition from the Dutch, who had originally settled New York. An act of 1715 made the Anglican church the established church in North Carolina, and earlier, in 1706, it was established in South Carolina. Georgia accepted Anglican establishment in 1758. Not until the American Revolution was this pattern changed.

The Society for the Propagation of the Gospel in Foreign Parts, founded in 1701 by Thomas Bray (1656–1730), the commissary of Maryland, made possible a more consecrated and spiritual ministry in the various established churches. Before that time the established churches had often been characterized by moral and spiritual laxity. The society sent over three hundred missionaries to the colonies. Thus the southern colonies developed state Anglican churches.

The official seal of the Society for the Propagation of the Gospel in Foreign Parts. Natives are shown coming to the beach to welcome a minister of the gospel, who stands in the bow of the ship with an open Bible.

B. The Planting of New England Congregationalism

Congregationalism became the established church in New England. Early in the seventeenth century, the Scrooby congregation, which had migrated to friendly Leyden in Holland to escape persecution because of their Congregationalist ideas, decided to migrate to America in order to prevent the eventual incorporation of their young people into the Dutch population. A London company of merchant "adventurers" loaned them seven thousand pounds to finance the voyage. The immigrants, who had nothing to contribute but their labor, were to repay the merchants by helping them build up a fishing industry. In August 1620 over one hundred colonists, known as the Pilgrims, set sail from England for America in the *Mayflower*. For some reason they landed at Plymouth in New England rather than in northern Virginia; so they had to get a new charter from the company in whose territories they were living. In order to prevent the unruly from disturbing the colony, they drew up the Mayflower Compact as an instrument of government before they landed.[2] It was really an extension of the covenant idea of the Separatists to civil government, and the compact remained their main constitution until Plymouth was incorporated with the Salem settlements into Massachusetts in 1691. The landing at Plymouth was providential, for if the colonists had landed in Virginia, they would have been persecuted as much as they had been in England. Elder Brewster served as their religious leader, and William Bradford became their first governor. At least fifty of the colonists died during that first hard winter; but from the next spring on, the fortunes of the colonists flourished, and they were soon able to pay off their debts. The church was the center of spiritual and social life in their community.

The larger number of non-Separatist Puritans settled in Salem and Boston after 1628. In 1626 John White, a Puritan minister of Dorchester in England, organized a company to settle a few people at Salem. About fifty of this company landed in Salem in the fall of 1628 and chose John Endicott as their governor. These people were either Puritan Congregationalists or, possibly, Anglicans inclined to Congregationalism before they left England.[3] This, more than the kindly medical services of Dr. Samuel Fuller, who came from the Separatist Plymouth colony to give them medical aid during the winter of 1628–29, led the Salem colony to set up the congre-

The *New England Primer* taught Puritan doctrine and values as well as the ABCs.

gational system of church government based on a covenant.

In 1629 White's organization was incorporated into the Massachusetts Bay Company. All the stockholders of the Massachusetts Bay Company who did not want to migrate from England withdrew, and about nine hundred sailed to America with the governors of the company and the charter in order to get away from the despotic personal rule of Charles I. In 1631 the Massachusetts General Court limited the right to vote to church members, and Congregationalism became the state religion. The colonists rejected episcopacy but upheld the principle of uniformity of faith. John Winthrop (1588–1649) was made governor of these settlements at Salem and Boston. Over twenty thousand Puritans came to these settlements between 1628 and 1640. The ministers for the increasing number of churches were university graduates, most of whom were educated in Cambridge. They interpreted the authoritative Scriptures to the people so that they would know how to apply them in their private and civil life. Although the polity of the churches was congregational, the theology of these Puritans was Calvinistic.

The desire to occupy adjacent fertile areas and the intolerance of the leaders of the New England Settlement led to what one might term the "swarming" of the Puritans. Thomas Hooker (1586–1647), appointed as minister of Newton in 1633, became irked with the limitation of the franchise to church members. He and his congregation petitioned the magistrates for permission to migrate to the fertile Connecticut River valley to the west. They were permitted to leave, and by 1636 three towns were founded. In 1638 the Fundamental Orders of Connecticut were drawn up as the constitution for the new colony. This constitution was more liberal than that of the mother colony because only the governor was required to be a church member,[4] and government was based on the consent of the people expressed through their vote for the magistrates.

The founding of still another colony may be credited to John Davenport (1597–1670), pastor of a church in London, and one of his members, Theophilus Eaton, who sailed to America with many members of the congregation in 1636. They decided that they would not be happy in Boston and set up the colony of New Haven in the southern part of modern Connecticut. They obtained land from the Indians by treaty and in 1639 created a commonwealth, based on the Bible, in which only church members could vote. In 1664 this colony was merged with the others to form the colony of Connecticut.

Unity of theology and polity was secured after the Cambridge Synod of 1646, at which representatives of the four Puritan colonies adopted the Westminster Confession as an expression of their theology and finally drew up the *Cambridge Platform*[5] in 1648. This platform declared that each church was autonomous but was related to other churches for fellowship and council. Each church was created by a church covenant linking the believers to one another and to Christ, the Head of the church. Pastors and deacons became the most important officials, and ordination was performed by neighboring ministers when a church wanted to ordain someone.

The early Puritans did not entirely ignore their pagan neighbors. John Eliot (1604–90), pastor of Roxbury Church, who began work among the Indians in 1646, organized his converts into towns. By 1674 there were fourteen villages with nearly twenty-four thousand Christian Indians. He also translated and published the Old and New Testaments in the Indian tongue in 1663 and 1661 respectively.

C. Planting the American Baptist Churches

The beginning of the Baptist churches in America was also associated with the swarming of the Puritans. Roger Williams (ca. 1603–83), who was educated for the Anglican ministry at Cambridge, soon adopted Separatist views. His independence of mind brought him to Boston from unfriendly England in 1631. He went from there to Plymouth because he thought the Boston church had not purified itself sufficiently. For two years he ministered at Plymouth. When the church in Salem called him as pastor in 1635, the General Court, inspired by John Cotton, interfered. It ordered him out of the territory under its jurisdiction within six weeks because he upheld the Indian ownership of land, opposed a state church, and insisted that the magistrates had no power over a man's religion. Leaving his wife and children in a mortgaged home, he plunged into the forest in the depth of winter and wandered until friendly Indians gave him aid. In 1636 he purchased some land from the Indians and founded Providence.

In the next year Mrs. Anne Hutchinson (1591–1643) fell under the ban of the authorities because she held meetings in her home where she proclaimed what she called a covenant of grace. This covenant was opposed to the covenant of works, which she said all the ministers but John Cotton proclaimed. Her inner-light concept and claim to full assurance of salvation also got her into trouble. Exiled from the colony shortly before her baby was born, she was forced to walk in the depth of winter to Rhode Island, where she and her followers settled at Newport and Portsmouth. John Clarke (1609–76), a physician and preacher, became a teaching elder of a church in Newport in 1638; but it is not certain that this was a Baptist church.

In 1639, a church was founded in Providence, and all of the members were rebaptized, including Williams. There is some question whether or not this was by immersion, but at any rate, the twelve members organized the church along Baptist lines. It was probably the first Baptist church in America. Although there was a church in Newport in 1638, the first distinct Baptist church in Newport appeared in 1648, according to the records. Both the Newport and Providence churches still dispute for the title of the oldest Baptist church in America. Williams later withdrew from the Providence church, but he continued to serve the settlement by securing a temporary charter for Rhode Island in 1644. This charter was confirmed by the charter of 1663 granted by Charles II.[6] Williams's greatest contribution was his emphasis on the separation of church and state and freedom of conscience; and the great Baptist fellowship of modern times has sprung from his early activities in Rhode Island.

Roger Williams, who organized what was probably the first Baptist church in North America in Providence, Rhode Island. He later withdrew from the church and became a "Seeker for Truth."

D. Planting Roman Catholicism in Maryland

Central and South America received a homogeneous, Latin, authoritarian Roman Catholic culture from Spain and Portugal; but North America, except for Quebec and Louisiana, received a pluralistic, Anglo-Saxon Protestant culture from northern and western Europe. In 1565 the Spanish introduced a short-lived Roman Catholicism into Florida and later into New Mexico, Arizona, and California. The French planted it in Quebec, but Catholicism did not take root in the thirteen colonies until 1634 in Maryland. Most of the Irish and Germans who came after 1850 were Roman Catholic.

The Lords Baltimore—George Calvert (ca. 1580–1632) and his son, Cecil Calvert (1605–75)—were successive proprietors of what became known as Maryland. Unlike the idealistic Roger Williams, the Calverts were interested in profits. From 1634, when the colony began, they permitted religious toleration so that Protestants as well as Roman Catholics would settle there. The strict political control by Calvert was balanced by religious toleration until Maryland was made a royal colony in 1692. Anglicanism became the established religion in 1702 when the English government finally approved the 1692 act of the Colonial Assembly.

E. Pennsylvania and the Quakers

Quakers appeared in Boston in 1656 but soon found that they were not welcomed by the New England Puritans because of their idea of separation of church and state and their indifference to doctrine. After 1674 New Jersey was divided into East and West Jersey until 1702, and West Jersey became a Quaker settlement. But it was Pennsylvania that became the great Quaker refuge, through the efforts of William Penn. Charles II owed sixteen thousand pounds to Penn's father and gave William Penn control of Pennsylvania in 1681 to pay the debt. Penn made the colony an asylum where oppressed of any belief might find refuge. This explains the great diversity of sects that is apparent in the study of the religious history of Pennsylvania. In 1683 great numbers of German Mennonites settled at Germantown near Philadelphia. In 1740 numbers of Moravians settled in Pennsylvania after a short residence in Georgia between 1735 and 1740. Zinzendorf, leader of the Moravians, visited Pennsylvania himself in 1741 and unsuccessfully attempted to unite the German sects. Bethlehem became a leading center for the Moravians. Although American Lutheranism had its beginnings in the Dutch colony of New Amsterdam and in the Swedish colony along the Delaware River, it had no definite organization until Henry Muhlenberg (1711–87) landed in America in 1742. He was able to form a Lutheran Synod in Pennsylvania in 1748. By the time of the Revolution there were about seventy-five thousand Lutherans in Pennsylvania alone. Religious diversity was the keynote of religion in Pennsylvania and the middle colonies whereas the Anglican church dominated the southern colonies and the Congregational church the northern colonies.

F. Presbyterianism in America

During the first half of the seventeenth century the Scottish Presbyterians, who were brought in by James I to displace the native Irish, continued to migrate to northern Ireland. Many of the Scotch-Irish migrated to the colonies after 1710 because of the economic discrimination practiced against Ireland by the trade laws of England. By 1750 about 200,000 had come to America. Many, after a short stay in New England, moved to New Jersey and to New York, where they populated Ulster and Orange counties. More went into central and western Pennsylvania and became influential in the Pittsburgh area, which became a leading center of American Presbyterianism. Others went south into the Shenandoah Valley of Virginia.

Francis Makemie (1658–1708), an Irishman who arrived in the colonies in 1683, became the father of American Presbyterianism. By 1706 he had organized a presbytery in Philadelphia, and in 1716 the first synod of the colonies was held. In 1729 the synod adopted the Westminster Confession as the standard of faith. The Presbyterians ranked with the Anglicans, Congregationalists, and Baptists as the largest churches in the colonies.

G. Methodism in the Colonies

Methodism was introduced to the thirteen colonies by Robert Strawbridge in Maryland and Philip Embury and Captain Webb in New York after 1760. John Wesley sent Richard Boardman and Joseph Pilmoor as official missionaries in 1768. The great circuit rider Francis Asbury (1745–1816) came in 1771; and in 1784, when Methodism was formally organized in the colonies, he became the first bishop.

In this manner the various churches created by the Reformation were transplanted from Europe to America, with England as the bridge, during the first 150 years of the history of the colonies. Except for a while in Maryland and the middle colonies, an established church held sway until the American Revolution. After the Revolution the separation of church and state made the churches of America dependent on voluntary support for money to finance their ventures and on evangelism to win the unchurched and children of members of the church into their fellowship.

II. EDUCATION IN THE COLONIES

After homes had been built, churches erected, civil governments set up, and means of livelihood secured, education was one of the earliest concerns of the colonists, according to the pamphlet *New England's First Fruits*. This interest was in the tradition of the Reformation because Calvin and Luther had emphasized the need of education so that the individual could read his Bible and so that leaders for the church and state could be trained. The Bible had first place in their curricula and that of the educational institutions of early America, and classical training took second place as an aid to the full knowledge of the Bible. Vocational education in the colonies was assured by the continuance of the apprenticeship system of England. By this system one was apprenticed to a master in a particular trade until one learned that trade. Elementary education was by law the concern of the government in the northern colonies, but in the southern the same end was secured in wealthy families by the hiring of a private tutor.

Secondary schools, known as Latin or grammar schools, were set up to prepare the student for university by giving him a grounding in the classical languages. Colleges were to provide civic and religious leaders.

Harvard was founded in 1636 to "advance learning" and to secure a literate ministry that could pass on the cultural and religious tradition of the current generation to that which was to succeed it.[7] The main end of life and study was to know God and His Son Christ so that He would become "the only foundation" of learning. John Harvard, after whom the college was named, willed about eight hundred pounds and his library of about four hundred books to the infant college.

William and Mary College in Williamsburg was founded in 1693 with the idea that one of its main functions should be "the breeding of good ministers." Shortly thereafter the Puritans of Connecticut opened Yale College in 1701 to give youth a "Liberal & Religious Education" so that leaders for the churches should not be lacking. In 1726 William Tennent, Sr. (1673–1746), an Irish minister, set up a "Log College" near Philadelphia to educate his sons and other boys for the ministry. Jonathan Dickinson secured a charter in 1746 for a school to continue this effort. This school, known as the College of New Jersey, moved to Princeton and was eventually known as Princeton University. King's College (Columbia) came into existence by royal charter in 1754. The Baptists set up Rhode Island College in 1764 as an institution that would teach religion and the sciences without regard to sectarian differences. In due course it became Brown University. Dartmouth was founded in 1770;

the present Rutgers came into being in 1825; and the Quaker school Haverford was founded in 1833. Each group sought to set up an institution of higher learning to provide godly leaders in the church and the state.[8]

III. THE GREAT AWAKENING

Recurrent revivals have been a characteristic of Atlantic Anglo-Saxon, Teutonic, and American Christianity. The need of reaching the unchurched as well as of stirring the believers seems to have motivated these spiritual awakenings. They appear to have occurred in several eras for at least a decade at a time, at times of crisis. Before 1865 they were spontaneous, unorganized, pastoral, and rural or village congregational awakenings. Some time before 1700 a decline of morals and religion, caused by the influence of the frontier, a dynamic population on the move, a series of brutalizing wars, and the tendency in some areas to separate the church and the state, became noticeable.

The more Calvinistic Great Awakening had its beginning in the preaching of Theodore Frelinghuysen to his Dutch Reformed congregations in New Jersey in 1726. The revival stimulated earnest moral and spiritual life among the people. Frelinghuysen's work influenced the Presbyterian pastors Gilbert Tennent (1703–64) and William Tennent, Jr. (1705–77), so that they became fiery evangels of revival among the Scotch-Irish of the middle colonies. Whitefield thus found the groundwork for revival soundly laid when he came to the middle colonies in 1739.

The revival fires that had started among the Calvinistic Dutch Reformed and Presbyterians of the middle colonies soon spread to Congregationalist New England through the efforts of Jonathan Edwards (1703–58). Edwards was a precocious student who graduated from Yale in 1720 at the age of seventeen, and became associate pastor at Northampton in western Massachusetts in 1727. Although he read his manuscript sermons, his earnest manner and prayer had a great effect on his people. His 1741 sermon "Sinners in the Hands of an Angry God" is an impressive example of his pulpit power. The revival, which began in 1734, spread throughout New England until it reached its high tide in 1740.[9] George Whitefield (1714–70) made his appearance at this time in Boston, and his preaching there and throughout New England was attended with great success. When Edwards lost his pulpit in 1750, he served as an Indian missionary until 1758. In that year he became president of Princeton, where he died of smallpox inoculation in the same year. He upheld a Calvinistic theology and believed that while people have a rational ability to turn to God, because of total depravity they lack the moral ability or inclination. This ability must be imparted by divine grace. He made much of the sovereignty and love of God in his work on *Freedom of the Will.* He wrote that God's love draws men to Himself and to His service after they have become Christians.

Presbyterians from the middle colonies carried the revival fires to the South. Samuel Davies (1723–61) became the leader of the revival among the Presbyterians in Hanover County in Virginia. This had grown out of Samuel Morris's reading of religious literature to his neighbors in his "read-

Jonathan Edwards, Congregational pastor, preacher of revival, missionary to the Indians, author, first president of Princeton, and, by the estimate of some, the greatest philosopher-theologian North America has ever produced.

ing house." The Baptist phase of revival in the South grew out of the work of Shubal Stearns (1706–71) and Daniel Marshall of New England. Their preaching was more emotional, and many were won to the Baptist church in North Carolina. Revivalistic Methodism also took deep roots in the South through the efforts of Devereux Jarratt (1733–1801), an Episcopalian minister, and lay preachers during the revival.

Whitefield unified the efforts of all these revivalistic preachers as he traveled in all the colonies in seven visits between 1738 and 1769. Though unusual phenomena often followed the preaching, it was a soberer type of revival than the Second Awakening, which was to come near the end of the century. It was the American counterpart of Pietism in Europe and the Methodist revival in England.

Such a movement was bound to have unusual results. Between 30,000 and 40,000 people and 150 new churches were added to those in New England alone out of a population of 300,000. Thousands more came into the churches in the southern and middle colonies. A higher moral tone was noticed in the homes, work, and amusements of the people. Colleges such as Princeton, King's (Columbia), Hampden-Sydney, and others were started to provide ministers for the many new congregations. Missionary work was spurred so that men like David Brainerd (1718–47) in 1743, with great personal sacrifice, engaged in missionary work among the Indians. Whitefield founded an orphanage at Bethesda, Georgia. Many other humanitarian enterprises also owed their birth to the revival.

The revival also brought schism as ministers took sides concerning the attitude of the church to the movement. New England clergymen split into the "Old Lights" (led by Charles Chauncy, who opposed the revival, the itinerant evangelists, and the Calvinism of many of the revivalists) and the "New Lights" (led by Edwards, who supported the revival and a slightly modified Calvinism). This schism led eventually to the development of an orthodox group and a liberal group. Out of Chauncy's group the Unitarians, which split off New England Congregationalism, emerged early in the nineteenth century.

The revival split the Presbyterians in the middle colonies into two groups in 1741. They were not reunited until 1758. The "Old Side," made up of the older ministers in and near Philadel-

phia, opposed the licensing and ordaining of untrained men to the ministry, the intrusion of the revivalists into established parishes, and the critical attitude of many of the revivalists toward the work of the ministers. The "New Side" supported the revival and the licensing of untrained men who showed unusual spiritual gifts to take care of the new churches. The Dutch Reformed of New Jersey and the Baptists of the South also both split for a time over what attitude the church should take toward the revival. But it cannot be denied that the revival was a valuable influence in the life of America and helped to prepare the people spiritually to face the problems of the French and Indian Wars of 1756–63.

IV. THE CHURCHES AND THE AMERICAN REVOLUTION

The American Revolution also brought many problems to the colonial churches. The Anglican church remained loyal to the revolutionary cause in southern colonies, such as Maryland and Virginia; in the middle colonies its loyalty was about equally divided between the revolutionists and the English; in New England it was generally loyal to England. Because John Wesley was a Tory and supported the ruler, the Methodists were accused of disloyalty to the colonial cause. Generally, however, they took a neutral position. The Quakers, Mennonites, and Moravians were at heart patriotic, but their pacifist principles kept them from any participation in the war. Congregationalists, Baptists, Lutherans, Roman Catholics, and Presbyterians espoused the cause of revolution; and in their sermons and teachings the ministers and educators amplified the idea of the church covenant based on the consent of the people into a political compact based on the consent of the people as necessary to the setting up of any state. The ruler cannot violate his contract or act contrary to God's laws, they reasoned, and not expect the people to revolt.

The ending of the war in 1783 had important results for religion. The influence of the church contributed to the development of a ban on any established church and of the right to a free exercise of religion as set forth in the First Amendment to the Constitution. It also brought about the separation of church and state in states where there had been an established church. Disestablishment took place in Maryland and New York during the Revolution; but not until 1786, through the efforts of Jefferson, did the Anglican church lose its privileged position in Virginia. New Hampshire in 1817, Connecticut in 1818, and Massachusetts in 1833 separated the Congregationalist church from the state.

The churches, following the analogy of the nation, which had created a national government by 1789, made constitutions and set up national organizations. The Methodists, led by Coke and Asbury, created a national church in 1784 which became known as the Methodist Episcopal Church. The Anglicans set up the Protestant Episcopal Church in 1789. The Presbyterians created a national church in 1788, and the first national General Assembly met in 1789. The Dutch Reformed created a national church in 1792, and the German Reformed in 1793. New England churches were not greatly affected by the tendencies to centralization and nationalization of organization. It is fortunate that the new national churches were given fresh spiritual zeal by the Second Awakening, which began about the time the new nation adopted its Constitution. The American churches had been tried by the fires of war and they were now ready to take up their mission to the new united nation.

SUGGESTED READING

Titles marked with an asterisk cover the entire period of American Church History.

*Ahlstrom, Sydney E. **A Religious History of the American People.** New Haven: Yale University Press, 1972. This is a well-written, scholarly, and encyclopedic account of religion.

Albright, Raymond W. **A History of the Protestant Episcopal Church.** New York: Macmillan, 1964.

Alexander, Archibald. **The Log College.** 1851. Reprint. London: Banner of Truth Trust, 1968. This book has short sketches of Tennent and his students.

Armstrong, Maurice, and Loetscher, Lefferts. **The Presbyterian Enterprise.** Philadelphia: Westminster, 1956.

Atkins, Gaius G., and Fagley, Frederick L. **The History of American Congregationalism.** Boston: Pilgrim, 1942. This is a standard history of the American Congregationalist churches.

*Beardsley, Frank G. **A History of American Revivals.** New York: American Tract Society, 1904. This may be consulted with profit.

*Brauer, Jerald C. Protestantism in America. Revised ed. Philadelphia: Westminster, 1965.

Bridenbaugh, Carl. Mitre and Sceptre. New York: Oxford University Press, 1962. The book discusses the fear of an Anglican bishop by the colonies before the Revolution.

Coen, C. C. Revivalism and Separatism in New England, 1740–1800. Nea Haven: Yale University Press, 1962.

Edwards, Jonathan. Edwards on Revival. New York: Dunning & Spalding, 1832. A Faithful Narrative, describing the revival at Northampton, and Thoughts on the Great Awakening are contained in this work.

Ellis, John T. American Catholicism. 2nd rev. ed. Chicago: University of Chicago Press, 1969. This briefly surveys American Catholicism.

––––––. Catholics in Colonial America. Baltimore: Helicon, 1965. This is an excellent survey of Roman Catholic missions in America.

––––––. Documents of American Catholic History. 2nd ed. Milwaukee: Bruce, 1962. This contains all the important documents.

*Ferm, Vergilius, ed. The American Church of the Protestant Heritage. New York: Philosophical Library, 1953. There are excellent discussions by denominational experts of the European background and history in America to the present of the leading American denominations.

Garrett, John. Roger Williams. New York: Macmillan, 1970.

*Gaustad, Edwin S. A Religious History of the American People. New York: Harper, 1966. This combines sources, pictures, and secondary accounts in one volume.

––––––. The Great Awakening in New England. New York: Harper, 1957.

––––––. Historical Atlas of Religion in America. Rev. ed. New York: Harper, 1976. This has excellent maps, charts, and graphs to illustrate American religious history.

Gewehr, Wesley M. The Great Awakening in Virginia, 1740–1790. Durham, N.C.: Duke University Press, 1930.

Glazer, Nathan. American Judaism. Rev. ed. Chicago: University of Chicago Press, 1972.

Grant, John W. A History of the Christian Church in Canada. 3 vols. Toronto: McGraw-Hill, Ryerson, 1966–72.

*Handy, Robert T. A History of the Churches in the United States and Canada. Oxford: Clarendon University Press, 1976. This first in a series of twenty volumes on the history of Christianity artfully links American and Canadian church history.

Hanzsche, William T. The Presbyterians. Philadelphia: Westminster, 1934. The story of the Presbyterians is described in this book.

Heimert, Alan, and Miller, Perry, eds. The Great Awakening. Indianapolis: Bobbs-Merrill, 1967. This contains pertinent sources for the Great Awakening.

*Hudson, Winthrop S. Religion in America. 2nd ed. New York: Scribner, 1973.

James, Sydney V. A People Among Peoples. Cambridge: Harvard University Press, 1963. This is a discussion of eighteenth-century American Quakerism.

Jones, Rufus M. The Quakers in the American Colonies. London: Saint Martin's, 1923.

McLoughlin, William G. Isaac Backus and the American Pietistic Tradition. Boston: Little, Brown, 1967.

Miller, Perry. Jonathan Edwards. New York: Sloane, 1949. This is scholarly and sympathetic.

*Mode, Peter G. Source Book and Biographical Guide for American Church History. Menasha, Wis.: Banta, 1921. This is the most valuable collection of source materials for American church history.

Moir, John S. The Cross in Canada. Toronto: Ryerson, 1966. This book has many relevant documents.

Nelson, E. Clifford, ed. The Lutherans in America. Philadelphia: Fortress, 1975. This is a detailed, scholarly history of American and Canadian Lutheranism.

Norwood, Frederick A. The Story of American Methodism. Nashville: Abingdon, 1974.

*Olmstead, Clifton E. History of Religion in the United States. Englewood Cliffs, N.J.: Prentice-Hall, 1960.

Pilcher, George. Samuel Davies, Apostle of Dissent in Colonial Virginia. Knoxville: University of Tennessee Press, n.d. This is an able biography.

Rudolph, L. C. Francis Asbury. Nashville: Abingdon, 1966.

Schlenther, Boyd S. The Life and Writings of Francis Makemie. Philadelphia: Presbyterian Historical Society, 1971.

*Smith, H. Sheton; Handy, Robert T.; and Loetscher, Lefforts A., eds. American Christianity. 2 vols. New York: Scribner, 1960–63. This includes both important documents and their historical background.

*Smith, James W., and Jamison, A. Leland, eds. Religion in American Life. 4 vols. Princeton: Princeton University Press, 1961. This work has a useful collection of interpretive and historical essays with critical annotated bibliographies.

*Sweet, William W. Makers of Christianity. 3 vols. New York: Henry Holt, 1937. Volume 3 has excellent brief biographies of the leading characters of the colonial and later periods.

_____. Methodism in American History. Nashville: Abingdon, 1954.

_____. Religion in Colonial America. New York: Scribner, 1942. This is the most useful work on colonial church history.

_____. Religion in the Development of American Culture, 1765–1840. New York: Scribner, 1952. This is a helpful work on the national era.

_____. Religion on the American Frontier. 4 vols. Chicago: University of Chicago Press, 1931–46. This contains accounts from church records of religious events in local churches of the Methodist, Presbyterian, Baptist, and Congregational denominations.

*_____. Revivalism in America. New York: Scribner, 1945. This is an excellent discussion of the various revivals.

*_____. The Story of Religion in America. 2nd rev. ed. New York: Harper, 1950. This is an excellent survey of church history in the United States.

Tanis, James. Dutch Calvinistic Pietism in the Middle Colonies. The Hague: Nijhoff, 1967.

Tappert, Theodore G., and Doberstein, John W., trans. The Journals of Henry Muhlenberg. Philadelphia: Muhlenberg, 1945.

Torbet, Robert B. A History of the Baptists. Rev. ed. Valley Forge, Pa.: Judson, 1963.

Walsh, H. H. The Church in Canada. Toronto: Ryerson, 1956.

Wentz, Abdel R. A Basic History of Lutheranism in America. Philadelphia: Muhlenberg, 1955.

Winslow, Ola E. John Eliot, Apostle to the Indians. Boston: Houghton Mifflin, 1968.

Wolf, Richard C. Documents of Lutheran Unity in America. Philadelphia: Fortress, 1966.

Ziff, Langer. The Career of John Cotton. Princeton: Princeton University Press, 1962.

Chapter 33

Rationalism, Revivalism, and Roman Catholicism

The sixteenth century was marked by the rise of Protestantism and the development of its basic ideas through the efforts of such creative leaders as Calvin and Luther. Unfortunately, during the seventeenth century Protestantism developed a system of orthodox dogma that one accepted intellectually. This system brought about a new Scholasticism, particularly among the Lutherans in Germany who became more interested in dogma than in the expression of doctrine in practical life. This cold intellectual expression of Christianity, coupled with the severe religious wars between 1560 and 1648 and the rise of rationalistic philosophy and empirical science, led to rationalism and formalism in religion between 1660 and 1730 in England, Europe, and, later, America. The distaste for cold orthodoxy among the rationalistic philosophers and scientists, the rise of natural religion, and the insistence that the church is a group of believers covenanting together with God and one another led to the rise of toleration and denominationalism.

During the late seventeenth and eighteenth centuries two responses to this Protestant Scholasticism developed. The one response was rationalism, which had its religious expression in the natural religion of Deism, and the other was revivalism. The latter expressed itself in some cases in an emphasis on what is called the theology of the inner light and in other cases in a stress on the importance of the Bible and personal piety. The diagram on the following page will illustrate the relationships between these various movements between 1648 and 1789.

I. RATIONALISM AND RELIGION

Modern thought has emphasized the importance of reason and the scientific method in the discovery of truth and has refused to be bound by traditions of the past. These ideas had their rise in the period between the

REACTIONS TO PROTESTANT ORTHODOXY

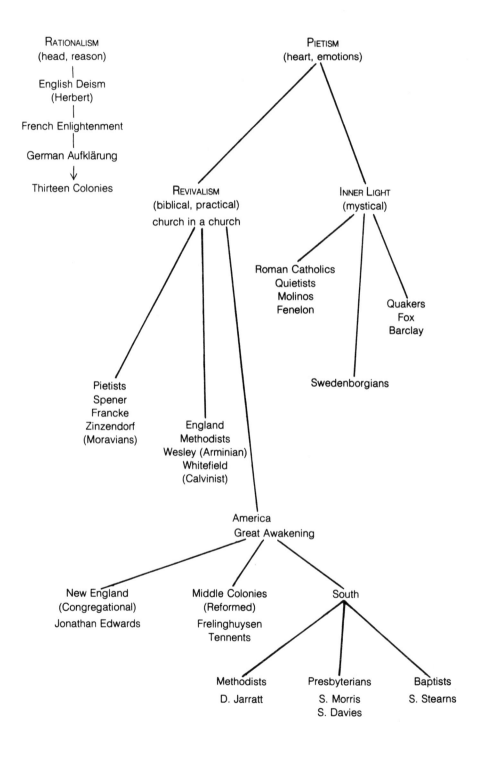

RATIONALISM
(head, reason)

English Deism
(Herbert)

French Enlightenment

German Aufklärung

Thirteen Colonies

PIETISM
(heart, emotions)

REVIVALISM
(biblical, practical)

church in a church

INNER LIGHT
(mystical)

Roman Catholics
Quietists
Molinos
Fenelon

Quakers
Fox
Barclay

Swedenborgians

Pietists
Spener
Francke
Zinzendorf
(Moravians)

England
Methodists
Wesley (Arminian)
Whitefield
(Calvinist)

America
Great Awakening

New England
(Congregational)
Jonathan Edwards

Middle Colonies
(Reformed)
Frelinghuysen
Tennents

South

Methodists

D. Jarratt

Presbyterians

S. Morris
S. Davies

Baptists

S. Stearns

end of the Thirty Years' War and the beginning of the French Revolution. Some attention should be given to the reasons for the rise and the results of these ideas because of their impact on religion.

A. The Origin of Deism

Several developments contributed to the rise of rationalism in the seventeenth century. The scientific horizon was greatly expanded by the work of outstanding scientists of the day. The old theory of a geocentric universe gave way to the theory of a heliocentric universe. This theory was developed by Nicholas Copernicus (1473–1543) and popularized by Galileo Galilei (1564–1642). Isaac Newton (1642–1727), while still a young man, became interested in the question of whether there were basic principles that operated throughout the universe. In 1687 he wrote *Principia Mathematica* in which he developed the idea of the law of gravitation. Gravitation provided the key to unify the phenomena of physics. Until it was replaced by Darwin's concept of biological growth, the principle of natural law was considered to be basic; and people came to look on the universe as a machine or mechanism that operated by inflexible natural laws. The principle of natural laws discovered by reason were applied to many other areas of knowledge, such as political science, economics, and religion.

Europeans also became acquainted with other cultures as adventurous traders went to the far corners of the earth to carry on their business. Knowledge of non-Christian religions was brought back to Europe, and scholars began to compare these religions with Christianity. They found similarities in principles. This led many to wonder whether there was a basic natural religion that all men had apart from the Bible or priests. In this way people were led in their thinking toward deism, which seemed to provide a religion both natural and scientific.

The new philosophies of empiricism and rationalism also challenged tradition in the name of reason. These philosophies substituted reason and man's senses for revelation as the main avenues to knowledge. They were earthbound in their concern for the knowing subject, man, rather than concerned for the reality to be known, God.

Empiricism provided science with a method that has been somewhat deified by positivists and pragmatists. Francis Bacon (1561–1626) published his *Novum Organum* in 1620. In this work he developed an inductive method of interpreting nature. This method, he thought, would replace the deductive method of Aristotle, so widely used by the Scholastics in the Middle Ages. Using the inductive method, which is also known as the scientific method, the scientist accepted nothing on the basis of authority alone. He developed a hypothesis, observed facts concerning his tentative idea, checked the facts by repeated experimentation, and only then developed a general law. In the older deductive method, men linked a general principle, accepted on authority, to a fact and drew a conclusion without testing the validity of the general principle.

The empirical philosophy of John Locke (1632–1704) reinforced Bacon's contention. In his *Essay Concerning*

Human Understanding (1690), Locke denied the existence of fixed ideas in the mind, such as time and space, and asserted that the mind of a baby is a blank. Knowledge comes to the baby as his senses present sensations to his mind, which by reflection on the sensations creates knowledge. This tying of knowledge to sensation created a materialistic approach to life. The combination of Locke's ideas with those of Bacon led to an exultation of the scientific method as the major way to get knowledge.

The rationalistic school of philosophers had also earlier exalted man's own ability to discover truth by reason without recourse to revelation. Natural theology was to be the starting point for theology. René Descartes (1596–1650) developed a philosophy in which his starting point was doubt of everything except his own consciousness and his ability to think. From this self-evident fact he built up a system of thought in which various axioms could be known with mathematical certainty. He argued that there were certain innate concepts in human reason, such as time and space, that enable the mind to organize the data that the senses bring to it. Although Descartes was a dualist who believed in the existence of mental and material worlds, he believed that by reason alone he could accept the existence of God and the soul. His ideas tended to strengthen man's belief in his ability to attain knowledge by unaided reason and scientific method. Rationalistic philosophy and the scientific laws of Newton gave rise to the view that by reason and the scientific method man could discover natural laws and could live in accord with them.

Deism was a natural result of the scientific and philosophic approach to knowledge that has just been described. It arose in England during the seventeenth century and spread from there to France, Germany, and America. It was a natural religion or a religion of reason. Deism (Latin *deus*, God) set forth a system of belief in a transcendent God who left His creation after He had created it to be governed by natural laws discoverable by reason. God thus became an "absentee God." The deist insists that God is above and beyond His creation. The pantheist tends to emphasize the immanence of God in His creation; but the theist has always insisted that the transcendent God is not a part of His creation but that He is immanent in it as Providence and as a Redeemer through Christ.

B. The Dogmas of Deism

Deism, a religion without written revelation, emphasized the starry heaven above and the moral law within. One of the main dogmas of deism—the deists also had their dogmas, the natural laws of religion discoverable by reason—was the belief in a transcendent God who was the First Cause of a creation marked by evidences of design. The deists believed that God left His creation to operate under natural laws; hence, there was no place for miracles, the Bible as a revelation from God, prophecy, providence, or Christ as a God-man. The deists taught that Christ was only a moral teacher and insisted that worship belonged to God. Another dogma was the belief that "virtue and piety" were the most important worship that one could give to God. God's ethical laws are in the Bible, which is an ethical guidebook, and in the nature of man, where they can be discovered by human reason. A person must repent of wrongdoing and have his life conform to ethical laws because there is immortality and each individual faces reward and punishment after death.

Deism dominated the thinking of the upper classes in England between the presentation of the basic tenets of deism by Edward Herbert, lord of Cherbury (1583–1648), in 1624 and the work of David Hume (1711–76). Herbert's belief may be summed up in the statement that God, who exists, must be worshiped by repentance and an ethical life so that the immortal soul may enjoy eternal reward rather than punishment. Charles Blount (1654–93) was another influential deist. John Toland (1670–1722), Lord Shaftesbury (1671–1713), and others insisted that Christianity was not mysterious but could be proved by reason. What could not be proved by reason should be repudiated. David Hume attacked biblical miracles.

Many rose to defend orthodox Christianity. William Law (1686–1761), who wrote the fine work concerning the devotional life of the Christian entitled *A Serious Call to a Devout and Holy Life* (1728), also wrote *Case of Reason* (1732) in which he argued that man cannot comprehend the whole of religion by rational processes because God is above reason. Joseph Butler (1682–1752), in *The Analogy of Religion* (1736), shows that the arguments the deists used against the God of the Bible would apply to the God of nature if reason were the authority. Butler used the argument from probability to demonstrate that orthodox Christianity answered problems better than

deism. William Paley (1743–1805) used the argument from design to prove the existence of a God who revealed Himself in the Bible, Christ, and miracles so that man might be led to a good life of obedience to God and of preparation for immortality.

C. The Spread of Deism

Because the English deists such as Herbert and Shaftesbury traveled in France, because deistic books were translated and published abroad, and because Frenchmen such as Rousseau and Voltaire traveled in England, deistic ideas spread to France where they found a favorable climate of opinion among the *philosophes* of the eighteenth century. Rousseau's deism was developed in his *Emile*, and Voltaire's deism permeated all his writings against the church and in favor of tolerance. D'Alembert and Denis Diderot (1713–84) edited the *Encyclopédie*, a large rationalistic encyclopedia of universal knowledge. The contest in France was between the Roman Catholic church and these deistic freethinkers. Because their deistic ideology provided a rationalization for the French revolutionaries in 1789, the freethinkers had an important influence on the coming of the revolution that was to bring such great changes in Europe.

Such things as the writings of the deists, Toland's visit to Hanover, and the residence of Voltaire at the court of Frederick the Great spread the religion of reason to Germany, where it found a congenial home despite the earlier work of the Pietists.

Immigration of English deists, deistic writings, and deistic officers of the English army in America during the war of 1756–63 helped to spread deism in the colonies. Franklin, Jefferson, Ethan Allen, and Thomas Paine were among the leading deists of America. Paine's *Age of Reason* (1795) helped to popularize the ideas of the deists. In this manner America as well as England, France, and Germany were exposed to the destructive influences of deism.

D. The Results of Deism

Deism helped to strengthen the idea of the omnipotence of the state, because men, such as Rousseau, insisted that the state was of natural origin. The state originated, so the argument went, in a social compact among sovereign people who chose their rulers. The rulers were responsible to the people to such an extent that if they failed in their duties, the people had the right to change them. The state, subject only to the sovereign people, is supreme in all areas of life. Deism helped to develop the concept of man's essential goodness and perfectibility so that continued human progress toward a more perfect order on earth could be expected. Deism was unduly optimistic because it tended to ignore human sin. Modern liberalism with its emphasis on rationalism in methodology owes much to deism. Deists also helped to create the modern system of higher criticism of the Bible.

However, some gains for Christianity came from deism. No one will condemn the rise of tolerance, and in this rise deists played a leading part because they believed that religious ideas that were rational should be held freely. The deists also cooperated with orthodox Christians in various humanitarian activities because they believed in the dignity of man as a rational being. The impetus to study also led to beneficial results in the field of textual criticism and exegesis. Scholars helped to develop an authoritative text of the Bible and to demonstrate that it has come down to us from the original authors in an excellent state of preservation. The application of grammar and history to a correct exegesis of the Bible was stimulated indirectly by the rationalistic movement.

Numerous revivalistic movements on the Continent and in England and America arose concurrently with the development of rationalism and deism. In some cases these movements were based on an emphasis on an "inner light" by which man could be illumined spiritually apart from or through the Bible. Roman Catholic Quietism and English Quakerism illustrated this tendency. Revivalism based on the Scriptures may be illustrated by Pietism and Methodism in the Lutheran and Anglican churches.

II. MYSTICISM AND RELIGION

A. On the Continent

Quietism was a mystical movement within the Roman Catholic church during the seventeenth century. It emphasized an immediate intuitional approach to God by the passive soul opening itself to the influence of the inner light. It was a reaction against the emphasis on the rationalization of dogma. Forerunners of the Quietists were the godly Charles Borromeo (1538–84), cardinal and archbishop of Milan, Ignatius Loyola, Theresa of Spain, and Francis of Sales (1567–1622) of France. The latter's *Introduction to the Devout Life* (1609) could be read by

Protestants today with profit. These mystics of the Counter Reformation were succeeded by the Quietists of the seventeenth century.

Michal Molinos (1640–ca. 1697) in his *Spiritual Guide* (1675) emphasized passivity of soul as the way to open oneself to the impartation of divine light from God. In such a state the human will was not even to be exercised. His ideas were adopted by Madame Guyon (1648–1717), who emphasized passive contemplation of the Divine as the method and union with the Divine as the goal of mystical experience. Francis Fenelon (1651–1715), the royal tutor, defended her from Bossuet's attacks and in his work *Christian Perfection* gave a positive note to Quietism. The work has been an aid to the devotional life of Protestants as well as Roman Catholics.

Protestant mysticism may be illustrated by the work of the great Swedish scientist Emanuel Swedenborg (1688-1772), who came to the conclusion that back of the physical world of nature was a corresponding spiritual world. He maintained that communication between these two worlds was possible through conversation with heavenly beings. He spiritualized the Bible to correlate it with the revelations that these heavenly visitants brought to him. By 1788 a church was organized in London and the denomination, The Church of the New Jerusalem, is still in existence.

B. In England

The Quakers appeared on the English religious scene during the chaotic period of the Civil War and the Commonwealth. They set aside the doctrines of an organized church and the Bible as the sole and final revelation of God's will in favor of the doctrine of the Inner Light, by which they meant that the Holy Spirit can give immediate and direct knowledge of God apart from the Bible. They resembled the Montanists, but their mystical tendencies were fortunately balanced by moral earnestness and a strong social passion.

George Fox (ca. 1624–91), who was born in a weaver's home and apprenticed to a shoemaker who was also a dealer in wool, started his search for spiritual truth in 1643 when he was challenged by two Puritans to a drinking bout in which the one who stopped first would have to pay the bill. In disgust he left the church, and not until about 1647 did he have a satisfactory religious experience that ended his seeking. Christianity then became a way of life to him, a mystical experience in which one could come directly to God. He began to preach, and a group of his followers, who called themselves Friends, was organized in 1652. They were also called Quakers. In 1652 Margaret Fell (1614–1702) of Swarthmore Hall was won to Quakerism, and her home became the unofficial center of Quakerism. Fox later married her in 1669. The expansion of Quakerism was rapid as missionary zeal and persecution by the authorities caused its adherents to seek new homes outside England. When Fox traveled in the thirteen colonies (1672–73), he found many Quaker groups. In 1666 monthly meetings were established to provide order and a means of checking on the conduct of the membership.

Robert Barclay (1648–90) became the theologian of the movement. He published *An Apology for True Chris-*

tian Divinity in 1678. His propositions give the essence of Quaker theology.[1] To him the Spirit was the sole Revelator of God and the Source of the Inner Light within man that gave him spiritual illumination. The Bible was but a secondary rule of faith, and the inspiration of the writers was placed on the same level as the inspiration of Fox or any other Quaker. However, revelations to a Friend should not contradict "the Scriptures, or right and sound reason." Because of the Inner Light, a professional ministry was unnecessary, and the two sacraments, being inward and spiritual, were separated from material symbols and ceremonies. Quakers were not to engage in war, and slavery was banned. Woolman, an American Quaker, was one of the earliest to speak and write in favor of the abolition of slavery. Oaths in court were banned, and human titles were not to be honored. This latter teaching got the Quakers into much trouble in class-conscious England where the upper class expected the use of titles and the doffing of hats from lower classes. Many Quakers suffered imprisonment, but the movement grew in spite or because of persecution. By 1660 there were about fifty thousand Quakers in England.

William Penn (1644–1718) was able to bring relief from persecution when Charles II gave him a large grant of land in America in 1681 as payment of a sixteen-thousand-pound debt to Penn's father. Penn organized Pennsylvania in 1682 on a basis of complete religious freedom and invited the oppressed sects of Europe, including the Quakers, to find refuge there. Both in Pennsylvania and West Jersey, Quakers became quite numerous.

The Friends have always em-

William Penn, founder of Pennsylvania, had a reputation for elegant dress, courtly manners, and eloquent speech.

phasized the spread of their faith by a strong missionary program in which social service plays an important part, but in doing this they have not neglected education. The excellence of Haverford and Swarthmore colleges, as well as many other schools, is a testimony to Quaker interest in education. But the movement has not been free from dangers of schism and the cooling off of spiritual zeal. The lack of interest in doctrine and the absence of an objective historical standard, such as the Bible, has sometimes brought excessive mysticism and at other times led to a vague theism in which the person of Christ is not sufficiently exalted.

III. REVIVALISM AND RELIGION

A. On the Continent

Quite different from the inner light mysticism just discussed was the

Pietist movement in Germany, which arose as an internal evangelical corrective to the cold orthodoxy of the seventeenth-century Lutheran church. Pietism emphasized an internal, subjective, and individual return to Bible study and prayer. Biblical truth should be manifested daily in a life of practical piety by laymen and ministers alike. Although there were other contributing factors, the movement was primarily a result of the efforts of Philip Spener (1635–1705), who became a Lutheran pastor in Frankfurt in 1666. In 1670 he organized what he called *collegia pietatis*, meetings in a home for practical Bible study and prayer. His *Pia Desideria* (1675) emphasized the "cottage prayer meetings" as an aid to the cultivation of personal piety among Lutherans. He also suggested that ministerial education should be biblical and practical, with internships for prospective ministers. In 1686 he went to Dresden as court preacher. From there in 1691 he went to an influential pastorate in Berlin where he remained until his death. Pietism flourished in Germany, Holland, and Scandinavia.

August Francke (1663–1727) and some friends at Leipzig University also founded a group for the study of the Bible. During a visit to Dresden, Francke was influenced by Spener, who was finally able to get him a professorship in 1692 at the University of Halle, which soon became a center of Pietism. Francke organized a free elementary school for poor children in 1695 and a secondary school two years later. He also set up a home for orphans and was influential in the creation of a Bible institute, founded by a close friend, to publish and to circulate copies of the Scriptures in 1719.

Pietism brought a new stress on the study and discussion of the Bible and its application to daily practice and the cultivation of a pious life. Stress was laid on the function of the Holy Spirit as the Illuminator of the Bible. Good works as an expression of true religion were emphasized. Fresh spiritual vigor was infused into the Lutheran church. Halle became a center of missionary effort. Pioneer work was done in Africa, America, Asia, and the islands of the Pacific by missionaries from Halle. The scientific study of languages and church history was stimulated in an attempt to get at the true meaning of the writers of the Bible for daily life. ːndifference to doctrine on the part of Pietists led some to adopt the philosophy of idealism.

In addition to its infusion of fresh spiritual vigor into the Lutheran church, Pietism resulted in the founding of the Moravian church by Count von Zinzendorf (1700–60), who studied in Francke's school at Halle and in Wittenberg, where he read law. Von Zinzendorf emphasized a life of vital personal devotedness to Christ. In 1722 Moravian refugees founded Hernnhut on Zinzendorf's Berthelsdorf estate, and in 1727 he became leader of their organization. The Moravian church was recognized as a separate church by 1742. It had a threefold organization of bishop, elder, and deacon by 1745. The movement had such a missionary vision that missionaries were sent to the West Indies, Greenland, India, and Africa by the middle of the century. After a short period in Georgia, the Moravians moved to Pennsylvania, where Zinzendorf during his stay in America in 1743 tried to unite all German Protestants under the Moravians. Zinzendorf's passionate, poetically expressed devotion to Christ was put into theological expression by August Spangenberg, the theologian of the movement. It is interesting to note that the circle of influence was completed when Wesley was helped to personal faith in Christ by the Moravians. Wycliffe's teachings had influenced Hus, the founder of the Bohemian Brethren, out of which the Moravian church, which was to have such an influence on the spiritual life of the Englishman John Wesley, emerged. It is unfortunate that the English influence on the Continent in the seventeenth and eighteenth centuries promoted deism and rationalism.

B. In England

The Methodist revival was the third religious awakening in England, coming after the sixteenth-century Reformation and seventeenth-century Puritanism. It was associated with the name of John Wesley (1703–91), who dominated the century as far as religion was concerned. Historians readily acknowledge that Methodism ranks with the French Revolution and the Industrial Revolution as one of the great historical phenomena of the century, and some subscribe to the idea that Wesley's preaching saved England from a revolution similar to that of France. Methodism was to Anglicanism what Pietism was to Lutheranism.

Even earlier in Wales, revival had come through Howell Harris (1714–73), a teacher at Talgarth, and Griffith Jones (1683–1761), a pastor. The Welsh Calvinistic Methodist church grew up out of this awakening. Jones also set up the system of circuits.

We have already seen that the rationalistic religion of deism was widely accepted among the upper classes. Sermons in the established church were often only long homilies filled with moral platitudes. The upper clergy were highly paid while the lower clergy, in over five thousand churches, had small incomes of twenty to fifty pounds a year and could hardly be expected to be efficient. Too often they became hangers-on of the local squire and joined in his coarse sports and drinking bouts. Morals were at a low ebb, too. In the first half of the century the death rate went up as cheap gin killed many and sent others to the "asylum." Gambling was rampant. Charles James Fox, a political leader, was said to have lost one hundred thousand pounds by the time he was twenty-four. Bull-, bear-, fox-, and cock-baiting were regular pastimes, and a series of executions by hanging on Tyburn Hill was a gala occasion for the whole family. It was indeed a "sick century," suspicious of theology and lacking fervor.

Wesley was the fifteenth of nineteen children born to Samuel and Susannah Wesley. He was narrowly saved from death when the Wesley home burned in 1709. Because of this experience, he often referred to himself as a "brand plucked from the burning." He entered Oxford in 1720 on a scholarship. From 1726 to 1751 he was a fellow of Lincoln College and was ordained a priest in 1728. After two years, during which he helped his father handle a second parish adjoining Epworth, he returned to his duties as a fellow. Wesley then became the leading spirit in the "Holy Club," which included his brother Charles. The members of this club were nicknamed Methodists by the students because of their methodical Bible study and prayer habits and regular attempts at social service in jails and homes of the poor. Between 1735 and 1737 Wesley was in Georgia as chaplain in Oglethorpe's colony.[2] His ritualistic ideas, strict churchmanship, simplicity, and frankness in his relations with women created such difficulties with his parishioners that he was forced to go home in 1737. On May 24, 1738, while listening to the reading of Luther's preface to his *Commentary on Romans*, Wesley's heart was "strangely warmed," and he trusted Christ alone for salvation from sin. His brother Charles had had a similar experience two days earlier. Because of the brave conduct of Moravians in a storm at sea on the way to Georgia, the words of Spangenberg in Georgia,[3] and the efforts of Peter Böhler,[4] all of which had been important influences in his conversion, Wesley paid a visit to Hernnhut to study the Moravian church more closely.

In 1739 George Whitefield (1714–70), with whom Wesley broke in 1740 because of the former's Calvinistic theology, asked Wesley to engage in field preaching at Bristol. Thus began John Wesley's career of field preaching during which he traveled over 200,000 miles on horseback in England, Scotland, and Ireland, preached about 42,000 sermons, wrote about 200 books, and organized his followers. He organized a Methodist society and built a chapel in Bristol in 1739. In that same year he also bought the "Foundery" building in London and used it as the headquarters for his work. Whitefield, who had become a Christian in 1735, began open-air preaching in 1739, organized converts into societies, used lay preachers, and had a social emphasis with his orphanage.

The fine hymns that Charles Wesley (1707–88) wrote were a great help in the meetings. Charles wrote over six thousand hymns, among which "Jesus Lover of My Soul," "Love Divine," and "Hark! The Herald Angels Sing" are still universal favorites. Following the path blazed by Isaac Watts (1674–1748), the Congregationalist theologian and "father of English hymnody," Charles wrote hymns other than rhymed passages of Scripture, which had been used up to that time.

Wesley did not want to break with the Anglican church, and therefore he organized his converts into societies similar to Spener's *collegia pietatis*.

John Wesley, the founder of Methodism.

The societies were subdivided in 1742 into classes of ten to twelve under a lay leader who had the spiritual oversight of the class. In 1744 the first annual conference of his preachers was held in London, and in 1746 he divided England into seven circuits. In 1784 he ordained two men as ministers and set apart Thomas Coke as superintendent of the Methodist church in America. In that same year, the Deed of Declaration legalized the conference to hold property such as their Methodist chapels. The church in America set up its own national organization in that year. Not until after Wesley's death in 1791 were the Methodists of England organized into a Methodist church separate from the Anglican church. The Anglican influence in the Methodist church was demonstrated by episcopal polity and the reception of the Communion while kneeling at the altar rail.

The Methodist church accepted an Arminian theology after Wesley's break with Whitefield, but the major doctrine that Wesley stressed was justification by faith through an instantaneous experience of regeneration. He also laid great emphasis on the doctrine of Christian perfection or perfect love. This was a belief in the possibility of absolute Christian perfection in motive in this life because the love of God so filled the heart of the believer that God's love would expel sin and promote absolute holiness of life. This progressive process was to be initiated by an act of faith. Wesley made it clear that this was not sinless nor infallible perfection but rather the possibility of sinlessness in motive in a heart that was completely suffused with the love of God. Mistakes in judgment might still result in bad moral consequences, but the possibility of achieving the ideal was there. This seems to be the teaching of his letters[5] and his book, *A Plain Account of Christian Perfection.*

Wesley insisted that the gospel should have an impact on society, and no one can deny the impact of the Methodist revival on English society. He opposed liquor, slavery, and war. There is some reason to believe that England might have had an uprising of the workers similar to that in France if they had not been won to Christ. Most of the later labor leaders got their training in speaking in the class meetings. The gin traffic was stopped, partially because of the influence of the revival. Wesley was an advocate of the abolition of slavery and a friend of the early abolitionists. His love of amateur doctering led him to establish the first free medical dispensary in England in 1746. He had an influence on Robert Raikes, the popularizer of the Sunday school movement, and on John Howard, the leader in prison reform. By the time of Wesley's death, a strong Methodist church was in existence in the United States. About seventy thousand followers in England were organized into a national church very soon after his death. This neat, almost dapper, little hardworking man had under God transformed the religious life of the workers of England. The Evangelical Revival within the Anglican church, a result of the Methodist revival, was to transform the upper class of England and to help England become the great leader of nations and the keeper of world peace during the nineteenth century. Whitefield was the prophet, John Wesley the organizer, and Charles the songster of the Methodist revival.

IV. ROMAN CATHOLICISM

The influential sixteenth- and seventeenth-century missionary thrust of the Roman Catholic church by the Jesuits, Dominicans, and Franciscans; the seventeenth-century Jansenist movement; and, in the same century, the mystical Quietist movement, as well as the expulsion of the Huguenots from France in 1685, have already been described.

During the period of royal absolutism from 1648 to 1789, monarchs sought to limit papal power in their countries. The Pragmatic Sanction of 1438 was an early French attempt along this line. Such a tendency in France was known as Gallicanism in opposition to Ultramontanism, the extension of the political power of the pope beyond the mountains over national hierarchies. The Gallican Articles of 1682, drafted by Bossuet, asserted that the king was not subject to the pope in temporal matters; that the pope was subject to general councils, his power being limited by the constitution of the French church and the kingdom; and that while they accepted his definitions of faith, he was not above correction. This French movement had its counterpart in the Holy Roman Empire in Josephism in the reign of Joseph II (1741–90), from whose name the term was derived. The term "Febronianism," the pen name of Nikolas von Hontheim (1701–99), was used in Germany for this same tendency to assert the royal power over church leaders while being obedient to the faith of the church. It represented the rising power of the rulers of new national states and the beginnings of a feeling of nationalism.

V. THE ORTHODOX CHURCH IN RUSSIA

The Russian church had in 1589 been granted the patriarchate for its archbishop. This made the Russian Orthodox church a national church with its head having an equal role with other patriarchs in the Eastern churches. The earlier Fall of Rome to the barbarians and Constantinople to the Muslims in 1453 led the Russians to think of Moscow as "the third Rome."

Shortly after 1650 the new patriarch Nikon sought to reform the church ritual by such practices as making the sign of the cross with three raised fingers instead of two as had been the former Russian practice. A group led by a cleric named Avvakum opposed this and other changes and were known as "Old Believers." When Avvakum was burned at the stake in 1682, his followers openly opposed the church and formed a new group, which still exists.

The church came more directly under the control of the state when Peter the Great in 1721 abolished the patriarchate and put the church under the control of the Holy Synod, which was led by a civil official responsible directly to Peter. Thus the church and the state were closely linked; and the church became a virtual department of the state until 1917, when church and state were separated by the Communists, and the church elected a new patriarch.

SUGGESTED READING

Baker, Frank. **From Wesley to Asbury.** Durham, N.C.: Duke University Press, 1976.

Barbour, Hugh, and Roberts, Arthur O. **Early Quaker Writings, 1650–1700.** Grand Rapids: Eerdmans, 1973.

Belden, Albert D. **George Whitefield the Awakener.** New York: Macmillan, 1953. This is an able presentation of the evangelistic and humanitarian work of Whitefield with documentation from the sources.

Bennett, Richard. **The Early Life of Howell Harris.** London: Banner of Truth, 1962.

Brailsford, Mabel R. **A Tale of Two Brothers.** New York: Oxford University Press, 1954. This is an account of John and Charles Wesley.

Braithwaite, William. **The Beginnings of Quakerism.** London: Macmillan, 1923.

_____. **The Second Period of Quakerism.** 2nd ed. Cambridge: Cambridge University Press, 1961. These two works provide a detailed, well-documented history of the Quakers.

Bready, J. Wesley. **England: Before and After Wesley.** New York: Harper, 1938. This also appeared in an American edition without footnotes under the title **This Freedom Whence.** Rev. ed. New York: American Tract Society, 1943.

Burtner, Robert W., and Chiles, Robert E., eds. **A Compend of Wesley's Theology.** Nashville: Abingdon, 1954. The theology of Wesley is described by well-chosen documents. The student should also consult Wesley's **Journals and Letters** to grasp his spirit.

Cameron, Richard M. **Methodism and Society in Historical Perspective.** New York: Abingdon, 1961. This work discusses the social impact of English and American Methodism.

_____. **The Rise of Methodism, A Source Book.** New York: Philosophical Library, 1954. This tells the story of Methodism through sources.

Cannon, William R. **The Theology of John Wesley.** New York: Abingdon-Cokesbury, 1946. This is a well-documented account of Wesley's theological views.

Clark, Elmer T. **An Album of Methodist History.** Nashville: Abingdon, 1952. The story of Methodism is presented in pictures and text.

Cragg, Gerald R. **The Church in the Age of Reason.** Harmondsworth, Middlesex: Penguin, 1960.

Dallimore, Arnold A. **George Whitefield.** London: Banner of Truth, 1970.

Davis, Arthur P. **Isaac Watts.** New York: Dryden, 1943.

Edwards, Maldwyn L. **After Wesley.** London: Epworth, 1935.

_____. **Methodism in England.** London: Epworth, 1943.

Fox, George. **George Fox's Journal.** Edited by Rufus M. Jones. New York: Putnam, 1963. This is invaluable to the student of Quakerism.

Gay, Peter. **Deism.** Princeton: Van Nostrand, 1968. This is a source collection of deist writings.

Gell, Frederick. **Charles Wesley the First Methodist.** New York: Abingdon, 1964. This is better than Wiseman's work.

Green, Vivian H. H. **John Wesley.** London: Nelson, 1964. The author used new sources in this critical biography.

_____. **The Young Mr. Wesley.** New York: Saint Martin's, 1961. This describes Wesley's life at Oxford from previously unpublished sources.

Harmon, Rebecca L. **Susanna.** Nashville: Abingdon, 1968. This recounts Wesley's mother's influence on his life.

Henry, Stuart C. **George Whitefield, Wayfaring Witness.** Nashville: Abingdon, 1957.

History of the Moravian Church. *Bethlehem, Pa.: Interprovincial Board of Christian Education, 1967.*

Lewis, A. J. **Zinzendorf, the Ecumenical Pioneer.** *Philadelphia: Westminster, 1962.*

Lunn, Arnold. **John Wesley.** *New York: Dial, 1929. This is an accurate and interesting account of Wesley's life and work, although the liberal bias is apparent.*

McGuard, Ina D. **Miss Hannah Ball, A Lady of High Wycombe.** *New York: Vantage, 1964.*

Moulton, Phillips P., ed. **The Journal and Major Writings of John Woolman.** *New York: Oxford University Press, 1971.*

Noble, Vernon. **The Man in Leather Breeches.** *London: Elek, 1953. This is a popular biography of George Fox.*

Orr, John. **English Deism.** *Grand Rapids: Eerdmans, 1934. The student will find this to be a helpful discussion of the development and expansion of English deism.*

Outler, Albert C. **John Wesley.** *New York: Oxford University Press, 1964. Wesley's main theological ideas are given.*

Rattenbury, J. Ernest. **Wesley's Legacy to the World.** *Nashville: Cokesbury, 1929.*

Ross, Isabel. **Margaret Fell, Mother of Quakerism.** *London: Longmans, 1949.*

Russell, Elbert. **The History of Quakerism.** *New York: Macmillan, 1943. This describes the world-wide expansion and contributions of the Quaker movement.*

Schmidt, Martin. **John Wesley.** *3 vols. Translated by Norman P. Goldhawk. New York: Abingdon, 1932. This work describes Wesley's spiritual development in detail.*

Semmel, Bernard. **The Methodist Revolution.** *New York: Basic, 1973.*

Spener, Philip J. **Pia Desideria.** *Translated by Theodore Tappert. Philadelphia: Fortress, 1964.*

Tuttle, Robert. **John Wesley: His Life and Theology.** *Grand Rapids: Zondervan, 1978.*

Tyerman, Luke. **The Life and Times of the Reverend John Wesley, M.A.** *3rd ed. 3 vols. New York: Harper & Brothers, 1876. This work is perhaps the best longer biography of Wesley's life.*

Vickers, John. **Thomas Coke, Apostle of Methodism.** *New York: Abingdon: 1969.*

Weinlick, John R. **Count Zinzendorf.** *New York: Abingdon, 1956. This is an interesting and scholarly account of Zinzendorf's life and work.*

Wiseman, Frederick D. **Charles Wesley Evangelist and Poet.** *New York: Abingdon, 1932.*

Wood, A. Skevington. **The Burning Light.** *Grand Rapids: Eerdmans, 1967. This is a sympathetic, yet well-balanced account of Wesley's life based on careful study of the sources.*

Chapter 34

Roman Catholic Victories
and Vicissitudes 1789–1914

The Roman Catholic church suffered the loss of her temporal possessions and much of her political influence between 1789 and 1914. The ignominious fate of the papacy during the French Revolution was in marked contrast to the advances made during the period of the Counter Reformation. During the Romantic reaction after the Napoleonic wars, she regained prestige and power until 1870. From then until World War I her story is one of loss of prestige and the rise of anticlericalism in many countries of Europe. These difficulties grew out of the problem of the relation of the national churches to the universal papal church.

I. REVOLUTION AND THE PAPACY,
1789–1815

Before the outbreak of the revolution in France, bad economic, political, social, and legal conditions; the successful example of the English Revolution of 1689; and the American Revolution of 1776 were fused by the development of an ideology that rationalized the right of popular revolution against Louis XVI. This ideology was the result of the teachings of the *philosophes*, among whom were Rousseau, Montesquieu, Diderot, and François M. Arouet or, as he is better known, Voltaire. While Rousseau and Montesquieu provided the political ideology for revolution, Voltaire criticized the Church of Rome and cried out for tolerance. It must be admitted that there were grounds for criticism of the Roman Catholic church in France. It owned much land, the revenues from which went for the most part to the upper clergy. Voltaire favored a religion of reason rather than the religion of the leaders of the Roman Catholic church in France. But these men wanted reform rather than revolution.

The National Assembly of France in November 1789 declared that church lands were public property, and it issued bonds that were redeemable in this land. Later these bonds were circulated as money. Early in 1790 monasteries were abolished by law. In the summer of 1790 the assembly passed the Civil Constitution of the Clergy[1] by which the number of bishops was reduced to eighty-three, a number corresponding to the number of provincial units. The bishops were to be elected by the voters who chose the civil officials, and the pope was merely to be notified of their choice. Clergymen were to be paid by the state and were to take an oath of loyalty to the state. The pope's power was reduced to that of stating the dogma of the Roman Catholic church. Churchmen did not object too strenuously to the loss of church lands, but they thought that this new act meant secularization of the church; and they were violently opposed to it. About four thousand clerics left France.

The Roman Catholic church and the French state were completely separated during the Reign of Terror of 1793 and 1794, when so many were executed for counterrevolutionary activities. At this time support of the church became voluntary. The more atheistic of the leaders even tried for a time in 1793 to force a religion of reason on France and they crowned a young actress the goddess of reason in Notre Dame Cathedral. Others, who would not accept this extreme, did accept the change in the calendar that made every tenth day rather than Sunday a day of rest. This calendar, adopted October 7, 1793, lasted until 1804. It was designed to eliminate Sundays and the numerous saints' days. Robespierre preferred the deist's religion of the Supreme Being. In this short period the Roman Catholic church faced tremendous opposition. Even the pope was captured and taken as a prisoner to France, where he died.

When Napoleon took control in 1799, he realized that the majority of Frenchmen were Roman Catholic in religion and he proposed a liaison between the Roman Catholic church and the state by the Concordat of 1801. In the concordat Napoleon recognized the Roman Catholic religion as "the religion of the great majority of French citizens," but he did not make it the established religion. Bishops were to be named by the state and consecrated by the pope. The clergy were to be paid by the state, but the property taken from the Roman Catholic church in 1790 was not to be returned to it. This concordat governed the relations between the church and state in France until 1905. But the Organic Articles of 1802 provided that papal bulls could not be published nor synods held in France without the consent of the government. The church was thus controlled by the state.

II. RESTORATION OF PAPAL POWER, 1815–70

Until 1870 the papacy was able to regain lost ground in Europe. Metternich, the chancellor of Austria, favored an alliance of the rulers of Europe with the Roman church to protect the *status quo* and to prevent national or democratic uprisings anywhere in Europe. Because of this reactionary viewpoint, he favored the papacy wherever possible. The Congress of Vienna, of which he was chairman, restored the papal states to the pope. Metternich wrote of the importance of religion as a bulwark of society in his "Confession of Faith" (1820).

The Romantic Movement also aided the papacy because it was a revolt from the rationalism of the eighteenth century. It emphasized an intuitional approach to life. Romanticists expressed themselves in poetry rather than prose; they emphasized content rather than form; they glorified the medieval past and nature; and they made their appeal to the heart of man rather than to his head. Wordsworth emphasized the presence of God in nature; Walter Scott and Hugh Walpole glorified the medieval past in their novels; Chateaubriand glorified the church in his literary works. Rousseau wrote that man was happiest in a state of nature. He expressed his belief in the fitness of the people to rule by his insistence on their right to choose their rulers through an expression of their general will, which was to be discovered by a majority vote. His *Social Contract* began with the words "Man was born free and is everywhere in chains." Painters also gave less attention to forms and rules in their work and they sought to express on canvas, not a copy of reality, but the impression that reality had made on them. Their paintings were an interpretation of nature rather than a portrait of it. Idealistic philosophy also emphasized the volitional and emotional side of man's nature. Kant built his arguments for God, the soul, and immortality on the sense of the right that man had within his nature. People also became interested in the past history of their various states. All these expressions of Romanticism, which held sway in Europe from about 1790 to 1850, strengthened the hold of religion on man. Particularly did the colorful, ritualistic, sensuous religion of the Roman Catholic church give rein to religious imagination and sentiment.

The Jesuits, who had been disbanded by Clement XIV in 1773, were reconstituted by a papal bull issued by Pius VII in 1814. They immediately began their work of educational missionary activities, although they interfered less with the political activities of states than they had earlier in their history.

The political disabilities that had kept Roman Catholics in Britain from voting and filling any public office were removed in 1829 by the Catholic Emancipation Act, the result of the work of Daniel O'Connell. The Anglican church was disestablished in Ireland in 1869 by Gladstone so that the people of Ireland no longer had to pay tithes to support the Anglican church as well as supporting their own Roman Catholic clergy by voluntary gifts. By the mid-nineteenth century similar disabilities had been removed in Prussia, France, and Austria.

The Oxford movement in the Anglican church also helped the Roman Catholic church both directly and indirectly. In 1845 Henry Edward Manning and John Henry Newman, leaders in the movement, joined the Roman Catholic church, and by 1862 about 625 important individuals— soldiers, professors, members of Parliament—and nearly 250 Anglican clergymen became Roman Catholics. Indirectly, the movement aided Rome by restoring in the High Church section of the Anglican church a view of the Communion not too far removed from transubstantiation, monasticism, ritualism in worship, and a sense of the importance of the church in man's life. Many made an easy transition from the High Church party of the Anglican church to the Roman Catholic church.

Pius IX (1792–1878), who occupied

the papal chair between 1846 and 1878, did not lose any opportunities to strengthen the Roman Catholic church. In 1854, in *Ineffabilis Deus*, after consultation with the bishops of the church, Pius proclaimed the doctrine of the Immaculate Conception of Mary, that is, that Mary was conceived without "any taint of original sin." All the faithful were henceforth to accept this doctrine as a part of the dogma of the Roman Catholic church that one must believe in order to be saved.[2]

Shortly after this event the pope began to take note of the nationalism and political liberalism of the day that seemed hostile to the Roman church and in 1864 he issued the *Syllabus of Errors*.[3] In this he condemned such new forms of philosophy as idealism, with its tendency toward pantheism, toleration in religion, separation of church and state, socialism, Bible societies, secular school systems, the view that the pope had no temporal power, civil marriage, and biblical criticism. He believed that such thinking was destructive to the best interests of the church of which he was pontiff. In 1863 in *Quanto Conficiamur*, appended to *Quanto Cura*, he upheld the idea of *Unam Sanctum*, that salvation is only in the Roman Catholic church.

The declaration of papal infallibility in the decree of the Vatican Council in 1870 marked the peak of the work of Pius. The declaration was approved in 1870 by 533 of those who were present. Two voted against it, and a minority of over one hundred had stayed away from the council that day. Evidently the heavy peals of thunder and the terrific flashes of lightning of the storm that raged outside were not reflected inside. The essence of the statement

accepted by the council was that when the pope speaks *ex cathedra*, that is, as the head of the church on the earth, concerning either faith or morals, whatever he says is infallible and must be accepted by the faithful as dogma to be believed if one is to enjoy salvation.[4] The doctrine made church councils unnecessary in the future because the pope was now the final authority concerning faith and morals. The Old Catholic Church emerged in 1871 under the leadership of Johann J. Von Döllinger (1799–1890).

III. RESISTANCE TO PAPAL POWER, 1871–1914

The declaration of papal infallibility and the loss of political power were not far separated in time. Almost immediately after the declaration in 1870 the papacy began to experience anticlerical hostility that brought losses in many countries. In 1870 the Italian armies took Rome when Louis Napoleon had to withdraw the French garrison protecting the papacy in order to meet the threat of the Franco-Prussian war, and the pope lost all his temporal possessions except the immediate area of the Vatican buildings. But the pope would not come to terms with the new national Italian constitutional monarchy despite the generous offer held out in the Law of the Papal Guarantees of 1871 by the Italian government. This law offered him an annual sum of $645,000 in perpetuity to compensate him for the loss of his temporal possessions; it allowed him to keep his possessions in the Vatican; and it provided for freedom of self-government in that area and no interference from the state. The pope refused to accept this settlement, issued an order forbidding

Roman Catholics to vote or hold office in the Italian government, and retired to a self-imposed imprisonment in the Vatican from which a later pope was only rescued by an agreement with Mussolini's government in 1929.

The Church of Rome also faced trouble in Germany with the Iron Chancellor, Bismarck. Bismarck thought that the internationalism of the Roman Catholic church stood in the way of full unification of the people of the new German Empire, which had been proclaimed in 1871 in the Hall of Mirrors in the Palace of Versailles. He thought that this "Black Internationale" was as much a threat to German national unity as the Red Internationale of socialism. In 1872 he expelled the Jesuits and in 1873 had the Falk or May Laws approved. These laws secularized education, put vital statistics under the control of the state, commanded civil marriage, and forced the clergy to be educated in state universities. Bismarck, who remembered Canossa where Henry IV had been humiliated in 1073, said he would not go to Canossa as Henry had done. However, he did have to give up his battle by the end of the decade and to repeal some of the disabilities placed on Roman Catholics, because he found that the Roman Catholic church was a valuable ally in the battle against socialism.

Anticlerical feeling was strongest in France in this period. In 1901 religious orders of nuns and monks were excluded by law from educational activities, but the severest blow came in 1905 with the passing of the Separation Law by the French Chamber of Deputies. The clergy were no longer to be paid by the state, and all church property was to be taken over by the state. Churchmen had to form themselves into associations in order to get permission to use the property for religious purposes. The state would no longer recognize any faith in a special manner. Thus the Roman church lost the privileged position that had been created by the Concordat of 1801. The pope denounced the new law, but his denunciation had no effect on the carrying out of the law.

Leo XIII (1810-1903), who was pope between 1878 and 1903, had been trained as a Jesuit and had wide administrative experience. He issued encyclicals opposing the power of the national states, especially in Germany under Bismarck. In *Immortale Dei* (1885) he asserted that both church and state were from God and each had God-given functions, but he denounced the state's failure to recognize God's authority through the church instead of trying to control the church and claim unqualified state sovereignty.

Leo also asserted the moral rights of the church in economics as well as politics by his issuance of *Rerum Novarum* in 1891. The state, he wrote, should recognize private property as a natural right and the legitimate existence of classes. Workers have a right to cooperate in unions, and the state should act to alleviate injustices against workers and to promote an adequate living wage. He criticized socialism and earlier had actively opposed it and Communism in his writings. In *Quadragesimo Anno*, (1931) Pius XI (1857-1939) restated and adapted to changed conditions the same principles, which were again reaffirmed and updated by John XXIII in *Mater et Magister*.

In theology, Leo in *Aeterni Patris*

(1879) urged the necessity of studying the theology of Aquinas in Roman Catholic schools and seminaries. He upheld biblical inerrancy in *Providentissimus Deus* (1893).

Pius X (1835–1914), pope from 1903 to 1914, continued the struggle against liberalism in all forms. Alfred Loisy (1857–1940), who was a teacher of biblical studies in France, wanted to move from biblical introduction and exegesis to historical studies in relation to the Bible. Special creation, messianic references, and the claim that Christ set up the Roman Catholic church directly were challenged. George Tyrrell (1861–1909) in England wanted to apply historical criticism to Scripture and thought that there was an evolution of theology in the Bible. They were both excommunicated, and in *Lamentabili Sane Exitu* (1907) and *Pascendi Dominici* (1907) the pope listed and condemned modernistic ideas. Because of this, liberalism was never the problem in Roman Catholicism that it became in Protestantism.

A new surge of devotion in the church was encouraged by the holding of eucharistic congresses, beginning with that in Lille in 1881; the new emphasis on the Virgin Mary at Lourdes after 1858; and Fatima in Portugal, with claims that Mary had appeared to people in those places. The veneration of the Sacred Heart of Jesus also encouraged this trend. The Benedictines encouraged stress on liturgy and put the liturgy for some of the sacraments into the vernacular.

Such were the fortunes of the Roman Catholic church between 1789 and 1914 in the major countries of Europe. Since 1914 the Church of Rome has found itself in increasing difficulties because of the expansion of Communism and the disorder that two world wars in the twentieth century have created.

SUGGESTED READING

Althoz, Josef L. The Churches in the Nineteenth Century. *Indianapolis: Bobbs-Merrill, 1967.*

Butler, C. The Vatican Council. *2 vols. New York: Longmans, 1930.*

Freemantle, Anne, ed. The Papal Encyclicals in Their Context. *New York: Putnam, 1956.*

_____, ed. The Social Teachings of the Church. *New York: New American Library of World Literature, 1963.*

Ratte, John. Three Modernists. *New York: Sheed & Ward, 1967.*

Readon, Bernard M. G. Roman Catholic Modernism. *Stanford: Stanford University Press, 1970.*

Vidler, Alec R. A Variety of Catholic Modernists. *Cambridge: Cambridge University Press, 1970.*

_____. The Church in an Age of Revolution. *Harmondsworth, Middlesex: Penguin, 1961.*

Chapter 35

Religion and Reform in Great Britain and Europe

English religious life during the nineteenth century was characterized by a practical manifestation of the forces of revivalism in the Anglican and nonconformist churches, by ritualism in the Anglican church, and by liberalism. The first produced a movement that fostered missionary activity and social reform; the second, a strong liturgical movement within the church; and the last, a liberal element in all the major denominations. The pattern in Scotland was the reunion of diverse groups that had left the Church of Scotland. In Ireland the injustice of supporting the established Anglican church by taxes and the Roman Catholic church by voluntary giving was eased by the disestablishment of the Anglican church in 1869. Similar developments occurred on the Continent.

I. RELIGIOUS LIFE IN ENGLAND

A. In the Anglican Church

1. *The Evangelicals.* The French Revolution made the ruling Tory party in England fearful of a similar revolution in Britain. From 1790 to 1820 the rising tide of reform was halted until religious and humanitarian liberal forces cooperated to force many reforms through Parliament between 1820 and 1852. The religious forces, generated by the Wesleyan and later evangelical revivals, produced such practical fruits of social reform and missionary zeal that Latourette, the great modern historian of missions, has called the nineteenth century "The Great Century" of missionary effort. Personal piety and devotion to Christ and the Bible were also stimulated.

The Arminian Wesleyan revival of the early eighteenth century had been most influential in bringing personal religion to the workers and farm people of England. Not until the end of the century, however, was the upper class in the established church affected by a more Calvinistic revival. Between 1790 and 1830 the influence of revival was felt in the Anglican church. The careless living of the Enlightenment gave way to personal piety, to faith in Christ, and to philanthropic and social activity.

The early evangelicals served as rectors in parishes scattered throughout England. One such was John Newton (1725–1807), the young infidel who sank so low that he became the slave of a slave trader. He was converted and, after a period of training, was ordained to the ministry. Becoming the minister in 1764 at Olney, he was soon recognized as a spiritual leader, and his help was sought by many even outside Olney. He wrote the hymns "Amazing Grace" and "How Sweet the Name of Jesus Sounds," and his influence inspired the shy, sensitive invalid William Cowper (1731–1800) to write great hymns also, including "There Is a Fountain Filled With Blood." Newton's successor, Thomas Scott (1747–1821), wrote a biblical commentary that was widely used by evangelicals.

The evangelical movement also had such scholarly leaders as Isaac Milner (1750–1820) and Charles Simeon (1759–1836), who made Cambridge University the center of the evangelical forces and who produced the Calvinistic theology that guided the group in its work and life.

The so-called Clapham Sect, made up of wealthy individuals who had their homes in Clapham, provided many of the lay leaders in social reform from 1792 to 1813 under the leadership of their godly rector, John Venn (1759–1833). This group of laymen often met in the great oval library of Henry Thornton (1760–1815), a wealthy banker who gave the greater part of his large income for philanthropy each year. Charles Grant, the chairman of the East India Company; William Wilberforce, who led in the fight for the emancipation of the slaves; James Stephen, whose son as head of the colonial office gave a large amount of aid to missionaries in the colonies; and other leading evangelicals lived in this fashionable suburb, which was just three miles from London.

Evangelical influence was also exerted on government through what was known as the Exeter Hall group. Exeter Hall in London was the building where most of the missionary societies held their annual meetings. These meetings so influenced evangelical public opinion that the government was often forced to act favorably on matters of interest to the missionaries. John Philip (1775–1851), who served as the capable superintendent of Congregationalist missions in South Africa from 1819 until his death, used Exeter Hall influence to win favorable legislation to protect the Hottentots of Cape Colony from exploitation. This influence was always exerted to prevent exploitation or oppression of natives by white settlers and traders.

The evangelicals were not so much interested in polity and doctrine as in the practical expression of Christianity in a redeemed life of piety that gained its inspiration from Bible study and prayer. William Wilberforce's widely read book *Practical View* (1797) expressed the evangelical interest in the Atonement as the only regenerating force, in justification by faith, in Bible reading under the illumination of the Holy Spirit, and in practical piety that would result in real service to society.

Followers of Adam Smith and the philosophical radicals, who looked to the writings of Jeremy Bentham and

John Stuart Mill for inspiration, promoted political reform because they believed in the dignity of rational human personality; but the evangelicals promoted social reform because they believed that man was a spiritual being who was either a potential or an actual son of God. Most of the social reforms between 1787 and 1850 were the outcome of evangelical effort for the poor.

William Wilberforce (1759–1833), who had led a dissipated life in the company of such distinguished persons as the younger Pitt, was converted in 1784 through Isaac Milner's efforts. He then dedicated his life to the abolition of slavery in the British Empire. In 1772 a court decision made the ownership of slaves impossible in England. In 1807 Parliament passed an act that banned Englishmen from participating in the slave trade. Evangelical public opinion, working through the English delegate to the Congress of Vienna in 1815, was able to bring about the outlawing of the slave trade by most European states. This was at great cost to the English taxpayer because Spain and Portugal gave their consent only when they were promised 700,000 pounds from the English treasury. Slavery was ended in British possessions by an act passed just before Wilberforce's death in 1833. The act provided nearly 100 million dollars to compensate the owners who freed 700,000 slaves. These achievements would have been impossible without the work of Wilberforce and his evangelical friends in Parliament.

Another evangelical of the second generation was Lord Shaftesbury (1801–85), who was the son of a socialite mother and a drunken politician. Having been led to Christ by his nurse, Shaftesbury dedicated himself to the service of the poor and oppressed at the age of fourteen. He always marshaled his facts carefully so that he would have an unshakable case when he asked the House of Commons for reform legislation. He refused high offices in order to carry on his work without compensation, although others on the same commission were paid by Parliament. In 1840 he secured the passage of a law that kept boys under sixteen from the arduous and dangerous work of the chimney sweep. In 1842 he succeeded in getting legislation passed that barred boys under ten and women from working in the mines. His work resulted in laws in 1845 that protected the insane in such asylums as Bedlam, where it had been the custom to charge a fee to admit the public to see the antics of the crazed. Crowded lodging houses, where disease and immorality abounded, became a thing of the past through his successful efforts in getting beneficial legislation.

Another evangelical, John H. Howard (1726–90), a nonconformist who had been influenced by the Wesleyan revival, devoted his life and fortune to prison reform. Before his death in 1790 from jail fever, which he caught while inspecting a vile prison, he traveled fifty thousand miles and spent thirty thousand pounds of his own money on prison reform. Through his efforts jailers were paid salaries and given budgets for food so that they no longer needed to extort money from the prisoners to keep the prison going. Prison sentences were emphasized as a corrective rather than as a punishment for crimes against society. Elizabeth Gurney Fry (1780–1845) continued this work.

The Sunday school movement, popularized by Robert Raikes in 1780, to give children religious training and elementary instruction in reading, writing, and simple arithmetic, was taken up by the evangelicals and introduced into the established church. The Religious Tract Society, founded in 1799, and the British and Foreign Bible Society, founded in 1804 with Lord Teignmouth of the Clapham Sect as its first president, were practical expressions of the interest of the evangelicals in the spread of the gospel through the printed page. The evangelicals were also the ardent supporters of the powerful missionary movement of the century.

2. *The Broad Church Movement.* If the evangelicals represented the spiritual force of revival, and if the Oxford movement represented the ritualistic segment, the Broad Church movement represented the social and the liberal or modernistic element in the Anglican church. The Broad Church movement began about 1830 and continued to attract followers during the century. These Latitudinarians, as they were often called, owed much to the Kantian idealism that Samuel Taylor Coleridge, poet and preacher, introduced into England at Oxford. They emphasized an intuitive consciousness of God and the immanence of Christ in man who was looked upon as a son of God. The Fall and the Atonement were either ignored or minimized.

One segment of the movement, led by Frederick D. Maurice (1805–72) and Charles Kingsley (1819–75), a clergyman and novelist, founded a Christian socialist group. They sought to bring the kingdom of God upon earth by social legislation that would give people economic and social as well as political democracy.

Another part of the group held ideas similar to those of Bishop John W. Colenso (1814–83) of Natal, Africa, who was led to question the Mosaic authorship of the Pentateuch when he could not satisfactorily answer the questions of a native in 1862. Deposed from office by the bishop of Capetown, Colenso was later reinstated by higher authorities. Thomas Arnold (1795–1842), the famous headmaster of Rugby, a private school for boys, and Henry Milman (1791–1868), the dean of Saint Paul's, were of the same group to which Colenso belonged—the group that adopted the theories of the German biblical critics. These two wings of the Broad Church movement thus fostered both liberalism in theology and a social gospel.

3. *The Oxford Movement.* The Oxford movement (1833–45), which was linked with Oxford University, emphasized the importance of the church and ritual in the religious life of the individual. In 1833 its leaders began to publish *Tracts for the Times*, in which they called attention to the importance of apostolic succession, baptismal regeneration, and the importance of ritual in the worship. Numerous Anglican churchmen accepted their ideas.

The movement was partly a protest against the domination of the church by the state. The grant of religious freedom to nonconformists and Roman Catholics by acts of Parliament in 1828 and 1829 and the grant of the franchise to the middle class in 1832 made many churchmen fear that the Anglican church might in time be disestablished by a Parliament dominated by dissenting forces. The Romantic movement, with its emphasis on the glories of the Gothic past and its love of beautiful ritual that would stimulate the aesthetic emotions in worship, contributed to the ritualism of the movement. People became interested in the history of rites and vestments and sought to restore more of the color of the past to the service. The group symbolizing these forces in the Anglican church has been known variously as the Oxford movement, the High Church movement, the Anglo-Catholic movement, the Puseyite movement—after one of the leaders, Edward Pusey—and the Tractarian movement because of the *Tracts for the Times*.

In 1827 John Keble (1792–1866) wrote a work called *The Christian Year*. This work, consisting of hymns in praise of the church and the value of Communion, made Keble the virtual author of the Oxford movement. His sermon on "National Apostasy"[1] on July 14, 1833, in Oxford, roused widespread interest in his ideas. Keble emphasized the real physical presence of Christ's body and blood in the Communion and maintained that the Communion was valid only when administered by ordained ministers in the apostolic succession.

John Henry Newman (1801–90) became the leader of the Tractarians after he issued the first of the *Tracts for the Times* in 1833. Newman, the son of a London banker, brought up under Calvinistic doctrine, went through a period of liberalism at Oxford before he joined the men of the Tractarian group. While he is perhaps better known for his hymn "Lead, Kindly Light," he was the real leader of the Oxford movement until he became a Roman Catholic in 1845. He wrote over twenty of the *Tracts*. The last of these, *Number Ninety*,[2] consisted of remarks on the Thirty-Nine Articles and the Prayer Book. In this tract Newman argued that these documents were not anti-Roman Catholic but simply condemned the abuses in that church. He believed that the Book of Common Prayer and the Thirty-Nine Articles showed the continuity of the Anglican church with the Roman Catholic church. His friend Henry Edward Manning and nearly 875 others, of whom nearly 250 were ministers or theological leaders at Oxford and Cambridge, followed him into the Roman Catholic church after 1845. Newman's greatest work was his *Apologia Pro Sua Vita* (1864), an autobiographical account of his life and work. Late in his life he was made a cardinal of the Roman Catholic church. He based his thought on the church fathers and accepted apostolic succession; a real, corporeal presence of Christ in the Mass; and baptismal regeneration.

After Newman's defection to Rome, Edward Pusey (1800–82), who was a professor of Hebrew in Oxford, became the leader of the movement until his death. The Oxford men were interested in upholding the spiritual nature of the church and its freedom from control by the state. They wanted to develop a middle position between an infallible ecclesiastical body and rampant individualism in the church. They emphasized both the real presence of Christ in the elements of the sacrament and baptismal regeneration. They came very close to the Roman Catholic exaltation of the sacraments as important factors in justification.

By advocating the use of crosses and

lights, the men of this movement brought a renewed stress on the importance of colorful ritual in the liturgy of the church. Gothic architecture, too, was favored as an aid to worship. The ascetic tendency created by the group found expression in the founding of monasteries and convents for men and women who wanted to pursue an ascetic life of worship and service. The Cowley Fathers was one such organization for men.

The movement also deepened the gulf between the Anglican church and the nonconformist churches by its emphasis on the sacramental nature of the Mass and apostolic succession. It also created within the Anglican church a new party that was at odds with the evangelicals. But it should be given credit for the service that its exponents rendered to the poor and the unchurched. To many it offered an appealing compromise between Roman Catholicism and the strong evangelical position, and it reminded Anglicans of their universal Christian heritage.

B. Among the Nonconformists

While these three movements were agitating or rejuvenating the established church, new developments were taking place among the free churches. The Salvation Army was begun by William Booth (1829–1912), a Methodist minister, to reach the down-and-outs by open-air evangelism and social work, which Booth had started in 1865. The name Salvation Army was applied to the organization, and in 1878 Booth organized it along military lines with a hierarchical organization and uniforms. It is now world-wide.

John N. Darby (1800–82), a lawyer who became a curate in the Church of Ireland, organized the groups known as the Brethren about 1831 in Dublin. The Brethren emphasized the priesthood of believers and the direct guidance of the Holy Spirit to such an extent that they did not accept an ordained ministry. They were, and still are, earnest students of the Bible and continue to manifest a practical piety in their lives. George Müller (1805–98), the founder of a large orphanage in Bristol, and Samuel Tregelles (1813–75), a great student of lower criticism—the study of the text of the New Testament—were both members of this group. The name Plymouth Brethren is often given to the group because Plymouth was the early chief center of the movement. Another member, Thomas J. Barnardo (1845–1903), from 1870 on founded many homes for orphan boys.

Edward Irving (1792–1834), a Scottish Presbyterian minister, believed that the church should enjoy the gifts of the Holy Spirit that it had had in the apostolic era. His followers emphasized "speaking in tongues" and the imminent return of Christ. Many joined the Catholic Apostolic Church organized in 1842.

In 1844 George Williams (1821–1905) founded the Young Men's Christian Association to meet the need of young men in the city for exercise, social life, and lodging in a Christian environment. The organization appeared in the United States in 1851. Its sister organization, the Young Women's Christian Association, was founded in 1855 to provide similar services for young women in the cities.

Charles H. Spurgeon (1834–92) became England's foremost mid-nine-

Charles Haddon Spurgeon, well known as a Calvinist, a Baptist pastor, and an eloquent preacher.

By 1859 another revival movement, which was related to the lay prayer revival of 1857 and 1858 in the United States, swept over England, reviving the churches and promoting social reforms.

The Welsh revival of 1904 and 1905, which began with the ministry of Evan Roberts in the mining town of Loughor, became the spearhead of a world-wide awakening. Both the revivals of 1857 and 1859 and that of 1904 to 1907 have been described and their social impact ably recorded in the many books of J. Edwin Orr. The 1907 revival in Korea was another major awakening related to that in Wales.

II. ENGLISH PROTESTANT MISSIONARY EFFORT

Protestant churches did not do much missionary work during the era of the Reformation because all their energies were absorbed in the work of organization and the struggle to exist. During the Counter Reformation the great missionary work was done by the Jesuits and other orders in the Roman Catholic church. But a combination of forces, beginning with the work of William Carey in 1792, led to such great missionary effort in the nineteenth century that this has been called the "Great Century" in Protestant missionary effort. The emphasis of the twentieth century has been on ecumenism or church reunion.

This missionary enthusiasm was the result of revivalism among the Pietists and Methodists and among the Evangelicals of the Anglican church. People wanted to convert others to the same joyous religious experience that they had had. The gaining of empires by such Protestant

teenth-century preacher. Increasing crowds brought moves to larger churches until by 1861 he moved into his Metropolitan Tabernacle, which had 4,700 seats and cost 31,000 pounds. Nearly fifteen thousand people were added to his church by 1891. He opened the Pastor's College, which trained about nine hundred preachers by the time he died.

The Keswick victorious life meetings each summer first began under the leadership of Canon T. D. Harford-Battersby in 1875. These meetings appealed to Christians in all denominations. Preaching emphasized the experience of instantaneous and progressive sanctification that would enable one to defeat sin and live victoriously. The Keswick type of meetings spread to centers in the United States and Canada.

nations as Holland and England acquainted Europeans with the spiritual need of people in other lands. Such missionary explorers as Livingstone, Grenfell, and Rebmann and Krapf, revealed the extent and needs of Africa to the world. The Reformation concept of the importance of the individual's relation to God provided a final motivating force for such work. Individuals rather than whole states were won.

India was opened to missionary work after 1813, when the East India Company was forced to admit missionaries. China was forced to accept missionaries by the 1858 Treaty of Tientsin, which ended the second Opium War. It is paradoxical that the war to force China to admit opium into her land should have resulted in opening China to missions.

Numerous missionary societies were organized after 1792. The Baptist Missionary Society was founded at Kettering, England, with an initial fund of a little over thirteen pounds, as a result of the vision of William Carey (1761–1834), the cobbler who taught himself several languages. Carey went to India, where he managed an indigo factory to earn a living until he moved to Danish Serampore in 1800, but he made missionary work and Bible translation his first interest. George Grenfell (1848–1906) was the Baptist society's greatest missionary explorer. He, rather than Stanley, should be given the credit for mapping the Congo River and its tributaries between 1884 and 1886.

A letter from Carey resulted in the founding of the London Missionary Society of the Congregationalists in 1795. John Philip, David Livingstone, Robert Moffat, and John Mackenzie, the man who persuaded the British government to annex Bechuanaland to protect the natives from exploitation by the Boer colonists, were among its greatest missionary statesmen.

The Scottish Missionary Society and the Glasgow Missionary Society were founded by Scottish Presbyterians in 1796 and 1797 respectively, and the Church Missionary Society was founded by the evangelicals in 1799. The latter's greatest missionaries were Pilkington (1865–97), the missionary translator of Uganda, and George Alfred Tucker (1849–1914), the missionary bishop who was largely responsible for bringing Uganda under the British crown and for instituting the progressive policies that made that country for a time one of the finest in Africa. The Methodists founded the Wesleyan Missionary Society in 1817. J. Hudson Taylor (1832–1905) founded the China Inland Mission as a faith mission in 1865, and by 1890 it embraced 40 percent of the missionaries in China. Other societies were founded in Europe in rapid succession, and missionaries were sent out to all parts of the world.

William Carey, whose motto was "Expect great things from God; attempt great things for God," went to India where he became a leader in the translation of the Bible into the tongue of the people. After India was opened to missionaries in 1813, such men as Henry Martyn (1781–1812), who was inspired to missionary effort by reading David Brainerd's Autobiography, began missionary work. American missionary effort was joined to British effort after the first American missionary society was founded in 1810. Many single women became missionaries in this era.

The London Missionary Society followed the Moravians into South Africa and did excellent work among the natives, though not without considerable friction with the Boer settlers. John Philip protected the rights of the natives by persuading the British government to grant them civil liberties. Robert Moffat (1795–1883) translated the Scriptures into the language of important tribes of South Africa. David Livingstone expanded geographical knowledge of central Africa from 1841 to 1873 and fought the Arab slave trade, which was destroying potential village preaching centers. His purpose in both was to promote missionary effort. The Scottish Presbyterians took up Livingstone's challenge to work in the region of the great lakes of central Africa. The evangelical Church Missionary Society provided the missionaries who started work in Uganda and became martyrs there.

Robert Morrison (1782–1834) studied the Chinese Mandarin language and provided a Chinese dictionary and a Chinese translation of the Bible that could be used as soon as missionaries were granted access to China after 1858. Adoniram Judson (1788–1850) made a dictionary of Burmese and translated the Bible into that tongue.

The results of missionary work have been tremendous, not only in the salvation of natives but also in many cultural accomplishments. Missionary explorers were often the first to inform the world of geographic conditions. Many names of missionaries are on the roster of the Royal Geographical Society of Britain because of their work as explorers. Others, such as Alexander Mackay and James Stewart, built the first roads in Uganda and Nyassa-land respectively. Missionaries have opened academic and industrial training schools such as Lovedale in South Africa, introduced new crops, and stimulated trade so that the natives could raise their own standard of living. Others have been empire builders because they thought that the British government would better protect the interests of the natives than the colonists who wanted the land. Such men as Moffat, Morrison, Pilkington, and Carey were used of God to give the natives of their adopted lands the Scriptures in their own tongue. The missionary movement was in some respects the ancestor of the modern ecumenical movement because, as natives could not understand the divisions among Christians, missionaries of many denominations began to work together. Christianity became a global religion.

This advance has not been without struggle. Nationalism in the Far East and the unfortunate linking of the missionaries with Western imperialism have created problems in China and other countries. Communism and Catholicism have often opposed Protestant missionary effort. Liberalism among many of the missionaries has become an increasing problem in our own time. In spite of these handicaps, however, any unbiased historian will admit the great contribution that the church has been able to make to the world through its missionary effort.

III. DIVISION AND REUNION OF THE SCOTTISH CHURCHES

After the Scottish church had rid itself of control by Rome by 1567, it faced the further problem of how to maintain the presbyterian system of polity and the Calvinistic theology that it had adopted. For more than a century the Scots opposed the attempts of the Stuart kings and bishops Laud and others to force the episcopal system of government on them. Not until James II fled from England and William and Mary took the English throne was the Presbyterian church securely established in 1690 as the national Church of Scotland.

From 1690 until 1847 the Scottish church was plagued with divisions over the question of lay patronage. Lay patronage meant that the crown or landlords could dictate the choice of a minister for a congregation. Patronage was made official by act of the English Parliament in 1712. Many divisions occurred as the Scots fought for the freedom of their church. Ebenezer Erskine (1680–1754) was deposed by the General Assembly of the Church of Scotland because he upheld the right of a congregation to choose its own minister. In 1733 he and others founded the Associate Presbytery, which in 1740 became the Secession Church. This church split again in 1747 into two groups, but by 1820 most of the two groups merged as the United Secession Church.

The problem of lay patronage also resulted in the founding of the Relief Church by Thomas Gillespie (1708–74) in 1761. The Relief Church and the United Secession Church united to form the United Presbyterian Church in 1847 because of the similarity of their stand against lay patronage.

A more important schism occurred when Thomas Chalmers (1780–1847), a great mathematician, preacher, and theologian, led a group in the founding of the Free Church in 1843 over the issues of the right of a congregation to choose its own minister and of the growing spirit of revival stimulated by the evangelical revival in Scotland. An earlier revival led by Robert (1764–1842) and James (1768–1851) Haldane preceded that led by Chalmers. Over a third, 474, of the ministers of the state church withdrew. The Free Church became an aggressive evangelistic and missionary body. By 1868 it had eight hundred churches and nearly one thousand clerics. It united with the United Presbyterian Church in 1900 to form the United Free Church. A small minority, sometimes known as the Wee Frees, refused to unite and continued to exist as the Free Church of Scotland. The United Free Church combined with the Church of Scotland in 1929 to form the Kirk of Scotland because the right of lay patronage, the main cause of division, had long since disappeared with the abolition of patronage by act of Parliament in 1874. Today the Church of Scotland is the major church of Scotland.

Liberalism was also a problem in the Scottish churches. Professor William Robertson Smith, who was deposed from his chair in the Free Church college in Aberdeen in 1881, was largely responsible for the spread of German critical ideas in Scotland and for the rise of liberalism.

IV. THE CHURCH IN IRELAND

Racial antagonism and the natural hatred of the conquered for the conqueror were intensified at the time of the Reformation because the English accepted Protestantism while the Irish remained Roman Catholic. When he became king of England, James I deepened the division by settling

Northern Ireland with Scottish settlers.

From a religious viewpoint, there were two major events in Ireland between 1689 and 1914. The first was the migration of about 200,000 Scotch-Irish of Northern Ireland to America from 1710 to 1760. There they became the backbone of American Presbyterianism. The later potato blight in the 1840s caused over a million people, mostly Roman Catholics, to migrate to the United States.

The second major event was the disestablishment of the Anglican church in 1869. Until that time Irishmen had to pay church taxes for the support of the Anglican church and to give voluntarily to the support of the Roman Catholic clergy, whom they accepted as their real ministers. They had been given civil rights earlier in 1829 by the Catholic Emancipation Act, which opened up all positions in local and national government to Roman Catholics except for the throne, the lord-lieutenancy of Ireland, and the positions of chancellor and the archbishop of Canterbury. Although these changes helped to relieve bitterness, religious hostility between the English and the Irish has persisted into the twentieth century. The Ulster revival of 1859 did bring spiritual renewal to Northern Ireland.

V. THE CHURCH ON THE CONTINENT

The Inner Mission in Germany and the Réveil in French-speaking western Europe occurred between 1825 and 1860, the Continental counterparts of awakenings in England and North America. Robert Haldane carried revival flame to Switzerland early in the century. Leaders such as Alexandre Vinet (1797–1847), César Malan (1787–1864), Francis R. Gaussen (1790–1863), and the church historian Merle D'Aubigne helped the Swiss development of the Réveil. Frederick and Adolphe Monod were the leaders in France.

The German Inner Mission awakening grew out of the work of Johann H. Wichern (1808–81). The Inner Mission began in 1848 to promote practical social outcomes of revival as well as evangelistic work. Wichern built "rough houses," beginning in Hamburg in 1833, as homes for orphan boys, homes for the aged, lodging houses, city missions, and institutions to work with prisoners and seamen. Theodore Fliedner (1800–64) organized deaconess houses for Protestant women to work in the social efforts of the church in the 1830s at Kaiserwerth. Groen Van Prinster led in a similar renewal in the Netherlands. Abraham Kuyper's (1837–1920) spiritual development led to his extensive theological writings and to the founding of the Free University of Amsterdam. Nicolai F. S. Grundtvig (1783–1872) in Denmark stressed pietistic awakening and channeled his efforts into the development of cooperatives and "folk schools." George Scott in Sweden and Gisle Johnson in Norway carried on the earlier awakening linked with Hans N. Hauge's (1771–1824) work in Sweden. The Continental movements seemed to be more socially oriented than those in the United States and the British Isles.

A remarkable spiritual awakening took place in Korea among the Presbyterians in 1907. The Presbyterian missionary John L. Nevius visited Korea and urged his idea of a self-supporting, self-governing, and self-propagating church on the missionaries who should make evangelistic tours with national workers, whom they would disciple. The resulting revival won thousands, beginning in 1907. In the 1970s there was another resurgence of the Christian faith, and today Korea is about 20 percent Christian.

Suggested Reading

Bacon, Ernest W. **Spurgeon, Heir of the Puritans.** *London: Allen & Unwin, 1967.*

Balleine, G. R. **A History of the Evangelical Party.** *London: Longmans, 1911. This is an excellent account of the evangelical revival and its results in the Church of England.*

Battiscomb, Georgina. **Shaftesbury.** *Boston: Houghton Mifflin, 1975. This is a well-balanced, documented biography.*

Best, Geoffrey, ed. **The Oxford Movement.** *Chicago: University of Chicago Press, 1970.*

Bready, J. Wesley. **Lord Shaftesbury and Social Industrial Progress.** *London: Allen & Unwin, 1926. This is a well-developed evaluation of Shaftesbury's life and work.*

Brown, Ford K. **Fathers of the Victorians.** *Cambridge: Cambridge University Press, 1961. The reforms of Wilberforce and his friends are discussed.*

Burleigh, J. H. S. **A Church History of Scotland.** *Oxford: Oxford University Press, 1960.*

Cairns, Earle E. **Saints and Society.** *Chicago: Moody, 1960. This describes the setting, ideals, and reforms of the evangelicals in England.*

Campbell, Reginald J. **Livingstone.** *New York: Dodd, 1930.*

Coad, F. Roy. **A History of the Brethren Movement.** *Grand Rapids: Eerdmans, 1968. This is an excellent account of the rise and development of the Plymouth Brethren movement.*

Coupland, Reginald. **Wilberforce: A Narrative.** *Oxford: Clarendon University Press, 1923. This is an excellent account of that evangelical's attempts to end slavery.*

Ervine, St. John. **God's Soldier: General William Booth.** *2 vols. New York: Macmillan, 1935.*

Fairweather, Eugene R., ed. **The Oxford Movement.** *New York: Oxford University Press, 1964. This is a collection of edited documents.*

Hinchcliff, Peter B. **John William Colenso.** *London: Nelson, 1964.*

Hodder, E. **Life and Times of the Seventh Earl of Shaftesbury.** *3 vols. London: Hodder & Stoughton, 1886.*

Hopkins, Charles H. **History of the YMCA in North America.** *New York: Association, 1951.*

Howse, Ernest. **Saints in Politics.** *Toronto: Toronto University Press, 1952. The author has given an authoritative and useful account of the private life and social activity of the upper-class evangelicals of the Clapham Sect.*

Ironside, Harry A. **A Historical Sketch of the Brethren Movement.** *Grand Rapids: Zondervan, 1942. This traces the development of the Brethren movement.*

Jeal, Tim. **Livingstone.** *New York: Putnam, 1973. This is an objective biography based on new data.*

Meacham, Standish. **Henry Thornton of Clapham, 1760–1815.** *Cambridge: Harvard University Press, 1964.*

Neill, Stephen S. **Colonialism in Christian Missions.** *New York: McGraw-Hill, 1966.*

Newman, John H. **Apologia Pro Sua Vita.** *London: Longmans, 1873. One who wishes to understand Newman's work as a leader of the Oxford movement can gain much from reading this autobiographical account of his life.*

Orr, J. Edwin. **The Flaming Tongue.** *Chicago: Moody, 1973. This deals with the revivals of 1901–10.*

_____. The Second Evangelical Awakening in Britain. *London: Marshall, Morgan & Scott, 1949.*

Scharpff, Paulus. History of Evangelism. *Translated by Helga B. Henry. Grand Rapids: Eerdmans, 1966.*

Searer, George. David Livingstone: His Life and Letters. *New York: Harper, 1957.*

Steer, Roger. George Muller. *Wheaton, Ill.: Shaw, 1975.*

Ward, Wilfred P. The Life of John Henry Cardinal Newman. *New York: Longmans, 1912.*

Wood, Arthur S. The Inextinguishable Blaze. *Grand Rapids: Eerdmans, 1960. This presents the events and impact of eighteenth-century revival.*

Chapter 36

Foes of the Faith

During the nineteenth century several influential movements appeared that threatened the faith that the church has endeavored to maintain throughout the ages. Biblical criticism grew out of the individualistic and humanistic climate that was produced by the Renaissance. This development was reinforced both by the rationalism and individualism of the eighteenth century and by the historical outlook of the Romantic Movement and German idealistic philosophy. The preoccupation with material goods, engendered and promoted by the higher standard of living made possible by the industrial revolution, also helped to turn the minds of all classes of people from the absolute authority of the Bible as a standard for faith and life. The biological dogma of evolution, when applied to the Bible by analogy, made Christianity nothing more than the product of a system of religious evolution. The denial of the authority of the Bible was a logical outcome of this point of view.

I. CRITICISM

People have usually followed one of three approaches to the Bible. Pietists have approached it from an experiential viewpoint in which the application of truth to daily life is the criterion. Others have approached it as a source book of doctrine. Still others have adopted a historical approach, which results in the conception of the Bible as an ethical guidebook only. This latter approach became the fashion in the nineteenth century because of the influence of German idealistic philosophy. When the historico-critical approach was combined with the application of the theory of evolution to religious phenomena, the background for a system of biblical criticism was completed.

Discussion between one who accepts the critical approach to the Bible and one who is a believer in the inspiration and the integrity of the Bible is difficult because each has a different set of basic ideas. The radical critic of the Bible assumes that the Bible is merely a work to be judged by the canons of literary criticism just as any other literary work would be; that there is an evolution of religion; and that natural explanations of biblical phenomena should replace supernatural explanations. Such individuals look on the Bible as a book written by human authors. They ignore the function of the Holy Spirit in the inspiration of the writers of Scripture.

A. The Philosophic and Theological Background of Biblical Criticism

The idealistic philosophy of Immanuel Kant (1724–1804), when combined with the views of Schleiermacher, Hegel, and Ritschl, created a philosophic background favorable to a critical approach to the Bible. Kant accepted Locke's emphasis on sensation and Descartes's stress on reason as the keys to knowledge concerning the phenomena of nature; but he argued in his *Critique of Pure Reason* (1781) that man cannot know God or the soul, both of which he classed as data of the world of "noumena," by the senses or reason. His pietistic background led him to the assertion that the sense of moral obligation or conscience in man, which he called the "categorical imperative," should be the starting point for religion. Because man has a moral sense, Kant argued in his *Critique of Practical Reason* (1781), there is a God who has provided that sense. The postulates of the soul and immortal life become essential, if those who obey the dictates of conscience are to be rewarded, because often the good receive no temporal reward in this life.

Because Kant denied that man can know the world of noumena, there is no place in his system for a historical and objective revelation of God in the Bible. To him it is only a man-made book of history, to be subjected to historical criticism just as any other book. There is no place for Christ, the God-man, in Kant's system. Man with his free will and his immanent sense of what is right becomes the creator of a religion in which he develops the morality inherent in himself. There is a logical line of continuity between Kantian idealism and modern liberalism with its insistence on the "spark of the divine" within each of us, which liberals insist we need only to cultivate to achieve good moral conduct and eventual immortality. In this fashion Kant helped to provide a philosophical framework for both biblical criticism and modern liberal theology.

Unlike Kant, who found the starting point for religion in man's moral nature, Friedrich D. E. Schleiermacher (1768–1834) made feelings or the emotions the element out of which religious experience develops. Schleiermacher was trained in Moravian schools and owed the subjective nature of his philosophy to them and to Romanticism. In his book *The Christian Faith* (ca. 1821) religion is presented, not as a set of beliefs and obligations based on the authority of the church, but as the result of man's feelings of absolute dependence in a majestic universe in which he is but a small entity. Christianity best brings man into harmony with God as man passively realizes his dependence on God. Religion thus becomes a mere subjective apprehension of Christ, who serves as the Mediator to reconcile man to the Absolute who is immanent in the universe. Thus man is freed from dependence on a historical revelation of the will of God and needs only to cultivate the feeling of dependence on God in Christ to enjoy a satisfactory religious experience. Because of his view that the essence of religion is subjectivity, Schleiermacher is often referred to as the "Father of Modern Theology."

George W. F. Hegel (1770–1831) also had a marked influence on both theology and the critical approach to the Bible. God was the Absolute who was seeking to manifest Himself in history by a logical process of reconciliation of contradictions, which Hegel called thesis and antithesis. The synthesis or reconciliation created a new pair of contradictions that were again merged in a new reconciliation or synthesis. Hegel thus held to philosophical evolution as the way in which the Absolute was manifested. His dialectic or logic was taken over by Marx, and his emphasis on the state as a manifestation of the Absolute was borrowed by Hitler and Mussolini in order to glorify both the state and the dictator who headed it.

Albrecht Ritschl (1822–89) was influenced by Schleiermacher's acceptance of religious feeling as the foundation for religion, but he insisted that religion was the social consciousness of dependence. The historical Christ of the Gospels brought the practical revelation of sin and salvation to the individual in the kingdom by faith. The Bible is simply the record of community consciousness, and it should therefore be subjected to historical investigation in the same manner as any other book. Thus Ritschl, as well as the other philosophers, made religion subjective and opened the way for extreme critical study of the Bible. He also promoted the social approach of love to religious problems.

B. Biblical Criticism

Rationalism of the Enlightenment and idealistic philosophy of the Romantic era were thus the parents of a criticism that tries to destroy the supernatural nature of the Bible as a revelation and that makes the Bible the record of the subjective evolution of religion in human consciousness. Opposition to such destructive criticism should not lead the reverent student of the Bible to reject all biblical criticism. Higher, or historical and literary, criticism, or as it is also sometimes known, introduction, which has come to be associated with the above destructive views, is simply the careful study of the historical background of each book of the Bible; and lower, or textual, criticism is the study of the text of the Bible in an attempt to ascertain whether the text that we have is the one that came from the hands of the writers. Lower criticism has resulted in the granting to the text of the Bible a high degree of accuracy so that we can be sure that we have the writings of the original authors of the Bible. Thus no doctrine or ethical teaching of Scripture can be called into question by the most radical critic. It has been radical higher criticism, rather than lower criticism, that has destroyed the faith of many persons in the divine revelation in the Bible.

The popularization of higher criticism has been associated with an eighteenth-century French doctor by the name of Jean Astruc (1684–1766), who in 1753 divided the Book of Genesis into two parts. He assumed the use of two documents as sources because he found the name *Elohim* (God) used in some places and *Jehovah* (Lord) in others. Johann G. Eichhorn (1752–1827), who laid down the dictum that the Bible was to be read as a human book and tested by human means, gave such studies the name of higher criticism. Eichhorn noticed other literary characteristics, besides the use of the names for God, that led him to believe that not only Genesis but also the entire Hexateuch (Genesis to Joshua) was made up of composite documents. Hupfeld in 1853 was the first to claim that the Pentateuch was the work of at least two different authors rather than a narrative composed from many sources by Moses. Graf and Wellhausen developed a well-elaborated theory, known as the Graf-Wellhausen theory, that has been adopted by the higher critics. According to this theory, the sections in which the name Jehovah is used constitute the earliest document; another part by another author is known as E; still another in Deuteronomy as D; and P. In this fashion the unity of the Pentateuch and its Mosaic authorship are denied.

Later critics divided Isaiah into at least two parts and advanced the date of Daniel to the Maccabean period so that it became history rather than prophecy and history. The development of doctrine in the Bible was explained along evolutionary lines. Critics emphasized the development of the idea of God from the primitive storm god of Mount Sinai to the ethical monotheistic God of the prophets. The work of biblical archaeologists has forced many critics to abandon their former radical positions and has tended to confirm conservative views of the Bible.

The beginning of higher criticism of the New Testament is usually associated with the name of Hermann S. Reimarus (1694–1778), who taught Oriental languages at Hamburg. In his *Fragments* (1778) he denied the possibility of biblical miracles and advanced the idea that the writers of the New Testament with their stories of miracles were pious frauds. Gotthold Lessing (1729–81), who published Reimarus's *Fragments*, argued that the Scriptures served man as a guide during the primitive phase of his religious development but that reason and duty were sufficient guides in the more advanced state of religion.

Ferdinand C. Baur (1792–1860) argued in 1831 that in the early church there had been a Judaism that emphasized the law and the Messiah. This earlier approach can be observed in the writings of Peter. Paul developed an antithesis in such books as Romans and Galatians, in which the emphasis was on grace rather than on law. The Old Catholic church of the second century represented a synthesis of Petrine and Pauline views. This synthesis is revealed in such books as the Gospel of Luke and the Pastoral Epistles. Baur then proceeded to date the books of the New Testament in this framework as either early or late according to the manner in which they reflected Petrine, Pauline, or Johannine tendencies. Thus historical data gave way to subjective philosophical presupposition in ascertaining the chronology of the books of the New Testament.

In the twentieth century New Testament criticism has successively focused on three different but interdependent approaches to the Gospels. Source criticism was concerned with the order of writing of the synoptic Gospels (Matthew, Mark, and Luke) and the extent to which one was dependent on another or on even earlier sources. In the 1920s and 1930s form criticism arose to investigate evidences in the Gospels for the forms in which the gospel was orally passed on in the earliest years before written Gospels. This approach claimed that the Gospels contain truth about Christ that can be found only after one peels off the layers of tradition and form in which the truth is hidden. Most recently redaction criticism has taken center stage. It proposes to analyze the manner and significance of the subtle changes the Gospel writers allegedly introduced into their accounts of Christ's life and work.

Some theologians, who adopt critical views of the New Testament, consider that the essence of the gospel is in the ethical teachings of Jesus and that Paul changed the simple ethical religion of Jesus into a redemptive religion. Destructive higher criticism has led many to deny the inspiration of the Bible as a revelation from God through men inspired by the Holy Spirit and to minimize or to deny the deity of Christ and His saving work on the cross of Calvary. *The Life of Jesus* (1835–36) by David F. Strauss (1808–74) combined all these views. Strauss denied both the miracles and the integrity of the New Testament as well as the deity of Christ, whom he saw as a man who thought He was the Messiah.

Germany, once the home of the Reformation, became the land in which criticism developed. The history of Hitler's Germany well illustrates the lengths to which men will go when they deny God's revelation in the Bible and when they replace revelation with reason and science as the authority for thought and action.

II. MATERIALISM

Another movement or viewpoint that threatened the faith during the nineteenth century, and that still threatens it today, was materialism. More subtle perhaps than higher criticism, materialism may be defined as the practice in modern society of emphasizing the material values of a high standard of living. To the extent that man's attention is concentrated on this life, he will neglect the spiritual values of eternal life. The abundance of goods, which has made a high living standard possible, is an outcome of the industrial revolution that occurred first in England between 1760 and 1830. Machine power was substituted for hand power so that great amounts of goods could be produced cheaply. Nowhere has this emphasis on a high material standard of living been as great as in America. Both Walter Rauschenbusch, the founder of the social gospel in America, and Karl Marx emphasized in their systems what they thought was the primary importance of material goods in life. Those who lay such stress on the distribution of material goods forget that "man does not live by bread alone."

III. CREATIONISM VS. EVOLUTION

If philosophical, literary, and historical criticism of the Bible destroyed faith in it as a revelation from God, and if the materialism induced by the industrial revolution created indifference to a future life, the views of Charles R. Darwin (1809–82) and his successors created the idea that there was no such thing as sin or that sin was merely the remnant of animal instinct in man. Evolution as a philosophical doctrine goes back to the time of Aristotle, but Darwin was the first to put it on what seemed to be a scientific basis.

Darwin spent some time in studying medicine and theology before he developed his inclinations to become a naturalist. A voyage around the world on the *Beagle* between 1831 and 1836 convinced him that differences between living animals and fossils on the mainlands and those on the islands that he visited could be accounted for only by biological evolution. He published his book *Origin of the Species* in 1859 after finding that Alfred Wallace had independently arrived at similar conclusions. In his book Darwin argued that the struggle for existence kept the population of the various species constant in spite of the fact that reproduction is geometric and that many more are produced than are essential for the survival of the species. In this struggle some individuals develop characteristics favorable to survival through a process of adjustment or adaptation to environment. These characteristics are passed on by sexual selection in which the favored males and females mate. Thus only the fittest survive. He thought that such a similarity as that of the body structure of man and animals substantiated his theory, but he forgot that this and other similarities might be evidence of design on the part of the Creator who gave His creatures similar body structures because of the similarity of their environment. Darwin applied his theory to man in *The Descent of Man* (1871) and argued that man was linked with animal life by common ancestral types.

Darwin's idea of continuity between man and animal has been summarized as "descent with change," or continuity. This view is opposed to the biblical concept of special creation by God, or discontinuity, with fixity in the groups thus created. In emphasizing similarities between man and animals, Darwin ignored the uniqueness of man's larger brain, his power of speech, his memory, his conscience, his concepts of God, and the soul. He admitted that the last three items were problems for his theory. No missing link that would conclusively identify man with animals has been discovered; in fact, crossbreeding between many groups is impossible. The use of the Hebrew word *Bara* for the act of creation is used only of the heavens and the earth, mammals and man (Gen. 1:1, 21, 27). God is said to have made each of the different groups reproduce "after his kind."

Although the theory of evolution denied the direct creation of man by God, the greatest damage came from the application of the theory to the development of religion. God and the Bible were looked upon as the evolutionary products of man's religious consciousness, and the books of the Bible were dated accordingly. The biblical eschatology, in which perfection would come into this world only by the direct intervention of God through the return of Christ, was replaced by the evolutionary view of a world that was being increasingly improved by human effort. Because man was not guilty through original sin, there was not need of Christ as Savior. Tennyson gave poetic expression to evolution in his autobiographical poem, *In Memoriam* (1850).

Evolution was also used to justify the idea of race superiority because that idea seemed to fit in with Darwin's concept of the survival of the fittest. It has also been used to justify having no absolute foundation or norm for ethics. Good conduct is merely those actions deemed suitable by each generation for the proper conduct of society. The doctrine of evolution has also been used to glorify war as the survival of the fittest.

All these conclusions have been reached by the application of a biological theory to other fields through an unwarranted use of the argument from analogy.

IV. COMMUNISM

The church has also faced the enmity of socialism in the twentieth century. This movement had its roots in the materialistic philosophy of Karl Marx (1818–83). From Adam Smith Marx borrowed his idea that only labor creates value; from Hegel, his method; and from the utopian socialists, his utopian goal. He and Friedrich Engels developed the major outlines of his view in the pamphlet *The Communist Manifesto* (1848). Marx had been attracted to the philosophy of Hegel, but he substituted materialism for Hegel's Absolute Being. Reality, he maintained, was only matter in motion. On this foundation he built the idea that all the religious, social, and political institutions of society are determined by the way people make a living. Class struggle takes place because the capitalist takes the surplus value or profits. Marx argued that the profits belong to labor because, he believed, it is only labor that can create value. Marx charted the progress of this struggle by the application of Hegel's logic. Capitalism generated its antithesis, the proletariat, which would destroy it and set up a classless society after a temporary dictatorship of the proletariat or workers. Lenin provided a set of aggressive tactics by which this system could be worked out. He emphasized the idea that a devoted, disciplined, small party of Communists could infiltrate democratic organizations, such as labor unions and government, and use a time of crisis or war to seize power. Stalin successfully combined this program and technique in the Russian state.

Marx and his followers believe that "man shall live by bread alone." They ignore human sin, which will always upset their ideal order unless they resort to brutal regimentation—which Communists have done everywhere. They also oversimplify human problems. There is no place for God, the Bible, or absolute standards in their system. They insist that "religion is the opiate of the people." While the emphasis on the importance of the economic factor has been an aid to the historian, recent history reveals the fundamental hostility of Marxism to all forms of religion. While the continuance of the Christian religion and the church is not dependent on any particular political or economic system, it must be recognized that socialism as practiced by the Communists finds it difficult to come to terms with the church.

Criticism of the Bible, Darwin's theory of evolution, and other social and intellectual forces created religious liberalism in the late nineteenth century. Liberal theologians have applied evolution to religion as a key that might explain its development.

They have insisted on the continuity of man's religious experience to such an extent that the Christian religion has become the mere product of a religious evolution rather than a revelation from God through the Bible and Christ. Christian experience has been emphasized much more than theology. Conservative Christianity has fought and the movement associated with the name of Karl Barth has opposed various forms of liberalism and socialism.

Suggested Reading

Bales, James D. Communism: Its Faith and Fallacies. Grand Rapids: Baker, 1962.

Daniels, Robert V. The Nature of Communism. New York: Random, 1962.

Hoover, J. Edgar. A Study of Communism. New York: Holt, Rinehart, and Winston, 1962.

Kenyon, Frederick C. The Text of the Greek Bible. London: Duckworth, 1937. This work describes the mass of texts of the Greek Bible and clearly presents their general confirmation of the integrity of the text of the Bible.

Klotz, John W. Genes, Genesis, and Evolution. St. Louis: Concordia, 1955. This is discussed from a Christian perspective.

Nash, Henry S. The History of Higher Criticism of the New Testament. New York: Macmillan, 1906.

Vincent, Marvin R. A History of the Textual Criticism of the New Testament. New York: Macmillan, 1903.

Young, Edward J. An Introduction to the Old Testament. Grand Rapids: Eerdmans, 1949. This work has more information concerning the history of criticism.

Zimmerman, Paul A., ed. Darwin, Evolution, and Creation. St. Louis: Concordia, 1959. Evolution is discussed from a Christian viewpoint.

Chapter 37

The American Church in the National Era

By 1789 the influence of the Great Awakening had been largely dissipated by the deism that had been brought over to the colonies by British army officers during the French and Indian War, by the import of deistic literature, and by the influence of the French Revolution. Yale University illustrates the decadent religious spirit in this period. Few students professed regeneration. Gambling, profanity, vice, and drunkenness were common among students, who were proud of being infidels. The Second Awakening, which improved this depressing picture, was the first of many revivals during the nineteenth century.

From the American Revolution to World War I, the United States was shaped religiously by a rural Protestant mold in which Protestantism was the majority religion. With the rise of Roman Catholicism by immigration after the Civil War, this country has become more pluralistic and even secular in its religious life. Protestantism has lost the monopoly it formerly enjoyed.

I. REVIVAL AND VOLUNTARY SOCIETIES

In 1787 a revival movement began at Hampden-Sidney, a little college in Virginia. The revival, which grew out of concern by three students for their spiritual condition, spread to Washington College and from there throughout the Presbyterian church in the South.

The New England Congregational phase of the revival began at Yale in 1802 under the leadership of President Timothy Dwight (1752–1817), whose earnest scholarly chapel messages on infidelity and the Bible destroyed the shallow infidelity of the students. About a third of the student body professed conversion during the revival, which later spread to Dartmouth, Williams, and other colleges. Another awakening at Yale came later.[1] Thus the eastern revivals began in colleges.

Revival also spread to the frontier, where great numbers of people had migrated. One quarter of the population resided outside the thirteen original states by 1820. Whiskey became a curse in these new settlements and was the cause of most frontier social and moral problems. The Presbyterians were the most influential in propagating revival on the frontier, the camp meeting having originated among them with the work of James McGready (ca. 1758–1817). The most famous camp meeting was the one held at Cane Ridge in August, 1801, with ten thousand people present, according to some estimates.[2] It was marked by strange physical phenomena such as falling, jerking, rolling, dancing, and barking. But there could be no question concerning the desirable results of the revival. The frontier areas of Kentucky and Tennessee were all helped by it. The frontier revivalism was much more spectacular than the quiet spiritual awakening brought about by the preaching of the Word in New England.

As was the case with the Great Awakening, one of the results of revival was division within the churches. Division came among the Presbyterians when the Cumberland Presbytery ordained men without the proper educational qualifications to minister to the increasing numbers of churches on the frontier. This division resulted in the formation of the Cumberland Presbyterian Church in 1810. Its use of the camp meeting and the circuit system and its advocacy of revival made it one of the strong churches of the frontier.

Another division was made by Thomas Campbell (1763–1854), a Scotch-Irish, anti-Burgher Presbyterian who came to America in 1807. When his church refused to permit him to administer Communion to those outside his own group, he de-cided to preach a noncreedal faith based on the Bible. He soon gained numerous followers among the Baptists; and, after his son Alexander came to America, he organized congregational churches that practiced baptism by immersion and emphasized the second coming of Christ. By 1830 these churches separated from the Baptists and were known as Disciples. In 1832 the Disciples united with the Christians who followed Barton W. Stone (1772–1844), and so the Disciples or Christian Church was formed.

The Second Awakening indirectly helped to precipitate the rise of the Unitarian church in New England. The first Unitarian church in America had been formed in 1785 when members of King's Chapel, Boston, voted to omit all mention of the Trinity from the service. Then in 1805 Henry Ware was appointed to the Hollis chair of divinity at Harvard in spite of his Unitarian views. Andover Theological Seminary was founded in 1808 by orthodox Congregationalists in protest against this appointment. In 1819 William E. Channing preached a sermon in Baltimore in which he developed Unitarian doctrine.[3] This sermon became the basis of faith for over one hundred Unitarian churches that soon appeared in Boston and throughout New England. These churches opposed both orthodox Christianity and the revivalist movement. The Massachusetts Supreme Court in the Dedham Decision of 1820 gave all voters in a parish, whether they attended church or not, the right to vote on calling a pastor. The American Unitarian Association, which came into being in 1825 with 125 congregations, held the doctrines of the goodness of man, salvation by character culture, the unity of God, the humanity of Christ, and the immanence of God in the human heart.

A second major result of the revival was the improvement of morals on the frontier. Drunkenness and profanity gave way to godly conduct as the Methodists and Baptists increased in number. Although the revival had begun among the Presbyterians, the Methodists and Baptists won more followers because they did not insist so strongly on an educated ministry and made extensive use of the camp meeting technique, which the Presbyterians ceased to use. In three years over ten thousand joined the Baptist churches in Kentucky.

From this time the midweek prayer meeting became an important institution in American Christianity. The American Sunday school was also started at this time. As early as 1786 Sunday school was held in a home in Virginia, and in 1790 it was introduced into a church in Philadelphia. Since then it has been an integral part of religion in America and enables a church to educate the young in biblical truth. Higher education was strengthened by the founding of over a dozen new colleges between 1780 and 1830 by the Presbyterians and Congregationalists in order to meet the need for more trained ministers. Andover Seminary was founded in 1808 to meet the threat of Unitarianism in Harvard. Others, such as Princeton Seminary (1812), Auburn, and Bangor, were founded soon after.

Missionary endeavor at home and abroad was another outcome of the revival. The founding of the American Board of Commissioners for Foreign Missions in 1810 was in part the result of the "haystack prayer meeting" of Samuel Mills (1783–1818) and other students at Williams College. Later, other denominational boards were created until missionary work by Americans swelled into a mighty tide by 1900. Nondenominational voluntary societies for mission, Bible distribution, and social purposes were founded in great numbers. To aid this effort at home the American Tract Society was founded in 1825, and the American Bible Society was organized in 1816. Beginning early in the nineteenth century, numerous denominations began to publish weekly religious papers for their people.

Revivalism did not end with the Second Awakening. Charles G. Finney (1792–1875), a lawyer who was converted in 1821, came to public notice as a revivalist in his campaign in 1830 and 1831 at Rochester, New York. His "new measures" of revivalism included protracted meetings, colloquial language in preaching, unseasonable hours for services, naming individuals in public prayer and sermons, and the "anxious bench" to which inquirers could come. He became a pastor for a time in New York City and later in Oberlin, Ohio. In 1851 Finney became the president of Oberlin College. His lectures on revival and systematic theology have had great influence.

A lay interdenominational prayer-based revival in 1857 and 1858 grew out of a noonday prayer meeting set up in Fulton Street in New York City by Jeremiah Lanphier on September 23, 1857, with six present. In six months, 10,000 were meeting in noonday prayer meetings in New York. It is estimated that between 500,000 and 1,000,000 people were added to the church, with the Methodists gaining most of the new members. This revival had its counterpart in Ulster and other parts of the world. In 1863 and 1864 a revival broke out in the Confederate Army before Richmond. Claims of 150,000 converts were made, and army churches were set up.

Dwight L. Moody, evangelist. Although he was never ordained, he was regarded by many of his contemporaries as the most influential "clergyman" in the last quarter of the nineteenth century.

After the Civil War, the nature of revival changed. With Dwight L. Moody's successful meetings in the British Isles from 1873 to 1875, revival became urban, professional, organized mass evangelism carried on outside the churches in great public halls. Moody helped organize the Chicago Evangelization Society in 1886, out of which Moody Bible Institute developed in the fall of 1889. His successors in this newer type of evangelism were Reuben A. Torrey, Gypsy Smith, and Billy Sunday. Since 1949 Billy Graham has been the most widely known evangelist.

II. SOCIAL REFORM

The church in America was also interested in social reform during the nineteenth century. Revivalism created an atmosphere antagonistic to the prevalent practice of dueling with pistols or swords. The tragic death of Alexander Hamilton in a duel with Aaron Burr, coupled with propaganda from the pulpit, soon brought the practice to an end. The interest of the church in social reform also slowly brought about the abolition of imprisonment for debt and promoted prison reform.

During the nineteenth century and earlier, the church became interested in the problem of liquor. In 1784 Benjamin Rush exploded the theory that intoxicants were beneficial to the body and called on the churches to support a temperance movement based on total abstinence. The Methodists, who have always had a keen interest in social problems, demanded that their members neither sell nor use intoxicants. Presbyterians and Congregationalists soon followed suit. Before long, numerous temperance societies were formed to promote abstinence and to battle the liquor interests. The Anti-Saloon League (1895), a federation of temperance agencies, was the most important of these. After World War I the realization that liquor incited crime, that liquor and modern machinery would not mix safely, and that thirty-three states had state prohibition aided the work of the league. The adoption of the Eighteenth Amendment in 1919 was the outcome of all these forces. From 1919 America was officially prohibitionist until the repeal of the Eighteenth Amendment in 1933.

During the first half of the nineteenth century, slavery became a serious problem that the churches had to face. As early as 1769 Congregationalists in Rhode Island spoke out against slavery in an attempt at *amelioration* of the condition of slaves between 1729 and 1830. John Woolman's *Journal* (1756–72) describes the devoted efforts of that godly Quaker to persuade others to emancipate their slaves. About 1833 Lane Seminary in Cincinnati became the center of an antislavery movement led by a student, Theodore Weld. This movement aimed at *abolition* of slavery from 1831 to 1860. When the seminary authorities attempted to ban the movement, the students migrated to Oberlin College. The American Anti-Slavery Society was founded in 1833. Inspired by such people as the editor of the *Liberator*, William L. Garrison; poet John Greenleaf Whittier; educator Jonathan Blanchard; and author Harriet Beecher Stowe (*Uncle Tom's Cabin*), the abolitionist movement grew rapidly. At the same time slavery was becoming an apparent economic necessity in the South for the production of cotton for the increasing number of textile factories in New England and England.

Attempts to end slavery by religious persuasion split several denominations. The Wesleyan Methodist Church was organized in 1843 on the basis of no-slave-owning membership after many people withdrew from the Methodist Episcopal Church. A Southern Baptist Convention was organized in 1845 because of the opposition of Northern Baptists to slavery. In the same year the Methodist Episcopal Church, South was founded. Southern Presbyterians from both the new and old school groups split in 1857 and 1861 over slavery and theology. They united to form the Presbyterian Church in the United States in 1864. The churches created by these schisms over slavery have not yet all reunited with their Northern brethren, though there have been recent overtures for reunion. But despite the schisms, one should remember that the church conscientiously faced the slavery issue as a social problem to be solved. When the Civil War came, churches on both sides of the line did their best to bring aid to the needy and suffering. The resort to *arms* in the Civil War and the Thirteenth *Amendment* ended slavery, but segregation was continued until the 1960s.

III. FRONTIER AND URBAN SECTS

In addition to the new denominations, such as the Cumberland Presbyterians and the Disciples or Christians, heterodox sects appeared on the American frontier and in American cities during the nineteenth century. The Mormons and Adventists appeared on the rural frontier, and Christian Science emerged in urban New England.

Joseph Smith (1805–44) maintained that in 1827 he dug up a book of thin gold plates on a hill near Palmyra, New York. After three years spent in translating, he published the book as the Book of Mormon in 1830.[4] Attracting many followers, he made Kirtland, Ohio, the headquarters for the organization between 1831 and 1837. Independence, Missouri, became the chief center until the Missourians drove the Mormons out in 1839. Nauvoo, Illinois, became the next center; but opposition to polygamy, which Joseph Smith sanctioned by revelation in

1843,[5] resulted in the death of Smith at the hands of his enemies in 1844 and in the migration of the Mormons under the leadership of Brigham Young (1801–77) to Utah between 1846 and 1848. Salt Lake City is still the center of the largest group of Mormons. Aggressive missionary work has won thousands of converts all over the world. This body of nearly three million members is known as the Church of Jesus Christ of Latter-Day Saints. A second group of about 160,000 repudiated polygamy and, led by Joseph Smith, the son of the original founder, built up a strong organization with headquarters in Independence, Missouri. This group is known as the Reorganized Church of Jesus Christ of Latter-Day Saints. Mormons, as well as Shakers, look to a future utopia.

The Mormons accept both the Book of Mormon and the Bible as Scripture. They look for an earthly Zion and do not give Christ His rightful place as Lord and Savior in their theology.[6] Mormons baptize living persons for dead persons. Until it came under federal ban, polygamy seemed to have been widely practiced among the Mormons as a means of having a large posterity in the future world.

The Seventh-Day Adventists, another frontier group, was founded by William Miller (1782–1849), a farmer who studied the Bible assiduously. Study of Daniel and Revelation convinced Miller that Christ was going to return to earth 2,300 years (Dan. 8:14) after Ezra's return to Jerusalem in 457 B.C. This gave him the date of 1843 as the year of Christ's return. Many thousands accepted his idea and began to prepare for the coming of Christ. When Christ did not make His expected appearance either in 1843 or

The Millerites, as the early followers of William Miller were called, were made fun of in this widely published newspaper cartoon. The Millerite is being held down by a dog tugging on the tail of his ascension robe.

1844, Miller's followers faced persecution in the churches and formed themselves into an Adventist denomination by 1860. Hiram Edson later explained the nonappearance of Christ in 1843 and 1844 by the theory that the sanctuary to which He came in that year was a heavenly rather than an earthly sanctuary. Ellen G. White (1827–1915) superseded Miller as the major leader. Although there are several Adventist denominations, most of them believe that the Sabbath (Saturday) is the correct day of rest, that the soul sleeps between death and the resurrection, and that the wicked will be annihilated. However, in most of their teachings they are orthodox.

Spiritualism also had its beginning in America in this period. In 1848 strange knocks and other noises occurred in the bedroom of Kate and Margaret Fox of Hydesville, New York. Both reportedly confessed years later that the noises were the result of childish pranks. But overnight they became a sensation and attracted numerous followers who later organized themselves into a Spiritualist church. Spiritualist mediums purport to communicate with the dead. Spiritualism makes a strong appeal to those who have lost loved ones by death and receives vigorous support following the losses of war. Such influential people as Sir Arthur Conan Doyle and Ella Wheeler Wilcox accepted Spiritualism as an authentic religion.

Christian Science, which appeared first in Boston in the post-Civil War era, was an urban sect with a philosophical twist. It was the brainchild of imaginative, moody Mary Baker (1821–1910). After the death of her first husband, Glover, she became increasingly subject to spells of hysteria. In 1853 she married Patterson, a dentist, whom she divorced in 1873. She later married Eddy in 1877. All through this marital career she was seeking help for her neurotic tendencies. In 1862 she met P. P. Quimby who emphasized healing by mental assent to truth that denied the reality of both illness and matter. She set herself up as a practitioner of the "new science," which she apparently gained from Quimby's manuscripts, and won many followers, to whom she imparted the secret of her method in a series of lessons. In 1875 she published *Science and Health*. This work now has an equal position with the Bible in all Christian Science churches. The Christian Scientists Association was formed in 1876, and in 1879 the Church of Christ, Scientist, was given a state charter. The First Church of Christ, Scientist, of Boston became the finest and most important of all their churches and has been known as the Mother Church since 1892.

Mrs. Eddy denied the reality of matter, evil, and sickness and held that these were merely delusions of the senses. God is all and all is God. One has but to realize one's identity with God or good to be freed from both evil and sickness.[7] This emphasis on healing has made the movement appealing to many sick people. New Thought and Unity are similar in their approach to the problems of health and prosperity, and no doubt they owe much to Mary Baker Eddy who, in turn, owed much to P. P. Quimby.

IV. THE PROBLEMS OF URBANIZATION

The increased industrialization of the nation during and after the Civil

War and the expanded immigration from southern and eastern Europe after 1890 to provide unskilled labor for the mills, mines, and factories of a developing America brought about an astonishing growth of great cities, such as Chicago and Detroit. This growth of urban communities created many new problems for the church in America during the nineteenth century, and these problems continue to confront the church in the twentieth century. Over two million Irish Roman Catholics and about two million German Roman Catholics migrated to the United States between 1840 and 1870.

Many rural churches lost so many of their young people to the city that their existence was endangered. These youths in the cities often neglected their religious life because the city provided them anonymity. Immigrant laborers settled in congested areas, and the native groups moved to the suburbs along with their churches. Because most of the immigrants after 1890 were Roman Catholic, the problem of the relations between that church and the dominant Protestant churches was raised. Immigrants brought with them loose ideas concerning the observance of Sunday. Material success also in many cases created an indifference to spiritual life that could only be characterized as secularism. The tendency of city life toward secularity was reinforced by the widespread acceptance of evolution and all the naturalistic ideology that went with that theory.

To meet the challenge of these problems was the task of the church after the Civil War. As early as 1850 city rescue missions were founded to meet the physical and spiritual needs of the down-and-out of the city. The Water Street Mission of New York, opened in 1872. It became the most famous of these missions, under the leadership of its founder, Jerry MacAuley (1839–84), who had been saved from a wasted life through the preaching of Orville Gardner in 1857 at Sing Sing. Chicago's Pacific Garden Mission began in 1877. Aid to tenement families; aggressive opposition to gambling, drinking, and vice centers; physical care for the outcast; and aggressive evangelism to reclaim souls were the major elements in rescue mission work.

In 1864 the New York Protestant Episcopal City Mission became the arm of that church for social service. Orphanages, missions, hospitals, homes for the aged, and other agencies were developed to meet the needs of the poor, the homeless, and the diseased.

The Young Men's Christian Association first appeared in Boston in 1851 to meet the social needs of young men in the cities. The movement grew rapidly as it provided lodging, exercise, Bible study, and social activities for such men. The Young Women's Christian Association was organized in 1855 to meet similar needs of young women in the cities. Both these movements became agencies through which Christians of various denominations were able to cooperate in social service.

Social settlements, of which Hull House in Chicago under the leadership of Jane Addams was the earliest, carried out social work similar to that of the institutional church; but they did not emphasize religious education. The dynamic behind the settlements was humanitarian and social, that behind the social work of the institutional church was primarily religious.

The institutional church itself was still another agency to meet the challenge of urban problems. By 1872 Thomas K. Beecher's (1824–1900) Park Church in Elmira, New York, was one of the early pioneers of the institutional church. The institutional church attempted to provide for the entire life of the individual. Numerous churches of this type were organized by the various denominations after the Civil War. Gymnasiums, libraries, dispensaries, lecture rooms, social rooms, sewing rooms, auditoriums, and other necessities for meeting the physical, social, mental, and spiritual needs of people were usually a part of these churches. Saint George's Episcopal Church in New York, with William S. Rainsford as pastor and with the financial aid of J. P. Morgan, became an institutional church in 1882 in order to serve the people in its own area. The various types of work were carried on in the adjoining parish house. Temple University in Philadelphia developed from Russell H. Conwell's Baptist Temple, which adopted institutional practices in 1891.

The Goodwill Industries, originated in the church of Edgar J. Helms (1836–1942) in Boston soon after 1900, was an attempt to provide employment for the poor and aged by having them repair discarded articles that could be sold cheaply to the needy. Thus the needs of both the unemployed and those who could not afford to pay for new articles were met. Religious and social activities were also provided. The movement was incorporated in 1905 and has grown to include many factories and retail stores.

The Salvation Army also met social as well as religious needs of people in cities. It began work in America shortly after its founding in England. Street meetings, social settlements, homes, nurseries, and many other techniques were devised to meet the needs of the neglected poor and the outcast.

The social gospel was an attempt to get at the causes of the evils that some were attempting to meet by the means mentioned above. It was felt that measures dealing with the symptoms of economic maladies were not sufficient because they left the causes untouched. Organized labor rose as one answer to the challenge of the capitalist who seldom considered the welfare of the consumer and worker in his heavy emphasis on profits. Thinkers began to study the social teachings of Christ to see whether there was not some way in which economic injustice might be righted. Basing their work on the theological dogmas of the fatherhood of God and the brotherhood of man, many turned their attention from the salvation of the individual to the application of the teachings of Christianity to the economic life of the state in order to bring the kingdom of God to earth.

Washington Gladden (1836–1918), a Congregationalist minister in Ohio, emphasized the need for applying the principles of Christ to the social order by using, if necessary, the force of the state to intervene for the well-being of society. The popular work *In His Steps* (1896), written by Charles Sheldon (1847–1946), showed in fictional form what the social outcome might be if everyone tried to act as Christ did in daily life. Walter Rauschenbusch (1861–1918), a German Baptist minister who taught from 1897 to 1917 at Rochester Theological Seminary, became the foremost American apostle of the social gospel as a result of his studying social ethics in the Bible and reading utopian books. His books *Christianizing the Social Order* (1912) and *A Theology for the Social Gospel* (1917) spread the social gospel widely. He emphasized the necessity of economic as well as political democracy as the way by which the kingdom of God could be realized on earth. He supported unions, government intervention, and a mild socialism as means that might accomplish that end. He argued that because labor was not a commodity, men should have the right to organize and bargain with the employer for better hours of labor, better wages, and better working conditions. He urged profit sharing as a good way to give labor a fair return for its work. He was opposed to a *laissez-faire* type of capitalism that emphasized competition above co-operative action in society. These views were predicated on the idea that the church must realize the kingdom of God on earth rather than to talk about a future millennial kingdom. At the beginning of the present century the social gospel was widely accepted by the liberal churches. The Federal Council of Churches was its main sponsor.

V. THEOLOGICAL LIBERALISM IN AMERICA

The development of Darwinian evolution, the appearance of biblical criticism upon the American scene through theological students who studied in Germany and Scotland under men such as Samuel R. Driver, and the importation of German idealism brought liberalism to American churches in the nineteenth century. Mention has already been made of Rauschenbusch's social gospel, which was merely the application of liberal theology to the social and economic spheres of life. Liberal theology emphasized the ethical message of a humanized Christ and the immanence of God in the human heart. Thus experience, rather than the Scriptures, was normative. Liberals were also greatly devoted to the scientific method and to natural law to explain miracles but were opposed to the doctrines of supernaturalism, original sin, and Christ's vicarious atonement. Many of the ministers trained by liberal teachers in the seminaries popularized these ideas from their pulpits.

Liberalism has had an impact on the great movement for Christian education in the churches through the work of Horace Bushnell (1802–76), the Congregationalist minister of North Church in Hartford. After completing the study of law, Bushnell turned to theology. In 1847 he published his book *Christian Nurture*, in which he emphasized the idea that the child merely has to grow *into* grace in a religious environment. Holding to a defective view of original sin and to the moral influence theory of the Atonement, Bushnell did not believe that the experience of conversion and growth *in* grace, as taught by the evangelical church, was necessary for the child. He wanted the child to grow up as a Christian so that he would never know himself as being other than a Christian. He emphasized divine love at the expense of divine justice and bitterly opposed the revivalism of his day.

These ideas influenced Christian education in the church. Uniform Sunday school lessons were developed in 1872 as a result of the work of John H. Vincent (1832–1920). He and Lewis Miller in 1874 started Chautauqua to train Sunday school teachers. The grading of the lessons became a part of this work as the idea of progressive development of the child in Christian truth was adopted from the ideas of Bushnell. A Religious Education Association was formed in 1903, out of which developed the International Council of Religious Education in 1922. Unfortunately, this movement, dedicated to ideas of Christian education similar to those of Bushnell, fell under liberal control. These various liberal organizations and leaders met strong opposition from the Princeton theologians, led by A. A. Hodge (1823–86), and other evangelical leaders.

VI. INTERDENOMINATIONAL AND NONDENOMINATIONAL COOPERATION

Cooperation with one another in various inter- and nondenominational endeavors was another activity of American churches during the nineteenth and early twentieth centuries.

The Young Men's and Women's Christian Associations were the result of the cooperation of people of various denominations to meet pressing social needs in the new urban society of the day. The 1801 Plan of Union and the American Bible Society in 1816 are other examples.

In 1881 Francis E. Clark, a minister of Portland, Maine, organized the first Christian Endeavor Society. This society speedily became an interdenominational organization, enlisting the interest of young people of various denominations. By 1886 over eight hundred societies were organized. These provided ethical, social, and religious training for young people. Later, denominational organizations along similar lines were set up to keep the movement within each denomination. The Epworth League of the Methodist churches is an illustration of this type of organization.

Organic reunion of denominations was another form of cooperation. The reunion of the Cumberland Presbyterian Church with the Presbyterian Church, USA, in 1906, is an illustration of ecumenical cooperation. Another was the Prussian Union of Reformed and Lutheran churches by royal pressure in 1817.

The Student Volunteer Movement, which began under Moody's auspices at Northfield, Massachusetts, in 1886, provided an interdenominational agency under the leadership of John R. Mott (1865–1955) to recruit missionaries by the stimulation of interest in missions. By 1945 it had recruited 20,500 missionaries. Denominations also cooperated in missionary activity along interdenominational lines after the founding of the Foreign Missions Conference of North America in 1893. A Laymen's Missionary Movement was organized in 1906[8] to interest laymen in missionary activity.

Samuel S. Schmucker (1799–1873), professor at the Lutheran Gettysburg Seminary, was an early exponent of church confederation in his 1835 "Fraternal Appeal to the American Churches." Interest in new social problems and theological liberalism and a desire for interdenominational cooperation and unity coalesced in the founding of the Federal Council of the

Churches of Christ in America. The council provided for cooperation among the denominations through a council made up of the representatives of autonomous churches. In 1905 the constitution of the Federal Council was drawn up at a meeting in Carnegie Hall in New York. It was accepted by thirty-three denominations at a meeting in Philadelphia in 1908.[9] This is an example of confederation.

The Federal Council has always had a strong interest in social problems and the application of the ethical principles of Christianity to the solution of those problems. Unfortunately, it fell under the influence of liberal leadership and at times seemed to subscribe to collectivism as the ideal economic order.

This survey of the history of the church in America between 1789 and 1914 has revealed the diversity of the problems and the variety of solutions that the church adopted to meet them. It is to be regretted that some of the churches in meeting many of these problems took positions that were hostile to the teachings of the Bible.

SUGGESTED READING

The suggested readings in chapter 32 also cover the era discussed in this chapter.

Anderson, Courtney. **Federal Street Pastor.** *New York: Bookman, 1961. This is a helpful biography of W. E. Channing.*

_____. **To the Golden Shore.** *Boston: Little, 1856. This is a biography of Judson.*

Atkins, Gaius G. **Religion in Our Times.** *New York: Round Table, 1932. Although written from a liberal viewpoint, this gives much helpful information concerning modern American Christianity.*

Bell, Aaron I. **The Urban Impact on American Protestantism 1865–1900.** *Cambridge: Harvard University Press, 1943. This is an account of the way Protestantism met the challenge of the city.*

Bradford, Gamaliel. **Moody, A Worker in Souls.** *New York: Doran, 1927.*

Brodie, Fawn M. **No Man Knows My Name: The Life of Joseph Smith, the Mormon Prophet.** *New York: Knopf, 1957.*

Cartwright, Peter. **Autobiography of Peter Cartwright.** *Nashville: Abingdon, 1956.*

Curtis, Richard K. **They Called Him Mr. Moody.** *New York: Doubleday, 1962.*

Dickson, D. Bruce. **And They Sang Hallelujah.** *Knoxville: University of Tennessee Press, 1974. This is useful for the history of camp meetings.*

Dorn, Jacob H. **Washington Gladden.** *Athens: Ohio State University Press, 1966.*

Ferguson, Charles W. **The Confusion of Tongues.** *Garden City, N.Y.: Doubleday, 1929. This is an interesting, critical, but somewhat satirical, account of the history and dogmas of the major American cults.*

Findlay, James F. **Dwight L. Moody: American Evangelist, 1837–1899.** *Chicago: University of Chicago Press, 1969. This is the definitive biography of D. L. Moody.*

Foster, Charles L. **An Errand of Mercy.** *Chapel Hill: University of North Carolina Press, 1960. This describes in a scholarly manner the rise and decline of evangelical reform in this country from 1790 to 1837.*

Garrison, Winfred. **The March of Faith.** *New York: Harper, 1933. This is an interesting survey of American Christianity since 1865.*

Griffin, Clifford A. **Their Brother's Keepers.** *New Brunswick: Rutger's University Press, 1960.*

Gundry, Stanley N. Love Them In: The Proclamation Theology of D. L. Moody. *Chicago: Moody, 1976. This volume corrects many current misinterpretations of Moody's message, methods, and significance.*

Handy, Robert T. The Social Gospel in America. *Oxford: Oxford University Press, 1966.*

Hirshon, Stanley P. The Lion of the Lord. *New York: Knopf, 1969. This is a useful biography of Brigham Young.*

Hudson, Winthrop S. Religion in America. *New York: Scribner, 1965. This has a well-balanced discussion of religion in the colonial as well as the national eras.*

Jacquet, Constant H., Jr., ed. Yearbook of American and Canadian Churches. *New York: Abingdon, 1978. This is a helpful volume on denominations with recent statistics.*

Johnson, Charles A. The Frontier Camp Meeting. *Dallas: Southern Methodist University Press, 1955.*

Martin, Walter R. The Kingdom of the Cults. *Grand Rapids: Zondervan, 1965.*

Mcloughlin, William G. Modern Revivalism. *New York: Revell, 1959. This is a helpful but sometimes inaccurate and very critical account of revivalists from Finney to Graham.*

Mead, Frank S. Handbook of Denominations in the United States. *6th ed. Nashville: Abingdon, 1975.*

Orr, J. Edwin. The Light of the Nations. *Grand Rapids: Eerdmans, 1965. Revivals and their results are covered from 1789 to 1860.*

Peel, Robert. The Life of Mary Baker Eddy. *New York: Holt, Rinehart, and Winston, 1966.*

Smith, Timothy L. Social Reform in Mid-nineteenth Century America. *New York: Abingdon, 1957. The author shows the link between revival and social action.*

Stone, Barton W. The Biography of Elder Barton Warren Stone. *Cincinnati: James, 1847.*

Strong, William E. The Story of the American Board. *New York: Arno, 1969. This is a history of the American Board of Commissioners for Foreign Missions.*

Sweet, William W. Religion on the American Frontier. *4 vols.* The Baptists. *Vol. 1. New York: Henry Holt, 1931.* The Presbyterians, 1783–1840. *Vol. 2. New York: Harper, 1936.* The Congregationalists. *Chicago: University of Chicago Press, 1939.*

Tyler, Alice F. Freedom's Ferment. *Minneapolis: University of Minnesota Press, 1944. This contains detailed discussions of social reform in America.*

Van Baalen, Jan K. The Chaos of the Cults. *2nd rev. and enl. ed. Grand Rapids: Eerdmans, 1956. This is a useful history of the cults that compares their doctrines with the teachings of the Bible.*

Weisberger, Bernard A. They Gathered at the River. *Boston: Little, 1938. This is a critical account of the revival period from Finney to the 30s.*

Weisenberger, Francis P. Ordeal of Faith. *New York: Philosophical Library, 1959. This covers the same period as Garrison's work.*

Woodbridge, John; Noll, Mark; and Hatch, Nathan. The Gospel in America: Themes in the Stories of America's Evangelicals. *Grand Rapids: Zondervan, 1979. This volume is one of the finest descriptions and analyses of Evangelicalism in print.*

Note: Edwin S. Gaustad's Historical Atlas of Religion in America *has been updated to 1975 in Jackson W. Carroll, Douglas W. Johnson, and Martin E. Marty,* Religion in America. *New York: Harper and Row, 1979.*

Chapter 38

The Church and the Social Order

The twentieth century since 1914 would appear chaotic to a European of the period between the French Revolution and Napoleon and the First World War. He would be dismayed by the disorder in international affairs and the insecurity people seem to feel in economic matters. The many religious voices clashing with historic Christianity would be a matter of deep religious concern.

This has come about because the period between 1914 and 1945 brought more drastic changes to the world than Europe faced in the era of religious ideological conflict in the Thirty Years' War. The world has gone through two global, impersonal, total, and mechanized wars that have brought tremendous loss of life and treasure to Europe. The German, Russian, Turkish, and Austrian empires were liquidated and replaced by either democratic or totalitarian states. Europe became eclipsed in world affairs by the two superpowers, the United States and Russia. Communist China and the Arab world, with its oil, may even threaten the hegemony of these two powers. Democracy has been replaced with totalitarian rule over two-thirds of the world's people.

Political nationalism seems to be promoting economic nationalism instead of the international cooperation that appeared after World Wars I and II. The Arab world with its large population, a renascent Islam, and its control over three-quarters of the world's oil threatens economic disaster if it should withhold its oil.

The national territorial state that had supported the Reformation settlements in Europe has become increasingly secularized. It has adopted in the United States a neutral attitude to religion as defined by the Supreme Court and, in the case of leftist and rightist totalitarian states, a hostile attitude and even in many cases severe persecution.

The global Christian church through missionary expansion has to cope with increasing external encroachment of the state on what the church had formerly considered to be its rights and privileges as well as its responsibilities. This growth of the power and functions of the secular state has been stimulated by the increase in social welfare legislation. Such legislation had its beginnings in England when the state was forced to give aid to those monks who had been dispossessed of their monasteries when the monasteries were broken up by 1539. The state was forced to help those whom the church had formerly served through the charitable work of the monks. The increasing political power of labor has forced the passage of legislation for its benefit, and the administration and enforcement of that legislation has increased the power of the state. Two world wars in the twentieth century brought complete regimentation of all the human and material resources of states to achieve victory. These necessary wartime powers have increasingly been extended into the postwar era. The all-powerful, secular, totalitarian state brooks no opposition and permits no division of allegiance on the part of its citizens. The threat to religion from the powerful secular and, in some cases, hostile state is one of the greatest external problems the church now faces.

I. THE CHURCHES IN TWO WORLD WARS AND IN REVOLUTIONS

During the nineteenth and early twentieth centuries, aggressive movements that fostered the idea of world peace arose. Liberal theology and the social gospel, with their emphasis on the fatherhood of God and the brotherhood of man, helped to promote this tendency to work for world peace. Pacifistic groups also threw their weight behind the peace movement. The American Peace Society (1828) united many state peace societies into a larger national unit to work for world peace. The society condemned any war but that for self-defense and supported the negotiation of treaties of arbitration so that nations could settle their problems peacefully. By 1914 American secretaries of state had negotiated nearly fifty such treaties. International peace conferences, supported mainly by the churches, were held annually from the time of the first important meeting in Paris in 1889 until 1913. One of the more notable peace conferences was held at The Hague in 1899. That conference founded a court for the arbitration of international disputes. Then in 1910 the Carnegie Endowment for International Peace was founded by Andrew Carnegie.

The position of the American churches was summed up by an editorial in the May 7, 1898, issue of the *Outlook*. The churches, after they had determined whether the war was righteous, were to strengthen national morale, to relieve suffering, and to work to prevent the usual postwar decline in morals.

Optimism concerning peace was somewhat dampened by the coming of war in 1914, but the American churches supported Wilson's declaration of neutrality. They held Germany and her allies responsible for the war, but at the same time they believed that general European mammonism, immorality, and neglect of spiritual values had contributed to the coming of war. While pity and aid were to be extended to sufferers through the Red Cross, America was to remain isolated from the war and even from the peace.

As propaganda increasingly interpreted the war in spiritual terms as the struggle to save the Christian civilization that the "Huns" were trying to destroy, religious opinion gradually changed. A poll of American Presbyterian ministers in 1916 indicated that a large majority favored armament for self-defense. A strong America, it was believed, could help to extend democracy when peace came. By the beginning of 1917 churches were beginning to put the national flag in the churches along with the Christian flag and to give it the place of honor on the right.

American churches supported the declaration of war by the president in the spring of 1917 and sought in every possible way to help the state win the war. The attitude of hostility to war and of neutrality speedily changed to one whereby the churches sanctioned the war and became agencies of the government. Notable clergymen gave their blessing to the bayonet as an instrument to bring about the kingdom of God. The churches provided chaplains for the armies that were coming into being. They supported the Red Cross by contributions and by such work as rolling bandages. Many preachers actively recruited young men for the army by expounding from the pulpit the religious nature of the war in Europe. Some ministers even sold war bonds in church services. Some also spread atrocity propaganda. One outstanding minister even called German soldiers such names as "rattlesnakes" and "hyenas." Even German classical music was under ban during the war. Conscientious objectors and defenders of free speech were attacked for daring to oppose the war effort. In short, the church blessed and supported the war as a holy crusade.

With the failure of the nations to secure peace after World War I, the growth of nationalism, the later repudiation by European states of their debts to the United States, and the revelations of the Nye Committee in 1935 concerning sales of arms during the war, the churches in America became disillusioned with war. Many liberal ministers and laymen became pacifists. In fact, in a poll taken in 1931, over twelve thousand of about twenty thousand American clergymen of all denominations who replied to the poll stated that the church should neither sanction nor support any future war. However, the task of aiding the impoverished churches of the Continent was not neglected by the churches of the victorious allies, and large sums were contributed for relief and reconstruction. The churches also supported disarmament and the outlawing of war between 1919 and 1939.

Even before World War II churches in such totalitarian countries as Germany were forced to keep silent concerning political issues and to concentrate on the spiritual message of Christianity, to syncretize totalitarian dogma with the Christian faith, or to oppose the totalitarian state and accept the resulting persecution. Many German churchmen, led by Niemöller, adopted the last course and suffered for their stand. Christians in these countries could well appreciate the plight of Christians who were persecuted by the Roman state in the early days of the Christian faith.

For their opposition to the Nazis, Dietrich Bonhoeffer was executed and Niemöller was imprisoned. Churches in Japan were forced to unite in the Kyodan in 1941. The Orthodox church in Russia supported the war effort.

World War II found the churches in democratic countries much more cautious in their approach to war than they were in 1914. There was no attempt as in 1914 to make it a "holy war." The church resisted the hate appeal. Many Christians in countries such as Norway and Holland, which were occupied by the Axis powers, suffered for their faith. Conscientious objectors were given more aid by the churches than they had been given in World War I. Reluctant support of the war was based on the idea of the survival of the nation rather than on any idealistic aim. A sense of the unity of all Christians, irrespective of which side of the battlefront they were on, was maintained throughout the war. At the end of the war, the major Protestant American denominations pledged themselves to raise over $100 million for relief and for the reconstruction of churches that were destroyed during the war in Europe.

Although the church in World War II did not surrender its conscience to the state as it did in World War I by approving the war as a holy enterprise but maintained the essential unity of all Christians everywhere and resisted the tendency to hate, the church did nevertheless provide chaplains for the armed forces and warmly supported the Red Cross. It also put greater efforts into serving the needy and suffering during the war and into the reconstruction of churches after the war. John Foster Dulles helped to integrate efforts of the American churches and the State Department to plan for a just peace. The churches looked on World War II and the Korean War as "just" wars, but many churchmen opposed American participation in the Vietnam War.

II. CHURCH AND STATE TENSIONS

A. In Democratic States

While the church has not endured severe persecution or martyrdom in democratic states, the working relations between church and state have often been tense as states have become increasingly secularized and through taxing and regulatory powers have gained more control over the individual. Patterns of separation or an establishment with toleration have developed.

1. The United States has followed a pattern of "a wall of separation" based on decisions of the Supreme Court on the First Amendment to the Constitution, which bans any established church or threat to the free exercise of religion. Article VI also bans any religious test for public offices.

The "wall of separation" principle was spelled out in the 1879 *Reynolds* v. *The United States* with the provision that the free exercise of religion would not lead to action violating the public welfare. The states in the 1940 *Cantwell* v. *Connecticut* case were declared by the court incompetent under the Fourteenth Amendment to make any law that would violate the First Amendment. In 1947 in the *Everson* v. *Board of Education*, the Supreme Court ruled that busing of parochial students at public expense was not a breach in the "wall of separation." It also outlawed the use of public school facilities during school hours for religious instruction by religious leaders in the 1948 *McCollum* v. *Board of Education* case. Even voluntary state-approved

Bible reading was disapproved in the 1963 *Schempp v. School District of Abington* case, and public prayers approved by the state were banned in the 1962 *Engel v. Vitale* decision. While these decisions have banned any established church, they have made the state and public education so neutral that a moral vacuum seems to have developed in public education; and the way has been opened for teachings inimical to the Scriptures.

2. Germany, England, and Scandinavia have followed the pattern of union of church and state with an established church and toleration for all dissenting denominations. The appointment of church leaders and any change in standards of faith must be approved by the government. This became apparent in 1928 when church leaders in England wanted to revise the Book of Common Prayer, and the government withheld its approval. While Canada does not have a state church, public funds in Quebec have been allocated both to Protestant and Roman Catholic schools on the basis of their size in the population.

B. In Totalitarian Countries

One should not forget that revolutions, such as those in England, France, and the thirteen colonies in the seventeenth and eighteenth centuries, were democratic and edenic in their desire to return power to people, which they held in a former idyllic system. The state was limited by a constitution and a multiparty system by which the people in elections could choose the party with the best policy. A Bill of Rights and a government of law left the individual with a free, private religious and social life.

While acts of conscription, rationing, and "defense of the realm" even led to limitations in wartime in democratic lands, the state was all-powerful in leftist and rightist totalitarian states that arose after World War I. These states looked to a future racial or imperial utopia led by one man or an elite group who made laws without any limitation. One party with unlimited government, coupled with mass control by propaganda and secret police, ruled with the welfare of the state as the end. There was no distinction between public and private rights nor any Bill of Rights. Even private producing property was banned in the leftist states. Leftist Communist systems, such as in China, Russia, and Cuba, were generally harsher with the church than rightist totalitarian states, such as Germany and Italy, where there were fewer martyrs.

The democratic world has not opposed either nationalistic communism, such as that in Yugoslavia, or the rightist South American states as much as it has the international aggressive Communism of Russia or the rightist racialism of Hitler's Germany, which threatened the peace of the world. This opposition led to World War II and the cold war.

The Roman Catholic church has suffered great losses all over the world except in Spain, Portugal, Quebec, and the United States. The Nazi dictatorship in Germany weakened the Roman church of that land despite the 1933 concordat. The Communist revolution in 1917 eliminated any influence that the Roman church had had in some parts of Russia. The acquisition by Russia since 1939 of the satellite states of Estonia, Latvia, Lithuania, Czechoslovakia, Poland, Hungary, Bulgaria, Rumania, and Cuba and the present Communist domination of China has resulted in the persecution of the leaders of the Roman church in an effort to break their hold on the people. In many Latin American countries the intellectuals deserted the church and became indifferent to religion. The workers and farmers are stirring in revolt against the social, political, and economic exploitation that they have undergone during the centuries. Because the Roman church is associated with the rulers of the state, people may also turn against it as they become educated and see that it has sided with their exploiters. The nationalistic government of Mexico in its desire to create a higher economic standard of life has severely limited the power of the Roman Catholic church and has sought to eliminate its political influence. The Roman Catholic church seems to be losing its centuries-old religious monopoly in Latin America; but many priests have begun to advocate and even support violent, usually leftist, revolutionary social and economic changes to redress grievances.

To offset this loss of communicants, the Roman Catholic church has endeavored to strengthen her position in the United States and in other democratic countries whose aid she can enlist. She knows that the United States must now assume responsibility for the maintenance of world order. Both the attempt to secure an American ambassador to the Vatican and the increase in the number of American cardinals in several recent consistories seemed to be aimed at winning the support of American Roman Catholicism.

Early in the 1940s an attempt was made to have the United States State Department refuse passports to Protestant missionaries seeking to enter South American lands on the ground that they were endangering the Good Neighbor Policy. This move was defeated by aggressive action on the part of the Protestants. The power of the Roman Catholic church in the United States is demonstrated by the way Hollywood has avoided antagonizing the Roman Catholic Legion of Decency when the legion objects to immoral or anti-Roman Catholic films. Seldom does any publicity unfavorable to the Roman Catholic church appear in the American press; on the contrary, much favorable publicity, beyond its numerical strength in the population, is accorded to the Roman church by many sections of the press. Over two hundred Roman Catholic colleges and as many seminaries are located in the United States. The Roman Catholic church in the United States and elsewhere has also courted labor much more assiduously than the Protestant churches have done.

The Roman Catholic church has always insisted that it, speaking through the pope, is the final authority in matters of faith and morals. It has also claimed that the papal hierarchy can give or withhold salvation through the sacraments, which the hierarchy alone can dispense. This authoritarian, hierarchical, and sacramental system is by its very nature totalitarian in its demands on its people. Allegiance to the pope ideally precedes any other allegiance, but in practice Roman Catholics in such countries as the United States have modified this position. Insistence on a prior allegiance to the church has brought the

Roman Catholic church under persecution in totalitarian states. Because totalitarian states are basically antireligious and because Rome demands at least a friendly state, peaceful coexistence is a problem. For this reason, the pope has used every possible weapon he can against aggressive totalitarian communism and has also sought to enlist the support of democratic states.

1. One should realize that Roman Catholic hostility to rightist totalitarian states is not hostility to totalitarianism as such. Where the state will recognize the rights of the papacy, the papacy will cooperate with that state even though it is totalitarian. This fact can be demonstrated by the recent history of the papacy in Italy. Pius IX, after the Italian state incorporated the papal states and Rome into the nation (1870), retired to voluntary "imprisonment" within the Vatican and forbade Roman Catholics to cooperate with the democratic monarchical state in Italy either by voting or holding office. Not until 1929 in the Lateran Accord with the dictator Mussolini did the papacy relax its hostility to the Italian state. Mussolini permitted Pius XI to set up a new Vatican State to receive and to send ambassadors and he recognized the Roman Catholic religion as the "only religion" of the state. In return, the papacy permitted the faithful to support the totalitarian state. The papacy supported the dictatorships of Franco in Spain and Salazar in Portugal. It also came to terms with Hitler in Germany by a concordat in 1933. The pope did criticize both states in his encyclicals but did not protest German attempts to liquidate the Jews.

Smaller rightist dictatorships as well as the larger ones have also interfered with Protestant religious life. While Hitler in the 1933 concordat with the papacy guaranteed the independence of the church and freedom for Roman Catholics to profess and practice their religion, he was not so generous with Protestants after 1933. The Deutsche Evangelische Kirche of the "German Christians" was set up in 1933 with Ludwig Muller as its presiding bishop. The German Confessional Church, led by such men as Karl Barth, Martin Niemöller, and Dietrich Bonhoeffer, protested and in May 1934 issued the *Barmen Declaration.* This was for the most part the work of Karl Barth. It reasserted the authority of Christ in the church and the Scriptures as the rule of faith and life and refused to accept the claims of the state to supremacy in religious life. Niemöller was imprisoned until after the war.

Hitler also persecuted the Jews and made them the scapegoat for German troubles. He embarked on a deliberate policy of genocide, and in extermination camps in Poland and elsewhere his minions killed about six million Jews. This was nearly a third of the world's Jewish population. Not until the Allies overran the camps did the world realize how horribly he had implemented his policy.

Protestants and Roman Catholics in smaller dictatorial states have also suffered. The Protestant churches of Japan were forced into union in the Kyodan in 1941 by the Japanese government. The archbishop of the Anglican Church of Uganda was killed by Idi Amin's men; and bishops, such as Festo Kivengere, and other Christians became refugees. The revival in Chad of "yondo"—older pagan religious practices—brought persecution to the church until the dictator was over-thrown. Christians in many parts of the world know what Christians in the Roman state went through in the days of Decius and Diocletian.

2. Leftist totalitarian communism has even more severely persecuted the church. Many have suffered martyr-dom, cruel imprisonment, and horri-ble tortures for their faith. Com-munism is as great a threat to or-ganized Christianity as war or the modern blight of secularism and materialism that blasts so much of Western civilization. The opposition of the Roman state to the early church and the spread of Islam at the expense of Christianity in the Mediterranean area during the seventh and eighth centuries are the only comparable threats that the church has faced. Communism is dangerous because it is essentially a faith or a materialistic religion with an international scope and because it claims to have the only solutions to the problems of modern civilization. Its conquest of China in 1949 has made its menace more ap-parent. The largest Communist parties in free lands are in Italy and France; and communism briefly ruled in Chile by the electoral process. Communism controls one-third of the world's people.

Communism is hostile to Chris-tianity because of the materialistic atheism that underlies its philosophy. To a Marxist, religion is an "opiate" that makes the exploited content with their present hard life because they have the hope of a brighter life in the hereafter. Russian communism has been antagonistic to religion also be-cause the Russian Orthodox church in the days of the czars was linked with the oppressive policies of the state. When the Communists destroyed the czarist state, they tried to destroy the Orthodox church because it was a part of the system that they hated.

Because the Communists, through the governmental structure and over 8 million members of the Communist Party, are able to control over 200 mil-lion Russians for their own ends, the attitude of the Communists in Russia toward organized religion is of impor-tance. In 1917 over 100 million people in Russia belonged to the Orthodox church, which was controlled by a wealthy bureaucratic hierarchy.

The Communists seized power in the revolution of November 1917; and from that time until the beginning of 1923 they attacked the church directly, even though the constitution of 1918 guaranteed freedom to proclaim both religious and antireligious propa-ganda. In 1917 the property of the Or-thodox church was confiscated and made state property without any compensation to the church. The state permitted the use of churches only for worship. In that way the church lost its means of support. Clergymen and monks were deprived of the privilege of the franchise, which often meant that they could not get work or ration cards for food. Religious instruction in any school was banned, except for seminaries for adults in which only theology could be taught. Marriage ceremonies were to be performed by state officials. However, the church was allowed to elect a patriarch again.

The economic failure of pure com-munism by 1921 forced the state to reinstate some features of capitalism in order to keep production going. This also helped to bring about a change in religious policy. The policy of direct attack gave way in 1923 to a policy that emphasized propaganda to discredit religion. Antireligious carnivals, in which objects used in worship were held up to ridicule, were organized. A League of Militant Atheists was founded in 1925 to circulate atheistic propaganda.

Neither the ridicule nor the atheistic propaganda of the 1923-to-1927 program was successful; so the Russian government adopted a program that included strangling Christian culture, direct attack, and antireligious education. It was carried out between 1928 and 1939. The few remaining churches were permitted to hold services of worship only and were deprived of the right to teach or persuade others to become Christians. Over fourteen hundred church buildings were closed in 1929 and used by the government for secular purposes. From 1920 to 1940 no one could go to church unless Sunday corresponded with the sixth rest day. The constitution of the state was amended in 1929 to provide "freedom to hold religious services and the freedom of antireligious propaganda." This meant that any attempt to win others to Christianity was banned, but atheism was given full rights to propagandize adults and the young in the schools.

The failure of militant atheism to eradicate Christianity, the persistence of belief in God, which approximately half of the Russian people expressed in the 1937 census, and the threatening international situation dictated the need for a strategic retreat after 1939. Churches were reopened, the antireligious carnivals were dropped, and the teaching of atheism in the schools was abandoned. In 1943 Sergius was permitted to function as the patriarch of Moscow and all Russia.

The seven-day week was restored, seminaries were permitted to reopen, and the Orthodox church was freed of many burdensome restrictions. From the viewpoint of the government, the wisdom of making these concessions became apparent when the church supported the government at the time Germany invaded Russia in 1941. At the most, the Russian church has toleration but not full freedom of religion.

Russian communism emerged from World War II with great new additions of territory in Europe and Asia. The three Baltic republics, Poland, Czechoslovakia, Hungary, Rumania, and Bulgaria have all come under Communist control. In each state the church has been persecuted. The persecution in some instances had the support of the people because the clergy had a bad record of clerical oppression of the people. Even the nationalistic brand of communism in Titoist Yugoslavia persecuted the church. The church in China suffered persecution from the Communist authorities.

The Roman Catholic church bitterly opposed communism. Pius XI in *Divini Redemptoris* (1937) criticized communism as he did Nazism in that same year in *Mit brennender Sorge*. Later the Roman Catholic church seemed to be somewhat accommodating itself to Communist regimes by having its people in Poland vote for the Communist Gomulka as head of the state, which was 80 percent Roman Catholic. The pope even on one occasion received the son-in-law of Khruschev in the Vatican. Vatican II documents have no condemnation of communism. Where such rulers will leave the Roman Catholic church free to work with its people, it seems willing to cooperate either with left or right dictatorships.

When Protestants have been in Communist states, they have not fared well. At first the regime seemed to cooperate with the churches, as in China, and urged them only to cut ties with the "imperialistic" world. The "Three-Self Movement" in China in 1951, while supposedly leaving the church free, led to the takeover of church property and the banning of Bibles and religious education. Some Protestants, such as Hromadka in Czechoslovakia, even urged submission to and cooperation with the state as scriptural and urged dialogue with the Communists by Christians. Communism with all its repression has not been able to destroy religion; and religion still is the comfort of millions in China, Russia, and other countries behind the Iron Curtain.

The Christian world must realize the nature of this new political faith by a study of its ideas so that people can discern the difference between truth and Communist propaganda. The church must support measures to end the evils that help to create communism. Communism flourishes best where there is poverty and suffering that it can promise to alleviate. The church must not let itself become the tool of any particular group and condone or encourage wrongs in society. While recognizing that it can flourish best in a free-enterprise, democratic society, it should preach and live the gospel rather than permit itself to become identified with any particular political or economic order. Above all, a consistent Christian life on the part of her members, whatever their status in society, is the most effective answer

of the church to communism or to the secular state.

III. ETHNIC AND RELIGIOUS STATE NATIONALISM

The churches in the United States supported the freeing of blacks from slavery by the Thirteenth Amendment in 1863, but they were indifferent to the problem of segregation in the next century. Black awareness developed with the rise of the NAACP in 1906. Blacks desired better economic and social conditions and an end to segregation. In 1949 President Truman banned segregation in the military and civil services. The Supreme Court in *Brown* v. *The Board of Education* in 1954 declared the end of "separate but equal education" schools for blacks in favor of integration in the schools. President Eisenhower had to send Federal troops to Little Rock, Arkansas, in 1957 to enforce the decision. Busing has become the present pattern of enforcement by order of the court. Rosa Parks's defiance of segregated bus seating in 1955 led, under the leadership of Martin Luther King, Jr., to a ban on segregated seating on interstate buses in 1961 by the Interstate Commerce Commission. Black sit-ins opened up restaurants, parks, and other public facilities to blacks. The 1964 Civil Rights Act reinforced this and banned discrimination because of skin color in unions. Another act in 1965 protected the right of blacks to vote. The 1968 Housing Act promoted open housing.

While many, especially of liberal theological persuasion, supported these movements, many churches were slow to admit blacks to white churches. Much progress has been made in this area since 1965.

Blacks in South Africa faced ecclesiastical opposition to their demands for an end to apartheid, or separate development of the races in black states. Some concessions have been made to them. People forget that both blacks and whites moved into southern Africa from different directions about the same time and that it is a homeland for both races.

Many blacks in Africa have rebelled against what they feel is white missionary paternalism and have created independent black churches. A fair estimate lists six thousand such groups in 290 tribes with over seven million followers in thirty-four states in 1967. They are often eschatologically oriented, charismatic, and under native leadership.[1]

Hitler's treatment of the Jews as an ethnic and religious minority has already been described. Arabs have bitterly fought the Jewish state. India had to be made into separate states of India and Pakistan because of Muslim-Hindu rivalry, which was a form of religious nationalism. Orthodox Greeks oppose Muslim Turkish people in Cyprus, and bloody conflict in recent years has made North Ireland a battleground between Roman Catholics and Protestants.

Many new states in Asia and Africa have either banned new missionaries or nationalized the missions' educational, printing, and other facilities. Many also have supported the revival of older ethnic religions as in Chad.

The problems of relations of church and state over war, the power of the state, and state ecclesiastical and ethnic nationalism are likely to continue. What progress has been made is gratifying, but there is much yet to be done by the church in standing for its own independence and against oppression of every kind.

SUGGESTED READING

Abrams, Ray H. "The Churches and Clergy in World War II." In **The Annals of the American Academy of Political Science** 256:110–19. *This discusses the role of the church in World War II.*

_____. **Preachers Present Arms.** *Scottdale, Pa.: Herald, 1969. This presents much information on the role of American churches in World Wars I and II.*

Blanshard, Paul. **American Freedom and Catholic Power.** *2nd ed. Boston: Beacon, 1958. This is a well-documented survey of the activities of the Roman Catholic church in the United States.*

Cochrane, Arthur C. **The Church's Confession Under Hitler.** *Philadelphia: Westminster, 1962. The author claims that the church was the only social unit to oppose Hitler.*

Curtiss, John S. **The Russian Church and Soviet State, 1917–1950.** *Boston: Little, 1953. A well-documented account of the history of the church in Russia since 1917 is presented.*

Fey, Harold E. "Can Catholicism Win America?" In **Christian Century,** *29 November 1944 to 7 January 1945. This series of articles presents the many ramifications of Roman Catholic ecclesiastical machinery in the United States.*

Hoover, J. Edgar. **A Study of Communism.** *New York: Holt, Rinehart, and Winston, 1962. This is an able discussion of contemporary communism.*

Howard, G. P. **Religious Liberty in Latin America.** *Philadelphia: Westminster, ca. 1944. The author presents the place of Roman Catholicism in Latin America.*

Hutten, Kurt. Iron Curtain Christians. *Translated by Walter G. Tillman. Minneapolis: Augsburg, 1967.*

Kolarz, Walter. Religion in the Soviet Union. *London: Macmillan, 1967.*

Patterson, George N. Christianity in Communist China. *Waco: Word, 1969.*

Pollock, John C. The Faith of the Russian Evangelicals. *New York: McGraw-Hill, 1964.*

Rehwinkle, Alfred M. Communism and the Church. *St. Louis: Concordia, 1948. The author ably discusses communism and the means by which Christians can develop a positive approach and program to meet its threat.*

Stokes, Anson D. Church and State in the United States. *3 vols. New York: Harper, 1950.*

Timasheff, Nicholas. Religion in Soviet Russia. *New York: Sheed, 1942. This book develops with adequate documentation the struggle between church and state in Russia.*

Chapter 39

Changes in Theology and Structure

Evangelical Christianity faced increasing attacks during the late nineteenth century and the early part of the twentieth century. Ideas of the once-for-all universal nature of Christianity; the absolute God known through His propositional, verbal, inerrant revelation inspired by the Holy Spirit; and the global validity of that inspired objective historical revelation concerning Christ were challenged. They were also later denied in favor of subjective, immanental, and humanistic approaches to the gospel. The nature of the church, biblical inspiration and inerrancy, the role of the Holy Spirit in the church, and eschatology have figured more in contemporary theological disputes.

Classical liberalism arose in the nineteenth century and peaked by World War I, when it controlled major seminaries, colleges, and pulpits. It broke down after World War I because of the horrors of war, major depression, and the rise of neoorthodoxy. Its doctrines of the immanence of God, subjective revelation, and a postmil-lennial future through human effort were too naive to meet the postwar challenges.

Neoorthodoxy dominated the theological scene from 1930 to 1950, but it lost momentum in the 1960s. It became more subjective and existential in the writings of Tillich and Bultmann.

During the past two decades it has been replaced by radical humanistic, relativistic, and secular theologies, such as the death-of-God theology, the secular theology of Cox and Robinson, Marxist-tinged theologies of hope by Moltmann and radical liberation, and black and feminist theologies. Sociological salvation through people in time rather than by the eternal God through Christ seems to be the vogue. A renascent evangelicalism, however, developed rapidly to replace liberal theology with its bias toward ecumenicalism.

In addition to these internal problems of the source and nature of theology, the church has faced the problem of the ecumenical movement,

443

which desires to reunite Christendom. This movement has in some cases sacrificed sound theology for structural union based on the lowest common denominator.

I. THEOLOGICAL DECLINE AND RECONSTRUCTION

A. The Dissolution of Liberalism and Neoorthodoxy

1. By 1900 the ideas of the universal fatherhood of God and brotherhood of man had spread from the seminaries to the laity as liberal ministers took over the pulpits of the land. Although some have tried to trace the roots of this theological liberalism to Stoic ideas, it was transmitted to America by American students of theology who studied German idealistic philosophy and biblical criticism in German and Scottish universities.

Kantian philosophy was a major source of liberal thinking. Kant held to two levels of truth and confined the Bible to phenomenal history as the subjective record of man's consciousness of God. The Bible was to be studied as a human book by scientific methods rather than as a revelation from God. Religion was rooted in the upper level of practical reason with the postulate of an innate human sense of right and wrong that demanded the acceptance of the existence of the soul, God, and immortality, with reward and punishment as practical religious ideas. This immanental approach to theology was amplified by Schleiermacher, who considered religion to be a feeling or consciousness of dependence on God in Christ. Darwinian evolution was also applied to religion so that it became an evolutionary subjective process of increasing knowledge of God and upward human progress.

Liberals had in common ideas of a God immanent in history and in each person to guarantee progress toward an ideal human order on earth. Perfectible man faced mainly the problem of an environment that would lead him to sin by choice. With Christ as his example, however, he could improve himself and the social order. The Bible, according to the liberals, contained only the subjective record of man's consciousness of God. Education and social action, sponsored by the church, would create an ideal social order to which Christ would return after the Millennium. College and seminary professors, the popular and religious press, and preachers proclaimed these ideas. Harry Emerson Fosdick became a popular exponent of these ideas from his pulpit in Riverside Church in New York.

The problems of World War I, the Great Depression of 1929, and the influence of the existential theology of Sören Kierkegaard (1813–55) on Karl Barth and his followers shattered the liberal idea of human progress through the efforts of man. God to Barth was transcendent rather than immanent, and man was sinful rather than born with a spark of the divine in him. By 1930, liberalism became less influential, and the old-line liberal denominations declined in membership, influence, and the number of missionaries they sent abroad.

Several theologians, meeting at Hartford Seminary in January 1975, criticized these liberal assumptions and called for a return to doctrines these liberally oriented men had earlier associated with evangelicals. This was a drastic reversal of the 1923 Auburn Affirmation, which 1,300 Presbyterian ministers had signed. This document had stated that biblical inerrance, the Virgin Birth, vicarious atonement, and Christ's resurrection and miracles were not "essential" doctrines.

2. Neoorthodoxy, the theology of crisis, or, as it is sometimes called, existential theology replaced the declining liberalism between 1930 and 1950. The study of Schleiermacher, Ritschl, and Harnack in seminaries gave way to the study of Barth's *Commentary on Romans* (1919) and his later books. Barth, Brunner, and Reinhold Niebuhr were later followed by the more radical and existentialist Bultmann and Tillich.

Two destructive global wars, the Great Depression, and the diabolic nature of right- and left-wing totalitarianism after World War I made liberalism increasingly irrelevant and neoorthodoxy more historically and theologically tenable. When his father told the Danish theologian Sören Kierkegaard that he had once as a boy cursed God and had been unfaithful in his marriage, when Soren's own engagement to Regina Olsen was arbitrarily broken off by himself, and when he saw the spiritual failure in the Lutheran state church of Denmark, he began to develop his existentialist theological system, which was to strongly influence neoorthodox thinkers. Human despair caused him to relate to a transcendental God in personal decision and commitment by a "leap of faith" rather than by any rational process. This idea of God confronting a person in crisis apart from human effort and reason reappears in neoorthodoxy.

Karl Barth (1886–1968), who initiated neoorthodoxy, was born in Basel, Switzerland, but received a liberal theological training in Germany. After a short period as a writer for a liberal German magazine he became a pastor in Switzerland. There the needs of his parishioners and the inadequacy of his liberal theology drove him to the Scriptures and the writings of John Calvin. He then taught theology in German theological institutions from 1921 until 1935, when his opposition to Nazi religious policy forced him to go to Basel. He taught at the university there until 1962, after which he retired to engage in writing his massive theological works.

He and his followers had certain common ideas. God was "wholly other" than man, an eternally transcendent holy being. Man was helplessly finite and sinful. The Bible is a human book subject to biblical criticism like any other book. It is a record of revelation and a witness to revelation rather than being an inspired, objective, historical, propositional revelation in itself. The Bible becomes revelation to the individual in the moment of crisis, when the Holy Spirit uses it to effect a personal encounter with God. In fact, revelation is understood to be encounter rather than communication of information. Divine history, or salvation history, is separate from the human sciential history produced by the historian. God is uninterested in human history or social salvation in it. People are in Christ, already elected to salvation, and need only to be made aware of this fact.

Evangelicals welcomed this reassertion of the sinfulness of man, the transcendence of God, and the emphasis on biblical theology by Barth, but they rejected his discontinuity between holy and secular history and his rejection of an objective, historical, propositional revelation from God. Except for Reinhold Niebuhr, neoorthodox thinkers have no place for social responsibility. Appeals to rational apologetics and Christian evidences were replaced by a description of faith as a blind leap. Elements of universalism were present in their soteriology. Although man was looked upon as sinful, it was more because of actual sin than original sin that was based on the "myth" of a historical Adam and Eve. Neoorthodox thinkers also retained the older liberal biblical criticism.

Although Emil Brunner (1889–1966) supported most of these ideas, he differed from Barth by accepting some general revelation of God in nature and by holding a less historical view of the Virgin birth of Christ. Reinhold Niebuhr (1893–1971) soon found liberalism inadequate to meet the needs of auto workers in his Detroit parish. In *Moral Man and Immoral Society* (1932) and *The Nature and Destiny of Man* (1941–43) he pointed up human sinfulness and its baneful political, economic, and social impact. He believed that God's love in the Cross gave an answer reaching beyond history, but he insisted that redeeming love in man would bring about proximate social answers to human social needs.

Paul Tillich (1886–1965), a German refugee and a professor for many years at Union Theological Seminary in New York, was more philosophical than Barth. His God was the ultimate nontheistic "ground of being" with whom human encounter was experiential and existential. He dissolved both the Bible and creeds into subjective expressions of human thought to be subjected to historical criticism. Religion was "ultimate concern" and a commitment to God as the ultimate ground of being, and, by having religion a person was able to overcome sin, which was merely estrangement from that ground of being. John Robinson (1919–), bishop of Woolwich, in his book *Honest to God* (1963) popularized some of Tillich's ideas about God but leaves us without a personal God and a historical revelation from Him.

Rudolf Bultmann (1884–1976) used form criticism to extract the kernels of revelation from the husks of myth and other literary forms in which he said the apostles presented truth. He concluded from his criticism that we can know very little about Christ's person, teachings, or life. Thus he "demythologized" the Bible and made experience and ethics more important than doctrine. His critical views became so radical that significant differences arose between him and Barth. Neoorthodoxy, while in some respects an improvement on liberalism, began to collapse in the 1950s. In the next decade it was replaced by radical theologies.

3. Several radical, secular, and humanistic theologies have risen and fallen since 1960. Each has proved inadequate to meet man's religious needs. Each exchanged a transcendent God for one who was immanent in history, and a Christ who was wholly God for a human Christ who was not God.

a. Theologians such as Thomas J. J. Altizer, Paul van Buren, and William Hamilton developed the ephemeral "God is dead" theology. These men were indebted to Nietzsche for their theology, which was first popularized in columns in the *New York Times* and the *New Yorker* in October 1965. It is not clear whether they intended to say that for many God is dead psychologically because He has ceased to exist in practice for them; or He is dead historically because He seems irrelevant in a secular world of wars, the Jewish "holocaust," and the Great Depression; or He is ontologically dead, according to Altizer, because He died in the death of Christ. Action in this secular world replaces theology. With Bonhoeffer, who was executed by the Nazis, they wanted a "religionless Christianity" with ethical meaning in action. This stress on activism and social action seemed to match the radical mood of the sixties. It would link the church with the world much as the older liberalism and its social gospel did.

Dietrich Bonhoeffer (1906–1945), who had been influenced by Barth and Bultmann, spoke of man as having "come of age" intellectually in a world of crisis in which theology was irrelevant and in which man must act responsibly in moral, "holy worldliness" in commitment to Christ as Lord. Such an existential "worldly Christianity" would link the sacred and secular in daily life. Bonhoeffer's books and letters from the 1930s and 1940s were widely influential in this period.

Harvey Cox, a professor of divinity at Harvard University, wrote *The Secular City* (1965), in which he argued that urbanization and secularization led to the demise of a God "out there." God is immanent in the world, especially in urban society, and man can find fulfillment in society, in which the hidden God may be discovered.

b. These secular theologies have fallen before the newer theologies of hope of Jurgen L. Moltmann (1926–) and Wolfhart Pannenberg (1928–). Moltmann emphasized the future action of God in history more than past revelation. Man's dilemma will be solved by the fulfillment of promise of future deliverance by God's will and action. These ideas in his *Theology of Hope* (1967) dissolve history into the future and the future into revolution in which Christ and salvation are related to social development in a system that has a Marxian tinge.

Pannenberg takes history more seriously and particularly the resurrection of Christ. History reveals God in action, and His activity can be studied historically. Revelation is act or event rather than proposition. Final meaning through Christ comes at the end of history.

c. Pierre Teilhard de Chardin (1881–1955) seems to be somewhat in the tradition of Lloyd Morgan's concept of emergent evolution or Henri Bergson's vitalism. He anticipates in some respects process theology with his involvement of God in the natural process of evolution. In Teilhard's evolutionary process the "alpha particles" are part of an upward development in a process in which Christ as the "Omega Point" draws these elemental units together creatively to form higher orders. God and His world are together evolving to a new, or more perfect order.

d. Process theology that is more philosophical than that of Teilhard is based on the thinking of Alfred N. Whitehead (1861–1947) and is propounded by Charles Hartshorne (1897–) of the University of Chicago and John Cobb, Jr. These men seek to develop a theodicy to explain evil in the world. The nature of reality is *becoming* rather than *being,* and both God and His universe are becoming rather than being. All living existents react to environment and to one another in free creative choice, which may cause suffering. The primordial God, who is also creative, is in love guiding creation to a higher level in order that He and His creation may overcome evil and avert chaos in a new order.

e. Liberation theology, to which radical black theology and feminist theology are somewhat related, emerged in Latin America in *A Theology of Liberation* (1973) by the Roman Catholic Peruvian Gustavo Gutierrez (1928–) and in the writings of Rubem Alves and, in North America, Roger Shaull. According to them, theology must start as did Christ with a commitment to the liberation of the oppressed as practice rather than theory. Theology grows out of the human situation in history rather than out of thought. This is also true of James Cone's black theology and the more recent feminist theology. Human history is the stage of theology and liberation, often conceived of in Marxist terms. This salvation is social, economic, and political liberation from all forms of oppression. As in the case of the Jewish Exodus, revelation is dealing with historical oppression and liberation by man led by the example of the liberator Christ rather than by the revealed Word of God. The eternal gospel is not simply contextualized by relating it to temporal culture but is divorced from revelation. Most of these attempts to end oppression and build the kingdom of God in a new liberated society flirt with Marxism and politicize Christianity in situation history.

These short-lived systems have flitted across the theological stage with increasing rapidity since 1960. They are attempts to solve the problems of man in history through the efforts of autonomous man and an immanent deity in a human Christ; but they do not do justice to God, Christ, or the Bible. A resurgent evangelicalism listens to the cry of need in these theologies but emphatically asserts the authority of the Bible, the existence of the transcendent God, and the relevance of Christ as God and Savior to man. Although he is aware of man's personal and social needs, the evangelical is also aware that the final solution to human problems is to be found in God and His revelation.

B. The Resurgence of Evangelicalism

Former stereotypes of evangelicals, such as "Fighting Fundies," "snake handlers," "bibliolaters," or "third-degree separationists," have been replaced by a growing understanding of the numerical strength and influence of evangelicals. George Gallup, Jr., after a 1976 poll revealed that about 34 percent of all Americans, or nearly 50 million people, classed themselves as evangelicals, declared 1976 the Year of the Evangelical.

A more recent poll by Gallup for *Christianity Today* showed that 20 percent of all adults over 18, or 31 million Americans—or if those under 18 are included, 44 million—call themselves evangelicals. Nearly one-third of all adults, or about 50 million Americans, speak of having had a life-changing spiritual experience related to faith in Christ. Of the 31 million adults mentioned above, about 4 million claim to be Roman Catholic, and about 10 million think of themselves as charismatic. All of these evangelicals generally hold to the Bible as God's Word, to the deity of Christ, and to salvation by faith.

Although these people are in the tradition of the Reformation, they also owe much to Puritanism and Pietism. At the beginning of this century evangelicals included the Princeton theologians and others oriented to Calvinism, the more Arminian Wesleyans in the Church of the Nazarene, and the Salvation Army. Premillennialists (some holding to dispensational theology), amillennialists, the classic Pentecostal groups, and the mainline denominational charismatics, as well as the Jesus people, must be included. Some are in independent churches; others in smaller denominations or in the older mainline denominations.

Most of these who are characterized as evangelicals hold certain ideas in common. They believe the Scriptures are the inspired, infallible rule of faith and practice. They believe in human depravity because of a historic Fall and original sin. They assert vigorously Christ's Virgin Birth, deity, vicarious atonement, and resurrection. A new birth and a life of righteousness become a reality through faith in Christ. Although they have insisted on the priority of the proclamation of the gospel, they have often been in the vanguard of social action in America. They have opposed biblical criticism, evolution, and the social gospel as taught by liberals of the past.

1. Until the end of World War I evangelicals fell into two groups, which often cooperated in some areas of religious activity.

a. The followers of the Princeton school of theology of Archibald A. Hodge (1823–86) and Benjamin B. Warfield (1851–1921), such Presbyterians as Francis L. Patton and Robert Dick Wilson, such Baptists as Edgar Y. Mullins, and the notable Greek scholar Archibald T. Robertson (1863–1934), were Calvinists who fall into this category. Several Arminian groups such as some of the Mennonite denominations and the Church of the Nazarene, should also be included.

The Nazarene denomination began in Los Angeles in 1895 under the leadership of Phineas F. Bresee. By 1908 many other churches who were dissatisfied with the Methodist denomination united finally under the name the Church of the Nazarene. They emphasize a second work of grace for sanctification as do most in the tradition of John Wesley.

b. A second large category in this period includes mainly premillennialists and dispensational premillennialists who were often called "Fundamentalists." This term was first used in the July 1, 1920, issue of the Baptist *Watchman Examiner* by the editor, C. C. Laws, to designate those holding to the fundamentals of the historic faith. The word was used later in a pejorative sense even of some of the amillennial evangelicals in the denominations who held to the common doctrines of the evangelicals.

Both categories of evangelicals often cooperated in Bible conferences such as one of the earliest, which was held in July 1876 at Swamscott, Massachusetts. A nondenominational prophetic conference gathered in 1878 in Holy Trinity Church in New York to discuss prophecy concerning the second coming of Christ. Meetings on this theme were continued annually from 1893 to 1898 at Niagara, New York. The premillennialism discussed in these meetings was wedded by some to the dispensational theology spread by J. N. Darby (1800–82). The so-called five points of Fundamentalism were usually linked with the Niagara conference of 1895, but the statement actually included fourteen points.

Some of the leading participants in these conferences helped to found Bible schools to provide biblical training for lay people. Nyack Missionary College in New York began in 1882. Moody Bible Institute opened in 1886 but did not engage in its present work until 1889. Toronto Bible College in 1894 and the Bible Institute of Los Angeles in 1908 were next to open. Many others have been added until in 1976 fifty thousand students were enrolled in four hundred Bible schools. Of this number, thirty-five thousand were in one hundred schools accredited by the American Association of Bible Colleges.

Cyrus I. Scofield (1843–1921) popularized dispensational premillennialism in the footnotes of his Scofield Bible, which was published in 1909 with the generous help of influential businessmen. It has been widely used by the laity and is the unofficial text of the Bible in many of the Bible schools.

A sermon in August 1909 by A. C. Dixon led the wealthy oilmen Lyman and Milton Stewart to give about $200,000 to publish *The Fundamentals*. This twelve-volume set included articles both by denominational and nondenominational evangelicals on both sides of the Atlantic. James Orr, B. B. Warfield, M. G. Kyle, R. A. Torrey, C. I. Scofield, and many other evangel-

ical scholars contributed articles, all of which helped to disseminate evangelical ideas. The first volume came out in 1910, and by 1915 the twelfth volume appeared. About 300,000 copies of each volume were sent free of charge to seminary professors and students, pastors and Y.M.C.A. secretaries in the United States, Canada, and Great Britain. W. E. Blackstone's (1841–1935) *Jesus Is Coming* and periodicals, such as *The Sunday School Times*, *Moody Monthly*, and *The Christian Herald*, helped to promote the ideas of the early evangelicals.

Billy Sunday, R. A. Torrey, and Rodney "Gipsy" Smith adopted the urban mass evangelistic campaigns developed by Dwight L. Moody. Professional evangelists with well-organized staffs held major meetings outside the church in large halls and added many to the evangelical ranks.

2. Between 1919 and 1945 this dual pattern of "Fundamentalists" and evangelicals, many of them in the older denominations, continued in opposition to liberalism. Increasing tensions over such theological issues as eschatology often created internal problems in these two groups.

a. "Fundamentalists" such as W. B. Riley (1861–1947), John B. Straton (1874–1929) of Calvary Baptist Church in New York, Henry ("Harry") A. Ironsides (1876–1951), and T. T. Shields (1873–1955) of Toronto opposed liberalism and, especially Riley, evolution.

Nondenominational colleges were formed by evangelicals. Wheaton College (1860) was joined by Bob Jones University (1926) and Columbia Bible College (1923). Dallas Seminary was founded by Lewis Sperry Chafer (1871–1952) in 1924 and became a center of dispensational premillennialism. Chafer wrote a multivolume *Systematic Theology* (1947–1948) setting forth dispensational premillennial thought, and J. Oliver Buswell developed a similar but more Reformed theology.

b.. Evangelicals who were not dispensational or, in some cases, even premillennial actively opposed liberalism in their denominations between the two world wars. J. Gresham Machen's scholarly *Origin of Paul's Religion* (1921) and his *Virgin Birth of Christ* (1930) ably met liberal challenges to these doctrines. Robert Dick Wilson excelled in his writings in the field of archaeology.

Mark Matthews (1926–) of the First Presbyterian Church in Seattle and Clarence C. Macartney (1879–1957) in Pittsburgh built up large evangelical denominational churches.

More militant evangelicals supported the evangelical cause both in civil and church courts. They responded to Baptist Harry Emerson Fosdick's sermon "Shall the Fundamentalists Win?" by action in the General Assembly of the Presbyterian Church, USA, to force him to leave the Presbyterian Church he was supplying. He became a popular liberal preacher in the Riverside Church in New York City, a church that John D. Rockefeller helped to build. The tables were turned in the 1930s when some evangelical preachers, J. Gresham Machen, for example, were put on trial by liberals in church courts and forced out of their denominations.

Those who were forced out of the liberal denominations formed new denominations and educational institutions. J. Gresham Machen (1881–1937) helped in 1936 to organize the Orthodox Presbyterian Church, having earlier (in 1929) helped to found Westminster Theological Seminary in Philadelphia, where Cornelius van Til and Edward Young did scholarly work. Carl McIntire broke with Machen in 1937 and organized the Bible Presbyterian Church and later Faith Seminary along premillennial lines. Later defectors from McIntire's group founded Covenant Seminary in St. Louis. Baptists broke with their liberal denomination to create the General Association of Regular Baptists in 1932 and the Conservative Baptist Association in 1947.

Bitter opposition to the teaching of evolution in public schools brought about the Scopes trial in 1925 in Dayton, Tennessee. William Jennings Bryan (1860–1925) was the prosecuting lawyer, and Clarence Darrow (1857–1938) defended John T. Scopes. Scopes lost the case, and several southern legislatures passed laws banning the teaching of evolution in public schools.

3. Between the end of World War II and the present the evangelical spectrum has widened into at least four major orientations. All uphold the authority of the Bible for faith and practice and the deity of Christ and other doctrines, but they differ on how these doctrines are to be conceived and how evangelicals are to relate to nonevangelicals. Evangelical parachurch organizations, charismatic groups, the Jesus People, and intradenominational lay groups must be considered a part of the evangelical spectrum.

a. *Evangelical diversity.* The older "Fundamentalism" is expressed by the contemporary right wing separatism of such groups as those led by Bob Jones, Carl McIntire, John R. Rice, and many others. *The Christian Beacon* of Dr. McIntire and the more evangelistic *Sword of the Lord* of John R. Rice represent these groups in the periodical press. The American Council of Christian Churches (1941) and the International Council of Christian Churches, which McIntire organized in 1948 at Amsterdam, links such people in the United States with like Christians in other countries.

Somewhat to the right of center are those who have been called the "Evangelical Establishment." They emphasize the verbal inspiration and inerrancy of the Scriptures and the priority of proclamation, without, however, excluding social action by Christians. These include such men as Carl F. H. Henry, Harold Lindsell, and Francis Schaeffer; such Bible schools and seminaries as Moody Bible Institute, Trinity and Dallas Seminaries; and such colleges as Wheaton. The National Association of Evangelicals with a claimed constituency of 10 million, the scholarly Evangelical Theological Society (1949), the periodical *Christianity Today* (1956), and the Billy Graham Evangelistic Association may also be understood to belong in this category. Many in the Southern Baptist Convention and in the Lutheran Church–Missouri Synod fit into the same category.

Another grouping to the left of the evangelical theological center looks to Fuller Seminary (1947) for leadership. Because Harold J. Ockenga, the first president of Fuller Seminary, coined the term, those who are of this viewpoint have often been described as neoevangelicals (or new evangelicals). While they hold the Bible to be an infallible authority for faith and practice, they raise questions concerning verbal inspiration and inerrancy and believe that biblical criticism can be used profitably; see, for example, Jack Rogers in *Biblical Authority* (Word, 1977). This viewpoint became evident as early as 1966 during the Wenham conference on inspiration at Gordon College. Harold Lindsell in his *Battle for the Bible* (1976) and its sequel, *The Bible in the Balance* (1979), opposed this tendency in favor of declaring the Bible to be verbally inspired and inerrant.

These two groups also differ on how far evangelicals should engage in dialogue with liberal and neoorthodox ecumenical groups, on the nature and extent of social action by evangelicals, and on whether any form of evolution can be reconciled with creationism. Certain leaders have adopted some form of theistic evolution, such as "threshold evolution." Jack Rogers, Dewey Beegle, Daniel Fuller, Bernard Ramm, and many other younger evangelicals support one or more of the less conservative viewpoints.

A smaller group of younger evangelicals is moving still further to the "left" over the issues of social action and feminism. Many of their leaders met in Chicago in November 1973 and issued a declaration that expressed repentance for past evangelical indifference to social and economic issues and called for greater political participation in solving social problems. Ronald J. Sider advocates a simpler lifestyle, and Paul Henry of Calvin College has been advocating increased participation in the political process to promote social justice. Magazines such as *Sojourners*, edited by Jim Wallis, express their concerns regularly.

Letha Scanzoni and many other young career women related to the above group have developed a feminist theology and helped to promote an evangelical feminist meeting in 1975 in Washington. They formed an Evangelical Women's Caucus to promote the interests of Christian career women, including those who opt for a single life. They claim a membership of over 2,000. They have applied some of the elements of liberation theology in the development of a feminist theology.

b. *Evangelical parachurch organizations.* The borders of these four groups of evangelicals since 1945 are somewhat fluid so that a person may fit in more than one group in regard to the various points of difference. All of them however, would want to be classified as evangelicals and, except for those on the right, cooperate in what have come to be called parachurch or extrachurch organizations. Parachurch groups cooperate with most of the denominations. These growing organizations constitute one of the more important elements to rise in the history of the church and have a variety of services or ministries that they offer to the Christian public.

The desire for evangelical cooperation is seen in the *ecumenical* organizations that have been formed. For those on the right there is the American Council of Christian Churches. Those in the center and some on the left have generally cooperated in the National Association of Evangelicals, which parallels the liberal National Council of Churches (see pp. 465–69).

With the exception of some persons to the right, evangelicals have worked together in various types of *evangelism* to fulfill Christ's Great Commission. Many organizations with creative leaders seek to reach youth with the gospel. Inter-Varsity Christian Fellowship, which began in England in 1923, was organized in Canadian universities by 1928. It developed in the United States until it was large enough to incorporate in 1941. The Student Foreign Missions Fellowship, created to spark student interest in missions, affiliated with it in 1945. It has sponsored the student missionary conventions at Urbana since the first one was held in Toronto during the Christmas vacation of 1945 with seven hundred students in attendance.

Campus Crusade was organized by Bill Bright in 1951 to present the gospel to students on the campus of U.C.L.A. This businessman and seminary student promoted a more aggressive type of evangelism and discipling process for converts. His organization set up Explo 72, which brought seventy thousand young persons together in Dallas in 1972 for intensive short-term training in evangelism.

Youth for Christ first appeared with a rally promoted by Roger Malsbury in 1943 in Indianapolis. Torrey Johnson became the first president in 1944, and Billy Graham its first traveling representative.

Young Life was created in 1941 by James Rayburn to reach high school students by the organization of Bible study groups.

The Torchbearers, with headquarters in Capernwray, England, was formed by Ian Thomas after World War II. Through personal witnessing of its members and short-term Bible schools, it has reached thousands all over the world.

Other organizations have been formed to meet the needs of special groups. The Officer's Christian Fellowship, organized in the United States in

1943, ministers to over 350,000 officers in the armed forces. Dawson Trotman founded the Navigators in World War II to win sailors to Christ and to disciple them in the Christian life. Billy Graham enlisted the aid of the Navigators in the development of the follow-up program for his converts.

In 1898 some businessmen founded the organization called the Gideons. They have given much time and money to placing copies of the Bible in hotels, motels, and schools. During World War II they distributed copies of the New Testament to young people in the various branches of the armed services.

The Christian Businessmen's Committee International began in 1931 and was incorporated in 1937 to help businessmen in evangelizing their colleagues and in the development of their own spiritual life. This organization now reaches around the world.

International Christian Leadership under the guidance of Abraham Vereide has through prayer breakfasts since 1954 sought to reach political leaders in all levels of government with the gospel and to support them spiritually in their lives.

Francis Schaeffer, through people studying at his home in L'Abri, Switzerland, and through his writings and movies, has reached many of the upper-class intellectual dropouts and disenchanted students with the gospel, which he presents at a high intellectual and philosophical level. He also stoutly defends a high view of the inspiration of Scripture both in meetings such as that at Lausanne and in his writings.

James Kennedy originated Evangelism Explosion in his Coral Ridge Presbyterian Church in Ft. Lauderdale, Florida. He trains the laity through teaching and practice in the art of home visitation and presentation of the gospel. The method has been widely used throughout the United States and abroad.

Donald McGavran, a minister in the Christian Church, combined evangelism, especially on the mission field, with scientific crosscultural research. In 1965 he became the head of the School of World Mission at Fuller Seminary. Colleagues continue his work, and graduates have used his methods to analyze the needs of a field and to develop a relevant message for church growth.

Organized professional evangelism in centers outside church buildings in large cities has been practiced in the United States since the days of Dwight L. Moody. The career of Billy Graham (1918–) was launched with his tent crusade in Los Angeles in 1949. During his 1957 crusade in New York nearly 57,000 of the 2 million attending the crusade made a decision for Christ. Over 3 million attended his five-day crusade in 1973 in Seoul, Korea. His "Hour of Decision" program on radio in 1950 and later on television, as well as films that his organization have made, has extended his evangelistic outreach. He has avoided the taint of commercialism by careful financial accounting and receiving only monthly salaries for himself and his colleagues.

Graham also supported the World Congress on Evangelism sponsored by *Christianity Today* in the fall of 1966. About 1,200 evangelicals from all parts of the world met to discuss and pray concerning the task of world evangelism. The relevance, urgency, nature, problems, and techniques of Bible-

Billy Graham, leading evangelist of the mid-twentieth century.

centered evangelism were considered. Asian evangelicals met in Singapore in 1968 to discuss evangelism in Asia.

The largest conference on evangelism was held at Lausanne in July 1974 with over 2,400 delegates, of whom one-third came from Third World churches. Delegates represented 150 countries, 135 of them Protestant. The resultant Lausanne Covenant emphasized loyalty to the inspired Scriptures as the infallible rule of faith and practice and also stated under pressure from the Third World delegates that social concern and action were a relevant part of the gospel. The Consultation on World Evangelization, with 600 participants and 300 others from 87 countries at Pattaya, Thailand, in June 1980, discussed both the present situation concerning evangelism in various

lands and techniques to reach 3 billion non-Christians with the gospel.

Evangelicals have successfully used both radio and television in evangelism. Both Charles E. Fuller's "Old-Fashioned Revival Hour" and Walter Maier's "Lutheran Hour" pioneered in gospel broadcasting. Billy Graham's "Hour of Decision," first on radio, then on television, has had an audience of many millions. Kathryn Kuhlman, Rex Humbard, and Oral Roberts saw and developed the potential of television in their ministries. Pat Robertson's "700 Club," Jim Bakker's "PTL Club," and Jerry Falwell's "Old Time Gospel Hour" reach millions of followers who contribute nearly $150 million annually. Thirty-six religious TV channels and 1,300 religious radio stations are estimated to reach an audience of 50 million each week.

Several evangelical parachurch organizations have promoted *social action*. World Vision International was organized in 1951 by Bob Pierce. It is ably led by Stanley Mooneyham. In 1979 World Vision had a budget of nearly $68 million of which about $47 million was raised in the United States. World Vision supports orphanages in many lands and has provided food, medicine, and shelter for refugees from war and natural disasters. The Medical Assistance Plan has also provided medicine and supplies for missionary hospitals and needy people after disasters in such areas as Pakistan and Cambodia.

Charismatic David Wilkerson's Teen Challenge in New York reaches young drug addicts. His organization claims that 70 percent of the drug addicts they help are cured. This is a much higher rate than that of any secular agency. His book *The Cross and the*

Switchblade popularized his work.

Missions or various forms of evangelism abroad have been well supported by evangelicals. A Congress on the Church's Worldwide Mission held in Wheaton, Illinois, in April 1966 discussed the state of missions and future strategies. It brought together 938 delegates from 150 mission boards representing 13,000 missionaries in 71 countries. The final Wheaton Declaration held up the Bible as the source of the gospel of the cross, which is the message of the church.

Recruitment of missionaries was stimulated by the deaths of five missionaries at the hands of the Aucas in Ecuador in 1955. Regular meetings of college students at Urbana, Illinois, since the initial meeting at Toronto in 1945, have raised many recruits. The last meeting in 1979 brought 17,000 students together to consider the Scriptures and the challenge of missions. Short Terms Abroad has recruited persons with needed specialties to serve in other countries for a term of one or more years.

Wycliffe Translators has since 1942 sponsored many missionary linguists who have reduced tribal languages to writing and translated parts or all of the Bible into those languages. Its abstention from politics under the leadership of Cameron Townsend has induced many governments to permit entry to tribes hitherto unreached even by their own government in order to reduce their languages to writing and to translate the Bible into those languages.

Missionary organizations have also creatively used radio and, in some cases, television to spread the gospel. The pioneer station HCJB in Ecuador; ELWA in Liberia, Africa, since 1950; and FEBC in Manila have been the leaders in reaching non-Christians by telecommunications.

Harry Strachan of the Latin American Mission developed Evangelism-in-Depth in 1960 in Guatemala—the first time it was tried in an entire nation. It involves enlisting national Christians in prayer bands and training them in how to reach their neighbors for Christ. This technique has since been used all over the world.

Theological Education by Extension (TEE) was first developed in 1962 by Presbyterian missionaries in Guatemala. This program permits the local lay pastor to study the Bible and related subjects from programed materials, supplemented by occasional visits from trained teachers, while he earns his living by a vocation and carries on the work of a pastor in the local church. The method has now been applied in countries all over the world and has proved successful.

Missionary endeavor has been strengthened by missionary societies cooperating in the Interdenominational Foreign Missions Association (founded in 1917 by nondenominational faith missions groups) and the Evangelical Foreign Missions Association (founded in 1945 by the National Association of Evangelicals). These organizations with relatively small amounts of money serve over a third of all North American missionaries. They provide information, services, and a coordination of missionary effort.

Third World Christians have begun to take an active part in missions. There were about 8,700 Third World missionaries in 1980.

Numerous *educational* institutions have been developed to meet the needs of various students for education under Christian auspices. Elementary and high schools both within denominations and in independent groups have been created to develop education that is biblical and not permeated with the humanism and secularism that seems to have developed in the public school system. Wheaton College and Calvin College are respectively representative of the many nondenominational and denominational colleges that are unashamedly evangelical and at the same time are scholarly institutions of higher learning. Seminaries, such as Fuller, founded in 1947, and Dallas, train evangelicals as pastors for churches in denominations or independent churches.

Evangelicals are also producing *literature* for both the layman and the scholarly specialist. *Christianity Today*, with about 200,000 paid subscriptions; *Eternity; Moody Monthly*, with about 300,000 subscriptions; and *United Evangelical Action* are all widely read by lay and ordained Christian workers. *Bibliotheca Sacra*, the *Journal* of the Evangelical Theological Society, the *Journal* of the American Scientific Affiliation, and *Fides et Historia* of the Conference on Faith and History are examples of scholarly periodicals appealing to different segments of evangelical scholars.

Edward T. Young in Old Testament, Carl F. H. Henry in theology, Cornelius van Til in apologetics, and Gordon Clark in philosophy are examples of the many who have been engaged in the writing of scholarly works that are also evangelical. Eerdmans Publishing Company, Zondervan Publishing House, Baker Book House, Channel Press, Word Books, Tyndale Press, and Moody Press publish scholarly works, as well as more popular literature, that are sold widely in 2,400 evangelical bookstores. Zondervan's *Pictorial Encyclopedia of the Bible*, Baker's *Encyclopedia of Ethics*, Zondervan's *New International Dictionary of the Christian Church*, and Eerdman's *Handbook of the Bible* and *Handbook of Church History* well illustrate some of the scholarly works that evangelicals are producing in cooperation with one another.

Evangelicals have also cooperated in the translating and production of new versions of the Bible that have met with wide acceptance. Nearly 20 million copies of Kenneth Taylor's *Living Bible* in part or whole, a paraphrase in contemporary prose, have been sold. The *New American Standard Bible* is an accurate translation incorporating the best results of biblical scholarship. The *New International Version* may in the future replace the King James Bible in popular use.

c. Both the classical Pentecostal churches and the newer charismatics in the denominations form a large part of what Henry P. van Dusen described in the June 9, 1958, issue of *Life* as the "Third Force." They increasingly cooperate with other evangelicals in parachurch activities while stressing the role of the Holy Spirit in individual life.

The earlier group emphasized speaking in tongues according to the experience of the early church as evidence of the baptism of the Holy Spirit. They drew their membership from Wesleyan holiness churches and in many cases from Reformed groups when they began. Perhaps the opening of Charles Parham's Bethel Bible College in Topeka, Kansas, in October

1900 began this movement. On January 1 the following year, students were studying the work of the Holy Spirit in Acts, and one student, Agnes Ozman, asked others to lay hands on her so that she would receive the Holy Spirit. She spoke in tongues, and later other students also spoke in tongues.

Parham opened another school in 1905 in Houston, Texas. William Seymour, a black student, later became the leader of a mission at 312 Azusa Street in Los Angeles in 1906. Speaking in tongues became common in the mission. People who came to visit had similar experiences and carried the message to other countries. The present Assemblies of God was founded in 1914 in Arkansas. A Sabellian group, insisting on baptism in Jesus' name only, broke off to form what became known as the smaller Jesus Only Church or the New Issue church.

Thomas B. Barratt carried the message and experience from the Los Angeles church to Norway, and Lewi Pethrus became the leader in Sweden. Pentecostalism spread in England through the work of an Anglican pastor, Alexander A. Boddy. Pentecostals in Chile, as a result of the work of the Methodist Willis Hoover, make up 80 percent of Chilean Protestants. Americans carried their message to Brazil, where Pentecostals now number over 4 million. They began world-wide cooperation, with their first world conference at Zurich in 1947. They now claim a following of 8 million world-wide—each one engaging in aggressive "every-member" evangelism.

Classic Pentecostals at first looked askance when the charismatic movement began in the older denominations in California in 1960. Dennis Bennett of Van Nuys spoke in tongues in 1949, and others in his Episcopal congregation had the same experience. Jean Stone, a member of his group, spread this teaching through her magazine *Trinity* (1961–66). Larry Christensen was the leader of charismatics in the Lutheran churches.

The Roman Catholic charismatic movement first emerged in a student-faculty retreat in 1967 at Duquesne University in Pittsburgh. Ralph Keifer carried the message to Notre Dame University in February 1967, and many faculty members and students spoke in tongues. When ten thousand met in Rome in 1975, Pope Paul spoke appreciatively to the assemblage. Cardinal Leo Suenens of Belgium is their major figure. In 1976 about thirty-five thousand charismatic Roman Catholics met at Notre Dame University for a conference to consider their growing power in the church.

Most charismatics have remained in their own denominations. The Full Gospel Businessmen's Fellowship organized in 1953 by Demos Shakarian, as well as the work of "Mr. Pentecost," David DuPlessis of South Africa, have helped to spread and popularize the movement. Charismatics are usually middle class, nonseparatist, urban, ecumenically minded, and theologically pluralistic in outlook. Classic Pentecostal churches originally were more often made up of workers meeting in storefront churches and were noisier in worship. They are fundamentalist in theology and aggressively evangelistic.

d. The Jesus People were young, middle-class dropouts from society in the 1960s but have now been partly absorbed into the churches. Many of them adopted communal patterns of living, stressed love, aggressively witnessed to Christ on the street and earnestly studied their Bibles. The movement was strongest on the west coast and especially in California. A rally at Morgantown, Pennsylvania, as late as 1975 drew a crowd of thirty thousand. Their enthusiasm was refreshing, but they lacked sound doctrinal teaching.

e. Evangelical organizations have emerged in many denominations in order to call the churches back to former evangelical doctrine and life. The Presbyterian Lay Committee, incorporated in 1965, and the Presbyterians United for Biblical Concern (1965) work within the United Presbyterian Church, USA. The Good News group with organizational headquarters in Wilmore, Kentucky, since 1967 are carrying on the same work in the United Methodist Church. The Lutherans Alert and the Fellowship of Witness in the Episcopal church have similar functions. These evangelicals seek to recall their denominations to earlier witness and faith.

This discussion shows the strength, zeal, and influence of evangelicals as well as their diversity. Hopefully all these groups, while maintaining their identity, will enlarge areas of cooperation and minimize their differences. If they succeed, they can helpfully link proclamation of the gospel with social action for the benefit of society.

C. Roman Catholicism

The small but influential Roman Catholic charismatic group and the relation of the Roman Catholic church to the state have already been considered. The 732 million Catholics throughout the world have been subjected to great changes since Vatican II. These changes are all the more remarkable because, from the French Revolution on, the papal leadership tried to maintain a closed society insulated from the liberal political, economic, social, and religious changes in Europe.

Benedict XV (1914–22) sought to develop more uniformity in the church with the completion of the codification of canon law by 1917. In 1943 Pius XII (1876–1958) in *Divino Afflante Spiritu* encouraged Roman Catholic scholars to make more use of the findings of archaeology and textual criticism. Bible reading on the part of the laity was encouraged by Vatican II decisions.

Pius XII, who became pope in 1939, reinforced the link with the past in 1950 by his proclamation of the bodily assumption of Mary into heaven by miraculous means after her death. There is also some tendency to associate Mary with Christ in His redemptive work.

Still greater change in the church was inaugurated in January 1959 when John XXIII (pope from 1958 to 1963) announced to his cardinals his plan to hold a new ecumenical council. The council, which met from 1962 to 1965 in four fall sessions, was, according to John, to advance *aggioranamento*, or "renewal." He said that he wanted Vatican II to be "pastoral" rather than doctrinal or governmental. Rather than bringing any immediate major change in doctrine or polity, it created new attitudes that have affected relations with Protestant and Orthodox denominations. Reflecting the new spirit, individual leaders, such as Hans Küng, even raised questions about papal infallibility. John's assertion that the content or substance of doctrine should not change but that forms are open to change may well open the way even to doctrinal change. Supporters of change and of reaction clashed during the sessions at which about twenty-seven hundred Roman Catholics and some Protestant observers were present.

The importance of the laity was recognized by many references to them as the "people of God" and assertions of their spiritual priesthood. They were encouraged to read the Bible and were even to be allowed to participate in the Mass, which was now permitted to be carried out in the vernacular of each country. The Bible and tradition were linked in a new way by considering them to be one expression of the Holy Spirit. Protestants were described as "separated brethren" rather than as schismatics and heretics as in the past. Cooperation in the ecumenical movement, forbidden earlier, was encouraged. Liberty of worship for all was accepted. Collegiality of the bishops with the pope was proclaimed, and Pope Paul called a council of bishops. Its acts were not effective, however, without the proclamation of its decisions by the pope. The pope opposed both birth control and clerical marriage.

Pope John Paul I seemed to follow the more free, informal approach of John XXIII. Pope John Paul II is a more colorful and popular pope, understands communism better, and is more conservative than his predecessors. He faces many problems, such as falling attendance at mass, Latin American liberation theology, the demand for the ordination of women, and scholars who question certain doctrines of the church. He has reacted vigorously against the more liberal tendencies of Hans Küng and Schillebeeckx with disciplinary measures.

Cooperation in ecumenical ventures, however, still continues. Pius XII in *Mortalium Animos* (1928) had forbidden ecumenical cooperation. If there was to be any reunion, he declared, it would come about by the return of the schismatic churches to the Roman Catholic church. In contrast, in 1960 Pope John created a Secretariat for Promoting Christian Unity under the leadership of Cardinal Bea. Five Catholic observers were allowed to be present at the meeting of the World Council of Churches meeting in 1961 in New Delhi. A Joint Working Group of Roman Catholics and representatives of the World Council have met several times since 1965 to chart paths of cooperation and possible eventual union. Protestant observers were cordially invited to be present at Vatican II. Pope Paul met with the Eastern patriarch Athenagoras in Constantinople in 1964. On December 7, 1965, Paul in Rome and Athenagoras in Constantinople revoked the mutual excommunication of each church by the other in 1054. All of these openings to the world are in sharp contrast to the closed church of the nineteenth and early twentieth centuries.

D. New Cults

Many unhappy souls, who were dissatisfied with the lack of authority in liberalism, turned to the message of theological or ethical absolutism proclaimed by various cults, many of which have arisen since World War I. The doctrines of cults are developed outside the pale of the church, and the leaders of cults seek to win converts from the church by proselyting and by meetings, home visitation, or correspondence courses. The cults not only claim to have final or absolute answers to the problems of health, sorrow, popularity, and success, but they also offer an authority that the hungry soul cannot find in liberal Protestant churches. They are often deceptive, exclusive, and negative toward culture.

Cults such as Spiritualism, Theosophy, New Thought, Unity, and Christian Science oppose materialistic interpretations of the universe and assert its unity and spiritual nature. Spiritualism in particular grew fast after World War I because those who had lost loved fathers, husbands, or brothers in the war sought to communicate with them through mediums. Both Unity and New Thought were developments of the Quimby process of mental healing that Mrs. Mary Baker Eddy had used to good advantage in building up Christian Science. Charles Fillmore, who had been a cripple from infancy, and his wife, Myrtle, who had had tuberculosis, developed the idea of their unity with God so that illness and poverty could have no hold on them. Their group grew so much that the leaders of the movement have built Unity City near Kansas City, Missouri.

The Russelites—or, as they prefer to be known since 1931, Jehovah's Witnesses—were founded in 1872 by Charles T. Russell (1852–1916), whose avid study of the Bible led him to oppose the churches and ministers as tools of the devil and to preach the doctrine of Christ's return and the participation of the "witnesses" in that event. Because they claim that their only allegiance is to God, members of Jehovah's Witnesses will not salute the flag nor serve in the armed forces. Their leaders were not recognized as ministers in World War II. Judge Rutherford (1861–1942), a Missouri lawyer, became the leader upon Russell's death in 1916. The movement which was incorporated as the Zion Watch Tower Tract Society in New York in 1884, distributes millions of books and tracts. It is estimated that there are about 500,000 adherents in the United States and over 2 million in the world.

The Oxford Group, or Buchmanites, do not constitute a particular organization but seek to work in the churches somewhat after the fashion of the Pietists who desired to rejuvenate Lutheranism in the seventeenth century. Frank N. D. Buchman (1876–1961), the leader, was a Lutheran minister in Pennsylvania who was dissatisfied with his spiritual experience. He tried to reach the well-to-do and educated through his gospel of the changed life; "sharing," or confession to the group; guidance; and the four absolutes of honesty, purity, love, and unselfishness. House parties for personal witnessing and public confession have been the method of operation adopted by the group. It has won many notable converts and even sought in Moral Rearmament, its new name, to prevent the coming of World War II by winning the leaders of states to Christianity. It has helped the educated and rich, whom the church often fears to challenge with the claims of Christ lest it lose their support. Two weaknesses of the group are that the lack of a sound theology may lead to the substitution of the feeling of release, after one has "shared" sins, for real regeneration, and confession may

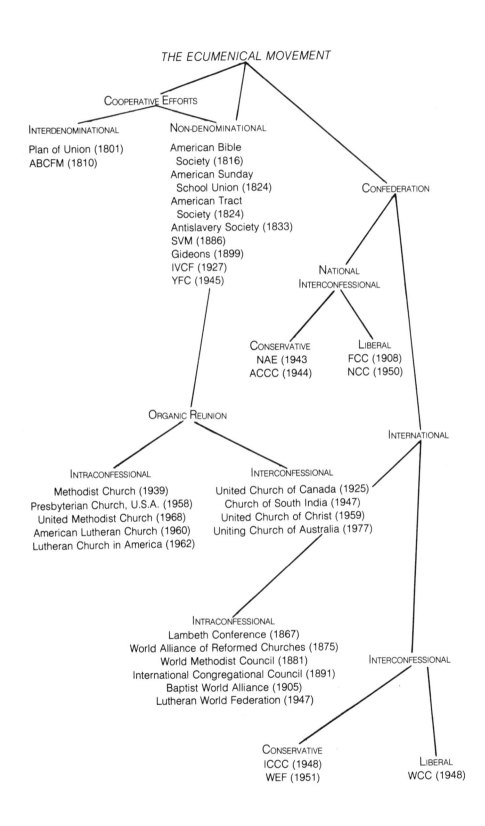

THE ECUMENICAL MOVEMENT

COOPERATIVE EFFORTS

INTERDENOMINATIONAL

Plan of Union (1801)
ABCFM (1810)

NON-DENOMINATIONAL

American Bible
  Society (1816)
American Sunday
  School Union (1824)
American Tract
  Society (1824)
Antislavery Society (1833)
SVM (1886)
Gideons (1899)
IVCF (1927)
YFC (1945)

CONFEDERATION

NATIONAL
INTERCONFESSIONAL

CONSERVATIVE
NAE (1943
ACCC (1944)

LIBERAL
FCC (1908)
NCC (1950)

INTERNATIONAL

ORGANIC REUNION

INTRACONFESSIONAL

Methodist Church (1939)
Presbyterian Church, U.S.A. (1958)
United Methodist Church (1968)
American Lutheran Church (1960)
Lutheran Church in America (1962)

INTERCONFESSIONAL

United Church of Canada (1925)
Church of South India (1947)
United Church of Christ (1959)
Uniting Church of Australia (1977)

INTRACONFESSIONAL
Lambeth Conference (1867)
World Alliance of Reformed Churches (1875)
World Methodist Council (1881)
International Congregational Council (1891)
Baptist World Alliance (1905)
Lutheran World Federation (1947)

INTERCONFESSIONAL

CONSERVATIVE
ICCC (1948)
WEF (1951)

LIBERAL
WCC (1948)

be directed only to man rather than to God.

Occult and Eastern cults from Asia have won many Western young people who are seeking inner peace and security. Astrology has become a religion to some, as the magazines on astrology on newsstands indicate, Satan worship and witchcraft cults have their devotees in Europe and the United States. Buddhism, forms of Hinduism, Hare Krishna, Transcendental Meditation, and assorted gurus claim the allegiance of many, especially young people. These groups, however, seem to have peaked in membership.

The Unification Church of Sun Myung Moon (1920–), founded in 1954 in Korea, now with about 200,000 followers; the Church of Scientology under the leadership of L. Ron Hubbard, with headquarters in England; and The Way International led by Paul V. Wierwelle, a Princeton Seminary alumnus, are reputed to practice something like mind control of their followers. The new convert is surrounded by loving concern; given much work, little sleep, and a low protein diet; and urged to listen to repetitious tapes and speeches by the leader. The PFAL course taken by all members of The Way in twelve three-hour sessions over three weeks costs $85.00. The denial of the essential deity of Christ and antinomian morals divide these cults from orthodox Christianity. Many young people seem to be attracted to them.

Neoorthodoxy, evangelicalism, and the cults appear to have risen to meet the need for a religious message with authority. To some extent, such movements are attempts to fill the spiritual void created by the theological bankruptcy of liberalism with its shallow message of a vague fatherhood of God and brotherhood of man. Liberalism taught morality but neglected the religious dynamic of the Cross, which alone can energize a life so that it conforms to Christian ethics.

II. THE RISE OF ECUMENICITY

The process of fission into new denominations that marked Protestant development since the Reformation began by 1800 to give way to fusion of denominations into new groups. Integration or ecumenism, beginning in the nineteenth century, replaced missionary expansion in the minds of many. The term *ecumenical* seems to have been used first about 1936 in a Faith-and-Order conference. Both liberal and conservative elements in the church have participated in it. On occasions, in order to attain consensus, theology has been the lowest common denominator in the drive for organizational unity.

Ecumenism has gone through three stages. Nondenominational and interdenominational cooperation began early in the nineteenth century. Organic reunion of denominations of like and unlike backgrounds proliferated in the twentieth century. Confederations on a national and international scale have multiplied in recent years.

A. Interdenominational and Nondenominational Cooperation

1. The Plan of Union by Congregationalists and Presbyterians to meet the shortage of pastors on the frontier lasted from 1801 until 1852, to the advantage of the Presbyterians. The American Board of Commissioners for Foreign Missions linked Congre-

gationalists and other denominations in *interdenominational* missionary endeavor.

2. *Nondenominational* cooperation was far more widespread. The American Bible Society was organized in 1816, and Christians from different denominations supported its work. The same principle was followed in the American Sunday School Union of 1824, the American Tract Society of 1824, the 1833 Antislavery Society, the Student Volunteer Movement of 1886, the Gideons in their distribution of Bibles, and Youth for Christ.

B. Organic Reunion

Organic reunion occurs when separate denominations give up a corporate existence to form a new denomination. It has been easier to achieve organic reunions when there have been similar backgrounds of theology, polity, and rites.

1. The northern and southern Methodist churches, which had separated over slavery, came together in 1939. The German Methodists of the United Brethren Church and the Evangelical Church united in 1946 to form the Evangelical United Brethren Church. This new body united in 1968 with the Methodist Church of 1939 to form the large United Methodist Church. The United Presbyterian Church and the Presbyterian Church, USA, formed the United Presbyterian Church, USA, in 1958. Several bodies of Lutherans merged so that two great Lutheran churches, the American Lutheran Church in 1960 and the Lutheran Church in America in 1962, became an important part of the American denominational scene.

2. Churches with unlike theological and governmental patterns have formed transconfessional reunions. The United Church of Canada linked Presbyterians, Baptists, Methodists, and Congregationalists in 1925. The 1927 Church of Christ in China included Presbyterians, Baptists, and Methodists. The Church in South India in 1947 brought Episcopalians with their episcopalian outlook into union with Congregationalists, Presbyterians, and Methodists, who had different forms of church government. Unitarians and Universalists united in 1961 to form the Unitarian Universalist Association. The Consultation on Church Union, proposed in a 1960 sermon by Eugene C. Blake in James Pike's Grace Episcopal Cathedral in San Francisco, initiated the most ambitious attempt at reunion to date. A plan of union was formulated in 1966 at Dallas, but the United Presbyterian Church, USA, withdrew in 1972. This union would, if it ever takes place, reunite about 25 million people of ten different theologies and polities. A Uniting Church of Australia was formed in 1977.

C. National and International Ecclesiastical Confederations

Calvin, Luther, and Cranmer desired to bring their respective groups together in a council to talk about union. Zinzendorf tried to unite Germans in Pennsylvania during his visit from 1739 to 1742. William Carey proposed a conference at Capetown in 1810 to unite the missionary efforts of different groups. Samuel S. Schmucker (1799–1875), a Lutheran professor at Gettysburg Seminary, formulated a call to reunion in his 1838 "Fraternal Appeal to the American Churches." An

Episcopalian, William R. Huntington (1838–1918), proposed in *The Church Idea* (1870) that discussion of reunion be based on the Bible as the Word of God, the universal creeds as the rule of faith, the two sacraments, and the historic episcopate. This "Quadrilateral" was adopted in 1888 at the meeting of the Episcopal Lambeth Conference. The ideas in these various proposals have been important in discussions concerning confederation.

1. In any system of ecclesiastical confederation thus far developed, the cooperating units maintain their sovereignty but cooperate to achieve ends of common interest to the participating groups. Different Protestant denominations have set up *national* confederations so that they can cooperate in service. In 1905 the Protestant churches of France created the Protestant Federation of France. The Protestant Federation of Churches in Switzerland came into being in 1920. But the most important illustration of national federation of different denominations is the Federal Council of Churches of Christ in America. It came into being in 1908 when the assembled delegates of about thirty denominations approved the constitution that had been drafted at an earlier meeting in 1905.[1] The words "divine Lord and Savior" constituted the only statement of theology in the constitution. The major interest of the Federal Council has been to have the churches cooperate in social action. The Social Creed of the Churches adopted by the council urged the churches to support such social needs as the abolition of child labor, the establishment of a minimum living wage, and provision for arbitration in industrial disputes. Various commissions were set up to carry out these and other programs. Because of this social emphasis and weak theological foundation, liberals have been able to seize and hold the reins of leadership firmly since the inception of the council.

On 29 November 1950 the Federal Council joined with other groups to become the National Council of the Churches of Christ. The International Council of Religious Education, the Foreign Missions Conference of North America, the Home Missions Council, and various other interdenominational boards united with the Federal Council in the new organization. Missionary, educational, social, and other activities were coordinated under this larger organization. Twenty-five Protestant and four Orthodox denominations became a part of the council. Southern Baptists, Missouri Synod Lutherans, and Pentecostals are not in the National Council with its forty million constituents. The British Council of Churches was set up in 1942.

The conservatives have not lagged in the development of cooperation by national confederations. The American Council of Christian Churches was organized in September 1941 to dispute the claim of the Federal Council to speak for all Protestants. Churches that are in any way related to the National Council are not eligible for membership. The American Council has been led by Carl McIntire, who has opposed the National Council in the pages of *The Christian Beacon*. This council claims to represent about two million Protestants.

The National Association of Evangelicals, which is more irenic than the American Council but no less true to the historic faith of Christianity, had

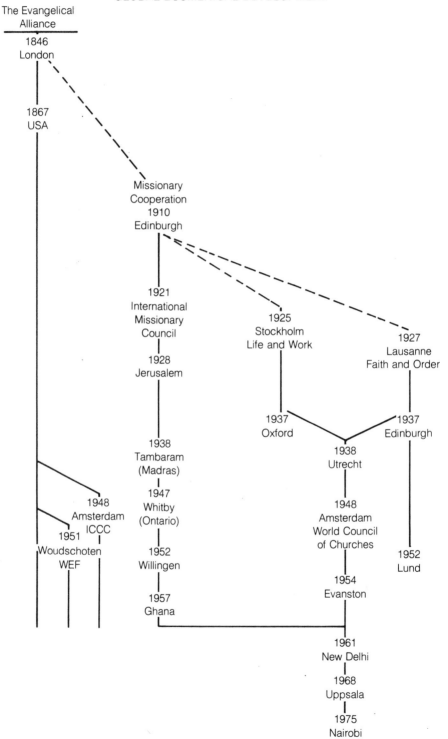

GLOBAL ECUMENICAL DEVELOPMENT

The Evangelical
Alliance

1846
London

1867
USA

Missionary
Cooperation
1910
Edinburgh

1921
International
Missionary
Council

1925
Stockholm
Life and Work

1927
Lausanne
Faith and Order

1928
Jerusalem

1948
Amsterdam
ICCC

1937
Oxford

1937
Edinburgh

1938
Tambaram
(Madras)

1938
Utrecht

1947
Whitby
(Ontario)

1951
Woudschoten
WEF

1948
Amsterdam
World Council
of Churches

1952
Willingen

1952
Lund

1954
Evanston

1957
Ghana

1961
New Delhi

1968
Uppsala

1975
Nairobi

its first annual meeting in Chicago in May 1943. The delegates accepted the provisional constitution that had been drafted at a meeting in Saint Louis of 150 evangelicals in April 1942. The organization has an evangelical statement of faith that denominations, local churches, and individuals accept. Thè NAE has commissions at work on various projects involving such matters as missions, education, evangelism, and social action. Annual seminars for ministers and for college students have created more interest in Christians in government. Its periodical, *United Evangelical Action*, gives regular reports concerning activities that are of common interest to the several million members that the organization claims to represent.

In many countries of the world these national Protestant federations have been formed to provide an agency for interdenominational cooperation. Each of them has stimulated the demand for an ecumenical council that will embrace the Protestant orthodox churches of the world.

2. Various denominations have set up *international* organizations in which the same denominations in other nations can work cooperatively to advance the interests of that denomination throughout the world. Ever since 1867 Anglicans throughout the world have met every tenth year in what is known as the Lambeth Conference to consider matters of common interest to Anglicans. The World Presbyterian Alliance was organized in 1875 and held its first meeting at Edinburgh in 1877. The International Congregational Council held its first meeting in 1891. The Baptist World Alliance came into being in 1905 to consider matters of interest to all Baptists.

The decisions of these councils are merely advisory and may or may not be put into effect by the member groups. The Lutheran World Federation, finally organized at Lund in 1947, has met several times since its inception in 1923. The Methodists also have a World Methodist Council, which began in 1881. These conferences, which bring together nationals of like faith from many countries, have given people a new sense of unity in faith and practice and have strengthened the idea of ecumenical federation of all denominations.

Not since the days of the ecumenical councils at Nicaea, Constantinople, and Chalcedon in the fourth and fifth centuries has there been such a wave of cooperation among churches as there has been in recent years. Founded in London in 1846, with nearly 800 present, the Evangelical Alliance had a definite theological statement that linked individuals rather than churches. Consequently, the alliance became inactive about 1900 as other organizations to promote interdenominational and international cooperation came into being. But it marked the first step in the development of a modern ecumenical body. The accompanying chart shows the development of the World Council of Churches.

The World Council of Churches owes much to the various international missionary conferences that began in 1854 in New York. There were fifteen hundred leaders from all parts of the world and from all Protestant denominations. The meeting at Edinburgh in 1910 brought together twelve hundred delegates from 160 societies engaged in missionary work. Representation at the meeting was by countries. Charles H. Brent (1862–1929), Nathan Söderblom (1866–1931), and William Temple (1881–1944) were so impressed with the ecumenical nature of the meeting that they dedicated their lives to the task of Christian unity. This meeting laid the foundation for the World Council of Churches. The publication of the *International Review of Missions* in 1911 and the formation of the International Missionary Council in 1921 were important results of the Edinburgh meeting. International meetings of missionary organizations and churches were again held in Jerusalem in 1928 and in Madras in 1938. At Madras, for the first time, some of the indigenous churches had representatives.

The first meeting involving the theology and polity of the churches was the World Conference on Faith and Order held at Lausanne in 1927. Bishop Charles Brent of the Protestant Episcopal Church of the United States, financed by a large gift of money from J. Pierpont Morgan, was largely responsible for the meeting of over four hundred delegates representing 108 denominations. The participants were conscious of their unity in one church under the headship of Christ and urged that another meeting be held. This meeting, which also dealt with Faith and Order, was held at Edinburgh in the summer of 1937. Over five hundred delegates from 123 churches and 43 lands conferred on theological issues. The idea of unity in diversity seems to have been uppermost in the minds of the leaders as they discussed the common faith, the sacraments, and the nature of the church.

Another group of international meetings during this period was devoted to the theme of Life and Work.

The first meeting to consider Life and Work was held in August 1925 in Stockholm through the efforts of Nathan Soderblom, the primate of Sweden. The program was devoted to plans for a better economic and political order. The six hundred delegates, representing over ninety churches in thirty-seven lands, did not adjourn until they had urged consideration of the creation of a universal council at Geneva. A second equally large meeting at Oxford in 1937 joined with the Faith-and-Order meeting at Edinburgh, which met later in that summer, to call for an international council of churches to unite the Faith-and-Order and the Life-and-Work movements.

The meeting of 80 leaders at Utrecht in the spring of 1938 resulted in the development of a provisional constitution,[2] a plan of organization for the World Council of Churches, and the creation of a Provisional Committee to bring it into being. Between 22 August and 4 September, 1948, over 350 delegates, representing about 150 churches from 44 countries, met at Amsterdam. This meeting completed the task of creating a world ecumenical council. The Southern Baptists of the United States, the Roman Catholic church, and the Missouri Synod Lutherans have never joined it. William Temple's dream of an international ecclesiastical organization came to pass as the delegates discussed "Man's Disorder and God's Design." Many of the major backers of the project were Americans who were also involved in the Federal Council of Churches. The major result of the meeting was the formation of the World Council of Churches with its headquarters in Geneva. The World Council is composed of an Assembly, which meets every seven years; a Central Committee, which meets annually; an Administrative Secretariat; and various commissions that work on major problems facing the organization.[3] Several Orthodox churches in Communist states joined the council, and the phrase "according to the Scriptures" was added to the doctrinal statement at the 1961 meeting of the council in New Delhi.

The World Council increasingly since its fourth assembly at Uppsala, Sweden, in 1968 has turned to the left socially, economically, and politically, making salvation earthly and physical rather than spiritual. Another commission meeting at Bangkok, Thailand, in 1973 interpreted its theme "Salvation Today" as the "humanizing of society" to free man from all forms of oppression and to create a new society on earth. The fifth assembly at Nairobi, Kenya, in 1975 supported "nonmilitary guerilla programs" of revolution and adopted what amounted to liberation theology oriented toward socialism.

Both the American Council of Christian Churches and the National Association of Evangelicals answered the attempt by the liberal forces to create an ecumenical church by creating conservative international organizations. The International Council of Christian Churches was founded in Amsterdam in 1948 two weeks before the meeting described above in order to oppose liberalism and to develop evangelical world spirit. At a meeting in Holland in August 1951, the World Evangelical Fellowship came into being to provide fellowship and to coordinate the works of the NAE with that of evangelicals throughout the world. Cooperation of the World Council of Churches and the Roman Catholic church has already been described.

As one objectively reviews this movement toward world ecclesiastical unity, one is constrained to wonder whether Christ had in mind unity of the organizational type described above when He spoke of the unity of His church, or whether He had in mind a spiritual unity that believers in the invisible church, the body of Christ, have through Him as their Head. The true church will always be a living organism, and no human organization or machinery should ever be a substitute for this spiritual unity that makes the church the only true international body in the world. Such a unity of spirit will never endanger orthodox doctrine, which the World Council has minimized to foster inclusiveness.

III. CHRISTIAN EXPANSION AND RENEWAL

Radical theologies that try to secularize the church with Marxist economics and existential relativism are in the process of disintegration as were liberalism and neoorthodoxy in previous decades. Ecumenism is in trouble because it has generally ignored evangelism in order to promote radical social and political revolution. Indifference and even hostility at the grass roots has hampered its work. Dean Kelley in his book *Why the Conservative Churches Are Growing*[4] points out the decline in membership of churches supporting radical theology and the ecumenism and the surprising growth of evangelical churches.

While there has been no world-wide

revival since that of 1901 to 1907, there have been regional awakenings that come more often among rural agricultural societies than in industrialized urban nations. The Anglican and other churches in Kenya and Uganda experienced widespread revival and evangelism after 1930, and revival still continues in that area. The Wallamo tribes in Ethiopia, with only a small number of Christians when the missionaries had to leave them because of the Ethiopian War in the mid-thirties, numbered about 100,000 in 1964. An awakening in Indonesia that began in 1965 has been overpublicized, but about 200,000 were converted from 1965 to 1967 in Timor. Revival continues in Korea, where about 20 percent are Christians.

The Western world has had some awakenings. The 1950 revival in Wheaton College and in Asbury College in February 1970 had wide impact through student witness teams that went to other campuses. The Saskatchewan revival of 1971, which began under the ministry of Ralph and Lou Sutera in William L. McLeod's Ebenezer Baptist Church in Saskatoon, brought awakening all across the Prairie Provinces of Canada. The work of Billy Graham and many other evangelists and the charismatic movement in the denominations as well as the Jesus movement testify to the continuing work of the Holy Spirit in the churches.

Africa has about 200 million Christians, which is nearly one-half of the population, and the number continues to grow. The greatest need is for trained leaders and the development of viable indigenous churches. Perhaps missionaries can make their greatest contribution by training national leaders.

While the oil power of the Muslim world and revival of aggressive Muslim missions make that part of the world, with its nearly 700 million Muslims, hard to reach, there are signs of change. Many Muslims in Indonesia have become Christians. Others in Africa are responding in considerable numbers. Through the work of the eye hospital of Kano, Nigeria, many in Africa have been reached with the gospel of Christ.

South and Central America are experiencing unprecedented Protestant church growth, particularly on the part of the Pentecostal groups in Chile and Brazil. Luis Palau has had many successful urban mass crusades in leading Latin cities.

Christianity in Communist Europe and Asia is very much like that of the Book of Acts. Christians in these countries meet and witness secretly, but the growth is steady and impressive. The Russian Baptist Church embraces over 500,000 people. Doors of witness are opening again in Communist China in recent years.

In spite of all this expansion, Christianity is still not a majority religion in the world. Christians of all kinds numbered over 950 million in 1978, Muslims numbered about 700 million, and Hindus over 500 million out of a world population of over 4 billion. Thus the quarter of the world's population that is Christian still has over three-quarters of the people of the world as its mission field.

SUGGESTED READING

Abbott, Walter M. A. Documents of Vatican II. *New York: Herder, 1966.*

Armerding, Carl, ed. Evangelicals and Liberation. *Nutley, N.J.: Presbyterian and Reformed, 1977.*

Bell, George K. A., ed. Documents on Christian Unity. *London: Oxford University Press, 1955.*

Berkouwer, G. C. The Second Vatican Council and the New Catholicism. *Grand Rapids: Eerdmans, 1965. This is an optimistic description and interpretation of the new Roman Catholic spirit.*

Betthge, Eberhard. Deitrich Bonhoeffer. *Evanston, Ill.: Harper, 1970. This is a definitive biography.*

Blanshard, Paul. American Freedom and Catholic Power. *2nd rev. and enl. ed. Boston: Beacon, 1958.*

Bloch-Hoell, Nils. The Pentecostal Movement. *Norway: Universitetsforlaget, 1964. This is a scholarly, documentary study.*

Brown, Robert M. The Ecumenical Dialogue. *Garden City, N.Y.: Doubleday, 1967.*

Burton, Katherine B. Leo the Thirteenth. *New York: Mackay, 1962.*

Cavert, Samuel M. The American Churches in the Ecumenical Movement, 1900–1968. *New York: Association, 1968.*

———. Church Cooperation and Unity in America, 1900–1970. *New York: Association, 1970.*

Claybaugh, Gary. Thunder on the Right. *Chicago: Nelson-Hall, 1974. This is an unsympathetic account of right-wing evangelicalism.*

Cole, Stewart G. History of Fundamentalism. *New York: Harper, 1931. This is a good account of fundamentalism, but from a liberal viewpoint.*

Conn, Harvie M. Contemporary World Theology. *Nutley, N.J.: Presbyterian and Reformed, 1973. Contemporary theologies are outlined and evaluated.*

Crow, Paul A., Jr. The Ecumenical Movement in Bibliographical Outline. *New York: Department of Faith and Order, National Council of Churches in the USA, 1965.*

Curtis, Charles J. Söderblom, Ecumenical Pioneer. *Minneapolis: Augsburg, 1967. This is a brief biography with much data on the ecumenical movement.*

Damboriena, Prudencio. Tongues As of Fire. *Washington: Corpus, 1969.*

Detzler, Wayne A. The Changing Church in Europe. *Grand Rapids: Zondervan, 1979. A useful account of contemporary religion in Europe.*

Dollar, George W. A History of Fundamentalism. *Greenville, S.C.: Bob Jones, 1970. This is a detailed, well-researched, militant account of the schools, leaders, and associations of the early twentieth-century fundamentalists.*

Elliot, Lawrence. I Will Be Called John. *New York: Reader's Digest Press, 1973.*

Erickson, Millard. The New Evangelical Theology. *Westwood, N.J.: Revell, 1968. This is an able account and evaluation of the neoevangelicals.*

Evans, Robert. Let Europe Hear. *Chicago: Moody, 1963.*

Fey, Harold E., ed. A History of the Ecumenical Movement, 1948–1968. *Philadelphia: Westminster, 1970. The period of 1517–1948 is covered in the work edited by Ruth Rouse and Stephen Neill.*

Fosdick, Harry E. The Living of These Days. *New York: Harper, 1956. This is an account of the author's theological pilgrimage to liberalism.*

Fraser, E. Franklin. The Negro Church in America. *New York: Shocken, 1964.*

Fuller, Daniel P. Give the Winds a Mighty Voice. *Waco, Tex.: Word, 1972. This is a biography of Charles E. Fuller.*

Furniss, Norman. The Fundamentalist Controversy, 1918–1931. *New Haven: Yale University Press, 1954.*

Gatewood, Willard B., Jr., ed. Controversy in the Twenties. *Nashville: Vanderbilt University Press, 1969.*

Gaspar, Louis. The Fundamentalist Movement. *The Hague: Mouton, 1963.*

Goodall, Norman. The Ecumenical Movement. 2nd ed. *London: Oxford University Press, 1964. The history and the work of the World Council of Churches is presented by the author.*

Gundry, Stanley N., and Johnson, Alan F., eds. Tensions in Contemporary Theology. *Chicago: Moody, 1979.*

Halecki, Oscar. Eugene Pacelli: Pope of Peace. *New York: Farrar-Strauss and Young, 1951.*

Hamilton, Kenneth. God Is Dead: The Anatomy of a Slogan. *Grand Rapids: Eerdmans, 1966. A helpful survey.*

Henry, Carl F. H. Evangelicals in Search of Identity. *Waco: Word, 1976.*

———. Fifty Years of Protestant Theology. *Boston: W. A. Wilde, 1950.*

Henry, Carl F. H., and Mooneyham, Stanley, eds. One Race, One Gospel, One Task. *Minneapolis: Worldwide, 1967. The proceedings and papers of the 1966 Berlin Congress are presented in this book.*

Hoke, Donald E., ed. The Church in Asia. *Chicago: Moody, 1975. The author gives the histories of Asian lands, missions, and the work of evangelicals.*

Hollenweger, Walter J. The Pentecostals. *Minneapolis: Augsburg, 1972.*

Hordern, William A. A Layman's Guide to Protestant Theology. *Rev. ed. New York: Macmillan, 1968.*

Horton, Walter M. Toward a Reborn Church. *New York: Harper, 1949. The important twentieth-century ecumenical meetings, including the Amsterdam meeting in 1948, are described.*

Hughes, Philip E. Creative Minds in Contemporary Theology. *Grand Rapids: Eerdmans, 1966.*

———. Pius the Eleventh. *New York: Sheed, 1938.*

Ironmonger, F. A. William Temple. *London: Oxford University Press, 1948.*

Kantzer, Kenneth S., and Gundry, Stanley N., eds. Perspectives on Evangelical Theology. *Grand Rapids: Baker, 1979.*

Kelley, Dean M. Why Conservative Churches Are Growing. *New York: Harper, 1972.*

Lightner, Robert P. Neo-evangelicalism. *Findlay, Ohio: Durham, n.d.*

Maier, Paul L. A Man Spoke, A World Listened. *New York: McGraw, 1963. This is a biography of Walter Maier.*

Marsden, George. Fundamentalism and American Culture: The Shaping of Twentieth-Century Evangelicalism 1870–1925. *New York: Oxford University Press, 1981. This is a critical reassessment of the Sandeen proposal.*

Menzies, William W. Anointed to Serve. *Springfield, Mo.: Gospel, 1971.*

Murch, James D. Cooperation Without Compromise. *Grand Rapids: Eerdmans, 1956. This describes the origin and work of the NAE.*

———. The Protestant Revolt. *Arlington, Va.: Crestwood, 1967. This describes the conservative reaction and organizations that rose in the older denominations against liberalism.*

Nash, Roland H. The New Evangelicalism. *Grand Rapids: Zondervan, 1963.*

Nichol, John T. Pentecostalism. *New York: Harper, 1966.*

Orr, J. Edwin. Campus Aflame. *Glendale, Calif.: Gospel Light, Regal, 1971. The author has chronicled campus awakenings.*

Pache, Rene. The Ecumenical Movement. *Dallas: Dallas Theological Seminary Press, 1950. This is an excellent survey of the rise of the World Council of Churches from an evangelical viewpoint.*

Quebedeaux, Richard. The New Charismatics. *Garden City, N.Y.: Doubleday, 1976. This is an able survey and evaluation.*

_____. The Worldly Evangelicals. *San Francisco: Harper, 1978. Excellent survey.*

_____. The Young Evangelicals. *New York: Harper, 1974.*

Reed, Walter, et al. Latin American Church Growth. *Grand Rapids: Eerdmans, 1969.*

Rouse, Ruth, and Neill, Stephen S., eds. A History of the Ecumenical Movement, 1517– 1948. *2nd ed. Philadelphia: Westminster, 1964. See Harold E. Fey for the sequel.*

Roy, Ralph L. Apostles of Discord. *Boston: Beacon, 1953. This is a critical assessment of right-wing evangelicals.*

Russell, C. Allyn. Voices of American Fundamentalism. *Philadelphia: Westminster, 1976. Biographies of fundamentalist leaders of the twenties are presented.*

Sandeen, Ernest. The Roots of Fundamentalism. *Chicago: University of Chicago Press, 1970. The Princeton-school-of-theology root of fundamentalism is presented by the author.*

Shelley, Bruce. Evangelicalism in America. *Grand Rapids: Eerdmans, 1967.*

Slosser, Gaius J. Christian Unity. *New York: Dutton, 1929. This is an excellent survey up until 1929.*

Stone, Ronald H. Reinhold Niebuhr, Prophet to Politicians. *Nashville: Abingdon, 1972.*

Stonehouse, Ned B. J. Gresham Machen. *Grand Rapids: Eerdmans, 1964.*

Surgrue, Frances. Popes of the Modern World. *New York: Crowell, 1961. This is a popular account.*

Synan, Vinson. Aspects of Pentecostal Charismatic Origins. *Plainfield, N.J.: Logos, 1975.*

_____. The Holiness-Pentecostal Movement in the United States. *Grand Rapids: Eerdmans, 1971.*

Tozer, Aiden W. Wingspread. *Harrisburg, Pa.: Christian, 1943. This is a biography of A. B. Simpson.*

Wagner, C. Peter. Look Out! The Pentecostals Are Coming. *Carol Stream, Ill.: Creation, 1973. The author discusses the phenomenal growth of Pentecostalism in Latin America.*

Wells, David F., and Woodbridge, John D., eds. The Evangelicals. *New York: Abingdon, 1975.*

Wirt, Sherwood E. The Social Conscience of the Evangelical. *New York: Harper, 1968. The biblical rationale is developed and possible areas for evangelical social action are suggested.*

Witmer, Safara A. The Bible College Story. *Manhasset, N.Y.: Channel, 1962.*

.

Conclusion:

Problems and Prospects

The church has always faced problems, but the scope and intensity of its problems now seem to be greater than at any previous time in its history. With large increases in world population and with conversions to hostile resurgent non-Christian religions outstripping conversions to Christianity, Christianity is becoming a minority religion in the world. Those who become pessimistic because of these problems should remember that revival has made the church resilient.

I. PROBLEMS

A. The Secular Warfare-Welfare Democratic and Totalitarian State[1]

Although the threat of world domination by totalitarian Nazi Germany, Fascist Italy, and imperialist Japan ended with World War II, right-wing totalitarian governments have been set up by revolutionary force in countries in South America, Africa, and Asia. These regimes have usually deprived the individual of free expression of speech and worship. Some have also

refused to admit missionaries or have expelled them. Many members of the Roman Catholic clergy have openly defied those governments in an attempt to end oppression and to set up new, often Marxist, governments. Liberation theology, which emerged in Latin America, claims to be Bible-based but is more often involved with Marxian ideas of revolution to end oppression. Missionaries are caught between their sympathy for the oppressed and poor and their status as guests in the country.

Contextualization of theology to escape "Western imperialism" has also become an issue in Latin America, Africa, and Asia. Should contextualization be an application of biblical principles to the indigenous culture or should theology always be worked out in the context of oppression and a new, often Marxist, order?

Totalitarian communism has been and still is a major threat to Christianity. It is comparable to the barbarian invasions of the Roman Empire and the surge of Islam in the seventh century. It is not only a social, economic, and political system; it also has religious overtones with its message of people unitedly seeking by violence a better world order whose coming is as inevitable in their thinking as the rising of the sun each day. Communists seize power through a minority of dedicated persons backed by armed force or the threat of such force. It now holds sway over more than one-third of the world's population through clever use of modern techniques of revolution and mass communication. It spreads from the Elbe River in Europe to the Pacific coast of Asia and from the Baltic to the Adriatic Seas in Europe and to the borders of Iran and India in Asia.

Because of its basic materialistic and atheistic premises, it has opposed Christianity wherever it has gained power. Leaders in Communist countries expel missionaries and persecute the national church by open or covert means.

The rise of the democratic warfare-welfare state in the West also has created problems for religious groups. Increasing discussion of limiting or ending tax-exempt contributions to Christian groups or charity would probably limit what might otherwise be given. Governmental regulation of schools set up by Christians has hampered them in the expression of their religion, in spite of the protection of the First Amendment to the constitution.

B. Missions

The threat of communism is related to the problems of missions because where communism controls a country missions have ended, and missionaries are expelled. This was true when in 1949 Communists took over in China.

Nationalistic reaction against colonialism in Asia, Africa, and Latin America has tended to identify missionaries with past imperial regimes, no matter how benevolent those regimes were or how much they helped to develop the economic potential of the area. Because the Treaty of Tientsin of 1858 forced China to open her doors to missionaries, missionaries were identified with Western imperalism. Not until World War II was that treaty abrogated. Many new Mongoloid nations in Asia and Negroid nations in Africa have gained their freedom since 1945. Restrictions have been placed on missions, and in certain areas—for example, India and Saudia Arabia—new missionaries have been refused admission. Contextualization theology and liberation theology have been attempts to create theological systems related to national needs.

The resurgence of Buddhism and Hinduism led either to restriction on missionaries or to a refusal to admit them. The new vitality of Islam coupled with the power of oil revenues in the billions has not only closed the Near and Middle East to missionaries but has created resources for Islamic missions and radio broadcasting of that faith. A magnificent new Islamic temple in London is another manifestation of Islamic missions in Europe.

Liberals have also opposed more conservative missionaries. In 1931 an interdenominational group set up the Laymen's Foreign Missionary Inquiry, which surveyed missions in India, Burma, China, and Japan. The report *Rethinking Missions*, put out in 1932 under the chairmanship of William E. Hocking, a Harvard professor of philosophy, suggested the continuance of missions along lines that would emphasize social effort through medicine, education, and other means apart from evangelism. In his view, missionaries should seek to link their faith with whatever common ideas they can find in pagan religions. This would involve syncretism. The liberals also urged ecumenicity in missions. Hendrik Kraemer (1886–1965) criticized the report in his book *The Christian Message in a Non-Christian World* (1938) and opposed any syncretism of the gospel with pagan religion.

The recession of 1980 and current high inflation with increasing costs for energy have increased the need for greater economic support of missionaries in other countries as American currency depreciates. Christians in Western countries have less money to give as high taxes and inflation erode the value of money. Inflation in 1979 averaged 13.3 percent in the United States. In spite of this, Americans in 1979 gave over $43 million to charity and religious causes. Nearly one-half was given to the latter. Over half of all missionaries in the world come from the United States, to whose religious people they look for support.

C. Moral Decline

An increase in sexual immorality, drunkenness, divorce, unmarried couples living together, and the low moral tone of many radio and television programs threatens the stability of the family in the West. Morality by those in public office seems to be at a low ebb. The average age of criminals has declined till most crimes in the United States are committed by young people, most of them in their teens. Crime doubled between 1961 and 1976. Over 10 million Americans are alcoholic, of whom nearly 3 million are women. Nearly two-thirds of all deaths by automobiles are linked to the use of alcohol. These problems seem to be common to all Western nations.

D. Urbanization

The general world-wide shifts in population from the country to the cities and the alienation of labor from the church offer another challenge to ecclesiastical leadership. Suburban living tends to isolate and insulate people from urban problems. Estimated population in 1980 in greater Tokyo was nearly 20 million; in Mexico City, about 14 million; and in New York City, nearly 18 million. It is estimated that two-fifths of the world's people live in suburban or urban areas. This creates crime and overcrowding in slums and, until recently, has caused the migration of the middle class to the suburbs. With the increase of urban black people and other ethnic enclaves in cities in South Africa and the United States, racial problems emerge. It is fortunate that the church is rapidly developing new urban ministries. A new interest in applying the gospel to racial and urban problems as well as to personal salvation is being manifested by Christians.

E. Institutionalization

The tendency to institutionalize and bureaucratize the church and make it a part of culture constitutes a threat to dynamic Christianity. Civil re-

477

ligion, a blend of blind chauvinistic patriotism with a distorted ethic and a nationalistic theology, further tends to tie the church to the status quo in the state and to cause it to lose the respect of those who really need its help.

II. PROSPECTS

What are the prospects for a Christianity faced with these and other problems? The student of church history will remember other eras when it seemed as if the problems and enemies of the church would overwhelm it. It surmounted the very difficult problems of the heretical Arian and pagan Germanic invasions from 375 to 500 and the threat from Islam in the seventh and eighth centuries.

A. Revival and Evangelism

The perennial recurrence of revival in Atlantic civilization in the church in times of crisis has renewed the church and helped it to serve its "own generation." Although revival on the scale of the great awakenings on the continent of Europe, in England, and in America have not been a part of the contemporary scene, there are many evidences of revival forces in the world today. Billy Graham in person and through radio and television has reached more people with the gospel than any other person in history. Movements to evangelize youth and to challenge them to missions, as well as movements to reach special groups, are at work. Efforts are being made to promote evangelism in the major denominations in spite of their preoccupation with the social gospel. Church growth, stimulated by the work of Donald McGavran of the School of

World Mission at Fuller Theological Seminary, has promoted evangelism by the church both in this country and abroad.

B. The Revival of Biblical Theology

The revival of interest in biblical theology—an interest that in liberal churches was to some degree stimulated by Karl Barth—is an encouraging development. More attention is being given to the study of the Bible in colleges and seminaries. This should help to develop a teaching ministry in the church by emphasizing the importance of sound biblical theology for evangelism and effective social action (1 Tim. 6:3).

C. Ecumenicity

While some may wonder whether the ecumenical movement represented by the World Council of Churches will result in anything but a unity based on organizational ecclesiastical machinery, there are encouraging signs that evangelicals throughout the world are beginning to realize their essential spiritual unity in the only true ecumenical and international organism—the church as the body of Christ. This may then likely be expressed in organization as a tool to promote common interests. Any sound ecumenical movement must be built on a unity of spirit based on the authority of the Bible as God's Word to us and an experience of Christ as the only Savior from sin.

D. Missions

Despite the fact that about two-thirds of the population of the world lives in closed totalitarian societies, there are still many fields open to missionary endeavor. Forty million Chinese outside mainland China attracted the attention of missionaries driven out of China in 1949, and many of these Chinese are now taking an interest in reaching other people. In addition, there is some relaxation of the restrictions on religion in mainland Communist China. The spread of vital Christianity in Asia, Africa, and South America has been encouraging.

The church has also been willing to adopt and adapt new techniques to reach the unevangelized. Shortwave radio and television, theological education by extension, and films have been used in the proclamation of Christ. The airplane has removed the barriers of space and has freed people from the rigors of long, hard trips to reach their field of service. Medical work, education, agricultural programs, and other services have helped to develop higher living standards, as well as opening the way for witness to Christ as Savior.

The student of church history who has observed the operation of the transforming power of the gospel over the span of centuries in remaking the lives of men and nations sees the problems only as challenges to renewed effort in the power of the Holy Spirit. He realizes that God is both providential sustainer of the universe and redeemer through Christ's work on the cross. Both history and its termination are in the capable hands of Christ as the Lord of history. With serene confidence in her risen Lord, the church will meet the challenges of the present as well as she has met the challenges of the past.

NOTES

Introduction

[1] 1904; reprint ed., New York: Scribner, 1930.

[2] New York: Knopf, 1939.

[3] Grand Rapids: Baker, 1979.

Chapter 1

[1] See also the *Epistle to Diognetus*, chaps. 8–9, and Origen, *Against Celsus*, 2.30, for the same idea.

[2] Some scholars in recent times have attempted to find in the mystery religions one of the main sources of Christianity. According to them, Paul developed the simple ethical religion of Jesus into a mystery religion. But it must be remembered that the church early fought these religions and refused to have anything to do with them (1 Cor. 8:5). Such action was in marked contrast to the Roman tendency to syncretism. As long as a Roman citizen fulfilled the obligations of emperor worship, he was free to follow other religions if he so desired. Furthermore, it was because the Christians refused to mix Christianity with any other religion that they were severely persecuted by the Roman state. One has only to read the various apologies to realize that it was the exclusive claims of Christianity on the life of the individual that brought severe persecution. The pagan Roman world was quick to realize that this new religion, unlike others, was uncompromising in its ethic and its theology. When one bears these things in mind, it is easy to see how impossible it would have been for Paul to synthesize Christianity with any religion prevailing in that day.

[3] Kenneth S. Latourette, *The First Five Centuries: A History of the Expansion of Christianity*, vol. 1 (New York: Harper, 1937), 1:8.

Chapter 2

[1] Shirley J. Case, *The Historicity of Jesus* (Chicago: University of Chicago Press, 2nd ed., 1928), pp. 39–61.

[2] Tacitus, *Annals*, 15.44.

[3] Pliny, *Epistles*, 10.96.7; 10.967.1.

[4] Lucian, *The Passing of Peregrinus*, 1, 11, 13.

[5] Flavius Josephus, *Antiquities of the Jews*, 20.9.1.

[6] Ibid., 18.3.3.

[7] J. Gresham Machen, *The Virgin Birth of Christ* (New York: Harper, 2nd ed., 1932). This is the best conservative and scholarly work on this subject.

Chapter 3

[1] Eusebius, *Ecclesiastical History*, 3.5.

Chapter 4

[1] Adolf Deissman, *Paul, A Study in Social and Religious History* (London: Hodder and Stoughton, 1926), app. I.

[2] Floyd V. Filson, *One Lord One Faith* (Philadelphia: Westminster, 1943). This work asserts the essential oneness of the gospel that Paul preached with the teachings of Christ. It answers those who claim that Paul transformed the simple ethical message of Christ into a species of mystery religion.

[3] Morton S. Enslin, *The Ethics of Paul* (New York: Harper, 1930). The writer has found this a most useful book for the study of Paul's ethical system, though Enslin's liberal bias is at times apparent.

[4] The author follows the line of reasoning that links the Jerusalem visit of Galatians 2:1–10 with that of the Jerusalem Council. This view is ably presented by William J. Conybeare and John S. Howson, *The Life and Epistles of Saint Paul* (New York: Scribner, 1897).

[5] For more about Gnosticism, see chapter 8, pp. 98–100.

Chapter 5

[1] See Ephesians (not to be confused with the Ephesians of the Bible) 2:2; 3:2; 4:1–2, 5:1–2; 6:1; 20:2; Magnesians 3:1, 4:1; 6:1–2; 7:1; 13:1–2; Trallians 2:1; 3:1–2; 7:1–2; 13:2; Philadelphians 1:1; 3:2; 8:1–2.

[2]Eusebius, *Ecclesiastical History*, 4.15.

[3]Allegory is the seeking of a symbolic, hidden meaning by reading into the literal meaning of the Scripture meanings in accord with moral or philosophical preconceptions. It distorts the meaning intended by the writer for the people to whom he was writing into what the interpreter wants to find in the Scripture.

[4]Irenaeus, *Against Heresies*, 5.33.3–4; 5.36.1–2.

[5]Eusebius, *Ecclesiastical History*, 3.39.3–5, 15–16. See 3.24 for Eusebius's view.

[6]The Muratorian Canon is a mutilated fragment containing a list of New Testament Scriptures, probably those recognized as canonical by the Roman church toward the end of the second century.

Chapter 6

[1]Eusebius, *Ecclesiastical History*, 2.23.

[2]Ibid., 3.18, 20, 23.

[3]Ibid., 3.1.

[4]Clement, *1 Corinthians* 44; *Didache* 15; Acts 6:5; 13:2–3.

[5]Pliny, *Epistles*, 10.96.7 in Henry Bettenson, ed., *Documents of the Christian Church* (New York: Oxford University Press, 2nd ed., 1963), pp. 3–4. The paperback edition (G.B. 324) is used for all references. See also *The Didache*, 7–15; Justin Martyr, *First Apology*, 65–67; and Tertullian, *Apology*, 39.

[6]*Didache*, 7–15; Martyr, *First Apology*, 65–67, in Bettenson, *Documents*, pp. 66–67.

[7]*Didache*, 7.1–3.

Chapter 7

[1]Justin Martyr, *Dialog*, 10.

[2]Tacitus, *Annals*, 15.44, in Henry Bettenson, ed., *Documents of the Christian Church* (New York: Oxford University Press, 2nd ed., 1963), pp. 1–2).

[3]Pliny, *Epistles*, 10.96–97, in Bettenson, *Documents*, pp. 3–4; Eusebius, *Ecclesiastical History*, 3.33.

[4]Eusebius, *History*, 4.15.

[5]Bettenson, *Documents*, p. 18.

[6]Eusebius, *History*, 6.29.

[7]Bettenson, *Documents*, p. 14; Eusebius, *History*, 8.2–12.

[8]Eusebius, *History*, 8.6.

[9]Bettenson, *Documents*, pp. 15–16; Eusebius, *History*, 10.5.

Chapter 8

[1]Irenaeus, *Against Heresies*, 1.23.1–5; cf. Acts 8:9–24.

[2]Arthur C. McGiffert, *A History of Christian Thought* (New York: Scribner, 1946), 1:28–29.

[3]Eusebius, *Ecclesiastical History*, 5.16.

[4]Ibid., 7.27–30.

Chapter 9

[1]Henry Bettenson, *Documents of the Christian Church* (New York: Oxford University Press, 2nd ed., 1963), pp. 7–8.

[2]Tertullian, *Apology*, 50; see also chapters 32 and 37 for his insistence on the loyalty of Christians to the state despite their rapid growth. It is in chapter 50 that his famous saying "The blood [of the martyrs] is seed" (of the church) occurs.

[3]Irenaeus, *Against Heresies*, 3.3.3; 4.26.2.

[4]Ibid., 1.10.1. See 3.11.8 for his views on the New Testament.

[5]Clement, *Stromata*, 1.5, also in Bettenson, *Documents*, p. 6. See Eusebius, *Ecclesiastical History*, 6.13, for a description of this work.

[6]Eusebius, *History*, 6.1–8, 16, 19, 23–27, 32.

[7]Ibid., 6.16.

[8]Cyprian, *Epistle*, 63.14.

Chapter 10

[1]Henry Bettenson, *Documents of the Christian Church* (New York: Oxford University Press, 2nd ed., 1963), pp. 71–74.

[2]Philip Schaff, *The Creeds of Christendom* (New York: Scribner, 3 vols., 6th ed., 1890), vol. 1, chap. 1. This is an excellent introduction to the whole topic of creeds of the church.

[3]Beresford J. Kidd, *Documents Illustrative of the History of the Church* (London: SPCK, 3 vols., 1920–1941), 1:117–18, 145–46.

[4]Eusebius, *Ecclesiastical History*, 3.25.

[5]Jack Finegan, *Light From the Ancient Past* (Princeton: Princeton University Press, 2nd ed., 1959), pp. 451–85.

Chapter 11

[1]This viewpoint is ably developed with an abundance of illustrative material by Charles N. Cochrane in his excellent book, *Christianity and Classical Culture* (New York: Oxford University Press, 1944).

[2]Henry Bettenson, *Documents of the Christian Church* (New York: Oxford University Press, 2nd ed., 1963), pp. 15–19. See also Lactantius, *De Martibus Persecutorum*, 48; Eusebius, *Ecclesiastical History*, 10.5.

[3]Bettenson, *Documents*, pp. 19–21.

[4]Ibid., p. 22.

[5]Frederic A. Ogg, *A Source Book of Medieval History* (New York: American, 1907), pp. 53–54; Gregory of Tours, *The History of the Franks* (Oxford: Clarendon University Press, 2 vols., 1927), 2:18–22.

Chapter 12

[1]Nicae (325) to settle the Arian dispute.

Constantinople (381) to assert the personality of the Holy Spirit and the humanity of Christ.

Ephesus (431) to emphasize the unity of Christ's personality.

Chalcedon (451) to state the relationship between the two natures of Christ.

Constantinople (553) to deal with the Monophysite dispute.

Constantinople (680) to condemn the Monthelites.

Nicaea (787) to deal with problems raised by the image controversy.

Manual of Councils of the Holy Catholic Church (Edinburgh: Grant, 2 vols., 1909) by Edward G. Landon contains descriptions of the problems, personnel, and main discussions of the councils. See map on page 184 for the cities named.

[2]Beresford J. Kidd, *Documents Illustrative of the History of the Church* (London: SPCK, 3 vols., 1920–41), 2:6–10; Joseph Ayer, Jr., *A Source Book for Ancient Church History* (New York: Scribner, 1913), pp. 297–356. The pages in Ayer contain most of the documents of importance for an understanding of the Arian heresy. See also Socrates, *Ecclesiastical History*, 1.5–9; Eusebius, *Life of Constantine*, 1.61–73.

[3]Kidd, *History of the Church* 2:21–25. This letter from Eusebius to his people includes both his creed and the one formulated at Nicaea.

[4]Henry Bettenson, *Documents of the Christian Church* (New York: Oxford University Press, 2nd ed., 1963), pp. 35–36.

[5]Bettenson, *Documents*, pp. 25–26; canon 1 of the Council of Constantinople is given in Ayer, *Source Book*, p. 353, and Philip Schaff, *Creeds of Christendom* (New York: Scribner, 3 vols., 6th ed., 1890), 1:24–34; 2:57–61.

[6]Bettenson, *Documents*, p. 25, n. 6.

[7]Ibid., pp. 44–45; Kidd, *History of the Church*, 2:84–86, 103, 108, 114, 147.

[8]Bettenson, *Documents*, pp. 46–48; Ayer, *Source Book*, pp. 504–11.

[9]Bettenson, *Documents*, pp. 49–51.

[10]Ibid., pp. 51–52; Ayer, *Source Book*, pp. 511–29.

[11]Bettenson, *Documents*, pp. 51–54; Kidd, *History of the Church*, 2:235–36, 246–47.

[12]Bettenson, *Documents*, pp. 76–83.

[13]Ibid., pp. 61–62; Kidd, *History of the Church*, 2:334–37.

Chapter 13

[1]Translations of his homilies may be studied in Beresford J. Kidd, *Documents Illustrative of the History of the Church* (London: SPCK, 3 vols., 1920–41), 2:102f., and in vols. 10 to 14 of Philip Schaff, *A Select Library of the Nicene and Post-Nicene Fathers of the Christian Church* (New York: Christian Literature, 1889, First Series).

[2]Eusebius, *Ecclesiastical History*, 1:1.

[3]Kidd, *History of the Church*, 2:176–77.

[4]Ibid., 2:146–47.

[5]Augustine, *Confessions*, Books 1–10. These books give the story of his life until shortly after his conversion. The account of his conversion is given in 8.12.29.

[6]Ibid., 8.7.17.

[7]Meredith F. Eller, "The *Retractationes* of Saint Augustine," Church History, 32:172ff. (Sept., 1949). This article discusses the value of this work in some detail.

[8]Augustine, *Retractiones*, 2:43.

Chapter 14

[1]Athanasius, *Life of Anthony* in *A Select Library of Nicene and Post-Nicene Fathers of the Christian Church* (New York: Christian Literature, 1892, 2nd series), 4:195–221.

[2]Joseph Ayer, Jr., *A Source Book for Ancient Church History* (New York: Scribner, 1913), pp. 402–5; Sozomen, *Ecclesiastical History*, 3.14.

[3]Ayer, *Source Book*, pp. 405–6.

[4]Henry Bettenson, *Documents of the Christian Church* (New York: Oxford University Press, 2nd ed., 1963), pp. 116–128.

Chapter 15

[1]See chapter 10 for further discussion of reasons for the rise of the bishop of Rome.

[2]Henry Bettenson, *Documents of the Christian Church* (New York: Oxford University Press, 2nd ed., 1963), pp. 82–83.

[3]Ibid., pp. 32–33.

[4]Ibid., pp. 113–14.

[5]Beresford J. Kidd, *Documents Illustrative of the History of the Church* (London: SPCK, 3 vols., 1920–41), 2:311–19.

[6]Cyprian, *Epistles*, 63:14.

[7]Frederick J. Foakes-Jackson, *An Introduction to the History of Christianity, A.D. 590–1314* (New York: Macmillan, 1928), pp. 25–27.

Chapter 16

[1]Jonathan F. Scott, Albert Hyma, Arthur H. Noyes, *Readings in Medieval History* (New York: Appleton-Century-Crofts, 1933), pp. 84–92. This is a fair account of Gregory's life and times.

[2]The Venerable Bede, *History of the Church of England* (New York: Putnam, 2 vols., 1930), 2.2.

[3]Henry Bettenson, *Documents of the Christian Church* (New York: Oxford University Press, 2nd ed., 1963), pp. 151–53.

[4]James H. Robinson, *Readings in Modern European History* (Boston: Ginn, 2 vols., 1904), 1:78–80.

[5]Ibid., pp. 80–82; see also Frederic A. Ogg, *A Source Book of Medieval History* (New York: American, 1907), pp. 91–96, for other extracts from this work.

[6]Frederick J. Foakes-Jackson, *An Introduction to the History of Christianity, A.D. 590–1314* (New York: Macmillan, 1928), pp. 25–27.

Chapter 17

[1]Charles H. Haskins, *The Renaissance of the Twelfth Century* (Cambridge: Harvard University Press, 1939).

[2]Frederic A. Ogg, *A Source Book of Medieval History* (New York: American, 1907), pp. 72–77.

[3]Beresford J. Kidd, *Documents Illustrative of the History of the Church* (London: SPCK, 3 vols., 1920–41), 3:54–58.

Chapter 18

[1]Henry Bettenson, *Documents of the Christian Church* (New York: Oxford University Press, 2nd ed., 1963), pp. 98–100. These pages give the text of the document. Valla's refutation of the *Donation of Constantine* is available in *The Treatise of Lorenzo Valla on the Donation of Constantine*, trans. Christopher B. Coleman (New Haven: Yale University Press, 1922).

[2]Jonathan F. Scott, Albert Hyma, and Arthur H. Noyes, *Readings in Medieval History* (New York: Appleton-Century-Crofts, 1933), pp. 149–66.

[3]Oliver J. Thatcher and Edgar H. McNeal, *A Source Book for Medieval History* (New York: Scribner, 1905), pp. 51–52; 55–56.

Chapter 19

[1]Frederic A. Ogg, *A Source Book of Medieval History* (New York: American, 1907), pp. 152–54.

[2]Ibid., pp. 154–56.

[3]Oliver J. Thatcher and Edgar H. McNeal, *A Source Book for Medieval History* (New York: Scribner, 1905), pp. 412–18.

Chapter 20

[1]C. Robinson, *The Conversion of Europe* (London: Longmans, 1917), pp. 437–84.

[2]Beresford J. Kidd, *Documents Illustrative of the History of the Church* (London: SPCK, 3 vols., 1920–41), 3:82–84.

[3]Noreen Hunt, *Cluny Under Saint Hugh* (Notre Dame: Notre Dame University Press, 1968), p. 18, n.1.

[4]Frederic A. Ogg, *A Source Book of Medieval History* (New York: American, 1907), pp. 247–49.

[5]Kidd, *Documents*, 3:92.

[6]Ibid., 3:86–91.

[7]Ibid., 3:115–17.

[8]See Robinson, *Conversion*, chap. 19, for an interesting account of the winning of Russia to Christianity.

Chapter 21

[1]Henry Bettenson, *Documents of the Christian Church* (New York: Oxford University Press, 2nd ed., 1963), pp. 101–2.

[2]Beresford J. Kidd, *Documents Illustrative of the History of the Church* (London: SPCK, 3 vols., 1920–41), 3:129–30.

[3]Bettenson, *Documents*, pp. 102–4; Frederic A. Ogg, *Source Book of Medieval History* (New York: American, 1907), pp. 270–72.

[4]Bettenson, *Documents*, p. 104.

[5]Ibid., pp. 154–55.

[6]Ibid., pp. 155–56.

[7]Ogg, *Source Book*, pp. 382–83.

[8]Bettenson, *Documents*, pp. 161–64.

[9]Ibid., pp. 112–13.

[10]See Kidd, *History of the Church*, 3:150–53, for relevant documents.

[11]Bettenson, *Documents*, pp. 113–15.

[12]Ibid., pp. 115–16.

Chapter 22

[1]Oliver J. Thatcher and Edgar H. McNeal, *A Source Book for Medieval History* (New York: Scribner, 1905), pp. 512–13.

[2]Ibid., pp. 513–21.

[3]Ibid., pp. 537–44.

[4]Frederic A. Ogg, *A Source Book of Medieval History* (New York: American, 1907), pp. 251–60.

[5]See pp. 307–97 of *Little Flowers of St. Francis* (New York: Dutton, 1910) for a medieval account of Francis's life and pp. 1–180 for the devotional work, *Little Flowers*, in which his deeds and words are recorded. Author unknown.

[6]Henry Bettenson, *Documents of the Christian Church* (New York: Oxford University Press, 2nd ed., 1963), pp. 128–32.

[7]Beresford J. Kidd, *Documents Illustrative of the History of the Church* (London: SPCK, 3 vols., 1920–41), 3:160–63.

Chapter 23

[1]Henry Bettenson, *Documents of the Christian Church* (New York: Oxford University Press, 2nd ed., 1963), pp. 137–38.

[2]See Jonathon F. Scott, Albert Hyma, and Arthur H. Noyes, *Readings in Medieval History* (New York: Appleton-Century-Crofts, 1933), pp. 334–48, for autobiographical data concerning Abelard's life, and *The Love Letters of Abelard and Heloise* (1908; reprint ed., New York: Cooper Square, 1974) by Pierre Abailard for the letters exchanged between Abelard and Heloise.

[3]Scott, Hyma, and Noyes, *Medieval History*, pp. 348–57.

[4]Anton C. Pegis, ed., *Basic Writings of Saint Thomas Aquinas* (New York: Random, 1945).

Chapter 24

[1]William E. Lunt, *Papal Revenues in the Middle Ages* (New York: Columbia University Press, 1934), 1:57–136.

[2]Beresford J. Kidd, *Documents Illustrative of the History of the Church* (London: SPCK, 3 vols., 1920–41), 3:190–91.

[3]Raymond B. Blakney, *Meister Eckhart* (New York: Harper, 1941). This book gives several of Eckhart's writings.

[4]Albert Hyma's *The Christian Renaissance* (New York: Century, 1924) is a scholarly discussion of the Brethren of the Common Life.

[5]Ibid., chapter 5 contains an able discussion of the authorship of the *Imitation*.

[6]Kidd, *History of the Church*, 3:201–2.

[7]Henry Bettenson, *Documents of the Christian Church* (New York: Oxford University Press, 2nd ed., 1963), pp. 173–75.

[8]Ibid., pp. 175–79.

[9]George M. Trevelyan, *England in the Age of Wycliffe* (London: Longmans, 1920). *John Wycliffe* (Oxford: Clarendon University Press, 1926), a two-volume work by Herbert B. Workman, is an interesting account of Wycliffe's life and work.

[10]Kidd, *History of the Church*, 3:213.

[11]Frederic A. Ogg, *A Source Book of Medieval History* (New York: American, 1907), pp. 391–92.

[12]Oliver J. Thatcher and Edgar H. McNeal, *A Source Book for Medieval History* (New York: Scribner, 1905), pp. 317–23.

[13]Ibid., pp. 327–28.

[14]Kidd, *History of the Church*, pp. 208–9.

[15]Thatcher and McNeal, *Source Book*, pp. 328–29; cf. 329–30.

[16]Ibid., pp. 331–32.

[17]Ibid., p. 332.

[18]Ogg, *Medieval History*, pp. 395–97.

Chapter 25

[1]Jonathan F. Scott, Albert Hyma, and Arthur H. Noyes, *Readings in Medieval History* (New York: Appleton-Century-Crofts, 1933), pp. 624–36.

Chapter 26

[1]See Preserved Smith, *The Age of the Reformation* (New York: Henry Holt, 1920), chapter 14, for an account of the interpretation of the Reformation.

[2]Ibid., pp. 20–25.

[3]Henry Bettenson, *Documents of the Christian Church* (New York: Oxford University Press, 2nd ed., 1963), pp. 182–83.

[4]Ibid., pp. 184–85; Hans Hillerbrand, *The Reformation* (Harper, 1964), pp. 41–46.

Chapter 27

[1]Henry Bettenson, *Documents of the Christian Church* (New York: Oxford University Press, 2nd ed., 1963), pp. 185–91.

[2]Hans J. Hillerbrand, *The Reformation* (New York: Harper, 1964), pp. 55–56.

[3]Ernest G. Schwiebert, "The Reformation From a New Perspective," *Church History*, 17 (March, 1948): 3–31.

[4]Bettenson, *Documents*, pp. 191–92; Hillerbrand, *Reformation*, pp. 65–76, on debate with Eck.

[5]Bettenson, *Documents*, pp. 192–97.

[6]Ibid., pp. 197–99.

[7]Hillerbrand, *Reformation*, pp. 80–87.

[8]Bettenson, *Documents*, pp. 199–201; Hillerbrand, *Reformation*, pp. 87–100.

[9]Philip Melanchthon, *Loci Communes Rerum Theologicarum*, trans. by Charles L. Hill (Boston: Meador, 1944).

[10]Clyde L. Manschreck, ed., *A History of Christianity* (Englewood Cliffs, N.J.: Prentice-Hall, 1964), pp. 35–40.

[11]Hillerbrand, *Reformation*, pp. 149–63.

[12]Philip Schaff, *Creeds of Christendom* (New York: Scribner, 3 vols., 6th ed., 1890), 3:1–73; Bettenson, *Documents*, pp. 210–12.

[13]Schaff, *Creeds*, 3:74–92; Bettenson, *Documents*, pp. 201–9.

[14]Hugh Thomson Kerr, Jr., *A Compend of Luther's Theology* (Philadelphia: Westminster, 1943), pp. 213–32.

[15]Schaff, *Creeds*, 1:258–307.

[16]Ibid., 3:93–180.

Chapter 28

[1]Samuel M. Jackson, *Huldreich Zwingli* (New York: Putnam, 1901), pp. 183–85; Clyde L. Manschreck, ed., *A History of Christianity* (Englewood Cliffs, N.J.: Prentice-Hall, 1964), pp. 67–70.

[2]Philip Schaff, *Creeds of Christendom* (New York: Scribner, 3 vols., 6th ed., 1890), 1:365–66.

[3]Henry C. Vedder, *Balthasar Hubmaier* (New York: Putnam, 1905), pp. 69–71; 130–36.

[4]Schaff, *Creeds*, 3:13, 17, 173, 291, 306, 433.

[5]Hans J. Hillerbrand, *The Reformation* (New York: Harper, 1964), pp. 235–38.

[6]See Wilhelm Pauck's article, "Calvin's *Institutes of the Christian Religion*" in *Church History*, (15 March 1946): 17–27 for an able discussion of the history of this great work.

[7]*A Compend of the Institutes of the Christian Religion by John Calvin*, Hugh Thomson Kerr, Jr. (Philadelphia: Presbyterian Board of Christian Education, 1939). This is an excellent condensation of Calvin's *Institutes*. It omits the mass of biblical references and the references to the Fathers, among whom Augustine is the most quoted.

[8]Hillerbrand, *Reformation*, pp. 188–96.

Chapter 29

[1]Philip Schaff, *Creeds of Christendom* (New York: Scribner, 3 vols., 6th ed., 1890), 3:356–82.

[2]Henry Bettenson, *Documents of the Christian Church* (New York: Oxford University Press, 2nd ed., 1963), pp. 215–16.

[3]Ibid., pp. 269–70.

[4]Schaff, *Creeds*, 5:307–55.

[5]Ibid., 3:436–79.

[6]Ibid., 3:383–436.

[7]Ibid., 3:545–49; Bettenson, *Documents*, pp. 268–69.

[8]James Arminius, *Works*, trans. by James Nichols and W. R. Bagnall (Buffalo: Derby, Miller & Orton, 3 vols., 1853), 1:329; 2:472–73.

[9]Ibid., 1:248.

[10]Ibid., 1:316–17.

[11]Ibid., 1:254; 2:497.

[12]Ibid., 1:254, 281.

[13]Ibid., 2:490.

Chapter 30

[1]Hans J. Hillerbrand, *The Reformation* (New York: Harper, 1964), pp. 310–15.

[2]Henry Bettenson, *Documents of the Christian Church* (New York: Oxford University Press, 2nd ed., 1963), pp. 217–18.

[3]Ibid., pp. 218–22.

[4]Ibid., p. 227.

[5]Ibid., pp. 233–34.

[6]Carl Stephenson and Frederick G. Marcham, *Sources of English Constitutional History* (New York: Harper, 1937), pp. 323–24.

[7]Henry Gee and William J. Hardy, comp., *Documents Illustrative of English Church History* (1896; reprint ed., London: Macmillan, 1921), pp. 369–72, cf. pp. 358–66.

[8]Bettenson, *Documents*, pp. 234–35.

[9]Ibid., pp. 235–39; Gee and Hardy, *English Church History*, pp. 458–67.

[10]Philip Schaff, *Creeds of Christendom* (New York: Scribner, 3 vols., 6th ed., 1890), 3:486–516;

Gee and Hardy, *English Church History*, pp. 477–80.

[11]Bettenson, *Documents*, pp. 240–41.

[12]Ibid., pp. 242–43.

[13]Schaff, *Creeds*, 3:707–29.

[14]Gee and Hardy, *English Church History*, pp. 508–11.

[15]Schaff, *Creeds*, 1:727–816.

[16]Ibid., 3:598–673.

[17]Gee and Hardy, *English Church History*, pp. 594–632.

Chapter 31

[1]Beresford J. Kidd, *The Counter-Reformation* (London: SPCK, 1933), pp. 12–14; Colman J. Barry, *Reading in Church History* (Westminster, Md.: Newman, 3 vols., 1965), 2:96–102.

[2]Paul Van Dyke, *Ignatius Loyola* (New York: Scribner, 1926), chap. 18.

[3]Henry Bettenson, *Documents of the Christian Church* (New York: Oxford University Press, 2nd ed., 1963), pp. 258–61.

[4]Ibid., pp. 261–63.

[5]Ibid., pp. 264–66.

[6]Ibid., pp. 266–68.

[7]See Philip Schaff, *Creeds of Christendom* (New York: Scribner, 3 vols., 6th ed., 1890), 2:77–206, for the canons and decrees.

Chapter 32

[1]Peter G. Mode, *Source Book and Bibliographical Guide for American Church History* (Menasha, Wis.: Banta, 1921), pp. 9–10, 26.

[2]Ibid., p. 49.

[3]Ibid., pp. 64–65. Cf. Perry Miller, *Orthodoxy in Massachusetts, 1630-1650* (Cambridge: Harvard University Press, 1933), chap. 5, esp. pp 127–31.

[4]Mode, *Source Book*, pp. 97–98.

[5]Ibid., pp. 76–77.

[6]Ibid., pp. 119–20.

[7]Ibid., pp. 73–75. See also E. E. Cairns, "The Puritan Philosophy of Education" in *Bibliotheca Sacra*, 104 (July-September 1947): 326–36.

[8]Ibid., pp. 20–21, 109–10, 244–50, 288–90. These pages give some of the charters of these schools.

[9]Ibid., pp. 214–21.

Chapter 33

[1]Henry Bettenson, *Documents of the Christian Church* (New York: Oxford University Press, 2nd ed., 1963), pp. 252–56; Philip Schaff, *Creeds of Christendom* (New York: Scribner, 3 vols., 6th ed., 1890), 3:789–98.

[2]In 1733 philanthropist James Oglethorpe founded Georgia as a refuge for debtors and for persecuted Protestants from Germany.

[3]When Wesley arrived in Georgia, he met the Moravian leader Spangenberg. The Moravian asked him, "Do you know Jesus Christ?" Wesley could only reply, "I know He is the Savior of the world." To this Spangenberg replied, "True, but do you know that He has saved *you?*"

[4]Böhler was another Moravian whom Wesley met. The three main points of Böhler's teaching were a complete self-surrendering faith, an instantaneous conversion, and a joy in believing.

[5]John Telford, ed., *The Letters of the Rev. John Wesley* (London: Epworth, 8 vols., 1931), 2:280–81; 4:213; 5:38, 223. Schaff, *Creeds*, 3:807–13.

Chapter 34

[1]John H. Stewart, *A Documentary Survey of the French Revolution* (New York: Macmillan, 1951), pp. 158–59; 169–81.

[2]Henry Bettenson, *Documents of the Christian Church* (New York: Oxford University Press, 2nd ed., 1963), p. 271.

[3]Ibid., pp. 272–73.

[4]Ibid., pp. 273–75.

Chapter 35

[1]Henry Bettenson, *Documents of the Christian Church* (New York: Oxford University Press, 2nd ed., 1963), pp. 315–18.

[2]Ibid., pp. 318–21.

Chapter 37

[1]Peter G. Mode, *Source Book and Bibliographical Guide for American Church History* (Menasha, Wis.: Banta, 1921), pp. 339–42.

[2]Ibid., pp. 336–39.

[3]Ibid., pp. 404–7.

[4]Ibid., pp. 491–99.

[5]Ibid., pp. 499–501.

[6]Ibid., 491.

[7]Ibid., pp. 653–55.

[8]Ibid., pp. 675–76.

[9]Ibid., pp. 669–71.

Chapter 38

[1]David B. Barrett, *Schism and Renewal in Africa* (Nairobi: Oxford University Press, 1968), pp. 3, 6.

Chapter 39

[1]Peter G. Mode, *Source Book and Bibliographical Guide for American Church History* (Menasha, Wis.: Banta, 1921), pp. 669–71.

[2]George K. A. Bell, ed., *Documents on Christian Unity* (London: Oxford University Press, 3rd series, 1930–48), pp. 292–97; Henry Bettenson,

Documents of the Christian Church (New York: Oxford University Press, 2nd ed., 1963), pp. 333–34.

[3]Bettenson, *Documents*, pp. 333–34.

[4]Evanston, Ill.: Harper, 1972.

Conclusion

[1]Edwin L. Frizen, Jr., and Wade T. Coggins, eds., *Christ and Caesar in Christian Missions* (Pasadena, Calif: William Carey Library, 1979). Part I, pp. 1–45, gives a fuller discussion of this problem.

INDEX

INDEX

Abelard, 224, 233, 235, 237, 240
Absolute Spirit, 16
Addams, Jane, 424
Address to the Greeks, 107, 111
Adeodatus, 146
Adolphus, Gustavus, 351
Adrianople, Battle of, 127, 165
Adventists, Seventh-Day, 421, 422
Adversus Haereses, 110, 422
Aeschylus, 40
Aeterni Patris, 393
Agabus, 81
Against Celsus, 112
Against Praxeas, 112
Agamemnon, 40
Age of Reason, 378
Agnes, 214–15
Agricola, Michael, 298
Aidan, 155, 177
Alaric, 157
Albert, of Mainz, 281, 282, 283, 290
Albigenses, 100, 216, 226–27, 348
Alcoholism, 477
Alcuin, 187, 243
Alexander, 133
Alexander, the Great, 39
Alexander II, pope, 212
Alexander V, pope, 255
Alexander of Hales, 233, 282
Alexandria, School of, 110–12, 135
Alexius, emperor, 220, 221
Allegory, 75, 110, 168
Allen, Ethan, 378
Allen, William, 333
Alopen, 136
Altizer, Thomas J. J., 446, 447
Alva, Duke of, 323–24
Ambrose, 18, 111, 145, 146, 162, 167, 168, 169
Amendment, Eighteenth, 420
American Anti-Slavery Association, 421
American Association of Bible Colleges, 450
American Bible Society, 419, 427, 464
American Board of Commissioners for Foreign Missions, 419, 463
American Council of Christian Churches, 453, 465, 469
American Peace Society, 432
American Revolution, churches in the, 368–69
American Sunday School Union, 464
American Tract Society, 419, 464
American Unitarian Association, 418
Ames, William, 335

Amillennialism, 51
Amin, Idi, 437
Ammoun, 153
Amsterdam, ecumenical meeting at, 468
Anabaptists, 283, 305–8, 318, 323, 353
Ananias, 57
Andover Seminary, 418
Andrew, martyrdom of, 81
Anglicanism: in America, 359–60; in England, 283, 324–35, 353, 395–400, 435; in Ireland, 331, 405
Anicetus, bishop, 103
Anne of Bohemia, 252
Anne of Cleves, 331
Anselm, 234–35, 239
Anskar, 200
Anthony, 152
Antioch, School of, 151–52
Antiquities, 47
Anti-Saloon League, 420
Antoninus Pius, 106
Apocryphal New Testament, The, 46
Apollinarius, 135–36
Apologists, 105–9
Apology, First, of Justin Martyr, 83, 106; *Second*, 106
Apology to Autolycus, 107
Apostle, definition of, 80
Apostles' Creed, 117, 135
Apostles, careers and deaths, 80–82
Apostolic fathers, 71–78
Apostolic succession, 117; Cyprian on, 163; Irenaeus on, 110
Aquinas, Thomas, 23, 169, 188, 226, 232, 235, 237–38, 240, 281, 394
Architecture: in the ancient church, 23, 121, 161–62; Gothic, 241–43; Romanesque, 241–42
Aristides, 106
Arianism, 127, 133–35, 171
Aristotle, 23, 106, 175, 231, 233–35, 237, 262, 289, 414
Arius, 131, 133–35, 143, 158
Armada, Spanish, 333
Armenia, 127
Arminianism, 324–25, 449
Arminius, James, 17, 324–25
Army, Roman, 37
Arnold, Thomas, 398
Arouet, Francois M., 389
Arthur, 329

491